GERMANTOWN DURING THE CIVIL WAR ERA

GEORGE C. BROWDER

GERMANTOWN DURING THE CIVIL WAR ERA

A REVERSAL OF FORTUNE

The University of Tennessee Press ♦ Knoxville

This book was originally published in a different form as *A Tennessee Town during the Civil War Era: Germantown's Reversal of Fortune* by Heritage Press, 2015.

Copyright © 2024 by The University of Tennessee Press / Knoxville.
All Rights Reserved. Manufactured in the United States of America.
First Edition.

Library of Congress Cataloging-in-Publication Data

Names: Browder, George C., 1939- author.
Title: Germantown during the Civil War era : a reversal of fortune / George C. Browder.
Description: First edition. | Knoxville : The University of Tennessee Press, 2024. | "This book was originally published in a different form as A Tennessee Town during the Civil War Era: Germantown's Reversal of Fortune by Heritage Press, 2015."—Title page verso. | Includes bibliographical references and index. | Summary: "Germantown's Civil War experience mirrored that of many small towns across the South: It ardently supported secession throughout 1861 only to undergo serious disruption in 1862 as Federal forces and Confederate raiders contested control of the area. Then, during 1863 and early 1864, the Tennessee town felt the mixed benefits of an obdurate Federal occupation as guerrilla warfare continued throughout the countryside surrounding the town. And although it began to recover shortly after the close of the Civil War, Germantown's fortunes changed again as Reconstruction took hold and emerging economic inequality mixed with racist fears of a newly freed slave population. Browder recounts the history of what is now a large suburb of Memphis, how it fared during the Civil War, and how its current demographic makeup began shortly after the close of the war"— Provided by publisher.
Identifiers: LCCN 2023058440 (print) | LCCN 2023058441 (ebook) | ISBN 9781621908142 (paperback) | ISBN 9781621908159 (pdf)
Subjects: LCSH: Reconstruction (U.S. history, 1865-1877)—Tennessee—Germantown. | Germantown (Tenn.)—History—19th century. | Tennessee—History—Civil War, 1861-1865. | BISAC: HISTORY / United States / Civil War Period (1850-1877) | HISTORY / United States / State & Local / South (AL, AR, FL, GA, KY, LA, MS, NC, SC, TN, VA, WV)
Classification: LCC F444.G47 B74 2024 (print) | LCC F444.G47 (ebook) | DDC 976.8/04—dc23/eng/20240108
LC record available at https://lccn.loc.gov/2023058440
LC ebook record available at https://lccn.loc.gov/2023058441

CONTENTS

Preface xi

Acknowledgments xv

Abbreviations xvii

Introduction 1

Part 1: Antebellum Germantown 7

1. The White Folks and Their Lives 11
2. Hierarchy and Harmony? 51
3. A Transportation and Economic Center 95
4. Growing Political Tensions 117

    PART SUMMARY 148

Part 2: The War Years 153

5. 1861: Germantown Goes to War 155
6. 1862: The War Comes to Germantown 179
7. 1863: Germantown Occupied 223
8. 1864: Germantown Returns to Anarchy 283
9. 1865: Winding Down the War 315

    PART SUMMARY 337

Part 3: The Aftermath 341

10   Reconstruction   343
11   Social and Economic Recovery   374
12   The Troubled Rebirth of a Community   416

Conclusion   453
Postscript   464

APPENDIX 1   Defining Germantown and Its People   481
APPENDIX 2   Identifying Men Who Served in the War   483
APPENDIX 3   Assessing Population, Wealth, and Property   486
Notes   493
Bibliography   543
Names Index   559
Subject Index   567

ILLUSTRATIONS

Illustrations

- ILL. 1   Taking the Census   16
- ILL. 2   Picnicking as It Might Have Looked at Nashoba   110
- ILL. 3   Women's Sewing Group for the Boys   161
- ILL. 4   Cotton Burners   199
- ILL. 5   Cavalry Raiders Attacking Union Wagon Train   199
- ILL. 6   Revenge Foraging   203
- ILL. 7   Provost Marshall Provides Supplies for Locals   245
- ILL. 8   Confederate Prisoners Coming into Town   246
- ILL. 9   Suttler's Store   260
- ILL. 10 Contrabands Coming into Camp   268
- ILL. 11 Contraband Camp, President's Island   274
- ILL. 12 Negro Recruits at a Depot   277
- ILL. 13 Yeoman Family Hand Grinding Corn Meal   304
- ILL. 14 Irving Block, Memphis   311
- ILL. 15 Confederate POWs, Camp Douglas   312
- ILL. 16 Guerrilla Robbers   317
- ILL. 17 Union Troops Sharing Rations with Defeated Confederates   328
- ILL. 18 Colored Orphan Asylum, Memphis   399
- ILL. 19 Quarantine Stop on the Railroad   465

Photographs

- PHOTO 1   Webb School and Home   26
- PHOTO 2   Masonic Lodge   31
- PHOTO 3   Presbyterian Church (Evans Chapel)   32
- PHOTO 4   Brooks Weekend Town House, Bridge Street   42

PHOTO 5   Town House, Bridge Street   42
PHOTO 6   Woodlawn, Brooks' Plantation   44
PHOTO 7   Log Planter's House   55
PHOTO 8   Planter's House, Poplar Pike   55
PHOTO 9   Dog-Trot Cabin   56
PHOTO 10   Two-Room Plank-Sided cabin   56
PHOTO 11   Cornelius House, Late Victorian Adaptations   57
PHOTO 12   Germantown Depot from South Looking across Tracks and Bridge Street   103
PHOTO 13   Track Crew   105
PHOTO 14   Two-Story Inn   108
PHOTO 15   Ridgeway Store, State Line Road near M&C Railroad   112
PHOTO 16   Confederate Mess   173
PHOTO 17   Robert Vinkler Richardson   215
PHOTO 18   Col. Benjamin Grierson   215
PHOTO 19   Col. La Fayette McCrillis   255
PHOTO 20   DeWitt Clinton Fort   302
PHOTO 21   Greenlaw House   382
PHOTO 22   Germantown Baptist Church   414
PHOTO 23   New Bethel Missionary Baptist Church   446

Maps

MAP 1   Counties of Southwest Tennessee   xviii
MAP 2   Approximate Area of Greater Germantown, 1860   3
MAP 3   Approximate Area of Incorporated Germantown, 1850   8
MAP 4   Nashoba Tract at Germantown   13
MAP 5   Germantown Center   30
MAP 6   Shelby County, Major Roads, 1839   96
MAP 7   Civil Districts, Shelby County, 1835   133
MAP 8   W. Kentucky, Tennessee, and N. Mississippi Theater of War   169
MAP 9   Guerrilla Warfare Theater around Germantown   197
MAP 10   Guerrilla Warfare Terrain   206

Tables

TABLE 1 Comparative Wealth, 1860 62
TABLE 2 Civil War Incidents in and around Germantown, 1862 180
TABLE 3 Civil War Incidents in and around Germantown, 1863 222
TABLE 4 Civil War Incidents in and around Germantown, 1864 284
TABLE 5 Civil War Incidents in and around Germantown, 1865 316
TABLE 6 Comparative Wealth, 1870 388

PREFACE

Among the vast Civil War literature, military and political histories are profuse. Increasingly, however, social and economic aspects have come into the picture, especially the African American experience, but also the daily life of the civilian population and the war's impact on them. So far, all such work covers broad topics or regions. What is offered here is a case study of one small community—both typical and atypical. It offers a detailed picture of life and the impact of war on that life. This town was intermittently, but often heavily occupied by Union troops in the midst of a theater of guerrilla warfare. Despite the extensive examination of that form of warfare in recent decades, Shelby County, Tennessee, and its civilian environment has not yet drawn much attention.

When an historian covers a topic or region that is broad, the available evidence is usually rich enough to paint a solidly based picture. To make that focus as specific as a particular community, however, one needs an unusually rich supply of source material: public records, census and tax data, extensive newspaper coverage of social, political and cultural affairs, personal diaries and correspondence. If one chooses a community regardless of those criteria, one must work with what is available.

For instance, Germantown's government records for the entire period have been lost. County records at least provide significant insights. Although state records about the town and its civil district are available, most are significantly limited. Of course, the usual federal census data is available as are the official records of both armies for the war. Memphis-based newspaper coverage was spotty except for one paper. All that coverage was, however, intriguing. Only one church has an archive of any consequence, while another rebuilt a fragmentary archive from district records. Only four personal diaries survive, one pre-war, one for one war-year and two post-war. Only two relevant Civil War veterans' questionnaires exist. Personal letters and family accounts have surfaced in several cases, plus fragmentary quotations for others. Outsiders' impressions have survived in many letters and diary references.

While coping with such a supply of sources, this book seeks to capture a picture of one town in south-central Shelby County, Tennessee. Why? After retirement, I began this adventure as a member of the city's Historical Commission. When I argued that the city should do more to advertise its position as part of Civil War tourism, I got pressured into doing the research to document historical markers. This drew me into the search for sources, but also into an unfamiliar and vast body of scholarly literature far beyond my former academic focus. I had worked entirely on research and writing in modern European history. As I rapidly became aware of the guerrilla warfare environment in which the town had been immersed, I saw the potential for a small book to reacquaint people with those aspects of local Civil War history that have not been a part of local understandings. I realized that the community also needed a broader context in which to place and test its popular and family traditions. Soon, I foresaw a book about people and their community amidst the turmoil of guerrilla warfare that just might interest anyone. As I fleshed out community life before the war, to set the stage, I found an equally interesting picture. That led to a search into post-war life to see what changes were brought about by the war, which yielded even more interesting results.

Unfortunately, there are only two voices plus two short notes revealing the personal experiences of the town's people during the crucial war years. What did the rest of the population think about what was happening to them? How did it impact them in the long run? Consequently, I have compulsively teased out every available detail about community life before and after. I had to develop as complete a picture as possible in order to uncover those aspects that were impacted by the war, emancipation, Reconstruction, and the yellow fever epidemics. Sometimes conventional ideas about Southern towns and their fates were confirmed; in others they are challenged.

To understand civilian life amidst guerrilla warfare, one needs a narrative of other military developments so essential to the context of that life. I have recorded details of Union troop presence and activities in and around the town and the Confederate raiding and guerrilla activities that embroiled them all. However, such a minimal military focus omitted the experiences of the majority of the town's men folk, Black and White. Consequently, attention is also given to the military side of their lives to flesh out the picture, for that too is inseparable from the town's story. Just as today, the physical and psychological effects of their war extended well into the peacetime decades.

One striking impression is the strong similarity to America's later involvements in places like Vietnam, Iraq and Afghanistan. The experiences of the occupying Union Army were in so many ways like those of modern American soldiers, unable to distinguish friends from enemies among the civilians. The civilian experience, therefore, resembled in some ways that of those countries we have sought to liberate or pacify. Of course, such an analogy should not be overdrawn, for Americans North and South were not ethnically or in any other significant way so different from each other. Nevertheless, Tennessee represented the classic problem for occupiers. They had to win the war against the enemy's army, while simultaneously trying both to control and to win the people.

The most striking impressions, however, were the indications that what we have learned about Post-Traumatic Stress from 20th century wars needs to be applied to the survivors in the post-war South. In the case of a guerrilla-war theater, total immersion affected both soldiers and civilians, men and women, Black and White.

A Note on Language

Because I must distinguish among those Americans whose ancestors came from Europe and those coming heavily from Africa, I choose the simplest conventional labels of "white and black" that have traditionally lumped a diverse population into two rigidly separated groups. At least this conforms to the social-cultural perceptions of then and now. It also avoids our contemporary, convoluted, and awkward efforts to find terms that do not offend.

Occasionally I will have to use the now-unacceptable language of the times, "colored," "negro" (not capitalized), "mulatto," and even the pejoratives and other epithets when they express the meaning they were intended to convey by the user. If one really wants to understand fully our ancestors and the complex historical contexts in which they operated, one has to forgo current sensitivities and listen to their words. But one must also remember that their insensitivity to such terms did not always express the same hostilities they do today. For instance the term "Twenty Nigger Rule" was more an expression of hostility toward privileged slave owners than it was a slur directed at African Americans.

Whenever I feel it necessary to use an insensitive term not embedded in a direct quotation, I put it in quotation marks to indicate that it was a commonly used term by people to which I am referring. I hope readers can accept the intention and not be offended.

Finally, to preserve the historical flavor of quotations, I usually ignore the convention of noting misspellings and grammatical errors with the insertion of (*sic*) that make reading tedious. Where confusion might result, I do note errors in the spelling or inaccuracy of names.

Revisions

New evidence plus comments by readers have demanded improvements and expansions. Fortunately, both new evidence and new techniques for analysis of sources speak to several of the questions my original text had raised. They have also produced major challenges to other local traditions that I had previously accepted. This has greatly enriched my pervious descriptions and strengthened support for my earlier conclusions and arguments

Sources and Authority

I have attempted to cite all my primary sources and most pertinent secondary sources for my statements. This may have already produced excessive footnoting. In many cases, however, I have made statements that are the conclusions of my accumulated impressions drawn from emersion in multiple primary sources and the secondary literature. It would be impossible to fully document them even with voluminous footnoting. Also, my context for those conclusions results from many years of scholarly involvement in the study of racism and related phenomena like antisemitism—even a lifetime of personal emersion in those phenomena. For more on the problems inherent in use of many available primary sources, see Appendix 3.

ACKNOWLEDGMENTS

Lucile Bagby, late chairperson Germantown Historical Commission.
Jennifer Baker, former Branch Manager, Germantown Regional History and Genealogy Center Library and Archive.
Katherine Bennett, Librarian, New Bethel Missionary Baptist Church.
Darla Brock, Archivist I, Tennessee State Library and Archives.
Vincent Clark, formerly Shelby County Archives.
Harry Cloyes, late local historian, collector of artifacts and records.
Wayne Dowdy and staff of Memphis and Shelby County Collection, Memphis and Shelby County Public Library.
Edwin G. Frank, former Curator of Special Collections and Mississippi Valley Collection.
Ned McWherter Library, University of Memphis.
Carolyn Gates, late chair Germantown History Museum Committee and for Kimbrough family traditions.
Sylvia Harris, Library Assistant, Germantown Regional History and Genealogy Center.
Elisabeth P. Hughes, late Shelby County Genealogist and local research historian.
Marilyn Bell Hughes, Archivist, Tennessee State Library and Archives.
Howard Johnson, late and formerly member Germantown United Methodist Church History Committee.
Jennifer Lynch, Senior Research Analyst, Postal History, U.S. Post Office.
Joyce McKibben for her invaluable indexes of local, historical newspapers.
Andrew Pouncey, City Historian and long-time activist resurrecting local history.
Jane Sanderson, for Mosby and Sanderson family traditions.
Frank Stewart, Shelby County Archives.

George Sunder, Germantown Regional History and Genealogy Center library and archive.

Tina Swanson, Branch Manager, Germantown Regional History and Genealogy Center library and archive.

Susan Thompson for Dr. Martin's family traditions.

Walter Wills, preservationist of Kirby Farms and Woodlawn and for Kirby-Brooks family papers and traditions.

ABBREVIATIONS

CSA RR Confederate Railroads (web site)
FB The Freedman's Bureau Online, Tennessee.
GBS Google Book Search
GM Germantown Museum, The (Virtual Museum)
GN *Germantown News*
GPC Germantown Presbyterian Church, Historical Display
GHPC Germantown Historical Preservation Committee
GRH&GC Germantown Regional History and Genealogy Center
GUMCA Germantown United Methodist Church Archive
M&SC Memphis and Shelby County Room, Benjamin L. Hooks Central Library, Memphis
MCA Memphis Conference Archives, United Methodist Church
MVC Mississippi Valley Collection, Special Collections, McWerther Library, University of Memphis
NPS *National Park Service Website, Civil War Soldiers and Sailors System*
NARA National Archives and Records Administration
OR *War of the Rebellion: Official Record of the Union and Confederate Armies*
SCA Shelby County Archives
SHS Southern Historical Society Papers
SOR *Supplement to the War of the Rebellion*
TCWSB Tennessee Civil War Source Book
THS Tennessee Historical Society Quarterly
TNGenweb Shelby County, Tennessee Genealogy and History
TSL&A Tennessee State Library and Archives
VRHC Valentine Richmond History Center
WTHS Western Tennessee Historical Society Papers

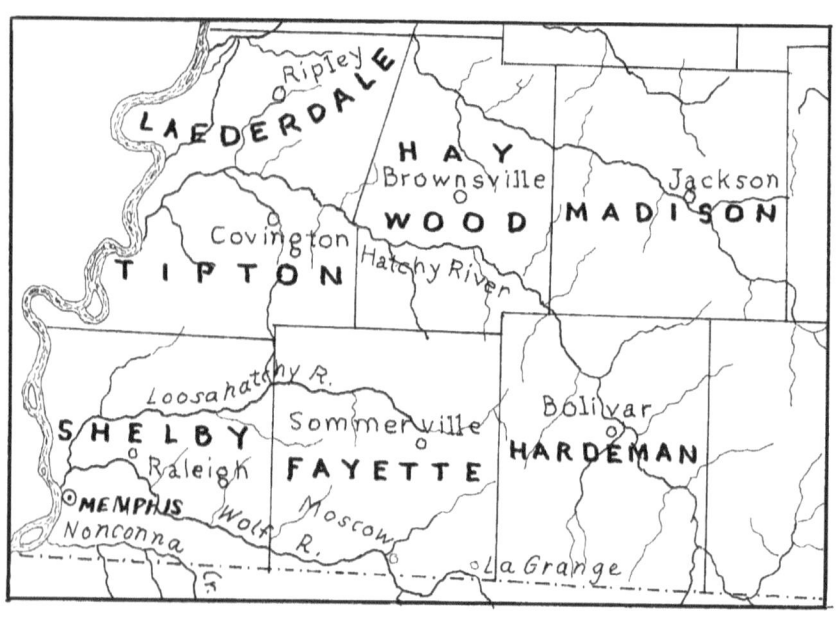

MAP 1 Counties of Southwest Tennessee.

INTRODUCTION

Our subject is the people who inhabited the area around Germantown, Tennessee. That area and the larger context in which it lay provided a special environment. Although today the present city of Germantown is almost surrounded by Memphis and its eastern border with the city of Collierville, in those days it was fifteen "country miles" from Memphis and surrounded by farms and plantations, dense woods and wild river bottoms. Although by no means a unique community in the mid-nineteenth-century South, its location had produced some promising opportunities and differences from our common perceptions of them. Unfortunately, however, life in that environment would also encounter a succession of overwhelming obstacles that sorely tested the inhabitants.

That location in the south-west corner of the state sets the stage. Tennessee is divided into three distinct "grand divisions," East, Middle and West. West Tennessee in particular has more in common with its three neighboring states than with the rest of its own. Settled latest, even by the 1840s it was just emerging from a wild frontier environment. For example, the county had recently been paying bounties for wolf scalps to end predation on livestock. Consequently, by the middle of the century, much of its adult population had been shaped by frontier mores. Under subsequent war-time conditions, lawless and violent proclivities would reemerge adding to the intensity of guerrilla warfare and its post-war residue. Also southwest Tennessee was the most committed to cotton farming and its connection with slavery. Bound by the Tennessee and Mississippi rivers and penetrated by several significant tributaries, even before the arrival of the railroads, large parts of West Tennessee had been more accessible to outside markets for cash-crop farming such as cotton, corn and livestock, and the lumber industry.

This western division was also very diverse. On the East, the rich Tennessee valley was separated from the rest by the hilly western Highland Rim, orienting the valley people eastward. West of the rim, one finds the dominant character of the region. Around the Mississippi and its many tributaries lay the swampy bottomlands with their frequent floods and unhealthy conditions. As a result, the higher bluff area around Memphis was the only part of the western counties that was densely populated by 1860. All the northern counties along the river were more sparsely inhabited. A few communities concentrated along the bluffs over the river and ridges between the streams. Even the fertile lands between these rivers developed differently. The northern counties, the Plateau Slope crossed by river floodplains, remained less densely populated, providing the ideal base for guerrilla raiders during the war. Its population was also more strongly divided over secession. The southern part, especially its south-west counties, was in the cotton belt. It would be a constant field of operations for both guerrillas and cavalry-raiders out of Mississippi.[1]

Lying in the southwest corner of the state, Shelby County was unique in the division (Map 1). The large urban center of Memphis provided the most prominent distinction. By 1850, it had given Shelby the second largest population in the state. Despite this urban center, Shelby was third in the production of cotton, behind only Fayette and Marion. It held the second largest number of slaves after Fayette. Yet north of the Loosahatchie River, it was more thinly developed. South of it lay a much more densely settled and developed area with Raleigh on the upper bend of the Wolf River, the county seat and second largest community. But specifically the southern high ridge running between the Wolf and Nonconnah Creek was well settled. There lay the towns of White's Station, Germantown and Collierville.

The area included in this study is more than that of the modern city of Germantown. The community "greater Germantown," was far more than just the chartered township. Specifically, it encompassed the much larger area served then by the Germantown post office. That included all of what was then Civil District Eleven, running from the Wolf River on the north to the state line in the south. The western side of the district lay well west of the present city's border almost to White Station, while the eastern border with Civil District Ten bisects the present city. Beyond into District Ten, the postal service included another fourteen households living along roads leading into Germantown from as far east as Bray's Station, including the settlement of Forest Hill. North of the Wolf in both Districts Seven and Nine lay a dozen or so households, also tied to Germantown as their social and economic center.

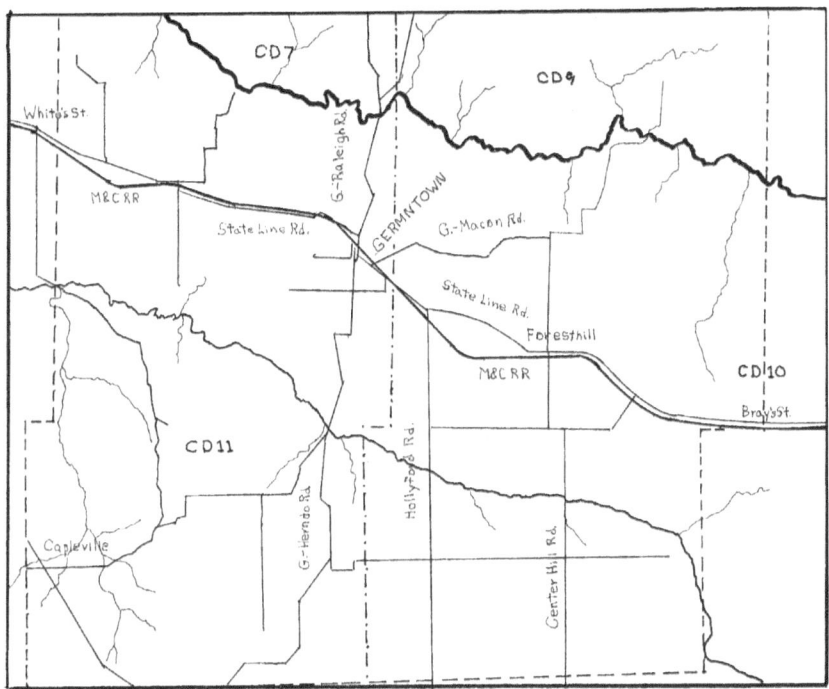

MAP 2 Approximate area of greater Germantown, 1860.

By 1860, this total area included a population over 900 white people and well over 1300 slaves.

◆ ◆ ◆

The entire South suffered from the war. Some places recovered, even thrived, while others did not. After starting to recover, Germantown nevertheless suffered the latter fate. There was a complete shift of the local economic and population center from Germantown to Collierville.

Before 1860, however, Germantown was the dominant economic and population center along the transportation lines from Memphis through Shelby and Fayette counties. Its advantage was being a crossroads positioned along those lines into Memphis. In 1850, Germantown, Collierville and LaFayette (present Rossville in Fayette County) were relatively equal in population, and theoretically had the same advantages. Germantown's total population was

245 including slaves; Collierville's was 236, while LaFayette's was 216. But the 1854 *New and Complete Gazetteer of the United States* was soon painting a very unequal picture. While it only gave Collierville and LaFayette simple one-line descriptions as post-villages, it described a more dynamic Germantown. "A thriving post-village of Shelby County, Tennessee, near Wolf River, and on the Memphis and Charleston Railroad, 15 miles E. of Memphis, is situated in a rich cotton growing district, and has an active trade. Population, about 400." This population figure indicated an explosive growth. Another indicator of preeminence—Germantown's post office was the second most heavily used in Shelby County. The town also provided much of the political leadership of county government. It was almost as industrial as agricultural in its economy, with three or four operations that could be termed factories, plus all the usual smithies, mechanic's shops, gins and mills. Not just a transportation hub, the town was also a cultural center with prestigious private academies and colleges. Consequently, it attracted many professionals and merchants.

Despite local traditions, it is impossible to access how extensively both Collierville and Germantown had been destroyed by war's end. Clearly, however, by 1870, that destruction had already added to changes in their relative positions. While Germantown's population had sunk to 197 white and "colored," and LaFayette's to 161, Collierville had 274. This shift in the balance would increase. Collierville emerged as the major center of economic activity for Shelby and Fayette counties and De Soto County, Mississippi. According to the Bureau of Agriculture, in 1874 Collierville had a population of 1,000, "quite a pleasant and prosperous village," that had "been built up since the war." About 1,200 bales of cotton shipped out of the town annually, and it had "about twenty-two business houses, mostly supply stores." In contrast, Germantown was simply "a pretty little village ... with a population of 350. It has three general churches, a cotton gin, and two groceries." While Germantown retained its simple prewar rows of shops, offices and industry, Collierville blossomed with a grand town square of storefronts, a two-story hotel, public parks, and a boulevard lined with fine homes. It consisted of many acres of neat residential town lots on a grid of rectangular streets running from above what would become Poplar Avenue to across the tracks, contrasting with Germantown's irregular, mixed-use lots. Although there had been considerable recovery in both communities before the great Yellow Fever epidemic in 1878, by 1888 that blow had brought Germantown's population back down to 200. Thereafter there was little growth, and it remained a sleepy little town until the 1970s.

Yet, the relative decline in the population and economic prominence of Germantown is not the most interesting part of the town's story. The impact of the war and emancipation on the community—on its people psychologically, socially and culturally, on its cohesiveness and the general character of life—though difficult to tease out, offers the best story. The impact of war and natural disaster went far deeper than economic destruction and loss of life.

◆ ◆ ◆

This is the story of Germantown, of the community's people, their vices and virtues, foibles and failures, secrets and successes. It paints a picture of a community that was mostly lost as well as changes in the life of its citizens before, during and after that war. Such a perspective is hard to recapture, for ordinary people rarely recorded their experiences. When they did, those records have rarely survived, or they remain buried in dust-covered boxes. Today, even the family traditions that were once recited and elaborated as everyone sat around in the evening are no longer being passed along. Such stories and records are badly needed to give this history more flesh and blood. I hope any readers who have such stories about Germantown and its people or any documents to share will contact me. But especially those with anything that challenges my impressions.

PART 1

ANTEBELLUM GERMANTOWN

As war loomed in 1860, Germantown was a rapidly growing but peaceful town. By the late 1830s, it and nearby Pea Ridge had already become sufficiently significant settlements to appear on local maps. The state legislature had offhandedly incorporated it in 1841, and then fully chartered it in 1850. During the 1840s and 50s, it outpaced the surrounding communities and emerged as a "place of note."[1] As it grew, it generated major crossroads with the State Line Road focusing local trade on the town. Then the arrival of the Memphis-Charleston Railroad made it even more economically vibrant and gave it a strategic importance during the forthcoming war. The town proper had become more than a typical Southern rural village serving an agricultural countryside. Nevertheless, it and the surrounding agricultural population formed a coherent community that has to be seen as a whole.

This extended community of "greater Germantown" is best defined as those served by the Germantown post office in 1860. All these people saw the town as the center of their economic, social and cultural life. They not only came to town for their mail and the news, but also attended its churches and schools, conducted business and legal affairs, used its stores, saloons, and professional services, belonged to its fraternal and political organizations, attended militia musters and a wide range of social and cultural events.

As a chartered entity, the incorporated town only covered about one half a square mile. It was governed by a council of mayor and aldermen. Outside the town, however, the majority of the population was served by the elected officials of Civil District Eleven seated at the town. (Map 2) Civil districts were the major governmental subdivision of a county and came under the

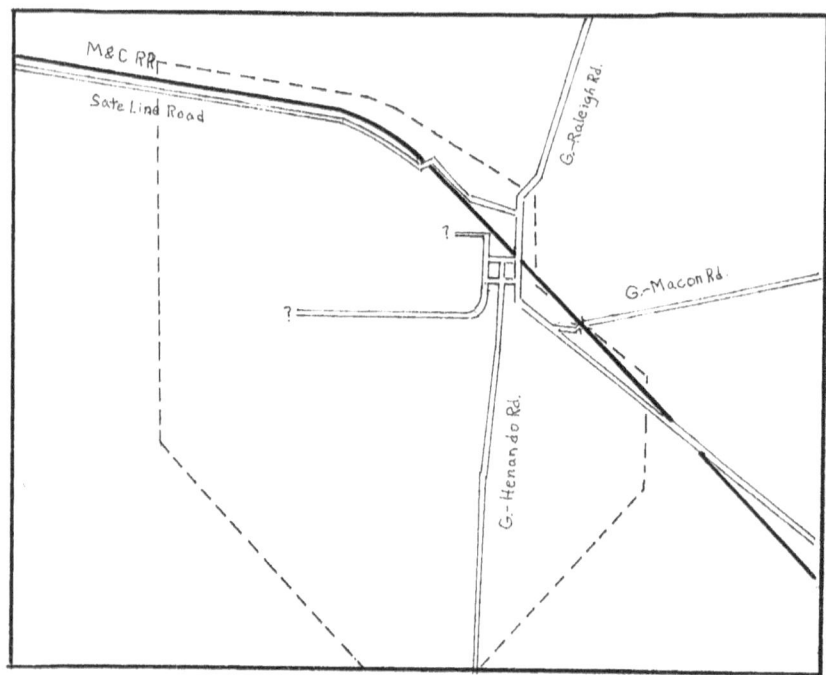

MAP 3 Approximate area of incorporated Germantown, 1850.

county governing body of the Quarterly Court. Since other members of the population of "Greater Germantown" lived in adjacent civil districts, especially District Ten, some of their political and legal affairs were managed in those districts. Nevertheless, much of their social, economic and cultural life focused on Germantown. Thus, people throughout the postal district identified themselves as "living near or around Germantown."

The town proper was defined essentially by the State Line Road, along which it ran for a mile. It spread from two-hundred yards north of that road to a half mile south.[2] Thus it encompassed little more than half a square mile straddling the State Line Road and running from its "town center" predominantly west toward Memphis. Its center was an irregular grid formed by three parallel streets and the intersection of roads connecting with practically every community in the adjacent counties of Tennessee and Mississippi.

Such a community lacked any clear urban versus rural, or any commercial or industrial versus residential divides. There was nothing like zoning. Even around the town center, homes, business and manufacturing shops mixed indiscriminately. Homes housed professional offices. Workshops were adjacent, if not part of family quarters. Along the major roads radiating out, homes were more widely spaced with townhouses indistinct from farmhouses, and also intermixed with industrial and commercial operations. Behind some of the houses near the roads or railroad tracks, lay farms of 40 to over 100 acres. Until one was well out of town, one could hardly know whether one had left the town's official limits and entered the countryside.

After its charter in 1850, there seem to be no records of an expansion of the town's corporate limits in either county or state archives, although numerous records of such expansions for other towns exist. Apparently, the leading citizens saw no advantage in expanding their jurisdiction, despite a burgeoning population. Or perhaps, the "country-folk" saw no advantage in paying extra taxes. Thus town-like shops and enterprises lay outside the official limits.

This prosperous community would soon find itself in the center of a theater of guerrilla warfare. It would undergo all the vicissitudes of war, pillaging, intermittent firefights, occupation, and emancipation and post-war Reconstruction. Many of its men "met the elephant," experiencing combat with all its physical and psychological effects that they brought back home. Comprehending the impact of a bitter local partisan and cavalry-raiding warfare on soldier and civilian alike requires a comparison of both antebellum and post-war society to reveal its consequences. Likewise for relations among the black and white citizens, for whom the heritage of slavery birthed some of the most brutal aspects of that war and exaggerated the smoldering racial tensions that followed.

The chapters of Part 1 will paint a picture of that antebellum life. We will explore every possible aspect of those lives, not just to experience their flavor and color, but also to establish a base line for revealing the full spectrum of change brought by the war and the post-war experience. We will see some stark contrasts in Part 3.

1

THE WHITE FOLKS AND THEIR LIVES

During the three decades prior to the war, what was a frontier area became fully settled. From the very beginning, the vast majority merely passed through. Mobility if not instability was a characteristic of the population. Those who moved on were replaced by others seeking opportunity.

There are no census data broken down for the town in 1860, only for civil districts. Census schedules fail to indicate town residence. Thus, it is impossible to know the exact population of the town proper.[1] A conservative estimate would be perhaps 85 households with 450 white citizens, although one resident remembered as many as 500 to 600.[2] The problem with such estimates is that, as already described, there were no perceptible borders between town and country. The town's population had at least doubled during the 1850s. It had literally burst its seams, expanding north, and east along the major arteries.

The rural community that focused on the town and was served by its post office consisted of all of Civil District Eleven and the western half of District Ten, plus a few families living along the northern bank of the Wolf River above those two districts (Map 2). From the Wolf, it ran to the Mississippi line. By 1860, the total population exceeded 900 white people and well over 1500 slaves.

The first settlers arriving by the 1830s were a diverse group. Many were self-sufficient yeoman farmers, Appalachian types from the east and hill-folk from the Deep South. Some were fleeing the growing money-market and eastern slave economies.[3] All brought their families and meager possessions by flat boat or over the rugged inland trials. They were repeating the story of their hardy frontier ancestors, too cash poor to acquire lands elsewhere.

Also in significant numbers, however, were planter families from the tidewater states or the Deep South. Although they also had to follow trails through the wilderness, they brought their slave labor, a more complete supply of equipment, livestock, and the material comforts of home.[4] Of course, this group varied greatly in degree of wealth. Some more closely resembled the Appalachian types, except for the possession of slaves to clear their land. They were attracted by the rich soil, not exhausted by decades of cotton farming. Some were also less comfortable in the societies they left behind for different reasons.

A third group formed a less agriculturally inclined "middle class," merchants to set up stores, professionals like doctors and lawyers, and mechanics to build mills and blacksmith shops of their own. They sought opportunities less constrained by competition.

Life in mid-nineteenth century America was far less stable than our romantic images. Only about 16% of the town's 1850 families remained in 1860, and mortality was not the cause. What seemed to have been stable businesses in a rapidly growing community had been turned over to newcomers. Most all the families of men who had worked for others, journeymen, shop workers, overseers, and laborers had moved on. Their greatest hope for advancement lay in relocation. Even farmsteads turned over surprisingly, for only 22% of the 1850 farm families in District 11 remained in 1860. Americans in general moved frequently in search of greener fields. To account for all this movement, there was a good deal of upward mobility out of western Tennessee. The opening of Texas and the fertile delta lands of Arkansas combined with veterans' bonus-lands offered desirable opportunities.[5]

The rural population of the district actually declined during the 1850s. For one reason, yeomen farmers again found it increasingly difficult to compete against growing slave-labor. Also an interesting argument put forth by Steve Baker contends that the massive influx of black slaves made whites uncomfortable. The almost universally held beliefs depicted blacks as inherently and dangerously savage. Fear of bloody slave revolts was widespread.[6] If true, there is nothing new about white flight.

For farmers, another cause was simply the vicissitudes of their life. For instance, in June of 1846, a hailstorm totally destroyed the cotton crops of even major planters. Within five miles of Germantown, it dumped a swath of destruction three miles long and a quarter mile wide, covering the ground to a depth of eight inches.[7] A yet more common problem—two years in a row, one small farmer lost much of his corn when cattle or hogs got into his fields, and once he lost seven acres of cotton.[8] Any new arrivals, like this man, who had

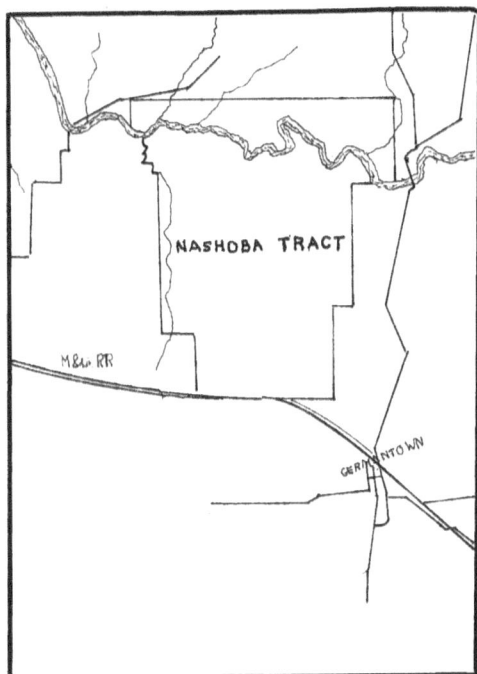

MAP 4 Nashoba tract at Germantown.

just put in their first crop and needed it to cover their startup expenses would be further in debt or go under.

Isham Howse is an example of a farmer who came and went between 1850 and 1860. He was not "typical" in that his major problem was such poor health that he could do little farm work himself. He relied on his older sons and four slaves, who were also older and infirm. He had given up as a merchant and farmer elsewhere. He owned acreage and town lots in several other Tennessee and Mississippi counties that he rented while trying to sell them. He was drawn to the area for its favorable communications with markets, and a favorable arrangement with Fanny Wright to operate her Nashoba lands. The large Nashoba Tract was a project of Frances Wright in 1825 intended to be a model for the emancipation of slaves. She soon had to abandon it as a failure.[9]

Howse, his family, and servants suffered from constant bouts of "chills". He was unable to make enough to cover his debts and left after the 1853 season. He had sold his other properties and could set himself up again as a merchant in Mississippi.[10] In that respect, his story was similar to that of others on their way through.

A common problem was clearing enough land—basically a function of affording enough slaves to do the work. Most farmers could improve less than half their acreage. Plowing new land was arduous, for the roots and stumps of trees endured for many years. The Kimbrough's Cotton Plant Plantation, with 89 slaves, 19 mules and 10 oxen to pull out the stumps, had only 700 improved acres of its 1600 total. Since cotton rapidly exhausted the land, the pressure was on to clear more, leaving the smallholder at a disadvantage.[11]

Finally, no matter how much farmers and planters liked to see themselves as independent, they functioned as dependents of the urban banking and market complex. Despite their status, most planters usually had to work through the cotton factors and bankers in Memphis. In a cash poor economy, they needed ready cash, especially to buy expensive slaves. Loans and debt were intricate parts of the cycle of planation operations. Also anyone trying to sell locally lost a considerable percentage of the value of his crop. Instead, he tried for market prices at places like New Orleans. Memphis merchants, as middle men, maintained warehouses to store the farmer's cotton and then negotiated shipping to market where their contacts sold it for the farmer. In turn, they or their affiliates imported manufactured goods the country folk needed. They kept open books with their customers who entrusted their crop to them when it came in.[12]

In contrast, to gain economic independence, the more entrepreneurial expanded into direct cotton trading. Men like Joseph Brooks managed their business directly with New Orleans. The Brooks family had been involved in mercantile activity since its arrival in the 1830s.[13]

Otherwise, through this complicated process, a percentage of the market value of the crop went to the merchant. To give the farmer money, he went to a local bank to draw a draft or bill of exchange on the firm, primarily in New Orleans, that would receive the crop. This was a bank loan that carried a fee plus interest until the final sale of the crop in three to four months. The agent also took a percentage, usually 2.5 percent, and sent the proceeds to the Memphis merchant who credited the remainder to the planter's account.[14]

The small farmer simply had to sell directly to local merchants. They filled his needs on credit until his crop came in. He was tied to them and took lower local market prices. He lived in a world of semi-subsistence that combined credit and barter.[15]

Part of this complex relationship was the instability of paper money, still in its early stages of evolution. There were a handful of private banks operating in Memphis. The federal government allowed such banks to issue their own paper money. Such bills could only be used for local business, however, and could only be redeemed at the issuing bank. If so many sought redemptions that they exceeded the bank's reserves, its bills could become useless until the bank recouped those reserves. There was no federal insurance, and Memphis operations had no backing elsewhere. Bank failures were common in the frequent depressions, threatening local farmers and businessmen who held their depressed or valueless notes.[16] The great world-wide depression of 1837 resulted in more than fifty foreclosures in the county.[17]

The expense of acquiring enough slaves for operations also required bank loans. Deaths and financial distress involved the banks in repossessions and resales. Thus, the banks were heavily and directly involved in slavery and its trade. The collapse of a bank could leave its debtors finding themselves in the hands of a new creditor.

Significant to this struggle for survival was the livestock of every farmer. With less than half the land cleared, there was plenty of woodland for the free ranging of pigs, cattle, and sheep. One could brand and let them loose until time to harvest them. The papers were full of notices of the apprehension of some widely ranged horse or cow that could be retrieved from the captor. Consequently, the farmer not the owner of livestock was responsible for protecting his fields. One was even legally responsible for having fencing that was "horse high, bull strong and hog tight."[18] If you did not have such "fencing-insurance," you operated at great risk.

With all of these problems facing both agriculturalists and town folk, there was a constant search for better positions. All this mobility makes the growth of Germantown proper seem that much more significant. Far more people saw opportunity around the town than did those who left.

Family Life

The 1860 census provides pictures of family life.[19] In a typical household, there were three children, but up to nine was not uncommon Mostly the number of children depended on the length of the marriage. For example, Job Lewis, age 38, had his own farm by at least 1850, with a twenty-five-year-old wife, Barbara, and four young children. By 1860, there were seven children.

ILL.1 Taking the Census. *Harper's Weekly*, 11.19.1870. A typical extended family household often included three generations plus siblings, cousins, nieces or nephews, employees, servants, and sometimes boarders.

It was also common for extended family members to be present, such as grandparents or siblings or cousins of the husband and/or wife. In addition, a household often included one or more boarders who lived and worked in the town or a farm. For example, in 1850 wagon-maker Lewellen (or Lon Allen) Rhodes and his wife Rachel housed his younger brother or cousin as an assistant. By 1860, this family with six children also included his older sister and an older gentleman, probably Rachel's father. The boot-maker family of Julius and Mary Resten had only one child, but included (probably) her mother, a carpenter as a boarder, and an eleven-year-old girl, who could have been a foundling taken on for service. The childless farm family of William and Elizabeth Brooks had three Mosby children, apparently orphans from her family.

Tennessee and Shelby County were conscientious about protecting apprentices and guaranteeing their rights. There were provisions against "immoderate correction," and apprentices had the right to appeal to the court against mistreatment or negligence. Since neighbors often helped bring the complaints, we have a measure of a community's sense of collective responsibility. In 1845, Thomas Bleckley, a farmer east of town, was forced to give up his apprentice, Mary Joyce, on an allegation of mistreatment.[20]

There were no records of apprentices in skilled labor in Germantown. They were all for farm or housework. Area residents seemed to prefer simply employing free children over contract servitude. They also had their hands full with orphans of family and friends. As for the orphans "of color" increasingly indentured during the 1840s-50s, locals preferred the long-range investment in slave children.[21]

For other measures of intimate relationships among the town's residents and their sense of communal responsibility, in 1850 the physician J. M. Cornelius and his wife Eliza cared for the four-year-old Louisa Ledbetter, perhaps an orphan. Ten years later, Edward Cornelius had inherited both his father's practice and Miss Ledbetter, attending a local school. The farm family of Julian and Virginia Bedford and their twin daughters hosted a five-year-old Edward, a seventy-one-year-old Ms. Lucy Kenney, a fifty year-old Mr. Haskins, and a twenty-eight year-old German immigrant, Mr. Angle. Mr. Haskins was titled a "gentleman," but was noted as "insane."

Germantown's families provided elder care, orphan asylum and job training, assisted-living and other social services. In some cases it was remunerated. In others, it grew from a sense of Christian duty and family responsibility. Overall, such a collective sense of social responsibility was typical of the pre-war community and requires comparison with post-war conditions.

♦ ♦ ♦

Also important for comparisons are gender relations. We see nineteenth century America, especially the South, as a rigidly patriarchal society in which women had no legal rights and played no public roles. Of course, Southerners rejected the classical model of patriarchy, believing instead that their familial relationships were based on Christian models of love and protection.[22] There was some truth to that. Studies of the letters and journals of Southern ladies reveal the female perspective. Reliant on their men for protection, security, and an appropriate status, they also expected such as part of the proper order of things. Theirs was the private world of home and family. With few exceptions, most accepted gender differences as absolutely clear and biologically determined, just like "racial" differences. Such a reality dictated life choices and aspirations. Women were subordinate, dependent, and drew no attention. Simply to have one's name in the paper for even an innocent reason was as bad as being the object of gossip.[23] There were, of course, exceptions.

No matter how clearly people accepted such ideals, generalizations obscure the subtle realities. First of all, young ladies did not always toe the line. We shall hear of their alcohol adventures in the Center Hill Academy, and of men having to defend the honor of their female relatives accused of improper behavior. As for genteel femininity, in 1863 a Federal officer would observe that the young ladies of Germantown "invariably . . . have some excessively vulgar habit. Yesterday two young misses of sweet 16 or 18 were in to get a pass and they were quite good looking & pleasant. But great scott, how they would spit half way across a good sized room was easily accomplished."[24] Undoubtedly-frontier crudeness and proper decorum mixed unevenly in local families.

The older generation of women had all survived a pioneer experience, mostly coming over the mountains in wagons or down rivers on flat boats. Such ladies were hardly "helpless females." The reality was mixed, but frequently more like that of the "steel magnolia," with the woman of the household exercising her own influence. Many women mastered the art of deferring to conventions while leveraging for their own space or even getting their own way. Ultimately the individual personalities of each partner determined real power and personal relationships. In the "household economy," the management of the house, food and clothing, its processing and production, and in matters of the arts and culture, of child rearing, family health and entertainment, the women ran things. A man might or might not criticize the results. Many found it more comfortable to be "above" involvement in the woman's world.

One well established planter remembers that his mother "in addition to usual household duties, did carding, weaving, spinning etc." In this, she was assisted by a cook and a house girl. Another remembers his mother as "looking after her household duties" with four or five household servants.[25] Ladies and women could be personally productive and self-reliant in many ways. In many households she also ran something like a bread and breakfast. Also Germantown society did not doom the mistress to the isolation of plantation life more typical of the Deep South, for she had access to more social support and extended contact.

Among agriculturalists, the man's world was the fields and the hands who worked them, the processing of the produce and their marketing. In the world of business and industry the same applied. For everyone, aside from the church, anything public was the man's world, business, politics, law, taxes and the defense of home and community. Defending family honor was especially the male's responsibility. More specific examples of complex gender relations locally will emerge below.

In Germantown, the profession of teaching was the only exception open to proper women. Otherwise, roles were limited to church work, charity, and cultural affairs, but even those were not performed with any public notice. Even teaching was seen as a mere "position" for wives and daughters living with their parents. In the census, women with teaching positions would not list an occupation, except wife or homemaker. Likewise, no midwives appear in the census, although experienced women often performed that function.

There reached a point, however, when a woman was "emancipated" and had full control over her affairs. When a widow inherited the estate, legally at least one-third, she might proceed as head of household with only legal niceties in the hands of a trustee. Such women in the Germantown area were the planters Sarah Jones, Maria Scruggs and Sarah Walker. For example, Mrs. Scruggs exercised the responsibility for providing her "hands" to do road work, and she took it upon herself to advance tuition for the Woodward orphans.[26] The one area in which women usually acknowledged incompetence was the management of recalcitrant field-hands. If she did not have an overseer, she called on an available male.[27]

Locally more progressive husbands allowed their wives to hold property in their own names and designated them as executors of their wills, while protective parents tried to ensure that property going to their daughters remained free from the debts or mismanagement of their husbands.[28] Unfortunately, we cannot measure future changes in such local "liberating" trends as consequences of the war. Nor can we compare them quantitatively against other regions. Nevertheless, they are a measure of the progressive side of the community.

Below the "genteel levels" of society, we have few pictures of the reality of gender relations. There again, however, much had to depend on individual personalities. A hard life made some women as tough as nails and unbending to male dominance. Others were broken into total submission. The typical yeoman wife certainly considered herself as much a model of respectability as any other. The vast majority of all women around Germantown were literate, putting them well above southern averages.[29]

In the more typical yeoman family or that of smaller merchants and mechanics, the wife had to participate in a much broader range in the family's economy. They might handle sales or clerical work in a business, or on the farm help in the fields, and deliver and negotiate the sale or barter of milk, eggs and cheese. They were more involved in the broader economy than the privileged. Nevertheless, no local censuses listed them as anything but "home makers" or "keeping house".

Yet at all levels, women were part of a changing world, and a few were aggressive about making those changes. In their capacity as models of morality, the pressure of their Christian consciences drove them to the fringes of the private realm. They openly joined their pastors in such righteous crusades as the temperance movement. Ladies' societies also involved them in other charitable and reform activities, including fund raising. Yet before the war, this was always under the supervision of pastors and laymen, and their names were not to be publicized. For Germantown, this "purely private" behavior would undergo post-war changes.

✦ ✦ ✦

Although "dependent" children were expected to work far more than today, even the yeomen and poor farm kids had some time for "play." Although the only recorded childhood memories for Germantown date from the 1870s, things could not have changed much. Before school and during recess, the school yard was a loud and boisterous gathering place. Indoor and outdoor games resembled today's. Parties for that part of society that held them were less fun—"there was too much formality."[30]

Of course, Christmas was a special occasion. Memphis papers advertised toys specifically for Santa Claus to provide. He was eagerly awaited by some, and children rushed to their stockings for special treats, of a sort not normally available. Families of means bought manufactured toys advertised in the papers or mail-order catalogs, but more typical was something simple and handmade. Torpedoes and firecrackers were essential ingredients, even for surprisingly young children.[31]

Girls of any class were hardly restrained, at least not before menarche.

Fathers took girls hunting and fishing. They learned to shoot and ride. Aside from playtime, they had to learn all the skills performed by their mothers. Of course, a respectable young lady had to live with constraints that protected her against all the "threats" to her respectability. Preserving the honor of the family was impressed upon them as strongly as upon boys, but with a significant double standard. By the same token, internal fortitude and toughness were essential qualities to develop. Learning to balance all that against the necessity of showing proper respect to male authority must have generated a great deal of ambivalence. Any gender equality in early childhood had to evolve into propriety.

Boys, of course, had more freedom, running through the woods and fields and swimming in the Wolf, where making it across was a rite of passage. As today, that river provided sand bars and beaches. A favorite gathering place in town was the platform of the depot, especially for those intent on mischief. Older boys enjoyed egging the younger into fights. No boy could refuse a dare that could lead to a fight. He would be "discounted and humiliated." It was rough and tumble with no rules, but few got seriously hurt. Boys of all classes were conditioned from early on for a manly defense of honor. Such fighting was essential to the mutual respect that produced life-long bonds of friendship and trust.[32]

Social and Cultural Life

Contemporary references do not paint a consistent picture. An 1846 add for a new private school boasted of "the health, intelligence and good morals of the surrounding community." According to an 1858 railroad handbook, "the inhabitants are generally moral, intelligent, and a reading people; supporting three churches. . . ." Yet in 1872, a witty proponent of the town reflected that "Germantown was once famous mainly for drunken brawls. It was filled with whiskey-shops, and there were roaring old debauchees about the village." Indeed, there were more than an ample number of saloons for the population, and in 1858, such establishments were castigated for being the source of liquor imported illicitly to corrupt the young ladies of Semple Broaddus College of nearby Center Hill, Mississippi.[33] How does one square such images?

Isham Howse also painted a mixed picture. He described a community of friendly and supportive people with an active social life, constantly visiting one another and attending church events, yet bemoaned drunkards of whom he sternly disapproved. As for the environment, he wrote

> It is a beautiful country to the eye, and remarkably convenient to market, etc., but it is sickening to the heart. Labor is not rewarded, and disease lurk about in ambush, ready to seize upon and devour the whole people. . . . This is a pleasant place to live, and possesses many rare conveniences; but I feel now that I would not accept the whole estate as a gift. . . .

He and his family suffered bad health on the Nashoba estate. He also noted that his planter neighbor, Britten Duke, shared his objections to the country, "its sickness, and its poor, unproductive soil."[34]

Again, in contrast, the earlier settler, Wilks Brooks, wrote, "we have the best country taking into consideration all the things that I have seen, we have the health, the climate, soil and near this grate river where we can git any thing from a northern or southern market at fair prices."[35]

Actually, the quality of the soil varied greatly.[36] As for sickness, "chills" were not unique to the area, but were common throughout those parts of the South. House's fixation on diseases probably resulted from his own condition. Given their ignorance of the causes of the various "fevers," people commonly believed that higher elevations were healthier and constantly sought refuge in Germantown from disease ridden Memphis. There was one point of agreement, however, the area was ideally situated for commerce. Unfortunately, Howse's apocalyptic prediction about disease devouring the people would come true after the war. Before that, however, we have plentiful evidence for balancing out the picture among the other contradictory images.

Education

Another area for interesting contrasts. Public education in Tennessee was always of unequal quality, but generally poor. State support and guidance were hampered by graft, indifference and opposition to taxes. Shelby County at least sought eventually to provide a modicum of "common" schooling. Generally, however, private schooling was favored, especially around Germantown, initially retarding public education, but gradually producing an environment with rich educational opportunities.

Since 1829, the state had authorized local taxes for the support of common schools and began to distribute funds gained from land sales. Yet, "common schools" remained underfunded into the 1850s. Then in 1854, the Legislature passed an act establishing Tennessee's first state tax for public schools, which seems to have promoted more interest in public education around Germantown, since they were already paying for it.[37]

Meanwhile beginning in 1851, women had been allowed to teach in Tennessee's common schools and to draw pay equal to the males. Regardless of gender, competence was a problem. Not until 1856, did the state finally impose a requirement on the counties to maintain one or more Common School Commissioners responsible for certifying the teachers hired for the common schools. The subjects of competency included primarily spelling (orthography), reading, writing, arithmetic, geography and English grammar.[38] From all indications, competence requirements were not well enforced, and particularly Shelby County was as late as 1860 in conforming.[39]

Most local historians report the tradition that from 1833 Germantown operated a school in a multipurpose log building. Needham Harrison remembered attending a "comfortable log schoolhouse," which should have been between 1847 and 1854. He described it as a private school.[40] It was probably a subscription school, whereby the community provided a building, while a teacher earned his living giving instruction for a fee per student. Apparently during the 1840s, county school funds could be used to pay such subscription fees as "tuition from the common school fund." In 1846, for instance, the district's school commissioners dispensed all its allotted funds to seven men and one woman for teaching, in some cases as few as two students.[41]

In addition to the tradition of a common log schoolhouse, surviving records mention only one school building by name, Dukes School House, named after Britton Duke and located on his land west of town nearer Pea Ridge. He had initially funded its construction and provided the land. The teachers commonly boarded with the Dukes, initially using the building as a subscription school.[42] Descriptions of it do not correspond with stories of a log school house, so initially there may have been two common purpose buildings serving as subscription schools. There are indications that by 1860 Duke's was the only dedicated school building.

As we shall see in the fourth chapter, the records of the county and district school commissioners are incomplete, and sometimes grossly contradictory, making it difficult to fully reconstruct the history of the earliest local public schooling. By 1850, it seems the district's commissioners had become more parsimonious with school funds, perhaps distributing them only for tuition for poor and orphaned students. For instance, in 1853 when Isham Howse arranged for his three oldest sons to attend the writing school of Samuel Holmes, Sr., Howse had to pay the tuition. His sons obviously were not getting county funds. Meanwhile, Howse's wife felt qualified to supplement their income with her own subscription school for younger children, apparently also without public funding. Holmes gave up his subscription school in the spring of 1853, finding that "his prospects about here are rather unpromising."[43]

By this time, the people of the district had apparently abandoned the idea of any publicly supported education. The district commissioners of the common school reported that for the years 1853/54 there had been no common school or teachers for the eleventh district. Neither had there been any commissioners in office until September 1854, so the community had acquired no funds.[44] Community leaders were probably satisfied with private schools, for Needham Harrison, remembered only private schools. He attended for seven years and five months to age nineteen, traveling two and half to three miles to get there. He remembered the schools as operating for ten months per year, the boys and girls attending regularly, although "sometimes during the press of farm work (they) aided in that work as they some do at this time."[45] His class-biased perspective led him to ignore the total absence of the propertyless.

Germantown's subsequent turnaround in attitudes related to two developments: the arrival in town of John W. A. Pettit in 1852, and the availability of state-tax money after 1854. Previously in Memphis, Pettit had been heavily involved in that city's efforts to establish a free public school system in the late 1840s, after which he was elected first superintendent. In district eleven, he would sit on the school commission from September 1854 to June 1856, bringing into being fully funded public schools.[46]

Before that, the system of subscription schooling had created an unstable instructional environment. Teachers commonly moved about among the districts from session to session, even month to month. When the district began its free common school in 1854, it operated sometimes two, one at the Duke School and another in a rented facility in town. From then until 1860, Pettit's young wife and oldest daughter and Achilles N. Plunkett carried most of the teaching load providing consistency. Earlier, Plunkett, a more established professional, had lived in the adjacent 12th district where he taught and boarded a number of students. He and his family had settled in Germantown by 1859.[47]

Finally in 1861, Miss Julia Pettit, twenty-year-old daughter of the Judge and newly certified, became the teacher at the common school. In October of that year, she instructed thirty-three "scholars," for which her pay varied from thirty-three to thirty-six dollars a month, depending on the number of students served. Providing fuel for heat was the collective responsibility of the parents, except any considered indigent.[48]

The significant presence of women among the district's teachers brings us back to gender roles locally. In most parts of the South, women had not been encouraged to teach before the war. Also women's education did not prepare them for competency examinations.[49] Yet the town's women had increasingly taken up the role as early as the 1840s. Another example of how local women seem to have been more progressive.

The annual survey of the "scholastic population" counted children of ages between six and twenty-one. The state based its funding to the county and district on this "scholastic population." For distribution in 1861, it allotted district eleven $133.25 for its total of 205, not all of whom were attending.[50] Clearly public education was poorly funded.

The education thus provided was basic, and it is unclear what constituted competency for advancement to an academy. There was no grading by age, and with attendance so irregular there could be little correlation between age and achievement. One teacher's pay record indicated that his students ranged from ages 5 to 14.[51]

Tuition could also be provided for the county academy. That academy was located at Raleigh, which obviously required boarding. There were two academies, one for boys, one for girls. A typical Tennessee academy had only two teachers and served 58 students.[52] Whatever the quality of education available, private institutions of "higher" learning were preferred. And that is precisely what gave Germantown its cultural status, achieved far earlier than the evolution of common schools.

One such private school had become available in the early 1840s when Randolph Webb opened the Webb School for Boys in his house east of town off State Line Road (present Nurnberger House, 2576 Germanwood Lane).

P. 1 Webb School and Home, built 1840s. The front contained two classrooms, behind was the family wing.

From the road it still looks like a typical plantation-cottage, white clapboards, porch across the front, and one full-length window on each side of the door. Two classrooms fully occupied the front wing. One chimney on each side serviced fireplaces, and in later years probably potbellied stoves. Behind lay the family quarters where they boarded students.[53]

After graduating from the University of North Carolina, Webb had become an English teacher. According to one tradition, he and his family settled near town in 1832 on their 36-acre farm east of town.[54] Unfortunately he does not appear in the 1840 census for Shelby County, but rather in that for Madison, Alabama. By the 1850 census, he is listed as having a farm of 173 acres in Civil District Ten, just east of town, the site of the Webb school house. That is consistent with another family tradition that he arrived in 1849. Although the 1850 census lists him as farmer, that second family tradition titles him Dr. Webb, apothecary and education entrepreneur.[55]

Webb's school operated first as a boys' school and after his death in 1851 under his son Monroe as coeducational. The 1858 railroad handbook described it as "an excellent school for boys and girls." By 1860, his daughter Mary also taught while married to the nearby farmer Louis Lycurgus Thompson.[56]

It would take a few years for the area to support more significant private schools. Several attempts failed. One launched in 1837 by Thomas Pittman, Jr. and another in 1846 by Brooks Trezevant, both located about a mile and a half east of town on the State Line Road. Both had abandoned their projects within a year or two.[57] For at least a year, 1851/52, there was also a Germantown Female Academy, one of the teachers being Mrs. S. W. Ferguson, joining the growing ranks of women entering this professional field.[58] Efforts to launch academies had to induce parents to send their young scholars. Prestigious competitors advertised regularly in the newspapers, and parents solicited more information before making a choice. The Dukes invested the equivalent of a small fortune in the tuition and board for their eight children.[59]

The final heir to ambitious local operations opened in August 1854 firmly establishing the town's academic reputation. The Shelby Male High School appeared "a half mile East of Germantown, and facing the road on the north," west of the Webb School. It was described "fronting the Railroad."[60] Initially the teachers were Reverend Richard R. Evans, A. M. Rafter and L. B. Johnson. A. M. Rafter was Alexander Rafter, the twenty-three-year-old son of farmer James Rafter.[61]

Reverend Evans was the town's Presbyterian minister. Since the Rafters were founders of his church, that is undoubtedly how they hit upon the idea of opening the school when the young man graduated with academic credentials.[62]

The *Appeal*, so impressed with the new institution, gave considerable coverage to its first public examination. The school had already attracted forty to fifty students from Arkansas, Mississippi and Tennessee, with many from Memphis. "It seems to be the object of their teachers, not only to make them good scholars, but high toned gentlemen."[63]

For the evening "exhibition," a large "delegation of ladies and gentlemen from Memphis came out on an extra train of cars." The assembly began with a prayer and singing of the national anthem. A quartet entertained with other songs interspersed among eight essays, declamations and orations by students. Three local families proudly listened to the exercises of H. M. Neely, R. F. Duke, and A. T. Cornelius.[64] We will learn much more about all three of these young gentlemen.

Within a year, the school had grown considerably. "A commodious building" had been added. The enlarged faculty listed specializations: Mr. Rafter was both Principal and Professor of Natural Science; Reverend Evans Professor of Mental and Moral Philosophy; plus a Professor of Mathematics and Principal of a new Commercial Department, a new Professor of Ancient Languages and another of Modern Language and Belles-Letters. Evans, a Princeton graduate, brought the school prestige. It now boasted of "a splendid Mathematical, Astronomical, and Geographical Apparatus" and an excellent, growing library. By 1859, it held 1,200 volumes.[65] In contrast to Webb's small house, this school required two or more sizable buildings. In addition to a library, several classrooms and other teaching facilities, there was dormitory space, a kitchen and dining hall.

Rafter's ambitions included hiring an additional professor to staff a new Agricultural Chemistry branch. To finance it, he would sell one hundred scholarships for two-year's tuition at $50. These served as bonds, redeemable for the future education of a son. Although the *Appeal* enthusiastically endorsed the idea, it may have caused problems if enrollments did not offset bond redemptions.[66] Rapid expansion obviously represented a heavy investment, but Rafter did not stop there.

In 1857, he expanded to include "military instruction and discipline." Again the *Appeal* waxed eloquent. The railroad handbook also asserted "This institution—which so advantageously unites a collegiate education with military discipline—enjoys an excellent reputation."[67] In February 1858, the state assembly officially authorized the Shelby Military Institute. Its Board of Trustees were empowered to raise funds in order to "erect buildings, purchase grounds, apparatus, books, or any other thing, which may be necessary...."[68]

Germantown was now poised to acquire a collegiate-level institution that granted not only degrees but military commissions. It was charged to pursue a level of educational quality comparable to the U.S. Military Academy at West Point. The Board was to elect a President and Commandant qualified to give instruction in such a course of studies. Furthermore, faculty and the students would constitute a military corp, "each student ... styled a cadet." The Govenor was "to issue the commission of Colonel to the President, of Lieutenant Colonel to the Commandant, and such other commissions to the professors and cadets ... and is authorized to cause to be issued to the Academy the necessary and suitable arms and equipment...."[69]

Although the 1860 census listed only one military college in Tennessee, there were at least two other more prominent such schools than Germantown's.[70] Pretensions to such high academic and military proficiency for the school make one wonder about its actual achievement. Certainly the elevation of young Alexander to the exalted rank of colonel seems specious. It seems unlikely he experienced any military training at Miami University. No references to a commandant survive. We may never know anything of the military qualifications of his instructors. Competing institutions at Lagrange and Nashville boasted more specifically of their programs including artillery.

Rafter's ambitions had apparently exceeded his reach, and something had gone wrong. Fund raising and tuition must have proved insufficient. Advertisements for the school soon ceased, and Rafter seems to have abandoned his post. In the 1860 census, the only names in residence formerly associated with the school were Evans and the elder Rafter. By that year, Alexander and his wife Elizabeth were living in Searcy, Arkansas.[71] However, he would be back in town in 1861.

Throughout the 50s however, both Rafter and Webb's schools lined up along the State Line Road east of town. Farther out, "on the North side of the road," was the Forest Hill College Institute for Young Ladies, which opened in 1856. It advertised itself as located "in the open country; very beautiful and remote from distracting influences; one hours ride (via Memphis and Charleston Railroad) from Memphis; thus ensuring the real advantages of both city and country." It offered a "corps of accomplished, faithful and experienced Teachers." It provided primary, preparatory and collegiate levels, plus piano, guitar and violin, French, German, Latin and Greek, painting and embroidering.

The state legislature granted it status as a collegiate institute with full power to confer degrees in 1858. The proprietor was Barnett Miller, a Baptist minister.[72] It was served by a "Professor of Music," Anton Shide, who also boarded five young ladies from New York as teachers. The Germantown area had become a seat of higher learning for both men and women.

Clearly the town's educational institutions put it on the map. Such a reputation continued to attract others, though less successful. In 1857, James Voorhees tried unsuccessfully to open a Male High School near Forest Hill Seminary.[73] Then in 1859, a Professor M. Solomon opened an "Academy of Music and Language", a mobile operation, for he offered to teach "every language and give instructions upon every musical instrument" within ten miles of Memphis or

Germantown.[74] This ambitious "Professor Harold Hill" was obviously quite mobile, and unbelievably versatile. His advertising campaign did not last.

Such failures aside, the full range of prestigious private schools from elementary, through academy to college levels provided the area's elite with ample choices for their children's' education. That of a Germantown lad or lass might involve moving up entirely locally.[75]

Since letter writing was a grace schools were expected to impart to young ladies, their mistresses insured that they wrote parents regularly. The young ladies suffered from the usual teenage girls' reluctance to reveal anything to her parents. Letters were limited largely to sentimentalities, greetings to friends and family back home, reports on academics, personal health, diseases circulating in the school, and formal excuses for not writing enough. Of course each letter usually included a request for a necessity or simple pleasure. Unlike today, a request for money was abnormal.[76]

The content of their letters to friends was generally vacuous. It was mostly limited to talk about visits to places like Memphis, but also some references to

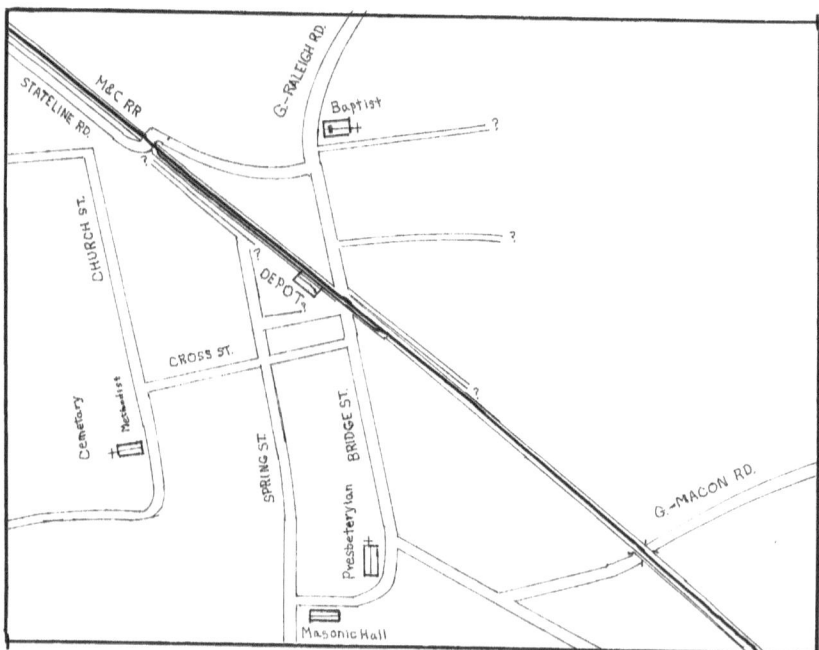

MAP 5 Germantown Center.

P. 2 Masonic Lodge, GHPC. Rebuilt after the style of the original, following a fire.

interesting boys. Nothing about politics or other public affairs, not even slavery or possible secession.

Other Social and Cultural Institutions

Among its social institutions, the town had an Odd Fellows Hall, about which there is no local memory, although it was still there at least as late as 1864. The inauguration of this hall in June 1851 was reported in the *Appeal*.

The town's Masonic Lodge, the Blue Lodge, formed in 1841 and met initially in the community's multipurpose log building. One wit claimed they were driven out by the nesting wasps. So in 1854, they built an impressive two-story lodge where Bridge Street intersected Spring Street. The November cornerstone-laying ceremony provided a gala occasion. Masons from the city and area lodges attended in large numbers. "A sumptuous Barbecue," and Hessing's Brass Band provided entertainment.[77]

Baptist, Methodist and Presbyterian churches also lay inside the town. From 1833, the town's multipurpose log building had served the different congregations. By the 1850s, each had its own fine little church building. Normally

THE WHITE FOLKS AND THEIR LIVES · 31

p. 3 Presbyterian Church, GHPC. In its original orientation and location; steeple added in the 1870s.

small-town churches did not have full-time pastors but shared men who covered several communities, so each congregation only held full services once or twice a month. In contrast, Germantown had other advantages. Some practicing pastors had taken up residence around Germantown as their home base, giving the town's churches a share of their time. In 1860, Joshua Cross, Baptist, and Phillip Tuggle (the local Methodist circuit rider) farmed outside town. Germantown's churches also had additional ordained ministers who had "located" or retired and could serve their congregations in the absence of the pastor. The Baptist Jeremiah Burns had retired to his farm. In addition, there was Reverend J. Dix Mills with the status of "local pastor," a unique Methodist commission. He was a traveling businessman, available to serve whatever community through which he passed. After receiving his doctorate from Princeton University in 1849, Reverend Evans had become pastor at Germantown in 1850, and was the only minister to remain in residence for well beyond the period covered here.[78] Like other professionals, pastors found their income insufficient, so they either farmed or had other ventures.

The last of the three buildings to appear, the Presbyterian Church was officially dedicated May 15, 1853, with guest sermons and a church dinner in between. The Sunday service included a lecture by the missionary, Mr. Wilson, "on the condition of the heathen in India," followed by an evening service. Actually it seems that when the pastor was in town, he held both a Saturday evening service as well as two on Sunday, at least this was the Presbyterian practice. One farmer attending complained about "the perfumed ladies and gentlemen. Sweet scents were too strong for me."[79]

All three churches had similar construction. Set on brick pillars, the exteriors were of white clapboards, and the high windows held only clear glass. Steeples were often later additions, as in the case of the Presbyterian Church. Steps led up to the doors, through which one entered the narthex, a small vestibule, and then the hall with its high ceilings. Heat was provided by a centrally located iron stove. The present Evans Chapel was the original Presbyterian building. The existing old Baptist church is a close replica of the original, which held 350 to 400 people. The Methodists apparently had a more modest church, described as a one-room building, perhaps with only four windows per side and a relatively low roof. There was another, more simple, Baptist church or chapel in Forrest Hill.[80] In 1845, the Methodists living well below Nonconnah Creek established the Chapel Hill Church off the Germantown-Hernando Road on what is today Richmond Road. In the same year, another congregation that had formed further east at what was called McCrosky's Schoolhouse built Bethlehem Church on what is today E. Holmes Road.[81]

Episcopalians had to meet in their homes or travel a few miles to Duke's non-denominational chapel. So too any Campbellites. The three local churches were also generous with their facilities for other denominations. Practicing Catholics had to commute to Memphis.[82] No surviving records indicate any Jewish presence.

Differences among the congregations were taken seriously, such as the proper form of baptism. The Baptists segregated the sexes in church. There were separate entrances to their building and separate seating in the hall. In addition to Sunday school, children of all ages were expected to sit through the sermons, although mothers brought distractions for the youngest.[83]

The churches were central elements in community life, with people coming from miles around on a Sunday. The better endowed even maintained townhouses where they spent the weekend, to observe the Sabbath, to socialize and to shop. Despite the great religiosity of the age, the entire population was not so devout. The religiously indifferent and the anti-religious were present, although few have left records of their attitudes. One thirty-three-year-old man freely confessed, "I was not then much of a churchgoer."[84] Indifference and greater priorities were undoubtedly much more common than atheism or hostility toward the "sanctimonious," with one exception—when the "temperance lecturers" brought too much pressure on the good-old-boys.

Across the South, only forty percent were church members. Typically the women were the backbones of the churches, with the men constituting only a quarter or less of the congregations and attending even less. Salvation and morality were more commonly female concerns. It was religious involvement and a sense of righteous imperative that drove women to be more assertive with their husbands, even at the expense of being accused of "trying to rule." Yet, although women might teach children's Sunday school, church offices and the exercise of authority and discipline remained the purview of the men.[85] The church was an area in which Germantown women played more typical roles in the complex gender relations.

Attitudes among churchgoers were hardly uniform about strong drink or other "vices." The town produced at least two or three stalwarts in the temperance movement. Some locals held hard-nosed positions on public impropriety—not just drinking but dancing. One once consented to take his children to a great barbecue, but lamented, "There may be dancing—I have heard there will be—but I have no love for that exercise, and of course, so far as I am concerned, I had rather there would be none."[86]

Other men were probably as firm in their religious convictions as this Isham Howse, but like him also independently minded about some conventions. Once he asserted, "Some go to church to see and be seen—for display; some to find fault with the preaching, but many I hope go to receive instruction, and to worship God in sincerity. When I cannot go for this last purpose, I would rather not go at all. It is but seldom that I hear a sermon which I approve in toto, but I always get some benefit. . . ."[87] Often Howse found excuses for not attending, instead sending his Presbyterian wife and children to her church.[88]

Poor Howse seems to have had a number of problems with Presbyterians, not to mention those of other faiths. He claimed to have been such a nonconformist on points of dogma that they called him "a heretic, and, sometimes, an infidel." He saw himself as alienated from the town people. Yet the only point about which he was specific was, that having been raised a Baptist, he believed strongly in immersion. He accused Reverend Evans and other Presbyterians of being "sectarians," but constantly belied these contentions with frequent, fond references to Evans and many church members regularly visiting and dining with his family and vice versa. It was not they who seem to have been judging.[89]

Christian morality, charity and service were certainly central to the community's self-image. It would be wonderful if we had statistics on church membership as a percentage of the local population. Obviously, however, the community supported its churches. The early settler, Wilks Brooks, had donated the land for the Baptist Church.[90]

Despite a few allusions to sectarianism, it seems not to have gone much beyond differences over issues like baptism. Although people did take such issues seriously, others prided themselves and their community on religious open-mindedness. One correspondent wrote to Emily Lucken, assuming such feelings were mutual. She bragged about the near total breakdown of it in her community.[91] Later in life, Emily and her Germantown friends spoke of sectarian differences as of little concern within their extended families. They also indicated, however, that there were nevertheless strong sectarian elements in the community. Undoubtedly, the various Campbellite groups were viewed as tainted, and Catholics were beyond the pale.

Society and Social Life

The town's educational institutions and their faculty enriched its social and cultural life. The Masonic and Odd Fellows halls, and the churches provided venues for cultural events, such as music performances, learned lectures, poetry readings and "appropriate" plays. Less tasteful events had to find other venues. Lucken's Inn was often preferred by politicians for delivering impromptu speeches to a lively audience that imbibed his lager.[92] The genteel families entertained small parties with music and singing in their homes. Since no homes had a hall large enough for even a small dance party, barns were decorated for ambitious gatherings. Large public events occurred outdoors, with temporary brush arbors erected and sawdust spread for a ground cover. Local organizations sponsored fundraising "fairs." Of course, events included a barbecue, dancing, and fireworks on such as the Fourth of July.

Until local militia drills were terminated, they also provided an occasion for public gathering. The company for District Eleven should have drilled in town or nearby monthly. Once a year, all companies assembled for regimental drills.

The regiments of Shelby and Tipton Counties had formed the 22nd Tennessee Militia Brigade. Of its five regiments, southern Shelby County fielded the 128th. Its last regimental muster occurred at Germantown in 1843. Things had become rather haphazard before the end in 1857, and company drills were irregularly held and poorly disciplined events, with some comic relief with drinking a major component of militia musters.[93]

The ladies of the Germantown Presbyterian Church advertised their fair to help fund construction. For their 1852, event, they advertised,"they will exhibit for sale many useful and fancy articles at reasonable prices. Also, on the same occasion, a dinner will be provided. The Fair will be continued at night."[94]

The *Appeal*'s reporter, who traveled to "the neat village of Germantown," described the event. The church had been handsomely decorated by fair hands, and that all the taste, tact and skill of the gentler and better sex had been brought into requisition, to attract the liberal purchaser. . . . Later, after some political speeches, the "viands" provided prepared "with a heartiness suggestive of the idea of good cheer."[95]

Some limited insight into the social circles of the upper classes can be found in correspondence between young ladies. Emily Lucken frequently mentioned family names of a fairly small circle, more reflective of girlish cliquishness than social snobbery. On the contrary, the milieu of a Germantown bell included the full range from planters to well-set farmers, merchants, businessmen, and professionals. Nothing indicates a limited upper elite, although it certainly did not go below the respectably comfortable yeoman farmer level. Contacts extended out to Fishersville and Lafayette as well as into Mississippi and Alabama.

A Germantown girl's "social whirl" consisted of winter balls at local hotels, cotillion parties and barn dances. But encounters with eligible young men were hardly limited to local opportunities. Frequent visits to friends in other towns as far away as Grenada, Mississippi, involved arrangements for her specifically to meet them. A daguerreotype sent ahead would be used by such match-making friends to attract their attention.[96] Thus the opportunities of the young people of the town extended well beyond the county.

The private social life of their families consisted primarily of hosting meals for a few friends on Sundays and holidays. Small parties for family and friends involved music and card playing. Elite and middle-class women met for tea, sewing and knitting or more refined arts, and readings. Undoubtedly some families had more exclusive social contacts, or, as in the case of the Dukes, their friendships could be egalitarian.

The humbler yeoman family's girl's social life must have centered more on church social events and the kinds of community gatherings described above. Although more geographically limited, it was probably less constrained when it went beyond the eyes of the church ladies.

Health Care, Illness and Death

Sixteen men around Germantown titled themselves physicians, but the low level of science in medicine provided no guarantees. Efforts to regulate the profession had been repealed. There were two ways to qualify. One could "read" with a practicing doctor, until he felt that the apprentice had learned all he could teach. One could attend a school of medicine and biology, usually for two years, involving little or no practical experience. The best physicians combined both routes.[97] The number of private medical schools had mushroomed, sometimes granting degrees after a few weeks.[98] For one glaring example, William Blair, the son of Germantown's hotel keeper and of the ripe old age of 19 was assigned by his proud parents the title of "physician" for the census.[99]

A few doctors resided in town. More lived in the countryside where they could also farm. Dr. Leonidas Richmond, who settled south of the town in 1840, was typical for making house calls on horseback—as far north as Cordova and as far south as Olive Branch.[100] As for fees, in 1854 when Britten Duke needed a night-time house call for surgery, he was charged $3.00. The next day for an office visit and prescription—$1.00. For a regular daytime house call—$2.00.[101]

Although fees were in terms of cash, the economy was still heavily involved in barter and reciprocity. Poorer farmers could pay in produce. Mostly local doctors apparently preferred to extend credit. One especially unhealthy family ran up $208.44 bill before the farmer could pay it off from the sale of land. The farmer gratefully noted, "Our doctor is a humane man, and will not distress us, but will have patience with us till we can pay him without feeling it badly."[102]

Despite the dismal state of medicine, area residents did have access to the best available. During the 1840s, Dr. R.L. Scruggs was a physician who not only kept on top of the latest medical advances, but who contributed regularly to medical journals, sharing experiences with other professionals. His published professional reports paint a vivid picture.

In May 1846, he treated a twenty-three-year-old man with severe and well-advanced pneumonia. In tune with the age, his first effort was to bleed the patient. Fortunately, Scruggs was astute enough to notice quickly that the treatment weakened the man, so he desisted. Scruggs described the physical aspects of the illness and diagnosed accurately.[103]

He was less successful in treating a pregnant woman suffering from a ruptured uterus. She had been in labor for three days before he was called. He found "an irregular practitioner in attendance, with several old women." Their brutal efforts to extract the child had only made matters worse. He could not save mother or child.[104]

More impressive were his successful diagnosis and treatment of a rarer condition described as "polypus of the uterus." In the spring of 1845, he was called in to treat a slave woman suffering from excessive bleeding. Initially, "a skillful physician" had treated the symptoms successfully but returned episodes had brought her to death's door. Not only was Scruggg's diagnosis right on, but without surgery and by a process we might call minimally invasive, he tied it off, starving the tumor, and removed it. In 1847, he reported, "She recovered rapidly, and has menstruated regularly ever since. . . ."[105]

In 1848, he reported on an epidemic of typhoid fever. He could detect the outbreak early because of previous experiences two years before. Of his twenty-two cases, only one was fatal because the patient refused treatment. With his readers, he shared his knowledge of early and advanced symptoms. As for its cause, he correctly ruled out contagion. For treatment, he had little to offer beyond the practices of the era, of which the most effective were rest and "moderate exercise and nutritious food."[106] Dr. Scruggs died in Germantown in 1853.

Nationally, except during epidemic years the major killers were "consumption" or tuberculosis, pneumonia and other respiratory diseases. For the Germantown area, in 1850 these two took only three, but in 1860, nine. Locally cholera and yellow fever were regular visitors. But the cholera epidemic of 1849–50 brought four such deaths. In 1860 east of town, an outbreak of typhoid hit especially hard taking a total of eleven.[107] Since 1828, yellow fever epidemics had threatened, the second hitting in 1855. Every summer, local papers reported on its approach coming upriver and speculated on its intensity for the season, which ended with the first hard frost. In 1860, it did not advance much beyond Louisiana. Germantown had always been spared its visitations.

The frequency of still births, early childhood deaths, and of women dying in childbirth is readily apparent in the letters to and from Germantown women. Between the 1850 and 1860 censuses, two of the five wives in permanent residence had died in the interim. Several other wives and small children had died in the countryside as well. The predominance of such announcements and attention to ever-present illnesses in their letters would signal anxiety and hypochondria in modern women. Then they were simply an overwhelming reality of life.[108]

It is no wonder that some women recorded in personal letters and diaries an intense fear of pregnancy. Although they talked about intimacy in ways indicating that they were not sexually repressed, some became so phobic that they forcefully requested abstinence and often got it.[109] Here again was another measure of the importance of individual personalities in determining the workings of female submissiveness and obedience—even to scriptural admonitions.

For children, the above diseases were especially fatal. Other major childkillers were diphtheria, dysentery, measles, scarlet fever, small-pox, typhus, whooping cough and worms. Scarlet fever hit hard in 1860. Six died in infancy and it took 12 children.[110]

Such deaths left families in mourning. Benjamin and Sarah Ellis lost two children and replaced them with four others between 1850 and 1860. Sarah had begun the joys and tears of motherhood at age sixteen, birthing a total of eight by age 35. The Kimbrough family lost a three-year old girl in 1859, a two-year old girl in 1860 and a one-year-old girl and two teenage boys in 1861.[111] In 1859, the Goodrich family lost two children. In the following January, they suffered another loss, a six-month infant.[112] One other family seems to have met a more terrible fate. In 1850, the family of the blacksmith William Stevenson and his wife Elizabeth, both in their thirties, had three children in ages nine to three. By 1860, only the youngest, little Josephine, remained, an apparent orphan, residing with Wiley and Feraby Rochelle.

Although doctors were generous with credit, a sizable part of the population was so pressed for cash that they turned first to alternatives. Folk remedies and midwives were often preferred over professionals, but they could also prove fatal, as we have seen. Isham Howse almost lost his wife when she took a "new remedy." Others like Howse dosed themselves regularly with injections of over-the-counter morphine for pain and quinine for "chills".[113]

Death was certainly a great presence. Burial and mourning were much more highly ritualized and far less commercial than today. Most of the local folk inclined toward the simple. The town had no funerary professionals. All arrangements fell to family and friends.[114] More typically, the women of the family washed the body with folk-recipes and then dressed them. The viewing was held as soon as possible. Although coffins could be bought from Memphis, the men usually made a pine box. In contrast, Britton Duke's family paid $60.75 for his coffin. Some of the elites were coming around to buying coffins, and within a few decades, Germantown would have its own coffin factory.[115]

Families that could not afford a newspaper death notice posted their own around town. The front door was draped in black. As family and friends arrived for the burial, they contributed with food preparation and even dug and filled the grave. Traditionally, the grave had to be dug on the day of the funeral.[116]

After the viewing, pallbearers carried the coffin to the grave, frequently on the family property. In town, the community cemetery was on the Methodist Church property. The coffin was loaded on a wagon and a procession followed it to the cemetery. At the grave site, there would be a short service, but for Masons, more elaborate ceremonies. There is no record of where pauper burials occurred.

After burial, came the period of mourning. A widower was expected to wear black for one month and a black armband for two more. Ideally he waited a year before remarrying, but the realities of life allowed him to find a wife sooner if he had young children. For a widow, the conventions were more restrictive, demanding up to two and one-half years of formal mourning in "widow's weeds." For the first four months, "a proper lady" could not go out in public, except for church.[117] Yet, widows still had to supervise all the work, or do it themselves unless there were mature sons. These elaborate conventions could not have extended much below the more comfortable classes.

Homes and Property

Rural and town life blended indiscriminately. Except for the very center of town, homes were widely spaced, and from there they spread out along the major roads and a network of little lanes radiating out from them. Spread throughout the two civil districts were several little communities. Further east lay the hamlet of Forest Hill. Its major feature was the two buildings of the girls' school. There was also a little Baptist chapel, plus one store and a few houses. Another crossroads settlement at a greater distance was High Hill (Afton), where a physician, a blacksmith and a carpenter served local farmers. It, Forest Hill and Pea Ridge to the west, were satellites of Germantown, although High Hill had a short-lived post office after 1852. The people of Capleville on the southwest fringe were often drawn to Germantown for legal business and amenities despite their easier access to Memphis on the Pidgen Roost Road.

The oldest homes in Germantown proper were either log cabins or plank-sided, two-room affairs with a separate cook house. Most log cabins were subsequently weather boarded over. By 1860, more commodious, professionally constructed townhouses prevailed. More typical were one-story town houses, with surrounding porches, peaked roof, and floor to ceiling windows. They still had plain undecorated exteriors. Gingerbread was added only later in the century. Almost all simply sat on brick pillars.

For construction, there was an ample supply of carpenters in residence. There was only one "brick layer," Jackson Lewis. Before the brick factory, any bricks involved in construction had to be fired on site. The lack of any construction craftsmen in the previous 1850 census indicates that most building was do-it-yourself until after mid-century. Their new presence by 1860 spoke to the greater rate of growth.

The porches, high windows and high ceilings helped residents cope with summer heat. Brick chimneys served each wing for fireplaces or iron stoves. Roofs were covered with wooden shingles. Over time a two-room house would grow, acquiring additional wings to accommodate the expanding family. The resultant footprint could have an L or T or even a C shape with additional porches off one or more of the wings. There were a few one-and-a-half and two-story houses. Only three had basements. Such town homes included a wide variety of wings, gables and porch configurations.[118]

For most town families, outbuildings housed one horse or mule, a milk cow or goats, and chickens. Small, one-room affairs usually housed the slaves who served homes and family businesses. Of course, each house had its own "necessary," one or two holes.

Nicer houses elevated on short piers were screened by laths. Respectable

p. 4 Brooks' Town House, Bridge Street, adjacent to the Baptist Church, built 1850s. Family usually came into town on a Saturday to shop and visit, and returned to the plantation Sunday evening after church services.

p. 5 Typical Town House, Bridge Street, built circa 1860.

ladies maintained profuse flower beds, and almost every family had a kitchen garden and fruit trees. Most had cisterns to collect rainwater for bathing, animals and gardens, and fighting fires. Buried terracotta pipes brought rainwater from collecting roofs, and a hand-cranked bucket chain brought the water up for use.

Farmers who lived outside town were very much a part of town life. Most of the Masonic leadership and many church leaders.[119] Their landholdings marched side-by-side along the roads radiating out from town. Unfortunately, this transportation network was easily navigable only in dry weather. Fortunately, that usually coincided with the harvesting of crops. When dry, however, the dust could be stifling.

The survival of "Cotton Plant," the Kimbrough home, until the 1950s, preserved an image of the grander homes of the wealthiest planters. Although a stereotypical southern mansion with Doric columns, nothing locally was comparable to the grand mansions of the Deep South—no grand ball rooms, no sweeping stairways. The home had been built by James Titus, one of the earliest settlers. His slaves had erected the two-story building from native poplar. After James Kimbrough arrived from South Carolina with his wife Mary Elizabeth, he bought the Titus estate for $22,000 in 1838. A long drive, lined with trees and flowering shrubs, led down from the Germantown-Hernando/Capleville Road (present Cotton Plant Road).[120]

A more typical plantation home is Woodlawn, which still exists, at 2000 Old Oak Drive. When completed, it consisted of only six rooms with a separate kitchen out back. A kitchen was almost always an outhouse to protect from kitchen fires. If located close to the house, rather than sitting on a permanent foundation, it might sit on a wooden sledge. A team of mules was in harness all day to haul the kitchen away if fire broke out.[121]

Woodlawn's builder, Wilks Brooks arrived from North Carolina in 1834. Brooks and son had originally built a two-room log dogtrot, and then expanded into a two-story, six-room building. It took them a year to make the house ready for the family. Construction began with hand-hewn timbers and round wooden pegs. The siding was sawed at a sawmill on the Wolf River. Both the bricks for the chimneys and the square nails were manufactured on site. Like other finer homes, interior walls were finished with a discordant patchwork of mixed-wood paneling, or with horsehair plaster over split hickory lathes. Building was a family operation in which father, son and slaves did the

p. 6 Woodlawn, Brooks' Plantation Home, built 1830s. Relocated; wing on left was added later.

work. Nevertheless, it ultimately cost him between two and three thousand dollars.[122]

In 1836, his family arrived. Brooks had originally built the home also with dogtrot between the two downstairs rooms to benefit from cooling ventilation. This did not suit the tastes of his wife, so he had to enclose the dogtrot into a paneled entry hall with only an inelegant, steep and narrow stairway. Around 1840, he had completed the home. The full-bearded Wilks and his beautiful wife became mainstays of the growing community and pillars of the Baptist church.[123]

A contemporary description of a planter's property emerges from an advertisement, rounding out our image of a typical plantation. He offered 872 acres, 250 of which were cleared, in good cultivation, and mostly bottom land. In addition to everything else, it boasted a cotton gin.[124] Planters originally ginned their own cotton. One who could not afford such equipment had to go to a neighbor or a commercial gin and pay a percentage of the crop. In addition to buying the machine itself, one had to have a two-story building to house it. Outside, one needed a giant wooden screw press to compress the cotton into bales. Both the gin and the press were driven by animal power, but more advanced planters were acquiring steam engines.

"All the necessary outhouses" included a carriage house, cotton sheds, a smokehouse, chicken coop, pig parlor, stock and feed barn, corn and potato barns, and for the more prosperous and independent, a smithy and a sawmill. In addition to the acreage for cash crops and extensive uncleared land for wood lots, there was a large kitchen garden, orchards with a wide variety of fruit and nut trees. Slave quarters concentrated along roads leading to the fields.[125]

Despite the usual descriptions of cotton as the cash crop, most farms and plantations were quite diversified, both for self-sufficiency and the market. About sixty percent of farmers produced cotton, some producing fewer than ten bales. Even when cotton was the primary cash crop, corn was secondary. Wheat, a little rye, sweet and Irish potatoes, beans and peas were also cash crops, while everyone produced much of the produce, eggs and dairy products consumed at their tables. Sheep and cattle, but especially swine found their way to market. Butter was marketed, but not milk, for it could not be kept. Buttermilk was leftover for consumption. A few swine herds were quite sizable, with some small farmers focusing almost entirely on the sale of pork. Herds of sheep, sometimes sizable, also provided wool. With the exception of honey which was purely for family consumption—all other sweeteners had to be imported.[126]

As an example of a "comfortable" yeoman family, we have Isham Howse again. In January 1853, his two older sons hauled the last three bales of cotton to Memphis, for about $99. With this, they paid off a $75 debt to Street, Daugherty & Co., but ran up a further debt for supplies, since they held on to $20 for some cash. In February, they delivered a load of wheat and paid another $75 off their debt. In May, they hauled in another wagon of wheat. They were also selling pork and sweet potatoes in Germantown and at White's Station, as well as trading sweet for white potatoes. Meanwhile, Howse, his friends, and neighbors were borrowing and repaying small amounts of cash among each other in order to cope. Son Andy also earned money hauling wood for the railroad from neighbor's woodlots.[127]

More needs to be said about property and relative wealth in the next chapter.

Some Unusual Disturbances of the Peace.

A clear understanding of post-war changes requires a picture of what was a relatively peaceful antebellum town. Although life there was not always quiet and convivial, even those exceptions cast further light on the color of Germantown life and society. Probably the most sensational act of violence occurred in 1845, but since that was a politically related confrontation between outsiders, the story is best told later. Aside from that, even political disputes were probably limited to saloons, and even there, probably good-natured.

On January 23, 1852, the only recorded homicide reveals some disorderly saloon life. A coroner's inquest was held in town and the jury ruled that William W. Joyce had fatally stabbed William Trammell. The incident occurred in the presence of fifteen male and female witnesses outside a saloon. Joyce was a twenty-six-year-old farmer who with his wife cared for three orphans. Trammel was a newcomer or visitor to town, but so were many of the witnesses. Being a family man, Joyce did not flee, but remained and surrendered. He was charged with first degree murder and pleaded not guilty. But, the ominous sounding indictment read that Joyce "feloniously willfully premeditatedly deliberately and of his malice of forethought did strike stab and thrust giving the said William Trammel ... one mortal wound." The papers went further, referring to repeated stabbings. In the face of all this, after posting bail, Joyce fled. By July, when the sheriff heard that he was back home, he rode with a posse, arrested and jailed him in Memphis. On October 8, the *Appeal* reported a mistrial, the jury being unable to agree.[128]

What a frustrating story! What led to the killing? Joyce just went home and hung around, with no one, the constable or the sheriff feeling compelled to do anything, allowing him to surrender. After a hearing and posting bail, surprised at the charges, he became fearful and fled, only to return soon. Either because of a chaotic court or because the cause of the incident was such that a jury could not agree, the trial was postponed. Indeed the court records are most puzzling. From September 27 through October 1, the court had met repeatedly only to adjourn each day because of jury problems. During that time, thirteen jurors refused to appear, and were fined. Then the deputy sheriff was fined for "failing to keep order in the court room." After continued jury problems, the case was held over until January. The court felt it necessary to bond the jurors and witnesses heavily.[129] Were Shelby County courts always so chaotic, or was there something special about this case?[130]

What is worse, there is no mention of the subsequent trial in either county court records or newspapers. Meanwhile, if Joyce's problems had not been enough, four creditors brought suit against him. They were handled by the justices of the peace, holding court in Germantown. Since he had pledged all his property as credit, Joyce was in danger of losing his farm. Both Drs. Morgan and Cornelius tried to come to his assistance.[131] All this indicates that he had the sympathy of some of the town's prominent citizens. Nevertheless, he was convicted, for he was serving a sentence in the Tennessee State Penitentiary in 1853.[132] To get this conviction, perhaps the prosecution sought a change of venue out of the county where local sentiments would not interfere. This might explain the lack of further newspaper coverage and local court records.

Perhaps this was not so unusual a murder trial for those times. "Honor killings" were part of the American culture, especially in the South or on the frontier. Among "gentlemen," an affront to one's honor often resulted in a formal duel. More ordinary men settled their disagreements with knives, whips, or whatever—their affair of honor being settled in the heat of the moment. Though officially illegal, prosecuted and punished, a violent defense of honor was still a widely accepted part of the culture. Howse, however, considered it homicide, no matter who or why.[133] Whether others would consider homicide as justified would have depended heavily on the individual's reputation. Apparently Joyce had a good one. Even Howse referred to him as "Captain Joyce," a popular title indicating local respect, someone elected captain of militia.[134] Orphaned as a teenager, while his younger siblings had been apprenticed, he had made the family farm work. It was his sister who had been mistreated as an apprentice by Thomas Blakely. This may be why he and his wife had taken in orphans. But none of this was good enough for whatever court settled his case. Furthermore, the fact that the sheriff felt it necessary to take a posse out to the town to bring in Joyce seems to imply a concern about something more than one man's possible resistance.

This incident tells us about the culture of which Germantown was a part. Attitudes about formal dueling were complex.[135] Frowned upon by the churches and illegal, duelists were barred from elected office in Tennessee. Yet the duels of gentlemen and wannabes usually escaped successful prosecution and were the subject of popular interest. Up to 1861, Memphis papers reported local duels several times a year, and more frequently from all over the South.[136] They were integral to the southern code of honor. There were clear double standards, however. While a gentleman planter could be excused for his dueling, a public confrontation involving a yeoman like Joyce ran the risk of government determination to maintain law and order.[137]

With only one of what may have been an honor killing and no other recorded acts of serious violence, one gets the impression of an unbelievably docile and law-abiding population for the times. Yet there was at least one man who harbored a serious vendetta. In October 1851, a Theophilus Hall from "somewhere near Germantown" rode to Monroe County, Arkansas, to try to kill one Edward Jackson.[138] Obviously, however, local people did not seem to have that much hostility toward each other.

Then there was the town's reputation for "drunken brawling." The pattern of combining grocery stores and drinking establishments created a shopping environment that seems strange today. Each of the two bondings for merchant and tippling was a separate process, so the combination was not assumed. As part of the tipplers license, the proprietor had to promise to keep tax records of his sales in "spiritous and vinous liquors," while maintaining "a peaceable and orderly house," with no gambling allowed. Although fines for violating this bond were common in the county, no records of any around Germantown have survived.[139] There was, of course, the previous mention of an owner using a black teamster to deliver liquor illegally to the ladies of Semple Broaddus College across the line into Mississippi, but if true, he seemed to have escaped detection by authorities. One would suspect that the combination of store, frequented by women and children, with "saloon" curbed excessive drinking and rowdiness, at least during the day. After all, it was only typically witty "contributors" to the papers who enjoyed singling the town out for excessive tippling. Yet, as we have seen, inebriation was a problem at least significant enough to mobilize some of the town's citizens for the temperance movement, but that also was hardly unique.

Unlike murders, small town accidents usually did not become news, but one that did tells us something more about town life. On March 25, 1852, P. A. Lewellin accidentally wounded James Kelly, Jr. Lewellin, concerned about his reputation, addressed a letter to the *Appeal* with a testimony signed by Kelly, his parents and other family members verifying that it was an accident.[140]

Obviously Kelly's wound was not serious. James Kelly Sr. was a laborer who had actually acquired a home in town for his family of five children. One was James Jr., by then 21. Previously Kelly had to move about considerably to find work to support his growing family. How long he had been settled in Germantown is unclear. The names on the testimony reveal that it was family connections that helped Kelly take up roots in town and have a house. His in-laws were William Clark a grocer, and Joseph Clark, a wagon maker. The Clarks had probably helped their sister, Elizabeth, whose marriage had proven less successful.

More tragic was a fire a few weeks earlier, which in a very indirect manner, indicates a relative lack of social uneasiness in the area. When Dr. Morgan's stable burned, eleven horses died in the conflagration. His stage office was in conjunction with his hotel. The fire was discovered too late to save the animals. It was blamed on the "carelessness of a negro boy." Despite this report in a rival newspaper, the *Appeal* observed that this was "the 3d instant, in the county."[141] Repeated fires always raised suspicions that a "barn burner" was afoot. Typically such spontaneous suspicions were a product of the better classes' fears of a dangerous, disgruntled underclass. In this case, however, such a rumor was apparently simply a journalist wanting a sensational edge to his report.

Fire struck again July 12, 1860, when the Southern Star Cotton Gin Factory was destroyed. The proprietors suffered a heavy loss, about forty gins amounting to about fifteen to twenty thousand dollars, none of which was insured.[142] They would promptly set about rebuilding. More about that later, and its significance.

Undoubtedly the goriest event experienced in the town occurred one month later. The mangled remains of an unknown black man were found on the tracks, run over by the train. Several local gentlemen had to view the remains and testify as a coroner's jury to cause of death. This was a shocking event, for unlike the people of Memphis, they were unaccustomed to finding bodies of vagrants and wanderers, the victims of homicides, accidents and exposure. Such people occasionally passed through town looking for odd jobs, but they had the decency to expire elsewhere. In this case, the man was probably a runaway. Fortunately, the county bore the expense of the pauper burial.[143]

In the weeks that followed, Germantown mothers undoubtedly used the occasion to admonish their children about the dangers of playing on the tracks. It was to little avail, however, for hopping a train became a favorite adventure.

When freight trains had to slow to enter a siding outside town, the boys could catch a ride into the station. Over the years, many took a painful fall, but there are no records of deaths or serious injuries.[144]

In summary, from all indications Germantown was a relatively harmonious and peaceful community, contrasting sharply with the crime-ridden and rowdy city nearby. It lacked the violent proclivities of an honor-bound elite. It suffered not from a threatening, hopeless underclass. Whatever crime there was, it was too petty to attract area newspapers. Clearly, no residents would draw attention to their proud community by sending indiscrete reports to the papers.

2

HIERARCHY AND HARMONY?

Despite the positive conclusion in the previous passage, an assertion about social harmony in a Southern community requires consideration of prevalent conventions about the antebellum South. Furthermore, understanding the impact of the war on Germantown also requires determining whether the antebellum community was truly socially harmonious or the rigidly divided and regressive society often attributed to the Old South. One problem is that the genteel discreteness of Southern propriety usually militated against public records of disharmony among the town's citizens. To uncover such, one must read between the lines.

For example, after the Southern Star Gin Factory fire in 1860, by May 9, 1861, Joseph Neely and Stephen Trueheart announced that the factory was back in production. Surprisingly, the very same issue of the *Appeal* also carried simultaneous advertisements for a new Hurt Cotton Gin, manufactured by Hurt, Shepherd & Co., Germantown.[1]

This event hints at a rift among the town's entrepreneurs. Barry Hurt was the former foreman of the Southern Star plant, now competitively marketing his own version of a gin. He claimed awards at the Memphis and West Tennessee fairs where it had proven superior to the conventional gin. What was more, "Capt. John M. Woodson, formerly connected with the above concern" (Southern Star), was given as reference for the good performance of Hurt's gin.[2] Woodson was deeply in debt for his involvement in the burned factory and must have withdrawn from the partnership amidst disagreement. Trueheart, Woodson's former partner, was now Neely's partner. The two companies ran competing advertisements for many months. Former partners and employees were now rivals. To make the story even more intriguing, a Nashville newspaper had reported that the Star Gin fire was "supposed to have been the work of an incendiary."³ No source for this supposition was given, nor repeated in surviving issues of local papers. Even if only a rumor, it speaks to what some locals were possibly thinking about those involved. This, unfortunately, is the only clue we have that this rivalry might have generated personal animosities or in any way divided the community. Whatever conflicts this story may reveal, it only speaks to personal business rivalries. On the other hand, the rise of the former "mechanic" Hurt to entrepreneur status seems to speak of a meritocratic environment. As we shall see, after the war members of the former elite will express great respect for his achievements.

◆ ◆ ◆

More relevant to our interests in the community, was there a social basis for more widespread disharmony? Relations among classes in the antebellum South have been a subject of debate since that time.⁴ Some insisted that theirs was a fully egalitarian, meritocratic society. Others argue that the planter class lorded it over disgruntled small farmers and poor whites. Pursuit of this controversy in regards to Germantown society produces many insights into the pre-war community and how its society might have subsequently changed.

Fred Arthur Bailey gives "some comfort to" the school that insists there were class conflicts in Tennessee. Even so, his conclusions are nuanced. Basically he argues that there were pronounced class distinctions and consciousness, but perhaps not tension and conflict. His method involved a highly detailed statistical analysis of a collection of questionnaires completed by Tennessee Civil War veterans.⁵

He describes planters, plain folk, and the poor living as neighbors, but with vastly different social patterns. Wealth, education, and family connections enabled elites to move in much wider circles than other whites. Tennessee's planters, professionals (attorneys, physicians, professors) and prosperous merchants were the important people. Many were vitally concerned with the defense of a southern culture based on slavery. They fought the political battles and wrote the proslavery polemics. Their community extended far beyond the confines of their rural environment, and their united self-interest caused them to lead their fellow Southerners into war.

Those fellow Southerners were primarily small landholders and tenant farmers. He argues that their worldview was much more restricted. Lacking extensive formal education, relying more on subsistence agriculture and less on a market crop for a living, the plain folk concentrated on the immediate needs of their families and close friends. The broader worlds of commerce or politics rarely intruded into their daily routines or consciousness. They were largely undisturbed by the nation-splitting debates over slavery and states' rights, focusing instead upon such narrow community interests as crops, marriages, births, baptisms, and deaths.[6]

Specifically relevant to our line of inquiry, Bailey concludes that it was mostly the war and their disproportionately greater suffering that "made the poor and plain folk painfully aware that their needs were in fundamental conflict with those of the planters, merchants and professionals. During and after the war, class resentment resulted."[7] Before the war, however, the classes simply lived in very different worlds, too preoccupied with their own to develop sharp animosities over those differences. Although Bailey's conclusions were based on questionnaires from all over the state, his statistical analyses often broke out the seven counties of Southwest Tennessee that clustered around Shelby—a more unique part of the state. Even so, Bailey's image may not be nuanced enough. All his arguments have to be tested against the primary evidence about the real Germantown to determine if it was even more different from the rest of Tennessee, much less the Deep South.

Area society certainly manifested socioeconomic distinctions among its citizens. Nevertheless, although everyone knew his "place," it was apparently not rigidly fixed. Notably, however, in 1861, an outsider, a Confederate officer stationed in the town, observed that one particular, nice lady "was one of the upper ten, rode in a carriage, and two mules to draw it, and a negro to drive."[8] It would be interesting to know if such a phrase as "the upper ten" was actually used in Germantown. If applicable to the area, was it just a loose label for the upper crust, or a literal list of ten families jockeying to maintain their status against new families? Most likely, given the constant turnover in population, a strong sense of old families versus outsiders could not have been easily maintained. In any case, the officer did not describe this "nice lady" as being either snobbish or offensively condescending.

As revealed previously and in subsequent chapters, the arrival of the Pettit family and its quick assumption of prominence bears this out.[9] Newcomers would have been quickly assessed and given an "appropriate place" among locals, sometimes regardless of landed wealth as in the Pettit case. Initially the reception would have been gracious, as long as the newcomers were equally obliging. Also the laborer family of the Kellys is an example of inclusiveness among the middle to lower ends of the scale. Otherwise very low on the scale, they clearly had access to the middle through family. (Chap. 1, p. 49) Given the closeness in time to the frontier experience, there was undoubtedly a sufficient sense of meritocracy for a newcomer to change any initial evaluation.

Following Bailey's model, below any "upper ten," but part of their social circle, were the lesser plantation owners, professionals and successful merchants. Together something like Bailey's "elite." Below them were the yeomen farmers who owned fewer than twenty slaves and less acreage. Included among their rank were property-owning respectable middle-class merchants and "mechanics" (well-trained and established craftsmen). Part of their identity was at least one household slave or having a live-in white domestic. Renters or lease holders could be included if of sufficient means. To continue with Bailey's categories, the lower yet still respectable strata of society included yeomen farmers and mechanics without slaves. Below them were the landless poor, with only their labor to improve their lot. Once burdened with a family, such a man could be hopelessly frozen.

In summary, according to Bailey's model, Germantown's social structure should have consisted of four classes: (1) an elite of planters, professionals and merchants; (2) yeomen farmers who owned fewer than 20 slaves, lesser merchants, and well-established mechanics; (3) yeomen farmers without slaves and small-scale business and craftsmen; and (4) the landless poor—farm, industrial and domestic labor.

Such generalizations are essential to statistical analysis, but they also have limited value. As we shall see, Germantown's society actually constituted more of a continuum of families and single men running from the wealthiest and most prestigious to the poorest and most hopeless, with no clear point of delineation between any such categories. We shall test the characteristics of his categories against specific examples.

Part of his analysis focuses on housing, since that is usually a barometer of social status. Nevertheless, he specifically noted complexities that apply to Germantown.[10] Many planters invested little in cosmetic improvements of their original log cabin, mostly adding extensions for more rooms and interior refinements. Being a planter was not always synonymous with luxury and gentility. Most of their houses, log or finished, were comfortable, but eschewed fine exteriors and fittings. They were satisfied with the rustic. Yet grand display is

p. 7 Log Planter's House, built 1850s, Davies Plantation. Original log structure, never sided over with finer white weather-boarding. Interior decorous but not pretentious.

p. 8 Town House, State Line Road at Railroad Crossing West of Town Center, built 1850s. Located on northern edge of town's chartered limits with farm lands behind.

p. 9 Dog-Trot Cabin, Davies Plantation. Typical for smaller planters and more prosperous yeomen farmers.

p. 10 Two-room, Plank-sided Cabin, Davies Plantation. Heating water for washing and some cooking done outside over an open fire.

p. 11 Dr. Cornelius's House, Stateline Road West of Town, original cabin built in 1830s. An example of finer town homes begun as a log cabin and expanded to meet family and professional office needs; frequently remodeled to keep abreast of latest styles up to Victorian gingerbread trim.

usually the means by which elites separated themselves. Most of their housing argues against any strong demarcations. Locally, there were no true mansions and none of them great. Simple practicality often prevailed over display, so these were people not easily classed by conspicuous consumption. The yeomen's houses or cabins at the upper levels were indistinct from the lower planters, while the rest simply ranged down in comfort and quality to whatever family and friends could help build. Perhaps the major delineator of "class" was a separate cookhouse. The poorer had to make do with their fireplaces, heating wash water outdoors over open fires.

Even in the town proper, it was not unusual for the 1860 homes of prominent citizens to contain within them the original log cabin from which they had expanded. One such was that of Dr. Cornelius, which was regularly brought up to date. Another was the Kirby farmhouse.

The truly poor lived in simple log cabins or shacks, only one or two rooms. This class moved about constantly, taking up residence in whatever housing available on the land they farmed.. In short, this aspect of Bailey's analysis shows that housing was not a solid barometer for separating either the elite from others or the slave-owing from the non-slave-owing.

✦ ✦ ✦

For testing Bailey's categories, there are a few contemporary statistics. Given the serious shortcomings in both the 1860 agricultural and slave schedules for District Eleven, only a good approximate analysis of the relative economic status of its agriculturalists can be made.[11] There were at least 23 who qualified as planters with over 20 slaves. Nevertheless, this is a misleading qualification, for at least 4 others holding fewer slaves were otherwise wealthier than others who qualified. The arbitrary dividing line of 20 between planter and yeoman is problematic for many were just on either side of that line, while several listed as having over 20 were actually hiring/renting some slaves rather than owning. In the entire Germantown area, altogether there may have been as many as 33 planters.

A review of landed wealth in District Eleven, reveals that there was not so grossly inequitable a distribution as elsewhere in the South. The top ten planters (10%) owned 39 percent of the land. The next eleven operating farms (12%) owned 28 percent. The next ten (10%) owned 14 percent. The next twelve (13%) owned 10 percent. The next twenty-one farmers (23%) owned 7 percent. The remaining twelve landed households (13%) held only 2 percent. The sixteen (17%) other agricultural households rented or leased. Since, however, renters were of wide-ranging means, if non-real resources are included, many renters join the higher orders, making the distribution even less inequitable, as we shall see. The frequently mentioned Howse, a renter, introduces the reality that such men could own property elsewhere, and could move back and forth between moderate yeoman status and that of mid-level merchant.

Poor is, of course, a relative term, for few of any status had much fluid wealth. Even many relatively poor were proud of their self-sufficiency and independence. All younger laborers aspired with some confidence to owning land. There was no large element that would have considered itself hopeless in the context of the times, as further analysis will show.

An indicator of how difficult meaningful categorization can be, the wealthy widow Sara Jones, who had a very sizable estate, had only 7 slaves and hired 4 more to farm only about 100 acres. The rest of her extensive landholdings, must have been rented to tenants. The Duke estate was now divided among the widow, Mary, and four sons and two daughters, some with their own families, all temporarily in the same household. They seem to have seriously reduced their total slave population. Only treating them as one household retains their status. Frances (Fanny) Wright, the largest landowner, but an absentee owner, is excluded from this analysis, because she was not an integral part of the community.[12]

Among the planters, a sizable majority had come west from the Tidewater states of Virginia and North Carolina. Presumably, this would have given them a patrician mentality unless they were from the Appalachian parts of those states. Three others were from the Deep South states with supposedly similar proclivities. The rest were from Tennessee or Kentucky with their more independently minded, anti-establishment and meritocratic characteristics. There was one anomaly, New York born William Bradley who had teamed up with Alabama born Columbus Stewart to hold a total of 31 slaves. The supposedly patrician tendencies of the majority were probably diluted by the fact that Tidewater planters and their sons had been steadily immigrating into the Appellation frontier since before the Revolutionary War, immersing themselves in that culture. In short, the planter class was probably less typical in its social consciousness than in the deeper South.

Among the yeomen farmers, Tidewater and Appalachian-born men were almost equally represented along with a slightly smaller percentage of deep-southerners. Any differences in origin among identifiable slave-owning versus other farmers were statistically insignificant. Whatever their regional origins, men of such modest means were unlikely to have brought any pretensions with them. Those who had left status-conscious societies sought more open opportunity.

Also the slave owning yeomen farmers cannot be numbered precisely, but there were at least 45, perhaps more. Some were active enough politically, socially and economically, for their names to crop up, George Sheppard (or Shepherd), John Gray, several Callises, and Jobe Lewis among them. To draw a clear line between slaveholders and the non-slaveholders is impossible, except for that one difference. The remaining yeomen farmers numbered at least 25, plus at least 3 renters who exceeded the resources of several yeomen owners. At least one renter had two slaves, and Isham Howse had four during the 1850s.

Bailey was clear that slave ownership did not constitute a real divide among yeomen farmers. The yeoman, whether slaveholding or not, renters or owners, were independent and proud of their work and what it brought them. A lack of slaves produced little difference in their sense of having had economic opportunity, which was generally quite positive. Blanche Clark's analysis of Tennessee's yeomen also presents them as essentially one class, running along a continuum based more on other wealth and resources than slaveholding.[13] The local census bear this out.

Bailey's generalizations about the yeoman need special testing for Germantown. He argues that the world of the yeoman farmer was distinct from either the class above or below. Highly self-sufficient, they had minimal contact with the commercial world. Their work-a-day life and their ties with family, neighbors and church theoretically consumed all their time, leaving little or none for politics or cultural pursuits. The typical local yeoman managed fifty to one-hundred and fifty acres, so his life certainly tied him inescapably to the seasonal rhythm of nature.[14] Although all of this was true, Bailey exaggerated the time consumed at farming. Most observed the Sabbath, sometimes including Saturday afternoon, even in the most demanding times.

He also exaggerated the isolated separateness of the yeoman farmer's world. Clark disagreed with Bailey's description. "The non-slaveholder took an active interest in politics and was usually better versed than his northern compatriot in political affairs of the day. This was partly due to the stump speakings and political barbecues so popular in the South."[15] Indeed Isham Howse was certainly not apolitical and uninformed. He subscribed to the *Eagle and Enquirer*, monitored international affairs as well as national politics and discussed them, attended and commented on political speeches, voted his Whig convictions, and worried over growing secessionist tendencies.[16] As we shall see, it was not the elite but the more successful farmers who usually held the elected political offices and served on commissions or juries and in appointed political roles. For Germantown, Clark's image of the yeoman seems far more accurate than Bailey's.

Despite his demanding lifestyle, Germantown's yeoman was not the "redneck" with narrow horizons. Most had moved from other states, and would move again, while maintaining contacts, often far afield. Although they may not get to great cities and resorts, they were not isolates. Neither were they uncultured or illiterate. Their four-room house might even contain a piano or a real violin, while the poorer manufactured their own instruments. They corresponded regularly with family and friends. They found time to be politically involved. The railroad leveled the playing field for easy access to the city. Memphis offered a wide variety of ordinary social, cultural, political and other experiences. The railroad also facilitated far-reaching contacts with distant family and friends. For business and visiting they traveled several times a year. Likewise they regularly received visitors coming to the springs.[17]

♦ ♦ ♦

When the non-agricultural population is added to the picture, the inclusion of other forms of wealth and prestige than land and slaves complicated perceptions of social rank and made the distribution of wealth even less inequitable by adding a considerable new, relatively landless elite and middle. The major merchants, "machinists," industrialists, and professionals moved in the circles of the elite. Many owned slaves for business or industrial labor as well as household service. They were often diversified, also owning farmland. Physicians and merchants ranged complexly in status, not just on the basis of wealth, but apparently also their families' roots in the area.

Some of the numerous physicians with less prestigious education or family undoubtedly fell outside the elite. But academy teachers and professors were a welcome addition as symbols of the community's cultural quality, regardless of wealth. Reverend Evans' academic credentials garnered him highest social status extending well beyond the community, while Pastor Tuggle stood among the rank of planters, but as a newcomer.

Table 1 reveals this more complex nature of the community's social and economic hierarchy, and its distribution of wealth.

This data further illustrates the composition of the community's social structure. The upper end of the curve is steep. The top six percent held 41% of the wealth. The next forty seven percent, however, a vast and wide-ranging middle, held 56% on a much less steep curve. From there the slope was gradual down to those with less than $100 of personal property. Even many households with no wealth indicated were earning income from professions and occupations.[18] Those without any such wealth or occupations were also earning income plus subsistence farming with hopes of rising socially and economically. In a cash poor economy, this 26% percent of the population were not as destitute as it would seem. The self-sufficient would have actually stood higher socio-economically. Without their incomes included, this chart still provides a slightly skewed picture. Few would have considered themselves an under-class.

Among the wealthy merchants, the largest group were Tidewater born, while the rest were almost equally distributed among deep-southern, Appalachian,

TABLE 1 Comparative Wealth, 1860 Census, Civil District 11

Over $100,000	3 households, 2%	$324,000	all planters (some with mercantile connections)
Below $100,000	7 households, 4%	$436,200	all planters (ditto?)
Below $50,000	42 households, 24%	$867,200	5 merchants, 1 physician, 1 minister-planter, 1 miller, 1 manufacturer, 1 renter-farmer
Below $10,000	20 households, 11%	$128,739	4 doctors, 4 merchants, 1 hotelier, 1 manager, 1 book agent, 1 mechanic, plus (+) farmers/renters
Below $5,000	15 households, 8%	$41,462	1 doctor, 1 merchant, 1 book agent, 1 overseer, +
Below $4,000	5 households, 3%	$13,825	1 merchant, 1 manufacturer, +
Below $3,000	10 households, 6%	$22,960	1 doctor, 3 merchants, 3 mechanics, 1 clerk, 1 student, 1 overseer
Below $2,000	9 households, 5%	$25,000	1 judge, 1 doctor, 1 dentist, 4 mechanics, 1 overseer
Below $1,000	8 households, 4%	$6,000	6 mechanics, 1 book agent, 1 peddler
Below $500	12 households, 7%	$2,075	1 grocer, 2 mechanics, 2 book agents, 1 overseer, 1 laborer, +
Total	74%		
Total	$1,867,461		(23 known property owning households or estates overlooked in the census)

3 households & 3 individuals,* otherwise of known means, listed as having none. Households in the above with no occupation included in the list were yeoman farmers.

Households with no Professional or Salaried Income Indicated

	1 household + 9 individuals* 1 real estate broker, 1 speculator, 1 gin worker, 1 RR conductor, 3 clerks, 3 teachers

Wage or Salary Earners without any Wealth Indicated

	1 household +3 individuals working as skilled labor*
	Overseers, Farmers** and Farm Laborers without any Wealth Indicated, 7 households +15 individuals*

With no Indicated Means of Income

	2 households + 3 individuals* (1 woman head of household) ***

Total Households and Individuals 178

	26% without any indicated wealth, living entirely on income and/or subsistence farming.

*"Individuals" refers to non-family members residing or boarding in a private home or boarding-house.
**In the census, "Farmer" was supposed to refer to one farming land owned or rented. If one held less than 3 acres, however, real wealth was not reported, complicating this analysis
***All adult and minor members of a household without any indicated occupation are not included in this analysis.

northern and foreign-born men. The Tidewater-born might have shared elitist pretensions, however, the western parts of those states were Appalachian, as were northern parts of Georgia and Alabama. Overall it is hard to suspect most professionals, merchants and industrialists of not leaning toward more meritocratic perceptions. The shopkeepers and mechanics were of almost equal distribution among regions of birth, but more probably of meritocratic dispositions. Of all the skilled and semi-skilled employees, half of whom were Appalachian-born, most were relatively young with hopes of securing a comfortable social-economic status. Again only a few might have seen themselves locked into a permanent underclass.

Teachers occupied a much more socially ambiguous status. For instance, the Pettit sisters shared their father's elite status. In 1850, the family of teachers in the Webb School was equivalent to the yeoman slaveholder category, which is probably why they titled themselves farmers in the censuses rather than "teachers." By 1860, however, Monroe Webb titled himself "gentleman," and was acquiring considerable means. His teacher-sister in both censuses listed no occupation, being first a proper daughter and then yeoman's wife.[19] Half of the others describing themselves as teachers were New-York-born girls at Forest Hill Academy, carefully guarded, respectable young ladies. Below them the other pedagogues descended to a humble social status. Such were the complexities of social perceptions.

✦ ✦ ✦

The local involvement of planters in non-agrarian pursuits contradicts the conventional argument that in the South the conservative, even reactionary, social influence of the planter elite mitigated against modernizing economic trends. The slave economy, traditional values and family pressures allegedly restricted the occupational horizons of their sons to agriculture. Supposedly, educational disadvantage made it even more difficult for young men below the planter class, so northerners and immigrants presumably had the edge in other careers.[20]

Here again, Germantown differed. In District Eleven, of the eighteen craftsmen or mechanics only three were born outside the South. Thirteen with careers in white-collar occupations ranging from merchant to clerk were all southern born. True, among the storekeepers there were five Germans, an Englishman and a northerner. In the book agent consortium, one southerner was outnumbered by four northerners and an Irishman. The professionals, however, including lawyers, physicians and ministers were entirely southerners. Especially notable were the four or five southern-born "industrialists," who were bringing their forms of employment to town.[21] On the other hand, one has to concede that once merchants and professionals established themselves, they frequently invested in farming and slave owning. There, however, they met the planter and more prosperous yeoman coming the other way, diversifying not just in real estate speculation and the cotton trade, but also other mercantile and industrial ventures. Among planters, professionals and businessmen alike, the popular speculation in railroad stock was probably common.

◆ ◆ ◆

The world of a wide range of craftsmen, mechanics and petty merchants was not that dissimilar from the yeoman in terms of time-demanding economic pressures. In the jargon of the age, "mechanic" seems to have mostly replaced the older guild-age terms, artisan or craftsman. Although blacksmiths and carpenters were essential to the community and generally respected citizens, some lacked the means to own enough of their own tools, much less to have their own shop. When they were dependent on others to practice their trades, they occupied a less clearly defined social position, "journeyman." In contrast, the independent blacksmith or carpenter could acquire wealth and property.

In 1860, the town's two wagon makers illustrate how widely such a family's economic status could vary. Lon Rhodes could run a business staffed by twelve slaves, adults and children. Well established, he and his business would survive the war, risen to the status of merchant. In contrast, James Helley (Kelly?) was on his own and had moved on by 1870. The two blacksmiths also differed in their establishment. John Slough had two male slaves for his work, while the family also maintained three women and a child in service. Telip or Telix Mendenall worked without slaves in his rural location but was also independently established.[22]

The status of such mechanics differed from that of yeomen. On the one hand, as a journeyman laborer the average mechanic could earn up to five hundred dollars per year, the equivalent of a plantation overseer or a clerk. Yet mechanic laborers were conventionally considered socially lower than the poorest independent farmer. Perhaps that is why the prominent miller, Mr. Molitor, labeled himself machinist rather than mechanic. This would seem to be a title falling somewhere between mechanic and engineer, the latter requiring higher-education credentials.[23] Locally, established mechanics could range along the social ladder from the equivalent of the small slaveholder to the slaveless farmer. Such status hinged on the ownership of property and equipment, not just slaves.

Given their portrayal in literature and film, overseers constitute an interesting intermediate class, socially well below the planter, and not independent like the yeoman. Locally, most were not "poor," but younger men aspiring to be upwardly mobile. Usually sons of farmers, they knew all the ends and outs of getting their particular crops through the entire process up to market.[24] In District Eleven, the planters provided houses for six overseer families who had also accumulated some non-real property. Forty-nine-year-old James Watson had $4000 worth, including slaves, one woman and three children. Two of them were old enough to work the fields. He undoubtedly moved on to better things. Although most generally aspired to becoming planters, the German immigrant William Essmann, who had acquired $2000, established himself in a grocery/saloon and would remain a local citizen. But forty-seven-year-old William Wells, with a wife and seven children, who had amassed only $150 in possessions, was clearly stuck. Similarly George Griffin at forty-five had a wife, four children and a mother-in-law to support with no accumulated property. Of the remaining six overseers who boarded with the planter, none had acquired any material wealth by 1860. Five of them were young single men just beginning.

Turning back to the farmers, further down the social ladder, in the seven-county block of Southwest Tennessee, 43 percent of the non-slaveholders held less than five acres. In District Eleven, however, only 16 farm families were so limited in property. Ten single men were obviously farm hands, boarding with their employer. Several men who listed no occupation were scattered throughout the population. Such young men anticipated acquiring the means to advance themselves. On the other hand, of seven men with no resources but with children, only three were sending any of them to school (5 out of 17 children). Their aspirations must have been lower, a self-perpetuating consequence of their position.

The seemingly incomplete agricultural census for 1860 probably results from large numbers of subsistence farmers whose production did not go to market or was below the $50 threshold for counting. Thus they are invisible in the statistics. Although they were poor in the sense of having no money, what they needed for consumption beyond what they produced could be had by barter. Thus they could still see themselves as proud, independent yeomen.

A simple farm laborer could earn as little as five dollars a month plus board. Twenty-five to fifty cents a day was good. Twelve dollars a month was extraordinary. Some farmers who rented land had to find such employment to make ends meet.

Itinerant farmers moved about regularly, owning only a mule and a cow. With little prospect for improving themselves or seeing their children advance, up against the wall of having to compete with slave labor, theirs was seemingly a life of squalor and depression. They could and would, nevertheless, pursue their aspirations elsewhere. Among the state's veterans of this class who completed questionnaires, almost two-thirds, felt that economic opportunity had been available to save enough to buy land or set up in business.[25] Almost all members of this class departed the area between every census. Once they acquired the means to advance, they went elsewhere. Bailey's argument that they "sank into the social background . . . largely ignored by both the yeomen . . . and the planters. . . ." is another overgeneralization.[26]

For instance, ostensibly near the bottom of the town's social scale in 1850, was James Kelly. That forty-five-year-old, previously-discussed laborer had no room to host boarders for extra income. The house they owned, valued at $50, offered no suitable space. But nothing better indicates the problems of using financial data to assess social status than Kelly's story. That shooting accident provided insight into a real case. Although his previous pattern of moving constantly to find work fits the poor-laborer model, his ability finally to own a humble house does not. He had ties to the Clark families, a grocer and a wagon maker, respectable families of independent means. Family ties escape statistical analysis and complicate efforts to define social relationships.

In town, laborers usually boarded. Again not all propertyless young laborers were of propertyless underclass origins. Many were of respectable yeoman or mechanic origins with no inheritance, beginning to establish themselves through honest labor. Their employers and neighbors often offered helping hands, encouraging the ambitious to better themselves. In such a process, the sons of "respectable" families, but without inheritance, had advantages over those of the "poor white trash."

The young female boarders were either domestics or employees. Their variable status depended on either having a skill or being placed with family or friends. Elite ladies might also provide a home for a "respectable" girl, providing training to prepare for a future in some proper "position" or as a respectable wife.[27] Daughters of the poor depended totally for their future prospects on the character of the family that employed them. Those "lucky" enough to be properly apprenticed had guarantees and some legal protection.

♦ ♦ ♦

With this picture of the positive self-images and relative wellbeing of the largest part of the population, lets return to the question did social and economic differences between them generate attitudes that fostered tension and hostility? Did those with some means disdain those who had only their own labor, and did the latter resent the former?

A few first-hand descriptions of local attitudes about social classes, work ethics, and the community's social relations have survived to enable us to test further Bailey's generalizations and the conventional image of a grossly divided population with resultant hostilities. The turn-of-the century responses of elderly Confederate veterans were subject to nostalgia and romanticizing. They must be read critically for class blindness. Also they were probably reacting defensively to the pointed questions designed to test negative beliefs about the slaveholding class and the South in general. Three such questions were:

> 18. Was honest toil—as plowing, hauling and other sorts of honest work of this class—regarded in your community? Was such work considered respectable and honorable?
> 19. Did white men in your community generally engage in such work?
> 20. To what extent were there white men in your community leading lives of idleness and having others do their work for them?[28]

Both former planters who participated in the survey insisted that their fathers "assisted in all necessary work" on their farms. They all asserted that honest physical labor was regarded as respectable and honorable." Only a "very few" idlers relied entirely on slaves for the work. As children, they also "did all that came to hand on farm, could and did do all kinds of farm work."[29]

They denied any form of social discrimination or snobbery relating to differences in slave ownership. Instead social relations were allegedly friendly and owners and non-owners met with equality in public gatherings. John Kirby did not think that slave ownership played a role in politics.[30]

Records of public meetings plus the elections of militia officers indicate a general sense of equality, at least above the level of landless farmers. Everywhere in the state higher political office was often the realm of the elite and comfortable middle.[31] But as we shall see in chapter 4, locally in Civil District Eleven, the elected offices fell mostly to professionals, mechanics and established yeomen. In the office of constable, Job Lewis, a modestly well-established farmer, became entrenched in a position of political standing. Such offices were never held by the small holder. None would have had the time or the resources to afford it.

Certainly within the full range of Germantown society, people would have made distinctions about whom to invite into one's home. Yet the Dukes of the early "upper ten" socialized freely with their neighbors, the yeoman family of the Howses. The wives regularly visited one another, while the children played together and slept over at one or the other house. The husbands discussed current events as well as their work. The Dukes provided neighborly assistance, not charity.[32]

As an example of support from social betters for upward mobility, Isham Howse described his future business partner's climb from very poor origins. His success grew from both hard work and the kind support of his "betters."

> Tom Brady . . . I have known him intimately for many years, from before he was grown. He has had cramped opportunities. Of indigent parents, he had to labor as a bond servant for his father. . . . His educational opportunities have been very scanty. Larkin Echoles was his early friend, and assisted him some, receiving in return, in labor upon his farm, as a common hand, full compensation. . . . Tom has lived with me, as a clerk, for a good while, and has boarded with me in my house as one of my family. . . . Although uneducated, he is a man of talents and of much promise. He is an honest man . . . honest-hearted in every sense of the word. It is therefore needless to add that he is a gentleman in the broadest sense of the word.[33]

This clearly describes a meritocratic society that would accept anyone who pulled himself up to the status of economic self-sufficiency. They assisted any who seemed willing and able. Yet Bailey's statistics indicate that a majority of the poor of southwest Tennessee, unlike the rest of the state, felt there had been some social conflict. A sizable percentage of them considered that conflict significant.[34] This needs to be addressed.

One barometer of social status was education. As we shall see in chapter 4, there the complex and contradictory nature of Southern elitism is more clearly revealed. Property owners dominated the school board, controlling the distribution of state funds, and determined what if any local taxes would be levied for additional support. The preferred private schools sufficiently served their own family needs, so their decisions were driven by their perception of how much the "lower" classes desired or appreciated education. Clearly the early 1850s hiatus in the district's common schools indicates a low point. Equally important, however, it turned around and they accepted public schooling as worthy of paying taxes.

Even from the beginning, the elite devoted unremunerated time to the management of the common schools and one had financed the construction of the local school building. For subscription schools, the school board provided tuition for the destitute. Also the private schools provided scholarships for "deserving" students with insufficient means. Finally, tuition at local private schools was below the average, lessening the barrier.[35] Certainly the commitments of the prestigious Pettit family are unquestionable. The elite seem to have subscribed to the principle of upward mobility through education for all classes., The necessities of life made it a self-fulfilling prophesy that the poor would often forgo the opportunity. Despite positive elite sentiments, educational opportunities for the majority of the landless poor and smaller yeomen were curtailed.

Yet according to Bailey's compilations, in southwest Tennessee the level of education was far superior to the rest of the state across all classes and far more equitable.[36] In the counties including Shelby, 68% of the participating total stopped attending at common school level while 32% went on to academies, as opposed to the rest of the state which averaged 92% and 8% respectively.[37] Memphis undoubtedly skewed these statistics. Across the state, higher education with its access to opportunity was also more common in the southwest.[38] The Germantown area with its academies and colleges undoubtedly offered a greater level of educational opportunity. Ironically, perhaps this greater educational opportunity in southwest Tennessee helps explain the greater differences in awareness of social conflict than elsewhere.[39] Those who failed to benefit felt it more.

Jennifer Boone, who has also analyzed the veterans' questionnaires, criticizes Bailey for being "most taken ... with those who emphasize distinctions and antagonisms." The strong majority from across the state were "not aware of differences." Mostly Tennesseans "mingled freely." "Showing benevolence to neighbors appears as a well-respected tradition. . . . More than one veteran mentions, for example, the custom of giving away fresh meat to poorer neighbors. . . ."[40] Again, the House-Duke relationship verifies this locally.

This example of what most contemporaries would have considered to be Christian behavior brings her to a strong argument. Most respondents "pointed particularly to two institutions, the local church and the community school, that clouded, and sometimes completely obscured, significant economic differences." Indeed in Germantown, the Baptist, Methodist and Cumberland Presbyterian churches "emphasized an individual and personal salvation and had few conventions, like pew rents, that distinguished between richer from poorer church members." All three were grass-roots religions that rejected the aristocratic assumptions of Episcopalians. Some respondents singled out church as the one place where everyone mingled on equal footing. . . ."[41]

There is no doubt that the services and the social events of these churches as well as their charitable outreach helped homogenize the community and provided moments of true Christian unity. One familiar with all three of these southern protestant churches knows both the strengths and weaknesses of this argument.

Unfortunately, her other argument about the leveling influences of the community schools holds less water. "Not only was at least a few months' attendance at one of the old 'field schools' a common experience for many of these veterans, but the values preached through antebellum schoolbooks provided ample encouragement for individualism and equality."[42] But the elitist preference for private schooling meant that the common schools provided less opportunity for social mixing. Finally it is naive to argue that ideals propagated in a hit-or-miss schooling were strong enough to undermine the lessons of the harsh realities of their lives.

Adding further to a more nuanced picture of Tennessee's antebellum life, Boone concluded that "Women noticed the differences, and the wealthier ones often made enough of them that more than one veteran pointed out that women did not mingle together as freely as the men did. 'Sometimes I have heard the women folks say of other women,' wrote one veteran, 'Oh, she is stuck up because she has a Negro.'" Others verified that women of slaveholding families discriminated against those without slaves. The working and sporting life of most men was still simple or crude enough that it provided for more bonding and leveling.[43] The surviving correspondence of a small circle of the town's young ladies contains some snobbery, for that circle was limited entirely to the elite and comfortable middle.[44]

In contrast, Isham Howse spoke constantly of wealthy neighbors like the Dukes and of professionals and businessmen who provided loans and assistance. Neighbors came to nurse them when illness struck especially hard. This sensitive man experienced no true social condescension. He had helped disadvantaged young men rise above their origins. He spoke admiringly of those who had pulled themselves up to be his equals. His journal complements those planter veterans whose memories were of a society of meritocracy and mutual support.

Unfortunately, Howse failed to mention any locals who were truly of the underclass, down and out, embittered or beat down. It was as though none existed, which confirms Bailey's picture of the truly poor. They, sometimes called "poor white trash," were distinct from the yeomen, mechanics, and "honest laborers." As Clark put it, they were "held in contempt by white people and Negroes alike."[45] Unfortunately, we cannot distinguish them from the respectable "poor" in the census data. Their absence from any contemporary descriptions of the area's prewar life implies social invisibility. If they had failed to rise through "honest labor," were they considered worthy of charity? Could their children expect anything more than pity? Were they feared as a possible source of crime or vandalism?

Boone went beyond Bailey's analysis to cast light on the social under-class. She included the data that contrasted the responses of Federal veterans to those of Confederates. Federal veterans showed a far stronger belief that they had little chance for economic opportunity (41%) than did Confederates (only 10%). As Boone points out, "These Federal veterans may have perceived themselves as locked in a society that afforded them bleak social and economic futures. Such a society would not be worth fighting for. Confederate veterans, on the other hand, were willing to fight for what they perceived to be a beneficial way of life."⁴⁶ This brings us to Bailey's arguments about the war and its effects. Wartime experiences, however, must wait until the later chapters.

Clark's conclusions about social conflict strikes one as more consistent with what one would expect to find in Germantown. "There were, indeed, social distinctions in (such a) society, the same ones which may be found in communities in any period of history. . . ."⁴⁷

Wyatt-Brown's analogy of social relations as being more fraternal then patriarchal also rings true for Germantown. If there was no rigid hierarchy, there were clearly significant social differences. With such came an expectation of deference, but not subservience. Deference would be duly given in the same vein as that towards one's elders. In return, as he puts it, "Being affable and condescending was required of the man with rank, but clearly the lower the subject of such attention the less solicitous one had to be."⁴⁸

In short, we can assume that before the war Germantown was not without some social tensions and resentments. It probably bubbled mostly below the surface with the more discontented pulling up stakes and going elsewhere. By and large, however, when times were relatively good there was considerable cohesion among the propertied classes, with Christian charity and neighborliness incorporating those below. The test of community cohesion would soon come, however. As we shall see, with politics there were other sources of tension as well, but what is more, the above focuses only within white society.

Slaveholders and the Black Folk's Life

The above account of relative community harmony has almost ignored the issue of slaves and slavery. It would seem they should have been more central to a picture of white people, whose cohesiveness was reinforced by threats to their "peculiar institution" and by fears of and prejudices about their "dependents." Indeed, owners seldom forgot their slaves and worried about proper management of a frequently troublesome, potentially explosive, but essential energy source.

Yet as Wyatt-Brown has argued in his study of Southern life and culture:

> White Southerners seldom forgot the presence of blacks; nevertheless, what mattered most to them was the interchanges of whites among themselves. That is what dominated whites' everyday life, no matter

how dependent so many were upon the unceasing toil of the unfree. Had it been otherwise, slavery would have been even more oppressive than it was. Whites' jockeying for positions in their own world gave the underclass some room for fashioning lives apart. Intrusiveness and over concern, sometimes well intentioned, must have been a serious vexation for those in the slave quarters. They preferred to be left alone.[49]

Nothing better illustrates the white focus on their own affairs than all the letters of Emily Lucken. She made only one reference to a slave, "I am sorry to say that Mr. Douglas lost last night one of his most valuable negroes."[50] Even such a tender young lady seemed only concerned with the owner's loss of property, or even a pet.

To fully understand the lives of their black "charges," we must further explore the complexity of white beliefs. That will give us specific insights into some local conditions not otherwise recorded.

Owners' Attitudes and Beliefs

The 1850 census, breaking out data on the town itself, listed 31 households with 163 whites and 82 slaves, many undoubtedly serving as domestics, others as workers in town. In the rest of District Eleven, 1,179 slaves were counted. By 1860 for the district, the slave schedules totaled only 1,157—not an accurate count.[51] Comparisons of the slave schedules and the property holdings of the white population make it appear that many slaves were absent from that total. The census taker may have missed entire plantations, not just small holders. Their numbers had probably grown by several hundred. In the greater Germantown area, there could have been 1500.

In 1860, living in the county outside Memphis there were only 78 "free coloreds," but none were recorded in the districts around Germantown in 1850 or 1860.[52] The absence of freemen resulted from the lack of opportunities for freemen, but they were also probably not allowed residence. The reason was white fears, at least according to the well-substantiated argument of Steve Baker. The laws in Tennessee at all levels limited the numbers of freemen.[53]

Indeed, earlier attitudes about "freemen" had been more complicated. During the early decades, opportunities for freemen in West Tennessee had been relatively good. Given the frontier lifestyle, many came west. Freemen could even vote. Tennessee had also made it illegal to import slaves into the state for sale. In Shelby County as elsewhere, the idea of eventual emancipation was widespread. Abolitionists were organized and campaigned freely for the cause. The mood shifted, however, as cotton farming became increasingly important, bringing with it a large population of slaves and generating strong economic incentives. Then with the hysteria unleashed by slave revolts such as that of Nat Turner in 1831, attitudes everywhere hardened. The 1834 Tennessee Constitution took away voting rights, restricted religious assembly, barred education and increased obstacles to manumission. Abolition became a dangerous pastime. A desire to remove all freemen prevailed. The legislature passed a law forbidding free blacks from immigrating into the state and required that newly emancipated men be sent out of state. All waivers required severe restrictions on the freeman's life. The state reversed its law against the importation of slaves for sale in 1855, and Memphis became a regional center for the trade.[54]

In the county, courts decided on the petitions of freemen to remain. Communities like Germantown could add their own constraints. The concern was the fear that their presence incited revolt and facilitated escape.[55] The County Quarterly Court did grant applications for freeman to reside in the county when there were local family ties and/or the freeman provided useful skills and an ability to support himself. For instance in 1853, District Eleven Magistrates Ledbetter and Bleckley happened to be sitting when a freeman applied, and they granted the petition.[56] Nevertheless, they and the town council must have denied any local residence.

✦ ✦ ✦

Slavery was actually a moral and psychological trap for the masters. To exploit slaves and to live with one's conscience, one needed justification. It is the business of the intellectual leaders of a society to provide such justifications for its institutions. During the eighteenth and nineteenth centuries, as products of these needs generated by slavery and imperialism the emerging natural sciences produced a pseudo-scientific "body of knowledge," a "racial science" that "proved" the inferiority of non-white "races," to reinforce the "common sense" knowledge of white superiority. Of course, lawyers and judges also made their contributions by treating slaves as property and appealing to constitutional and common law guarantees about property rights. Laws written by slave owners made anyone who sought to undermine them in any way a criminal instead of a moral role model.

The Dred Scott decision probably approached the high (or low) water mark in legal justification. Although the decision increased North-South divisions, the language of the majority opinion written by Chief Justice Taney probably captured the racial beliefs and attitudes of most white Americans with an original-intent argument. He attributed his opinion to the founding fathers deeply rooted beliefs that denied citizenship to blacks.

> (Negroes) had for more than a century before been regarded as beings of inferior order, and altogether unfit to associate with the white race, either in social or political relations, and so far inferior, that they had no rights which the white man was bound to respect; and that the negro might justly and lawfully be reduced to slavery for his benefit. ... The opinion was at the time fixed and universal.... It was regarded as an axiom in morals as well as politics, which no one thought ... to be open to dispute, and men in every grade and position in society daily and habitually acted upon it in their private pursuits, as well as in matters of public concern, without doubting for a moment the correctness of this opinion.[57]

Although opposition to slavery had grown since the founding father's time, beliefs about the races had changed little.

My references to "justifications" should not be taken to mean that slave owners consciously concocted a mythology they did not believe. Every society is held together by a "consensus reality," that body of self-evident, common-sense knowledge that every "reasonably rational" member of that society can plainly see. For one obvious example, once it was believed that the world was flat, and the sun revolved around us. Then as now, to question any consensus reality raises doubts about either one's rationality or motives. In this case, such racial thinking was nearly universal in the Western world, even where no longer used to justify slavery. In Christian slaveholding societies, it constituted a world view that one embraced and defended against obviously subversive ideas. Upholding such a God-ordained order was a Christian duty.[58]

Most Southern theologians offered biblical proof for both slavery and specifically the place of black Africans as slaves, ordained by God. In the South, the major denominations were all guilty of such justifying. Over disagreements about slavery in 1844, the Methodist Episcopal Church Convention split into two separate bodies to avoid conflict in their assembly, and as a result in 1845 the Methodist Episcopal Church South emerged. Most Baptist churches seceded from the northern churches with their abolitionist tendencies and formed a separate Southern Baptist Convention in 1845. Shelby County's Baptist Big Hatchie Association joined them in 1849. The positions of the Presbyterian and Episcopalian Churches were more complex. As the question of slavery had become increasingly divisive, the general assembly of the majority old school of the Presbyterians interdicted forever agitation on the subject. Silence cloaked the moral dilemma. Only in 1861 did the Presbyterian Church and the Protestant Episcopal Church in the Confederate states secede from their mother churches. Specifically, the Presbytery of Memphis seceded on June 14. In 1862, Lutherans split over the issue of secession rather than slavery. Despite Pope Gregory XVI's condemnation of slavery, Southern Bishops continued to justify it.[59] Likewise, Southern Jews found ample support for slavery in the Torah.[60]

Reverend Phillip Tuggle, who served the Germantown Methodist Church and its sister churches in the Hernando circuit, must have taught and firmly believed in the biblical justifications. He first began riding the Hernando circuit in 1854 and settled near Germantown where he bought and ran a plantation with 52 slaves. Previously he had served in a couple of the church's "colored missions."[61] As we shall see, from all appearances, Tuggle preached the proper Christian roles of both slaveholders and slaves to both his black and white congregations.

Isham Howse, who owned four slaves, subscribed to biblical and other theological justifications, but was still conflicted about holding slaves.

> But our slaves are well-fed, and clothed, and are happy, in comparison with the poor white slave, either in Europe or in our northern states.... I do not believe that slavery in itself is sinful. God has decreed a difference in mankind, and some men are born inferior to others, some to rule and some to be ruled. Servants need disciplining, and I am incompetent to enforce it. My feelings are too tender.... And, O Lord, if such is thy will, hasten the time when the children of Africa may go home civilized and Christianized! Or if that cannot be done in my day, so order my destiny that I might have nothing to do with slaves as their master. I do not say that the relation of master to slave, even as it exists in these states, is sinful. On the contrary,

> I believe that God in his providence has sent the black man here for wiser and benevolent purposes—that he may, in the fullness of time, be the means of doing good to the race in their native land. But I am unqualified to discharge a master's duty, and if it would please God, I would rejoice to be so situated as to have nothing to do with slavery. . . . I had rather live poor all my natural life than have slaves. . . . I must take care of them. It would be a curse to them to free them. How long, Oh, how long will it be before they all will return to their fatherland?[62]

Poor Isham—equally conflicted about other things as well and long suffering.

The churches certainly felt a responsibility for the spiritual well-being of blacks. All three Germantown churches had slave members. In some, within services seating was separated. Others held entirely segregated meetings, as did the Germantown Presbyterians, with the black service either following the white or being held in a nearby brush arbor. Black membership in the Memphis Presbytery averaged only about 10 or 11 percent of the total congregation during the 1850s, while in 1854 the Methodist circuit that covered Germantown had a ratio of 445 white to 492 "colored."[63] Blacks preferred the Baptists and Methodists to the Presbyterians as more expressive, and owners generally did not force their own denominations.

Baptist leadership was sensitive to the desires of their "black brethren" for their own instruction. In 1856, the Big Hatchie Association acknowledged that it was less successful among blacks than it should have been, because of "a strong prejudice against white teachers." The Association encouraged white pastors to train blacks to lead blacks, to reach them "through their own color." Thereafter the Association reported great success. Of course, white pastors maintained control of that instruction. Sometimes white children would sneak out of their service to enjoy the more spirited African American style at an assembly in a nearby brush arbor.[64]

For each of their circuits, such as the Hernando circuit that served Germantown, the Methodists maintained a "colored mission," with one pastor in the circuit exclusively serving slaves unable to attend a regular church. They held services at the larger plantations or central locations. But where a white church served a community like Germantown, it also had its own black members. In 1860, Germantown became the seat of the colored mission for the Hernando Circuit.[65]

Slave owners were especially concerned about controlling their slaves' access to religious instruction. They feared slaves who were assertive enough to seek their own "liberation theology" in secret services where subversive gospel songs promised liberation. The more blacks made Christianity into their own religion, the more complicated its effects on them became. It fortified their spirits and helped them cope, without leading them to accept slavery as proper. It provided them with a personal and communal morality that was not immune to the necessities for dissimulation and the "acquisition" of property their labor created. The realities of their situation required such. It also provided a moral scale for judging their masters.[66]

The concern that local slaveholders had for the spiritual development of their "dependents" varied greatly but was clearly circumscribed by practicalities of control and their racist ideology. For instance, although slave holders did not necessarily respect family relations, they had frequently encouraged them, because it made the slaves more likely to accept their lot and gave the owners leverage. Owners usually did not encourage formal church marriage but allowed the slaves to devise their own ceremonies. A full Christian wedding was not often desired, because it implied an inviolability that a Christian master should observe. When a pastor did preside, the phrase, "till death do you part," was never included in the ceremony, for masters had the power to part them.[67]

During the war, when escaped slaves ended up in the freedmen camps, Union authorities, often clergymen, became interested in their morals. The information they gathered in the camps in which former Germantown slaves resided casts light on the regimen under which they had lived. These clergymen were especially concerned when they learned that conjugal relations did not exist within "proper Christian contexts." Chaplain John Eaton, Jr., the general superintendent of contrabands in Grant's command, circulated a questionnaire to the superintendents of each camp. In the camps at Memphis, none of the 681 men and women were listed as married, which was unusual compared to the other camps. Of course, the local superintendent may have simply been narrower in his definition, accepting only a service provided by a minister.[68] As we shall see in Germantown, housing arrangements and the incidence of single mothers with children imply that most owners hardly concerned themselves with the sexual activities of their "charges."

Nevertheless, everywhere the liberated blacks quickly and gladly accepted the legal and religious trappings of a socially approved marriage. It both affirmed their full status as citizens and created a legal basis for property, inheritance, and custody within their families. Whenever full marital status became available, they sought it without any compulsion.[69] Subsequent censuses prove this for Germantown's later residents.

Differences of opinion among the whites over the proper management and treatment of slaves were a source of tension. When Wilks Brooks left North Carolina to settle at Germantown in 1835, he was allegedly motivated to escape problems created by such differences. There, as a member of the General Assembly and where memories of the Nat Turner Revolt were so vivid, he had argued strongly for the education of slaves to better civilize them. The fear of slave revolts also divided owners over whether to employ progressive or repressive methods. After his progressive ideas were voted down, he felt that life there was increasingly unsafe. This allegedly motivated him to move his family.[70] He brought with him from North Carolina only four of his slaves, but gradually accumulated several dozen more.[71]

The Unique Life within that "Left-Alone" Slave Community

Consistent with Wyatt-Brown's important observation, the preferred separateness of the slave quarters from white life provided the only elements of "freedom." Unfortunately because of the scarce evidence for any specifics of slave life around Germantown, we will have to tease out as much as we can about the slaves and their subculture from what is available. (Appendix 3) To begin, we may assume that it had much in common with what has been studied elsewhere. That culture was as rich as any other ethnic subculture of nineteenth century America. Nevertheless, its relative isolation from the rest of American culture in general certainly produced unique qualities and strengths.

There were several types of slave communities. The larger the farm or plantation the more separate or "independent" the slave culture would be. It could range from one extended family to a veritable village on a plantation. The smaller the "holdings" of the slave owner the more limited the possibility for a specific separate culture "at home." There a few slaves were entwined with the white family as subordinates, in a status ranging from pets to livestock. At an intermediate level, however, when there were a dozen or more slaves, they could become a veritable extended family. Furthermore, slaves living in Germantown proper had different opportunities than those more isolated in the countryside when limited to the confines of the plantation. In town, at least during the day, slaves might move about freely in order to do their assigned chores, with greater opportunities to "goof off" and intermingle. Beyond that, in all environments, a certain freedom of expression was often encouraged. The rich mix of African heritages survived in the form of vibrant music, dancing and storytelling. This simultaneously entertained the whites and assured them that their "charges" were happy and content.

The social structure within whatever community blacks developed would have been as complex as any extended family or village. There would have been patriarchs, but especially matriarchs. Relations among house servants and field hands must have been complex. Cooks and body servants had privileges. A favored mistress could get and share little treasures, or just be another especially exploited woman. The roles of such a diverse group of "privileged" individuals in the community could be positive or negative.

Beyond that, the previously mentioned common practice of the entire slave population of regularly visiting the infected speaks to a strong sense of community among the slaves of a plantation.[72] Even under the worst conditions in West Tennessee, the slave quarters became a community center. Storytelling and music lightened the spirits and news of the outside world came in.[73] By 1860, several generations of immersion and mixing left most speaking only English. Nevertheless, a wide range of cultural colors were preserved among those separated by generations from their origins. Such infectious spores would spread into the white world, enriching Southern culture.

✦ ✦ ✦

In addition to field work, women and children did the productive household labor: tending animals, gardening, food processing, cooking, carding, weaving, sewing, washing, and cleaning, from sunup to sundown. Nurses for children, personal servants for the women, and body-servants for men were the only privileged and relatively light labor, but nevertheless on call around the clock, and almost always more directly under white supervision. They often slept on the floor outside the bedroom. Grooming horses and driving, blacksmithing, working mills and gens, and processing special produce and meats were the equivalents for men. The larger the household, the more such employment.[74] The skills of local freedmen after the war, grew from such special labor "opportunities."

Collective and collaborative women's work such as clothing production and washing provided an opportunity to socialize and share information. When the slave wife's workday was over as slave, she returned to her cabin to work as wife and mother. That is, if she had sufficient energy left. Family life in the cabins was certainly problematic. Beyond that, small children spent most of their time under the supervision of slightly older girls or the aged.[75]

No traces of local slave housing survive, so it can only be deduced from clues in the slave schedules. For many plantations, these lists are such random mixes of gender and age that they provide no clues to housing except the total number of buildings. Fortunately, some owner-listings present patterns that seem to have been based on their housing. Many groupings of working-age males or females imply that barrack-housing was the most common. In one such case, only 6 buildings served a population of 41. In other cases, there are paired mature men and women with one to several children. This implies single-pen family units, and owners who encouraged at least family situations among their slaves. A single pen was a cabin, typically 16 by 18 feet. Some were double or multiple pins. In larger cabins, groups of single men or women were collectively housed. Other groups consisted of up to a dozen children, under 10, of mixed gender usually under one mature woman. These were barracks for children separated from parents by sale, but also day-care units from which infants might return to their mothers in the evening. This had to have been the case for true infants of nursing age in such groups. In the smaller holdings, paired couples and their children were common, but other unrelated children brought away from their mothers were often living with them. This seems apparent when one of the adults was mulatto, and children were listed as black.

Statistics for the three counties around Germantown indicate that more population growth came from purchases rather than local births. The relative scarcity of single-family units on local plantations versus gender concentration in barracks suggests that most owners were not supporting family living arrangements.[76]

Anything like the development of true paternal authority within a family depended heavily on this situation. Denial of any opportunity to protect wife and children, even suffering humiliation in front of them, required a man with extraordinary fortitude to display any model of fatherly dignity. Motherly women could provide the bonds and support needed by the many children, whether parts of intact families or torn from them. During the long workdays, the elderly or infirm acquired the roles of aunt or uncle. Otherwise the care of the infants fell entirely to girls too young for the fields. Indeed, it took a village to raise the children, but one in which normal relationships were seriously disrupted.

In town, the slave schedules paint a picture of diverse living arrangements. Whether the owner was a mechanic, professional or merchant, they might hold either intact families, or their work force was gender biased for specific labor. The wagon maker had 6 males 10 years or over, and 2 females, plus 1 child under 10. Only that seven-year-old may have been the child of the one adult female. One fifty-five-year-old stands out among them. They were all housed in two units, perhaps one couple having a family unit.

The foreman of the gin factory had 2 females and 3 children, two under one year of age. Obviously both women were bearing children without live-in fathers. All were housed in one unit. Since the children were not designated as mulatto, those men were slaves living in town.

The merchant Boardman had two women and one man sharing one cabin. Henry Massy apparently had an adult couple with an infant in one cabin, while two teenaged girls shared another. They were all probably house servants.

The physician Moore had on older male and two females in their thirties, apparently for mixed domestic and farm work. They and 4 children were housed in his home. Dr. Cornelius had 4 adults, probably working in both his home and on his land. They were apparently two families living in separate pens, each with a child.

On the plantations and farms, for example, Sarah Walker had 16 working males and 9 females with 7 children under ten years. In contrast Sarah Jones had 7 females and 3 such children, but only 3 working males. Of course, women worked as field hands, and/or house workers as needed. Joseph Brooks had 13 under ten, out of a total of 44. Richard Goodwin carried an equally high percentage of children. Both men either benefitted from their slaves' fruitfulness, or they bought children as an investment. Reverend Phillip Tuggle owned 16 children out of 34, housed with their parents in 5 buildings, indicating he encouraged properly married couples. Several of these couples would remain in the area after emancipation, at least three with fully intact families of multiple children.

The planter, William Harrison, had one cabin for an older couple who cared for six children ages from 11 to 7 months. They might not have all been theirs, one may have been Andrew, son of Mack, who resided in one of the four barracks. One other younger couple may have also had a single pen, the woman perhaps being Lydia. Ten men and four teenagers and two women and three teenagers housed in separate barracks. The women's quarters also housed and/or day-cared for five children, one of whom may have been nine-month-old William.

George Small, a yeoman, housed six men in one barrack and two females with one teenager and two children had another. The women's barrack also held an adult male classed as "idiot."

This mixed picture of living arrangements and childbearing indicates that most owners were not overly concerned about intimate relations among their men and women. A minister like Tuggle would be a clear exception. Other owners either respected or were indifferent to their slaves' private lives or were no more concerned about their sexual activities than they would be about the family dog.

✦ ✦ ✦

Aside from acknowledging the inherent evil and inhumanity of the institution, we need to be cautious about oversimplifying the slave experience. The recorded memories of former slaves are replete with examples of experiences that confound efforts at generalization. Not only were the owners individuals whose personalities greatly affected the experience of slaves, but the slaves were equally individuals with unique personalities. Although a bold, aggressive, cocky, or ill-tempered personality could often prove fatal, in others they proved advantageous. A few got away with unbelievable acts of defiance or simple self-assertion. Sometimes, they were even protected by their masters from punishment by others zealous to enforce controls.[77] Of course, the vast majority had to adjust their temperaments to reality or suffer serious consequences.

Southerners like to believe that their ancestors were good to their slaves. Some undoubtedly were. But being "good" to slaves was a relative term. It usually meant employing incentives rather than brutal enforcement and offering rewards or treats beyond just providing the most basic needs. Yet neither paternalism nor Christian kindness compensated for the degradation of enslavement.

During the war and occupation, slaves would have the opportunity to take their future into their own hands. As we shall see, Germantown slaves responded diversely when the opportunity came, revealing a lot about their treatment. Those who stayed or returned probably had mixed motives. A few had enough compassion for their owner families that they stayed out of concern for the welfare of the women and children left alone. Some preferred the relative comfort or security of a known working-living relationship, especially if the owner offered incentives. Others had been successfully suppressed and unable to visualize opportunities elsewhere.[78]

Since both master and slave were human beings, close relations could develop among them despite the barriers. Household slaves could acquire the status of "members-of-the-family." Of course, that was usually a status more like a "pet" rather than relative. A personal or body servant had often grown up with his or her master/mistress. Compared to the alternatives, someone with little hope might be content with such a status, but not grateful.[79] One extreme example, however, was the relationship between Randolph Webb and his servant Amos. When Webb died, he left Amos his gold watch in appreciation of his service, and when Amos died, he insisted on and was buried by his master in the family plot. The inscription of the headstone read, "Well Done. Thy Good Faithful Servant."[80] Such warm relations depended on the continued subordinate status of the slave, and the incidence of such were greatly exaggerated before and after the war to sugarcoat the realities of slavery.

As another side of "intimacy," slave women or girls frequently bore the offspring of masters or overseers. Of course, white wives and mothers usually considered this a moral morass for the men folk.[81] The black woman's place in such relations varied from outright rape through calculated consent to some degree of attachment. The offspring of such relations also fared differently. In Shelby County in 1860, 2,783 of the 16,953 slaves were mulatto, but there were distinct variations in District Eleven, where mulattos were reportedly rare.[82] In a few cases, however, high concentrations of mulattoes, especially children, on a particular farm may indicate the presence of one or more exploitative white men.[83] When such children were not doomed to a life of slave labor, the father provided some education and training, and perhaps a small stake, emancipated them and sent them elsewhere to earn a living. Since the 1860 census reported that 64 percent of the free Black population was mulatto, while only 16 percent of the slaves were, it appears that owners who sired children emancipated them far more frequently than their other slaves. Specifically, Shelby County's ratio of freed mulattoes was 178 to 2,783 mulatto slaves. This was a far higher ratio than among freed "blacks" at 98 to 14,170.[84]

Siring children with one's slaves was not uncommon around Germantown, and one particular case provides unique, specifics.[85] Schuyler H. "Kirk" Roberts was a most unusual "family" man.[86]

Born in Virginia in 1804, he had arrived with slaves about 1830, settling in what would be the Germantown area. Efforts by genealogists to assemble a record of his marriages and children are a confusing mess. In addition to three legal marriages, they attribute as many as twenty-two legitimate children. Records do not correlate well with the names given or these numbers. His first marriage in 1824 to Mary Keener was in Virginia, where they had two children. After arriving in Tennessee, they had more, one at Germantown in 1838, and the last in Memphis in 1840 when Mary had apparently left him, but there is no surviving record of divorce. There is no further local record of his first wife and children, although someone by her name died in 1849 in Arkansas.

He was next married in 1841 to Missinah Pass, by whom he had four children, the last in 1848.[87] She is also supposed to have died in 1849. In August of that same year at age 44, he married his third wife, German-born Maria (Mary) Louise Kuner, age 20. The Kuner family had just arrived in New Orleans from Germany in 1848, reaching Germantown in December. In the 1850 census the new couple were residing on his 635-acre plantation with two of the children of the previous marriage, Waddy and Iris. Maria would bear eight children, five of whom would die at birth. His growing plantation was located on Hollyford Road (present Hack's Cross) around its present-day intersection with Winchester Road. He owned somewhere between 45 and 50 slaves, but records and memories are inconsistent. One of his slave women and her children constituted Robert's "other family."

Sometime in the 1830s, he had bought a teenage girl, Mahalia. He needed a housekeeper. She became his mistress, giving birth to seven children between 1833 and 1847. One can only speculate about the feelings of either "partner," but surely the permanence of their relationship says something. Also it probably had something to do with the disappearance of his first wife and all her children. Either Missinah was naive or tolerant for nine years. As soon as his last wife discovered the situation, however, Roberts found it necessary to ship Mahalia and children off to a family plantation in Paris, Tennessee. By one account, they allegedly slipped back, and Roberts found them discreet accommodations somewhere back "home." In another version, Mary had them brought back after his death for distribution to the heirs.[88]

Roberts died December 1859 at age 55, reportedly chocking on a chicken bone. Mary promptly married T. G. Kincannon (later shortened to Cannon), and in 1860, Roberts' 49 slaves, including Mahalia and her children were divided among Robert's white children and Mary.[89] Apparently Mahalia found a relatively comfortable place in Mary's family. She was fondly remembered as "Aunt Mahayley." As we shall see, the subsequent history of her children indicates they were better equipped to cope with adjustment to the post-emancipation economy.

✦ ✦ ✦

Slaves did have some "free-time." In addition to the Sabbath which usually included Saturday afternoon, masters also allowed their slaves respite on some holidays. Some attended the whites' events but celebrated in segregation when not serving the whites. If the whites had music and danced under the shelter of a brush arbor on a prepared ground covered with sawdust, "the negroes had a dancing place to themselves—in the open air."[90] When the trains were still a new experience, young Caroline Burns brought some slave children to throw cotton bolls and flowers as it passed.[91] Black children had playtime up to about age six, while white children's needs for personal servants, playmates or smaller children to serve as play things affected that "playtime." Opinions varied widely on the age at which a slave should be put to work. Some believed they should learn early to do their life's work, but most thought it should begin with light chores around age six. Field labor could begin between eight or ten.

Expenses for upkeep were simply kept to a minimum, and lucky slaves supplemented their family's diets with fish and game, garden plots, woodland gathering or stealing. Likewise, masters and overseers realized they could thwart slow-down tactics best by granting some freedoms, privileges and opportunities. The alternative was brutal punishment. Perhaps the worse fate, however, husbands and wives, mothers and children were torn apart through sales. Threats to do so could be used to control slaves, but ultimately their fate depended on the economic needs of the master. It has been estimated that perhaps one quarter of all slave families in Tennessee were disrupted despite any laws to the contrary.[92]

Although Germantown was hardly a market in the local slave trade, occasional auctions did occur in town, usually at the railroad depot. For instance, to settle an estate, a slave named Sam was auctioned there for the sum of $1,070.

The heirs of Sam's owner were apparently opposed to the sale, which had to be forced through court order.[93] One can only guess what kinds of relationships Sam was torn from by this sale.

One aspect of slavery that is rarely mentioned was the several ways they were managed as property. Their purchase was often handled exactly like real estate bought on credit. Banks gave loans for the purchase of slaves, and they also accepted slaves as collateral for other loans. As we have seen, slave owners, especially those heavily involved in getting their cash crops to market, were totally enmeshed in bank loans and bank instability. This often resulted in bankruptcy and repossession when owners were unable to make payment. Loans also had to be repaid on the owner's death. When banks or other debtors "repossessed" slaves, they went on the market with total disregard for family ties. Even sensitive owners had no say.

By the same token it was common practice to rent out one's slaves to generate extra income. In the year of the 1860 census, of the 1426 plus slaves in the Greater Germantown area, 304 were rented by planters, yeomen, merchants and professionals. The consequences of this for the slaves would have been variable, but heavily determined by the renter's needs and character. One problem, the renter might believe he had little interest in the "maintenance" of a rented "item."

The renters had the advantage of cheap labor without the cost of purchase or the debts that usually entailed. A few yeomen actually achieved the prestige of "planter status" by renting. Renting also drew non-owning yeoman into the world of ownership with all that entailed.

❖ ❖ ❖

Scholars generally agree that the life of slaves in Tennessee was better than in most of the rest of the South. Despite plantation slavery's heavier presence in the western part of the state, that was true there as well, evidence of which we shall see in post-war statistics. The memories of a young soldier, who had grown up in Mason about twenty-five miles from Germantown, provide some insight into the relative condition of area slaves. When he encountered conditions in southern Alabama, "I left this place with a different view of slavery." The treatment of slaves there contrasted sharply with his view that they were "the most treasured servants and, aside from a human standpoint, a good strong negro was valuable property."[94] Of course, he said this in 1912, by which time such sentiments had become a key point in Southern romanticizing. Whatever, personalities determined the slaves' fate. Sadism, cruelty, or simple fits of anger were the prerogative of master, mistress, sons, daughters, and overseers.

The previously recounted story of Dr. Scruggs treating a slave woman for "polypus of the uterus" cats light on local attitudes. When she was about age 43, she began severe hemorrhaging. The first doctor was called in promptly and succeeded in stopping the bleeding. Over the next two years, the mistress had been treating her with remedies, but ultimately the woman had wasted away and seemed near death. Then Scruggs was called in and successfully treated the problem. The owners had been generous with the medical expenses, two doctors and a third as consultant, plus medications and a final treatment.[95] Many white families relied on even less medical treatment for their own members. So, one must speculate about motivation.

The doctor's concluding remarks seem pertinent. "She recovered rapidly, and has menstruated regularly ever since, notwithstanding she says she is 48 years old and has given birth to twelve healthy children ...; she has perfectly recovered her health and may yet have several children."[96] In one respect, the woman had served successfully as a brood mare. Were the owners merely protecting an investment? Considering the woman's age, that seems like a long shot. A woman who had survived 12 childbirths and 2 years of debilitating illness must have seemed a poor gamble. Humanitarian or moral concerns, perhaps even affection, seem among the motives.

Britten Duke is another example of area planters who at least treated their slaves as valuable investments worthy of medical care. In 1854, he paid $3.00 to have a physician make an emergency house call and perform a surgery. The next day he paid another $1.00 for a follow-up office visit and prescription.[97] The expense accounts contained in the individual Shelby County Probate Court records of Germantown area slave owners indicate that many area plantation owners did not subscribe to the minimum maintenance theory attributed to the deeper South. . Many had made frequent payments for the medical attention of their slaves.[98]

Another indication of humane attitudes about maintaining slaves is the slave schedule listings of impaired slaves. Although the aged, even into their 80s, were never listed as impaired by the census taker, in 1860 he did note two designated as "idiots" and one other undefined. Presumably "idiot" meant unable to perform simple takes.

Across the South, slave life involved enough deprivation to have consequences. According to the 1860 census, the average slave's life expectancy was only 33.7 years, a full ten years less than whites or free blacks.[99] Local conditions were purportedly better, but to what level we'll never know. In the area around Germantown, several slaves were in their 60s, still considered of full working age, baring serious disabilities. There were only six in their 70s. None had achieved octogenarian status.

❖ ❖ ❖

On the plus side, slaves were not totally without rights and legal protection in Tennessee. Much of Tennessee's slave code and judicial precedent had been set in the earlier years of more ambivalence about slavery. Although they often remained the letter of the law, such sentiments eroded over time, and the slaves' legal recourse depended on many variables. Even so, as late as 1858, a court ruled that slaves were not just simple property, but also persons. "That as persons they are considered by our law, as accountable moral agents, possessed by the power of volition and locomotion. That certain rights have been conferred upon them by positive law and judicial determination, and other privileges and indulgences have been conceded to them by universal consent of their owners."[100] On the one hand, they were punishable, though more severely, like whites for their actions under law, but they also had enforceable "rights."

There were legal limits on corporal punishment. Mutilation and torture were illegal, and a slave could not be killed except by proper judicial processes, or extenuating circumstances. Otherwise the killer, even an owner could be charged with murder. In Germantown, when a slave died of any cause, a magistrate serving as coroner conducted an inquest.[101] There are no local records of whites being held responsible, however.

The state Supreme Court was diligent in encouraging humane treatment by masters. It held that families could not be broken up and sold to settle debts against an estate, although this ruling was frequently violated without consequences. Masters were legally responsible for providing wholesome food, adequate clothing and shelter.[102] Of course, recourse to the law was not easy for an aggrieved slave.

Probably the most important rights for most slaves were the above mentioned "privileges and indulgences ... conceded to them by universal consent of their owners." Such rights actually acquired common law status, but the slaves simply understood them as traditional rights to be withheld only as punishment. Whatever "common law rights" the slaves could claim had to be based on long-standing traditions on a particular plantation, subject entirely to the owner's wishes. The Sabbath and holy days like Christmas were free days, sometimes Saturday afternoons and nights were also free for family and communal time. They were to be left alone and given freedom of movement within limits, including visitation with family on other plantations. Such travel off the owner's lands required a written pass, but it was a presumed right. When there were no vigilance patrols, there was no enforcement. Gifts, treats and feasts for special occasions, even small cash payments as rewards could become entrenched traditions. Hunting, fishing and garden rights, even the opportunity to market their own products were incentive strategies employed by owners. Once granted, such privileges could become entrenched. Slaves would exercise subtle or even overt forms of protest when they felt such rights were violated.[103]

One example of slaves earning income was Charles, one of Reverend Phillip Tuggle's slaves, bought at auction in New Orleans and fortunately brought back north. At age thirteen he and his mother were sold from their Virginia home and separated at that auction. Tuggle put Charles to work as janitor at the little church he had erected on his plantation to serve Methodists living south of Nonconnah. Charles reportedly endeared himself to the congregation who rewarded his services with tips. Typically, Tuggle allowed his slaves to keep whatever they managed to earn on the side. Charles saved some $500 that he would invest in land.[104]

◆ ◆ ◆

Under even the best conditions, the human spirit rebelled against enslavement in a variety of ways. One example, petty theft which slaves easily justified was common. Owners usually had to accept it as part of the price of operations. It only became a serious concern when it involved someone else's property.

By its very nature, slavery compelled one to attempt escape. One early attempt from Germantown provides details of how the underground railway worked locally. In 1825 when a slave escaped from John Lewis Phillips, he sought assistance from the freeman, John Bennett in Memphis. To get him upriver to freedom, the plan was to seal him up in a wooden box to be shipped by steamboat. Unfortunately the box sat on the wharf in the heat of the summer sun until he had to cry out for help. Newspapers found this story humorous.[105] Nevertheless, there were similar attempts at this method over subsequent years.

This 1825 attempt represented one of the three alternative routes of escape for area slaves. Two were through the underground railway base at Memphis. Aside from the river route, there were two railroad possibilities, directly north on the Memphis and Ohio, or crossing the river and going north or west from there. These all required forged travel papers or help camouflaging oneself to pass as white for the duration of the trip. The other route was north overload through other way-stations.

According to the 1860 census, runaways not only declined in Tennessee during the previous decade, but the escape rate was never very high. In 1850, the reported rate of runaway was 1 in 3,491, and by 1860 had fallen to 1 in 9,509.[106] Yet the Germantown area during the 1850s stood in stark contrast to these official statistics. At least seven slaves ran away in a five-year period, a much higher rate than this purported average. Considering the total number of slaves in the area, this would have been an extremely high escape rate compared to the reported overall average for the decade.[107] It is likely that in a cotton-growing plantation area, they were more desperate than elsewhere in the state. It is also possible that owners could be embarrassed by such incidents and not report them to the census taker.

For instance in 1857, an anonymous gentleman living near Germantown offered $40 reward for his two runaways, John and Simon. Rather than posting an ad in his own name, the owner was using A. R. Cartwright and Goodlet, Nabers & Co. as agents.[108] Perhaps this indicted some embarrassment?

Any form of slavery was onerous, and when a slave's conditions improved, he might develop "dangerous" higher expectations. In fact, runaway rates were higher among skilled and educated slaves, perhaps because freedom offered them even brighter opportunities. Such was the case of one of the two slaves, Henry and Taylor, who ran away from Dr. J. M. M. Cornelius in 1860. Henry was a bearded man of about 30, "intelligent, can read and write, and is very pompous in his language and actions." Such an educated slave was one groomed for service work of the sort that a doctor might need as a receptionist and assistant, butler or gentleman's servant. In this case, the slaves' confidence was also high enough that each took with him a carpet bag and some changes of clothing.[109] Neither were reported as escaped in the 1860 census.

An elaborate attempt occurred in 1860. A woman escaped from "a gentleman by the name of Merrick who lived near Germantown." She went to Memphis where she found support for her flight. An effort to board a boat north proved futile, so under disguise she boarded a Memphis and Ohio train. A "useful citizen," of Brownsville suspected her as she boarded.[110]

Few slaves probably spent their entire lives in total submission to the indignities they endured. Short of overt acts of defiance, most resorted to slow downs, "accidents," and theft. Polluting the food or drink of an especially hated master or mistress was a satisfactory revenge. Some simply snapped, refused to obey an onerous order or to submit to continued abuse. That or attempted escape resulted in painful punishment or sale into a worse life.

Finally, there was one much greater display of resistance. What slaveholders feared most was slaves so badly abused that they would take something more than petty revenge on their owners. The *Appeal* reported that on October 19, 1858, the Germantown area was in an uproar when a plot "conceived by the slaves" was uncovered to destroy the home of "a planter in that neighborhood." Arson was more common than revolt. "Two or three arrests of parties had been made, and the authorities were in pursuit of others connected with the conspiracy."[111] Notably, these were plantation slaves, and the *Appeal* rather thoughtfully failed to report the planter's name. Once ignited, slave revolts had the dangerous potential to spread their vengeful destruction against surrounding plantations, and even towns. The *Appeal* failed to report on the fate of the arrested.

Such an event must indeed have generated an uproar, for everyone had heard of a far more frightening story two years previously in nearby LaFayette. A slave girl reported a conspiracy to her mistress. The owners had 32 of them arrested, of whom 23 were considered sufficiently guilty to be jailed at Somerville.

These slaves allegedly planned to take advantage of the election of 1856 when the men would be away from home voting. They would kill all the women and children, seize money and arms, and waylay the men as they returned. They hoped to rally all the slaves in the surrounding counties. Such a story extracted from the culprits was so formulaic that it reminds one of how the Inquisition extracted confessions that confirmed their hysterical fears. Vigilant Patrols fanned out to insure all was safe. Rumors spread that the ringleaders had been lynched by an angry mob, but W. E. Eppes protested this slander of the town's "law-abiding citizens."[112] No punishments were published.

The reference to vigilance patrols raises the question of whether Germantown's district had maintained regular slave patrols. An act of 1806 provided for the appointment of patrolmen by the district militia captain, "for the regulation of the colored population." Each chartered town was also to maintain a nightly patrol. The work was so unpopular that it frequently fell to poorer men. They were to seize weapons, break up unapproved meetings and arrest slaves loose without passes. They became notorious for exceeding their authority to punish.[113]

Quarterly court records have a few surviving entries for patrol payments from the 1830s, ceasing thereafter. It would seem that regular patrolling had lapsed in most of Tennessee. But in 1856, the House and Senate reinstated patrols in each county.[114] After the outbreak of the hysteria of 1857, Shelby County resumed regular payments for patrols that lasted through 1861.[115]

♦ ♦ ♦

One of the more lasting scars of slavery was the frequent severance of family ties. The girl who would become Mrs. Margaret Scales was placed on a stump at the age of 12 and auctioned off. Brought to Germantown, she never saw her mother again.[116]

The 1870 census provides more varied stories. Out of 330 black households, 153 contained families that went well back into slavery. Many seemed fully intact, but some may have lost older children to sales. Others were obviously mere fragments. For some examples, William (Carter) was born in Virginia in 1824, while his wife was born in Missouri in 1830. When and where they came together is unclear, but by 1846 they had their first son, James somewhere in Tennessee. They would bear and keep 7 more children while in slavery. Lewis (Tuggle) was born in 1833 in South Carolina, while Margaret was born in Virginia in 1835. Phillip Tuggle brought them to Shelby County when he settled there. Reverend Tuggle undoubtedly formalized their Christian wedding before they had their first son Collins in 1853. Thereafter they had three other children under slavery on his planation south of Germantown. An example of unsettled early lives followed by a few settled years were James (Daily), born in 1826 in Virginia, while Chaney was born in Alabama in 1850. Whoever bought them took them to Mississippi, where Mary was born in in 1857. The three of them were living next on a plantation in Tennessee where they gave birth to three more children. All lived together at Germantown by 1870. Among the less fortunate, Martha (Jenkins), born in Alabama in 1810, was able to hold on to only her granddaughter, Emily, born in 1859 in Mississippi. Who knows how much turmoil and how many losses she suffered in between those years.

Although none of these slaves could have known how near emancipation was, the process would bring them great elation, but no great reduction of hardships. For most, the war-time transition would prove even more grueling and dangerous than for their former masters.

3

A TRANSPORTATION AND ECONOMIC CENTER

Today, locals seem most intrigued by the question of how and why the town got its name.[1] But that begs the question of why there ever was a town. According to tradition in 1834, George Shepherd had the 67 acres belonging to his wife Nicey surveyed to lay out lots for a town center. There is no clue why they thought "if we build it, they will come." The lots were well away from the Wolf River. Only after the town was established did it become the crossroads of three post and stagecoach roads. At the time, only the crude State Line Road passed through the surveyed area, connecting Memphis with points to the east and southeast. This was apparently sufficient to encourage settlement by men with plans for plantation-based market cropping. The subsequent crossroads and the final arrival of the trains in 1852 would make the town a transportation and economic center, but that was all after the fact. There was little reason to believe that its particular location on the State Line Road offered any superior advantages. Earlier the first little settlement in the area had already begun at Pea Ridge three mile west on that road. It could just as easily have become the area's crossroads. Indeed, it had already spawned at least one county crossroad. For unknown reasons, Germantown had quickly eclipsed it by 1836. Was the simple availability of town-sized lots sufficient to inspire business and professional settlers? If so, the enterprise of the Shepherd's paid well. One wishes to know how they advertised it.

The only memories of what this settlement offered were published in 1873 by a man known better for his sense of humor than accuracy. According to his "aged" oral sources, "Then, the principal improvements were a horse-mill (presumably grist), a store, three dram shops, a church subscription and a two-story

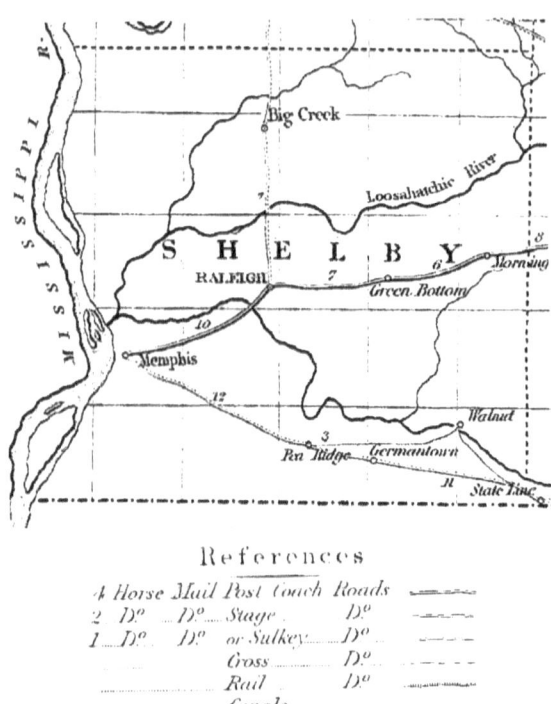

MAP 6 Major Shelby County roads, 1839.

log house.... A hotel was kept in the lower rooms," and the upper story was used for public meetings and other community building purposes.[2] Humorists of his ilk loved to emphasize the number of saloons always available throughout the town's history. "A church subscription" may be a reference to the two-story log building that traditions mention as a multipurpose community building. It should have been available for the congregations emerging at that time that did not prefer house meetings. Aside from some log-cabin homes, housing a doctor and a lawyer (Justice of the Peace), this is a very likely picture of the little community that coalesced in the 1830s to serve the surrounding farm families.

The Pre-Railroad Era

In 1826, the first wagon loads of several hundred bales of cotton had arrived in the little community of Memphis from as far away as Fayette County. The extraordinary quality of this cotton signaled the potential of the agricultural area and the development of a major port on the Mississippi. Men intent on plantation-style crops like cotton and corn were drawn to south-west Tennessee. It was apparent that a transportation network would have to evolve around the city to carry these crops.

Before the State Line Road was available, the only means of shipping to Memphis had been the Wolf River. (see Map 1) Earliest settlers like William Twyford, came down the Mississippi and up the Wolf to settle on its northern back opposite the future Germantown. H.S. Tanner's 1834 *The Immigrants Guide to the West* touted the availability of shallow draft steamboats on the Wolf to bring crops into Memphis. Settlers had hoped it would prove a reliable avenue as far up as La Grange, and indeed keelboats had been plying the river from there in 1829, encouraging settlement along the Wolf. Most of the earlier settlements, such as Raleigh, Neshoba, La Fayette, Moscow and La Grange located on the river. Unfortunately traffic was limited to periods of high water. Although by the 1840s, it had become more problematic, advocates for its navigation persisted. In March 1844, one "Commodore" Briggs brought down from Moscow 83 bales in his aptly named keelboat *Forlorn Hope*. After demonstrating its continued navigability, he argued that with "a small appropriation by Shelby and Fayette counties" to clear the river of snags, it could be kept navigable to Moscow. Petitions to county and state for clearing apparently ran afoul of other interests, such as the new railway craze.[3]

Soon it was so badly snarled with snags and silting that travel beyond Collierville had been abandoned. For a while, a tug hauled barges to Collierville and back, but eventually the river was only navigable below Germantown. In 1847, a small sternwheeler served visitors to the resort springs around Germantown for only one season. Commercial navigation of the Wolf was abandoned.[4]

Old maps show that before engineers channeled the river, a deep bend brought it closer to the Shepherds' town lots. There was a gentle slope down from the ridges to that point, and its topography may have made it more suitable for both landings and a ferry crossing than were other surrounding wet lands or high embankments. If such conditions were already being exploited by locals, that might have encouraged the Shepherd's venture. A near conjunction of river and crude road may have set the ball rolling.

For it was roads rather than the river that determined the appeal of Germantown. After it drew the intersection of three "highways," the town won its place. The State Line Road ran out from Memphis to the south-east corner of the county and from there into towns across Tennessee, Mississippi and Alabama. Originally, an Indian trail, the Cherokee Trace ran along the ridge between the Wolf River and Nonconnah Creek. In 1823 work began improving its first ten miles out of Memphis as a public county road. Citizens along its route were responsible for providing the labor to "cut it out."[5] That required removing huge numbers of trees and stumps. This was initially a second class road at least twelve feet wide, usable by wagons with bridges and causeways over low areas. This Alabama or State Line Road was supposed to become a first class post road in terms of construction and maintenance. This meant it had to accommodate stage coaches and was designated a post road.[6] Nevertheless as late as 1839, a map still indicated it was suitable for only a one-horse sulky carrier for the mails.(See Map 6)

By 1841, Germantown had become the first along that road to be significant enough to be chartered, increasing its chances of becoming a crossroads. So at some point, a road was cut northward out of town across the Wolf, connecting with the rest of the county, and it too would become a post road. In 1845, another post road was approved to run from Macon, Tennessee, to Hernando, Mississippi, specifically through what was then the newly chartered town.[7] The significance of these intersections was enough to make the town a transportation hub.

Since the county could never finance maintenance of the State Line Road at an appropriate level, in 1842 it chartered the La Grange and Memphis Turnpike Company to build and maintain a first-class road. That venture collapsed, so in 1847 it chartered the Memphis and Germantown Turnpike Company. It was to take over, straighten, improve and maintain the road bed between Memphis and Germantown and then on to Collierville. The state act that established several such turnpike companies provided standards for the road beds.

They were to be at least thirty feet wide, with sufficient ditches, on each side. There had to be a substantial covering of stone, gravel, sand, wood or charcoal. Substantial and sufficient bridges where necessary, to be "completed in a faithful and substantial turnpike manner."[8] Within its corporate limits, Germantown was required to maintain all public roads like the Pike that passed through it.[9] (See Map 2)

For the road system radiating from the town, the bridges across the Wolf were built in the mid-1840s, followed by a few over the Nonconnah. Before that, one could have forded the Nonconnah at numerous places much of the year, but the Wolf had to have a ferry. South of town, the Nonconnah remained a barrier on many smaller roads when the water was high.[10]

All roads, no matter how well maintained, were chokingly dusty in dry weather and impassably muddy when wet. Western Tennessee lacked the better built roads of the east. Historians contend that this was partly because the area was deficient in the raw materials for the preferred macadam base (a mix of clay and gravel). In fact, the entire area close around Germantown used to be pockmarked by gravel pits, not to mention plentiful clay. The presence of these gravel domes may not have been known until the late 1850s, however. So given the abundance of hardwood forests, the preferred alternative was to lay planks across the road bed, greatly benefiting the local lumber industry. The thick, twelve-foot planks lay on top of stringers, logs embedded in the mud, and provided a surface that prevented wagons from sinking up to their axles.[11]

So the section to Germantown was known as the Germantown Plank Road.[12] Riding on it was something like a trip down a washboard. One could hear the loud rumbling of wagons and stages for some distance as they rolled over the boards. And we think road noise is a modern problem.

Among the gentlemen who organized and subscribed to the Memphis and Germantown Turnpike Company were several residents who saw the need and expected the benefits. In Germantown, the sellers of stock were E. W. Kenny and Britton Duke. They set up shop at the town's post office.[13] By 1849, planking had been completed to Germantown.

There were toll gates every five miles. Number 4, lay between Germantown and Collierville, apparently near Forest Hill. Another west of town was near modern Ridgeway. For loaded wagons and carriages, the toll was ten to twenty cents, depending on the number of animals drawing. Horseback riders and empty wagons paid five cents. The fee was paid for each gate, with stiff fines for trying to sneak around. Farmers hauling grain to a grist mill were exempt, also family travel to church and that of militiamen to a muster.[14] For bringing in the cotton harvest, huge caravans of ox-drawn wagons passed along this road carrying bales on a drive of several days, rumbling through town.

The arrival of the railroad may have contributed to the collapse of this turnpike company in 1854, but a second company by the same name was chartered in 1855. Germantown citizens and area planters got themselves elected as commissioners of the Turnpike Company to guarantee their interests.

In 1859, they entirely dominated the commission with the planters W. C. Harrison and James Kimbrough, and Dr. John Stout, a gentleman well invested in transportation enterprises.[15]

Meanwhile, the road bed was realigned to parallel more closely the M&C Railroad, beginning just past White's Station. Running close by the tracks made the turnpike more profitable for transferring cargo to and from the stations along the roads running from the rail line.[16]

In 1860, a state act required the Germantown Plank Road Company to open its beds to at least twenty feet in width, although it still allowed planking. Consequently in June, plans were announced to regrade the road to Germantown and cover it with gravel to produce what would have been the best road out of Memphis. Completion of the project was expected before winter.[17] Unfortunately, there seems to be no record of how successful this project might have been, but this proposed development shows that the abundant gravel domes of the area were being exploited.[18]

Several stage lines served the town. The lines through Germantown served to connect Memphis with all the towns along the southern tier of West Tennessee. To the South, "L. Sims & Brother's daily line of four horse post coaches for Holly Springs, Ripley, Tuscumbia and Decatur." Dr. Morgan ran the stage office in town and maintained its livery stable.[19] Stages came twice daily from points east and west along the State Line Road, three times a week on the two other stage roads.[20] In addition to passengers, they carried the mail including the newspapers, keeping the town in touch with commercial activities in the city and the world. More than half of each issue carried advertisements for the growing number of products available in Memphis.

For casual passenger travel between Memphis and Germantown, two local gentlemen, George Furber and Samuel W. Ledbetter, maintained a "hack" service every day except Sundays, their carriage left the town at 7 A.M. and returned at 3 P.M.[21] Most families also had carriages or wagons for travel on their own schedule.

Through the network of public roads in the district flowed the lifeblood of the business and agricultural community. Their maintenance was assigned by the county court to local citizens as overseers who had responsibility for a section of each particular road in which they had a personal interest. For instance, in January of 1861, the section of the Raleigh-Germantown Road from the town to the Wolf River bridge was assigned to William B. Walker who lived along the road. In 1856, James Kimbrough had responsibility for the section of the Germantown-Capleville (Hernando) Road that ran through his lands. For each such section, the overseer and several other local men were responsible for the labor to be provided by their "hands," meaning slaves. Although non-slaveholders shared this legal obligation, none ever appeared in the list of "hands" assigned.[22] Thus non-slaveholders were placated, thus avoiding resentment.

The demand for more second and third class roads to serve local farms was met by the county in response to petitions. Such requests required review by a "jury of view." One would think such a review would involve disinterested parties, but quite often petitioners constituted more than half the jury.[23] County politics concerning the roads was usually a congenial collaboration of all vested interests, respecting each other's needs. Sometimes, however, when one party managed to sneak by an approval for changes contrary to truly collective interests, the affected parties mobilized to petition for a reversal. Majority interests prevailed.[24] Landholders of all sizes were too aware and involved in county and district business to be easily outmaneuvered.

In contrast to roads, bridge maintenance was farmed out to special contractors. In 1860, when major maintenance was performed on the Wolf River bridge, the contractor discovered a rotten "trussel." The bridge was in danger of collapse. Unfortunately, his repair raised one end two to three feet higher making the approach awkwardly steep and abrupt. He earned $300 only for the work for which he had contracted.[25]

A Railroad Town

The arrival of Memphis and Charleston train service amplified all this commerce. On September 16, 1852, an enthusiastic crowd turned out for the inaugural event. People threw cotton bolls and flowers. Passengers arrived on the excursion train from Memphis. But only 19 people made the trip out, which hardly compared to the hundreds that had ridden the four special trains to Eppy White's grand celebration of the arrival of service at his station.[26]

In fact, the Germantown inaugural was probably anticlimactic. Train service had approached incrementally every day. By August 2, a daily train was within a mile of the town and could be heard from there. Anyone wishing to take it into Memphis simply walked out to the end of the line until service finally reached the town center.[27]

The first engine was the new LaGrange, the familiar long-bodied American-type engine with a bell-shaped stack, a front truck of four small wheels behind a cowcatcher and ahead of four large drive wheels (4-4-0), followed by a tender for the fire wood.[28] The engines were bedecked with polished brass, while the cab and wheels usually sported bright colors, mostly red. Despite the high stack, smoke, sparks and cinders frequently wafted into the cars. Even after the advent of enclosed cars, tiny cinders in one's eye were a common problem until the end of the era of steam.

The inaugural ceremony disappointed many, which is probably why only 19 made the trip out. The reporter for the *Appeal* bemoaned, "It had been expected by many of those who shared in the hospitality of Col. White, at the celebration of the road reaching his house, that the people of Germantown would make a demonstration of their joy by giving a festival. But, as yet, we have heard of no such affair being on the taps."[29] White had thrown a mammoth barbecue.[30] Our disappointed reporter seems to have needed another barbecue fix. In any case, he went on to express an enthusiasm for the new convenience felt by all except Luddites, perhaps another dig at the parsimony of the people of Germantown?

By September 9, the M&C announced that passenger service would begin soon.[31] On September 18, came the notice, "A daily Passenger Train will leave the temporary Depot, on Beale Street, at 7 A.M. for Germantown; returning, will leave Germantown at 8 A.M." The fare would be 50 cents. Half price for children under twelve and servants. "Negroes must have permit to be delivered to the Conductor . . . without which they will not be carried."[32]

On September 15, 1852, the M&C delivered its first three bales of cotton to the city. It was Collierville rather than Germantown that provided the first load. Soon, however, both towns were bustling terminals for the year's crop. With only the LaGrange making the 24 mile trip to Collierville and back each day, the carrying capacity was still not sufficient. Yet in November, the LaGrange had generated $4459.20 in freight and passenger service. In December, the line had reached Lafayette, and the arrival of a new engine provided two trains per day.[33] In the month of October alone, the line already carried 5,589 passengers even before this expansion of service

For decades, the railroad ran special trains to Germantown or other places for occasions that attracted significant numbers from the city. Train travel was such a novelty that everyone took advantage of the slightest excuse for an excursion.

P. 12 Germantown Depot, GHPC. Rear view from south looking across tracks and Bridge Street; store front on right was on street connecting with Spring Street (see Map 5). Passenger wing on right side of depot; large freight wing to left where loading ramp was located.

The depot was built in 1855, which became the central focus of the town.[34] As the railroad quickly realized the need for depot buildings, Germantown got one of the first on the west branch. It was wooden, while later towns like Collierville got brick buildings. The facility was larger than the present structure, for it had two wings. One served passengers and their luggage, the other freight, with a platform at wagon level for loading and unloading. One observer described it as a "little jewel box," for its ticket office was adorned with a stained glass window. Probably, the exterior was a bright yellow with white trim and the roof was green. Under the cover of the broad eaves, passengers mounted the train.[35]

During harvest season, the station turned the surrounding roads into a network carrying heavy traffic from all around, providing time in town for other business. And from there almost everyone would soon be using the train to visit the city and other towns along the line.[36] The railroad turned out to be a bigger boon for passengers and the mail than for freight.

By 1860, Andrew Allden of Germantown was a conductor operating out of its station. He was only one of several by then. Another resident, William Moore, was clerk and railroad agent, which meant that he managed the station and was also telegrapher.[37]

The M&C announced that for the period March 1853 through February 1856, it hauled 51,340 bales, while over the next twelve months it increased to 61,816.[38] One would love to know the percentage of this traffic that came out of Germantown.[39] These numbers speak of a significant increase in wealth flowing through the area.

By 1855, passengers complained that only one train specifically served them.[40] A second passenger run was needed. How quickly they had become jaded. On the plus side, there was a generous free baggage allowance of 75 pounds per passenger. The railroad even promised to reimburse for lost luggage up to $100. Passenger service was clearly a high priority. Finally on October 14, service improved further. One could now travel both ways along the line twice a day.[41]

The line was finally connected with Charleston, Richmond, and Washington in 1857. By 1860, Germantown was one of a string of stations feeding passengers and freight into a network connecting all of the eastern United States.[42]

By 1861, the M&C was operating 50 engines, some specialized for either passenger or freight service. The newest first class freight engines boasted ten wheels (4-6-0). The strongest had hauling capacities of 18 cars, while the older and smaller were limited to 8. There were 30 first-class passenger cars and 9 for second class, plus 2 for branch line service. Unlike today, freight did not constitute the major part of railroad income. In fiscal year 1861, passengers and mail generated over a million dollars, while receipts for freight were only $729,885.[43]

Along with the new convenience came new dangers. Within the first month, the LaGrange derailed between Collierville and Germantown. Fortunately, only the engine was damaged, slightly. In fact, locomotive speeds were not all that great yet, twelve miles per hour initially, but eventually rising to thirty.[44] The problem was that tracks were simply laid on leveled dirt beds, and it could take two to four years for subsidence to abate. Until then, rail beds were unstable requiring reduced speeds and causing accidents.

p. 13 Track Crew, Library of Congress. Road bed and crude ties, laid on dirt bed.

In January 1853 after leaving Germantown, an overly adventurous passenger, a Mr. W. B. Nunnemaker, left the passenger car and was climbing on the tender when he fell. His arm had to be amputated. The equipment itself was not yet the safest either. Again in September 1854, a couple of miles out of Germantown, three of the wheels of the forward passenger car "gave way." Although the car was badly ripped up—timbers and wheels coming up through the floor—no one was hurt.[45] Four reported accidents in the Germantown area alone in the first five years of operation was probably a pretty good "track" record in those days. The worst accident came in 1860, however. Three miles from town, the night freight derailed killing the fireman and breaking the conductor's legs.[46] Yet if passengers had initially felt a spirit of adventure, by 1859 service was already a routine part of life.

Although the M&C was as well built as other southern lines that did not necessarily make for a lot of comfort. Ties could be up to two and one-half feet apart and the settling bed made for a rolling ride. The original ties were of inferior quality and lying directly on the ground encouraged rotting within five years. Extensive replacement became necessary during 1860. In the same year, other mechanical improvements created a ride that was "smooth and free from jar and rattle," ending accidents caused by bad rails.[47] Consequently for the next year, the superintendent could boast that only one passenger had been killed during the entire year—one out of 353,646. Two crewmen had been injured.[48] That was probably another enviable safety record.

An early officer of the road described passenger travel rather colorfully. The coaches seated 46 passengers, and were lighted with oil lamps. Platforms between cars were open."(W)hen the engine made an unusually quick stop, everyone... simultaneously bowed.... Similarly when the engine started, unless the (engineer) paid attention to the successive slack, the passengers felt that the back of the seat was the only thing that kept him from going heels over head backward." There were only hand brakes with wheels on each platform of the car. After setting up one, the brakeman "would rush madly through the isle to reach the wheel on the next car. Experienced mothers... hurriedly gathered their children from the isles to keep them from destruction in the wild flight of the brakeman.[49] The new fifteen-ton, eight-wheeled passenger car was ten feet wide and forty feet long, and through sleeping-car service to Charleston or Washington was an heretofore unimagined luxury with upper and lower berths and dressing rooms.

For most Germantown folk, the train served primarily as a local commuter service. Almost 77 percent of passenger traffic was local or "way" passenger. One paid extra to use the "flag" stops that served many, retarding the speed of travel. Between Germantown and Collierville lay the flag stations at Forest Hill, Nevil's (Nevelle's), Bailey's and Bray's. Traveling westward there was Ridgeway (old Pea Ridge) before White's Station, then the wood and water station at Buntyn and another flag station at McGehee's. For better or worse, the combination of laid-back lifestyle and southern manners resulted in trains running well behind schedule. As long as passengers consented, the conductor might hold a train at a station out of consideration for a lady's tardiness.[50]

Another impact of the railroad was on property values and use along its tracks. Rather than being shunned as today, the tracks became a desirable location for homes. As early as 1853, the *Appeal* rightly predicted that property along almost the entire line as far as LaGrange would be cut up "into 50 to 100-acre lots by fine family residences."[51] The process was incremental, but it soon happened in the Germantown area with some planters relocating their homes close to the tracks and new residents buying up the subdivided lands. The route was soon being described as having a "suburban" appearance out to Germantown. The State Line Road and the M&C ran parallel from White's Station to Germantown, and all along that length one could see plantation. farm and residential houses within walking distance of the line.

✦ ✦ ✦

Mail was no longer delivered by coach. On the eve of the war, Germantown's post office had become the second busiest in the county. Of course, the difference between the Germantown and Memphis offices was great. Postmasters were paid on a percentage of business basis. While Memphis' postmaster drew around $2,000 per year, Germantown's got a little over $200. Out of this grand sum, he had to pay all expenses for the office and its operations.[52]

Consequently the town's post office was usually the home or place of business of the postmaster. The first such was Dr. James M. M. Cornelius. Like almost all small towns, there was no designated post office building, rather it moved about as postmasters changed. During much of the 1840s Samuel Ledbetter and Job Lewis alternated the burden between themselves. Thereafter, the worthies of the town agreed that it was a responsibility to be shared among them annually.[53]

There was no home delivery. People came to the post office for their mail. When it arrived on the morning train, the postmaster sorted it. No matter how far from town one lived, one had to come to town, at least until 1852 when a little substation was finally set up at a place called High Hill, probably below Nonconnah Creek for those that far south.

Train service had greatly improved Germantown's communications with all the eastern states. After 1855, at the price of one three cent stamp per half-ounce of weight, one could communicate with almost anywhere in the country. In the eastern states delivery took about a week or two. Westward, of course, was more difficult, taking easily up to four weeks to reach the west coast by ship and much longer overland. Truly urgent communications could go by telegraph throughout the eastern half of the country.[54] People who had settled

P. 14 Two-Story Inn, Wolf House Arkansas. A building that Germantown's 1840s two-story inn may have resembled.

in Germantown could communicate easily with those left behind. They could receive news of the world, stay professionally and commercially connected, conduct business and legal transactions reasonably and reliably, and order and receive merchandise from far afield.

The Town as Commercial Center

According to an 1858 railroad handbook, there were in town two hotels or inns. A. H. Lucken was owner of the oldest establishment. His Germantown Tavern (Lucken's Place) sat on Bridge Street near the State Line Road. Originally a log structure, it had been expanded into a weather-boarded and whitewashed hostel. In the 1840s, Carson's Tavern, a two-story building, had been another such operation. East of Forest Hill, the Neville home also served as an inn for some years.[55] By 1860, Alexander Blair's family ran Dr. Morgan's hotel, which was undoubtedly also located near both the station and the State Line Road.[56] It may have been a continuation of Carson's Tavern, but undoubtedly an updated accommodation.

The 1849 advertisement for Ledbetter and Furber's Hack Line indicates clearly the presence of professional boarding facilities plus room-and-board in privat homes. In addition to travel between Germantown and Memphis, they offered hack service on demand "from Germantown to the Nashoba Sulphur Springs and back—distance two and a half miles." To entice customers, they advertised,

> To those who might wish to leave the city . . . after the business of day, to return the next morning, this arrangement will prove advantageous. And also for those who, singly, or by families, would like a pleasant day or two in the country in the hot season, with opportunities to visit the Springs as often as wished. The Hacks will be kept running during the season to Germantown.[57]

Even before the railroad, Germantown was already something of an area resort town, competing with the more prominent waters at Raleigh.[58] The 1858 railroad handbook touted the presence of three "favorite resort springs . . . delightfully located in groves of evergreens, within a distance of two miles." In addition to Nashoba, it listed "White Sulphur" and "Brunswick." Brunswick Springs lay one mile east of town on the ridge off the Germantown-Macon Road. There are no local memories of a second White Sulphur Springs. (See Map 4)

During 1845/46, Madame d'Arusmont, (Frances Wright) had advertised her Nashoba Farm "to rent or lease for a term of years." A large tract of land spanning the Wolf, its major attraction was its mineral springs. The *Appeal* saw fit to trumpet their value as a great opportunity for development.

> This land is valuable on many accounts; and especially on account of the medicinal qualities of several springs. Of the curative properties of which we have heard more than one of our physicians speak in the highest terms. . . . (W)e should suppose . . . that the leasing the farm for a term of years, with the view of establishing a *"watering place,"* would be a profitable investment. . . .[59]

This sparked hopes around the town that it could develop a prominent attraction. Farmer and entrepreneur Benjamin Mosby leased the springs with plans for developing a resort with picnic grounds and cabins to rent . . . an "eating house and confectionaries, together with such other refreshments as may contribute to the enjoyment of visitors." To encourage such a grand attraction, interested parties tried to drum up public enthusiasm for a gala Fourth of July

ILL. 2 A Picnic by Land, 1858. Clark Art Institute. Picnicking as it might have appeared at Nashoba or Brunswick Springs.

barbecue at the springs. They expected local approval and called for a county meeting To help with preparations. Mosby built a small, flat-bottomed sternwheeler to ferry passengers from the city to his summer resort.[60]

Unfortunately, country support never materialized. Worse, his little sternwheeler and the resort he had so hopefully erected were destroyed by a severe flood. All was swept away.[61] This disaster discouraged efforts at developing a serious resort at Nashoba for over a decade.

Meanwhile the undeveloped springs continued to be an attraction for city and area residents, but simply as "watering holes" for bathers, with adjacent groves suitable for picnicking.

Residents with homes around Germantown hosted visiting friends and relatives from miles around, especially during the hot months of July and August. Some canoed across, while others took carriages around, across the bridge, making an almost steady stream of traffic on some days. Real estate ads continued to refer to the "celebrated Nashoba Springs."[62]

After 1852, Eugene DeLaugutery contracted a purchase of Nashoba from Sylvia d'Ausmont, the heir. On the eve of the war, he would resurrect the scheme of a summer resort, complete with a hotel and a railroad spur from the M&C, but that also came to naught.[63]

◆ ◆ ◆

On the north side of town lay the Baptist church, Lucken's grocery/saloon and inn, a store featuring medicines, homes and shops, including the blacksmith. The depot was located on the south side of the tracks. The middle of the town (see Map 5) was the perennial location for stores, shops and offices alternately containing the itinerant post office. Most of the various establishments were either clustered in the center along two of the north-south streets, Bridge Street (modern Old Germantown Road) and Spring Street (present West Street south of the tracks) or spread out along the State Line Road. On the south side of town lay the Presbyterian Church, the Masonic Hall, and Molitor's mill. On the west side sat the Methodist Church and communal cemetery, appropriately located on Church Street (present McVay). The locations of the two gin factories and the commercial cotton gin are unknown. Without any such thing as a commercial district, town houses were interspersed among all this commerce and industry.

Somewhere there was a town commons or "the green." It is only mentioned in passing in a few surviving documents, and there is no record of its location.

The town had grown during the 1850s to be a bustling center of commerce and industry. Although a few of the town's business establishments may have been substantial enough to have been brick buildings, most shops were the sort of one-story clapboard affairs one still sees in old country towns. Situated directly on the street, they offered a covered porch. The entry sat in the middle of the porch with one or more windows to each side. The building was usually long with a low pitched roof. The facade or false-front often rose above the peak of the roof. Unless the building included a dwelling or shop in the rear, the only heat source was a centrally located pot belly stove. Wilks Brooks described the interior of his store built in town around 1840. "The store house is 24 by 32, so arranged as to have two rooms besides the store room, 24 by 10 shelves on both sides."[64]

The records of the substantial yeomen and planters indicate that the bulk of their purchases, and subsequent debts were with Memphis merchants. Such firms advertised extensively as providing everything the planter needed, and the credit network among the banks, cotton factors and merchants facilitated bulk purchasing with payment made when crops came in. The town's stores

p. 15 Ridgeway Store, courtesy Walter Wills. A store like many that were in Germantown proper; located on State Line Road near crossing over M&C Railroad.

were simply more convenient for small and frequent purchases—an individual item of manufactured clothing, a bolt of cloth, or needles and thread, a comb or brush, some produce, cured meat, cheese, candy, tobacco or a bottle of "spirits." Even then, much of this business was also done on credit or barter. The poorer yeoman and landless made purchases almost entirely at this level.

♦ ♦ ♦

Among the professions in and around town were numerous educators, a lawyer, a dentist, and sixteen who titled themselves physicians. Such professionals typically practiced from offices in their homes. Since the merchant William Miller would later describe himself as a druggist, it is likely his stock already included patent medicines and drugs.

The previously described large number of physicians suggests the presence of numerous "quacks," but apparently such conditions were hardly unique to Germantown. A surplus of physicians and the presence of "irregular practitioners" were common in rural America. At least Drs. Morgan and Cornelius were considered very distinguished physicians.[65] A later comer, Dr. Richard Martin settled on a large farm just north east of town in 1859. He was a graduate of Davidson College and had attended medical school in Philadelphia.[66] In addition to owning the hotel, Dr. Morgan had a sideline managing the stage office and livery stable.[67] Sidelines were common for most physicians. Their glutted ranks kept fees low, so even the most reputable earned hardly enough to live off their practice. For instance, Thomas H. Todd was heavily involved in road construction and overseeing outside the district.[68] Established doctors like Cornelius owned or rented enough farm land to maintain milk and beef cattle and pigs, raising the corn to feed them.

Squire S. W. Ledbetter, in addition to running his hack line and being sometimes postmaster, had been one of the justices of the peace during the 1840s and early '50s. He was succeeded by John W. A. Pettit, who eventually became county judge. The district constable, Jobe Lewis, had a sizable farm outside town. Other services were provided by William Tate, Real Estate Broker, and two speculators, William Warmell and Jonah Deloach, whose new presence spoke of rapid growth.

The two homes of Isaac and Hosea Bliss contained as many as six men listing themselves as "book agents." The term usually applied to men who sold books on commission for a publisher. These men, all from out-of-state, mostly New York, must have been providing books primarily for area schools, but were, however, of some means.[69] This combination of facts seems to imply that they constituted a book marketing establishment in addition to being a group of independent traveling salesmen- certainly an office and storerooms, perhaps even a bookstore. Their location in Germantown speaks to the cultural prominence the community was acquiring with its private schools. These 6 men constituted 18% of the 33 booksellers in the entire county, most of whom were concentrated in Memphis.[70]

One of the more interesting business families was the Molitors. Francis and his wife Cordelia, both born in Westphalia (Prussian Germany), had come to the states by way of Philadelphia where their first son Charles was born around 1833. From there they joined several German settlers seeking their fortunes in the Mississippi Valley sailing to New Orleans. Family memories of a storm at sea, undoubtedly in the Gulf, tell that the ship was forced into Galveston, and some children were lost. They spent years in Mississippi, where sons Joseph and Francis were born in 1838 and 1848. They finally settled in Germantown, sometime between the 1850 and 1860 censuses. Francis owned a significant mill operation, steam powered, and titled himself a "machinist," as did his younger son, Joseph. That label apparently applied to anyone who ran "machinery" such as a mill. They also acquired some considerable land holdings, and some slaves. Charles was an engineer.[71] The term, "engineer" was a prestigious title implying formal education, frequently in a military academy. This relatively wealthy family, including Mrs. Cordelia, played a prominent role in town through the 1860s.

One of the two "hotels," Lucken's Inn was famous for the high quality beer he brewed in his basement and was one of four "saloons" that Germantown hosted. Most of them were "grocery stores" rather than separate establishments for drinking. Nevertheless, they sold alcohol by the drink as well as by the bottle. When Harrison and Noland opened their Wholesale and Retail Grocery and Produce Business, they advertised, "a large and well selected stock of Groceries, fine Wines, Brandies and Whiskey; Hardware, Queensware, Tinware, and a general variety of merchandise."[72] In November 1860, the town gained an additional grocery/saloon when William Essmann acquired merchant and tippler's bonds. A German immigrant, Essmann and his family of five had been in this country for about four years, and by working as an overseer he had managed to save enough to go into business.

Among the town's other residents, Barry Hurt, John M. Woodson, William B. Jones, and Stephen D. Trueheart described themselves as "Gin makers." Hurt and Woodson were men of some property, while Jones and Trueheart were boarders, Jones boarding with Hurt.[73] What Trueheart was doing did not keep him from being a sufficiently respected citizen, an elder of the Presbyterian Church from 1858 to 1904.[74] In fact, one must not be misled by the word "gin." These men were not manufacturers of the "spiritous liquor," but rather the cotton-processing machinery by that name.

Apparently from 1849, Germantown had industry to produce just such a machine. There was a "factory in full operation with steam power, machinery and workmen sufficient to make any number of gins required." It apparently started as Burdine and Moore's Southwestern Cotton Gin. But by 1854, Neely, Goff & Co., Cotton Gin Manufacturers, were operating the factory that they had renamed the Star Cotton Gin Manufactory. Their market was the cotton planters of the tristate area, to whom they offered "Cotton Gins of the best

Manufactory, with all of the late improvements. - Our work is propelled by steam, and we are prepared to do all work in our line as well and as cheap as it can be done any where in the United States, not excepting Yankeland." Joseph Neely, oldest son of local planter Moses Neely, was the J. C. Neely of Neely & Goff.[75] Within a year, their product was called the Southern Star Cotton Gin. The Star Gin was endorsed as being the "the best Gin in general use" among others by Ja's Kimbrough and Wesley Cole, planters of Germantown. The *Appeal* saw fit to emphasize this venture as "a home manufacturing establishment (that) deserves encouragement." "Their Gins, we believe are equal to any imported. . . ."[76]

John Woodson, who had given up farming in Mississippi for Germantown in 1855, was apparently running the mill by that date. It seems Woodson and Trueheart had bought out or partnered with Neely, and were running the operation by 1857.[77] The factory had at least two white employees, Jones plus Hurt, who was the foreman. The factory was undoubtedly also staffed by slaves. Moses Neely's youngest son, Hugh, joined the partnership, serving as salesman and collector.[78]

According to the 1860 census, there were only 57 gin factories in the entire country. The average gin factory employed eleven people, paying them $432 each per year. It generated an average of $20,216 including $4,669 in labor costs.[79] Germantown's operation was average, supplying only a regional market, but added significantly to the town's economy.

Meanwhile more industry had come to town by 1855. One Henry Rehwoldt chose Germantown as the site for his Tennessee Terra Cotta Works and Pottery. There were clay sources nearby, and the railroad eliminated the transportation problem to the market. Rehwoldt offered every imaginable form of pipe and tile for functional and ornamental architectural and water management purposes, plus statues and fountains, which were popular for the lawns and gardens of planter homes. The pipes were essential for collecting rain water and sending it to the cisterns that every decent home and farm house relied upon. He also touted his earthenware cooking pots.[80] Rehwoldt's absence from the 1860 census implies that either his enterprise failed or he sold out to someone else. His works may have been converted or expanded into a brick factory that was soon in operation.

There was also a commercial cotton gin on the western fringe of town, with a factory for manufacturing cotton scrapers or seed planters, an item patented in

1859 by former town resident Jonathan H. Mitchell. Francis Molitor's mill was on the south. It is unclear where W.C. Harrison's steam-driven sawmill was located, but the town proper had two steam-mills. Among the other "mechanical establishments," were a cabinet maker, a machine shop, two blacksmiths and two wagon manufacturers. By 1860, the other shops included three dry-goods, three groceries and a drug store. Other craftsmen who may have had shops were a cobbler, a tailor, several carpenters, and a mason.[81] The city that today eschews industry was by 1861 almost as industrial as it was agricultural.

Most of this industry and commerce were products of the 1850s. By then, Germantown must have seemed almost like a boom-town. Away at school only a semester, Mattie Duke wrote to a friend who must have described some of the changes, "I know I will not begin to know Germantown when I get home." By the end of the year, she made a reference to "the *great city of Germantown*" (emphasis in original).[82] Although it was a tongue-in-cheek comparison to Memphis, it also reflected the image the townsfolks had of their rapidly expanding community.

The explosive growth of the area emerges when one compares an alleged 1850 Property Map of Shelby County with the 1860 census. In reality, the map reflects conditions earlier than 1840.[83] Almost all the lands bore the names not of landowners in the 1850 census, but many clearly land speculators. Lot sizes are usually above 200 acres and up to 800. Many of those around the town had become town and commercial-sized plots by 1850. Below the old state line, all the tracts, many of several thousand acres were either unowned or in the hands of land agents. By 1850, these larger, undeveloped tracts of land had become medium sized farms and plantations.

This economic growth constantly brought visitors to the area to interact with the population. Real estate investors were undoubtedly the most frequent. The agents of various other firms with agricultural dealings constituted the upper crust of traveling businessmen, while the drummers who came to town to hawk their wares were the more typical traveling salesman or huckster. At the bottom were the peddlers and tinkers who went from house to house in town and country. Apparently all were received with hospitality as long as they seemed about honest business. One August evening, Isham Howse, recorded that, "A little German peddler, named Gant, dined with us today. He is from Prussia; and is 17 years old. His whole stock of goods was tied up in a common-sized pocket handkerchief—yet from this small start he may grow rich."[84]

4

GROWING POLITICAL TENSIONS

Local politics must be understood in its larger contexts—national, regional, state, and divisional. From the 1830s, the American two-party system was Democratic Party versus the National-Republican or Whig Party until the Republican Party displaced the Whigs outside the South during the decade before the Civil War. During this entire period, the most contentious issue was slavery, or more specifically whether slavery would be allowed to expand into territories birthing new states. Slave-owning Southerners felt threatened by the abolition movement which ultimately sought to outlaw slavery nation-wide. If not enough new states were slave-states, the slave-holding states feared they would be significantly outvoted in Congress, and if legislative and executive power were combined against slavery, slavery could be strangled to death, despite purported constitutional guarantees.[1] Slave-owners would be denied their "property rights" by a "tyrannical majority" imposing its convictions on a "helpless minority."

The rhetoric employed by these threatened slaveholders infected even those with little or no human-property rights to defend. It evoked the same sense of oppression as taxation-without-representation had in their ancestors. They frequently compared themselves to those Patriots and their opposition to Tory tyrants. Throughout history, the responses of those who felt threatened with such loss of autonomy have been similar—receptiveness to conspiracy theories, and righteous threats of resort to force if necessary to protect their endangered rights.

At the heart of the problem, almost all Americans subscribed to contemporary beliefs in the inferiority, even savagery, of "the Negro." They could not exist on equal terms in a white society. In the South, where blacks constituted a significant part of the population, there was universal fear that emancipation would result in the liberation of a dangerous horde. In the North, many shared this phobic racism enough to sympathize with the Southerners on that point and to have doubts about the desirability of abolition. Even many abolitionists favored a "return to Africa" as the solution so blacks would not be living among whites as equals. Nevertheless, a growing majority of the national population increasingly saw slavery as an unjust and inhumane institution. Even so, that majority also saw no clear way to a solution. Most politicians preferred to "kick the problem down the road."

The response of some Southerners to the threat of losing their "rights and freedoms" to a "tyrannical" federal government was resort to the presumed states' right to secession. Since the formation of the Union, states both North and South had espoused such an untested right. Consequently by mid-nineteenth century, both the firebrand southern-rights advocates and the radical abolitionists were widely perceived as *disunionists*—threats to the political stability of the nation. The majority of the population, North and South, watched with trepidation, as the polarized became increasingly intransigent. Unfortunately, not enough were politically focused on demanding a workable solution to the problem of slavery itself rather than simply maintaining a balance of power between the factions. The more vocal extremes increasingly took the stage.

✦ ✦ ✦

Within Tennessee, the grand geographical divisions differed significantly in their involvement in slavery. In the East there were fewer slaveholders. Middle and West Tennessee were more heavily involved, with some counties largely committed to tobacco and cotton plantations. Even there, significant parts of the population were yeoman farmers and mechanics, disadvantaged by competition with slave labor. Consequently in Tennessee, few states-righters were as rabid as in the coastal and deep South, such as the South Carolina firebrands. Nevertheless, the above mentioned racist phobias made most people fearful of widespread emancipation. Laborers were even more threatened by the prospect of competing with a mass of freed slaves. At the same time, among the vast majority of Tennesseans, there was a commitment to a strong national Union as essential to their security and economic well-being. Commitments to the Union and to Southern Rights coexisted in tension within both political parties throughout Tennessee.

Tennessee's two-party system had emerged during 1837-39 and remained relatively stable until the secession crisis, although Whig dominance gradually declined. At the state level, Whigs increasingly lost control of the legislature to the Democrats after 1847.[2] Whigs and Democrats both appealed consistently to Tennessee's deep (little "r") republican commitments. There was a strong suspicion that centralized presidential power would fall under the control of powerful vested interest groups, undermining government by elected representatives who answered to other interests than the people.[3]

Aside from polemics about the threat of abolition, a key issue dividing them was the problem of currency and banking in an era when paper money was still in its infancy. At a time when West Tennessee was still transitioning from a subsistence-barter, frontier economy, except for the relatively secure and successful, the bewildering effects of the expansion of the market economy was generating populist fears and suspicions among most local citizens of all classes. Although it is usually argued that this was truer in rural then urban environments, it was more complicated than that.[4]

In Tennessee, Jacksonian democracy had created a more democratic constitution and voting structure than that in the tidewater areas from which many settlers of all classes had come. They had brought with them a distrust and resentment of the truly wealthy patricians who had held control there. The Jacksonian Democratic Party ethos appealed to those who cherished the freedom and independence of self-sufficiency. Yeomen and middling planters, small merchants and mechanics all felt threatened by the mysterious pressures of the growing market economy, and especially their dependence on the system of finance and indebtedness. This generated a populist perspective of conspiracy theories. The network of truly successful planters, factors, insurers and bankers constituted a conspiracy against their independence. Beyond the local seat of this "network" in Memphis, the true "string pullers" lay in the northern cities, and the industrial and banking Yankee elite. These "plutocrats" were more of a threat to cherished freedoms and the Southern way of life than even the abolitionists. Although the local economic and social elite might be resented, when the specter of powerful Yankee economic influences combined with that of the abolitionist threat, the collective interests of all classes could unite to plaster over local resentments and produce a united front.[5]

The local rivalry between the two parties during the 1840s and 50s is a complicated story. The political-economic ideology espoused by the Democrats tied one's economic independence and self-sufficiency to one's freedom.

Political and economic institutions and movements constituted an elitist, anti-democratic threat. In contrast, the Whig ideology was more in tune with the progressive liberal ideas of the century which believed the liberating expansion of knowledge and opportunity being generated by capitalism were the sources of true freedom.

These basic differences in world view generated different ideas about the proper role of government. Whigs espoused programs to bring progress and prosperity—governmental support for roads, railroads and canals, protective tariffs, public schools, and other public services and regulations. Very specifically, they favored central government regulation of banking and the currency. Whigs saw themselves as crusaders for improvement of the public wellbeing. Jacksonians suspected elitist paternalism. They opposed taxation to finance public works, factories and banks, and tariffs that benefitted industrialists. Were suspicious of elitist efforts to indoctrinate their children with non-traditional values and to regulate personal behavior. They especially saw banks, wealth based on bonds, and paper money as instruments of powerful elitist threats to their independence.

Given these socially-loaded appeals with economic undertones, Whigs initially found more support in areas of stronger urban and commercial development with market crops, while Democrats originally found theirs in more isolated subsistence-farming areas. For instance, in the gubernatorial and presidential elections between 1839 and 1851, Shelby County returned Whig majorities. As the community moved ever more to market production, mercantile and mechanical endeavors, and a cosmopolitan culture, one would have expected that political alignment to intensify rather than decline.

For much of the decade of the forties, the town had been the seat of a local Whig party organization and the locus for rallies drawing from many miles around. For such a rally in 1840, some 250 people traveled by horse or buggy through heavy rains and over problematic roads. In 1848, after a series of local meetings, persons from the neighboring counties of Tennessee and Mississippi met in Germantown to ratify the nominations of the Whig presidential ticket. Typically on such occasions the local Whigs provided cider and barbecue. Local leaders were William P. Vaden, a farmer from district 10, and James Kimbrough, a major planter of district 11.[6] In the Germantown area, political orientations had never been as rigid as traditional class analyses argue. The yeoman (sometimes small merchant) Howse was as Whigish as his neighbor the prominent planter Duke.

Nevertheless, Germantown was gradually becoming a bastion "for the Democracy" as the *Memphis Appeal* put it. In the gubernatorial election of 1843 and again in 1845, the Whigs took Germantown by only seven votes compared to more sizable margins elsewhere in the county. Nevertheless, in the much larger turnout for the 1844 presidential election, the Whig margin was again more substantial.[7] In August 1844, for that fight leading citizens in the vicinity had formed the Democratic Association of Germantown "to advance the cause of Democracy," and to promote the election of James K. Polk and the annexation of Texas to the Union. At least 179 local men joined, prompting the *Appeal* to label them "a little band of patriots," and "as examples to most associations in this part of the country." Germantown's Dr. William W. Morgan was elected president, with Dr. John R. Evans and Captain James Boren as vice presidents. H. F. Hammer, Joel H. Hall, farmer, and Henry Jackson, planter, became secretaries, and George C. Furber was standing orator. A list of worthies formed a Committee of Vigilance: Breton (*sic*; Britton) Duke, local planter, Job A. Lewis, farmer and constable, John Wilson, plus seven other farmers and planters."[8] The Democrats now drew from all levels of local society. In the gubernatorial election of 1851, the Whigs still won 53%. By the next year's presidential election, however, the tide had turned when 54% voted Democratic.[9]

This transition to Democratic Party allegiance involved a number of local factors as well as evolutions within the parties. For one thing, the shift was part of a self-perpetuating cycle. As the Whig party broke down in the 50s, which was hardly the result of local developments, the Democrats filled the vacuum. Among them, a younger generation of party leaders was replacing the older Jacksonians.[10] Some aspects of that will become clearer as our narrative continues. Another was the growth of Germantown and the arrival of the rails. Without being threatening, the growth of small mercantile, industrial and mechanical operations and the enlarging professional population shifted the composition of the community. But perhaps community was the key word. As previously argued, the interdepenance of almost all elements of that community and its meritocratic embrace, bound together everyone from elites down through middle and lesser planters to the more truly independent yeoman, and the upward-bound sons of such classes starting as laborers and clerks. The railroad was drawing the yeoman increasingly into the market economy with all the conveniences it offered. Such changes eroded the more hardline Jacksonian positions of the Democratic Party. As we have seen, that most Democratic rag, the *Appeal*, began castigating its followers for opposition to taxes and bonds to finance the railroads that brought such obvious progress. All of the papers with their truly urban, market-economy base propagandized more progressive views. Opposition to free public schools shifted to support, and even a willingness to pay increased taxes for them.

The presidential campaign of 1852 reflected the significance of Germantown and Collierville (the seats of Civil Districts 11 and 10 respectively). The campaign lasted from August 10 to September 18, with the electoral candidates for the 10th Congressional District from both parties going together from community to community,. They started at Memphis, but were promptly at Germantown on August 11 and Collierville the next day.[11] Candidates stumped routinely at Germantown and Collierville during all elections.[12] The two towns were clearly the centers for politicking in the rural southern tier.

Such occasions called for food, drink and a festive atmosphere. Traveling together and speaking in tandem, the candidates for elector normally maintained gentlemanly decorum, and an air of good humored but often sharp confrontation prevailed over invective. The *Appeal* criticized any disrespectful language, especially attributing it to the opposition. It seems, however, to have occurred more commonly in partisan assemblies and published formats than in the tandem stump speeches. By modern standards, speeches generally went on interminably with each candidate giving attention to details that would exceed the attention span of modern audiences.[13]

A different kind of political rally in Germantown, more spontaneous and locally organized, occurred on the occasion of the Presbyterian Ladies Fair in September. Nevertheless, it had the same format. The *Appeal* reporter rendered his less than objective observations. Before dinner, the crowd "proceeded to the ground selected for the political discussion," where a speech "seemed to please his (Winfield) Scott friends." The reporter found it "wide of the mark." After dinner, the real speechifying got under way, with two men addressing the crowd on the part of each party.[14] The speakers were all county or regional politicians, and no local worthy took advantage of the occasion.

Informal political discourse was reserved for Lucken's tavern, or the porch and cracker-barrel assemblies of the stores/saloons. Who knows whether it always retained its atmosphere of "friendly persuasion" when lubricated by "spiritous liquors." Perhaps not. To quote a contemporary referring to Lucken's Inn in particular, "... on its piazza the politicians, when they were wont to harangue crowds, used to gather noisy mobs to listen to stale jokes and boisterous eloquence.... the people ... (amused) themselves by listening to bald polatitudes and bald-eagle oratory.... I have listened to Dave Currin, Walter Coleman, Fred P. Stanton, Governor Jones and many others at different dates ... while they stood before the Lucken and set the country in an uproar."[15] Whenever in the area, even prominent politicians took time to hit the Germantown audience at Lucken's Inn.

With several of Germantown's postmasters being Democratic Committee of Vigilance members, the town's subscribers were assured of regular delivery of the *Appeal*, coming by mail. From elsewhere, however, during 1849 the *Appeal* got regular complaints that the paper was going lost at their post offices, while "the other papers of our city (Whig rags implied), having the merit of fast and regular travelling." After investigation showed the papers were leaving the Memphis post office on time and that the problem "lay elsewhere," service suddenly improved. But after things cooled off, papers started going lost again.[16] Nothing is new in the dirty tricks department.

Aside from stumping by the candidates, locals relied on the Memphis newspapers for political insights. By the 1850s, there were several with distinct points of view. These papers appeared in both daily and weekly formats with the weeklies serving the entire tristate area. Among them, the popular *Appeal* was challenged after 1855 by the *Bulletin*, and the *Avalanche* after 1858. The *Eagle and Enquirer*, which had fused in 1851, reduced to a weekly after 1858. The *Argus*, after 1859, was the city's official newspaper for publishing public notices. Although it never endorsed any candidates, it ultimately called for unity to defeat Lincoln in 1860. The *Appeal* and the *Avalanche* competed with one another in espousing Democratic Party and Southern-rights perspectives, with the *Avalanche* being outright secessionist. Though allegedly non-partisan, the *Bulletin* put forth a moderate Whig perspective. The more overt *Memphis Daily Whig* ran only from 1852 to 1856. The Whigish *Eagle and Enquirer* endorsed Know-Nothing candidates for a short period.[17]

Regular subscribers got their copies by mail, delivered by the morning train, or one could also arrange to pick up copies at the depot. The habit of private subscriptions grew during the 1850s. In 1852, as a subscriber to the *Eagle and Enquirer*, Britton Duke regularly shared its news with his neighbors. By the next year, even some of the more cash-pressed yeomen farmers were shelling out the $2.00 for their own subscription.[18] One had to go well down the economic ladder to find locals who were not politically informed by the printed word.

♦ ♦ ♦

The division of Germantowners into Democrats and Whigs, and the gradual shift reflected a wide range of attitudes over a variety of hot issues. In the presidential election of 1844, Henry Clay, of the Whigs was running against Polk. Clay opposed the annexation of Texas because he feared it would reignite the slavery issue, which he had recently helped to defuse. He also predicted that it would lead to war with Mexico. Most southerners favored bringing in Texas as a slave state. Other issues, however, complicated things. Polk's hard line stand on the border between Canada and the U.S. was also popular, helping him win.

Two resolutions passed by the Democratic Association on its formation reflect other issues that probably divided the people of Germantown.

> *Resolved*, That in supporting, as we will with all our hearts, the nomination of Polk and Dallas, we believe we are taking the only ground to avert the direst misfortunes to our land: and farther, that *Disunion*, which as Democrats we do condemn and repudiate, can only be produced by foreign influences, at present making most unhappy strides in the present course of the followers of Henry Clay.
>
> *Resolved*, That we will preserve as far as we can the perpetuity of our Union, by opposing all foreign influences showing themselves in the present opposition to the annexation of Texas; and by the election of JAMES K. POLK and GEORGE M. DALLAS.[19]

The peculiar references to "foreign influences" threatening the Union may have been a shot at Northern abolitionists, which seems a strained use of "foreign." Probably it related also to a different, growing paranoia. Since the creation of this country, every new wave of immigrants from countries or regions "alien" to Americans has led to hostility. During the 1840s and '50s, the perceived threat bordered on hysteria. American society would be overwhelmed by Catholic but especially Irish Catholic immigrants fleeing their home country in great numbers. They were perceived as hostile to American values because of their presumed obedience to the Pope. Pius IX had helped put down the recent liberal and nationalist European revolutions and was an outspoken advocate of opposition to liberty, democracy and legal equality. This fueled a conspiracy theory that he would subjugate this country through Catholic immigrants controlled by Irish bishops.

Indeed during the '40s and '50s large numbers of poor Irish-Catholics and Germans of Lutheran, Catholic and Jewish persuasions flooded into Memphis. By 1860, over one third of the white population was foreign-born—4,100 Irish and about 1,500 German. The Pinch district became the equivalent of northern tenements. The Irish became the primary target of hostility.[20]

Memphis newspapers carried stories of ethnic gangs and crime, fueling local nativism. There were also disturbing reports of violence directed at specific ethnic groups whose presence "provoked" such disorder. Although rural areas were far less infected, nativist feelings spread out from the city. All this fear even disrupted the Democratic Party's deepening roots in Tennessee, because the party's leadership included Irish-Americans elsewhere, which also "proved" their intentions to infiltrate and take over.

These fears split both parties and gave birth to the Native American Party in 1845, which became the American Party in 1855. This movement was known as the Know Nothings, because of their original secrecy about membership. When suspected members were asked about the movement, their canned response was "I know nothing." In 1854, the party won major victories in northern cities and states. By that year, the Whig Party, so badly drained of support by the Know Nothings, was nearly defunct nationally. Thus, in addition to abolition, nativism was part of the confusing mix in national and local politics.

In the early phases, Germantown was introduced to the potentially violent side of xenophobic fears. During the campaign of 1845, the Democrat's candidate for the Tenth District, F. P. Stanton, was accused of being a Roman Catholic.[21] Fierce exchanges ensued in area newspapers, especially between the *Appeal* and the *Eagle and the Enquirer*. Between 1844 and 1845, civility evaporated as polarization mounted. Differences of opinion over issues allegedly threatening the country were no longer respected. Former friends and neighbors became either fools or villains. Eventually, the radical nativists would go so far as to proclaim, "the time will come when we will have to rise in arms, and massacre the foreigners ... in order to preserve the free institutions of our country...."[22]

Nevertheless, in Germantown, the expectation was that decorum would prevail. When its Democratic Association held a meeting in August 1844, it announced specifically, "Every body—the LADIES *especially*—are invited to attend."[23] Clearly, it was assumed that women wanted to be informed about political issues, despite traditional assumptions about women. It was indeed common for women to be interested in politics, but they were not to discuss the subject publicly.[24] Since this was a partisan assembly, elsewhere, such as in Memphis, agitators could be expected. But the good people of Germantown considered their community immune from the likes of what ensued the very next year. So it was thought safe for women to attend.

On July 31, 1845, however, while in Germantown debating his opponent, Phineas Scruggs, Stanton was shot by Dr. J. R. Christian, one of his more outspoken nativist critics. The incident occurred as the speakers were milling about beside Carson's Tavern and his adjacent store. While in Justice Ledbetter's nearby office, Scruggs had told Christian that Stanton had accused him of lying. Christian set off to confront Stanton. The conversation that followed suddenly erupted into violence. Christian drew his pistol, but apparently it went off accidentally while he attempted to hit Stanton in the face with the gun. Christian then retreated from the scene. He walked calmly back into the tavern, went upstairs to the room where he had boarded overnight and subsequently surrendered to Constable Lewis, allegedly appealing for protection from the angry crowd gathered outside. Fortunately, the bullet had only struck the side of Stanton's face. He rested in town for several days, attended by Drs. Cornelius and Morgan. Although Stanton could not continue stumping, he went on to win.[25] One wonders what impact this violence had on the atmosphere in Germantown amidst growing nativist hostilities.

Previously in August 1844, even if the founders of the town's Democratic Association seems to have expressed nativist concerns in their resolutions, the Democratic Party in general and that of Shelby County in particular denounced nativist extremism and the Know-Nothings. As the Democratic position crystallized during the 1850s, the controversy added further to political divisions around Germantown. After the Shelby County Democrats took a hardline position against nativism in December 1855, among the delegates it sent to the state convention was Job Lewis, who must have represented the element that stayed true to the party.[26]

Nativist preoccupations have generally been considered insignificant in

Southern politics.[27] Nevertheless, during the 1855 elections, Germantown area voters (District 11) swung away from the Democratic Party to vote 58% for the outspoken nativist, gubernatorial candidate, Meredith Gentry. In contrast, however, next-door neighbors in District 10 stood by the Democrats by a margin of about 63%. While the ethnically divided Memphis wards went both ways, only the district around Raleigh matched Germantown's defection in favor of the American Party.[28] Of course, with many issues such as slavery and prohibition involved in this election, it would be unwise to assume that nativism was the deciding factor for Germantown voters. The very democratic Democrat, Andrew Johnson, may not have been as appealing to propertied voters.

The Party's hardly differed over slavery. The *Whig*, which lamented the Democratic victory elsewhere, warned voters that under Van Buren the Democrats were betraying the South. That true conservatives and "Union-loving men of the country, and particularly of the South," would find the American Party the savior of the South and its interests. Both Democrats and Americans in the South sought to distance their party from the abolitionist voices in their northern branches.[29]

Meanwhile, the stage was being set for the next year's presidential race. One citizen of Collierville specifically claimed that many Whig and Know-Nothings were shifting their votes. Reporting on the debate of July 27 in that town, he quoted Mr. Holmes as holding forth "in the usual strain of Know-Nothing orators, abusing Foreigners, Catholics and the Democratic party." In contrast, Colonel Tilman allegedly "made decidedly the most telling speech of the canvass" in which "he did not indulge in abuse or epithets, but in a quiet, good-natured way, completely dissected (Holmes') *carcass*." In such an atmosphere, Germantown's district eleven votes swung back to the Democrat Buchanan. Its 259 voters supported him by a margin of 13. Yet this was still weaker than Collierville's 96 to 41.[30] All this talk of foreigners and Catholics clearly indicated that nativism had reared its ugly head around Germantown, but its relative significance waned rapidly.

❖ ❖ ❖

Since nativism may have affected Germantown area voters for a short while, that raises the question of whether it also agitated any local social tensions. In 1850, the local foreign-born were mostly men of some means. Furthermore, both Germans and Irish had been among the earliest settlers. The Germans were merchants, propertied farmers or mechanics. The town's two new Irishmen would have been suspect only if Catholics. If not, they simply fit in with the rest of the areas' old Irish settlers. Also two wives of prominent men were Irish-born.

One resident demonstrated both strong attitudes about Catholicism and Jews in general, while being open and friendly toward particular individuals of both faiths. He once wrote,

> Catholics, the Pope as their head, say that Peter was the prince of Apostles, and Vicar of Jesus Christ, upon earth, and that the Popes are his regular successors; and they claim for him sovereign and infallible power over the whole church, that in Christ's stead he is as Christ upon earth. This, of course, is all mere assumption. But as successors of St. Peter, they would follow him in one particular, if in no other; they will when they can, use the sword in defense of their rotten system.[31]

A solid Whig, he was among those captured by phobic nativism. On the subject of Jews, he subscribed to the stereotype of Jews exploiting their young gentile serving girls. "Those who will deny and persecute Jesus will misuse and persecute his disciples." Yet this same man spoke of several "Irish friends." There were others he liked whom he feared were "idolaters," probably meaning Catholics. "God preserve them," he noted.[32]

Since immigrants had been accepted from the very beginning, the community probably adopted new immigrants without the tension that occurred elsewhere. The percentage of foreign-born local residents was 50 percent greater than in the state overall and almost four times greater than its comparable rural communities. It was even greater than other established states in the union. Only the newly opened western farm lands drew more.[33] Most likely, local nativist fears were directed at the abstract "foreign threat," those Irish Catholics or other stereotypes also not neighbors. They lived in Memphis, but especially in the North. If the anti-immigrant phobia created any tensions locally, nativism probably had no effect on the local sense of community harmony.

◆ ◆ ◆

The political and social interests of Germantown's Democrats must indeed have been complex. In 1848, several Northern newspapers chose to run a short interest piece on Germantown's political climate. Northern papers always liked to cast a light on the peculiar behavior of Southerners. In October, the *Boston Investigator* reported, "Madame Darusmont (*sic*), formerly Fanny Wright, made a speech at a Hunker meeting at Germantown, Tennessee, a short time since. A Democratic meeting, we presume, is meant by the term 'Hunker'—that being the political nickname of the Democratic party."[34] Like many other tantalizing snippets about Germantown, this one leaves one wishing for a more detailed report of the address and the audience's reactions. At least, she must have been accepted politely, since the papers reported no angry demonstrations of the sort that occurred elsewhere when she spoke.

In addition to being a critic of slavery, Fanny Wright, then a part-time resident of the area, a famous lecturer, author and publisher of a radical journal, espoused feminism, anti-clericalism, interracial marriage and other radical social and religious ideas—scandalous to many minds. Locals viewed her with a combination of awe and disapproval. Her original first neighbor, William Twyford, considered her "a little teched," and "with more money than she knew what to do with."[35] As a boy, Robert Duke, whose father had once managed her lands, remembered her as "the most beautiful woman he'd ever seen. . . . He'd never seen anyone that compared with her. She had a magnetism and a charm that was unbelievable. But people were horrified at her modern ideas. . . . She was not accepted at all in the community."[36] Nevertheless, locals approved of her charity and good intentions, while fearing "that she accomplished more evil than good" by her irreligion.[37]

It was apparently curiosity that drew a large crowd rather than the appeal of her message, a conclusion she herself had drawn.[38] In Memphis, on a previous occasion, one listener remarked that she "disbelieved in the othanticity of the Bible, and say it is a Book that will not bear investigation. . . ."[39] It amazes one that such a speaker would have even been invited to speak at Germantown by a local political group in mid-nineteenth century rural America. Such a controversial speaker sponsored by a political party today would produce such loud protests that the program organizers might be forced to resign. Yet presumably, she received a polite welcome, if a chilly response. This tells us something about local curiosity and hunger for intellectual and cultural stimulation.

Predictably, taxation was a political lightening rod locally. In July 1852, as the railroad building boom was really getting underway in Shelby County, Germantown became the seat of the third in a series of local meetings in opposition to a tax for the construction of the Memphis and Louisville Railroad.

Jacksonian prejudice still prevailed. They described the $250,000 tax burden as "both inexpedient and impolitic" in light of "the present depressed condition and indebtedness of our county. . . ." The opposition movement had started in Collierville, with Germantown citizens in attendance, and was followed by a second meeting at nearby Fisherville. Each meeting amended the published responses of the first with increasing intensity.[40] By the time the outraged worthies had gathered in Germantown, their rhetoric foreshadowed the indignity of the secessionists. They vehemently resolved:

> First, That the operations of this law, if carried into effect, would be oppressive to many, would do them injustice and would be unequal in its benefits.
>
> Second, That this law establishes a dangerous precedence, not sanctioned by the Constitution of the State, in giving to an irresponsible majority the right to dispose of the money of a minority.
>
> Third, That all men are free and equal, and that each should have the right to invest his money in railroad stock or not as he chooses, and that the Constitution of the State teaches us truly, that "the doctrine of non-resistance against arbitrary power and oppression is absurd, slavish and destructive of the good and happiness of mankind."
>
> Fourth, That we are opposed to the enforcement of this tax and will resist it at the ballot box, and by all means within our power.[41]

Among the elite participants of Germantown were, as usual, the planters James Kimbrough and Britton Duke, joined by Dr. T. H. Todd, uniting both Democrats and Whigs in a fusion of local concerns across party lines.

Germantown folks evinced yet other seemingly contradictory concerns. In August 1854, locals incited a meeting at Germantown that drew "more than one hundred citizens of Shelby County, Tennessee, and North Mississippi." They joined popular local efforts to prevent the Memphis Navy Yard from being turned over to the city. They saw it as a premier, "Government-run" facility for the production of rope and naval supplies and the repair of naval vessels, essential to national interests. It "ought not to be allowed to degenerate into a consideration of mere local interest or advantage, but should be determined alone as a national question." Their effort was for naught, because the facility had never been able to develop significantly and was expensive to operate.[42] It is interesting, however, that they opposed the "privatization" of a "big government" operation. Concern about "national defense" apparently prevailed once again to draw people together across party ideologies.

Finally, two other issues either interested the local population or infected both political discourse and social evolutions. Although neither women's rights nor suffrage acquired much significance before the war, local women were indeed attentive to political issues. Yet the idea of women voting seemed so outlandish that even some feminists rejected it, or at least considered it premature in their campaigns. Beyond the suffrage issue, however, women's rights were being discussed. This laid a foundation for the wartime experience of enforced self-sufficiency to embolden some. After the war, Elizabeth Avery Meriwether began speaking publicly in Memphis in favor of women's suffrage.

In contrast, the temperance movement, which was giving birth to the feminist movement, was truly vibrant before the war, and an obvious point of strong disagreement in a community with so much interest in the sale and consumption of alcohol. Temperance was the kind of public moral-improvement campaign the Whigs supported and Jacksonians abhorred as intervention in private lives. The town's temperance society had formed including members of the Baptist congregation by 1841. By 1853, the Friends of Temperance Reform had become such a forceful movement in Tennessee that it decided to run single-issue candidates for the legislature. The county's candidate was Germantown's Judge J. W. A. Pettit. Soon, however, they realized the error of trying to compete with one issue in an election involving other important matters, and sought instead other techniques.[43]

In their final pre-war campaign, they expected the press to jump on the bandwagon, despite the well-known habits of many journalists. Predictably, although the *Appeal* encouraged a well-informed vote on the issue, it avoided taking a position. Among the speakers officially chosen to stump for the cause was Germantown's Reverend Evans. All ministers in the county were called upon to preach one or more sermons for the cause,[44] so one also must wonder how mixed the reception must have been. Alcohol, tobacco, gambling and dancing had always been such important parts of popular Southern culture that the major denominations had been slow coming down against them.[45]

In any case, the cause failed, and over the next two years, the Friends began a campaign to get the state's legislators to impose prohibition despite the apparent lack of enthusiasm among voters. In Shelby County once again, Reverend

Evans participated in the convention that ardently pressured state Democrats to select temperance candidates.[46] That was an even more forlorn hope. One suspects the cause was taken seriously by only an impassioned minority. Isham Howse spoke strongly against drink and approved when his son went with William Duke to a temperance meeting a few miles north of the Wolf. Since this political assembly typically involved barbecue and probably attracted young women, it is hard to be sure what really drew the two young men on a Saturday afternoon.[47]

The movement appears to have been merely a great frustration locally for a few ardent crusaders, a nagging nuisance for those who could not ignore it, and the object of ridicule for the more boisterous imbibers. The cause ultimately lost its edge. After 1855, it almost disappeared from the pages of the papers.

One can be certain that many local women were among the supporters of the ministers. Even if their names never appeared in the papers, their physical presence would have been prominent. Their acceptable sphere of religious conviction spilled into the public and political sphere. In private, the men undoubtedly got an ear full, and the limits of deference and subordination were being tested. Well before the war, the movement was drawing women out and providing a unique experience in active public involvement, testing gender relations.

District Government and Politics

Even before Germantown was chartered, it acquired a political role that probably accounts among its earliest appeals as a settlement. By 1837, it became almost simultaneously the seat of local political and legal activity and the place for militia musters in Civil District Eleven and of a post office that served everyone south of the Wolf from east of White's Station to Bray's Station. It increasingly played a prominent role in county government.

Shelby County was governed by its Quarterly Sessions Court, composed of each district's justices of the peace. To it fell responsibility for law enforcement, legislation, taxation, the certification of voters, teachers, and lawyers, and judicial and other legal matters such as apprenticeships, estates and wills, slave emancipation, and freeman petitions and their bonding. In addition, it also provided or supervised most of the public services, such as bridges and roads,

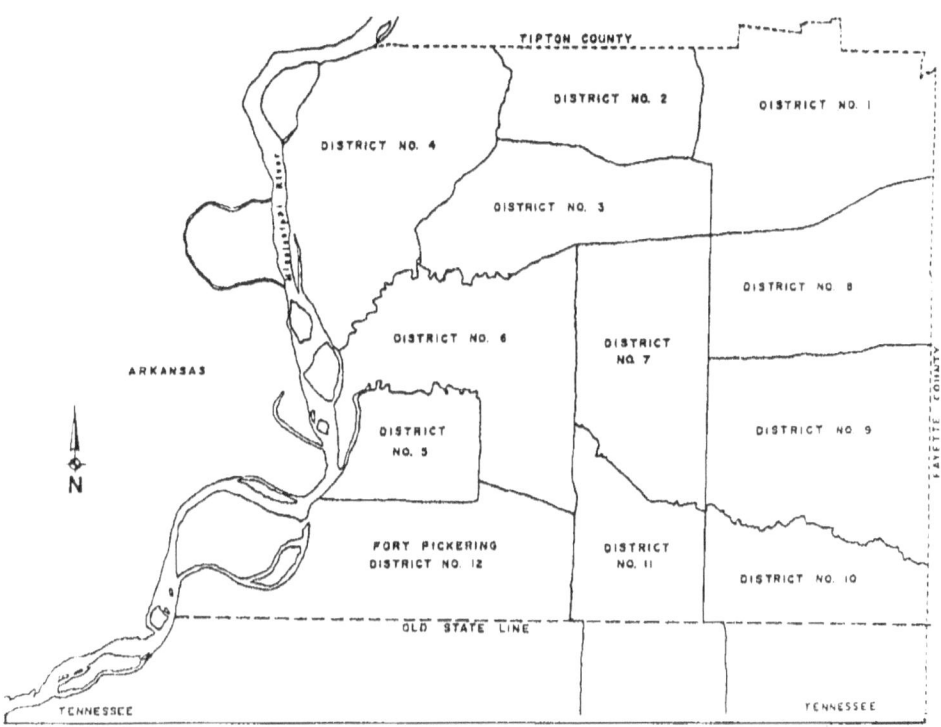

MAP 7. Civil Districts, Shelby County, 1835.

river maintenance, public buildings, public education, pauper burial, and the bonding of a variety of public officers and private businesses. It operated on taxes which it levied on property, plus fines and fees. With an annual budget of less than $5,000 on average, a county maintained its roads, bridges and public buildings, cared for the poor, and paid salaries and fees for services to the county.[48]

The civil districts that divided the county had grown out of the original militia organization of frontier times. They constituted an area that was expected to mobilize a company for its defense and the maintenance of law and order. Although this military responsibility had been suspended, it would resume with the reestablishment of an organized militia in 1861. When an act of 1836 had regulated the districts, they were to form the lowest level of rural government. Each elected its own justices of the peace and a constable, all of whom were responsible for prosecuting petty offenses too low for the court's attention, collecting fines, and the general maintenance of order.[49]

The original seat of Civil District 11, Pea Ridge was probably little more than a general store at the juncture with the State Line Road of a second class country road. Perhaps there was also a black smith and or a doctor living there. Eppy White's former house had served as the seat of the civil district and the post office. In 1836, that post office was relocated to Germantown at the home of the new post master Dr. Cornelius. In the next year, the citizens of the civil district voted unanimously to move the precinct and polling station to the house of Mrs. Fraziers in Germantown. By at least 1840, both county magistrates, had offices and homes in the town.[50] To carry out functions within the district, such as tax assessment, supervising elections, and managing the district's public school, citizens from the district were appointed or elected according to the nature of the job.

Germantown figured prominently in the Quarterly Court government. Each district elected two justices of the peace or magistrates who served as members of the court. In 1849, one of District Eleven's long-standing magistrates, Samuel W. Ledbetter presided as the court's chairman for a twenty-one day session. As a member, he drew three dollars per day, and as chairman another two dollars. As justice of the peace, Ledbetter had to post a $500 bond to insure that he forwarded to the county all the fines that he collected for petty offenses. In 1850, he was also elected county coroner. In 1854, he was succeeded as magistrate by John W. A. Pettit, who assumed his role in the court. After 1857, a judge was to be elected to chair the Quarterly Court and run the monthly court that handled the county's judicial business. When Pettit rose to the status of county court judge in January 1860, he presided over the court until its dissolution during the war.[51] With Pettit as judge, two magistrates from District 11 and a third representing the Forest Hill area in District 10, Germantown exercised considerable influence.

Occasionally townsmen would run for and hold other county offices such as sheriff, or coroner.[52] The most important of these was sheriff, who enforced state and county laws, made arrests, managed the jail, supervised elections (along with the coroner), and collected state and county taxes. As the most lucrative office in terms of commissions for services, its seat could be bitterly contested and a source of corrupt politics.[53]

✦ ✦ ✦

Contrary to the allegation that the planters controlled politics, local politics appearto have been a complex interaction among them, professionals like Ledbetter and Pettit, and the smaller planters and established yeomen farmers. Prominent among planters from 1841 through 1860 were Britton Duke, James Kimbrough, and John Gray. They served consistently in appointed positions such as judges for elections, as district tax assessors, and as grand and petty jurors for the court, but rarely in elected office.[54] Both planters and farmers shared appointed responsibilities for overseeing maintenance of the roads, just as the professionals and merchants of the town rotated the office of post master. While the preeminent justice or magistrate was often a professional, the secondary seat went to men of middle or mixed status. In 1860, William Walker won the preeminent position as justice and a role in political leadership that would continue after the war. The son of a planter, he described himself as a farmer, but also operated as a merchant. Likewise for adjacent District 10, T. C. Bleckley, a slave owning yeoman, with lands near Forest Hill assumed the same positions of prominence.[55] They represented the lowest level of economic achievement that could afford to hold office, and probably also that would be trusted by the land-owning voters who formed the majority of the electorate. Increasingly it was men of Walker's rank, plus professionals, who held most elected offices at district, county, and even state levels, with planters rarely entering the lists.[56]

Law enforcement in the district became a sinecure for an established farmer. Below the level of the county's sheriff, law enforcement was the responsibility of the district constable. Elections occurred every two years. To hold the office, a constable, usually with the help of several other citizens, had to put up a bond of $6,000 to guarantee his propriety. Duties included enforcing the law, executing legal actions, and collecting fines.[57] Jobe Lewis, respected yeoman, held that office from at least March of 1842. Then from January 1845 to August 1848, while Lewis served a deputy Sherriff, Jeremiah Shetter. Shetter, who boarded in Lewis' home, acted as constable.[58] In other words, he was Lewis' factotum. Then in August 1848, Lewis resumed the post of constable and was regularly reelected to his sinecure thereafter.[59]

✦ ✦ ✦

Education had become a significant focus for local politics, in ways hinting at local socioeconomic divisions and related political alignments. Although the state financed an elementary education, such schooling was managed by a district board of common school commissioners under the authority of the county. The few surviving election results for commissioners provide our only glimpse into political alignments inside the district. Conflicting attitudes about public education were exaggerated by the limited state funds available and the need for local taxes to finance anything significant. Most who could afford it preferred the expense of private schooling to taxes that supported an untrustworthy, plebeian, common school. Those below them financially, who might otherwise have preferred a publicly financed education, were counterbalanced at the polls by peers who doubted the value of more than minimal formal schooling. Jacksonian suspicions of public education mitigated their possible support.

The earliest records of local "education politics" are very sketchy. It seems that at first it was almost entirely the interest, and therefore, the business of the elite. The planter Britten Duke, a committed Whig, is the only known school commissioner for District Eleven from as early as 1837 until sometime in the late 1840s. His personal correspondence reveals that he managed the affairs of the district's "field school" for most of this period.[60]

As soon as the Duke family had settled near Pea Ridge in 1830, he assumed a position of local leadership, providing assistance in the affairs of his illiterate neighbors. Apparently always committed to education, such an involvement enhanced his commitments to the need for basic education. Perhaps as early as the late 1830s, he personally undertook the building of a school house to serve the community. The small, one-room building would serve the double purpose of school room and interdenominational chapel. He provided the initial costs of construction in agreement with unnamed neighbors who would apparently later defray some of the costs. He advertised for the teacher, hired and certified him, and handled the purchase of books and supplies. He even provided room and board for the teacher in his home.[61] For the duration of his tenure, this school functioned as a subscription school, the teacher's tuition being paid by the parents, and other expenses being reimbursed, at least in part, by the county's school funds. This was no free public school.

Initially, the election of commissioners generated limited interest, probably because county financing seemed so minimal. For instance, in 1848, there were only twenty-four who voted. In contrast, a much larger turnout in Collierville's

District Ten elected their school commissioners. By 1856, District Eleven's involved voters had risen to fifty-three, still less than a quarter of the electorate.[62] Nevertheless, this represented an increase of interest.

Since they served without compensation, commissioners had to be citizens of means with some commitment to education and/or concern about the taxes to support it, therefore attracting both Whigs and Democrats with opposing concerns. They conducted the annual scholastic census that justified the state and county funds for common schooling that they dispensed. They certified the pay of the teachers, and decided on their employment. How else they intervened in the instructional process is unknown, but since textbooks and classroom supplies were provided, they certified such payment.[63]

Although available funds from 1846 into 1852 had been expended for tuition at subscription schools, it is impossible to determine if it went for more than the support of destitute children and orphans. There were also suspicious peculiarities in accounting. In 1852, the commission stopped dispensing funds, no elections were held to replace commissioners, and no scholastic censuses were reported, so the district received no funding for 1853, nor initially for 1854. Yet in stark contrast, the state school fund trustee in Nashville reported that District Eleven had received $148 for 370 students, a grossly inflated number. When in September 1854, the newly elected district commission actually reported its census, there were only 216 students. Despite the lack of any records of investigations into this anomaly, one has to suspect corruption at some level, which must have fueled Jacksonian suspicions.

This peculiar period terminated with the establishment of the free common schools in District Eleven. That transition from "private" subscription schools, only partially supported by commission funding, to fully funded common schools generated political controversy. The final settlement was heavily influenced by the availability of regular state funding in 1854. It was also reflected in that heavier participation in the election of commissioners.

During the period leading up to 1854, there had been some political jockeying. In that poorly attended commission election of 1848, the farmers, A.L. Yancey, J.P. Winford and Elijah Brooks had overwhelmingly trounced T.M. More, Dr. Cornelius and Britten Duke, with his patrician dedication to public education. Voters had dumped More from his previous position on the commission, to be replaced by Winford. Squire Yancey, was a prominent citizen and local politician—justice from 1848 through 1854, and tax accessor. John S.

Dennis and A.J. Mattlock would later serve as commissioners.[64] From all appearances, district yeomen, possibly concerned over taxes and suspicious about stories of corruption, prevailed over those more dedicated to public education. They managed expenses tightly until that complete popular break with support for schooling had occurred by 1852.

In the summer of 1854, following the hiatus in commission membership and common instruction, Lewallen (Lonallen) Rhodes, wagon maker, J. Cole and Moses Neeley, planter and businessman, had been elected commissioners to get things going again, encouraged by the advent of attractive state funding. In July, Neeley resigned, and was replaced by John W.W. Pettit, who also assumed the office of commission clerk for the district.[65] Why Neeley resigned is indeterminable. Pettit was the county's leading exponent of free public schools. Strangely, Cole (Neeley's partner) seems to have been a short-term resident with no school-age children. Rhodes, now dabbling in local politics, represented the town's middle-class mechanic element.

Throughout 1855, Pettit pushed through the reform, perhaps against opposition. Both Rhodes and Cole resigned to be replaced by Pettit's appointees, John Dennis and Matthew Brown.[66] Pettit did not stand for reelection in the following year, but the primary reason was probably his involvement as newly elected magistrate for the district and heavy involvement in county court business. Regardless, thereafter the commission and its management of the new common schools seem to have run relatively smoothly.

Commission elections now became more hotly contested, with a larger number of voters, indicating increased community interest. In 1856, James Kimbrough began his running tenure, with the largest number of votes. William Harrison and Henry Jones, small planters or established farmers joined him. Thereafter, Joseph Clark and John Winford, farmers, served as commissioners.[67] Whatever the local elite still thought most appropriate for their own children's education, by 1857 majority attitudes about the need to finance free public education were strongly in favor. Locals voted almost unanimously (82 to 4) in favor of an additional tax for school purposes.[68] The agrarian alliance of planter and established yeoman would manage the funds and supervise the schooling.

As another related aspect of district politics, one has to wonder about the consequences of having the taxable property assessed by a local resident. For this purpose, the court appointed a citizen of each district, and paid him one hundred dollars. For instance in 1860 and 1861, it was the planter John Gray.[69] Was the listing so transparent that everyone knew so well how everyone else was taxed that no accusations of preference would result? Previously in 1853, the assessor, Esqr. Yancey, had not even called upon the people in their houses, but relied upon them to report their own tax list. He was so lax that it was not unusual for one to fall a year in areas without being harassed. How was the assessor protected from the pressures of friends and neighbors? Yancey, at least, had simply relied on their honesty and good citizenship.[70] No higher elite would impose taxes on the little man. As a matter of fact, even at the state level, tax laws and practices favored the little man over the planter and capitalist.[71]

Town Government

The loss of the town's archives makes it impossible to reconstruct town politics. Since the town had been first incorporated in 1841, the standard state requirements for the structure and authority of a town government had applied. There were seven aldermen, elected by the eligible voters living within the town. They held office for one-year terms, with annual town elections. They, chose from among their number, one to serve as mayor. A town constable was to be appointed by the council, to perform the relevant duties within the town itself. An appointed recorder and a treasurer rounded out the town's officialdom.[72] Unfortunately, I have not been able to uncover any records concerning any of these officeholders. For as long as a town remained chartered, the maintenance of a Board of Mayor and Aldermen was required by law so the town would fulfill its legal obligations to the county and state. That required the levying of taxes and collection of fines. The penalties for failure were sufficient to guarantee compliance.[73]

Since the original 1841 charter was veritably an addendum to another town's charter, it specified no official geographic town limits. One can merely conjecture how the community determined who held property inside it and who, therefore, could vote until the 1850 charter defined those borders.

The authority of a town government was extensive, but confined entirely to its borders. Any business or event outside those borders was under district jurisdiction. The obvious value of having an incorporated town was the services it could provide beyond the limited services of the county. In 1850, its authority and services were defined as:

full power and authority to enact such by-laws and ordinances as may be necessary and proper to preserve the health, quiet, and good order of their several towns; to prevent or remove nuisances, to establish night watches or patrols; to punish breaches of good order . . . ; to ascertain and declare, when necessary, the boundary of streets and alleys . . . ; to provide for licensing, regulating and taxing auctions, theatrical and other shows and exhibitions; to restrain and prohibit gambling; to prohibit the exhibition of stallions and jacks . . . ; to pass by-laws and ordinances for the paving of streets, alleys and side walks; to establish and regulate markets and inspection; to provide for the establishment and regulation of fire companies, and the sweeping of chimneys; to dig wells and to erect cisterns; to erect pumps on the streets and public grounds; to impose and collect fines and forfeitures for breaches and violations of the by-laws or ordinances . . . ; to collect taxes upon all property and privileges within their several corporations, which are taxable by the laws of the state . . . to tax ball, nine pin and ten pin alleys; to pass all by-laws and ordinances, necessary and proper to enforce the powers granted.[74]

This not only reveals what the town's citizens wanted to control and maintain in their community, but also something of popular and sometimes problematic pastimes. There is, however, one strange omission from the 1850 charter when compared with the powers originally granted town governments in 1841. There was no mention of restraining tippling houses, which had been specifically included in 1841.[75] Was this a deliberate oversight?

There was no town hall or any other public building, except perhaps the two-story, multipurpose log building mentioned in town traditions. How long it existed is not a matter of record. Duke's multipurpose school-chapel lay outside the town limits. If an alderman's home or business was not sufficient for council meetings, they may have met in the Masonic or Oddfellows' Hall. There was no jail or other holding facility for anyone arrested by the town constable. If one of the alleged "roaring old debauchees" got out of hand, the constable probably merely escorted him home. Since the town's only shooting incident, Stanton in 1845, was handled by the District's Constable Lewis, that may indicate that the town relied on him for double duty.

The right to vote in the town's elections fell to any male over age twenty-one owning property in the town, or who had resided there at least six months prior to the election, and to anyone otherwise entitled to vote for members of the state's general assembly.[76]

Local Politics and Power

Given all information accumulated so far, we have some basis for examining the contention that the planter aristocracy not only shaped the culture but controlled politics, which was becoming less democratic as the war approached.[77] First of all, one must note regional differences—not only those of the more western border states like Tennessee, but also in specific communities like Germantown. Tennessee had gone further with Jacksonian democratic reforms than the older states in terms of voter qualification, office holding requirements and an increase of elected versus appointed offices. At the state level, although real property holdings among legislators had increased between 1850 and 1860, the vast majority remained in the middle range. The same can be said of other forms of wealth. Although slave-owners had taken over 90% of seats by 1861, planters remained a distinct minority among them, and there were no large planters at all in the legislature. Lawyers, merchants, and small holders, had assumed the majority.[78] In Tennessee given its diverse demographics, the socioeconomic middle was forming the political majority, as in any modernizing democracy. . Of course, one would also expect wealthy and influential interest groups like planters to be able to exercise disproportionate political influence. Nomination processes can be manipulated, and both elected officials and voters can be bribed, cajoled or intimidated. No democratic constitutional process can be immune to such, but it is tricky to assert that one particular class "controlled" such a system.

More importantly, the insights we do have into county and district politics raise doubts about possible "control." Voting rights and the resultant pollings were certainly democratic. Any man in residence for six months and over the age of twenty-one could vote, and they certainly exercised that franchise enthusiastically in federal and state elections. In the turnout for district offices, especially the more seemingly petty school board, the vote was clearly dominated by a majority of the middle-sized property holders and men of other means. They and their sons of-age outnumbered both the great landed and the landless.

As the early alignment of the propertied with the Whig party shifted, the planters who stayed true to their party lost control outside their party. Those who joined the Democrats allied themselves with the more (little-d) democratic elements of society, who were by no means easy to manipulate.

Either party's positions, especially locally, seem to have been more a matter of a community of consensus than of influence—a consensus that could be marshaled to make persuasive political arguments. To argue that the Southern values and interests that this community shared were shaped mostly from above by its elite requires a "vulgar Marxist" set of assumptions. To argue with more sophistication that the economic system of slavery generated a common set of interests is easier, especially when one adds the racial fears and prejudices that it entailed inherently. Finally regional pride, suspicions and prejudices were deeply entrenched in that culture. They bound together those who benefited from slavery with those who did not.

Both Germantown voters in particular and county voters in general displayed the typical Southern distrust of government and resentment of taxes. Nevertheless, it did not result in the blocking of taxes, regulations and legislation that favored modernization, especially railroad building.[79] They were certainly a source of political contention locally, but usually insufficient to thwart development. The same was true for increasing taxes for education, although again never as generously as truly needed. There, private or business initiative usually exceeded government initiative, as it had in the case of roads. The belief that government existed primarily to protect private property, not to run or regulate it was a cornerstone. Otherwise its role was to protect national interests and provide defense. In the latter case, the federal government was perceived as more trustworthy than local or private interests, for example, the Memphis Navy Yard controversy.

With the exception of a few professionals, especially lawyers, the social and economic elite avoided the political hassle of running for office. Instead, they often served in the kinds of offices that involved community service, which did provide some influence in issues like taxes and expenditures for education and roads, but they shared these offices with the middle strata. An office like post master was passed around as more of a shared burden, usually among the town's professionals and businessmen. On the other hand, the important district offices of magistrate and constable became something approaching middle-class sinecures. We certainly cannot assume that these men were the tools of an elite few. Constable Lewis may have simply had a personality and style with which everyone was comfortable. He had undoubtedly built a base of personal power that reached beyond the district. By 1860, the men who were magistrates had become political scrappers. It seems unlikely they were simply the tools of the elite. More likely they built and maintained a majority base that may have run well down the socioeconomic scale, which is not to say that they would be easily indifferent to influential interests.

Issues like temperance, taxation and finance could be contentious but not seriously divisive. Phobias generated by Know-Nothing Americanism could temporarily disrupt voting trends, but not enough to rend the community. Likewise, consensus over the necessity of slavery did not easily produce agreement over secession. As we shall see, that was a crack that could only be patched over temporarily by community pressures responding to overwhelming external developments. In that regard as in all others, it seems that politics around Germantown were shaped more by a sense of community and common interests than by any one element.

The Clouds of War Gather

The Kansas-Nebraska Act had exacerbated divisions within both the Whig and Democratic parties. Since this act would settle the decision over slavery in each new state by popular vote, Democrats unanimously endorsed it as a victory of republican principles over potential congressional nullification of slave-owner property rights. Unfortunately, the consequence of the 1854 act unleashed the bloody confrontation in "bleeding Kansas" that would plague the nation up to the Civil War, doing much to set the tone of that war in West Tennessee.

In the northwest, the demise of the Whig party and the confrontation over the Kansas-Nebraska Act gave birth to the Republican Party. Southerners saw that party with its opposition to the expansion of slavery as a purely regional party threatening national unity. For its support of the act, in the North the Democratic Party also suffered severe losses in its congressional seats, thus making southerners feel doubly threatened.[80] Meanwhile, however, the emergence of the "Know-Nothing" movement had temporarily curbed the threat of the new Republican Party.

In Tennessee, as we have seen the American movement divided the Democratic Party and essentially absorbed the Whigs. Each party appealed to voters as the true national party for defense of the Union, but the Democrats had a stronger southern-rights position. The shift of old Whig leaders and voters to support Buchanan gave the Democrats victory in Tennessee, but especially in West Tennessee where they triumphed in former Whig territory. Democrats swept the state in the 1857 elections, putting the planter and Southern Rights advocate Isham G. Harris into the governor's seat and sending democratic Unionist Andrew Johnson to the Senate. They were indeed a temporary set of strange bedfellows, and a perfect example of the complexity of Tennessee politics and sentiments. The Dred Scott case and the fight over the admission of Kansas had kept the expansion of slavery issue center stage, cementing the Democrats' position as defenders of southern rights and preservers of the Union against "Black Republicanism."[81]

In October 1859, as word of John Brown's Raid spread, tensions mounted. Of course, the idea that he seized the Harper's Ferry Arsenal with plans to arm a slave insurrection fanned the racial phobias of all dwellers among the plantation lands whether slaveholders or not. Eventually, even relatively moderate papers like the *Appeal* began to argue that Brown was merely the cutting edge of an increasingly nasty mood among abolitionists whose teachings would incite further threats against Southern lives and property. The abolitionists were seen as pushing the country toward insurrection and war for which Southerners should be preparing.[82]

As the next presidential election approached, however, Tennessee Democrats became split over the candidacy of Steven Douglas. His role in the defeat of Kansas' admission under the Lecompton Constitution made him suspect in the eyes of many Southern-Righters. More pragmatic Democrats, such as the editors of the *Appeal*, argued he was the best bet to unite the Democrats, defeat Lincoln, and preserve the Union. Isham Harris and his organ, the *Avalanche*, however proposed a different candidate, while staunch Southern-Righters pushed for a hard line on slave owners' rights. The upshot was the state convention's nomination of Andrew Johnson as their candidate.[83]

Then at the national Democratic convention in Charleston in April 1860, both the national and state parties split hopelessly. When the Party reconvened in Baltimore, a fight over the seating of deep-South delegates resulted in their secession to a separate convention. The majority of Tennessee's delegates joined the secession, while the Douglas wing of the national Party succeeded in his nomination. Despite their firm commitment to the maintenance of the Union, Tennessee's Democrats supported the southern Democratic candidacy of John C. Breckinridge.

Tennessee's Democratic Party was now split into those who supported Breckinridge and those who stood by the national party. The Opposition became the Constitutional Union Party, nominated John Bell as its candidate, and once again presented itself as the staunch defender of the Union. Although Bell ultimately carried the state, Douglas drew over 20 percent of the votes in West Tennessee.[84] In Shelby County, he drew almost 44 percent.

In Germantown's 11th District, 229 voters divided into 100 for Bell, 94 for Douglas and only 35 for Breckinridge. In the 10th District, 148 voters split into 68 for Douglas, 50 for Bell and 30 for Breckinridge.[85] This late in the game, Unionist Democrats still had stronger support around Germantown than the secessionists, and a very sizable percentage voted for the Opposition Unionists. The secessionists were a distinct minority.

The town's Whigs had mostly been staunch Unionists. One once proclaimed,

> I have no patience with secessionists. He who would willingly see a separation of the states of this union, is a traitor to his country and an enemy of God and man, and deserved to be hung upon a gallows as high as that of Hamon.... But I have faith in God, that He will put down all evil plottings, and every unhallowed scheme of Northern abolitionists and Southern states rights hypocrites, who, under false pretenses, would destroy the fairest fabric of human government ever established.[86]

As in most of the Southern states, there were no ballots for Lincoln. The Republican Party was still a regional phenomenon, and without the Electoral College system, he could not have won. As has been the case in all such elections, the losers proclaimed the winner without a popular majority to be illegitimate. Southerners had one more justification for secession and defying the President. Lincoln had won, so South Carolina seceded on December 20.

✦ ✦ ✦

Without any relevant primary sources, one is left to conjecture about the social consequences of political divisions within the community. Were they a source of disharmony that disturbed the otherwise relatively harmonious society depicted so far? One has to use this last election as a barometer of the divisions, and then speculate using all the other indications of social relations in the community. Adding this to all the literature on prewar attitudes in Tennessee, one can conjure a portrait without violating the historian's responsibility for interpretation based on primary evidence rather than logical deduction. At least if one will grant him a little literary license.

One can assume that by the end of 1860, there were no covert radical abolitionists, and voting records make it evident that there was a minority of secessionists on the other extreme. The rest spread out on a spectrum ranging from firm Unionists to those torn between States Rights and a commitment to the Union. The divisions among those who accepted slavery as the natural order, those who wished for some release from its "burden," and those intellectually or morally opposed did not necessarily determine one's place in the political spectrum. Of course, such differences would intrude themselves into discussions and debates during the secession crisis, but subsequent political developments would be more decisive than those differences.

Outside influences came in two forms. Over the years, state and local politicians had held forth in every venue from stumping in election campaigns, partisan assemblies, and impromptu gatherings at such places as Lucken's Inn. The other sources were Memphis newspapers and mailed subscriptions for other periodicals. Purveying the generally Unionist opinions was the *Memphis Bulletin*, and at the other extreme, the *Avalanche*, the secessionist mouthpiece of Governor Harris. The *Appeal* was probably the most popular, and had been evolving from a firmly states-rights toward an increasingly hard line Southern-rights and finally a secessionist stance on the eve of the war. It probably reflected the transition among the majority during the upcoming winter and spring.

As the men discussed these various sources in their gatherings, one has the impression that such exchanges would have been restrained, despite the amount of alcohol consumed. Even at gatherings like Lucken's or other "saloons," though more voluble, they would have remained short of insulting, for that could have led to deadly violence. There would have been much talk of "honor," for that was every gentleman's responsibility to uphold. "Rights" were of equal importance in deciding where that honor might be challenged. All could agree there could be no violations of their state's rights and especially their homes and property. Under what conditions could these concerns require them to stand against the Union? Did "honor" require them to stand in defense of their neighbors in Mississippi who soon seceded? Although national patriotism was more ambivalent a concept than today, was not one honor-bound in its defense? One's patriot forefathers had shed their blood in its creation.

The younger men might have focused on more romantic martial posturing about how they should behave in the face of an increasingly likely war, with less concern about the issues involved. Valiant struggle is where their "honor" would be tested. The more literate had been immersed in images of brave derring-do and heroic sacrifice. All would boast of how good Southern boys could easily thrash and repel a horde of barbarous Yankees.

The women, often interested in politics, could only discuss among themselves in private, or in the intimacy of the home. There, if the woman was not allowed the last word, we can be sure that did not settle the issue. All would be fearful of invasion and wanted protection from every imaginable evil. Many would also have been ambivalent, however, given the prospect of the loss of husband or son.

As for the young ladies, a few may have shared their mother's interests and opinions, but most seemed to have been too involved in their social concerns than to do more than share in the young men's romantic imaginings. The thought of their beaus attired in the dress of the fancy uniformed militia companies must have set their hearts aflutter. Even an unfortunate result would have cast them in the role of the tragic heroine in one of their Victorian novels.

The non-slaveholding yeomen, small merchants, mechanics and clerical workers and their wives would have held wide-ranging attitudes about slavery, but shared in the common fear of an emancipated black mob. They would have also shared in the common regional fears, pride and prejudices. They could have seen no advantages in war, but would have been willing to fight in defense of hearth and home.

Below the level of informed discussion, the poorest farmers and landless laborers may have worried about a future over which they had no control, knowing it was unlikely to benefit them one way or the other. An end of slavery offered them no advantages without the removal of the blacks from the land. They might hope to be left alone by a distant war, but feared an invasion as much as everyone else. The women and girls could have seen absolutely no advantages for themselves.

Thus everyone drifted toward the precipice with no control over their fate.

No control over whatever position they would soon be driven to take. The course of American history had already come too far. In the following year, they would all find themselves sliding into a world in which there was no longer room for debate.

PART SUMMARY

On the brink of the war, Germantown hardly resembled typical stereotypes of the Old South. Images of a community of slaves and "rednecks" presided over by WASP ladies and gentlemen distorts a more complex reality. The old town was almost as cosmopolitan as the City of Germantown today. Although the majority of its inhabitants had come from southern states, a sizable minority had arrived from northern climes, while an equal share of immigrants provided a truly international spectrum. In addition to English, Scottish, Irish, and Welch, there were Germans, French, and Italians, present in greater proportions than in most of the rest of the country.

Despite its location in the midst of a plantation-agricultural community, nothing had impeded industrialization and trends toward modernity. The tendency of the majority of the population, smaller planters, comfortable yeomen, professionals, machinists and mechanics to diversify and enter into entrepreneurial and industrial ventures counterbalanced the alleged stifling of planter hegemony. The railroads and the proximity of Memphis not only encouraged such enterprise, but had a similar effect on social and gender relations. There is certainly no indication that southern traditionalism was being overthrown, but by the same token, Germantown society was not far behind the northern bourgeoisie in modernization. It was perhaps even more industrialized and commercialized than typical farm towns in the border or Northern states.[87]

Germantown certainly had its socioeconomic hierarchy, but the distribution of property and wealth was not disproportionate comparatively speaking. There was a high elite of wealthy planters and merchants. But they blended almost imperceptibly with an "under-elite," who in turn blended with the comfortable yeomen and mechanic, which in turn simply flowed down to the lowest level of independence among them. Below them were the poor, propertyless whites, but there was still no absolute social and upward-mobility barrier against them until one reached that small underclass of "poor white trash."

Of course, even below them were the slaves, whose experiences were also closer to those of the border states than the coastal and deep South. To say the least, slavery was the true seat of gross inequality supporting the elite, but they were outside the world of social relations. The black and white worlds were entirely separate worlds. That generated an entirely different set of social tensions.

From all appearances, the entire society above the poorest whites and slaves experienced less social tension than often attributed to southern society, though certainly no perfect harmony or egalitarianism. There would have been resentment of arrogant and condescending snobs, but no significant presence of them has appeared in the surviving evidence. Nothing indicates any class-based as opposed to individual resentments. As one historian has noted, the agrarian community "fostered communalism." Planter and yeoman, professional, businessman and mechanic were bound together in a tight economic relationship. Although each was proudly independent, they all relied on each other. The agriculturalist needed what the others provided. The others needed the food and raw materials the agriculturalist provided. They helped each other with public building projects such as church raisings. They ministered to each other in illness, communed spiritually, and shared public holiday gatherings. "It was the *community* that was self-sufficient, and all individual self-sufficiency was a product of mutual assistance." [88] Even the "respectable poor" were included, although they could feel some inequality and constrained opportunity.

Those below largely escaped our picture of Germantown life. They and the more marginal yeomen constituted smaller minorities than in other parts of the South. Although there are a few hints that the privileged may have suffered rare acts of hostility, "barn burning," property crime and robbery were not prevalent. Ladies were always accompanied in public, especially young ladies, but mostly to protect their reputations rather than to guard against evil threats. There is no indication that the local elites had to accommodate and coexist with a dangerous underclass as described elsewhere.[89] There were very few reports of gentlemanly violence in defense of honor, so common elsewhere in the South. Violence was mostly reserved for the management of slaves.

The real source of tension was the presence of that large black slave population. Despite the romantic image of happy and faithful slaves, most blacks resented their status, even if they generally avoided displaying it. Yet the black bogyman, the unrestrained or escaped slave, or worse the threat of revolt lurked in the shadows. Slavery created that which was most unique about the

South, and Germantown could not escape that pressure. The combination of community with the ideology of white supremacy formed two pillars of white social harmony.

One possible insight into the social and political attitudes developing within the area's population may lie in a unique analysis of America's social-political character. Colin Woodard proposes that our country has been divided into ten or more "nations," or distinct cultural entities each with its own set of political tendencies.[90] Three of them would form the bulk of the area's population, plus the "Midlanders" and Yankees (both being Northerners, 5 percent total) and immigrants (7 per cent), probably constituting a disproportionate presence among the elite. Among the two, however, most Northerners and almost all foreigners had become well integrated into the area's version of Southern life. The largest of the three purported cultural entities were Appalachians (39 percent), mostly born somewhere else in Tennessee. Rivaling their predominance were settlers from the Tidewater states (31 percent), many of whom were from their Appalachian regions, complicating our analysis. The Deep Southerners (20 percent) were clearly a minority. These percentages plus the very diverse population of the city of Memphis raises serious doubts about one of Woodard's contentions—that the south western most part of Tennessee belonged to the Deep South versus "Greater Appalachia." Although Memphis' was focused "down river" it was counterbalanced by commerce also focused "up-river."

That element from the Tidewater states who were not Appalachian would have brought an aristocratic social and political proclivity, tempered by immersion in the frontier environment. Nevertheless, they provided the leadership for the initial Whig majority. Although some brought with them plantation slavery, the majority may have shared the fears of that variety of slavery which generated so much potential for violent slave revolts. When the Appalachian elements from the Tidewater and the southern Mid-West mixed with other Appalachians, a majority probably emerged. Their ambivalence about slavery and greater tendency toward yeoman farming would account for the shifting diversity of attitudes toward secession, both before secession and later during Federal occupation. Such Appalachians allegedly inclined toward a more rugged individualism, anti-elite distrust of government and authority, acceptance of a social strata based on achievement, an aversion for taxation to support communal needs, and even lawless tendencies. This Appalachian predominance well-integrated with northern and foreign immigrants accounts for the lack of political control by the large planters and the ultimate prevalence of yeoman and professional domination of local Democratic politics. The Deep Southern minority might have brought a stronger commitment to plantation slavery, but any dirt-farmer elements among them were also seeking a refuge from that environment. Nevertheless, all three "nations" shared the general American racist assumptions plus a hostility toward Yankee self-righteous disdain for things Southern, especially campaigns for radical abolition. They were involved in an alliance in what Woodard describes as a struggle against "Yankeedom" for control of the country.

Despite what one might consider overgeneralization in Woodard's characterizations of the "nations," the clear regional mix of the area's population casts light on the mix that was antebellum Germantown. Regardless of its position in the cotton-belt South, it deviated from its purported social, political and economic patterns. By the same token, however, the heavy non-Appalachian mix would account for the relatively peaceful and law-abiding, literate, tidy and cohesive community that contradicts Woodard's generalizations about the people of the "Appalachian nation." The less domesticated elements of the frontier wave of Appalachians had moved on by 1860.

✦ ✦ ✦

Even radical secessionist rhetoric did not persuade many owners, especially not in Tennessee, as we shall see. Most eventually came around, but some never supported secession. Small owners and non-owners usually subscribed to white supremacy, and could feel threatened by the freeing of blacks. Most, however, were ultimately won for "the cause" by appeals to honor, the defense of home, community bonds and peer pressure, especially when war fever spread down from legitimate authority, like the pulpit and respected public leaders. All of this will play out around Germantown.

We shall see whether social harmony prevailed during and after the war or if the alleged Appalachian tendencies toward disdain for authority and lawlessness would reemerge. If white supremacy and related fears had plastered over resentments generated by social and economic inequalities, a society based on a slave economy that financed social and economic inequality constituted a vulnerable flaw.

Although often described as pleasant or lovely, Germantown was no sleepy town, but a bustling transportation hub for business, industry and recreation.

It boasted graduates from the nation's prestigious universities, renowned professionals, industrious entrepreneurs and inventors, and enviable institutions of higher learning. It provided political leadership in the county. Local folks had every reason to believe in a positive and progressive future as participants in nearly a decade of uninterrupted advances in their wellbeing. It had taken about twenty-five years for frontier settlers to build this thriving community. More than one hundred years would have to elapse for a similar environment to reemerge after the war.

PART 2
THE WAR YEARS

5

1861 · GERMANTOWN GOES TO WAR

Secession and Mobilization

Secession was a hard decision for the people around Germantown, as it was in the rest of the state. Throughout the winter months, Unionist Democrats and Opposition leaders called for voters to stand behind the Union, as a new Union party formed around them. On the secessionist side, Governor Harris called for a state convention to define the position of Tennessee. Unionists suspected secessionists would use demagogic tactics to stampede voters in their direction. So they engineered a popular referendum to require approval of whatever position the convention took. On February 9, although West Tennesseans and Shelby County approved holding a convention by a strong majority, it was rejected state-wide out of fear that it would force secession. But even West Tennesseans expressed opposition to secession. The vast majority voted for Unionist candidates over secessionists.[1]

Nevertheless, secessionists persisted, expecting that Tennesseans would lose confidence in the Union. They waged a hot campaign of pro-secession propaganda. The result was reflected in two of Memphis' major Democratic newspapers. The *Appeal* initially favored moderation and compromise and supported the National Democratic ticket. The *Avalanche* espoused secession radically, supporting the States-Rights wing. The secessionists, fueled by the *Avalanche*, argued that the inevitable war would require Tennessee to defend the South against "Northern invasion." By February, the *Appeal* changed its tune, advising promptly joining secession as the way to avoid war by a show of strength through unity. It was soon unrelentingly secessionist.[2] It had already removed the American flag from its masthead, and within the month replaced it with that of the Confederacy.

As the debate raged, secessionists constantly blurred the language, turning "abolitionists" and "Northerners," into "enemies" and "aliens". The illegitimate and usurpatious "black Republican regime in Washington" sought to coerce and subjugate the South. Their language was scripted with an eye toward inciting fear and calling for unity against oppression. Such appeals cut across class lines. Plantation owners, yeomen farmers and tenants, financiers, merchants, artisans responded alike.[3]

The people of Germantown, divided over developments, read the local presses that persistently beat the drums of war. They read the *Appeal's* calls for action that depicted the South as put upon and threatened with invasion to impose Northern interests.[4] It directly challenged the honor of Southern manhood to assure their women that their honor and safety would be protected.[5]

Then came the confrontation at Fort Sumter on April 12. Union efforts to hold and supply the fort were followed by Lincoln's call for troops, seen as a threat of "Northern aggression," that undermined the Unionist Party's support. The tide shifted radically, and martial fervor prevailed. While reading of pending invasion, the citizens of Germantown also learned of enthusiastic local displays of Southern patriotism.[6] On trips to Memphis, they attended entertainments designed to stir secessionist ardor.[7]

After Lincoln's call to arms to suppress the revolt, the die was cast for most Tennesseans. Throughout Shelby County, the civil districts held meetings to appoint delegates to a county convention to nominate candidates for the legislature. Those of Germantown's District Eleven met on April 15 at the store of Messrs. Cole and Co.[8] One would certainly like to have a report of those proceedings. Unfortunately, the Germantown meeting published only its nominations. They may have expressed the same sentiments as those of District Ten, many residents of which were part of "greater Germantown." They accused the "Black Republicans" of inciting the slaves to insurrection and murder and launching a war of aggression against the Southern states already in secession. They resolved to "resist unto the death the aggressive policy of Lincoln's administration."[9] Intolerance of any pro-Union sentiments completely replaced coolness toward secession. Those active in the Germantown's meeting represented a true cross-section of society, from planter to mechanic and yeoman, including many formerly reluctant secessionists.

On April 20, General Gideon Pillow, military consultant to Harris, called upon Tennesseans to form companies "for the defense of the Southern States against invasion." He called for "official reports from all organized corps of the State" to be sent to him, and concluded with an assertion that "I speak not without authority." Indeed, he had already visited President Davis to promise a division of Tennessee troops.[10] Secessionists were now confident that they controlled events.

Governor Harris proceeded to lead Tennessee into a de facto secession. On May 1, the General Assembly agreed to military alliance with the Confederacy. On May 6, it passed a "Declaration of Independence". The vote would also decide to join the Confederacy. The Assembly also passed the Military Bill of the State of Tennessee, empowering the governor to create a state army of 55,000 volunteers "for the safety of the State." Vote to approve all of this was set for June 8.[11]

The secessionists of Memphis organized a county meeting to mobilize voter turnout for secession. Germantown's district representatives included its political leadership, Judge Pettit and Constable Job Lewis, William H. Walker, L. A. Rhodes and T. W. Trueheart, who were to call meetings of district voters, organize political clubs, and liaise with the county organization.[12]

Even before formal secession, developments in Memphis went to extremes, while folks in the countryside followed the press reports attentively. To prepare for Northern invasion, and to ward off spies and treasonous subversives, the mayor and board of aldermen appointed committees of Military Affairs and of Vigilance. The Military Committee sought to coordinate the spontaneous burst of energy by amateur organizers to raise money and form military companies.[13] The Vigilance Committee responsible for policing , promptly issued orders establishing curfews for free blacks and slaves. Simultaneously, the *Avalanche* ran an inflammatory article about agitation among the city's slave population, spread by freemen.[14]

On April 19, a Committee of Safety proclaimed assumption of executive authority for security for Memphis and its suburbs.[15] As news of these committees of safety spread, some citizens must have reflected uneasily on the similarity to the French Revolution and Terror. Constant references to "Tories" also established clear parallels with American committees of safety and their tar-and-featherings of Tories.

What followed might well be described as a "Terror." Accounts in Northern newspapers paint such a picture, while the Memphis press handled affairs with much more circumspect reporting. The number of northerners reported to have fled varied wildly in the northern papers. Charles Lufkin has estimated, however, that during the months of April through June, about 3,000 Northern-born residents fled the city. Others from surrounding areas followed. Yet he estimates that only about 20% of the northern-born fled.[16] In Germantown's civil district, of the seventeen men and single women of northern birth reported in the 1860 census, seven were still present for the 1870 census. This was actually a much higher retention rate than for southern-born citizens. Aside from Isaac Bliss, however, all the men involved in the Bliss book-agent operation were no longer present for whatever reason. They, after all, were probably men far less well integrated into the community, owning no property.

Despite the air of terrorism in Memphis, and intolerance toward antisecessionists expressed in Collierville's resolution, there is no reason to believe that Germantown's erstwhile Unionistslived lived in fear. The Confederacy's August law to expel all "alien enemies" excluded such persons who were "citizens of the Confederate States".[17] Although a few staunch unionists may have fled, most who had opposed secession joined the cause preserving a sense of community cohesion that protected former unionists. The pressures that converted them to the cause were probably grown less of fear and more of conformity. Later that sense of community would help Germantown avoid the local Unionist retributions against former persecutors that occurred elsewhere during Federal occupation. Its unionists had not been terrorized, so they did not resort to acts of revenge. Nothing resembled Memphis' terror.

In contrast, one clearly outright act of intimidation by the Memphis Committee of Safety that affected Germantown voters was denial of a secret ballot during the county's final vote on secession. They required the election clerks to assign a number to each name on their voters list, with a corresponding number placed on each voter's ballot. No one could cast a secret vote against secession.

After West and Middle Tennessee voted overwhelmingly for secession, East Tennessee almost seceded from the state, seeing the elections were rigged. Prounion voters had been intimidated at the polls. In Memphis, where 5,613 votes were cast, only five men had the courage to vote for the union and were stigmatized in the press.[18]

In fact, these were the only five such daring voters in all of Shelby County.

The votes from every civil district like Germantown's were unanimously for secession.[19] For what it is worth, on May 21, based on intelligence that he had Union General George B. McClellan had identified Memphis as a stronghold of secessionists, but in other West Tennessee counties pro-union feeling was reportedly predominant. There were indeed many unionists "who are now outwardly secessionists," but who could be rallied if supported.[20]

A mini-civil-war soon erupted within the state when unionists in the east formed partisan units and initiated guerrilla warfare. They were in open, armed revolt by November. Fully aware of pro-union sentiments in Tennessee, in June, Federal Secretary of War, Simon Cameron ordered recruitment officers into Tennessee to raise 10,000 men. Although most could only be raised in the East, a recruitment officer was specifically dispatched into West Tennessee.[21] Undoubtedly, he could have achieved little before occupation. Eventually, however, at least thirty-thousand Tennesseans joined the fight for the union.[22]

✦ ✦ ✦

Meanwhile, cities like Memphis always had several volunteer, "uniformed militia companies" with colorful flags. They had continued to function even after the regular militia had terminated in 1857. They quickly coalesced into a rebirth of the 154th Regiment. As secession approached, new volunteer militia companies blossomed along with the flowers of April and May. Hardly a day passed without the newspapers proclaiming such a formation. Names like the Independent Southern Guards or the Tennessee Cadets were supplemented by companies for each of the immigrant nationalities, for many Christian denominations such as the Methodist Military Company, and also for the Jewish community.[23]

The infection spread to the countryside prompting the men around Germantown to meet on April 20. The published record of their assembly provides a list of those involved as well as a picture of their mood. They immediately formed a committee to consider forming two military companies.

> In view of the perilous dangers by which we are surrounded, and being determined to defend our firesides and country to the last extremity; therefore,
> *Resolved*, That a military company of the citizens of Germantown and vicinity be forthwith formed for the protection of our friends, to be called the "Home Guard."

Any member would be free to withdraw in order to serve in a second company for "active service abroad."[24]

Their language demonstrates the fear of invasion by Northerners intent upon harm. "Bloody Kansas" had ignited fears of lawless rape and pillage. Locals read sensational reports of how "jayhawkers" operating in Kansas, Missouri and Arkansas already used the war as a front for acts of murder, outright pillage and robbery.[25]. Such fears would prove not entirely unfounded. The unionist guerrilla activities in the east and the local militia-self-defense mood in the west set the stage for what West Tennessee would experience as guerrilla warfare spread throughout Tennessee.

Germantown had responded to the state's call for the formation of volunteer companies, one for home protection and one for service in or out of state.[26] A motion of Dr. John M. Gray was approved to form them. When those present were requested to enroll, about one hundred immediately joined the home guard. "The other company with many names" was also reported as "in process of formation."[27] Eventually, the Secession Guards were recruited with Germantown as its base. To the east, Collierville's Civil District Ten, including the community of Forest Hill, was becoming the nucleus of the Wigfall Grays.[28]

Another committee was formed to solicit subscriptions to purchase arms and equipment for the home company. Again it consisted of a representative spread of the planters, professionals, businessmen, and farmers. They approved a motion that those present who wished to subscribe money should do so. William Walker responded that since his broken arm prevented his service, he would contribute. "Mr. Fresstenheim (*sic*; Furstenheim), merchant, and many others, made liberal contributions."[29]

The meetings ended with expressions of enthusiasm Mr. A. M. Rafter read some patriotic lines of poetry. . . ."[30] One must wonder why "Colonel" Rafter did not play a more prominent role in the town's mobilization.

Newspapers told how city ladies enthusiastically began sewing the uniforms for their heroic young men.[31] Soon the papers filled with appeals for them to form auxiliary organizations to support the troops. The women of Germantown announced, April 26, 1861,

> Editors Appeal: We, the ladies of Germantown and vicinity, in consideration of the troubles that are brooding over our native land,

ILL. 3 Women's Support Committee. *Harper's Weekly*, 6.29.1861. North or South, they all looked the same.

have resolved to aid to the best of our ability our relatives and friends who shall engage in the approaching conflict. We, therefore, offer to the soldiers of Germantown all the assistance in our power with our needles, and promise also to aid in the care and sustenance of their families during their absence. And should the war approach our own homes, we will watch over the sick and wounded (though strangers) as our own brothers or fathers.

[Signed] Mrs. Maria L. Pettit, Mrs. E. B. Cornelius, Mrs. Mills, Mrs. Moliter, Mrs. Morgan, Mrs. Rhodes, Mrs. Harris, Mrs. Hicks, Mrs. Boardman, Mrs. Burnley, Mrs. Goode, and many others.[32]

After several months, the good ladies followed their Memphis counterparts by staging a fund-raising entertainment.

Exhibition at Germantown.—The ladies of Germantown and vicinity will give a concert with tableaux, at the Presbyterian church, Thursday evening, the 3d inst., for the benefit of our volunteers.
 Miss Adie Plunkett. Sec'y.
 Germantown, Tenn., Oct. 1, 1861.

The prominent ladies of the town and countryside exhibited very early such uncharacteristic behavior for rural Southern ladies. They created their own organization, elected officers, and published their names in the papers. Although Southern women elsewhere made this same transition, Germantown's ladies did so with greater promptness.[33] Perhaps they were already in the habit of organizing themselves, but without publicity. Undoubtedly their close social ties with the city had involved them in similar lower-key activities before the war. Their "suburban" environment had exposed them to far more than typical plantation ladies.

This experience converted what had been their private household activity into a public operation. They coordinated their own talents, employed their slaves, and put any personally owned sewing machines into teams producing the clothing. They purchased the cloth for uniforms and flags, and although working from patterns, added their own unique decorative touches. Their weavers and spinners also produced the coarser materials for equipment. Germantown area ladies may have fully dressed the entire Secession Guards Company.[34]

It's hard to find descriptions of the uniforms of local volunteer companies, but fortunately, a fragmentary description of the Secession Guards' uniform has survived. Such volunteer company uniforms could be quite flamboyant, but the Guards were more conventional, "made of gray jeans, trimmed with three stripes red, white, red."[35] Jeans referred to the approved cloth for the uniform, a cotton and wool blend. It would have been of the conventional Confederate uniform cut, a short jacket with small upright collar, and straight pants legs. The stripes would have covered the coat collar and shoulder straps, but perhaps also trimmed the cuffs and even ran down the pants legs. If they wore a kepi cap, it might also have had such a trim, added by the ladies after purchase from a Memphis supplier of military uniforms. The buttons would have also been purchased from such suppliers who had quickly begun running ads in the newspapers.

Area women surely responded to mobilization as women always do—with mixed emotions. Not wanting to lose their men, even temporarily, but also wanting to provide them with psychological support in defending their way of life. The elite and middle class ladies uniformed them, cheered them as they departed, and wrote supportive letters while they were gone.[36] The wives and mothers of small farmers and the landless poor had everything to lose and much less to preserve by sending their breadwinner off to war. Their support was more ambivalent.

Beyond romantic sentimentalizing about "our brave young men" dying heroically on the field of honor, the good ladies had little sense of how much they would soon be sacrificing or the horrible realities they would eventually experience.

After the initial outfitting, knitting and sewing continued to supplement official military supplies. As the war unexpectedly dragged on into the cold weather, they provided wool socks and underwear, perhaps even uniform capes or overcoats, if the men were lucky. But they were only able to continue such support until occupation.

♦ ♦ ♦

On May 15, the Shelby Grays and other volunteer militia companies from the city took train for rendezvous at Germantown where they, including the Wigfall Grays from District Ten, were sworn into the Tennessee Army as the 4th Tennessee Infantry Regiment. Due to high waters, the original encampment site, "the Sulphur Springs" at Nashoba, had to be changed to the Brunswick Springs, one mile north east of town.[37] From the Germantown area, the 4th drew some recruits. At least five area men served, but perhaps as many as fifteen. Among them was William H. Moore, the railroad agent. John A. Kirby, who would later become a prominent Germantown resident, had recently settled in Memphis in 1860 where he had entered the wholesale grocery business. In May 1861, he promptly enlisted in the Shelby Greys and fought with the regiment until Missionary Ridge, where he was wounded in the leg and captured.

On May 16, the Secession Guards, recruited at Germantown, were mustered into the service of Tennessee by its magistrate William Walker. They joined ten others from surrounding counties, rendezvoused on the old fair grounds at Jackson to be formed into the 13th Tennessee Volunteer Infantry Regiment.[38]

The 13th should be called a Germantown regiment more than any other, for it may have contained as many as 40 Germantown men. Thirty can be absolutely identified. Most of them clustered in companies C and H, indicating a strong preference for a community of friends and family. The captain of the Secession Guard's (Company C) elected by the men was J. H. Morgan of Horn Lake. William D. Harrison, the son of the plantation owner, Carey Harrison and wife Elizabeth, was elected lieutenant and later became its captain. Thompson Tuggle, 20 year-old son of plantation owners John and Martha, was elected corporal. He was joined by his 18 year-old brother, George, and cousin, 16 year-old Joseph Tuggle, son of minister and plantation owner Phillip and Mary. Joseph's younger brother Phillip joined them, probably lying about his age so he could go along. Needham Harrison, heir to a small plantation, would rise to Sergeant-Major and then Lieutenant. With them were at least several other friends or neighbors, the Ellis brothers, Adolphus and William, sons of Benjamin and Sarah, long-time plantation owners, John Buster, owner of the adjacent plantation, Robert Ford, and Sam Winford or Wainford, farmer and son of John and Martha. There was Richard Small, son of the planter, George and his wife Mary. Undoubtedly their parents felt some comfort at the idea that their sons were being watched over by men they knew. There was James Rodgers, a young student living in the home of Lewis More, overseer, while James Slough, was an overseer himself..[39]

Also in Company C were William B. Duke and his brother, Rolfe T. Duke. Confusion exists in service records, because a "Robert T. Dukes" was originally listed in Company C. Robert actually remained at home to manage the affairs of the plantation. He and "Rolfe" may have decided to change places. Boelif (variously written as Roelif and Rolfe) later became a lieutenant in the company.[40]

Company H, the Yancy Rifles of Fayette County, had at least 7 Germantown boys, Cleon or Clem Callis, William Dunlap, Andrew Moore, but perhaps also David Dunlap. Henry Woodson was later transferred in from the 34th Mississippi. James Lamb, Lucius and Robert Miller and Richard Small also served among them. Waddie Robards, living across the line in District 10, apparently joined Company A, the Fayette Rifle Grays. James, another of the Duke plantation, served with Company K, the Dyer Greys. The Thirteenth's commander later described these men as "the 'flower of the South' young men, most of whom were fresh from the best institutions of learning—aspiring, hopeful and ambitious—the very best material for volunteer service."[41]

Meanwhile, the 154th Tennessee (Senior) Regiment had been recreated as soon as the state government and its citizens became alarmed about developments in March 1860. It was formed from the standing uniformed companies of Memphis, to be available to the mayor or sheriff for the suppression of "mob, insurrection, riot or invasion." Such regiments were also on call by the governor for first service to the state.[42] On April 16, 1861, its officers sent out a call for volunteers and contributions to fully arm it for "the defense of Memphis". It consisted initially of the five, then six uniformed companies of the city and the Steuben Artillery. Three newly formed volunteer companies for "foreign service" were soon added.[43] Wiley Rochelle, his son William, and Richard Trueheart served together in Company F, joining perhaps 8 other Germantown area men. These three early regiments were among the first to draw the community's men who would soon find themselves well away from the defense of family and home.

The rest of Germantown's early enlistees were scattered among several other volunteer regiments. Specifically Robison's 2nd Tennessee Infantry which was organized in Nashville, May 1861, but for some reason contained men recruited in Shelby County, specifically the Shelby Riflemen. It fought initially at First Manassas or Bull Run before being sent back west for Shiloh.

Colonel Nathan Bedford Forrest's 3rd Tennessee Cavalry was organized in Memphis between July and October 1861 and may have had as many as 16 area residents in its ranks. Company C, the Forrest Rangers, then Company K, McDonald's Dragons, and Company D under Jesse Forrest were raised in Shelby County as the unit expanded to a regiment.

Another six independent companies of cavalry had also organized in South-West Tennessee, and under the command of Lieutenant Colonel Thomas Logwood were mobilized in April to join the army at Columbus, KY. Among them were three companies, the Memphis Light Dragoons, the Tennessee Mounted Rifles, and the Shelby Light Dragoons, drawing men from the county.[44] They were mustered into Confederate service as Logwood's Battalion in May. These units eventually became the 7th Tennessee Cavalry Regiment in 1862 which definitely contained Germantown men.[45] Its men, unlike those of the other regiments, would serve relatively close to home for much of the war, playing a direct role in the impact of war on the town itself.

Aside from the volunteers who entered the regiments, several of the town's professionals undertook special service. The physicians, Robert H. McKay, John Johnson and Leonidus Richmond, served as surgeons in the Medical Staff, C.S.A. Even that formerly 19 year-old "physician" William H. Blair served as Assistant Surgeon, perhaps an insight into the qualifications of army surgeons. If they served in field hospitals, their service would have been brutally traumatic, for the work was more like butchery involving amputations without benefit of anesthesia or sterilization. On the other hand, in base hospital service they would have treated more cases of resultant infections and disease. All had to face the trauma of inability to prevent high death rates.⁴⁶

On both sides, far more men died of disease, given the harsh conditions under which they would live, but especially the exposure to contagious disease in close quarters and the general lack of sanitation. Accidents took another high toll. If a man succumbed to serious illness or infection, they either languished in a hospital awaiting whatever fate, or were paroled home.

Anton Shide, the music professor of the Forest-Hill girl's Seminary, joined Memphis' Steuben Artillery, composed heavily of Germans like himself. He continued to serve in other Tennessee artillery units after it was disbanded. Shide's departure also relates to the fate of Germantown's schools. With the outbreak of war, most of the higher schools were abandoned by male students and teachers like Shide. The New-York-born lady instructors of the Ladies Academy undoubtedly fled north. Teaching at all levels was left mostly to the local women.

Another Germantown professional who did special service was A.M. Rafter, former head of the military school. His colonel's commission did not result in his being chosen to raise a regiment or even a company. For some reason, he was assigned to the General and Staff Regiment. For the duration of the war, he served with the title of "agent." Such a designation is too vague to define his actual role. Did it imply secret service employment? If he had been an agent for dealing with civilian contractors, his position should have been with the quartermasters. He remained in whatever service and surrendered with a command at Grenada, Mississippi in May 1865.

None of the area's residential ministers served, even as chaplains, although many ministers were firebrand rebels. For instance, the Memphis Conference of the Methodist Church listed large numbers of its pastors who served, including some who had once ridden in the circuit serving Germantown. A camp journal of the 13th Regiment recorded an exhortation from a Rev. Mr. Tuggle while they were still at their initial Jackson camp. Probably this was Germantown's resident circuit rider on a visit with his sons and nephews at that camp. He expounded on the irreligious North and how God intended "us to punish them for their infidelity

✦ ✦ ✦

The war brought a mobilization of the town's industry as well. In June, the Neely and Trueheart Southern Star Gin Factory converted to the manufacture of ordinance supplies. It would continue this work until December when it closed operations. One presumes something similar occurred with Hurt's factory.

As for other local developments, Goodspeed's history of Shelby County described militia formation. The entire county became a military organization. The men in each civil district were organized into (Home Guard) companies that elected their captains and lieutenants. "$30 were allowed for three months' guard service. Special taxes were levied for military purposes."[47]

The original Germantown Home Guards became part of the county militia. Its one hundred volunteers would have been greatly augmented, since all white males between the ages of eighteen and forty-five were required to serve, with exemptions for public officials, and essential occupations.

On April 23, the military board in Memphis had already called upon all volunteer militia companies being formed to report themselves, identifying officers, enrollments, whether infantry, cavalry, or artillery, head-quarters, and "what arms it has." They would form the Memphis Legion, to consist of two regiments, one of the city, one its suburbs.[48]

The Memphis Legion became part of the 23rd Militia Brigade, comprising the counties of Shelby and Fayette, and J A. Carnes of Memphis was elected Brigadier General, despite a strong preference for a Mr. Farabee in District Eleven. By July, expansion had Memphis contributing three regiments, while the civil districts formed another two. The company of Germantown's District 11 was part of the 2nd Battalion of the 1st County Regiment, while District Ten's was in the 1st Battalion of the 2nd County Regiment.[49] Reorganizations changes such alignments frequently.

The 23rd Militia Brigade was supplemented by an additional formation as adjuncts to the companies of each district. As part of an Act passed on May 6, the Assembly authorized the County Courts to raise semi-annually, a Home Guard or Minute Men. Shelby County complied on May 20 by creating small companies of Minute Men for three-month service, one company per civil district, appointed from the ranks of its militia company. The county supplied them with arms, and paid them ten dollars per month.[50]

With so many men going into the service, there was concern about security at home. That was the role of these Minute Men. One concern, given initial unionist sentiments, was spies, subversives, and saboteurs, and even terrorist acts. The company officers were charged with procuring warrants and arresting "all suspected persons," for trial. The primary concern, however, was maintaining control of the slaves. The officers were responsible "to see that all slaves are disarmed; to prevent the assemblage of slaves in unusual numbers; to keep the slave population in proper subjection. . . ."[51] The war against an allegedly abolitionist government heightened the perennial fears of slave revolt.[52]

These "companies" of Minute Men were initially small, fifteen men, and very heavily officered (one captain, two lieutenants and a secretary). Perhaps intended to provide more disciplined supervision than the notorious vigilance patrols. Each "company" elected Judge Pettit and the Commander constituted a committee to provide the arms and munitions, with the judge empowered to issue credits for payment by the treasury. In June, the Court expanded the size of the companies for Districts Ten and Eleven to sixty-four, rank and file. In July, it extended their term of service for three more months.[53] Perhaps the M&T rail line was deemed especially vulnerable.

District Eleven's Minute Men consisted initially of John J. Tuggle, farmer age 48, elected captain, Benjamin Ellis, farmer age 46, T.J. Stratton, A.C. Stewart, farmer age 27, James Sims, William Myrick, farmer age 35, H. Boardman, merchant age 30, C.F. Molitor, engineer age 27, William Carter, farmer age 40, I.W. Bliss, book agent age 42, S.D. Trueheart, gin maker age 30, S. Thompson, R.W. Turberville, farmer age 38, L.A. Rhodes, wagon maker age 39, James C. Anderson, farmer age 25. Stewart, Myrick, Carter, Truehart, and Anderson soon went into regular service and had to be replaced.[54] Thus most Germantown men remaining in Minute Man service were older, late 30s or above. By October, at the end of their second three-month tour, those who had not already enlisted for active military duty, promptly requested release to return to their regular lives. Nevertheless, the court decided to extend their term another three months. Domestic defense anxieties prevailed.

The presence of the former New Yorker, Isaac Bliss, in Germantown's Minute Men illustrates the allegiance of local northerners to the South. Bliss had owned and employed ten slaves in his operations. He was just a little too old for early conscription, but his local identity remained strong. He and his wife would remain to be counted in the 1870 and 1880 censuses, even though he lost everything in the course of the occupation.[55]

In addition to paying taxes and doing militia service, those still at home experienced regular visits from recruitment teams and war bonds drives. On August 19, an gent of the Treasury Department, C.S.A., would deliver an address at the town "on the subject of subscribing to the LOAN of the Confederate

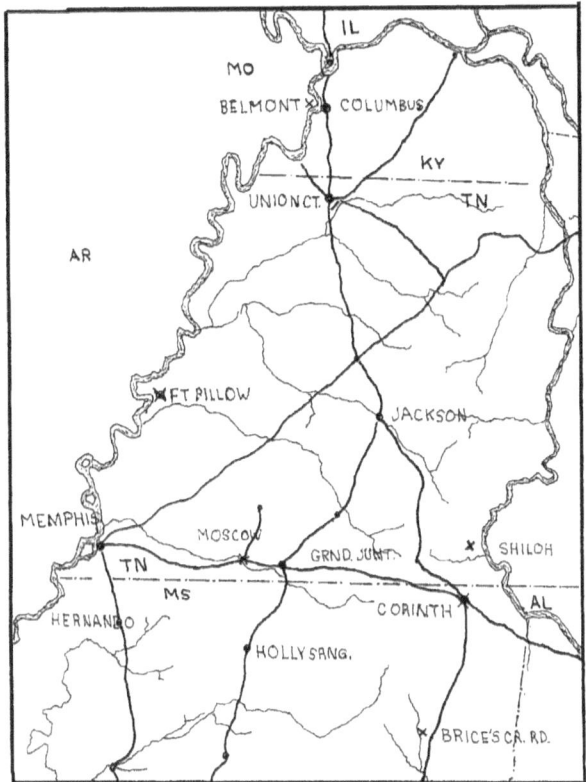

MAP 8 W. Kentucky, Tennessee, and N. Mississippi Theater of War.

States." He felt compelled to announce, "The Farmers are especially requested to attend."[56]

Germantown's first known casualty came at the same time as the bond drive, dampening the attendance of one farm family. The death was accidental, which was not untypical. While the Secession Guards was steaming up river, Robert L. Ford fell overboard. In newspaper notices, Mary and M.L. Ford offered a reward to anyone who found their son's body.[57]

Men at War—Life back Home

For the families at home, and the men off to war, their new lives required adjustment. The first months involved both parties in major transitions.

The enlistees of the 13th Tennessee had a typical introduction to military life. After drilling and training for weeks, on July 26, they shipped to New Madrid,

Missouri, and were mustered into the Confederate Army. While marching back and forth for more weeks in hot weather, they experienced several alarms, but missed all the skirmishes - always disappointed. Individuals frequently furloughed home to recover from fevers and diarrhea. Finally they joined General Pillow's occupation of Columbus, Kentucky. From September to November, they dug fortifications, and relentlessly drilled—bored by monotonous camp life. On top of all that, they were not receiving their pay. Disillusioned, many of the young men became rebellious. Worse, their first enemy was a plague of measles, which along with other illnesses brought the regiment's next casualties to be buried far from home. One victim was apparently Thompson Tuggle, Germantown's second death. Equally frustrating, they had yet to get proper weapons- only antique muskets. Finally, their colonel managed to get them proper .69 caliber rifled muskets, fired by percussion caps. For this privilege, they would pay a price.[58]

The men were not hesitant to display dissatisfaction. Nothing had prepared them for this. For a decade after the suspension of the militia, young men had experienced no military discipline. When Americans thought of military glory, it was the independent frontier rifleman, or romantic paintings of historic battle scenes. Nothing of the monotony, endless drilling, poor food, uncomfortable camp life, and long marches in bad weather. Soldier's journals tell of rebelliousness, insubordination and desertion, and the severe punishments that resulted as officers sought to turn such boys and men into disciplined troops. Many of the democratically elected officers and NCOs were unprepared for such roles. As time dragged on, it became obvious their sacrifices would not be of short duration.

Furthermore, parents like those from Germantown were disrupting discipline. Parents regularly took train to Columbus to visit their boys. This created such a severe disruption of control that the commanding officers had to forbid civilian visitation within the lines. Even this failed to impress the more persistent. The phenomenon of today's helicopter parent is not all that new. They were incensed at officers who failed to perform the same fatigue and night-time guard duties that their sons endured. Whenever one of them took ill, they insisted that he be allowed to come home to recover.[59] Soon, however, they learned that such wishes were totally inappropriate, and they could only hope for a son's return on furlough or as an invalid. Thereafter, they could at least send regular "care packets."

On November 7, the men of the 13th were finally called out for action—"all were excited and anxious to meet the enemy." Their brigade crossed the Mississippi to block Grant's advance on Belmont, Missouri. Partially because they were so well-armed, the 13th was given a prominent position in the line, which thanks to General Pillow's misjudgment, put them "in an open field without cover," exposed to "a galling fire" for an hour and a half. Before the day was over, they had lost 27 killed, 73 wounded, and 49 missing out of the 400 engaged—twenty-five per cent of the total Confederate casualties for the entire day. From Germantown, privates William J. Dunlap of Company H and James Rogers (Rodgers) of Company C were killed, and Richard Small was wounded. William was the son of David and Frances Dunlap, a local farm family, and he fell in the very first volley of fire. James could have been one of two area young men of the same name: a single young clerk who had been boarding with the Buch family; or an eighteen year-old of some means living with the family of the overseer Lewis More on the Thomas Goodrich plantation. In any case, this James was quoted as saying as he lay dying, "Tell my mother I died in discharging my duty; that was all I could do." Despite its initially heavy losses, the regiment rallied and played a prominent role in the final victory.[60]

From now on, combat deaths became a Germantown experience. One wonders how families learned of their losses. Telegrams and or men in uniform bearing sad news were not yet a phenomenon of war. Neither federal nor state governments had any system for notification or even burial of the dead. Although regimental commanders were expected to tend to such matters, they were overwhelmed by unexpected numbers and the frequent necessity to abandon the dead when the field was lost. Men frequently wrote their family on the eve of battle, so they knew of their involvement and anxiously awaited another letter, while perusing the casualty lists in the papers which were relatively prompt but often unreliable.[61] Often, the bad news arrived in a letter from a fellow soldier. The black wreaths of mourning began to bloom on Germantown doors.

As for the men themselves, a study of Civil War letters confirms that their first combat experience changed them. Before they had been anxious for action and honor. After having experienced the reality, they never again looked forward to combat. Even so, a sense of honor and duty kept them going in the face of constant death or disfigurement. They were now veterans—changed men.[62]

As the two armies squared off in September, General Albert S. Johnston, Confederate commander in the western area, had already called on Governor

Harris for an additional 30,000 troops. After Belmont, General Pillow raised the alarm that he would soon be cut of, and West Tennessee and the Mississippi valley would fall to the enemy. He and General Johnston called on Harris to mobilize Tennessee's militia yet once more.[63]

These two calls increased recruitment pressures on the population. The militia call-ups seriously disrupted the lives of those who had not anticipated service. Selected numbers from each militia company were sent into the ranks. Militia mobilization quickly revealed the limits of commitment to the cause. One Tennessean wrote, "I had no idea until the militia was called that we had so many afflicted persons in our community.... (I)ndeed almost every disease the human family is heir to have presented themselves to the surgeons for certificates of exemption."[64]

Men from the militia companies were simply drafted into the Confederate Army. From a population unaccustomed to such emergency measures, voices of dissent arose. Many objected to what they perceived as an autocratic tone in the governor's call, even labeling it Czarist in style. Although area papers joined the criticism of the governor's political insensitivity, they impressed upon the public the wisdom of the governor and General Johnston in warning that the state was in imminent danger.[65]

◆ ◆ ◆

Since we know the most about men who served in the 13th, it seems appropriate to return to them to pursue the questions raised about social relations. That will also add much more to our picture of their wartime experiences and post-war consequences.

Even when volunteer regiments were raised by officially designated, prominent men, all officers and NCOs were actually elected by the men. This militia tradition created a uniquely egalitarian situation for armies. All men enlisted as privates, and among the Tennessee veterans in the surveys, a surprising 66.5% of the social-economic elite served throughout as privates.[66] This did not mean that their social status counted for nothing. As before, social relationships were complex.

Experience, known leadership skills, self-confidence as well as charisma and congeniality would be compelling factors when soldiers chose their leaders. Many knew each other. The educated and socially prominent had advantages on all counts. Indeed, only the the elite (1 percent) and slave owning farmers (1.2

p. 16 Confederate Mess. This image depicts all the members of a Confederate Mess; the standard 6 Confederate service men; 2 former body servants, serving as mess servants or "mess stewards." Where the Black members slept is unclear. Another surviving photograph shows only 4 mess members, 2 White plus 2 Black men, implying they all shared the same tent.

percent) rose to officer's rank at the regimental level—that is, major through colonel. On the side of what must have been meritocracy, however, 3.5 percent of the poor became captains and lieutenants, while 5.3 percent of non-slave-holding farmers did also. At non-commissioned officer (NCO) levels, the range was 11 percent poor, 14.2 percent non-slaveholding farmers, 19.1% small-scale slave owners and 16.3% elite.[67] The rank of sergeant generally required record keeping. Regardless, all classes had to stand, work, march, eat and sleep side-by-side. They were locked together in the brotherhood of combat soldiers.

In the 13th, only three local men rose to officer's rank. William Harrison was elected lieutenant initially, Boelif Duke became a lieutenant, and Needham Harrison rose through the ranks to sergeant-major and then lieutenant. The only other known NCO was Corporal Thompson Tuggle. William Harrison, Duke and Tuggle were sons of families ranking among the wealthy planters.

Needham was from a more marginal slave owning family. Among these area men, class seems to have influenced election.

The basic "family" unit in a regiment was the "mess." Beginning at the camp of instruction and thereafter, a small group of men slept together in a tent, usually accommodating six men. With no regimental cooks and chow halls, each mess cooked its own food and did all the chores—shared equally. If the social classes were mixed randomly in such messes, social equality would have prevailed. Whether messes were assigned or self-selected among friends and relations is unclear.[68]

One thing is clear, among the elite, military rank frequently played little role in personal relations. Privates visited officers who were their old school chums, socialized and dined with them as equals.[69] Such fraternization would not have occurred between officers and men of significantly different status.

One important distinction belonged to slave owners. They had the unique opportunity of having servants to do the menial chores of their mess. One son of Mississippi made a request to his mother.

> (T)here is one thing I want very much, that is somebody to do my cooking. I can stand a soldiers duties very well, but that of a menial does not come so handy, it is pretty much of a bore after standing guard all night to have to cook breakfast, wash up dishes &c. A great many messes have servants and it helps along amazingly. You might very easily send Stephen down ... he would not only be of great service to me, but he could make a good deal for himself....[70]

For Germantown slaves, there is a record of them as "mess servants." After the war, many bore the family names of their former owners, we can even surmise whom they served. In Company C, Baltimore and Dick accompanied some of the sons of the two Tuggle households. Mull probably served William Harrison. Alf must have served the Ellis brothers, who probably shared a mess. In all, at least thirty-three slaves served the regiment.[71] One man's body servant became a paid servant for the entire mess, which made it somewhat egalitarian.

Obviously if the messes were socially mixed, men without slaves would benefit greatly from their messmate's status. Members of a less fortunate mess would, however, have developed a strong sense of inequality and unfairness. Also the well-off got a steady supply of food, clothing and other amenities from home until occupation severed their connections. Again, members of a less well-off family would have been more acutely aware of social differences than they had before the war, especially if the beneficiaries of such benefits did not share freely.

Finally, the departure of a father or son from a slave owning family had far less effect on the well-being of his family than did that of a farmer whose family depended almost entirely on his labor. Such a distinction weighed heavily on the minds of the poorer family men. Thus Fred Bailey is undoubtedly correct in arguing that the wartime experiences of the lower classes greatly increased their awareness of social differences and injustice.[72] The lack of surviving correspondence from the less educated explains why we remain largely unaware of how such great social differences might have affected the tight bonds formed among combat soldiers. Social problems were also enhanced by militia drafting.

♦ ♦ ♦

Meanwhile disruptions were also affecting attitudes and living conditions at home. Occasional newspaper articles reveal a growing public perception that the privileged escaped service and sacrifice. Early in the war, Memphis' mayor uttered a scathing attack on privileged shirkers. By August 1861, the commanders of the Memphis Legion, the remaining not-drafted members of the militia, sought to remain in the city "for the defense of Memphis and immediate vicinity (with the understanding that when not on duty our members may be allowed the privilege of attending to their ordinary business)." As "men of prominence and influence, who have large amounts invested in the commercial and manufacturing interests of this place and cannot leave without great pecuniary sacrifice." They had to stay home to continue supplying the area's needs.[73]

Secession began to disrupt business and communications. At first the major agricultural business, the cotton trade continued to flow south down to New Orleans, and there was much speculation in the cotton market. Business ties with the north became problematic. They either terminated soon or had to become surreptitious.

Likewise, mail services gradually broke down. The Confederate government established its own Post Office Department in February. Tennessee's secession did not immediately sever all ties with the north. Finally in May, the Federal Postmaster ordered the cessation of mail service to the South. Thereafter

Confederate service would have its ups and downs.[74] Rates rose steeply,[75] but that would soon be irrelevant to Germantown.

The war had increasingly significant effects on travel and traffic on the M&C Railroad. All four railroad companies out of Memphis had rallied to the cause, providing service at half-price rates for soldiers and munitions, to be paid in Confederate Bonds. Their presidents had to complain to General Polk that disorderly soldiers were interfering with the conductors, disrupting service and even endangering other passengers. They begged him to impose more discipline on the lines.[76] Regular passenger service continued to July, but was then terminated to accommodate military needs. In November, freight service to the town was nearly terminated. "Owing to the demands . . . on the road," the M&C announced it would stop receiving goods for transit.[77] Any remaining cotton and goods purchased had to move by wagon.

It became quickly apparent that the absence of the men folk brought hardships to their families, but especially those less well off. As early as May, the County Court established a tax to support the indigent families of volunteers. Each wife was to receive $12 for herself and each child over age twelve, plus $6 for each younger child.[78]

But problems immediately arose.[79] By July, funds had run out.[80] Then they realized that legislation only covered the families of soldiers on active duty. Once they had made the ultimate sacrifice, there was nothing for their widows and orphans.[81]

By the October Court session, some of these problems were solved, with an unfortunate reduction of payments. On the plus side, the evaluation of eligibility was brought down to the civil district. For the Eleventh, Magistrate William Walker was responsible.[82] Applicants henceforth received local, personal attention. By early 1862, the Court had finally worked out funding, for it made several successive appropriations thereafter.[83]

At least the more intimate life of a small town and its church congregations guaranteed that the poor were not invisible and the better-off were pressured to help. The promises made by Germantown's ladies to help soldiers' families were undoubtedly honored, but their ability to provide such help would not last long.

✦ ✦ ✦

The autumn mustering of the militia drew even more area men into newly formed regiments. The title "volunteer regiment" lapsed. The 32nd organized

October 28, 1861, was primarily a Middle Tennessee regiment, but drew some Shelby residents. James Harrison and James Kimbrough were certainly two such. As many as eight area men may have served with this regiment.

The town eventually became the site of a mustering and training camp known as the Camp of Instruction at Germantown or Camp Sam Hays.[84] Although in May, Germantown had already been on the radar of Union intelligence as a "rendezvous ... undoubtedly occupied" by troops, this may have merely referred to the 4th Regiment's rendezvous there.[85] The grounds may not have become an official camp of instruction until October when Colonel W.T. Avery announced that he had been authorized to establish "a CAMP as a rendezvous for the new regiment being raised by me at Germantown, Tenn. ..."[86] The actual location of this camp is unknown. It was probably on the east side of town at the previous rendezvous site at Brunswick Springs, just inside Collierville's Civil District 10, but less than a mile from town. This seems likely since a General Order of October 25 referred to Jackson, Trenton, Collierville (not Germantown) and Savannah as West Tennessee's rendezvous.[87]

By October 19, General William H. Carroll reported that portions of his brigade were assembling at the camp—his former regiment the 37th, plus the 38th and 39th.[88] It seems to have operated until late in the year. The last reference to a full regiment indicates it left in November. By then the soon-to-be renumbered 37th Tennessee Infantry, with perhaps 9 area men, represented a severe case of the problems Tennessee regiments had getting proper armament. It had sat at Camp Hays since September awaiting arms, not to be adequately supplied until January.[89]

The 38th had formed in September in Fayette County. It recruited heavily at Camp Sam Hayes. Perhaps because of connections formed with the brigade at Germantown, Hugh Neely enlisted along with his business partner Steven Trueheart, as did the son of their competitor, A. F. Hurt. After his Star Gin Factory ceased military production, Neely enlisted. He would eventually rise to captain and finally assistant brigade adjutant before resigning for chronic rheumatism in 1865.[90] The 38th also drew as many as 16 other Germantown men.

Thus for some time, Germantown was surrounded by many freshly minted Confederate soldiers. Business in the shops must have boomed, the good ladies of the town got another chance to provide the support for the boys that they had pledged, and the finer homes provided many an entertainment for regimental officers. One Lieutenant Colonel Barbierre had pleasant memories of his stay in September and of the leading citizens, Judge Pettit and Mrs. Cornelius whose "attentions I will never forget."[91]

Like Miss Scarlet, the young ladies must have been in heaven. Apparently many of the women and girls regularly attended the parading exercises. Undoubtedly their parents saw all this as a mixed blessing. Although no records survive for Germantown, letters and diaries from other camp towns relate a vibrant social life, marriages, including social misalliances.[92]

There are other references to the Camp of Instruction coming from letters. They cast light on the soldier's lot while living among Germantown's citizens. In October 1861 writing to Tullahoma, Captain A.O. Edwards reported,

> Several of the boys is sick with measels, there is ten of twelve in the hospital that is in the Methodist Church. They gave it to the Regiment for a hospital, and the ladies come every day and bring them something to eat. I believe there is some of the cleverest ladies here I ever saw. The drill field is full (of them) every evening and they bring some of the nicest boq'ts. I ever saw. I got one last evening from a nice lady.[93]

In all the camps of instruction, measles hit hard those who had grown up in rural isolation. Other contagious diseases were at work as well—chicken pox, mumps and small pox, but measles might have been the worst. Adults often suffered serious aftermath—pneumonia, deafness and various infections, sometimes death or invalidism. One of the purposes of a camp of instruction was to give the new troops time to get through such diseases before going into the field.[94] At least, the ladies of the town were living up to their promise to aid all soldiers in need. Of course, their first ventures into "nursing" were visitations and gifting. The coarse side was left to slaves and orderlies.

Perhaps this donation of their building by the Methodists began its ultimate demise. Commonly the early hospitals set up by the Confederate medical service to handle the overwhelming load of illness proved unmanageable. Samuel Stout, regimental surgeon of the 3rd Tennessee, described the conditions he abandoned on leaving Camp Cheatham. "The very ground has become in spite of the efforts of the officers to prevent it, odorous with effluvia from the secretions and excretions of sick men."[95] Captain Edwards' description indicates that Camp Hays' little hospital was neither so overwhelmed nor as poorly maintained as Stout's tent hospital, but the little church would soon experience more serious assaults on its structure.

6

1862 · THE WAR COMES TO GERMANTOWN

Undoubtedly expressing the sentiment of most locals, the *Appeal* welcomed the New Year with a martial ardor and optimism that would soon be dashed.[1] By spring, Tennessee was being cut in half. After the fall of Forts Henry and Donelson in February, Nashville fell and Governor Harris moved his government to the safety of Memphis. Federal gun boats mounted the Tennessee River and the Federal army moved to Pittsburgh Landing to threaten Corinth, Mississippi, with its strategic rail junction of the M&C Railroad with supply lines from the North to the South.

As the northern armies approached, Memphis began to anticipate its fate and troops in West Tennessee were repositioned in Mississippi. In March, the remaining militiamen of the 23rd Brigade were enumerated, including males between the ages of eighteen and forty-five. One quarter of every company had been called into active duty on March 3, another de facto draft. The remainder was called up for regular drills. Rural companies like Germantown's were to drill twice a week, and once a week for a regimental drill.[2] Memphians had to consider the prospect of a city under siege. On March 24, Governor Harris ordered all county court judges to have each civil district to form a Reserve Military Corps. Those under 45 constituted the active militia of the corps. Those over 45 were reserved for "invalid service" such as guard duty.[3] The remaining militia speculated about the possibility of combat while Germantown had to wonder about its place in such an environment.

Meanwhile, the continued military demands on the M&C further strangled the movement of freight into and out of town. Government demands occasionally

TABLE 2 Civil War incidents in and around Germantown, 1862
Aside from a few significant benchmarks, all these incidents were relatively minor skirmishes:

6/7 April 1862	Battle of Shiloh
30 May 1862	abandonment of Corinth
6 June 1862	capture of Memphis
18 June	skirmish at Germantown
25 June	guerrillas derail train near Germantown; sporadic Federal occupation of Germantown begins until July 18; legal foraging and searches for arms, and unsanctioned thefts become routine
17 July	Grant assumes command of the Armies of the Tennessee and Mississippi; Sherman of the Department of West Tennessee.
18–19 July	Sherman and Hurlbut's divisions pass through Germantown; sanctioned pillaging.
28 July	expedition through and skirmish at Germantown
August	another short occupation of Germantown
3–4 October	Battle of Corinth.
12 October	raid through Germantown
22 October	running battle from Germantown to Collierville
November	small-scale, permanent occupation begins at Germantown
25 November	Smith's wing of expedition into Mississippi staged at Germantown
20 December	Sherman departs Memphis to begin assault on Vicksburg.

consumed all rail traffic for days. Consequently by January, freight was piling up on the Memphis wharfs. Goods that had been bought and paid for by Germantown planters, farmers and merchants sat in warehouses.[4]

Consequently to centralize control of traffic, martial law was declared in Memphis and measures were taken to tighten security. The railroad was brought under the Quartermaster's Department, and civilian use was restricted. Farmers shipping cotton into the city required permits, and on the M&C in particular, only "a limited amount of family supplies" were being accommodated.

Details of one officer and five men were assigned to each passenger train. The obvious concern was sabotage.[5] An inspector recommended "placing a sentinel at the door of each car, subjecting all persons to a proper surveillance before entering . . . (and) preserving due decorum among the soldiers *en route*, who frequently, I regret to say, are guilty of the grossest misconduct."[6]

Martial law brought another damper to Germantown business. It stipulated, that the sale of intoxicating liquors within 5 miles of any station occupied by troops or within 1 mile of any public highway used for military purposes is prohibited. All saloons within such limits were closed. "Any violation of this order will be followed by prompt arrest of the offender and destruction of all his stores of liquor."[7]

Germantown's position on the State Line Road qualified it for this prohibition. Of course, it also suggests that drunken disorderliness had been part of the town's experiences, with many troops moving through the area. So this order might have come as a relief to some. Others undoubtedly found an opportunity to bootleg.

The state finally stepped in to assume responsibility for indigent families of soldiers, widows and orphans without any other means of support. As before, commissioners for each civil district ascertained eligibility.[8] Whatever assistance families of the Germantown area received, it would not last for long.

As the Federal army advanced down through Tennessee, the civilian population experienced the depredations always inflicted by an occupying force, but especially like the poorly disciplined, green civilian soldiers who formed both armies. The *Appeal* advised citizens on how to prepare for occupation. Parties subject to federal arrest and prosecution should leave for safer locations.

All other persons, however, especially the aged and infirm, and such as have been prevented . . . from engaging actively in the war, should remain at their homes. . . . If they have any slaves, they should be sent to a place of safety, and their cotton and such other produce as the enemy may desire, should be destroyed. By remaining at their homes they may manage to support themselves and families, and protect the little property they have. . . .[9]

Locals would soon find themselves considering whether, how and when to respond to these instructions. Unfortunately, with few exceptions, no records survive to tell us who left and when.

✦ ✦ ✦

Meanwhile in response to the Federal threat to Corinth, the Tennessee regiments with their Germantown men marched to meet them at Shiloh or Pittsburgh Landing. (See Map 8) The 4th Tennessee with the Shelby and Wigfall Grays was in the advance. Officer's reports tell us about the experience of Germantown's men. According to Lieutenant Colonel Strahl, the 4th Tennessee charged "against a battery of heavy guns, which was making sad havoc in our ranks, and was well supported by a large infantry force." According to Lieutenant-Colonel Strahl,

> at the order forward they moved at a double-quick to within 30 paces of the enemy's guns, halted, delivered one round, and with a yell charged the battery, and captured several prisoners and every gun. These prisoners reported their battery was supported by four Ohio and three Illinois regiments. It was a brilliant achievement, but an expensive one. In making the charge the . . . [regiment] lost 31 killed on the spot and (over) 150 wounded. . . .[10]

The 13th with its Company C, Germantown's Secession Guards, was there as well, now a veteran unit, also distinguishing itself in an assault on a Federal battery. Their Colonel A.J. Vaughn, described it.

> The next morning I advanced upon the enemy, who was strongly posted with a battery of six guns, commanding every avenue of approach, and supported by strong detachments of infantry. While in this position I was told by General Bragg that this battery . . . must be taken at all hazards. . . . I had proceeded but a short distance when I discovered that I could be exposed to a heavy fire from two of the enemy's camps. I therefore ordered an advance to be made directly forward. . . . (U)nder fire of their batteries, I soon engaged a heavy body of infantry, which, after a severe conflict and a desperate charge, I succeeded in putting to flight, and captured their battery. The ammunition being nearly exhausted, I supplied myself with that found in the enemy's encampments.[11]

This time, they charged through canister and grape, losing two officers, one NCO, 20 privates and 114 wounded and a number of prisoners. For Company C, their report stated, "We went into action on the morning of the 6th with forty men and came out on the evening of the 7th with only twenty, having one-half of our number killed and wounded, five of whom were killed and fifteen wounded."[12]

Among them, William Duke was the first of that planter family's losses. Also fell William Stokes, a twenty-nine year old landless farmer. He left a twenty-seven year-old widow and a four year-old daughter with only about $300 worth of possessions. She was lucky if that included a mule and plow, or a milk cow and a few chickens.[13] If death was a great equalizer, its impact on survivors was not. The yeoman and landless classes would increasingly feel the pain far worse.

After having fought heroically through a terribly bloody day, seeing comrades destroyed around them, they bedded down with a sense of a victory that could repel the invader from the doors of their homes. Depressingly, the next day brought a complete reversal. After another bloody day of fighting, they were forced from the field.

Although we always want to honor our veterans, the reality is that a significant number find ways to avoid the dangers of combat. Company C's report included, "In this engagement all did their part nobly, except Sergeant W. H. Bedee, William T. Lewis and W.D. Hawkins. They ingloriously deserted their company in the first engagements. . . ."[14]

The reports of other regiments give clues to the same effect. In addition to its 183 killed and wounded, the 154th reported 11 missing, while in addition to its 37 killed and wounded Forrest's Cavalry reported 12 missing. Men missing-in-action (MIAs) were as common as in all other wars. As opposed to families that knew their son or husband was dead, being told he was missing left them with uncertainty. They might wait indefinitely for a report of his capture or his return to ranks. Neither the modern technology for identifying remains nor the political motivation that exists today to find them were present. What is more, at Shiloh, because of the early heat, Federal burial details simply dumped Confederate bodies in trenches for mass burial.[15] There was not even a known grave to visit for the bereaved. Of course, there was always the possibility the missing had simply "gone astray." If the "missing" turned up at home, emotions must have been mixed, at least at this early stage. Soon, however, wives, especially of the yeoman and poor would increasingly encourage such behavior.[16]

The retreat to Corinth was another depressing ordeal. The city was overwhelmed by some 5,000 wounded, who were joined by 18,000 sick.[17] Trains dropped them off along the line in towns like Germantown, because the main hospitals at Memphis had filled to overflowing.[18] Towns along the railroads became one widespread hospital. The Presbyterian Church preserves the memory of the wounded being laid out on its pews. The Methodist Church surely resumed that role, and certainly the Baptist Church as well. Those of the town's physicians who had not gone off to war found their hands full. The women now saw the very unromantic side of war as they witnessed amputations, suppurating wounds and death. They tore cloth to make bandages and prepared food, while some of the tougher souls may have even performed real nursing duties, a chore generally considered unsuitable for ladies. Of course not all wounds were terrible, and disease was the more prevalent problem. The citizens were encouraged to take the less severe cases into their homes.[19] Undoubtedly the good citizens of Germantown did just that. Until the fall of Corinth, trains would continue to haul the sick and wounded for distribution.[20] We do not know how many died at Germantown. William Duke, who is described as having died of wounds may have been among these, for he was buried in the family grave yard.[21]

As for the survivors of the early bloody battles, they soon endured worries about their families and friends under Union occupation. Locally raised infantry regiments fought the rest of the war away from home, mostly to the east, rarely coming west of the Tennessee River. Since they had enlisted for only twelve months and had risked their lives, some felt they had a right to go home with honor and failed to reenlist as their regiments were reorganized in the spring of 1862. However, they soon found themselves back in ranks. A succession of conscription laws extended their commitment to "from three years or the duration."[22]

Conscription quickly added more distress to the lives of soldiers and civilians alike. It became clear to both sides that reliance on volunteers was insufficient. Although mobilization of the state militia had constituted a veritable draft, Confederate conscription laws, the first in April 1862, made it a reality. It initially applied to most able-bodied men between the ages of 18 and 35.[23] By February 1864, the situation would become so desperate that its reach ranged from 17 to 50. By the end of the war, draftees counted for up to one-third of the troops.

Conscription changed the social composition of the ranks. It drew more heavily on the smaller farmer and unskilled laborer who had felt less incentive to volunteer.²⁴ Conscription was not popular with anyone. Volunteers looked down on conscripts, while conscripts bore the stigma of being coerced slackers.²⁵

Conscription may have done more than anything else to raise the consciousness of the poorer parts of the population. As soon as Confederate leadership realized the danger inherent in removing all able-bodied males from the plantations, in the Second Conscription Act of October 1862 exemptions were added for overseers or one adult male per household for every twenty slaves held. One man could even be exempted for any two nearby farms totaling twenty slaves. A massive protest arose from small-holder to landless poor against what they called the "twenty Nigger rule." Anyone not heavily invested in slavery felt the injustice. That epithet spoke of hostility toward both the privileged and the slaves. The popularity of "the cause" came into serious question. for men of families that did not benefit. It also heightened racial tensions.²⁶

Consequently, desertions became increasingly a problem. The defeats of 1862, the occupation of their homes, conscription and the twenty slave exemption, provided enough justification for large numbers of area men. After Forrest had made several sweeps back through West Tennessee by 1864, he would report that he had rounded up about 1,000 men who had deserted in the spring of 1862.²⁷

The same developments also had a crushing effect on civilian moral. Many began to have second thoughts, and the citizens of Germantown were surely affected. A full year later, General Chalmers opined that after Shiloh the people of Tennessee "are now much depressed, and it will be some time before much assistance can be received from them. . . ."²⁸

In the midst of this chaos, the accidental deaths of warfare were again brought home to the town. Men, probably deserters, risked danger hopping freights to travel unobserved. On both the third and the tenth of May, the bodies of two soldiers were found near the tracks where they had been run over. As before, William Walker conducted townsmen in inquests at the gruesome sites.²⁹

Meanwhile Union forces had descended the Mississippi, taking Island No. 10 on April 7. After the Confederates evacuated Corinth on May 30, the Federal Army divided its forces with those portions under McClernand and Sherman moving west. The Confederates abandoned Fort Pillow on the Mississippi on June 5, opening the way for the Federal fleet to assault Memphis. Federal forces quickly spread out across the western parts of the state.³⁰

✦ ✦ ✦

In the subsequent campaigns, much West Tennessee cavalry had a different campaign history than the infantry. Some even saw service frequently close to home. Thus, after the occupation, they still had opportunities for contact with family and friends. This contact with the local, sympathetic population was one of their major sources of intelligence and collaboration in raiding operations. This was especially true for Germantown. There, the story of the town folk and the armies of both sides became totally enmeshed.

Specifically, the 7th Tennessee Cavalry frequented the Germantown area. Their early roots and history were complex. In April, General Polk had consolidated Logwood's independent cavalry companies, previously described, into Colonel William H. Jackson's 1st Tennessee Cavalry Regiment. The Memphis and Shelby Dragoons would become companies A and C respectively. In the summer of 1862, the regiment would be renumbered as the 7th, because delays during reorganization would cost its priority. Such regimental renumbering causes much confusion in the records, but perhaps as many as 9 Germantown area men served with this regiment.

Before the regiment could even form, a surprise attack on their base on March 31 cost them all their equipment. If this first experience under Jackson's leadership had not shaken their confidence, the conditions under which they were regimented upset those who had enlisted for independent service. Jackson's nomination as commander by Polk also did not go down well. Even a subsequent election won by Jackson left many unsatisfied. Morale and discipline were undermined. By March, General Beauregard had been forced to issue orders threatening severe discipline for pillaging the property of their fellow citizens.[31] These setbacks were serious blows to morale and produced an atmosphere of undisciplined behavior that ran rampant when they operated independently in the countryside. This history combined with looser command over cavalry units operating on the border with Mississippi resulted in irregular warfare.

During the Union invasion, Jackson's Cavalry moved to defend West Tennessee along Grant's western flank, covering the Confederate withdrawal from Fort Pillow. After the fate of Western Tennessee had become obvious, Jackson's Cavalry began burning cotton in local counties and removing potential military equipment to keep it out of Union hands.[32] Occasionally resistant civilians further compounded moral and discipline problems.

During the short Battle of Memphis on June 6, while crossing the M&C between Germantown and Collierville, they could hear the cannons. That night, they camped at Germantown and shared in the bad news from the city. Thereafter, they operated from bases in Mississippi, relying on constant contact with area citizens for information.[33]

♦ ♦ ♦

That night of June 6 must have been one of great suspense and concern among townsfolk. The withdrawal of all troops and the burning of their cotton created great unease. Theoretically the militia was to take up local defense against the invader. The departure of all necessary military leadership, however, deterred all but the more determined who contemplated guerrilla resistance. County and district officials turned over authority to the conqueror and would try to continue government and maintain order. Many southerners anticipated the worst at the hands of a brutal Yankee horde. Some fled if they could afford to. The more level-headed anticipated an uneasy period of accommodating and negotiating with a strange but not inhumane authority.[34]

Women had to consider preventive measures in the face of imminent invasion by the anticipated hoard of barbarians. They accurately expected undisciplined looting. They tried to calculate where best to hide valuables. Livestock were moved into the woods or creek bottoms. A part of romantic memories is how trusted slaves helped bury treasures and secreted livestock. However, some would be quickly disillusioned when vengeful servants betrayed them. As slaves became restive and more opaque in their demeanor, the illusion that benevolent mistresses had created a loving staff of child-like servants turned to suspicion and even fear.[35]

Following the capture of Memphis, some communities came incrementally under Union occupation, but much of the surrounding countryside was contested for the duration. Throughout rural West Tennessee, Confederate officers could even enforce conscription laws and punish deserters under the noses of the occupation forces for most of the war. The result was endless skirmishes. Shelby County was one of the few in Tennessee to experience almost continual action throughout the remainder of the war, though none were truly major battles. It was mostly guerrilla and lightening cavalry warfare. Although its primary railroad supply lines came south from Columbus, Kentucky, through Jackson to both La Grange and Corinth, the Union objective was to open and maintain the M&C with its river connection as an east-west route of supply.³⁶ All the rail lines, however, received the constant attention of guerrillas and raiders, disrupting operations.

Consequently for the remainder of 1862, Germantown would be veritably cut off from outside connections in the midst of a no-man's-land. Telegraph service resumed immediately, and rail connections followed soon, but even after reestablishment, rail connections were frequently disrupted and dangerous.

Of course, Germantown's connection with the newly established Confederate mail service was severed, and with it communication with men away from home.³⁷ Mail smuggled through Union lines was delivered through a succession of handlers until it reached its destination. Copies of the *Appeal*, its press also moved to Mississippi, had to be smuggled in as well. Papers coming out of Memphis were entirely subject to army convenience or the occasional citizen traveling from the city. Rumors replaced news coverage.

Even commerce with Memphis became extremely difficult. Not only was travel to and from dangerous, one could not go through the picket lines around the city without a pass. Officially, only persons who took the oath of loyalty to the Federal government could receive such a pass. To encourage farmers to bring in their cotton, a modified parole oath as opposed to an oath of loyalty was offered "people of the country," specifically "persons within the Federal lines north (of) and east (along) the Memphis and Charleston railroad, and inside of the outer line of pickets south." It merely required a promise not to support the Confederate cause in any way. Otherwise people living outside the city "would be endangered by taking the oath." Finally, civilians were forbidden to carry firearms within the city.³⁸ – a serious problem, considering the need for self-protection moving to or from the city.

Aside from the impact of isolation, severance of all connections with their men in service was an emotional blow. Formerly they could visit the camps, and the men could return home easily on furlough. Wives had communicated with husbands for advice on how to manage family business. All this ended when Memphis fell. Families now suffered from being denied the former opportunity to send their men supplies.³⁹

✦ ✦ ✦

Initially only a couple of regiments occupied Memphis. On June 10, General McClernand ordered General Lew Wallace, occupying Bolívar, to move his command toward Memphis and the Memphis and Ohio Railroad. He marched thorough Somerville toward Raleigh. His superiors ordered him to halt within eleven miles of Memphis at Union Depot, where he arrived on June 14. From that base, he was supposed to repair and secure the Memphis & Ohio RR.[40]

Nevertheless, some of his troops were the first Federals to visit Germantown, well to the south. On June 16, he sent out cavalry to the town, "a village 13 miles distant from that point, negroes having informed me that rebel troops had encamped there." This story offers insight into the effectiveness of a slave grapevine that helped Federal intelligence. Confederate pickets were indeed driven from the town, and civilians informed the officer in charge that a large enemy force lay nearby, preparing for an attack on Memphis.[41]

Usually such tantalizingly brief reports are all that tell about conflicts in and around Germantown. For some days, surely the townsfolk had gladly fed and supported whatever Confederate troops were in and around, anxiously sharing rumors with them. One can only imagine what they experienced as they heard the shots, saw the Confederate pickets retreating quickly through town with Union cavalry in pursuit. Everyone must have snatched up the children and ducked for cover amidst the galloping horses and firing carbines. On this and subsequent occasions, bullets crashed through windows and embedded themselves in walls where they remain to this day. The threat to civilians was like today's drive-by shootings.

The Union troops did not pursue much beyond town, fearing the presence of "a large enemy force." Instead they consulted someone they thought trustworthy, who confirmed their fears. Reports related that Forrest and Jackson were preparing to raid Memphis on the night of the eighteenth, so Wallace moved much of his division into Memphis.[42] Wallace's concentration of his forces in the city left Germantown still outside Federal lines.

Probably the troops reported were little more than Colonel Jackson's, 1st (later 7th) Cavalry. They would hover between Germantown and Lafayette south of the M&C and always within striking distance of any vulnerable target. Jackson had constant intelligence from locals who sought him out anytime they heard of an opportunity. One occurred when General Grant was on his way to Memphis on June 23, traveling west with "a very insignificant escort" along the State Line Road. Alerted by a Dr. Smith that Grant had stopped at the house of Josiah Deloach at Bray's Station between Germantown and Collierville, Jackson narrowly missed capturing the general.[43]

While the Confederates sought to deny the Federals use of the railroad, one event set the stage for unpleasant experiences for Germantown, as we shall learn later. It has long been reported that on June 25 Jackson's cavalry succeeded in derailing and destroying the first supply train to be sent out from Memphis, capturing a Colonel Kenney and 9 men, "one mile above Germantown." That would have been a little beyond the crossing of State Line and Holly Ford roads (present Hacks Cross). The Confederates bragged that the raid was "well-planned."[44]

In fact, the derailment was undoubtedly the work of locals acting as guerrillas. Before its arrival, the track had been torn up to derail the train and the telegraph wires were cut. Both Colonel Kinney and a Colonel Pride, who had also been on the train, reported that a considerable time elapsed before Jackson's cavalry arrived—up to an hour and a half.[45] This implies the derailing was the work of local civilians who called upon Jackson's men to take advantage of their handiwork. The second in command of the 56th Ohio accused a local plantation owner, a Mr. Davis (perhaps Charles Davis of District Ten), of being an informant.[46]

Such an early, overt resort to active civilian resistance was encouraged by the spottiness of the occupation, but also implies an initially high level of local resistance. Lacking any organized government leadership, local diehard members of the militia were determined to strike a blow. Railroad employees at the town's depot, must have gotten wind of the pending shipment from Memphis, so they had a ripe opportunity.

This incident planted the seeds in Sherman's mind that the citizens of Germantown were especially culpable, and that they needed to be taught a lesson. On June 26, he informed General Halleck, "that is the place of mischief."[47] On June 28, he wrote, "Had we not better clean Germantown, a dirty hole? There is where was planned the cutting of the wire and destruction of the road. I am told they openly boast the Yankees will never run a train over the road."[48]

Generals Halleck, Grant and Sherman had already experienced especially intense guerrilla harassment in the Trans-Mississippi Theatre and now behind their lines in Kentucky and Middle Tennessee. Realizing it represented deeply rooted civilian opposition, they resorted to measures designed to suppress civilian support. Property was confiscated or destroyed, civilians arrested, and families expelled from their homes. Of course, this produced heightened civilian resistance and guerrilla determination to take vengeance on Federal troops and local unionists. Once in Memphis and desperate to protect their vulnerable supply lines and mount the continued advance toward Vicksburg, the generals intensified their efforts to suppress civilian support, while at the same time hoping desperately to win over former unionists and less dedicated secessionists to a restoration of the cotton trade into Memphis and to stabilize the local environment.[49]

Following the incident on the M&C, Grant sent a cavalry patrol out to Germantown which reported that Jackson's men were hovering along the line in squads burning cotton around the town.[50] Grant stationed the 56th Ohio Infantry Regiment, 429 men, and five companies of cavalry, 382 men, at Germantown to secure the line. From the east, Sherman posted two regiments to guard the line between LaFayette and Germantown, and assigned the Indiana Railroad Regiment to accompany the 56th. The 52nd Indiana and 58th Ohio were apparently Sherman's other two regiments, describing their camps as being at and near Germantown. This was the first, short occupation of the immediate area, a sizable force totaling over 800 men and almost 400 horses specifically at the town, plus an equal number of soldiers nearby, not much less than the size of the pre-war, white population of the entire area. The cavalry companies were those of the 6th Illinois, which arrived in Germantown on June 28 and did picket duty and scouting.

Although there are no records of what ensued at the town, the commanding officers undoubtedly took approved actions against citizens suspected of supporting the guerrillas. What must have been the mood of the town's citizens suddenly outnumbered by the presence of so many men in blue? They may have doubted the wisdom of their former boast of being able to defy such a formidable foe with impunity, but they righteously resented confiscations or arrests. Little did they know how much Germantown would soon pay for such acts of resistance when Sherman had an opportunity to vent his spleen.

✦ ✦ ✦

Topography around Germantown played a significant role in what followed. (see Map 2) The town was situated on the hilly ridge that ran from the Memphis bluffs eastward. To the north and south lay the densely wooded bottom lands of the Wolf River and Nonconnah Creek respectively. These two miner tributaries of the Mississippi wound back from Memphis like slithering serpents threatening to converge on the town, then separating again to wend separate ways into Mississippi. The forests of the bottoms were entangled in vines and pockmarked with ponds and marshes left by the ever-shifting stream beds. Tranquil for most of the year, even diminishing significantly during late summer, they could host fierce winter and spring floods, filling the bottom lands to overflowing, uprooting huge trees and sweeping away any manmade obstacles, flushing them forcefully downstream. The safely high and dry ridge between them formed the strategic route along which ran the Memphis-Charleston Railroad and the State Line Road. The ridge itself was heavily wooded, hilly and scarred with frequent creek beds and drainage channels running down its sides, cutting sharply through the hills. The thickly grown river bottoms provided excellent cover for raiders, partisans and guerrillas to assault the transportation lines. Only local guides could enable Federal troops to penetrate guerrilla lairs, a service former slave dared to risk more often than loyal unionists.

Union forces in Memphis, responsible for the repair and defense of the railroads, had to operate along four main roads: The Raleigh Road north to the county seat and then across to the east (present US 64); the Hernando Road (present US 51) into Mississippi, the Pidgen Roost Road (present US 78) crossing the M&C and running to Byhalia and beyond, and that State Line Road, weaving through Germantown, and then just south-west of Collierville forking south into Mississippi (present US 72) or running due west as the La Grange-Memphis Road (present TN 57).[51]

Although on June 29, General McPherson, superintendent of railroads, had announced that the line from Memphis to Grand Junction, 49 miles, was fully operational, that did not guarantee its security.[52] The State Line Road was equally vulnerable. On June 30, Grant considered it necessary to have two companies of infantry and one of cavalry simply to escort a supply train as far as Germantown.[53]

Cavalry Colonel B.H. Grierson was in command of the cavalry temporarily at Germantown, specifically with responsibility for protecting railroad and wagon-trains between Memphis and Sherman at LaFayette. From his base, he was expected to monitor threatening Confederate cavalry movements. His orders were that citizens in the area "undoubtedly giving information to the enemy" were to be arrested and sent to Grant "with the charges against them stated." Grierson was admonished, however, not to annoy "peaceably disposed citizens," and to take no property from arrested citizens except fire arms.[54]

Grierson was left with the problem of deciding who were peaceable and who were Confederate collaborators—a perennial problem for local commanders of occupation forces in all wars. Likewise Grant's imposed constraints guaranteed little for the actual behavior of troops in direct contact with suspected collaborators. There are no records of which area citizens came under suspicion. Grierson's cavalry soon returned to Memphis, since Grant needed them elsewhere. All troops seem to have been gone from Germantown by July 18.[55] As soon as they withdrew, the Confederates returned.

The newly arrived Charles Bliven, Superintendent of the Railway Department, was less optimistic then McPherson. "Rebel pickets and scouting parties were reported within three to five miles of the city, and many fear an attack from them." Occupation forces were insufficient to prevent an attack. Col. Jackson actually sent letters into Memphis "to a large number of secessionists" allegedly warning them "to move their families from the city." Worsening such fears, federal authorities warned residents that if an attack came, the two gunboats anchored off shore would fire on the city, and "will not cease until Memphis is destroyed." Bliven also noted, "Railroad connection with the east is not yet open and it is very doubtful when it will be, guerilla parties are scattered along the Memphis & Charleston and the Memphis & Ohio railroads, who alternately burn cotton and bridges."[56]

On July 28, some companies of the 6th Illinois returned to Germantown on a scout and had a fire-fight with Rebel pickets. Once again the town was terrorized by a running battle. The 6th apparently returned again and remained at Germantown for another short period during August.[57] Townsfolk must have felt awash in the tides.

Meanwhile, Grant and Sherman's dispatches revealed considerable alarm over the insecurity of their communications, with much attention focused specifically on the area around Germantown. Grant had to concentrate all his cavalry on the State Line Road.

Confederate cavalry raiders ranged freely over the countryside, cutting wires, damaging the rails, burning cotton, and intercepting large Union wagon-trains. Consequently, from June into September, the railroad from Memphis through Germantown to Corinth required extensive pacification and reconstruction. Local planters were required to provide slaves as laborers in railroad repair.[58] No matter how important the railroad was to Union supplies, the line itself was capable of only limited carrying capacity. As a result, the State Line Road provided an alternative supply line through Germantown. Even so, that road seemed so insecure that following the incident of June 25, Sherman was avoiding it, sending his wagon trains by "back roads," north of the Wolf, guarding them with a full regiment.[59] Sitting at LaFayette, Sherman's supply lines from Memphis were dangerously tenuous.

Grant and Sherman were totally frustrated by the swarm of Confederate hornets that required the deployment of so many regiments, distracting them from their goal at Vicksburg. From the South came the legitimate Confederate cavalry raiders. But around them everywhere were the civilian guerrilla bands plus a new third element, Partisan Rangers who claimed legitimate Confederate military status, but fought and behaved indistinguishably from the wild guerrillas. From its new base in Grenada, the *Appeal* boasted of several successful raids by partisans and cavalry raiders often working together.[60]

The Partisans and Life in No-Man's Land

In 1862, as it became obvious that the South could lose control of much of its territory, including West Tennessee, the Confederates began authorizing independent partisan units to disrupt occupation. In Shelby County as early as March, the first such authorized unit was the Independent Scouts under "General" Edward "Ned" Sanders, formerly a commander of "rangers" in California during the Mexican War and second in command of a filibustering expedition in Nicaragua. He had returned from California to serve the Confederacy in the irregular capacity to which he was accustomed. On March 14, the *Appeal* announced that he was empowered to raise "the *only independent rangers* which have been authorized by the War Department." The commission authorized him to accept volunteers for such a company. When mustered into service, it would be "considered an INDEPENDENT COMPANY, not to be incorporated into any regiment or battalion."[61]

The paper recommended it, for "There is perhaps no branch of service which offers such attractions to young men who are ambitious of distinction, and who prefer active, vigorous campaigning to the ennui and inactivity of the usual routine of camp duties...." A subsequent advertisement promised that young men will "receive fifty dollars bounty and the same pay as regular cavalry, but are far more free, and under fewer restrictions, with greater chances for individual distinction."⁶² Sanders certainly had local support.⁶³ grew rapidly.

Soon however, he ran into the professional military's rejection of guerrilla operations. When Sanders reported to General Albert Sidney Johnston, commander of the Western Department, he told the general he had been informed that he would receive "any number of independent companies," and that "he would give them a general order to scour the country, destroying in every possible manner our enemies and their property . . . and that all the spoils consequent on such mode of warfare and everything captured by such guerrilla parties would be the property of such company, to be sold or used for their private interests."⁶⁴

Johnston was put off by Sanders' flagrant interest in booty and he was not yet informed of developing Confederate policy. He firmly responded, Sanders was "wholly misinformed." No independent companies would be received into service, and all companies would be assigned to regular units. There never be any branch of the army of such character indicated in your letter. "All troops in the service must be subject to the Articles of War, to discipline. . . ." Sanders was told that he had to report to Johnston's headquarters.⁶⁵

Sanders was respectful and patriotic enough to abandon his buccaneering instincts. He organized his recruits into a company on April 26 and reported as ordered. He was commissioned a captain of the "Confederate Rangers." In September, his obedience was rewarded when his command was expanded to form Sanders' 17th Tennessee Cavalry Battalion. It was attached to Armstrong's Brigade and saw service with Forrest.⁶⁶ Sanders and his men's aspirations had fallen between the cracks.

Nevertheless, J.P. Benjamin, the Secretary of War, aware of the pending government approval of Partisan Rangers, had endorsed Sanderson's unit in West Tennessee, patterned after the model that had been evolving for service in the Virginia state forces.⁶⁷

Soon the Confederate Congress passed the Partisan Ranger Act, and on April 23, the War Department issued General Order No. 30, an Act to Organize Bands of Partisans. President Davis was authorized to commission such bands.⁶⁸ The act provided "that for any arms and munitions of war captured from the enemy by any body of partisan rangers and delivered to any quartermaster . . . , the rangers shall be paid their full value. . . ."⁶⁹ Nothing was said about whatever else they might "capture" to support themselves. Thus the opportunity to capture booty provided that additional incentive for partisan as opposed to regular service. The offer to "requisition" legitimately was conducive to outright plundering.

The *Appeal* continued to extoll the benefits of guerrilla warfare and recommended another unit to locals. "It is expressly stipulated that it shall be an independent command, unattached to any battalion or regiment." There were only to be four or five in the Mississippi valley. "It is complementary to our city . . . that one of these should be held by one of our fellow citizens." Captain E. E. Porter was commissioned "to raise and muster into service a company of this kind. . . . We submit to our fellow citizens if it is anything but right to share with him the expense of arming and equipping the brave young men who are peculiarly unable to provide for themselves. Contributions of horses, money or cotton will be judiciously appropriated. Do not wait to be solicited personally."[70]

There were several assumptions implicit in the orders and the editorials. There would be few such units, commanded by carefully selected officers. They would operate totally independently and within limited parts of the state, close to their homes. Despite the romantic imagery, however, knowledgeable persons were fully aware of the potential for such operations to slip easily into brigandage, to incite retaliation and escalate into inhumane brutality on both sides. Indeed this was already happening because of the numerous unsanctioned guerrillas afoot in all occupied territory. When caught, they could be executed as many were, and the civilians, men and women, who supported them could be legitimately and severely punished.

Confederate legislation was an attempt to solve such problems created by spontaneous civilians intent on fighting the hated occupiers. They were embarrassing to the Confederate government and its legitimate military. Their lack of coordination with regular military commands often made their energy counter-productive. Worse, their appealing prospects drew men away from the ranks of the regular army. With the creation of officially mustered units, they could also insist that they could not be executed for "crimes," but had to be treated as prisoners of war.[71]

Such partisan units became a major alternative to service for Germantown men. There was much dissatisfaction in the ranks of those militia and volunteer "independent" companies that had found themselves incorporated into

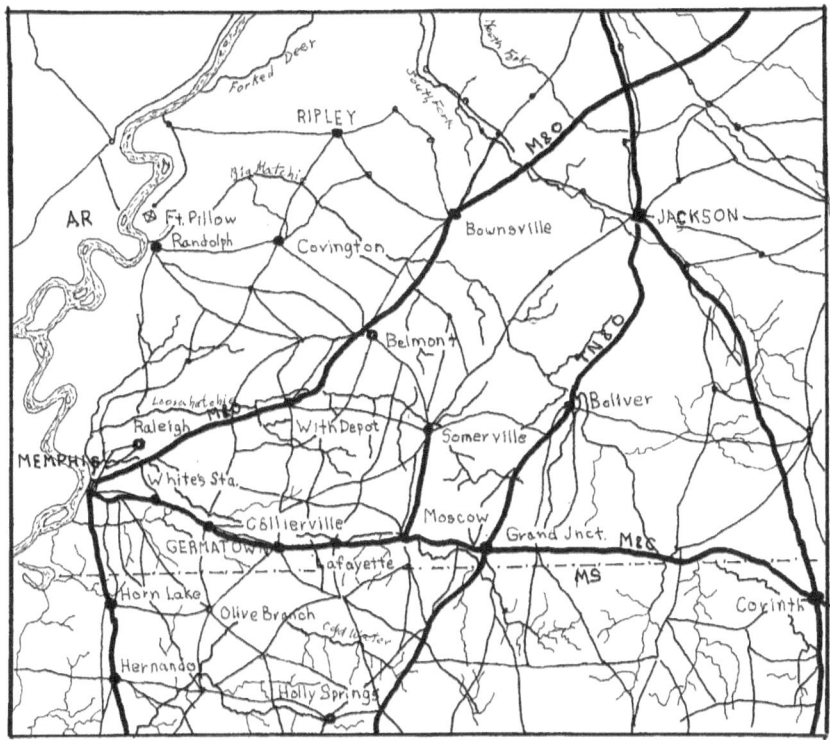

MAP 9 Guerilla warfare theater around Germantown.

regular service and marched off to fight far from home. Partisan service offered the opportunity to avoid call-up while feeling that one could still be giving protection to loved ones. Soon there would be the opportunity to take revenge for the abuses and for losses of home and property. For some, there was also the prospect of adventurous criminality under the guise of righteous revenge. The remark at the end of the *Appeal*'s editorial is surprising, coming so early in the history of these operations. "Do not wait to be solicited personally." It was like a veiled warning about how such units might have to "appropriate" their supplies.

Captain Porter began accepting applications in Memphis and in Somerville in Fayette County. He claimed that his recruits represented an elite corps of gentlemen of the most patriotic element.[72]

Among its earliest activities in the face of the Federal advance into West Tennessee, Porter recorded:

> *May 18.*—We were ordered into [service] by General [Pierre Gustave Toutant] Beauregard, since which time we have mostly been engaged in burning cotton in Fayette and Shelby counties of Tennessee and Marshall and De Soto counties of Mississippi.
> *May 28.*—We left Somerville, Tennessee for Holy Springs, Mississippi taking with us a large lot of government harness and also the bank assets of that place.
> *June 1.*—We landed safely at Holy Springs.[73]

By June 6, Porter reported that he had already recruited 150 men, "almost all from large planters." He told General Beauregard that his Partisans had ranged through all the western counties and DeSoto County in Mississippi, burning "upwards to 30,000 bales of cotton," encountering "but little opposition" from the planters.[74]

> *June 24.*—Then moved toward Byhalia burning all the cotton in our route. We continued burning cotton until June 24. We learned that by going into the enemy's lines we could inflict great damage upon them. We went as far as the Memphis and Ohio Railroad, capturing a number of drays laden with cotton; destroyed the drays and cotton. Brought the mules. We then attacked a wagon train guarded by the Fifty-ninth Ohio Regiment. Broke up a large number of wagons and took some mules.[75]

Memphis papers reported this ambushed wagon train as near Morning Sun about fifteen miles north of Germantown. Soon he and others would be burning the bridges and water towers on the Memphis & Charleston and Memphis & Ohio railroads. The *Appeal* and the *Avalanche* gave contrasting claims about the success of such guerrilla operations, but it is clear they were more than a nuisance.[76]

The Germantown area saw its share of partisan action, but both newspapers and local Federal officers, being unaware of any ostensible distinction, routinely reported most such events simply as guerrilla attacks. For instance, on July 21, 1862, a "Captain Sherwin" and his "independent scouts," a squad of eight men operating around Germantown, reportedly raided as far as White's

ILL. 4 Cotton Burners. *Illustrated London News*, 8.9.1862. Initially both Partisans and Confederate Cavalry scoured the countryside to deny the enemy private and public property they could use.

ILL. 5 Cavalry Raiders Attacking Union Wagon Train. *Leslie's Weekly*. A Partisan attack near Morning Sun.

Station before being stopped by Union forces. They took prisoner a team of men bringing cotton into Memphis, and burned their cargo. They also captured two Federal soldiers, who were soon "shot attempting to escape."[77] As late as November, "Ballentine's guerrillas," reportedly including Porter's Rangers, were operating between Germantown and White's Station stopping the delivery of cotton to Memphis.[78] Independent Scouts usually referred to legitimately commissioned cavalry, but the papers were not concerned with such details. Making Porter's Rangers a component of a band of guerrillas was clearly a product of such confusion, but such collaboration between guerrillas and partisans added to the problem

Thus local Union commanders were among the first to confront a test of the legitimacy of Partisan Rangers. Since they had to avoid battles with Union units unless they had greater numbers or some other advantage, partisans resorted to harassing tactics that violated orthodox conventions of war. Their snipers killed sentries and pickets. They bushwhacked small groups of soldiers who had wandered from camp. They killed or captured civilian teamsters and their animals. They fired on trains and boats and derailed trains that contained civilians, without concern for "collateral damage." They terrorized collaborators.

Pro-Union papers were full of accounts of criminal acts by the partisans, allegedly indifferent to the political sympathies of their victims. They were described as caring "very little for the success of the Southern Confederacy, their sole object being to plunder the weak and helpless." Their unionist victims harbored plans for revenge.[79] As an evil reputation grew around the partisans, animosity developed dividing West Tennesseans.

Initially Union commanders acknowledged no difference between partisans and guerrillas. From headquarters in Corinth, General Halleck had ordered that every man caught in guerrilla activities be hanged.[80] Soon, however, Federal commanders began to appreciate the situation, especially when Confederate authorities threatened retaliation against their men in Confederate captivity.[81] Halleck sought a legal opinion from one Francis Lieber whose legal treatise discomforted Halleck. Nevertheless, Halleck circulated the document as guidance that might help his officers. Lieber distinguished between partisans as the legitimately commissioned, properly commanded and paid forces of a government and guerrillas who operated without any legal sanction or control by military authorities. This led ultimately to Lincoln's Code that codified the rules of war, incorporating Lieber's argument.[82] Now Union commanders had to accept commissioned partisans as legitimate, as opposed to renegade guerillas.

By August, frustrated by the mask of partisan legitimacy, Sherman observed, "All the people of the South are now arming as partisan raiders, daring not to be guerrillas."[83] Although partisans were supposed to be uniformed, they often lacked true uniforms and could melt back into the civilian population. Theoretically, they should have had papers to identify themselves. As a partial solution, by November, Grant was refusing to allow partisan POWs exchange or parole like regular prisoners.[84] At least they could not return to their old ways while in prison camps.

Furthermore in response to civilian support for "guerrilla" operations, occupation authorities searched homes, confiscated all weapons, plus other civilian property as compensation.[85] Civilians did not benefit from arguments over distinctions. As raids continued around Germantown, its citizens and area farmers were visited frequently by Federal officers with a legitimate excuse for confiscations.

Caught in the middle, locals had to provide support for their own men both as a matter of patriotism and conscience. If caught supporting "guerrillas," they faced at least confiscation of all movable property. Accusations could come from vengeful slaves or local white informants. The need to obscure any evidence of collaboration became important. According to family tradition, a wounded Confederate rode up to Woodlawn, the house of Joseph Brooks. While they were nursing him in their home, he left tall-tale bloodstains on the floor. After he was gone, word came of a federal patrol headed toward Germantown searching for partisans and supporters. The family, unable to remove the stains, used hot coals to singe the floor boards, obscuring evidence.[86] To this day, descendants display the scorched boards, retelling the story.

With Germantown at the fore in the minds of Union commanders as a center of opposition, the town was targeted for retributive actions. Meanwhile it would suffer from simply being located in a contested no-man's land. Perhaps the first event to occur, according to the *Appeal*, happened early in June near Germantown.

Two Federal soldiers entered the house of an old citizen, and demanded his money. "One of the ruffians" leveled his gun at the old man. "The old lady interposed herself between the gun of the miscreant and her husband, and while the coward hesitated to shoot, a daughter of the aged couple came from an adjoining room . . . seized a double-barreled shot gun, with which she shot the ruffian through the head. . . ." His companion fled.[87]

Unfortunately, reports of such incidents survive exclusively in newspapers and family traditions, all of which glamorized and exaggerated heroic female resistance. Newspapers were notoriously unreliable and biased. Family traditions and memories are problematic. Nevertheless, they bear reporting for the mood they convey and the likelihood of some truth. A more likely example of proper Southern ladies involved the daughter of the above mentioned Brooks family. Her family's plantation west of town suffered heavily from pillaging. Unwilling to use inappropriate language herself, she instructed their slaves to curse Sherman "to their hearts' content."[88]

From beginning to end, despite Union efforts to prevent soldiers from pillaging, it was inevitable that they suffered from the affliction known as "cramping." This practice got its name because witty soldiers explained that when they happened to touch an appealing object, their hands "cramped" and they just could not let go. Sherman observed that "Stealing, robbery and pillage has become so common in this army that it is a disgrace to any civilized people. . . . This demoralizing and disgraceful practice of pillage must cease, else the country will rise on us and justly shoot us down like wild beasts."[89] It must be noted that Confederate officers had similar complaints and problems protecting local citizens' property from their own troops. Such chaos was always worse where there were no established occupation headquarters with clearly defined spheres of responsibility and sufficient staff to prosecute violators. Located in no-man's-land, the Germantown area would suffer from such a lack of responsible occupying authority for the bulk of 1862, during which it undoubtedly sustained much of its damages.

✦ ✦ ✦

Meanwhile, Federal commanders were trying to figure out how to control occupied West Tennessee and exploit its railroads while General Grant focused on an overland assault through Mississippi to take Vicksburg. Initially, Sherman commanded the area south of the Hatchie from Memphis to the east as far as Bolivar and Grand Junction, with responsibility for defending the railroads.[90] By June 21, Major General H. W. Halleck, over-all commander, believed that the best line to defend West Tennessee was across north Mississippi.[91] Sherman agreed that it was best to hold the Confederates well back from the railroad. He

ILL. 6 Revenge Foraging. *Leslie's Weekly*. More thoroughly destructive than either sanctioned or renegade foraging; as at Germantown, troops could be let loose on the population to pillage freely as a punishment for special cases of collaboration with guerrillas and Partisans.

proposed the Coldwater as their front line, with encamped divisions operating from bases along the railroad. He suggested that McClernand hold the Junction and La Grange, Hurlbut hold Moscow and Lafayette (Rossville), while he "be in front of Collierville and Germantown. It is there all roads toward Memphis debauch on this line of road."[92]

Rather than being allowed to pursue such a forward position which would have required a constant heavy presence in Germantown, on July 15 Sherman was placed in command of "Memphis and vicinity." On his way from Moscow, Sherman camped his division at Collierville on July 18, and marched the next day through Germantown to White's Station. On the nineteenth, Hurlbut's division camped at Germantown before going on to Memphis to join Sherman.[93]

Shortly thereafter, the *Appeal* got wind of a story from the *Bulletin*, now a Federal-supported newspaper in Memphis. For two days, soldiers encamped a few miles from Germantown had pillaged the town. They broke into stores and homes and carried off or destroyed whatever they could find—furniture, clothing, books, jewelry, silver, and anything else "that suited their fancy." They broke down fences, destroyed gardens, stripped the trees of fruit, green and ripe, "and seemed bent on doing all the malicious mischief in their power." Only one house in the community escaped pillage, but none were burned, contrary to some early reports.[94]

Such willful destructiveness sounds more excessive than random pillaging. It was extremely focused on Germantown. Indeed, one of the participants reported to his hometown newspaper:

> As we passed through Germantown, which is a perfect hotbed of secession, the soldiers did considerable plundering, and for the first time since leaving Pittsburgh Landing, the officers paid no attention to it. I was glad of it, of all the 'se-e-d' holes, Germantown is the most bitter I have ever seen. This is the place where the train of cars from Memphis was thrown off the tracks and captured. . . . I would rejoice at seeing the inhabitants of Germantown stolen poor, and the town burned.[95]

Sherman's opinions had been passed down to the troops and they had been given tacit permission to teach Germantown a lesson. Fortunately, however, nothing in town was burned despite initial newspaper exaggerations.[96]

For the federal troops involved, it was not just an outbreak of righteous violence, but also an opportunity to compensate themselves for a long period of deprivation—cut off from supplies from Memphis, specifically by the derailing of the train precipitated by Germantown-supported guerrillas. An observer noted that when they reached Memphis, "they made a ragged and dirty appearance. Some had on overalls for pants, others nothing but their drawers." In the field since Corinth, with transportation cut off, they had received no clothing and undoubtedly no desirable food.[97] Their Germantown adventure offered a badly needed respite, but they also had a bone to pick.

This was Germantown's singularly most traumatic event, an introduction to the following months of existence in the no-man's land of guerrilla warfare. In 1864, J. Dix Mills, who was not present in the town at that time, wrote a vivid description based on what he had been told.

> Shops, Factories Groceries, Stores, Dwellings, Lodges, and churches have been gutted, and their contents carried off by Soldiers and Yankee

negros, or scattered upon the street; the finest fabric of ladies ware tied about the bodies of soldiers and negro's. Soldiers with clubbed muskets cleared the shelves of the Druggest and in one heterogeneous mess tramped beneath their feet showcases, glass, medicines and perfumes. Shoulder-Strapped gentlemen looked on complacently: and little thought by the passive act that they were carving so deeply their names in the tablet of inglorious fame that the hand of time could not efface them....[98]

As we shall see later, Mills had a penchant for embellishing righteously the suffering of the South at the hands of a bestial enemy.

After this event, the defense of Memphis now being Sherman's primary responsibility, the closest to Germantown that his troops were to be stationed was for one brigade to guard the State Line Road three miles out from Memphis, patrolling as far as White's Station. Typically, when he heard rumors of infantry and some cavalry in Germantown, on July 27 he merely ordered the 6th Illinois Cavalry under Colonel Grierson to scout out to Germantown and Collierville. No matter what he thought of the strategic importance of Germantown-Collierville, he had to abandon hope of permanently occupying them. Within a few days after his march through Germantown, a Confederate force had reoccupied the town. Sherman repeatedly sent out expeditions "to clean out the countryside."[99] Among Sherman's command at Memphis, only 1,340 cavalry (12 companies) were available.[100] Thus he remained mostly in a defensive posture at Memphis.[101]

Federal intentions to operate the M&C constantly ran afoul of partisan raiders. By August 20, those "guerrillas" operating within Union-held territory in West Tennessee had become such a problem that Grant had to request more cavalry.[102] Meanwhile, he pressed down from between Jackson and Corinth into Mississippi toward Vicksburg, leaving Sherman to his own devices. It took a while to realize the necessity of the sort of permanent defensive line of occupation that Halleck and Sherman had originally conceived.

✦ ✦ ✦

Two factors shaped the character of guerrilla warfare, the terrain in which they operated and an inevitable proclivity to an almost complete lack of military discipline. Both these factors were indispensable to their effective operation,

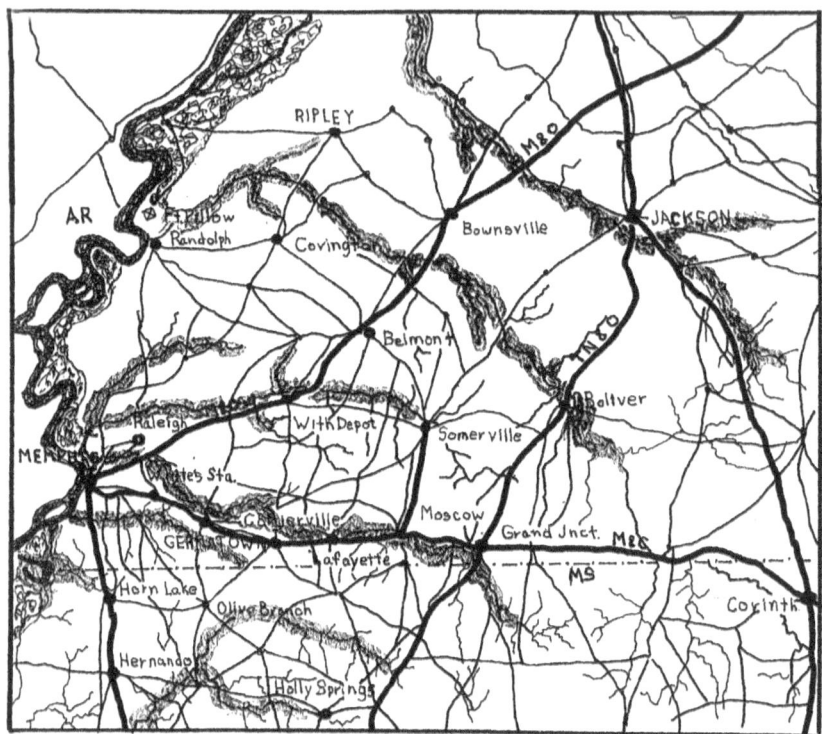

MAP 10 Guerilla warfare terrain.

but simultaneously, they imposed strict limitations on the nature of their effectiveness.

Map 10 imposes the key features of this terrain on the map of the theater of local guerrilla warfare. The most densely impenetrable river flood plains and the Mississippi River flood plains stand out. The occasional patches of rough terrain are not easily illustrated, but even along the ridge running out through Germantown, they could impose rugged barriers to conventional military operations. Even the seemingly open farm lands on the map were thirty to fifty percent heavily wooded.

Anyone old enough to remember the thick bottoms and woodlands around the area even as late as the middle of the twentieth century knows how easy it would be to stay hidden or lie in ambush. Many tributaries of the Mississippi snaked back through the counties of west Tennessee. From the Forked Deer in the north down through the Loosahatchie and the Hatchie, to the Wolf and

Nonconnah Creek, they provided a network for concealed movement throughout the counties and down into and back out of shelter in Mississippi. During flood season, they were dangerous and impassable for all but the most-local denizens. The terrain varied from swamps filled with cypress and tupelo to normally dry ridges and hummocks interspersed with creeks and small lakes. The seasonally dry areas hosted a high-canopied forest of hardwoods. Even before the modern invasion of privet, the native undergrowth could be impenetrably dense and entwined with brambles and vines hanging from the trees. Elsewhere the ground could be almost clear of undergrowth shaded by the high canopy and arching vines. Except where an occassional road cut through and a bridge crossed, only the seasonal fords were known to the natives. Likewise equally obscure footpaths and trails led to fishing spots and hunting camp sites. Only locals could help the Federals penetrate these networks and ferret out partisan camps. Operationally sized units could base themselves in such an environment, to be ferreted out by only a concerted search-and-find operation. When confronted by an overwhelming threat, the partisan unit could simply disburse and go home, the men hiding their equipment and arms, any semblance of a uniform, and going back to a daily routine.

Given the very nature of semi-military formations, partisan officers had to have both the respect and the tolerance of their men. According to one regular Confederate soldier,

> There was one thing that could be said of the private Confederate soldiers that could not be said of any other set of soldiers. While they had great respect for the officer they were under and would fight and obey orders when called on, the officer knew, or would soon learn, that he must not get too bossy, for the privates thought they were as good as Mr. Captain or Lieutenant, and if they got too big and bossy they would be thrown up in blankets or something worse.[103]

In the partisans, authority was even more tenuous, with even the NCOS and field officers being more inclined to infringements of the rules of war and having little respect for civilian property.

One problem lay in their need to operate as small units, even after they had been formally organized in partisan battalions under senior officers. Even on the occasions when a command actually operated as a battalion or regiment, it was the rare officer who could control such men. Lack of control combined with a "noble cause" against a "venomous enemy" and "traitorous neighbors" provided all the justification they needed to brutalize, kill, and confiscate property. They easily crossed the line to bandit behavior. Their enemies had an excellent opportunity to accuse them of the worst.[104]

Meanwhile, fully independent guerrilla units continued to blossom without properly issued political commissions. The net effect of legitimate and illegitimate guerrilla-like operations were having negative consequences. The political leadership of the Confederate government and area commanders issued directives to curb and control them.[105] As early as August 1862, both the District of Mississippi, which ostensibly commanded West Tennessee, and the Confederate Secretary of War revoked all authority to raise partisan rangers and ordered the muster of their conscripts into regular state units, many of which still retained the title partisan rangers.[106] In November, the Secretary of War instructed all district commanders to require the alleged commanders of Partisan Rangers to provide "a copy of their authority for raising their corps." Those failing to comply would be disbanded.[107]

Despite efforts to legitimize partisans, some local commanders issued orders that clearly crossed the line. For instance, Captain Porter's Partisan Rangers received orders that instead of destroying railroad bridges that might be useful later to the Confederacy, "the road may be rendered useless to the enemy by frequently firing into trains from places of concealment by small parties of your command *or by citizens*."[108] He was ostensibly to encourage, even solicit, civilian guerrilla participation contrary to the rules of war.

✦ ✦ ✦

There were consequences for the town within this theatre of irregular warfare. Typically, on July 13 when General Sherman reported a guerrilla raid "seven miles south of the Wolf River" against a forage train, killing one man and wounding three, he arbitrarily arrested twenty-five local men. He knew he could not identify the men involved, so he had to take an action that held the entire community responsible.[109]

By September, he had hardened his convictions that the population could not be wooed by conciliation. He wrote his brother, "It is about time the North understood the truth, that the entire South, men, women and child stand against us, armed and determined. . . . They are more confident than ever, none seems to doubt their independence. . . ." The women and children needed to suffer along with the men. It was a total war. He was soon confessing confidentially to his brother a depressed sense of their predicament. "(T)hough our armies can pass across and through the land, the war closes in behind and leaves the same enemy behind. We attempt to occupy places, and the people rise up and make the detachments prisoners."[110]

Sherman increasingly employed the pattern of retaliation against any community suspected supporting "guerrillas." On September 8, after an encounter south of Germantown, Colonel Grierson's' cavalry forayed out of Memphis and returned by way of White's Station where they arrested five prominent citizens.[111] On October 12, a raid through Germantown surprised and captured a captain with his company in a camp a few miles beyond the town.[112] On October 21, a sizable Rebel force had to be driven from Collierville.[113] No record of arrests survives for those incidences, so Federal responses were probably not being officially reported for the record. Sherman developed the firm conviction that the war had to be waged against the entire enemy population. He ordered that for every boat in the Mississippi fired upon, ten families, identified by lot, would be expelled from the city.[114] Well into autumn, Sherman's strategy was to dispatch his cavalry out State Line Road to Germantown and/or Collierville, seeking out guerrillas.[115]

Even when the town was spared a firefight, the passage of Federal expeditions could be onerous, as one participant described it to his hometown paper:

> The route of the force can probably be traced for some time. Chickens, turkeys, geese, hogs and sheep, found themselves legitimate objects for capture, and it would be difficult to estimate the number that "fell" to feed the expedition.... Some of the planters, who admire the work of treason, will look upon farms turned into commons, the fences being used for camp fires. In some instances horses and mules were taken and brought away. Many contrabands came in with the army.... In short the rebels were treated with anything but tenderness.[116]

On August 31, the infamous 7th Kansas Cavalry, the Kansas Jayhawkers, was at Germantown long enough to be mustered and paid.[117] At Jackson on their way west, they had established a reputation for undisciplined pillaging and expressions of hostility toward secessionists that disturbed even Federal officers.[118] That must have been a fitful day or two for the townsfolk. The worst of enmity born of the Bloody Kansas years had arrived, but no record of any incident requiring the attention of superior officers has survived concerning that short visit.

Then on October 22, Sherman sent Grierson out again through Collierville, where he disbursed a group of guerrillas, and up the northern route scouring "the country all the way to Randolph...." Instead of returning by land, he took steamship from Randolph. "The enemy hoping to intercept Grierson on his return, interposed a heavy cavalry force at Germantown, their scouts coming in as far as White's Station...."[119]

At the beginning of this expedition, it was actually at Germantown that the federal cavalry had first encountered about thirty of Captain O'Neil's cavalry from Alabama. During the ensuing skirmish, three of O'Neil's men were captured and one wounded, while "two Yankees were made to bite the dust. . . ." Badly outnumbered, O'Neill was forced to retreat. Grierson then made his turn north across the Wolf, "taking with them negroes, horses and mules to any number."[120]

Once again Germantown was the site of "a short engagement."[121] A Confederate report stated that some forty cavalrymen had been in the town until forced to retire." Afterward, the *Bulletin* told a colorful story of town life amidst this. It reported that O'Neal's men had set up camp east of the town blocking cotton delivery to the city. The townsfolk were preparing them breakfast, and their captain decided to have his in one of the hospitable homes. While the son of the house was on his way to school, he spotted the approaching Yankees and ran back to give warning. The captain seized his host's horse and barely escaped.[122] Throughout the autumn months, such incidents made the town the site of hot little fire fights.

Once Federal presence was firmly established in West Tennessee, new economic realities confronted the local residents and those of North Mississippi. The center of their market economy had always been Memphis, and nothing could change that. But, the city was now a complicated place of business where all the realities of the war collided. The economic infrastructure for the cotton trade remained intact. Only its links to the South were broken. West Tennessee connections into the city remained too essential to everyone's lives despite the new barriers created.

Initially both governments sought to shut down all trade. The Confederacy sought to build self-sufficiency, free from economic dependency on the North. They needed direct contact with world markets. The Federal government hoped to strangle the South by cutting it off entirely from trade with the outside world. Consequently, both Lincoln and Davis tried to outlaw all trade with the enemy. Nevertheless, economic realities made it impossible for either side to sever the economic ties at local levels. They were too much a part of everyone's lives. Both sides were almost immediately forced to make accommodations.[123]

For the North, finance, trade and industry were too tightly tied to the South's cotton, no matter how it was produced. Also local occupation officials soon realized that both to pacify and reintegrate the population, those not directly involved in outright support of secession had to be allowed to bring in that badly needed cotton. Humanitarian considerations also prevailed, for without trade, starvation would ensue. The problem was preventing contraband materials from going out to support the Confederacy.

From the very beginning, Lincoln allowed exceptions to his ban on commerce. In 1862, he allowed regulated trade with the population loyal to the Union in occupied territories. Trade out of West Tennessee and Mississippi had begun soon after the occupation of Memphis. Local commanders had the power to regulate this trade, but Grant and Sherman were especially concerned about the opportunities for corruption it generated and the supplies that could flow to the Confederacy. Consequently, efforts to find a balance between these concerns with the need for cotton, and to pacify the local population and meet its legitimate needs would produce constant vacillations in restrictions. The resultant uncertainty added greatly to the strains of life for the people around Germantown. Furthermore, the corrupt occupation officials in the city and opportunistic middle men on both sides would reap the lion's share of the profits. They had motives to facilitate illicit trade.

In the South, President Davis deferred direct regulation to his Secretary of War, James Seddon, and local commanding generals. At all levels, Confederate officers were torn between the benefit to the Union of cotton trade, on the one hand. On the other, they clearly understood that the people had always been dependent on trade through Memphis. Nothing the South offered could replace that dependence. For instance in 1863, Inspector General Jacob Thompson would implore President Davis to sympathize with the residents doing business with Memphis. It was not treasonous for them to trade with the enemy out of sheer desperation.[124] As with the Federals, however, responsibility for deciding what trade to encourage and what to block fell to local commanders. They too had to worry about the temptations for corruption at all levels of officialdom. But, it was a way to acquire supplies for their troops not otherwise available.

Initially they enforced harsh policies for the disloyal who seemed to betray the patriotic cause, and required the burning of all cotton and confiscation of all things useful to the enemy. Generals Chalmers and Pemberton cracked down hard on involved traders. In contrast toward the end of 1863, state Judge Alexander Clayton, tacitly supported by Governor Charles Clark, tried to block military confiscations in favor of supervision by civil authorities.[125] This state of confusion applied to the Confederate cavalry raiders coming under Chelmer's command, but operating at the outer limits of discipline. Even less subject to control were the partisan rangers, as vendettas against native Unionists and ostensible traitors would grow increasingly hotter.

Such ambiguity shaped the specific environment of the no-man's-land around Germantown. Local farmers trying to bring any surviving cotton into Memphis to buy food and supplies were frequently intercepted by the partisans. In October, a detachment of the 2nd Mississippi Partisan Rangers reported "a considerable amount of cotton in route to Memphis was burned near Germantown."[126] Then after Grierson's October 22 raid, the road was open long enough for thousands of dollars' worth of cotton to get through.[127]

Confronted by the economic realities of survival, area planters sought to sell their cotton in Memphis. If they had willingly let it be burnt before, such patriotic zeal had rapidly evaporated. Family survival trumped any qualms about disloyalty. For all involved in this dangerous trade, the opportunity for tremendous profits made the conflicted feelings less troubling. Where cotton had sold for thirteen cents a pound in 1860, it was at $1.00 a pound by early 1863.[128] Of course, it was not the local farmers who reaped the bulk of this windfall, but the merchants and corrupt officials sitting safely in Memphis. The planters and farmers bore the risk of getting the cotton to town, and took what they were offered. Sherman later remembered that by August he had established payment sometimes by Confederate script or in bank notes. But also by promissory notes to be paid after the war, or by deposits with trustees that could only be collected in Washington.[129] All promissory notes had to be sold locally at significant discount. Perhaps Sherman had made such diverse provisions at different times. Since some forms of payment were far more advantageous to the seller than others, perhaps form varied with the shifts in his ideas about encouraging commerce versus distrust of the local population who might be supporting rebel forces.

Farmers and planters were now hiding it for some hoped-for opportunities. The cotton burners had to resort to all sorts of subterfuge to get the hoarders to disclose their hiding places. They even held suspects in custody until they revealed their stash.[130] All this within occupied territory. In October, Sherman expressed the opinion that the partisans were almost an asset for the occupation. "The band of guerrilla or partisan rangers are doing us much less harm than our enemies." The farmers "are getting heartily tired of it." He told of a train of 40 wagons brought in by farmers desperately needing money to buy supplies for their needy families. When guerrillas tried to stop them, the farmers threatened to fight and the guerillas let them pass. "I think many of the farmers are tired of the war, and especially of guerrillas."[131] Similar incidents with various outcomes occurred along Germantown Road.

Sherman vacillated between seeing the local population as hopelessly rebel and optimism about turning their attitudes.[132] Such sentiments were always in tension in his mind with a "burning" desire to take revenge on the actively disloyal. The frustration of his hopes that the locals could or would stop the guerrillas mounted.

The cycle continued despite proclamations of martial law over West Tennessee.[133] Germantown did not benefit from the protection supposedly provided. Rather the town suffered from its restrictions. By October, the Nashville *Daily Union* reported that "The people east of Memphis, near Germantown, are said to be suffering for the necessities of life. Cotton is their only support, and it has been all destroyed by guerrillas."[134] November 7, the *Bulletin* reported that the Confederates had been able to throw up a screen around Memphis from the Nonconnah to White's Station.[135] This was soon broken by a major expedition through Germantown into Mississippi.

✦ ✦ ✦

Amidst all this, the town remained isolated. We may never know how long the town government continued to function trying to provide legal authority. News of the outside world came in sporadically. Letters had to be brought in through the lines. When Memphis newspapers reached town, that news was increasingly shaped by occupation authorities. All newspaper editors and owners in the District of West Tennessee were required to take the oath of allegiance. Since the

Appeal had been moved south before the occupation, it continued publication but had to arrive under cover. Nevertheless, it still circulated in the area. An innovative press in Grenada, the *Rebel Picket*, was a single broadsheet that could be more easily smuggled and in posted surreptitiously for public consumption. This tri-weekly focused on war news from the Confederate perspective.[136]

The adventures of one young man of the town provide another picture of the trials of life in no-man's-land. Henry Woodson, the son of the Gin manufacturer, at age sixteen joined a company raised by his uncle in Mississippi in March 1862. Like many, he succumbed to disease rather than combat, and was severely ill from June. On leave, he returned home to Germantown on November 1 for a few day's visit with his parents. He related what followed.

> But in the midst of my visit the Sixth Illinois Cavalry came along and made me a prisoner of war. To console and reassure my distressed parents, Captain Starr, the adjutant of the regiment, told them that if I would give my word of honor that I would not make any attempt to escape, I should go with the first batch of prisoners to be exchanged. The solemn promise was given and I was taken on to Memphis, and placed as a prisoner in the old Irving Block on Second Street. My parents and eldest sister came several times to visit me.... A few minutes after they had gone, I stepped out into the hallway and to my surprise, the guard was not there.... I walked lightly to the head of the stairs and looked down on the street. There seemed to be absolutely nothing to prevent an easy escape from that place. At that moment the recollection of my promise came to my mind and I stepped back into the room, closed the door and remained a prisoner a few days longer when I, with a large number of others, was sent by boat to Vicksburg, Mississippi, and exchanged. So the Federal officer, Captain Starr, kept his promise too.[137]

In contrast to the barbarities that were developing around them, such stories paint a much more civil picture. Woodson rejoined his unit at Shelbyville, Tennessee, and was subsequently transferred into the 13th Tennessee.[138]

Furloughs home for recovery were common, even when it involved return into semi-occupied territory. The soldier had to carry with him a furlough form that specified where he was to go and how many days he had before rejoining his command, "or be considered a deserter." The Quartermaster's Department provided him transportation where possible. Beyond that, he was on his own.

p. 17 Robert Vinkler Richardson, Wikipedia. Commander of the 1st West Tennessee Partisan Rangers, 1862, then, 1863, Brigadier General and Commander of Richardson Brigade of Confederate Cavalry; 1864 removed from command.

p. 18 Col. Benjamin Grierson, Smithsonian Institute, 6th Illinois Cavalry Regiment; Commander Cavalry Brigade, primary opponent of guerrillas, Partisans, and Confederate Cavalry in Mid-South; especially Richardson.

Upon arrival at home, he was to report to the nearest enrolling officer.[139] Apparently around occupied Germantown, the local Confederate conscripting officers operating behind enemy lines would have gotten a soldier's name sooner or later if he did not return.

✦ ✦ ✦

By the end of the year, the most significant and notorious of West Tennessee's partisan leaders had emerged to conscript and wreak havoc behind enemy lines—Colonel Robert Vinkler Richardson, a prominent citizen of Memphis. During the Mexican War, he had served Tennessee in raising and organizing volunteer units, and had resumed such a role under Pillow in 1861. On September 6, 1862, the Confederate Secretary of War authorized Richardson to organize a regiment of Partisan Rangers in Tennessee, vesting him with "large discretion" in his operations. Subsequently, Lieutenant General J.C. Pemberton, commanding the Department of Mississippi and East Louisiana, also authorized Colonels Robert F. Looney and Richardson to organize partisan regiments "within enemy lines in Tennessee." Since the approval of Governor Harris was required, he instructed them to apply to him. He was to designate their counties of operation.

Without gaining this proper recognition, Richardson proceeded to rally two existing guerrilla bands to his flag, Captain John Green's "Company of Tipton County," and Reuben Burrow's from Shelby. Quickly three other companies from Fayette County joined him plus Captain James Hazelwood's from Shelby. He titled his unit the 1st Tennessee Regiment of Partisan Rangers, C.S.A, and began work centered at Galloway Switch in Fayette County. During the four months it took him to recruit and organize, he had to operate constantly around the Union bases. He actually claimed that he was "able to hold all of Tipton and Fayette Counties and parts of Haywood, Hardeman, and Shelby Counties."[140]

Richardson did not get the bands he had cobbled together properly commissioned. To make matters worse, each band was provincially oriented, consisting mostly of men focused on defending home and community against menacing invaders, and staying close to those homes to do so. While attempting to get these men and companies to accept his command, Richardson allegedly promised them they would remain a state unit purely for local service. Although they accepted the command of this politically well-connected man, they naturally insisted on electing the remaining regimental and company officers. All such positions were filled, resulting in a complete command structure long before any appropriate numbers were recruited to fill the ranks.[141] Companies often had as many officers and NCOs as privates, almost all friends and neighbors.

If they had acquired the official status that Richardson's appointment should have given them, they would become official Confederate units subject to service wherever they were ordered regardless of his promises. If controlling such independently minded men was not difficult enough, they would become resentful and rebellious when ultimately required to serve in larger conventional commands far removed from home. Officers and men resented and distrusted "outsiders" exercising authority over them.

But that development lay in the future, and until then, Richardson was loose about communicating with his erstwhile superiors. As late as November, Pemberton noted that neither Richardson nor Looney had informed him of having received any authorization by Harris.[142] His military status was tentatively accepted by Pemberton, pending political approval by the governor, which never accrued. It is also difficult to evaluate accurately Richardson's achievements, because his reports were boastful and disingenuous. Which is not to say that his bravado was unusual among the reports of officers on both sides.

Meanwhile by December, according to the Federal commander at Bolívar,

> Bands of guerrillas still infest the neighborhood under Street, Richardson and others, carrying away citizens, stealing horses, and subsisting by plunder. At present they harbor in the bends of the river, a few miles above here, in the neighborhood of Somerville. They watch our forage trains and assail such of our men as stray beyond our lines, making occasional captures.[143]

Several Germantown men were attracted to Richardson's service.

♦ ♦ ♦

Elsewhere for Germantown's men with the Army of Tennessee, the rest of the year's experiences after Shiloh and Corinth affected morale and motivation. General Kirby Smith's Autumn campaign into Kentucky, ultimately became a disaster. Overextended, they encountered unionist guerrillas cutting their supply lines and then strong opposition forcing retreat. It "was one of greater trial and hardship than any march made during the war. Over a rough and barren country, without shoes and thinly clad, with scarcely anything to eat, the suffering was great, yet it was born with fortitude and without murmur." Or so the commander of the 13th memorialized it. At least no Germantown men of the 13th lay dead in Kentucky this time.[144] The 4th, however, was so badly reduced that it had to be united with the 5th into the consolidated 4th/5th Regiment.

On December 30, the 13th suffered its next bleeding. On the first day of the Battle of Murfreesboro, once again its men advanced in the face of heavy resistance. Of its 226 officers and men, it lost 110 killed, wounded and missing. Again, Company C's report elaborated the experience of Germantown's men.

> The company was also in the battle of Stone's River in front of Murfreesborough, Tennessee. In this engagement we lost half killed, wounded and missing. Lieutenant Rolfe (sic) T. Duke was killed. Wayne Holman and P. P. Tuggle, Orderly Sergeant P. B. Cash and Private J. W. Wright were missing and supposed to be killed, as they have not been heard from since the battle.[145]

Duke was the second loss for that planter family. Palmer Tuggle died of a severe wound in the left forearm, which probably required amputation. William Ellis was slightly wounded in the foot. From an unknown cause, following the war he would become paralyzed for life. In March, the badly depleted regiment was fused with the 154th as the 13th/154th. The two regiments had fought side-by-side since Belmont.[146] Thereafter, the war took them ever farther from home.

The "Burning" of Germantown, 1862/63

1862 was a year of severe trauma for the town. Occupation had been sporadic with no clear strategy other than a wacka-mole effort to defend the line and to end local support of raiders and guerrillas. That would soon change. The end of the year and the beginning of the next involved events that local traditions and misinformation have almost hopelessly distorted. This is a good point in the narrative to attempt clarification.

There is a well-established tradition that Germantown was thoroughly burned in July 1862, but as we have already seen, this story grew from an erroneous newspaper report that was subsequently retracted. That was Sherman's sanctioned pillaging, but no burnings. Undoubtedly the town had suffered considerably more by the end of the year, but precisely because eye witness descriptions are contradictory, we may never know how much serious damage had occurred. The two cotton gin factories, converted to manufacture supplies for the Confederate army, were torched. Possibly also grist mills were broken up to deny flour to Confederate troops. A few private homes succumbed to incendiary vandalism or even sanctioned retribution. However, the town's public buildings seemed to have survived the year, contrary to tradition.

There was at least one specific occasion toward the end of the year when the town suffered more indiscriminate destruction. On November 25, Sherman made a major foray into Mississippi, ordering Brigadier General M.L. Smith's 1st Brigade, containing the 8th Missouri Infantry Regiment, to pass through town and then down to Byhalia.[147] By early December, various northern newspapers were reporting that Germantown had been burned by soldiers of the 8th Missouri, and that *the division commander had shot the offenders*.[148] This report was grossly exaggerated. If there had been executions, official records should have survived. The relevant reports mentioned none. Nevertheless, if this version of burnings in Germantown grew out of any actual incident, it occurred around the days when the 8th was in Germantown, but probably specifically November 27, on their departure. Any such house burnings or other vandalism were acts of renegade soldiers and camp followers who would have been free to wreak havoc only after the troops under disciplined control had left town. One other source indicates that there might have been only one house burned. Contrary to local traditions, neither the Baptist nor Methodist Church buildings were burned at any time during this year, for their fate was yet to be settled.

Heavy and continuous occupation of Germantown would begin in January 1863. Since this was another time when traditions tell of burnings, we must look ahead briefly to finish this analysis of local traditions. Colonel Ephraim R. Eckley's 2nd Brigade headquarters, Colonel Samuel A. Holmes' 10th Missouri Infantry, and Lieutenant Colonel Thomas P. Herrick's 7th Kansas Cavalry settled into occupation of the town proper. Other infantry and cavalry regiments bivouacked at Forest Hill and in the surrounding countryside.[149] This may have been the context in which the most popular tradition about the fate of the churches must be set. Unfortunately, by the time the stories about the churches had been recorded in popular histories, they had undergone oral transmission through several generations, creating many problematic details. As we shall see, even recorded accounts of church burnings by contemporary residents were not based on eye witnesses.

According to the Presbyterian tradition, mostly based on a version handed down by descendants of Moses Neeley, at some undefined date Reverend Evans came to him disturbed by a report that the Federals were going to burn the public buildings, including their church. They went together to meet with the Federal commander to plead with him to save their building. Years later, stories told at a marriage between decedents of Neeley and Union Colonel William L. Sanderson expanded the tradition, misidentifying Sanderson as the commanding officer in question. When Evans and whatever officers involved discovered that they were fellow Masons, they allegedly agreed to save both the church and the Masonic Hall. According to the more popular version, the church was then used as a stable and the hall as headquarters, which is how they both survived. Another version among Presbyterians was that the church was used as a commissary, which would be more likely, since use as a stable would have ruined the building, especially the floor, far more extensively than the surviving original floors indicate. In any case, the tradition holds erroneously that the Methodist and Baptist churches were immediately burned.[150]

If Sanderson was involved in this meeting, then it had to occur between January 11 and 19. He had been in command of the units stationed at Boliver until the end of 1862, but never at or near Germantown.[151] In early January, his units were on the road to Memphis, arriving in Collierville on the evening of the 11th where he remained until the nineteenth.[152] Presumably he would have visited his fellow officers at Germantown, with whom he had previously campaigned. There he could have only been simply present at the fabled meeting. As we shall see, however, this was far too early in the year for any of the churches to have suffered their ultimate fate. Perhaps, however, such a meeting did occur at the beginning of the occupation.

In fact none of the church buildings were literally burned. Furthermore, it is highly unlikely that a commander establishing a permanent base of occupation in a town would have burned its public buildings. They were too useful for the occupiers and burning churches was certain to alienate the population they needed to live with and win over. Instead, deliberately burning public buildings was most commonly punishment for unoccupied communities suspected of aiding Confederate forces.

Evans and Neeley's purported fears of their building being burnt, may have grown from rumors, since during January, the town would have been anxious about its fate, and church burnings were not uncommon.[153] Evans may have established at whatever meeting both his Masonic credentials and pro-Union sympathies. We shall see what may have followed from that. Indeed the Masonic Hall survived intact because the commanding officers had decided to use it as headquarters for the duration. The Baptist and Methodist buildings may also have been used initially, perhaps roughly, as some traditions have it. Whatever the case, they ultimately succumbed.

Nevertheless, according to the traditions of the Germantown Baptist Church, their old building was burned by Federal troops in 1862. This belief seems partially supported by a single eyewitness account of Sallie Walker, residing across the street from the church at the time. In one subsequently recorded version, she described a very methodical process, with the soldiers removing all the furnishings and then building fires inside. Through her slave, she intervened with the officer in charge to save the pulpit Bible. Although this sounds like an official burning, there is no reference in the tradition of her actually describing the burning, only the burning of papers.[154] Such oral traditions, not recorded until much later, were subject to distortions. Only the story of the Bible appears true, for it remains in the hands of the minister's descendants. Subsequent retelling of the story predictably assigned the order for the burning to Sherman, and the 1862 date is probably a result of confusion with other erroneous traditions. Finally stories that the Yankees "destroyed our church" easily morphed into burnings through assumption. Probably, creative retellings explain even Walker's alleged description of fires being set inside the building.

Actually, the tradition that the Baptist Church was burned, stands in the face of the fact that in the early twentieth century, their deacons succeeded in getting compensation for the officially ordered dismantling of their building to provide lumber for the federal camps. The base commander might have had less sympathy for the Baptists, especially if his Provost Marshal determined that the congregation were unrepentant secesh. Many of those who testified regarding the destruction of the church agreed it occurred under the command of Col. La Fayette McCrillis, which fell between April and August of 1863. As we shall see, the only eyewitness account of conditions in Germantown up to June 1863 mentions no damage to any of the churches during that period. In the deacon's application, two eyewitnesses reported how the building was disassembled piece by piece and hauled away over a period of several weeks under supervision. The lumber and furnishings were used for camp construction. The continued insistence by the Baptists that their church was burned despite their own records is testimony to the needs of so many Southern communities to have as a badge of Confederate legitimacy the burning of their churches or their desecration by use as a stable.[155] Of course, it is likely that debris that remained and records (the papers of Ms. Walker's account) were burned. The remaining ash provided evidence of a church burning for subsequent observers.

A different fate befell the Methodist building. Regardless of any temporary use, it was not guarded. It fell prey to salvaging for firewood by soldiers encamped in the adjacent graveyard during the two severe winters of occupation. Immediately after the war, it was so badly damaged it had to be dismantled and rebuilt.[156]

Whatever, by the beginning of 1863, some observers would describe Germantown as completely in ruins with all shops and mills and many homes destroyed. Such statements may have been a bit of hyperbole, for the Webb school and apparently others survived, and most shops, the inns, and almost all homes as well. Even the fate of all three churches was unsettled until later. Nevertheless, the town had suffered damage.

TABLE 3 Civil War incidents in and around Germantown, 1863
January 1863, full, regular occupation of Germantown begins

10 January	Grant moved his headquarters to Memphis; mid-January, Vicksburg campaign.
27 January	engagement near Germantown.
28 January	skirmish south of Collierville by 7th Kansas Cavalry out of Germantown.
23 May	skirmish at Germantown.
3 July	fall of Vicksburg.
8 July	scout for guerrillas launched from Germantown.
16–20 July	scout launched from Germantown.
18 July	skirmish at Germantown.
11 October	Battle of Collierville; raid at Germantown.
3 November	Second Battle of Collierville, Col. Edmund Hatch counterattacks from Germantown.
November–December	Forrest's conscription raid into West Tennessee, passing by Collierville

7

1863 · GERMANTOWN OCCUPIED

The Impact of Federal and Confederate Forces

After seven months of being caught in a no-man's-land, suffering from the Confederate policy of denying the Federals any resources, suffering from Union reprisals and from pillaging by Union soldiers, during 1863, Germantown would "benefit" from a year of heavy occupation in and around the town itself. It became again an army camp town, but overflowing with men in blue. This was a mixed blessing. There would be many benefits from restored order, but the rule of alien authority and the presence of so many troops was a heavy burden.

Especially at first, locals were treated with suspicion as an occupied enemy and suffered the consequences. Federal forces felt threatened and suspicious of local collaboration. Pressure on Union forces in West Tennessee was maintained well into 1863 by the cavalry of Major General Earl Van Dorn headquartered at Spring Hill, Mississippi. Their object was to preoccupy possible Union reinforcements for the Vicksburg campaign. Thereafter, even though major military operations were usually focused elsewhere in Tennessee that did not reduce the local partisan threat.[1]

To counter those ubiquitous pests, Grant proclaimed that he would clean out all "guerrillas" from the country between Holy Springs and Memphis. "If it cannot be done in any other way I will be compelled to take and destroy the last bushel of grain between the Hatchie and the Tallahatchie, and all the stock. I will make it the interest of the citizens to leave our lines of communication unmolested."[2] Federal troops had a writ to confiscate and destroy. Only one company, F of the 59th Indiana Infantry, had been encamped at Germantown since November 1862,[3] in an attempt to discourage collaboration with guerrillas. In response to the combined threats of partisans and Confederate raiders, Union commanders revised their operations, establishing regimental and brigade strength bases all along the railroad. The forces in West Tennessee were redistributed along more stable defensive lines. Brigadier General Isaac F. Quinby (7th Division) was sent from Lafayette had orders to secure the State Line Road westward. By January 3, his orders had turned into establishing a stationary defense of the railroad. His 2nd Brigade under Colonel Ephraim R. Eckley guarded the road from Collierville to Germantown; the 3rd Brigade under Colonel George B. Boomer from Germantown to White's Station.[4]

The new disposition put Colonel Eckley, headquartered at Germantown, with five regiments: the 56th Illinois, the 17th Iowa (perhaps north-east of town at Brunswick Springs), the 10th Missouri (specifically in Germantown under Colonel Samuel A. Holmes[5], and the 80th Ohio east of town at what it called Camp Forest Hill. The right section of the Springfield Light Artillery Battery (Illinois) held a position described as "encamped within the fortifications, commanding Germantown, Tennessee." Also from the Cavalry Division under Colonel T. Lyle Dickey, the 7th Kansas Cavalry camped at Germantown until April.[6] Artifacts uncovered indicate its primary camp was north of the tracks around what is today the New Bethel Missionary Baptist Church. This placed a brigade headquarters and five full regiments, plus an additional cavalry regiment and artillery closely around the town. Life was drastically changed by an occupation several times that of the local population. Although constant rearrangements would reduce this force gradually, for the rest of the year it would remain an overwhelming presence.

Initially, for these occupation forces, settling in and around Germantown was a little like camping out under a hornet's nest. One member of the 10th Missouri recalled, as they came out of Memphis on December 31 escorting a wagon train to Collierville, "a great many of the stragglers had been taken prisoners by the guerrillas. The Eighteenth Ohio, lost four of their officers...." On January 2nd, they started "out after a body of guerillas who had attacked some of their brigade. Our regiment went out on the road, where we arrested a few citizens, who were supposed to know more of the whereabouts of the gang than they chose to reveal. In the afternoon we moved back to Germantown where we went into camp. I learned that some of the Eighteenth Ohio killed three guerrillas today. This country is infested with these bands, and it is not safe traveling fifty yards from camp."[7] Unable to tell peaceful citizens from the enemy, unsafe even in small groups, the men resented the local people and were likely to take revenge at any opportunity.

Local historian Elisabeth Hughes remembers being told that "The real damage such as looting and burning was not primarily done by Union troops but mainly raiders called Kansas Jay Hawkers.... In my grandmother's day to call a person a Jay Hawker was the worst insult imaginable."[8] However, Kansas Jayhawkers was specifically the nickname of the 7th Kansas Cavalry, as opposed to simply jayhawkers. Traditions mistakenly confused the clandestine marauding or jayhawking by undisciplined individuals and renegades with a regular regiment that had that moniker. The term "jayhawker" became the Southerners' equivalent of "bushwhackers," which was the Union epithet for Confederates operating outside the conventions of war.

Nevertheless, the 7th Kansas Volunteer Cavalry, recruited under the title of "Independent Kansas Jay-Hawkers," undoubtedly contributed enough to local damage to encourage the indiscriminate mixing of names in local tradition. They had been involved in the early phases of the war in Missouri and Arkansas which descended into vicious guerrilla fighting, and they brought with them behavior conditioned by that environment.[9] They revealed that side of their character when they sacked Somerville, Tennessee. In early January, before arriving in Germantown, while the 7th was pursuing partisans it had encamped at Somerville. After several hundred troopers became intoxicated, they not only plundered the town, but in the chaos that ensued, a drunken captain shot two of his own men and was shot in turn. In his later report from Germantown, Colonel A. L. Lee insisted that such behavior was not typical but resulted from an extended period of exhausting service followed by the unique availability of large quantities of intoxicants.[10] From December 31, 1862 to April 14, 1863 Germantown hosted these 7th Kansas Jayhawkers.[11]

On January 6, General Hurlbut became commander of the 16th Corps, seated at Memphis and in command of the entire area. Drunken, venal, and unscrupulous, he became notorious in the eyes of local southerners. His corruption included confiscated property.[12] He became the primary authority over the area as Grant began taking McPherson's 17th Corps for the Vicksburg siege, leaving Union defenses further reduced.[13]

Slowly Union occupation and control settled into a territorial division. Specifically for the defense of the M&C Railroad, Union efforts at "control" ended with their picket lines at Nonconnah Creek. Confederate lines lay along the Coldwater in Mississippi. In between was a no-man's land over which patrols and major raiding forces from both sides operated. But even behind Union lines and around its occupied positions, Rebel forces, regular cavalry and partisans, operated almost with impunity. Fortunately, full occupation of Germantown would at least keep Rebel raiders, guerrillas and the resultant firefights out of town.

On January 12, the *Bulletin* had boasted that they had the M&C repaired and they were bringing trains safely through, confident that the line could be "kept clear of guerrillas and track destroyers." Nevertheless, those repairs were not the best, for one train, coming too rapidly around the infamous curve east of Germantown, derailed when the ties gave way.[14]

As Grant continued to reposition defenses of the line from Memphis, their presence in and around town shifted. Both Hurlbut's 5th Division (Laumann's), described as "near Memphis," and his Cavalry Division under A.L. Lee, headquartered at Germantown, were now defending the line.[15] With brigade headquarters at the town, it became a center of intelligence operations. Its provost marshal received all prisoners for interrogation.

The area remained densely bivouacked by a shifting array of Union troops throughout the spring, continually rearranging positions.[16] This constant shifting, abandonment of old camps and establishment of new ones, meant that the soldiers were regularly looking for flooring, furnishings and amenities for their tents. Abandoned homes would be pillaged. Outside town, farms and houses were more vulnerable to unauthorized confiscations.

Meanwhile, Union concern about a hostile population supporting guerrillas and providing the Confederates with intelligence had already resulted in reprisals. In early January, the mood in the Union Army was clearly revealed in a series of orders that Grant issued to Quinby and Hurlbut. "Citizens on the road to Memphis" were to be subjected to severe penalties as reprisals. All males between eighteen and fifty years of age were to be arrested and paroled. This would have made them theoretically ineligible for legitimate conscription or enlistment in the Confederate army, and, therefore, subject to severe treatment if subsequently captured. He ordered Hurlbut that for every raid or attempted raid by guerrillas on the road, he was to arrest ten families of the most prominent secessionists.[17]

Ultimately, as partisan pressures increased, by April, Colonel W.W. Sanford, by then in command of the 4th Brigade at Germantown, would be ordered to expel "six rebel families" living near Buntyn Station for an incident.[18] Given the number of incidents near Germantown, one suspects that residents of the area must have also been subjected to expulsions. Such pressure on the civilian population never had any effect on the partisans.

In early January, Hurlbut reported to Grant that the road from Memphis to Germantown was full of guerrillas and warned that since he could not spare any guards, the road needed to "be strongly guarded.... I require more force than the ordinary guards, and especially cavalry, to beat up these guerrillas. Major Blyth (a Mississippi partisan leader) is within 14 miles on the Hernando road. Richardson near Wolf River, about Germantown."[19] He even made a dash into Memphis suburbs as far as Chelsea and the Fair grounds.[20] Richardson did indeed get around within the territory he claimed "to hold," coming close enough to the town to be able to pick up boys from the nearby farms. Although we will never know how many Germantown men rode with his Partisan Rangers, some did, and several would be with him later. Their wartime experience was different from that of regulars.

By March, he was such a threat that Colonel Grierson launched a successful operation against him. Although his reports minimized his defeat, Richardson's force was never so concentrated that it could be totally destroyed. Its ability to disburse into swamps and woods made them much less vulnerable. His language, however, provides one clue to what bothered his Confederate superiors. While his strength reports of 150 or 100 men in a particular engagement were possibly accurate, he constantly talked about his "regimental command." He claimed that he had successfully raised ten companies (no strength given), with five more in process of organization. Although cut off from contact, "We have fought two general engagements and have had innumerable skirmishes."[21] Inflated strength reports were only one thing that disturbed his superiors. He omitted reference to activities that raised serious charges. Each side's versions of the other's acts elicited accusations of criminality. Although often exaggerated, there was truth to the stories. The viciousness of guerrilla warfare had fully arrived in West Tennessee.

As he exercised "his discretion" to confiscate, harass and occasionally kill Unionists, especially the families of men serving the Union cause, he was denounced by his erstwhile superiors. General Hurlbut announced, "I am assured by high Confederate authority that they act without and against orders, and are simply robbers, to be treated as such. The gang must be exterminated, and the sooner the better." Given the enmity among the opposing sides within the population and the opportunities for vindictive actions, his men had deteriorated into undisciplined bands. Confederate command had become increasingly concerned with the negative side-effects of uncontrolled partisan rangers like Richardson, who was "cut off" from contact with his commander to the south.

During the March sweep against Richardson, Confederate Colonel Robert F. Looney was captured and sent back to Germantown for interrogation. Although citizens reported accurately that he and two other officers were there to recruit and organize a different "cavalry brigade" in West Tennessee, Looney professed "to have been sent there for the purpose of investigating the complaints of citizens against Richardson and his command."[22] Both versions were true. As we have seen, both Richardson and Looney originally had the same kind of commission to raise partisan rangers, but Richardson was now under investigation.

General J.E. Johnston, Confederate Department of the West at Chattanooga, directed that whatever authority Richardson had should be withdrawn, because he was "accused of great oppression."[23] He asked Pemberton, Richardson's purported commanding officer, to send Colonel Looney to arrest Richardson. While Richardson's forces had been raiding and recruiting from Germantown up into Haywood County, Looney had been recruiting from Collierville across Fayette County before his capture. One additional problem was that Richardson's conscripts had not been forwarded to the Confederate army but kept exclusively with him.

Pemberton was informed that Richardson's authority had expired. He reportedly had a "full regiment" organized, but not properly mustered into Confederate or state service. "Since he has got these men together, there seems little doubt of his having exercised authority never intended to be given. . . . It is thought best . . . the power granted to him to raise partisan rangers be revoked; at the same time, the services of the men collected ought to be secured."[24]

From the Union side came an ever greater determination to bring Richardson down. On March 15, Hurlbut ordered Grierson to use Richardson's captured muster rolls to identify his men. Then they would be unable to slip in and out of civilian status. Since high Confederate authority had defined Richardson's men as "simply robbers, to be treated as such," he ordered that "The gang must be exterminated. . . . The prisoners received are not held as prisoners of war, but as robbers and murderers, and will be so treated."[25] They had lost the legal distinction of partisan status.

Meanwhile during March, Federal cavalry kept Richardson under heavy pressure in Tipton County, provoking him to attempt a major counterattack. Although both sides were bloodied, several of Richardson's officers were killed or wounded, including Richardson himself. While he was recovering in hiding, on April 1 his officers disbursed the companies to escape heavy pursuit. Nevertheless, more than two dozen officers and men, including Lieutenant Colonel Green, were captured. As a coherent unit, the Rangers were in shambles.[26]

On April 17, the cavalry commander operating out of Jackson, reported, "I am informed by reliable citizens ... that Richardson ... crossed the Mississippi River in a canoe, with a fortune, robbed of citizens of Haywood, Tipton and the adjoining counties."[27] Although pure fiction, this was the essence of Richardson's reputation and some of the complaints being investigated by Confederate high command.

Meanwhile on April 1, Hurlbut had received reports that the partisan bands plaguing him, including Richardson had actually been ordered by Chalmers to report to him at Panola.[28] In fact, Chalmers was to "assume command of all the partisan corps in West Tennessee, organizing and reporting the same." He was ordered to ascertain if Richardson's command has been mustered, and even if so to arrest him.[29]

Then between April 17 and 18, Richardson's fortunes underwent a sudden shift. On the 17th, Richardson was an illegal guerrilla, still threatened with arrest. His command was almost non-existent. But on the very next day, Pemberton sent a scout to Richardson to tell him to cut the rail communications from Jackson to Corinth.[30] All of a sudden, Richardson was given an official assignment. As part of Grant's operations against Vicksburg, on April 17 he had sent a major cavalry expedition down through Mississippi from Corinth. In desperation, Pemberton called on Richardson to assemble a force from units in the field and to pursue Grierson's cavalry expedition, taking pressure off himself at Vicksburg.[31]

We may never know the details of this transition, or why Richardson, without an operational unit, was called on for this mission. On April 27, the *Appeal* at Grenada, Mississippi, reported an interview with Richardson, who was "at present in this city for purposes of answering some charges that have been preferred against him."[32] For the rest of the year, the *Appeal* would lavish praise on him. It was the desperate need for cavalry against the Union raid into Mississippi that undoubtedly explains the sudden willingness to ignore doubts about him.

Meanwhile, the cavalry expedition that Grant had sent into Mississippi had resulted in more changes at Germantown. The 7th Kansas went, to be replaced at Germantown by the 9th Illinois.[33] By the end of the month, the reshuffling of units was complete. Under Hurlbut, the 1st Division, headquartered at La Grange, stationed its 1st Brigade at Collierville and its 4th under Colonel William W. Sanford at Germantown. This placed the 48th and 119th Illinois Infantry around the town and the 49th Illinois (Colonel Phineas Phease) in town. In addition, the 2nd Brigade (Colonel La Fayette McCrillis) of the 1st Cavalry Division was also headquartered at Germantown with its 9th Illinois (Major Ira R. Gifford) specifically in town.[34] The garrison around the town had been reduced.

Soon, Grant's endless demands for troops against Vicksburg required yet another rearrangement. This required Major General Richard J. Oglesby (at Corinth) to shift his front as far west as Germantown. On June 10, Oglesby reported that he had two companies at LaFayette, six companies of the 50th Indiana at Collierville with a section of artillery, and Phease's 49th Illinois Infantry still at Germantown with a section of artillery, but its companies were spread out along the State Line Road as far as White's Station. The Cavalry Division (now Colonel John K. Mizner) was again headquartered at Germantown, also with its 1st Brigade (Colonel McCrillis) still covering LaFayette, Collierville and Germantown.[35]

Despite reductions, for the entire year, Germantown remained a heavily occupied headquarters. As regiments rotated in and out of town, they arrived sometimes by rail. They disembarked in the middle of town at the depot with all their equipment and supplies to march off to their encampments.[36] A steady stream of wagon trains carrying equipment and supplies also rolled through town. With their noise and danger to pedestrians and ongoing damage to property, life in and around town included all the hubbub and animal waste of a busy city.

Despite such a presence, Confederates repeatedly managed to penetrate Oglesby's defenses and tear up the rails and telegraph lines between Germantown and Collierville.[37] Characteristically, Hurlbut complained to Grant, "My line of railroad is not tenable. If attacked by a respectable force, it must be broken.... I will do the best I can on the line to keep it up and repel an attack, but am liable to be cut off ... at any time."[38]

The force that threatened the area from Mississippi was that of Chalmers. His command of the 5th Military District in Northern Mississippi headquartered at Panola included many West Tennessee cavalry and artillery batteries, tracing their formation back to Shelby County.[39] Chalmers' command sent parties into West Tennessee to recruit and conscript more. To build its strength, the 7th Tennessee Cavalry would draw constantly on men who had not previously enlisted and served, or who had left service for a variety of reasons, or even those who had been captured and paroled back home. By July, compared to the previous year when he opined that the people of Tennessee "are now much depressed," and unlikely to provide recruits, Chalmers now believed things were changing. "On the other hand, the people of those districts of which the enemy have had possession for some time, are, I am informed, now willing to enlist. West Tennessee is beginning to rally.... The number of them will be increased by the extension of the age of those liable to conscription to forty-five...."[40] This optimistic picture had probably been painted for him by men like Richardson. In fact, conscription generated most recruits rather than any "rally" of secessionist zeal.

Meanwhile, Richardson had resumed operations in West Tennessee where he had left behind most of his disbursed Rangers, whom he intended to reassemble. On June 26, the *Bulletin* reported that he had returned to his haunt "in the region of the corner of the three counties of Tipton, Shelby and Fayette." Now titling himself a brigadier, he would "carry on his old trade of robber, or at least, its equivalent...."[41] By July, refugees fleeing the area reported that he was still near Shelby Depot, with rolls estimated to contain names of 2,000 recruits and conscripts. There were still no more than 200 cavalry in his camp.[42]

Colonel McCrillis left Germantown on July 16 to hunt him down. Unable to catch him, he reported squads totaling about 400 men (conscripts) had been moving north across the Big Hatchie into Lauderdale County to join Richardson. Only about 100 were actually armed and low on ammunition.[43] Then on August 6 came the report that Richardson was again back down at Okolona, Mississippi. The will-o-the-wisp had gone back into Tennessee, not to raid but to recruit and conscript men. Now under tighter command,

Richardson had an official appointment for conscription for the army, into which his formerly independent Partisan Rangers were now integrated.

The *Bulletin* published what it alleged were conscription orders issued to "his serene demonship" Richardson by the Confederate Adjutant General. The Bulletin compared Confederate policy to the Russian treatment of the Poles.

> Every white man between the ages of eighteen and forty-five in the District of West Tennessee is hereby ordered to report immediately at such places of rendezvous as may hereafter be designated.... If a man should absent himself from his home to avoid this order, burn his house and other property, except such as may be useful to this command. If a man is found to resist the execution of this order, by refusing to report, shoot him down and leave him lying. If a man takes refuge in his house and offers resistance, set the house on fire and guard it in order the recusant may not get out.[44]

Until a copy of such an order turns up, the accuracy of the alleged draconian instructions cannot be tested. They, nevertheless, give a sense of the pressures under which some men existed while trying to live in peace around Germantown, and of the terms under which some had to serve.

The truth about responses to Confederate recruitment efforts fell short of their claims. Some men responded to the conscription notice dutifully. Others responded out of fear of retribution, or were even dragooned. While bringing large bands back through the lines, the conscription teams routinely had to keep them under guard like prisoners.[45]

On September 30, Chalmers received command of all troops in North Mississippi, with Richardson as his cavalry commander. Richardson reported

> I found a lively feeling of patriotism to prevail among the people, which was greatly stimulated by the knowledge of my appointment as chief for the Bureau of conscription of West Tennessee, and my proclaimed intention to put the laws in force without delay. Very soon there were not less than forty company organizations on foot throughout West Tennessee, some of these were soon formed, others dragged.[46]

Orders forbade independent companies or battalions to leave Mississippi or to attach themselves to any organization without permission.[47] Not only was command putting together a sizable force for Chalmers, but they sought to control their recruits for better use. Richardson's increased contingent of former Tennessee partisans needed to be officially incorporated into the army in North Mississippi.

Richardson and his men received official status as regular Tennessee cavalry regiments. They became the West Tennessee Cavalry Brigade and his 1st Tennessee Regiment of Partisan Ranges became the 12th Tennessee Cavalry under the command of his former Lieutenant Colonel James U. Green. The additional troops they had raised became the 13th under Colonel J. J. Neely (later renumbered the 14th), and the 14th under Colonel F.M. Stewart (which would become the 15th).[48] For a while, they had to cool their heels in North Mississippi. This transition did not go down well with many of the early partisan recruits who had been reassembled, including the original regimental and company officers. They were no longer serving independently near home as originally promised. With the addition of often unhappy conscripts, the brigade represented a problematic force. Anger over abuses during Federal occupation provided some a motivation. But if a conscript did not report for duty at the specified place, the process could be more like dragooning. They, like Dr. Zivago during the Russian Civil War, might simply disappear one day to serve the cause.

Although we may never know which Germantown area men rode originally with Richardson, some rosters have survived from after they became Tennessee regiments. In the 12th (Green's), perhaps as many as 25 area men served. Among them, 15 have entry dates indicating service in the Partisan Rangers. While Joel Harrison, and Henry Massey probably rode with Joel Duke to Fayette County to join in 1862, James Neely, about age 40, was likely a late conscript into the 12th in November 1863. Even the 14th/15th had area men. Of all the possible members identified, more than a third were in their forties and twenty percent in their teens. Such were the men who were swept up to ride with Richardson.[49]

One story that provides color to the lives of soldiers and civilians involves Joel Duke. He had enlisted with Richardson at age 15 and later described himself as one who "rode with Forrest." In 1863, he was captured in Fayette County and registered as with "Co. A, 1st Tenn.," which seems to have been a reference to the 1st Tennessee Partisan Rangers. A friend of the family, a Mrs. Willett, visited him at the Irving Block prison in Memphis. One of those indomitable southern women, she was on a mission to help him escape. She blackened his face and provided clothes to dress him as a waiter. In this guise, he escaped. After sneaking thorough the picket lines around Memphis, he rejoined his unit. Since there was no entry in the Provost Marshall's records of his final disposition as a POW, they may not have wanted to admit his escape. Unfortunately no more of his story has been told.[50]

♦ ♦ ♦

Throughout the summer, such men continued to harass the occupation. Confederate regulars and guerrillas could operate consistently behind Union lines. Occupation forces had been reduced, and there were constant complaints about insufficient numbers.[51] On August 13, McCrillis' troopers were so dispersed at the time of an incident that he had difficulty cobbling together enough men to mount the interception force that failed.[52]

To counter the raider threat, for the duration of its stay in Germantown Colonel McCrillis' brigade, either alone or as part of larger operations, aggressively invaded north Mississippi. Germantown thus remained a seat of Union efforts to neutralize those Rebel threats.[53]

In late summer, the establishment around Germantown again underwent changes. On August 20, the cavalry of the 16th Corps was reorganized and redistributed. Colonel Edward Hatch's 3rd Cavalry Brigade, replaced McCrillis' in Germantown. The 6th Illinois and the 2nd Iowa was specifically camped at Germantown, the latter on what is today's Festival Grounds.[54] Hatch reported his brigade as headquartered "1½ miles from Germantown, northwest, one-fourth of a mile from Wolf River, 1 mile north of the railroad, on what is known as the Nashbora [Nashoba] tract."[55] Grant again drained off troops, further reducing forces around Germantown. On September 14, Hatch's brigade headquarters relocated to Memphis.[56] All infantry regiments had left by October 29.[57]

Thereafter cavalry became the primary occupiers. The 6th Illinois was the most consistent presence from August 1863 to March 30, 1864 when it was furloughed to Illinois. Nevertheless, it was away at least twice on major expeditions against Forrest. Company K of the 1st Illinois Light Artillery, occupied the fortifications.[58]

The constant pressure on the rural population from guerrillas, Confederate partisans and raiders, Federal confiscations and retributions, and jayhawking were bad enough. To them, unfortunately during 1863 the Federals added the equivalent of their own partisans—state regiments of cavalry. Among them, the 1st and 2nd West Tennessee Cavalry quickly earned reputations as evil as those of Confederate partisans. Specifically, Colonel Fielding Hurst of the 1st became Richardson's counterpart in generating the ire of the opposite side. Likewise, he was as adored by the *Bulletin* as Richardson was by the *Appeal*.[59]

From January to autumn, the area had experienced a constant shifting of occupation forces, gradually diminishing. Always hovering around them were swarms of mounted raiders. Such were the problems of the Federal forces defending the line from Memphis through Germantown and Collierville on the eve of the only significant battles fought near the town.

The Battles of Collierville and Forrest's Raid into West Tennessee

In the run-up to the first battle of Collierville, both sides had their agents scouting the area. On September 1, a Confederate agent, J. A. Harrell, operating near Germantown, reported that he had just visited Memphis to gather intelligence. There were only about 3000 troops and a battalion of cavalry there—a sizable force having been sent into Arkansas. He suggested that a diversionary force be sent up between La Grange and Germantown to draw the Federals out of Memphis and engage and hold them at Germantown. Then a force of no more than 1000 cavalry could charge in and take the city. Major General S. D. Lee, commanding cavalry in North Mississippi, rejected the idea.[60] Germantown was thus spared becoming the battlefield.

Then on October 4, Hurlbut's long feared attack by a "sizable force" materialized. Chalmers launched his raid to break the rail line, but primarily as a diversion for a larger raid to the east. He planned a surprise attack on Collierville. Hurlbut had sent his cavalry against an expected attack well to the east, but had positioned a brigade at White's Station from where it could move to reinforce Collierville just in case.[61]

It was Richardson's Brigade combined with Chalmers's that launched the first Battle of Collierville, with Richardson commanding the entire force in combat. During the night of October 11, two detachments, succeeded in cutting the lines and rails east of Collierville, severing communications. Two other detachments from the 12th and 14th Tennessee were sent to effect similar cuts between Germantown and Collierville. Opposing Richardson at Collierville were only 240 men. The cavalry ordered to encircle the fortifications and attack from the rear foundered in its mission precisely because of its lack of discipline and penchant for looting. Nevertheless, except for a coincidence, Collierville would have been captured.[62]

Unknown to Chalmers, Sherman had returned to Memphis with orders to proceed east along the M&C to Chattanooga. Since the railroad was insufficient to move large forces, he began moving his entire force toward Corinth on the roads, but personally coming by rail from Memphis ahead of them with his headquarters and 260 men. His train reached Collierville at noon shortly after the attack had begun.[63]

Sherman organized the defense of the depot. The firefight was brisk and lasted a couple of hours. By three in the afternoon, the Confederates withdrew in the face of major reinforcements from Germantown and LaFayette. Hurlbut had dispatched a regiment and battery from Germantown, followed by the troops from White's Station.[64]

◆ ◆ ◆

Germantown's involvement in the Battle of Collierville has largely gone unreported. In fact, the little information available is both confusing and interesting. Although Chalmers reported that detachments of the 12th and 14th had failed to cut the lines between Germantown and Collierville before his raid, they apparently struck in time to do damage. At least one large and two small "culverts" had been burned blocking the line after Sherman's passage. Major Burrow's of the 12th claimed that he actually hit the railroad "about daylight on the morning of October 11 . . . half way between Germantown and White's Station . . . burned one trestle, tore up the railroad, and destroyed some 500 yards of telegraph wire. . . ."[65] The Nashville *Daily Union* reported "that a rebel force of some importance made an attack on Germantown at about the same time" as Collierville, apparently circling back from the west. Indeed, sometime after the Federal forces at Germantown had been dispatched to Collierville, Hurlbut received word from the town. "We were attacked in camp to-day at about 12 o'clock by enemy's cavalry in overwhelming numbers, and our effective force having been ordered from camp some days hence, we were driven from the camp, which was mostly burned. Losses as yet not known, but large." This was the camp of the 6th Illinois Cavalry which had been sent east. It was located on the Nashoba Tract.[66]

One is especially troubled when trying to correlate these various reports, especially Burrow's, with the timing of the movement of Federal reinforcements from White's Station. One can do little more than report them. One also wonders how Germantown's citizens felt as they watched Tennesseans, even local boys, riding rough-shod over the Federals around their own town.

One observer accompanying the expedition reported to the *Appeal*,

> We were cordially welcomed and cheered as we passed along, and on our return their patriotism was further evinced by having large baskets of edables on the roadside for our soldiers. Their loyalty has been wrongly impugned. There may be some Union proclivities, but as far as we could observe (and we had abundant opportunities) they were a unit. These people have, by fortune of war placing them in such close proximity to the enemy's lines, probably been reduced to the alternative of having to deal with the enemy to procure the necessities of life, but their condition is more deserving of sympathy than the unjust charges against them are of credence.[67]

Although he did not specifically identify the people of Germantown, their actual experiences and the likely mix of emotions and responses would have been the same. Clearly the town and the entire area had earned the reputation among Rebels of having defected. A Nashville paper reported that in Germantown, the rebel force burned some houses.[68] If true, it could have been targeted reprisals against collaborators. Whatever, none of the few surviving contemporary references to the town mention any such reprisals.

The local civilians had become chameleons, adapting their colors to the uniforms around them. Selectively collaborating to avoid retribution, leaving the military on both sides uncertain whom they could trust—whom they should punish.

✦ ✦ ✦

Sherman, however, was in high dudgeon. As usual he was especially irked by what he considered the perfidy of unrepentant secesh. "Citizens who travel the road betray us; I would restrict their travel." In his determination to make Chalmers and his civilian supporters feel his wrath, he ordered Hurlbut, "Instruct your cavalry to take all horses and mules between the railroad and the Tallahatchie, burn all mills and corn fields.... Several of the dead at Collierville had your oath of allegiance and all sorts of passes on their persons."[69] Some may have enthusiastically violated their parole, but conscripts may have had no choice.

Hurlbut actually ordered no such reprisals. In fact, when he sent reconnaissance parties into Mississippi, he ordered them to leave receipts for any confiscated feed.[70] Yet Hurlbut was certainly set back by the raid.[71] By October 20, he feared that Chalmers and Richardson had been sufficiently reinforced to attack again. In the event of a heavy attack, he timidly planned to have the troops at Collierville and Germantown fall back to Memphis.[72]

Indeed, Chalmers sent a spy, Charles Pierson, to reconnoiter the entire line. He arrived in Memphis on October 14, and visited Germantown and Collierville on the nineteenth. He reported that the Germantown garrison consisted of the 52nd Illinois Infantry and a few cavalry totaling 500 men. He was obviously unaware that the 6th Illinois Cavalry and the artillery battery were out on patrol.[73]

Chalmers got another assignment to harass Sherman's rear as he was moving east and to cut the rail lines to disrupt his supplies. He suggested a move against either Germantown or Collierville as a distraction while Richardson could cut the lines to the east. He concentrated his forces 16 miles from Germantown and 19 from Collierville to threaten both. His scouts, deployed along the rail line and the Germantown Road, reported that the Federals had evacuated the railroad and removed all infantry from the Germantown-Collierville area. Only one cavalry regiment defended each town, the 6th Illinois at Germantown. Believing his scouts, Chalmers decided to hit Collierville again on November 3, but with disastrous results.[74]

Forewarned, Colonel Hatch concentrated a force at Germantown to best defend both villages. He took Chalmers by surprise and drove him steadily south. Hurlbut dispatched the 25th Indiana Infantry to garrison both Germantown and Collierville.[75] They wanted no repeat of the destruction of the cavalry camp at Nashoba. The 25th was specifically ordered to occupy the fort and area around Germantown and to guard the railroad.[76]

◆ ◆ ◆

When Chalmers made his attack, Richardson was unable assist. His Brigade had been reduced to the 12th and 13th of only 300 and 200 men respectively and one battery of six-pounders. The rest of his command was

Mississippi cavalry. They had been thrown out on the east flank, headquartered at New Albany and defending as far as Tupelo.[77] This was too far from Richardson's preferred field of action, and his officers and men continued to be disgruntled.

On October 28, he wrote a long carping letter to headquarters which is worth quoting for its vivid picture of the condition of his West Tennessee cavalrymen and its Germantown men.

> It is known to you that my Tennessee troops were raised for service in West Tennessee.... The design of all of which was to enable me to raise as large a mounted force as possible in West Tennessee....
>
> I collected together parts of three regiments in August last, and came through the lines to this neighborhood to arm and equip my men; then to return to West Tennessee, collect the balance of my three regiments (in all about 2,000 men), and add to the forces.

He then described how, instead he was assigned to Chalmers' command and

> Although not equipped and fully armed, I was ordered to the front, and with my men half naked and half starved, I have earnestly endeavored to serve the country in the late campaign. I was placed in command of the Northeast District of Mississippi, and under the orders of Brigadier General Chalmers, and now I am back here. My men, nearly destitute, have deserted and are deserting me to go home and get clothing and bedding.

"If I am to protect this district and Mobile & Ohio Railroad, you must give me more men, arms, equipments and ammunition." They were not even able to do their own cooking, dependent on begging citizens."It leads to straggling and demoralization.... I want clothing, shoes, and blankets for my naked freezing men."[78]

Indeed, According to Chalmers,"Colonel Richardson's command had been greatly reduced by details sent after clothing and by desertion.... Colonel Richardson was unwell, and the force thus raised, which amounted to only 270 men, were placed under command of Colonel J.J. Neely."[79]

Then on November 13, he begged General Johnson "to permit me to move on the line of ... (M&C RR) and destroy it; at the same time execute my orders with reference to enforcing the conscription laws in West Tennessee and collect my command, the larger part of which is now in West Tennessee. . . . I can destroy the road and hold West Tennessee until I can get all my command together."[80]

Several developments encouraged such dreams. For what it's worth, the map company of James T. Lloyd produced one of its 1863 railroad maps purporting to reveal the areas actually controlled by Union forces, and those still "in Rebel hands," which presumably meant, for Tennessee at least, that sentiments had turned so strongly against the occupiers that support for guerrillas and raiders was nearly total. It contended that by October there was just a narrow band running down the Mississippi River and along the M&C in Federal hands. Everything above and below that line was "in Rebel hands," with Germantown and Collierville on the fringes of Union control.[81]

Richardson had also picked up reports that the Federals were abandoning all their defenses along the railroad.[82] They soon realized, however, that what was occurring was a major relocation of troops defending the rails. As part of this redeployment, in November, the 72nd Ohio under Lieutenant Colonel Charles G. Eaton occupied Germantown. Hatch's 3rd Cavalry Brigade remained in place there, patrolling from Memphis to La Grange.[83]

Then came the most significant change for the local scene. On November 14, President Jefferson Davis assigned Nathan Bedford Forrest to command in West Tennessee, and Richardson was ordered to report to him. When Forrest arrived to take command, he had brought only a small force of 271 men. Forrest immediately assessed the situation, including the weakness of Richardson's available force, and decided that he should descend on the rail line and scour West Tennessee for conscripts.[84]

Richardson's reports to Forrest provide another picture of the state of his West Tennessee troopers, unfortunately clouded by his constant claims of a ghost-like component extant across the border. His ordinance-sergeant's report indicated that none of the men were well equipped. There was 1 ambulance and 6 wagons with 22 serviceable mules. Everything else was unserviceable.[85] In another ordinance report of November 20, there were only 247 serviceable horses. Armaments represented another problem.[86]

His picture of West Tennessee men was revealing. There were always small, independent teams wandering the countryside, recruiting, foraging and harassing the enemy. Men who had gone home on their own initiative, who would normally be considered deserters from regular units, were given the benefit of the doubt since they did indeed need to replace clothing and attend to affairs at home. They had enlisted in the expectation of being close to home and able to do so. Consequently, Confederate commanders were not generous in issuing supplies. Regardless, Richardson, with a force still little more than irregulars, would soon penetrate West Tennessee under Forrest's command, intent on consolidating his army of ghosts and expanding it into a major combat arm.

General Johnston ordered Lee and Forrest to launch a joint raid "to break up as much as possible of the Memphis and Charleston Railroad." Then Lee was to return to Mississippi while Forrest moved into West Tennessee with only about 500 men. Forrest headed north with Richardson, arriving in Jackson on December third. Lee and Chalmers hovered in north Mississippi always threatening to move on the railroad as a distraction.[87]

From the surviving communications, the impression one gets of the entire expedition is that of a swirling dance among the armies of both sides. Federal commanders constantly exchanged intelligence and rumors of Forrest's whereabouts and his intentions. They dispatched units in an effort to box him in. He in turn maneuvered to cross the icy streams and avoid major Union forces, while striking where he hoped to break through.

By December 4, Union intelligence reported Forrest ranging as far as Kentucky, threatening all the railroads.[88] On December 5, Hurlbut, always easily intimidated, ordered the commanders at Germantown and Collierville to destroy the bridges over the Wolf to prevent him from attacking Memphis.[89] On December 12, all reports placed Forrest at Jackson, assembling all his forces for an attack on the line. Initial estimates put his growing force at 4,000, while straggling parties of conscripts were crossing the line west of Germantown headed south. Conscripts and volunteers were drawn to Forrest, fifteen hundred of them reportedly unarmed. Federal cavalry was dispatched to come at him from all directions.[90]

In late December, he crossed the Hatchie and moved south to LaFayette. On the 25th Hurlbut repeated his command to destroy the bridges over the Wolf and to picket all crossings. All men at Germantown and White's Station were to be mounted on mules to ensure thorough coverage of the Wolf.[91]

On December 27, Forrest's troops took the inadequately dismantled bridge across the Wolf at Lafayette (Rossville) and drove the Union forces advancing from Collierville back into their fortifications. He rapidly got all his unarmed men, wagons and captured cattle across and moved off south.[92] Richardson was apparently still roaming around West Tennessee at year's end.[93] Forrest had so badly shaken up Federal defenders that they abandoned all efforts to operate the M&C Railroad until February of the next year.[94]

Richardson's units spread out conscripting, bringing his brigade up to about 1000. Some entire units apparently remained to operate north of the railroad, while Forrest claimed to have brought out about 3,300 men.[95] It would seem West Tennessee would have been thoroughly drained of men suitable for service. Once again one wonders about the mixed emotions among the civilian population when for the third time in the year, full-scale war came so close to home. Was their enthusiasm reignited? Or were they just experiencing more depressing disruption and uncertainty?

Life in Germantown during 1863

This is a good point to attempt a picture of the town's experiences during the year. It had begun with a very heavy occupation by a suspicious and nervous Federal force. Despite the constant pressure on those forces, their coexistence with the locals gradually bred a familiarity that eroded much of the tension. Local enthusiasm for the cause became less supportive. By the time of the raid on Collierville, Confederate troops had the impression that the locals had succumbed to collaboration. We need to turn back to the beginning of the year to trace the experience of the townsfolk.

Life around town experienced uneven improvements over the previous year's rollercoaster ride in no-man's-land. One problem had been the breakdown of local government. With union occupation in June of 1862, county government had withered rapidly. After the Quarterly Court adjourned in May of 1862, it did not resume again until October 6, when Judge Pettit reconvened it. Grant's orders establishing martial law in February replaced most court authority with military jurisdiction. Its authority was limited to appointing road overseers and handling estates. It ended its autumn session on December 2, and never met again.

Soon, General order 100, 1863 terminated any ambiguity about Grant's authority over criminal and civil law.[96] In April 1863, a Civil Commission for the District of Memphis would perform most duties of the former court, and city administration.[97] However, its governmental attentions never extended as far Germantown.

The town and district magistrates were on their own. Then, after occupation of the town, anyone serving as either district or town officials had to take an oath of loyalty. So Judge Pettit, Justice Walker and Constable Lewis were removed. The effect of martial law was to suspend town charters and their government. Nevertheless in Memphis, wherever they had taken oaths of loyalty, the district justices of the peace and the Memphis police court seem to have continued functioning.[98] Consequently, Civil District Eleven's justices and constables could have taken the oath and fallen in line. It would take time for them to feel confident to do so.

Federally sponsored efforts to restore any form of responsible government were frustrated by their lack of control over the area. By the beginning of 1863, the first efforts to elect a unionist government for the state under the appointed military governor Andrew Johnson had completely foundered. The House of Representatives voided the December 1862 Congressional election in several West Tennessee counties. They were so infested by guerrillas that holding an election was dangerous. General Hurlbut proclaimed Shelby and surrounding counties as areas in which a fair vote could not be obtained. A significant factor was Forrest's December raid of 1862, for its disruption of the election frustrated hopes of restoring self-government.[99]

Throughout 1863, the county east of White's Station remained outside Federal efforts to establish and maintain any civil government and law enforcement despite heavy occupation. Since the failed December elections had produced no county officials, by June, General Veatch found it necessary to appoint a sheriff and coroner for Shelby County.[100] Such an appointed sheriff undoubtedly avoided risking his neck outside the city.

By August, federal tax collectors had arrived in Memphis to assess and collect property taxes. In 1862, Congress had applied to the "insurrectionary districts" the 1861 tax levied to support the war. However, since the collectors' reach did not extend into the county, it would not be collected in Germantown until after the war.[101] Nevertheless, all land owners would have to pay such taxes eventually, and then their property could be seized and sold to pay arrears. That threat heightened after Governor Johnson ordered that state taxes could only be paid with United States notes rather than the rapidly depreciating Tennessee State notes or illegal Confederate money.[102] Everybody's Confederate bonds and bills might still be exchanged locally, but at considerable discount. The mixture of the other notes that were available must have been chaotic. All this added further to everyone's sense of uncertainty and foreboding.

At least, the establishment of brigade headquarters at Germantown brought the presence of a provost marshal, Captain W.P. Moore, to establish some semblance of law and order. In addition to disciplining marauding and thieving soldiers, any locals who created serious problems would come to his attention and fall under military law. Citizens sabotaging military forces would go before a courts-martial, and could be executed. He had the power to arrest citizens suspected of spying, or smuggling, and hold them indefinitely or send them to Memphis for incarceration. Since all civilian courts were suspended, other crimes such as theft or acts of violence against fellow civilians were tried by a military commission. Locals could register complaints about the offenses of soldiers, and perhaps get some justice. The marshal also assumed responsibility for more routine civil affairs.[103]

In essence, he was both sheriff and judge for the entire area, completely independent of the local commander. Local memories of always appealing to the commander for help or grievances represent a lack of knowledge about relations between citizens and federal authority. Nevertheless, brigade and corps commanders also made decisions that affected citizens and carried out orders to punish locals for supporting partisans. Outside the town where regimental camps were located, citizens would have made appeals against his troops to the regimental commander. The brigade commander at Germantown granted passes to go through his picket lines. Of great importance, however, most marshals also concerned themselves with the wellbeing of needy women, children and the elderly. Supplies were issued to those in need, and passes were provided for local farmers who had food to bring into town for sale at regulated markets, and for anyone who needed to go to Memphis.

Of course, the corollary to such efforts to maintain peace and order was a determination to stamp out opposition. Marshals collected intelligence on the local population. The orientation of every household was of interest, and relief and just settlements could be doled out as rewards for compliance. Those identified as die-hard secesh became candidates when local guerrilla activities warranted expulsions and confiscations.[104] Perhaps intelligence about the attitudes and behavior of preachers and their congregations determined the fate of their churches. Also, the marshall's presence brought a steady stream of Confederate prisoners for an initial interrogation before being dispatched to

ILL. 7 Provost Marshall Provides Supplies for Locals. *Leslie's Weekly*, 11.29.1862. A common humanitarian practice, it may have been available on occasions of near famine during the period of heavy occupation at Germantown.

Memphis. Although disheartening to locals, it offered a chance to give succor to captured friends and relatives. Townsfolk scanned the faces of each arrival hoping to see someone alive and well.

After the fall of Vicksburg, Grant sought to restore a greater sense of peace and order. On August 1, he issued General Order No. 50 applying to Kentucky, West Tennessee and Northern Mississippi west of the Mississippi Central Railroad, all of which he proclaimed to be free of "regularly organized bodies of the enemy." Since it was to discourage "the presence of armed bodies of men among them," he announced that he would impose "the most rigorous penalties" on all irregular cavalry not mustered and paid by the Confederacy, all persons conscripting or apprehending deserters, all citizens aiding them, and anyone firing on unarmed trains or boats.[105] Obviously his threat applied to any civilian playing guerrilla, scout or informant. The assertion that conscription was forbidden was, however, an ineffectual claim. Most importantly, he strongly reiterated prohibitions against troops molesting peaceful civilians and restricted the confiscation of property to that approved by a "corps

ILL. 8 Confederate Prisoners Coming into Town. *Harper's Weekly*, 4.25.1863. As a point for initial interrogation, it was a common event at Germantown during 1863; residents had an opportunity to look for and succor friends or family members.

commander" and with provision for reimbursement to loyal citizens. Such an order was unrealistic, because decisions about confiscating needed supplies had to be made at the brigade and regimental levels, or even lower, depending on the disbursement of the unit. It was probably just a gesture at restraining undisciplined pilfering.

Under the authority of the brigade commanders at Germantown, the local quartermasters ordered confiscations of food, fodder and firewood from area planters. Nevertheless, William Hack had $330 of corn, meal and meat requisitioned for the commissary without receipt. In December, the troops burned 8,000 of his fence rails for firewood. As they were decamping, a soldier took away a mule, claiming to be under orders to do so.[106] It would only be after the war that things became settled enough for him to apply for and get reimbursement. Long after the war, Joseph Brook's widow, Agnes vainly made a huge claim for over $11,000 in damages.[107]

At least occupation ended the necessity to go to Memphis to apply for restitution, for the Provost Marshall or the commander over the offenders could be easily approached. One incident, however, clearly reveals the limited effectiveness of efforts to curb unauthorized confiscations, especially petty pilfering. A story told by the men of the 9th Illinois Cavalry reveals what they thought was a clever trick on a local planter. A few members of Company F

> corralled a negro who was cultivating cotton, and set him to digging potatoes, while they sat on the fence overseeing the job. Soon the old planter came out complaining "He had no potatoes to sell," but finally said they worth a dollar and a half per bushel. When they got the potatoes they wanted, the boys handed him a Confederate bill for five dollars. The old fellow asked "If that was a greenback." And was told "No, that he being a rebel should be willing to take that."
>
> He went to their captain. "Captain Perkins gave them a sever lecture in the presence of the old planter, but when the rebel had left, he told the boys, "They might steal all they could from the rebels, only they were to be sure that they were not caught at it."[108]

✦ ✦ ✦

Whatever peace and order occupation might have provided, it was limited to within the fortress island of heavily occupied Germantown. In addition to the headquarters and the regimental camps at the heart of town, a regimental camp lay tight by the eastern side, another to the north-east at Brunswick Springs, and another further east at Forest Hill. On the north, the cavalry sat in the Nashoba Tract. South of town a camp occupied the lawns of a planter, probably Kimbrough's. Just to the west of town, a camp was on the Brooks plantation. Well into the twentieth century, one could see the remnants of trench-works around this campsite.[109]

With the ever-present threat of raiders, such light fortifications were essential for camp security. Furthermore, in January Grant had ordered that at every military post or station, stockades be built. General McPherson promptly elaborated, "at all the points to be guarded, defensive stockades must be constructed to render the command safe against a sudden cavalry dash."[110] The artillery fortification that "commanded Germantown" was one such. Facing overextension along his new line, General Oglesby apparently felt that the defenses already constructed were inadequate. On June 3, he ordered, "Wherever you post detachments, you will immediately have them entrench themselves, by earthworks or stockades, in commanding positions, and so that they will cover the works they are to defend."[111] Shortly thereafter, Colonel Pease constructed an earth-work redoubt on the curve in the rail line east of Germantown that had been a frequent target.[112] Beyond these fortified perimeters, a line of pickets extended out to about two miles to provide advanced warning of attack.

Around these islands of security, guerrillas, partisans and raiders buzzed like angry hornets. Even the picket lines were porous, so small units could get close in. As we have seen, spies wormed their way into town, and even the camps themselves. Union soldiers who sneaked out of camp to pilfer risked the vengeance of partisans. If the townsfolk experienced the mixed blessing of occupation protection, the farmers further out were still in no-man's land. Country women rarely ventured from home to get into town.

The locals actually lived in three zones with different degrees of security. Except where the Wolf River bottoms provided cover for partisans, the northern section of the district along the State Line and M&C at major concentrations such as Germantown and Collierville was ostensibly secure from renegade pilfering, but not "official" federal confiscations. Outlying farmers could at least reapply what resources they still had to cropping. Unfortunately the fences were gone, so fields remained unprotected from wandering livestock. South of that line down toward Nonconnah lay a second zone of less security, though more secure than before. Confederates could not so easily forage and Federals were restrained. South of Nonconnah was still a true no-man's-land.

◆ ◆ ◆

In any case, by January 1863 full occupation had begun. Germantown had been damaged, but eyewitness descriptions paint different, conflicting images of the degree of destruction and the attitudes of Germantown folk. Comparing these images produces a mixed bag of first hand impressions that simply demand presentation with some effort at critical evaluation. They cannot be easily squared.

The first was recorded in the diary of Fletcher Pomeroy, a trooper of the 7th Kansas Cavalry Regiment (Jayhawkers) which had just taken up residence. It was dated Monday, January 26.

> This town is fifteen miles east of Memphis on the Memphis & Charleston Railway, and but a short distance from the Mississippi and Tennessee State Line. Like most southern towns it has suffered much

from the War. Some houses have been burned, and others are deserted and are used as soldiers' barracks. This country around is the best I have seen in the south.[113]

On the thirtieth, Captain Harvey Greene of the 8th Wisconsin arrived to defend the line until March.[114] He described a more severe desolation.

GERMANTOWN, TENN., JAN, 30.

We are fifteen miles from Memphis. This was once a little town, on the railroad, of a few hundred inhabitants; but it is all but depopulated, except by soldiers. The houses have been demolished, mostly, and there is not a vestige of a fence or stake or board to be seen. One brigade only is here. We have a circular earthwork, but there is no enemy near.

NOTE. The ladies came and remained two or three weeks. . . . We had a boarding place at a rebel woman's house, just outside of our camp—the men of the household all being in the rebel army.[115]

His wife wrote a letter home. She was prone to romanticizing, dramatic embellishing, and denigrating the locals. She described the train ride from Memphis as "through a suburban country" with "magnificent suburban homes," typically "of brick, large and beautiful, with a world of verandas above and below, statues scattered about the grounds, a large fountain, and the remains of trees, shrubs and banks of flowers." But we "cannot realize what war is till we see it." The homes were occupied by Union soldiers, who had put them to rough use, confiscating whatever they needed. "Can we blame them?"

Captain B. and wife, Harvey, Nelly and I are boarding in a secesh house. The hostess is a widow with a spinster sister. O, but they are rebels, they would be glad to cut our throats or poison our food if they dared; but their bread and butter depend on what they can get from Union soldiers. Such a desolate place I never dreamed of, not a tree, fence, or post—not anything that could be utilized as firewood remains. Not a sign of anything like gardens or field of grain—nothing but ground, flowering shrubs, and a few houses remain of what was once a prosperous village. Every mill, shop or factory lies in ashes; their sites are occupied by a brigade of Union soldiers. It is a hard sight, but it is one of the curses of war.

If *"every* shop and factory" had not been destroyed as Mrs. Greene stated, certainly some were. The Southern Star Gin Factory was totally burned. As we shall see, however, Mrs. Green's images of total destruction were overdrawn.

Other passages tell us about relations between occupiers and citizens. One grew from her indignation about slavery. "The widow still keeps a few negroes; but the most of them had run away. All the cooking is done in the quarters, as they call them [cook house?]. Mrs. B. being quite ill, I have to go out there frequently for little things for her comfort. How those two old cats watch me."

She had befriended "a cute little darkey girl named Becky, about twelve years old. . . .

> She would follow me around and every chance she gets she will say, "Dear Missus, won't you take me with you to the Norf?" I gave her one of Nelly's picture books. . . . I tried to teach her the alphabet from it, but the old cat caught me at it and took her book away.[116] We were all standing on the front porch to-day surveying the lovely weather and enjoying the sweet fragrance of the roses and honeysuckle. The two rebel women of the house joined us. While chatting away, we heard the low rumbling of an approaching train. The railroad runs directly in front of the house a few rods distant, with quite a deep cut a short distance before reaching the house. As the train steamed by, loaded with Union troops on flat cars, the officers' wives waived their handkerchiefs. The secesh women stood and glowered and hoped the train would go to pieces and kill them all. I wanted to wring their necks. . . .[117]

Mrs. Greene's veracity is undermined by her colorful references to blooming spring and summer flowers during the "two or three weeks" she was in town, January through February. She seemingly had a penchant for embellishment. Of course, puzzling internal contradictions in letters and journals are not uncommon, especially when the temporal references buried in them could be inaccurate or misleading. They are hard to explain, and leave us uncertain how to handle them. Some of the equally stark contradictions between her writings and those of different persons that will follow really confound efforts to reconstruct town life accurately. The experience of the trauma of war has vastly different effects on observes and their memories.

One more of her stories completes a vivid picture of the hostilities generated by the war, and the inability of women on either side to empathize with the other. The officers and their wives were housed in a wing of the house, with its own exterior door opening on to a porch in the rear. One night a Confederate soldier, "dressed in butternut from head to toe," let himself in, but was driven off by her husband. Of course, they assumed the worst. "He was evidently someone sent to get what information he could of the two women of the house, and had gotten into the wrong side of the house."[118] Neither his light-brown homespun butternut uniform nor his intrusion identified him as a spy.

Of course, she could have been correct. Women were key players in Confederate intelligence, and one boarding officers would have been a good source. Whatever, as she simply assumed the "glowering" face of the widow meant she was conjuring a train wreck, she also assumed stories about secesh women was true in this case.

Not only was it easy for Mrs. Green to condone the confiscation and abuse of property by her "boys," she was totally unable to empathize with a *nameless* woman, widowed and without means, having to house self-righteous and privileged officers' wives. She wanted to throttle this woman because she did not rejoice at the sight of more Union troops rolling on to fight and kill her loved ones. War does more than destroy lives and property. It warps minds. The occupier can always minimize the suffering of the defeated with the idea that they brought it on themselves by supporting the war, as though that were a unique quality of only the enemy population.

That diary of Fletcher Pomeroy provides a more sensitive picture of local conditions. He related the suffering of the citizens. Spring came late in 1863, and planting had not begun. The lack of available labor prevented any significant farming. The consequent lack of food and income would bring a hard year, with nothing left to fall back upon. Not only were many slaves and men folk gone, but so too were the draft animals for plowing. Their cattle, hogs and poultry had been eaten, their hay and feed-corn confiscated. After less than a year of Union presence, locals faced conditions bordering on starvation.[119] The poorer the family, the worse their fate. As we shall see, this description was more accurate at the beginning of full occupation.

Pomeroy emphasized the mixed nature of the early occupation experience. It was not entirely one of mutual suspicion and hostility. Not only had they been able to establish rather comfortable quarters in their camp, but they had also developed pleasant acquaintances in the neighborhood.[120]

Most sources contend that initially contempt was what women felt toward Yankee occupiers. Overt displays of hostility lessened, however, at least out of necessity. Extended periods of occupation led to fraternization. Most such were merely amicable, for one soldier compared their departure in April to almost like leaving home.[121]

As time wore on, many relationships became warmer. For instance, there was at least one lasting romantic liaison. According to a version as told by his comrades, Captain Louis F. Booth of the 9th Illinois Cavalry married a Germantown belle on August 6. While recuperating from an illness, he had "boarded at the house of a citizen by the name of Molter (Molitor)." The lady in question was their "daughter, a Mrs. Carroll, a young and handsome widow, whose husband had been killed at Corinth the previous summer in the rebel army." They fell in love, but she was already engaged to a lieutenant of an Ohio regiment. "Her parents favored the Lieutenant and were determined she should marry him at once." So the couple decided to elope one evening after all were abed. She climbed out the window and they rode off. "The Rev. R.J. Lockwood, Chaplain of the Forty-ninth Illinois Infantry, was summoned. The inmates of 'Crinoline Avenue' were awakened from their slumber, the circumstances explained, and there . . . the twin were made one . . . , just at the hour of midnight."

> The parents knew nothing of this until the next morning, when they found their daughter missing. . . . (F)inally they heard a rumor that she was in camp, when they came down post haste, and were met by Mrs. Gifford of whom they enquired, 'If their daughter was in camp?' The reply was, 'She is.' 'Where is she?' 'With Captain Booth.' 'What right has Captain Booth to have her in camp?' 'A very good right, she is his wife,' replied Mrs. Gifford. When the old couple heard this they whipped up their horse and left camp much displeased, and without any effort to see their offending daughter, whose unsuitable conduct they never forgave.[122]

The camp was well removed from town, so boarding in town was limited to invaliding personnel. The unexplained reference to Crinoline Avenue, must have been to an area in the camp reserved for the wives of the regiment. Mrs. Gifford was the wife of the regiment's Major Ira Gifford. Clearly the Molitor's did not object to their daughter marrying a Yankee, but rather her violating her pledge to marry the lieutenant. She must have left permanently when Booth's regiment was relocated.

To continue the contrasting descriptions of the town's condition, when this 9th Illinois had arrived in the area in April, they were ordered "to move out on the Memphis & Charleston Railroad, and we marched fifteen miles to a pleasant little place called Germantown. The camp here was situated in woods one mile from the town." Neither in this passage nor any other in the regiment's history written after the war were there any references to severely damaged property. Perhaps beautiful spring weather and improvements of property produced different perceptions.

In another contrast, a third observer, a headquarters staff officer of the 52nd Illinois Infantry painted another picture. Things had improved further by August when he was writing. He clearly contradicted images of great destruction, depopulation and hostility. "There are a good many citizens here. The majority of them very well disposed.... The ladies have arranged to board at a very fine house available by a very pleasant appearing lady whose husband is a surgeon in the rebel army. The officers here say she is now loyal and is urging her husband to come home. I think we shall find it very pleasant here." And a couple of days later, "There are a great number of citizens inside the lines and command is going to be full of perplexities. These people are living quietly at home and ought not to be molested." He went on to confirm that unauthorized confiscations by the rank and file continued to cause problems. Also, "There is a band of cut throats hanging about our lines robbing citizens and soldiers that I am going to try to exterminate." Finally, "I think this is a very healthy place and a pretty pleasant one. Ladies are as abundant as blackberries some of them good looking and intelligent and nearly all very chatty and free."[123]

Aside from occasionally boarding Union officers, which provided some income, families might be forced to share their homes. For instance, Woodlawn, the Joseph Brooks home, well west of town off present Poplar Pike served temporarily to house sick and wounded of the regiment encamped on their land. Although they remained in residence, Mrs. Brooks found it suitable to play her piano "to sooth the soldiers."[124]

Compared to such impressions provided by outsiders, there is only one record left by a resident during 1863. Emily Lucken Mills kept a journal beginning in April that describes her everyday town life until she left in mid-June.

One reads about a mundane daily life that greatly contradicts traditional sources. She had always been preoccupied with her personal social relations and comforts in her pre-war letters, and that continued throughout the war. Such a minimal concern with the world around her undoubtedly affected the content and focus of her entries.[125]

Emily made absolutely no reference to any destruction of property or of Federal pillaging. It was as though she had forgotten all the traumas of 1862 amidst a more tranquil life. Yet it would seem that the Baptist Church must have been dismantled before her departure, for McCrillis and Sanford's troops would have needed its lumber for their camps well before their departure in August. Could she have been so indifferent to its fate?

Except for references to the presence of boarding officers in her family homes and those of the friends she frequently visited, there seems to have been little inconvenience. She belonged to a circle of twenty-somethings who constituted young adult society. Her husband had left on business shortly before the Federal capture of Memphis in 1862 and could not return, so she may have been living with her parents. Her father, Anton Lucken, ran the inn that continued to serve travelers, but also as a privately run 'officers' club,' where they dined. Her circle of friends visited each other daily, slept over, dined at neighbors' homes, entertaining themselves, and occasionally even officers, with piano music and singing. The young ladies moved about freely, often unaccompanied even at night, without any fear of harassment. Only one disadvantage—travel had to be on foot, since almost all horses and mules were confiscated except for the doctors, who needed their buggies to do rounds. They ate well, even deserts, on which she commented. They played girlish tricks, escaping the older people who tried to chaperon ineffectively. In short, Emily especially still led the life of a frivolous antebellum Southern belle. Her father's business guaranteed access to adequate food and other supplies.

Her picture of relations with the Federal officers is more complex, however. References to the boarders indicated little more than inconvenience. Her personal impression of the commander Colonel McCrillis, was that he was "a clever sort of Yankee." That of his adjutant is unfortunately illegible, but probably not flattering. She also revealed the fabled disdain of Southern ladies for the Yankees, but primarily for their alleged lack of manners. Noting that since occupation, she and most ladies had stopped attending church, she proclaimed

P. 19 Col. La Fayette McCrillis. Commander, 3rd Illinois Cavalry Regiment; 1863, Commander 2nd Cavalry Brigade and senior officer at Germantown.

I consider it under present circumstances not altogether the proper place for our ladies particularly young girls for the Yankees' impudence will be seen without any ceremony whatever step up to them as they leave the church doors and walk home with them. I know this has been done, they visit without an invitation which if they waited for they never would get, enter your house without knocking, seat themselves without being asked and do everything that is despicable and which a Southerner would never do.[126]

What is especially surprising, however, is her reference about attending church. All traditions insist that church services were forbidden like all other public assembly. The Presbyterian Church was purportedly confiscated for Federal use. Yet she specifically wrote, "Sunday 24th another Sabbath, Rev, Evans preached today." She also referred specifically to the girls leaving by "the church doors." If not at this early date, as we shall see, during the next year Reverend Evans would take the loyalty oath, so knowledge that he had always been a unionist might have resulted in his freedom to preach services. Yet Emily indicates that services had continued from the beginning of occupation. Had the occupiers not yet occupied the church building? Had that occupation been terminated? Once again, historians encounter sharp contradictions in the sources that are impossible to square. However, primary sources, such as Emily's, must trump undocumented traditions.

Equally surprising is the liberality of Colonel McCrillis and his kindness in considering the wants and needs of the town's civilians. When Emily received word that her husband wanted her to come out and join him "in Dixie," she went to McCrillis to request a pass through the lines for herself and friend Julia Pettit Cornelius and child, who would also join her husband. It is unlikely, however, that she made it clear that Mrs. Julia's husband was perhaps a partisan. With only a few perfunctory questions, he consented not only to her pass, but to allow her husband to come in close enough to take care of some business and wait outside the lines to meet them the next day.

Most curious is McCrillis' seeming indifference to the enforcement of stringent guidelines to prevent persons passing through the lines to attend to personal affairs or business without taking the loyalty oath. The distress of a lady still played effectively on "a Yankee gentlemen's" decisions. This same episode casts light on the intrigues and covert behavior of the occupied folk. People who moved back and forth from Memphis on the M&C conveyed messages into the town that had come through some underground route. Reverend Mills, her husband, was at least afraid to come to their house and lurked somewhere outside the camps until Emily executed her departure through the pickets. He was an ardent secessionist and probably involved in contraband trade.

♦ ♦ ♦

Despite her failure to mention it, the pilfering of household property had been a serious problem. Those "comfortable quarters" that occupation troops constructed were at the expense of local homes. According to a Federal officer, when establishing a camp, the men immediately requisitioned "some sort of fireplace, a floor, bedsteads, writing tables, stools, carpets, etc."[127] John Woodson allegedly lost every possession that was "movable or destructible." But he contended that at least his home survived because it was "frequently occupied" by Federal officers, probably meaning that he boarded them.[128] Family memories make it sound like their home was confiscated, though in reality "shared." The duration of the indiscriminate pilfering is unclear.

As opposed to officially ordered burnings, stragglers simply torched homes for the fun of it. Once, a rider tossed a burning fagot onto the porch of the Brooks home, Woodlawn. Only a prompt response saved their home.[129] Perhaps this was the sort of event residents experienced at the end of 1862 when Smith's Brigade reportedly "burned" Germantown.

There was actually some modicum of protection during the heavy occupation. Numerous accounts indicate that the extent of that protection may have depended on personal relations that developed. Some fragments relating to one case survive in the Woodson family's records. A Mrs. Walsh was visiting at Germantown during the summer of 1863, when some silverware in her wagon was stolen. Not only were outsiders now free to "visit" the town, but two Union officers independently involved themselves in the effort to retrieve her stolen goods. They had apparently become acquainted with Mrs. Walsh socially. William Walker became a go-between in the return of her property.[130] Why the records ended in the Woodson papers is unclear. Since we know Woodson was a Unionist, likely he, Walsh and Walker all had established good relations with officers housed in his home.

Having to rely on commanding officers for protection was certainly a hit-or-miss proposition. Discipline and control varied greatly among the units. Although the presence of a higher headquarters usually minimized the depredations, the variable character of high ranking officers offered no guarantees. Germantown witnessed one proof of that. In November, Major Thomas Herrod of the 6th Illinois Cavalry murdered his commanding officer, Lieutenant Colonel Loomis. After a dispute over a reprimand, he shot him three times at Lucken's Inn where the officers had been dining. Colonel Hatch had to prevent the troopers from lynching Herrod.[131] Witnessing such a complete breakdown of discipline among one's protectors certainly added little to anyone's sense of security.

Any initial hostility toward the occupiers had gradually diminished for reasons other than necessity. Some considered hatred and hostility simply unchristian. Former unionists sought accommodation. If the notorious men of the 7th Kansas had experienced some friendly relations, when the townsfolk encountered officers of better backgrounds, or fellow Masons, it was easier to develop civil relations. All over the occupied South by late 1863, families began to extend to their "visitors" something of the hospitality they would have before the war.[132]

Meanwhile, however, in many cases the determined resistance of one woman had dissuaded some vandals or reversed an officer's orders to burn or destroy property. Mary Thompson allegedly saved the old Webb school and family home twice. Once she simply stood in the doorway and forbade any soldiers to enter for pillaging. On another occasion, she persuaded a young Union cavalry officer, who had also been a school teacher, to rescind an order to burn the building. He allegedly did so out of respect for her courage.[133]

Ladies often had leverage against their occupiers. They discovered that most Yankee soldiers like Southerners respected white womanhood. Frequently all women had to do was to insist on being treated like ladies who had rights to certain property. Practically every area family tells stories of women almost forcefully preventing the confiscation of a horse or even retrieving it. Ladies felt free to assert themselves against the Yankees in ways their men could not dare. Women who suffered brutality at the hands of regular soldiers were rarely of "respectable" status. It was servants who received unwanted attentions.[134]

By 1863, the Federal Army had in place regulations and procedures for prosecuting offenders who committed felonies such as robbery, assault, rape and murder. They had every intention to prevent crimes against civilians that would disrupt discipline, but also to protect helpless victims in a theater of war, where rape is inevitable.[135]

Consequently, occupation gradually brought the abatement of the greatest fear that Southern women had felt at the approach of Federal forces. Rape by the soldiers was not common considering the potential. When it occurred in an occupied environment, the provost marshals and reviewing judge advocates honored the victims' testimonies and treated the culprits more severely than is often common in civil jurisdictions today, producing severe punishment. Military courts are always less respectful of the concept of "innocent until proven guilty," and enlisted men, the most frequent culprits, rarely had legal representation. Nevertheless, any unprotected woman in occupied territory was vulnerable, regardless of social standing, or race. Lower class whites and all black women, especially those whose worked near camps, were less respected by soldiers who assumed their status as camp followers. Even so, an unfortunate "respectable" woman could be ravished.[136]

Although one local event did not likely happen near Germantown, a member of the 7th Illinois Cavalry reported, "Yesterday, I was out to witness a scene of seeing three men shot for committing rape on a girl 12 years old. The girl has died since I understand in hospital."[137] The execution in front of assembled troops was intended to put an end to such atrocities.

Given the constant threat of guerrilla attacks and lightening cavalry raids, the occupation forces were always anxious to punish any local guerrillas who resumed civilian status by day. This put in jeopardy any adult male who had remained at home. One such was Robert F. Duke, the son who had stayed to manage the estates and protect the women while his brothers were away. They lived west of town and closer to the Wolf River. All the brothers reportedly had such strong family resemblances that they were easily mistaken for each other, and that almost got Robert hanged. The Duke lands adjoined Nashoba where Federal cavalry were encamped, so he was known by the soldiers. When his youngest brother Joe participated in the October raid on that camp, the troopers thought they identified Robert among the culprits. The commanding officer dispatched men to arrest him, and allegedly to "string him up immediately." He was lucky enough to stay under cover until the matter was settled somehow.[138]

◆ ◆ ◆

Solutions to problems facing civilians are revealed in a letter of W.R. Hackley, Federal Treasury Agent in West Tennessee, responsible for the seven counties around Memphis.

> The country has not been cultivated the past season and the people are suffering for food. My duty will be to grant them permits to purchase from Stores in this place. Small quantities of clothing groceries provisions &c—such as will last them two month and only on application of the head of the family.[139]

This system allowing families outside Memphis to purchase necessary foods and supplies had been established by the Treasury Department in June. The "loyal citizens of Shelby" had to apply for permits to purchase at the customhouse in Memphis.[140] This provided access to supplies greater than those available around the town, such as that needed for a large plantation. To qualify, however, one had to take the oath of loyalty and had access to the city.

By the time occupation had begun in January, anything in the town's shops that had survived the pillaging had been consumed. Since one could bring out of Memphis only supplies limited to their own family's use, merchants had no way to restock. To replace the local merchants, there was a licensed suttler who served the Federal troops. To provide items not supplied to the troops, these suttlers bought wholesale in Memphis and set up shop at the camps. Any townsfolk not allowed to deal with them directly could have done so through soldiers black-marketing or just being friendly. But to do so, one had to have greenbacks. They earned them by providing services to the soldiers,

ILL. 9 Suttler's Store, *Harper's Weekly*, 11.29.1862. Licensed private businessmen set up such stores to sell the troops non-issued items. Some local citizens with greenbacks could be given permission to make purchases.

but especially room and board to officers, like Mrs. Green's hostess, or Herr Lucken and Mr. Blair who ran inns.[141] An ostensible slave, Philip Cornelius, who described himself as working as "hotel boy," went every day to get provisions from the suttler's shop. He also went regularly into the regimental camps to sell milk and butter, perishable goods not available at the suttler's or through commissary issue.[142] There was a two-way commerce that benefitted the community and even its slaves who "stayed home." Only a few merchants, however, were able to benefit enough from such commerce that they survived the war.

Another advantage of occupation was the resumption of more reliable communications with the outside world. Passenger service out of Memphis resumed on the M&C, which had previously been limited to military use.[143] Mail service resumed through federal post, but of course, only to loyal states and occupied territories. There was some concern about expressing any political sentiments in one's mail. One correspondent from Kentucky warned, "I do not think a letter can be sent to us from Memphis or Germantown but that it will be opened."[144] Indeed it was the responsibility of the local Provost Marshal to know the attitudes of individuals among the population. However, J Dix Mills responding from Germantown seemed to think there was no opening of the mail in the occupied South, but rather by self-appointed Copperhead hunters in the North.[145]

Apparently almost as soon as full occupation had been established, ostensibly persons were free to travel from the North either for personal matters or to do business in Germantown. Boarding for such civilians was available at Lucken's Inn, so inns were not limited to providing for the needs of Union officers.[146] Presumably travel out of town through Memphis to the North for personal reasons would have been far more constrained and required a loyalty oath. Business with the North remained officially proscribed for Southerners.

Although rail service on one mail-passenger train had been resumed, unlike for the M&O RR, there were no advertisements for passenger service on the M&C in Memphis papers. Nevertheless, civilian traffic on that line was possible, but those who traveled ran the risk of the same guerrilla attacks that plagued the Federals. In May, Union officers' wives traveling to visit their husbands in Collierville had a fright just after leaving Germantown. The train had traveled slowly to avoid derailments, when word came that the line had been torn up just ahead. Several ladies became near hysterical, "expecting to be shot or taken prisoner." They took shelter in a nearby house, and learned that only about thirteen rebels had been in the vicinity. After less than an hour's delay, they resumed and soon crossed the picket lines two miles outside Collierville.[147]

Unlike Emily Mills, women burdened with responsibility for family and farm experienced much more stress. Diaries and letters confirm that by 1863 women and children in the occupied South were plagued by anxieties other than personal needs and safety. The difficulty of communication among family members on opposite sides of the lines added greatly to feelings of loneliness, abandonment and despair. The women had to assume burdens previously reserved for the man. Particularly onerous was the problem of controlling their slaves. Many simply "abandoned" their mistress, while others became increasingly demanding in return for continued service. Women who had subscribed to the old myth that their "charges" loved them, felt betrayed and even increasingly fearful. Thus was born a resentment grown from shattered pre-war illusions.

Undernourishment added to the risk of the common diseases that struck with added force. Nevertheless, people asserted their will to survive. During the tumultuous year of 1862, at least three women had given birth to children who survived.[148] On the other hand, the more frequent mention in correspondence of the deaths of children and miscarriages testifies to the effects of wartime privation.

Since Federal authorities considered medicines as contraband, women had to travel to Memphis and smuggle them out, concealed in their clothing.[149] Health-wise, a woman's visit to Memphis to get medicine was a risk in itself. A New York observer described the occupied city as unparalleled in its "filth, squalor, discomfort, disease, dirt and destruction." Unbelievably filthy streets and the risk of small pox greeted them.[150]

Another consequence of the Provost Marshal's presence was a check point at the town depot. Arriving passengers were subjected to search thorough enough to net women with contraband hidden in their voluminous skirts. Soldiers' wives or black women were employed for the searching. One victim, sixteen year-old Ginny McGhee, was headed home to Collierville with a bolt of gray cloth. Arrested and sent to Irving Block in Memphis and then a prison camp, she would die in custody. Subsequently area women abandoned the railroad and resorted to carriage trips by roads where searching pickets were more easily intimidated by an offended lady.

Also, Mrs. L.G. Pickett, got caught smuggling out of Memphis "one pair of citizens boots, and six or eight wool hats." For this, she was sentenced to six months in military prison at Alton, Illinois, and fined one thousand dollars. She would not be released until the fine was paid, perhaps an indefinite imprisonment.[151]

Of course, given the suspicion of partisan participation, it was always dangerous for an adult man to be moving about any distance from his home. In September, Mr. C.L. Huskey of Eads was visiting near town for unknown reasons when he was turned over to Provost Marshall Moore. After examining him, and extracting an oath of allegiance and a bond, Moore released him.[152] When an unnamed gentleman from Mississippi came under suspicion, he was also arrested. In his case, he was held at Lucken's Inn until cleared.[153] Both men were lucky to escape imprisonment.

As previously related, even the limited renewal of commerce was a fluctuating benefit. By the fall, Sherman's dreams about the willingness of locals to collaborate, resume the cotton trade and resist partisan efforts seemed to have come true. In September, the *Bulletin* reported the arrival of cotton caravans of up to one hundred bales. They had organized armed wagon trains. "We hope the time will come when trade can be freely carried on without fear of guerrillas." With income from their cotton, they could buy needed essentials.[154] Another encouragement was the elimination of a ten percent tax formerly levied on all merchandise delivered to the city.[155]

Many a planter or farmer had secreted away his bales, worth up to $500 each. Aside from the problem of avoiding the cotton-burners, the desperate farmers only got part of what speculators and merchants would reap on the inflated market. But by October, once again only small quantities were coming into the city.[156] Increased raider activity like Chalmers' raids greatly reduced federal control of the countryside. Then came Forrest's first incursion.

Whatever trade Germantown farmers may have been able to conduct with either Memphis or with military encampments was shut off almost completely in November, when Sherman again issued more stringent orders for martial law. He ordered the lines of pickets around the military posts of this command in Tennessee and Mississippi be closed. No citizen with goods was to pass in or out, except firewood and provisions, without the written order.[157]

Germantown fell within such a line of pickets. Now only the bare minimum of subsistence was allowed in or out. Some of the former benefits of occupation dried up. One could only take something out with a permit granted by the provost marshal. Clearly, whatever benefits that had accrued from improved communications with Memphis fluctuated throughout the year. Occupation authorities became almost capricious. Some days the lines would be open, others they were closed.[158]

Nevertheless, the people of Germantown tried to maintain some modicum of normal life, but the right to pursue some activities essential to maintaining life required one to take the oath. In Germantown, the provost marshal administered it. There it read,

> I do solemnly swear in the presence of Almighty God, that I will bear true allegiance to the United States of America, and will obey and Maintain the Constitution and laws of the same, and will defend and support the said United States of America against all enemies foreign and domestic, and especially against the Rebellious League Known as the Confederate States of America.[159]

❖ ❖ ❖

Formerly closeted unionists could now enlist in the Union Army. So far, only two or three can be positively identified. Joseph and James Hacher, an overseer and a farmer, living just across the Wolf in Civil District 7, joined Company D of the 2nd Tennessee Cavalry Regiment, U.S.A. Interestingly, a Galloway family and the Hachers formed a cluster of apparently related, slave owning, yeomen farms. Predictably by 1870, the Hachers were gone from the area, but the Galloways remained.[160] Families divided over unionism despite their ownership of slaves.

As many as nine other men may have served in Union regiments, seven of whom were no longer residents at the next census. Then in November, General Sherman issued impressment orders. "All persons residing under the protection of the United States . . . are liable to perform the same in a country under martial law." He ordered all officers commanding district, division, and detached brigades to impress such able-bodied persons" to fill up the existing regiments and batteries to their maximum."[161]

Although he meant this order especially to remove undesirables from Memphis, it clearly applied to the brigade commanders at Germantown. Regimental commanders were reluctant to acquire men of doubtful loyalty. Nevertheless, the remaining "able-bodied men" could end up in the regiments occupying Germantown. A member of the 7th Illinois, which had been recruiting up and down the M&C, reported in July 1864 that, "There had been a good many soldiers joined since we have been here."[162]

Area men now had to choose either to risk staying home or to flee south and serve there. From its base in Mississippi, the *Appeal* received reports of Shelby County men fleeing in "large numbers" to escape impressment. Men who had left the Confederate cause for whatever reasons were caught on the horns of a dilemma. Serve against their former friends and neighbors or return south to serve.

❖ ❖ ❖

In summary, we can construct some images of daily life in Germantown. War and occupation reshaped the work life of women in proportion to their place on the social scale. If they had no men or boys, they were entirely on their own. Some slaves remained, depending on what they were offered to stay, but unless they were children, they were not easily "controlled." If a woman of some education had connections in the city, she might find work there as nurse, clerk or teacher. Any other woman who fled to the city without family to shelter would have been thrown into a glutted labor market that offered many less desirable opportunities. The wife of a landless laborer had to find some sort of employ or lucrative craft, if not in the city then at the camps.

Those who stayed continued to produce whatever food and goods they could. They had to defend their kitchen gardens, fruit trees, milk cow and chickens. When animals were lost, there was no replacement. They continued to make their own clothes, often a patchwork of scraps. Even during this period of comparative security, women and girls living only a few miles from town ventured cautiously onto the roads, making no visits to town for the entire period. Those with nicer homes living near regimental camps boarded officers and their families. Some did sewing and cleaning for the troops. They sold things they still had, or they manufactured crafts for sale. In town, some tutored local children or ran small schools, clandestinely when necessary.

Doing business with the camps was an opportunity for the desperate yeoman wives. Selling and bartering milk, eggs, cheese, and any surplus produce had always been part of their lives. Unlike women of the respectable classes, they had never been relegated to the "proper" status of women. Trading into towns or Memphis had been part of regular life before, and it had always been an economic necessity. Initially seen and treated as disloyalty by Confederate patrols, even they began to tolerate it for the desperate. Pickets probably let them through Union lines.

Life would have been hard for the children, both physically and psychologically. The skirmishes that ran through town had been dangerous but brief. Only a few saw anyone killed, but undoubtedly others saw bodies, and the wounded. They may have heard the screams of amputations in the makeshift hospitals and seen discarded limbs. They suffered hunger and cold, and their workloads were increased at every social level. If teaching in school buildings was forbidden as traditions insist, clandestine schools like Mary Thompson's and home schooling survived, at least in literate families.[163]

The permanent loss of fathers, brothers or other relatives was the greatest shock a child could suffer, unless he or she actually witnessed violence against a loved-one. Even the absence of a father for the duration had its effects. The political posture of the family greatly determined the degree to which the child was infected with animosities that would linger.

On the brighter side, just as they had when the town was occupied by the mobilizing Confederate troops, the children were drawn to the drilling and parading of Union troops and their colorful bands. Soldiers are usually friendly and generous toward children, especially those who are suffering. Although I have found no records of commanders complaining of problems keeping children out of the camps, they were probably a nuisance and at risk whenever wagons and equipment were being moved. The northerners brought the game of baseball with them, and probably coached the boys in its play and in other sports as well.

If not occupied, the churches were damaged or destroyed. Ministers were closely watched, for many had been ardent supporters of secession. At least two partisan leaders had been ministers in other local communities. Nevertheless, the Methodist Reverend Tuggle managed to continue serving the southern part of his Hernando circuit throughout the war. However, he could not cross the picket lines on Nonconnah to visit the church in Germantown. At least he served the Bethlehem Church at Capleville near the Mississippi border, as well as his Mississippi charges. His plantation was located below the Nonconnah and outside Federal picket lines, so he could at least do his work south of the creek. Even missionary work to the slaves south of the lines continued under Reverend Jere Williams out of Mississippi.[164]

Except for the Presbyterian minister, Reverend Evans, Baptists and Methodists were probably deprived of their customary spiritual support, at a time when it would have been ever more important. Under these circumstances, women left alone organized house prayer groups and Sunday school classes—yet another example of the erosion of traditional ideas about woman's place. Whatever sectarian differences existed evaporated into truly ecumenical gatherings.[165]

Although Memphis' cultural activities and entertainments resumed during occupation, with all public buildings closed or occupied in Germantown, none such were possible there. Only in private homes did the old social entertainments of card games and parlor music, recitations and readings resume. Perhaps on special holidays like the Fourth of July, the troops held celebrations that the townsfolk could attend.

As previously reported, the depot witnessed the frequent arrival and departure of men, supplies and equipment. The roads were clogged with wagon trains and lines of pack mules. All this greatly eclipsed even the prewar traffic of seasonal cotton wagon trains. The accumulation of manure would have equaled that of a sizable city. Likewise, the human waste and garbage of a regimental camp created new sanitation problems

How badly the pains of the war and the conflict of loyalties had strained personal relations inside the community is not a matter of record, and little evidence casts light on the subject. During 1862, as loyal secessionists were actively supporting Confederate raiders, they still seemed to maintain civil relationships with former Unionists. Or so it seems from the story of Grant's close call with Jackson's cavalry in 1862. Dr. Smith was making a friendly visit to Josiah Deloach when he was shocked to discover Grant sitting on the porch. Knowing that after Smith departed he would make a hasty trip to report to Colonel Jackson, without actually warning Grant, Deloach simply terminated the visit with a slight discourtesy. Deloach, though an anti-secessionist, typically had a son, a son-in-law and three stepsons in the Confederate army. There is no indication that he suffered any consequences for his continued pro-Union sentiments and contacts. He still owned his home at Bray's Station as late as 1869 and probably continued using it as a summer or weekend escape from the city. Such were the differences within and among families and friends. Unlike the counties to the east and north where blood feuds erupted, convivial personal relations in southern Shelby County seemed to have survived. All shared the same hardships. Since locals collectively had reservations about secession until early 1861, during the course of the war, as divisions reemerged, each side was seemingly less intolerant of the other than was true elsewhere.

By December, a letter from the 72nd Ohio, camped south of town, reported that the town's former population of several hundred had shrunk to "probably not fifty." This was another excessively dark picture since other sources reported about one hundred, although even that represented a considerable flight. The total occupation force in town now consisted of only the 72nd, the 6th Illinois Cavalry and a light battery, all under the command of Major Eaton.[166]

From Slavery to Freedom

The war had not begun as a war for emancipation, but by 1862 Union occupation provide safe havens for escape. De facto emancipation began for thousands, and with it rising expectations. The result was rarely like the long-awaited jubilee. There was no planning or preparation for a mass of freed slaves with no ready means for integration into the economy, and no government agencies

ILL.10 Contrabands Coming into Camp, *Harper's Weekly*, 1.31.1863. Arriving in groups or individually, they wanted protection and hoped to find opportunities.

to care for the needy. Union field commanders would bear the initial burden, while fully preoccupied with the more pressing war. They made ad hoc policy while awaiting guidance from Washington. The guidelines that emerged were more politically motivated than by any real comprehension of the problems. As Federal agencies were created, they were staffed by well-intentioned officials whose judgment was colored by racial misperceptions. Throughout the war and into Reconstruction, the consequences for the liberated could be disastrous. The price of freedom was far greater than usually understood.[167]

Of course, numerous slaves sought freedom, left their owners and flowed into Union camps. Their initial jubilation confronted unexpected realities. At first the government and commanding officers vacillated over how to deal with the overwhelming numbers. They represented an impediment, and a sanitation and supply burden. Their persistence, however, resulted in some accommodation, and many found employment among the troops. Ominously, the designation applied to them was "contrabands," the same term used to describe goods that could not legally be sold to Confederates. That implied that they were still property, and they were often treated as such. Worst still, letters home from soldiers often indicated that many of their erstwhile liberators did not see themselves that way, and often doubted the desirability of the consequences.

Other slaves simply found themselves cut adrift as their owners fled the approaching army. They only took valuables they could carry and their most able slaves. The rest they abandoned with instructions to fend for themselves.[168] We will probably never know the extent to which this happened in the Germantown area, but the odds against former slaves trying to survive independently in no-man's-land would have been steep.

Memphis was the most likely haven for local slaves fleeing or abandoned. As late as September 1862, however, Sherman carped, "Not one nigger in ten wants to run off." Although he estimated there were 25,000 slaves within twenty miles of Memphis, nevertheless "all could escape & would receive protection here, but we have only about 2000."[169] It would seem that local slaves were cautious about their great opportunity. For whatever reasons, they were wisely weighing their options, even during the euphoria of the first months of disorder. Good reasons for doing so would increase, and they were close enough to Memphis to be well informed.

Shortly after occupying the city in 1862, Sherman had decided to employ as fortification labor all blacks who applied. Although they would be fed and clothed and given a tobacco allowance, they would not be paid unless their status as freemen was established. Officers were forbidden to employ them as personal servants, but a regimental commander could hire them as cooks and teamsters. But what is worse, the post quartermaster was allowed "when necessary, to take them by force" when not enough applied. Guards shot at them for trying to escape. Respecting the legal rights of slave owners, Sherman ordered, "The negroes employed as laborers will be allowed to return to their masters at the close of any week, but owners are not allowed to enter the lines in search of slaves."[170]

The Confiscation Act of 1862 merely empowered Union commanders to liberate and employ the slaves of men in service to the Confederacy. Otherwise when they encountered slaves of ostensibly loyal or neutral owners, they were theoretically required to respect "the owner's property." By January 1863, the preliminary Emancipation Proclamation had permanently freed the slaves of Confederates, but still not the others. Even after the final Emancipation Proclamation, most slaves were not automatically free in Tennessee. Lincoln had agreed to exclude Tennessee from his final proclamation. The presence of so many unionists slave holders militated against alienating them by abolishing their "property." Thus emancipation did not change the local situation. Slaves were not automatically free, and a slave owner could take legal action to have a runaway returned.[171]

In order to hold their slaves, only the shortsighted resorted to the old methods. The wiser increased practices of leniency, freedom to hunt and fish, rights to household garden plots, and less arduous hours. Slaves were free to earn money on the side. Most importantly, owners extended to slaves the system of share-cropping. Slaves who remained loyal might receive either cash payments, or a share of the crop. Numerous records indicate how prevalent this practice was in Shelby County. According to one local planter, at the end,

> it was almost a universal thing for all farmers, to give those negroes who still remained with them, a cotton Patch for their fidelity, in remaining with them, - Cotton, that season commanded a fabulous price, a small cotton patch made considerable money—there were other planters that gave money, which amounted to the same thing.[172]

Obviously the popular image of all slaves simply running to freedom is too simplistic.

According to recent studies, many if not the majority did not abandon their owners' lands, or at least stayed nearby. Others returned during or immediately after the war.[173] Some simply preferred the security or certainty of the place they knew, farms or homes where they had been treated relatively well—perhaps just the devil they knew. Some had even been successfully acculturated to their lot in life. Young Ned Kearney, who reported that "Mr. Kearney was good to his slaves and wouldn't let an overseer whip us," continued to work at the "Big House" throughout the war. Whenever Union soldiers came near, his job was to help hide the valuables in the river bottom, "to keep the Yankees from stealing them." Ned saw the Union Army as "the enemy." Of course, Ned had yet to achieve adolescence.[174]

Booker T. Washington argued that some slaves actually put a personal sense of responsibility above the lure of freedom. They literally stayed to protect their mistress and her children who had been left in their care. Their self-respect and sense of humanity prevailed.[175] What we have dismissed as post-war stories romanticizing slavery or as evidence of some slaves' lack of self-worth was actually a sign of great dignity.

The local census schedules of 1870 contained numerous black families with the surnames of former planters and smaller holders. For whatever reasons, such men and women chose either to stay or to return. The surnames of other slave masters are notably absent. That may reflect differences in the management style of former owners.

Most who remained, however, were hardly cowed. Everywhere owners complained of their growing "insolence and laziness." They were proactive in demanding concessions, and whenever contracts were negotiated or an owner resorted to physical punishment, around occupied communities like Germantown the erstwhile slave could turn to the Provost Marshal for enforcement and protection. On the other hand, the farther from town the more the owners had an ally in the partisans and guerrillas who loved to punish troublesome and escaped slaves. Even worse, they confiscated them for labor service to the Confederacy.[176]

Whatever, the lot of the blacks who remained in or around town was greatly improved during the period of intense occupation. For instance, Philip Cornelius, age 36 at the time, lived in the town. Presumably he was one of the Cornelius family's slaves. As previously related, he worked as a hotel boy, and went every day to get provisions from the suttler's shop. Philip also had free access to the camps to sell milk and butter to the cooks. Cornelius was marketing his owner's produce or that of another party for a share of the profits.[177] He would emerge at the end of the war with sufficient funds to buy land.

Quinton Roberts, age 25 at the time, was living three-quarters of a mile from town, perhaps at his new owner's farm. But he was free to come into town every night to be with his wife. She was owned by the planter Sallie Walker who resided for the duration on Bridge Street across from the church. Roberts also seemed to have had opportunities for free employment or enterprise.[178]

One phenomenon that also emerges from the 1870 census is the apparent movement by owners of their slaves from out-of-state into the area around Germantown. For instance, Rhoda (McKever), aged 39, had been a slave in Arkansas from at least 1857. She birthed her third child in Tennessee in 1864. It seems unlikely that she could have pulled off an escape from Arkansas to Tennessee with two children in-tow. More likely, her owner had moved them to Tennessee where they would be immune from emancipation. Similarly, Jane (Malone) and her children had been moved from Alabama about the same time.

✦ ✦ ✦

As for Germantown-area slaves who ran away, the ordeals they faced often made the price of freedom high. During the fall and winter of 1862/63, Grant's Department of the Tennessee organized camps for the "contrabands." More specifically, to bring under control the large black population that had gathered in Memphis by the summer of 1863, occupation officials needed a system of monitoring. The Provost Marshal required the registration of all blacks, whether free or contraband, and their registration was the responsibility of the white person in charge of them—"his lawful property . . . or is regularly employed by him." A subsequent order clarified by requiring "every free negro or mulatto, and every contraband" to enter "into the employment of some responsible white person," who would be required to get the registration. Without possession of a registration certificate, they were subject to arrest as vagrants and removed to the contraband camp. Apparently even the formerly self-sufficient freeman was now forced into a form of bonded labor. The most self-sufficient contraband could hope for nothing better.[179]

The officers and civilians responsible for the contraband camps were confronted with confusing legalities and complicated social issues. For instance, as occupation increased the problems of managing slaves, some masters actually evicted their slaves selectively, keeping only those they could use and control. This practice especially resulted in fracturing families.[180] Consequently, Union authorities had to deal with legal conflicts between freedmen and their former masters over family members. An owner could send troublesome parents to a freedmen's camp and keep their more controllable children. If the parents stole them away, the officer in charge of the camp would have to return them to the owner, "amid the tears and protestations of the mother."[181]

Despite all efforts at regulation, unregulated settlements persisted, clustered in Memphis and around military camps. Living conditions were horrendous in shanty towns of makeshift lean-toes and huts. Sanitation and potable water were non-existent. It was hard to find sanctioned work. At least some industrious men and women found ways to live by providing services to the troops, or setting up markets for crafts and such. By April 1863, some 2500 contrabands still tried to make it on their own, neither fed nor cared for by officials.[182] In the pursuit of freedom and self-determination, the ex-slaves had given up "security."

Those who had found work in Memphis were subject to more harassment and authoritarian controls. In October 1863, the Provost Marshal issued a new order revoking all previous passes for blacks. Presumably the earlier passes had become compromised. Again the white citizens who legitimately employed blacks had to give an affidavit for new passes. The theory being that if employers were held responsible for their servants' behavior, they would discipline them better. All those caught without passes would be arrested and sent to Ft. Pickering.[183]

As for those who were corralled into the camps, the superintendent of contrabands was busily assigning men, women and children to work on abandoned plantations under opportunistic entrepreneurs who contracted with the government for a sizable percentage of the profits. By the same token, planters who had stayed in place but who now needed labor also contracted to hire contrabands.[184] As one scholar has put it, "The contraband camps performed a similar function to antebellum slave pens where auctioneers held people until they were sold...."[185]

Of the 1380 men, women and children in the Memphis camps, 1236 were hired out as field hands, including all the children. Only 44 men and 70 women found work as craftsmen, teamsters or in domestic or camp service work. The system under which the camp laborers worked was described as

> One man regulates camp—another directs the working men, who are divided into squads of eleven; - the most intelligent selected as leader. Each three of four squads are under a white foreman, who directs and credits their work, notes and supplies their necessities.
>
> Erecting cabins, - preparing camp, ... sometimes most grossly abused—as, for instance, worked all day in water, drenched, nearly frozen, and then driven to tents for shelter, to sheds for sleep, without covering, and almost without fire and food, they come back to die by scores. Wages seldom paid—none in hospitals. The services of a large number have been stolen outright.[186]

At first, in these camps there was no shelter, the people were housed in tents while cabins were being built. During the first four months of the camp, 21 women had given birth, 103 men and women had died, and another 184 had taken sick. About medical care, Chaplin Eaton reported,

> Hospital not under charge of Superintendent. Its condition wretched in the extreme. Lack of medicines, of utensils, of vaccine matter. No report of admissions, of diseases, of deaths, or discharges. No attention

ILL. 11 Contraband Camp, President's Island. Tent shelters and poor services characterized all such camps.

to sick in camp by surgeon. Sent assistants out of my own office, having no Knowledge of medicine, but surgeon refused vaccine matter & medicines. Improvement to date. *Diseases*—Pneumonia sic, fevers, small pox.[187]

Not only were conditions inadequate in the camps at Memphis and the one subsequently established on Presidents Island, they only got worse. On January 12, 1864, Memphis papers reported that 356 of those settled on Presidents Island had frozen to death during a spell of unusually harsh weather.[188] It would seem that everywhere the camps deteriorated into deadly, uninhabitable compounds. Inadequate food, shelter and medical care, poor sanitation and insufficient clean water turned them into death camps.[189] The white people around them, whether Northerners or Southerners, were not especially sympathetic. Blacks were targets of contempt, and abuse.[190]

When the slaves who had stayed on around Germantown got word of these conditions, they probably preferred to negotiate for better conditions at home. Owners spread the word and offered a more paternal environment as preferable to the insecurity of freedom. The only other alternative for the men was enlistment.

◆ ◆ ◆

1863 would be the break-through year in which they were allowed to join the Union Army in great numbers. Local African-Americans would serve in units originally designated as "of African Descent," abbreviated A.D. to distinguish them from white regiments. Later they would be redesignated as "U.S. Colored Regiments." Among these, the 11th, 59th, 61st, and the 88th were specifically raised in Shelby County. Artillery units were also recruited there, the 3rd and 6th Heavy Artillery Regiments, and Batteries D, F and I of the 2nd Light Artillery.[191] For such men, the war became one for emancipation.

Whatever their attitudes about slavery, most Union officers initially had little respect for "coloreds" and certainly did not consider them suitable as soldiers.[192] At Memphis, however, General Hurlbut was desperate to man his artillery defenses. Encouraged by the report that the Navy had discovered that "blacks handle heavy guns well," he endorsed their service. On April 15, he launched recruitment for eight companies to man the heavy guns at Fort Pickering. They would be officered by whites, but NCOs would be drawn from black recruits. They would also receive the same pay and allowances as other artillerymen, in sharp contrast to the general practice of paying black troops lower wages. By December, it had expanded into two regiments (the 1st and 2nd Tennessee Heavy Artillery [A.D.], the 1st of 1,153 men, the 2nd of 878), and the Memphis Light Battery of 99 men.[193] The Memphis Light Battery, would eventually became Company "D," 2nd U.S. Colored Light Artillery Regiment; while Battery I of the 2nd was also formed in Memphis in April 1864. The 1st Regiment of Tennessee Heavy Artillery (A.D.) was renumbered the 2nd and then 3rd Colored Heavy Artillery in the spring of 1864.[194] The 6th Colored Heavy Artillery, which had originally been raised as the 1st Alabama Siege Artillery, was also stationed and further recruited at Memphis.[195]

Listed in 1870 census were at least 19 men who served in the 3rd Heavy Artillery who also bore the names of Germantown area owners in 1860. There were also 5 such in batteries E, F and I of the 2nd Light Artillery.[196] These cannot be identified precisely as former area slaves because names were not recorded in the 1860 slave census. Nevertheless, these names indicate probable involvement of some in these artillery units.

However, there is one former Germantown slave who can definitely be identified in the 6th USCHA. Allen James Walker who belonged to the widow Sallie Walker. When he enlisted at age 18 in the 1st Alabama Siege Artillery, Captain Lionel Booth refused to enlist him under his mistress' name, so he recorded him as Allen James.[197]

In December 1863 to further augment his corps, Hurlbut decided to raise one regiment of black infantry at Columbus, Kentucky, and four at Corinth, Jackson and along the railroad route to Memphis.[198] Thus began the recruitment of blacks specifically at Germantown. The 1st West Tennessee Infantry Regiment (A.D.) mustered in at La Grange in June 1863. It was first reported in the *Official Records* on October 31, 1863, as the 1st Tennessee Infantry (A.D.), with 815 men in Hurlbut's 16th Corps, where it spent its entire term of service in West Tennessee and North Mississippi. It would ultimately become the 59th U.S. Colored Infantry Regiment.[199]

Captain Jesse H. Darnell enrolled part of its Company I at Germantown, June 27, 1863. In this company, about 20 men bore surnames common among the slave owning families of the area. Among them, Henry Ellis, and Isaac Johnson would return to district eleven by the 1870 census.[200]

The first mention of the 2nd West Tennessee Infantry Regiment (A.D.) in the records occurred on September 16, 1863, listed as 2nd U.S. Tennessee Volunteers (A.D.). It too had mustered in La Grange during June through August 1863. Captain Malte Stuth, enrolled Co. D at Germantown in June, while Captains Henry Sturges and Charles S. Graff enrolled companies G and I at Collierville. By October 31, the regiment had 610 men. It was still at Moscow on December 4, when attacked by Lee and Chalmers. It was these men who held the bridge, ultimately repulsing the Confederate cavalry on that day.[201]

That action first brought local black troops the recognition they deserved. Such commendation by Union officers was progressive by the standards of the times. On December 17, Hurlbut's General stated,

> The recent affair at Moscow, Tenn., has demonstrated the fact that colored troops, properly disciplined and commanded, can and will fight well, and the general commanding corps deems it to be due to the officers and men of the Second Regiment West Tennessee Infantry, of African descent, thus publicly to return his personal thanks for their

ILL. 12 Negro Recruits at a Depot, *Leslie's Weekly*, 5.7.1864. Events like this occurred all along the M&C line, as they did at Germantown in 1863.

gallant and successful defense of the important position to which they had been assigned....²⁰²

Other commanders added their praise.²⁰³ It would eventually become the 61st U.S. Colored Infantry Regiment.²⁰⁴ At least ten area men with surnames of slave-owning families of Districts Ten and Eleven were in Company D alone.²⁰⁵

The Union Army avidly began recruiting freedmen and contrabands. Some gladly volunteered, others were tricked by unscrupulous recruiters, and some were simply dragooned to meet quotas. Regardless, without them, the Federals might not have won the war for lack of manpower. Nevertheless, there was no sense that bringing them into service required any commitment to their families, who either had to be left behind in slavery or without provisions. No one realized how much family support was needed to compensate for the service of blacks from the occupied South.

After the formation of black military units, their families became part of the flood of contraband refugees. By the spring of 1864, large numbers of such women and children had been concentrated at the camp at Memphis where at first they were getting government support. Adjutant General L. Thomas pressed for an end to this practice. He noted that some women were allowed to find work, but that none were entitled to government rations. The families of soldiers had to support themselves. Occupation officials at Memphis developed plans to send as many as 2000 women and children down river to Helena, Arkansas where they could labor on plantations. Needless to say, the men of other black regiments became "seriously alarmed."[206]

Rather than submitting to the regimentation and poor conditions in the contraband camps, many families tried to settle illegally close to the camps of their men. They were frequently seen as the worse kinds of camp followers. The complaint of the commander of one Colored Regiment stationed at Memphis was typical of such attitudes.

> There are several hundred negro women living in Temporary huts, between the camp of this regiment and the city, who have no visible means of support, and who are, for the most part, idle, lazy vagrants, committing depredations, and exercising a very pernicious influence over the colored soldiers of this Post. They are generally in a destitute condition, and their wants are partially supplied by soldiers of colored regiments who claim them as wives. The influence of these women over the members of my regiment is such, that I have great difficulty in keeping my men in camp nights, and have to be . . . vigilant to enforce the severest penalties, in order to maintain any thing like satisfactory discipline. . . . I earnestly request . . . that these families be removed to Presidents Island where they will be much better cared for, and where they will be no detriment to the service, and society at large.[207]

Captain T. A. Walker, the local Superintendent of Freedmen, was instructed to execute the proposal. He assigned the 63rd Colored Regiment to do the moving, but encountered serious resistance. The women refused to cooperate. "The husbands swear their families shall not be moved to the island and in some instances have come out under arms to prevent it."[208] Nevertheless, the order seems to have been carried out.

As for the men who enlisted, service in the African-American units would be at least as dangerous as in others, or more so. Official reports noted that of the 20,830 men enlisted in the Mid-South during 1863, probably 5,000 had "either died of disease, been captured by the enemy, or have become lost to service by other casualties.... The number of desertions have been few."[209] They were proving far more reliable than white soldiers on either side.

Of course, the Confederacy saw the enrollment of blacks in the Union Army as a threat. On October 30, 1863, General Johnston ordered General Chalmers to head off the problem. Chalmers sent detachments into the "Country adjacent to the enemies lines to arrest and remove within our lines all able bodied negroe men who are liable to be Captured by the enemy." Out of respect for the needs of the owners, only "those Capable of performing military duty will be taken." They could leave behind "Old men women & children." Thus any men immediately south of Germantown were likely to be impressed into Confederate "Govt work."[210]

Worse, the Federal recruitment of blacks to fight against Confederate troops, but especially to serve as occupation troops over the people who once held them as slaves, created both anxiety and hostility among Southerners. As the first formation of African-American troops began in the North in 1862, the *Appeal* forcefully affirmed the accuracy of a prediction made in the Chicago *Times*.

> ... in the event of negroes being employed as soldiers, the Confederates, "not recognizing him as a legitimate antagonist, will massacre the negroe when or where found in arms, or transport him to the cotton fields of the extreme South; they will not regard him as a prisoner of war, but subject him to all the penalties used in the case of the most uncivilized foe."[211]

Such were the brutal conclusions inherent in the racist arguments that had evolved to justify slavery. Many Southerners were locked into such logic and its conclusions. Although many would recoil from the idea that massacring blacks was justified, the prediction reflected the prevalent mood.

Thus, the presence of African American troops added to the growing hostilities between the two sides which would reach a fever pitch in the following year. One observer voiced a shrill warning to the readers of the *Appeal*.

> It is positively certain that the Federals are drilling four thousand negroes at Corinth. They are soon to be turned loose, to murder defenseless women and children in North Mississippi. The very

thought of the inhumanity and cruelty which is to follow, makes the blood run cold through the veins.[212]

Many black soldiers would suffer the consequences of becoming involved in developments that would bring the theater around West Tennessee to the point of explosion.

Army Life away from Home

1863 was also a year of attrition and hardship for the town's infantrymen fighting ever farther from home. Anderson Kirby of the 4th Infantry summarized his experience as "hard time," especially the Battle of Missionary Ridge as "devilish bad." It seems to have impressed him more than Shiloh. The wound he got there would pain him for the rest of his life.[213] For the remainder of the war, he rotted away in a prisoner of war camp.

The remainders of the 4th and the 13th participated in major battles like Chickamauga, Missionary Ridge and down through Georgia into the battles around Atlanta. No other Germantown men of the 13th fell until Joe Tuggle died at Peach Tree Creek, Georgia. A.B. Ellis had also been wounded in the leg at Missionary Ridge, while the then sergeant-major Needham Harrison, severely wounded at Chickamauga, was subsequently promoted to lieutenant.

In contrast to the images of hungry and ill-clothed troops, a description of Confederate prisoners of war coming through Memphis after Chickamauga paints a different picture. "They were mainly large built, coarse, blousy fellows, looking very healthy and illiterate. They were dressed in the whitish gray jackets and pants, and various patterns of hats, shoes and boots."

The appearance of these prisoners indicated anything but starvation or suffering from want of apparel.[214] The prejudicial assumption of illiteracy was unfounded. Up to eighty percent of Confederate soldiers were literate, as were the vast majority of those from Germantown.[215]

But conditions got worse as the year progressed. William Yates, who lived about six or seven miles north of Germantown in what is now Cordova, served in Company H along with Germantown men. He left a vivid description of what service was like in the 13th throughout the war.

> Lived very well first part of war—got pretty tough in latter part.
> Clothes were pretty scanty. Slept on grass or anything we could get to.

Had vermin so bad at one time, although I only had one more suit of clothes, took off the one I had on and burnt it to try to get rid of some of the lice.... One night it was so cold, and I had so little to keep warm with, I lay so close to the fire that when I awoke I found part of the tail of my coat (the only one I had) was burnt off. At another time, I only had one shirt and as it was so awfully dirty, decided to wash it. Had no vessel to wash it in, so went in the creek (and it was snowing too) and washed it—then took it to the fire to dry.[216]

Such snapshots of conditions at one moment illustrates how the quality of supplies varied greatly both at times and over the duration of the war Innumerable variables dictated when troops got supplies and when they had only what they could forage. As late as October 1863, men in the Tennessee infantry had been reasonably well supplied. Standardization was far less possible than for the Union army, but quantity and quality was probably only a little worse.

As for their morale, as described in the above account, "... they looked dispirited, and sick of the fighting business." James McPherson's study of soldiers' letters addresses the question of what kept so many of these men fighting with ferocious determination. He argues convincingly that what motivated them throughout the war were "the complex mixture of (Southern) patriotism, ideology, concepts of duty, honor, manhood, and community and peer pressure."[217] These were reinforced by the camaraderie that develops with combat among 'a band of brothers.' It is often said that slavery was certainly part of the ideology they fought to defend, but more accurately for most, it was opposition to abolition and its perceived consequences. Liberty was more uniformly the "ideology"—the need to defend both family and hearth and Southern society from the invader who would reshape everything of value. Also the religious revival that swept through both armies during 1863-64 ironically kept them going.

McPherson also examined the issue of broken morale and desertion. Relentless exposure to the horrors of combat, though harsh for all, break some but not others for reasons beyond comprehension. Many ultimately broke. The growing numbers of less motivated conscripts contributed disproportionately to desertion. Heavy attrition undermined unit cohesion. The defeats of 1863, the resultant loss of confidence in Braxton Bragg, and retreat from their home state resulted in hundreds of desertions.[218]

For instance, eight members of the 13th Tennessee Infantry show up on the

Memphis Provost Marshall's list of POWs during 1863, captured far from their regiment's field of operations. Unfortunately details of their capture or disposition were provided for only four of them. None were listed as deserters, so possibly they were ashamed to admit their status, which was a mistake. While two others were sent through the lines for exchange, those denying desertion were sent to Alton Prison. In contrast, one self-proclaimed deserter from the 12th Tennessee Cavalry caught at Germantown was released, apparently free to go home.[219]

✦ ✦ ✦

1863 had brought developments that enmeshed soldiers and civilians of both races ever deeper into the violence and hate that any war, but especially a civil war, can generate. It had seen the full birth of the irregular cavalry who plagued civilians so badly. In West Tennessee, first had come the partisans on the Confederate side. Then the Unionist government of Tennessee created its volunteer state cavalry to help combat that guerrilla threat. These two less disciplined and poorly controlled components vented their spleens on each other, and civilians on either side. Many charges and counter-charges were thrown around about the other's atrocities and depredations. Each alleged that the other side's special formations had no rights as soldiers when captured. Gradually, in an effort to gain some control over these irregulars and state troops, each side upgraded them to regular units in their armies, brigaded and integrated into corps with regulars. Nevertheless, they continued in their old ways whenever the opportunity allowed. During the next year, the mutual escalation of hostility created by their actions and by growing racial hostilities also infected the regulars on each side and would bring both sides to the verge of a veritable blood feud. It would leave a lasting legacy that would plague Tennessee and the Mid-South for generations.

8

1864 · GERMANTOWN RETURNS TO ANARCHY

Year of Blitzkrieg and Blood Lust

The New Year around Germantown involved some delayed fireworks—another attempt to derail a train. A group of "about 40 rebels" placed a shell under the rails to the east of town, but could not get it to explode until the last car of the train had passed over. Having only succeeded in breaking the rail, they fled south, soon to be pursued by 200 cavalry from Germantown.[1]

The story of 1864 has to be told shifting back and forth between accounts of the area's men in arms and the effects of the war on the community. Although the majority of the town's men-in-arms remained far from home, locally the soldiers' experience and the effects on the civilian population became totally intertwined. Not only did cavalry and guerrilla warfare continue to impact the town, but the area's men fighting on both sides, black and white, confronted each other in increasingly bitter and murderous enmity close to home.

During the previous year, Germantown had experienced the "protection" of a heavy Union military presence. For the next, its status would vacillate between that and the returned anarchy of a no-man's-land. The effects on local morale and commitment to the Confederate cause were complex. By the end of 1863, the *Appeal* had noted that there was once again "a marked feeling of depression in the popular mind in reference to our cause and its prospects." Even such an enthusiastic supporter of the effort was beginning to raise questions about management of the war and the Confederate government infringing freedom and rights. As the conscription expanded to boys of sixteen and men over forty-five, it was equated with a European *levy en masse*. Matters were

TABLE 4 Civil War incidents in and around Germantown, 1864

January 1864	Forrest raids Middle & West Tennessee, conscripting
March 7–April	Forrest's major raid into West Tennessee
late March 1864	Federal occupation of Germantown temporarily broken
late March – April	elections to reestablish government rigged at Germantown
28 March	McCulloch's sweep reaches Germantown
12–15 June	remnants of Sturgis' Expedition rescued at Collierville and Germantown
24 July	skirmish with guerrillas 5 miles east of Germantown on M&C RR, near Collierville
21 August	Forrest's raid on Memphis
September–November	sporadic Federal occupation of Germantown
9 and 15 November	running fights through Germantown into Collierville

made worse by a loss of faith in Confederate money, especially when letters came from the troops complaining how devalued currency affected them.[2] The occasional destruction of their property and the great difficulty of getting an income from their land was a severe tax. Worse, local men and boys remained subject to Confederate conscription.

From the beginning of its operations, the pro-Union *Bulletin* had painted an ever more extreme picture of defection. Wherever there was the protection of Federal troops, it reported that large numbers of loyal and grateful unionists had reemerged and rallied to the national cause.[3] Another northern correspondent painted a more contrasting picture,

> Weekly meetings are being held here relative to re-organizing the State and county governments of Tennessee; but there is yet a spirit of bitter opposition to the Federal government, and many reluctantly submit because they know there is no other way. . . . Many who have taken the *oath* of allegiance have not changed their views. . . .[4]

The best guess that one can make is that the pre-war mix of unionist and secessionist sentiments had resurfaced among the citizens of Germantown, while most simply resigned themselves to a Union victory.

❖ ❖ ❖

The only available description of conditions in Germantown during this year came from Reverend J. Dix Mills who had returned with his wife sometime in early 1864. Writing in February to his sister in Kentucky, he was living in the midst of the temporary encampment of Griersons' Cavalry Division in preparation for the expedition against Forrest described below. The area was temporarily occupied by thousands of men and horses and heavily trafficked by guns and wagons. Nevertheless, Mills mentioned none of this but focused on venting his spleen at the Yankees.[5] This makes his letter disappointing for valid insights into the town's experience at the time of writing.

For instance, he described the pillaging and destruction the town had suffered in 1862, as told to him by witnesses, for he had been absent. He did not identify the actual event and presented it as on-going. He completely garbled an alleged transition from an early conciliatory commander to a succession of "petty tyrants, continuing to this day." His picture of endless pillaging implicitly occurring in the area may reflect conditions that had returned since the end of permanent occupation. Strangely, he made no mention of any of the churches having been destroyed, although surely the Baptist Church building was gone by then. Instead he reported

> The Masons and Odd Fellows Lodge both have been robbed of their jewels, and their papers and their charts destroyed: - Two of the churches have been converted into horse stables: and in the third has been quartered soldiers on the walls of which their vile thoughts are penned and figures so obscene as to make an harlot blush: - desolation is universal.

Perhaps the well-known tendency of soldiers to leave behind graffiti makes that element accurate, but the rest totally contradicts other accounts, exposing his version as almost pure hyperbole.

Instead, as a representative of the staunchest advocates of the cause, he reflects starkly their perceptions, including how they viewed the motives and fate of those among them who had either abandoned or never fully embraced the cause.

> Our village certainly prior to the war some five or six hundred in [illegible]; has now of those less than one hundred.—These few have

been detained here influenced by various causes—Some by Old-age, and Decrepitude—others by a lack of pecuniary means to get away—In some has existed a greater love of real and personal estate; than love of country, and have stayed to protect property. And a few remained behind when the Confederate forces withdrew: to see again "The Star Spangled Banner"—That glorious old flag unfurled to the breeze—this few have waited, and beheld again planted on [illegible] soil. "The Flag of the Union!! and in exultant-glee get close under the shadow of its folds; seeking there safety, and protection—but "Such protection as vultures give to lambs" . . .

Union men—for there were some union men, before union troops came—waited [illegible] for Uncle-Sam's troops—but since have with an anxiousness akin to terror sought—and sometimes vainly sought—the daily bread of hungry wife and starving little ones—This is the present condition of men who were union men—These men have no longer "The flag of our Union"—no longer trust to its champions for protection—no for the men who brought the Flag, brought ruin. They have robbed their friends; and beggared their children.[6]

Notably, he did not express hostility toward such benighted Unionists. Rather they were also victims of Yankee abuse. They were misguided parts of the community.

His descriptions contrast starkly with those his wife had written during the previous year of a seemingly tranquil civilian life under occupation. Who knows how much that had changed. He even admitted that their families were all well and referred to nothing like deprivation or starvation among them. He voiced a martial fever and predicted the South would hold out for at least another year, extracting a negotiated peace with desirable terms. No recorded utterances from the Unionists or fence-straddlers around Germantown have survived.

✦ ✦ ✦

By spring, there were some very peculiar signals about political sentiments coming from Germantown. As part of Governor Johnson's efforts to reorganize the state's government, in March elections were held for county officials. The contest was primarily between the moderates, labeled the Lincoln Abolition candidates, and the Johnson radicals, the Unconditional Union ticket. In initial results for the county, the moderates led by a margin of two hundred and fifty. Meanwhile, the return of the Germantown district had been withheld for some reason. When they were brought in, the *Argus* reported, "the precinct was made to poll seven or eight times its usual vote," nearly all for the Johnson ticket. Indeed something was obviously rotten in Germantown. Although there were only 20 legal voters, Germantown fielded up to 343, all but three of whom voted radical. In sharp contrast, only those three voters bothered to cast votes for the local district offices of justice of the peace and constable. The rest only voted for county offices, suspiciously having no interest in their district's affairs.[7]

There the candidates of the "Unconditional Free State Union ticket" for justices of the peace were A.G. Bowen and James Hall, and for constable, W. Koch.[8] Typically, none of these men resided in the district during the censuses of either 1860 or 1870, but men of similar names did live elsewhere in the county.[9] In contrast, the winners for the Germantown offices were locals, J.M. Gray and W.H. Walker for justices and J. Lewis constable, moderate candidates who beat the Unconditional Unionists.[10] All three had held these offices before the war and must have accepted the inevitable and were working with occupation authorities to provide order. For some reason, the remaining seventeen legal voters did not participate.

Even the loyal *Argus* cried foul. It published the affidavits of several officers of the 6th Tennessee Cavalry who observed that only soldiers voted at the poll site. Soldiers' votes were counted separately from the district's. Other allegedly loyal papers in the state denounced "the election as a shameful jugglery." More conservative northern papers distanced themselves from the controversy, distrustful of both sides in Southern politics.[11] Unfortunately no records concerning this election survive in the state and county archives, but apparently another election for county officers was ordered and held.[12] All this tells us, beyond radical skullduggery, is that there was at least a small openly and ostensibly "pro-Union" but Conservative presence, the foundations for a restoration of the pre-war political establishment.

The *Bulletin* editorialized, without comment on the fraud. Nevertheless, it went on to make a defensible argument about the long-term interests of area citizens. "Those who have stayed away through dislike to the amnesty oath will find that they have done ill for themselves. . . . (A)mnesty will not continue to be offered . . . if the people . . . refuse to take part in elections, they will gain nothing by their error in postponing the reorganization of the state, until harsher terms ... are the only ones they can get."[13]

The *Bulletin* was correct in its analysis of how Tennessee would fare in the future. Those who continued to hold to the "lost cause" would suffer. Those who accepted defeat could survive with something. Germantown residents were weighing these considerations by the spring of 1864. Occupation alone had already made the prospects clear enough to some of the wiser heads. The newly elected district officials, among a few others such as Reverend Richard Evans of the Presbyterian Church, had already sworn the oath.[14] The conversion of prominent citizens must have had a strong effect. The above reference to legal voters may indicate that by the spring, at least twenty men had signed the oath.

Among them, a minister like Evans had to play a balancing act. For instance, the Woodson family in his congregation had originally opposed secession, but typically joined the cause, and their son was fighting for the Confederacy. When, in 1864, he wrote home in a state of despondence, Evans had to console the family and wrote Henry a letter intended to sustain him spiritually, an act that could technically have been construed as communicating with and supporting the enemy. Apparently he was not able to dispatch it.[15] Unless the records of the Provost Marshall become available, we will not know how many others transitioned during the following months, but the list of loyalty oaths was growing, and some were bold enough to openly participate in governance.

The general reluctance of the majority to defect from the cause, even *pro forma*, retarded Federal efforts to shift responsibilities to local government. The formation of a Tennessee Home Guard had been authorized by General Hurlbut in September 1863. By January 1864, however, for the entire state, only seven companies had been fully formed.[16] Outside Memphis not much progress was being made toward establishing effective self-defense forces in the county. Tipton County had done so, and benefitted. They were free from seizure of property. Shelby failed to do so.[17]

Nevertheless in early March, Federal headquarters in Memphis reinitiated an open period of trade. The six main roads into the city were declared open again for bringing in cotton and other produce and taking out goods and supplies. Of course, the State Line through Germantown was one such.[18] This relatively favorable situation did not last long, however. Forrest launched his disruptive campaign, returning the area to a state of turmoil.

What had been a relatively stable situation Forrest turned into a roller coaster ride for the rest of the year. On July 2, Washburn imposed martial law in Memphis and suspended the municipal government for its lack of cooperation. By August, the *Bulletin* was reporting, "The prohibition of trade has checked every avenue of business.... Regular business on cotton has been out of the question." Many people from the country could sell at 75 to 80 cents per pound, but whatever came in had to be stored with the government. Efforts to get around such controls in order to get cash instead of promissory notes could result in confiscation. Inflation was putting pressure on the currency, and gold was forbidden. Security became so tight that neither persons nor merchandise could leave the city except on the six, controlled roads. Everything was in limbo.[19] The town was again in a no-man's-land.

Military Operations

Paralleling the frustrated efforts at recreating orderly government and commerce, military operations once again threw the area into chaos and threatened escalation to an even more viscous internecine warfare.

From the beginning of the year, the citizens of Germantown had watched the Federals depart on raids in all directions to pacify the countryside. On January 11, Grierson dispatched Fielding Hurst's 6th Tennessee Cavalry to Purdy as a base of operations.[20]

They continued to expand their evil reputation, contributing to growing tensions. Complaints even came from Unionists. "Col. Hurst burned 3 establishments belonging to 3 of the best Union men about Brownsville." Area victims had been forced to flee to Memphis and Peoria, while their personal property was being pilfered and wantonly destroyed.[21]

Even more serious charges against Hurst were leveled by Forrest. They included the murder of six captured Confederate raiders, even torture and mutilation. On February 12, under threat of burning the city, Hurst extorted $5,139.25 from the citizens of Jackson. Forrest proclaimed Hurst, his officers and men outlaws not entitled treatment as prisoners of war.[22] Blood feud and vendetta threatened.

January had proven an unnerving month for the Federals, chasing willow-the-wisps all over Tennessee and Kentucky. In reality, Forrest and Richardson's recruitment teams were simply all over the place conscripting.[23] Before being forced back to defend Mississippi, his forces had torn up the undefended M&C

RR from Corinth to La Grange, and he had planned to continue west through Germantown, but Federal cavalry came against him. Once again, Germantown was spared being the site of a significant confrontation. Federal control of West Tennessee and North Mississippi was so disrupted that solid Union occupation was limited to Memphis and Germantown.[24]

Then Sherman made a move that deflected Confederate raids away from West Tennessee for a couple of months, and put the Confederates on the defensive. His objective was the complete disruption of the Confederate supply system centered on Meridian. He launched his campaign on February 3. The immediate impact on the Germantown area would be the withdrawal of sizable forces along the rail line for his campaign, followed by the relocation of units into the area to replace them. Germantown would also become a major center for troop concentrations for one wing of his attack.[25] This bold offensive put Forrest and Richardson on the defensive.

In preparation, Sherman had cobbled together a sizable force, removing almost all of Hurlbut's seasoned, regular regiments. Sherman ordered significant reductions at "Memphis to two black and two white regiments."

> I wish, therefore ... all the men put into camp or bivouac as remote from towns as possible. The present garrison at Memphis, save the negro regiment, should form the nucleus of one of the infantry divisions named and encamp, say, at Germantown, where they can march inland or into Memphis for embarkation on one day's notice.[26]

Hurlbut did nothing to execute these directives. So Germantown did not become a base for concentrating an entire infantry division.

Instead, by January 26, General Grierson began concentrating his cavalry division around Germantown and Collierville, with 2nd Brigade at Germantown, where he also established his headquarters on February 6. The 2nd Brigade was an effective force of 2,900 men plus artillery. Grierson was to join Brigadier General W. M. "Sooy" Smith's expedition into Mississippi to hit the Confederates on a third front. That was a complete flop. They did not leave Germantown until February 11, far too late. By February 21, Sherman had completed destruction of Meridian and pulled back. Forrest was free to concentrate on Smith's column forcing him back to Germantown.[27]

As a result from late January and throughout February, several thousand men and horses had been concentrated in and around Germantown, and even during their temporary absence in mid-February, the town served as a major concentration point for supplies. All life would have been consumed by their presence, especially on the roads through town. For instance on February 7, a train of 200 pack mules arrived. As a point of interest, the bridge across the Wolf had apparently remained disassembled since Forrest's last raid.[28] Civilian traffic had to ferry, seriously impeding all movement.

By the end of February, Hurlbut's forces for the defense of West Tennessee had been reduced to about 11,500 effectives, plus Grierson's cavalry division, about 8,800 effectives.[29] Raiders had totally wrecked the M&C Railroad in the Germantown-Collierville area, abandoned since Sherman's expedition. Although temporarily reopened as far as Germantown on February 26, they abandoned it again by March 26 in the face of Forrest's next raid.[30] Federal defenders were so disoriented that they were giving up the idea that they could maintain the line.

◆ ◆ ◆

While the civilians of Germantown were experiencing all these disruptions, their men in Forrest's cavalry participated in the continued escalation of civil war at its worst. Forrest decided it was time to pursue his grandiose plans to liberate West Tennessee. On February 5, he reported his ambitions directly to Jefferson Davis. "The people of West Tennessee are generally loyal to the South," and I "am confident I shall be able to raise and organize at least four more full regiments of troops."[31]

Forrest commended the two Tennessee regiments that had accompanied his previous expedition "especially the new troops from West Tennessee, who considering their want of drill, discipline, and experience, behaved handsomely. . . ." These volunteers and conscripts had been thrown into battle without benefit of training. Among them was Richardson's West Tennessee Brigade, now under Colonel Neely.[32] Forrest had tightened his command.

Despite his praise of the troopers, Forrest had become thoroughly dissatisfied with the irregular nature of so many of his units. Many problems involved Richardson's command, still made up of an excess of officers and so many men who came and went as they saw fit.[33] So, Forrest regularized things, eliminating many unit commanders from their inflated numbers. When the dust settled, the West Tennessee formations in particular had become standardized cavalry regiments of the Tennessee line. Richardson was one of those who would soon disappear.

On March 16, Forrest moved north, east of Grierson's cavalry, through

Jackson, cutting the rail lines into West Tennessee all the way to Paducah Kentucky on the Ohio River before being checked.[34] While Forrest was moving north, Chalmers's division temporarily under Colonel Mo McCulloch, was sweeping west through North Mississippi arresting stragglers and deserters.[35] This land south of Germantown had been heavily infested with wandering bands of brigands, robbing indiscriminately. McCulloch was to move "up as near to Germantown as possible." He was to threaten Memphis and divert troops from moving against Forrest.[36]

The Federals had completely abandoned Germantown in the face of Forrest's threat. On March 28, rumors had it "Mo. McCulloch captured Germantown," and, "The rebels occupied Germantown Wednesday morning last."[37] We will probably never know what actually transpired in the town. Since whatever happened did not involve any combat, there are no military records. As late as April 9, a Confederate force drove Federal pickets in at Germantown, again the outer-most fringes of Federal presence by that date.[38]

On April 4, Grierson reported significant encounters with the 12th Cavalry. In the city, Hurlbut fearfully predicted that Forrest might try to cross the Wolf at Germantown, join McCullough and move on Memphis.[39]

Escalating the Blood Feud

Instead on April 14, his troops took Fort Pillow. Much ink has been spilled on the subject of the massacre, especially of African-American troops, and about Forrest's personal responsibility.[40] It is not possible here to improve the picture, although the consequences of this brutal massacre must be explored. Something about moods on both sides in West Tennessee emerges from the report Forrest wrote before he became defensive about charges of war crimes. On April 15, he reported

> The victory was complete, and the loss of the enemy will never be known from the fact that large numbers ran into the river and were shot and drowned. The force was composed of about 500 negroes and 200 white soldiers (Tennessee Tories). The river was dyed with the blood of the slaughtered for 200 yards. There was in the fort a large number of citizens who had fled there to escape the conscript law. Most of those ran into the river and were drowned.

The approximate loss was upward of 500 killed, but few of the officers escaping. It is hoped that these facts will demonstrate to the Northern people that negro soldiers cannot cope with Southerners. Large numbers of the Tories have been killed and made away with, and the country is very near free of them.[41]

The bottom line is that the previous year's conflict in West Tennessee had escalated Confederate hostilities toward the "homegrown Yanks" and blacks who had betrayed everything sacred and had allegedly pillaged, terrorized and murdered good Southern people. If the abuse and atrocities that each side had inflicted on the other had not been enough, wild and exaggerated versions spread as rumors, and sensational newspaper reports made matters worse. Official accusations were lodged by both sides. Both armies were infected with a drive to revenge insult and injury, real or imagined. For some Confederates it had become almost pathological. In their eyes the treachery and evil acts of Tories, but especially the alleged abuses of savage black soldiers and their white officers, demanded retribution.[42]

Afterwards, Forrest's defenders described the background to the massacre. He had been deluged by reports from locals "of rapine and atrocious outrage upon non-combatants of the country by the garrison at Fort Pillow." They pleaded for protection. The civilians in the fort were known to be deserters and "men of the country who entertained a malignant hatred toward Confederate soldiers, their families and friends." The fort's garrison had allegedly been scouring the country, stealing everything and insulting the women. The families of many of Forrest's officers and men had been "grievously wronged, despoiled and insulted, and in one or two cases fearfully outraged."[43] All this reportedly motivated Forrest's attack and the behavior of his men. Of course, the implication was always that bestial blacks were the worst participants.

Witnesses to the massacre on both sides were hardly dispassionate. The Federal version was replete with sensational images. Washburn asserted that "Men (white and black) were crucified and burned; others were hunted by bloodhounds, while others were made the sport of men more cruel than the dogs by which they were hunted."[44] A Confederate participant's words, though damning, probably provide a more accurate description. "Our troops, maddened by excitement, shot down the retreating Yankees, and not until they had attained the water's edge and turned to beg for mercy, did any prisoners fall into our hands. Thus the whites received quarter; but the negroes were shown no mercy."[45] It was admittedly a massacre. Major Bradford, the hated commander of Tennessee cavalry, was "summarily executed" and his body left to rot.[46] They were all swearing revenge on one another.

On each side, hostility toward civilian "traitors" had produced increasingly vicious retribution. When Federal troops were present, those suspected of secesh sentiments suffered, while Unionist confidence was buoyed and many men enlisted with Federal units, often hoping to defend their own towns against Confederate raiders. When Forrest experienced one of his successful liberations, he elicited enthusiasm and drew recruits, but neutrals, and even unionists were subject to Confederate conscription or worse. When possible, they fled to safety.

More emerged from Forrest's report to President Davis on April 15.

> The bands of guerrillas, horse-thieves, and robbers which infested this region have been broken up and dispersed, and many men heretofore Union in sentiment are openly expressing themselves for the South. There are as yet large numbers of men in West Tennessee who have avoided the service, and there is but little prospect of adding to our strength by volunteering. Conscription, however, would ... give us from 5,000 to 8,000 men. ...

Regarding the Tennessee Federal regiments, he had broken them up.

> "Their acts of oppression, murder, and plunder made them a terror to the whole land. For murders committed I demand that Fielding Hurst and such of his men as were guilty of murder should be delivered to me. ..."[47]

As for the victims of the massacre, they had recently arrived to occupy the old fort. In early February, Colonel William Bradford's 13th Tennessee Cavalry (officially the 14th) were the first to settle in. He had originally recruited irregulars in south-west Kentucky and northern counties of west Tennessee where hostilities between unionists and rebels had become intense. About ten percent were Confederate deserters seeking refuge. Such a motley crew soon gained the same foul reputation that plagued Hurst's men. After being designated an official Tennessee regiment, Major Bradford tried with limited success to enforce proper discipline.[48]

Next, an officer and forty men of Company A of the 2nd U.S. Colored Light

Artillery (USCLA) arrived to install two field guns. Since Bradford's men refused to be housed near blacks, segregated facilities may have added to the fortification's vulnerability. Typically black troops were to be kept inside the fort and away from the local population, while only the white cavalry were allowed to forage the countryside.[49] Federal efforts to keep the black troops away from white civilians never managed to staunch hysterical stories of black atrocities.

In late March, Hurlbut sent Major Lionel Booth with his 6th USCHA to reinforce the fort. He assumed command. Even after this addition, the total garrison consisted of only 536 men fit for duty. The 13th Tennessee had been hemorrhaging from desertions. After the able Major Booth was killed early in the siege, Major Bradford was too inexperienced to maintain an effective command.[50]

After the blood-rage of the victors finally abated, they had brutally killed well over 200 men, but a precise count is impossible.[51] Among the only 62 survivors of blacks taken prisoner, 13 would escape while being led away, in a couple of cases because they had been left by the side of the road to die. About half these men had been deliberately and viciously wounded, often while trying to surrender. The wounds inflicted were obviously unnecessary and deliberate. Once taken prisoner, the fate of any black was enslavement. The fate of white prisoners was ironically worse, Andersonville Prison.[52]

An unknown number of black survivors were kept by their captors for personal use, which was officially forbidden. One such was a former Germantown slave. Allen James Walker, the escaped slave of Sallie Walker who was serving in the 6th USCHA, had the good fortune of being captured by a Texan. Unlike the more bloodthirsty units, the Texans tried to curb the bloodbath, with little effect. His captor got him out of his uniform into Confederate clothing, and kept him as a personal servant. He traveled with his new master until early 1865 when he sent him to Texas to work as a field hand. After he was finally told of his emancipation in mid-July, he traveled by an unbelievably circuitous route back the Memphis by November to be reenrolled in the 11th USCI.[53]

The most likely presence among the attackers by a Germantown man would have been in the 15th Tennessee cavalry, in which only one Germantown man, John Hughs, can be definitely identified as serving plus four other possibilities. None of the Germantown area men riding in Richardson's former (1st) Brigade could have been involved. Under Colonel Neely, they were making a feint against Memphis to preoccupy the Federal cavalry. Forrest then granted the men of the 13th, 14th and 15th six-day furloughs to go home for clothing, horses and supplies. This time, Germantown may have joyfully welcomed a few of its men, but any locals faced a dilemma. The brigade swept the area for conscripts.[54]

Meanwhile, Forrest had received orders to return to Mississippi. By this time, the mutual recriminations between commanders on both sides had reached the point of unleashing an even more terrible blood feud. A select committee of the two houses of Congress drew up a report elaborating the atrocities at Fort Pillow. Hard-line politicians and journalists added fuel to the flames by calling for severe retribution, not just against all perpetrators, but even prisoners of war. The most important truth was that the massacre ignited ever greater animosities.

Northern newspapers reported that afterwards in Memphis Union officers threatened "that unless the government take retributive steps, they will consider it their duty to shoot every man of Forrest's command they meet, and take no prisoners. Soldiers even threaten to shoot Forrest's men then in Irvin prison, if they get a chance."[55] Black troops had drawn the conclusion that in future conflict they would be butchered rather than being allowed to surrender. So they took an oath among themselves that they would neither surrender nor give quarter to Confederates.[56] Each side was set to murder *en mas* those on the other.

♦ ♦ ♦

Meanwhile, Forrest had thrown Hurlbut into total panic over a possible attack on Memphis. He withdrew all his forces and financial resources into Fort Pickering. Except for cavalry, the rest of the county was so abandoned that Germantown could be visited by regular Confederate troops. Hurlbut was disgraced and removed. His successor would be under pressure to bring Forrest down.

Consequently Major General C.C. Washburn, Hurlbut's replacement, ordered out a large force under Brigadier General Samuel D. Sturgis to draw Forrest out. His third brigade included the 55th and 59th Infantry (A.D.) and the 2nd Light Artillery (A.D.). The 59th and the artillery contained men from the Germantown area. They had taken the oath not to surrender, and all the troops were allegedly exhorted by their officers to remember Fort Pillow. But, the expedition was a disaster from beginning to end, with most of the blame lying on commanding officers.[57] The blacks suffered the most. They had honored their pledge not to surrender. Even if they had, it would have availed them little.

The two armies collided in the Battle of Brice's Crossroads or Tishomingo Creek on June 10. Colonel P. Bouton, commanding the black brigade, threw his entire force into the line, where its "unflinching resolve" prevented immediate route. It repeatedly made orderly withdrawals, constantly reforming the line, while other regiments crumbled. The fighting was often hand-to-hand, "with bayonets and clubbed muskets." At one point, according to Bouton, "I was left entirely cut off and surrounded by several hundred of the enemy. My men, gathering around me, fought with terrible desperation. Some of them ... unyielding, died at my feet, without a thing in their hands for defense." The remainder escaped and rejoined the retreating column.[58]

Their ordeal had just begun. As the army retreated from Ripley, Mississippi the next day, the black soldiers were again guarding the rear. They resupplied their ammunition by scavenging what the white troops had dropped. In the desperate, hand-to-hand fighting that ensued, they became badly dispersed, retreating back to Collierville in three separate groups along different roads. Bouton with about 170 survivors, mostly disarmed and many severely wounded, reached Collierville on June 12. They were the luckiest. The larger number, about 600 under Captain Foster of the 59th remained under attack during its retreat. Again Foster's troops formed the rear guard, and according to Wilkins, "the imperturbable coolness and steadiness of the colored troops" kept the attacking cavalry in check and prevented confusion. They reached Collierville on June 13, only to find the town abandoned by federal troops. Sturgis had fled to safety in the city. They had to be rescued by a special train. The last group under Captain Reeve of the 55th, did not reach safety before June 15.[59]

Reeve's account of their ordeal was hair-raising. At Moscow, severely harassed by cavalry and completely out of ammunition, they scattered into the woods,

> every man going in for himself. From this point until we reached Germantown the loyal citizens of Tennessee turned out and hunted us with bloodhounds as we passed along. I reached Germantown on the 15th, about 4 o'clock in the afternoon. A good many of my men got in about the same time. We there found some of our cavalry.[60]

Only when Reeve's group finally filtered through to Germantown did they encounter the safety of Grierson's patrols, sent out to round up stragglers.[61] The civilians of Shelby and Fayette counties had allegedly joined the pursuit of the fleeing black troops as though they were escaped slaves. By June 15, Germantown was only sporadically inside the patrol lines of Grierson's cavalry.

The background of Sturgis' expedition casts further light on the experience of the black troops. To add insult to injury, at the beginning of the expedition, Colonel McMillen had placed guards at houses along the route ahead of the 3rd Brigade to prevent the black troops from entering even to get drinking water from their wells or cisterns. When Colonel Bouton complained to him, he responded that they did not need to get water from the houses, for there was standing surface water from the rains.[62] White commanders felt that the civilians needed to be protected, specifically from the black troops, for whom any puddle of water was good enough.

Federal commanders obviously feared that their black troops might take extra revenge on Southern civilians. Although Federal records do not indicate that anything extraordinary occurred in that regard, hysterical rumors had spread throughout the South. The Columbia *Daily South Carolinian* reported falsely that from the beginning at Germantown and all along the route of Strugis' march, only those who fled escaped a horrible fate. Allegedly refugees fleeing before Sturgis' army had brought tales of horror to the West Tennessee cavalrymen,

> detailing incidents which made men shudder who were accustomed to scenes of violence and bloodshed. I cannot recite the stories of these poor frightened people. Robbery, rapine and the assassination of men and women, were the least of crimes committed while the "avengers of Fort Pillow" overran and desolated the country. Rude unlettered men, who had fought at Shiloh and many subsequent battles, wept like children when they heard of the enormities to which their mothers, sisters and wives had been subjected by the negro mercenaries of Sturgis. The mildest, most placeable of our soldiers became maddened when they heard how the persons of their kinswomen were violated.... In one instance, the grand-mother, daughter and grand daughter were each, in the same room, held by the drunken brutes and subjected to outrages by the bare recital of which humanity is appalled.[63]

The author's pornographic imagination ran wild as he detailed other alleged specifics, all of which were intended to justify his report of the fate of the black troops.

Very few negroes, it seems, have been captured. Perhaps not more than forty or fifty have appeared at headquarters. Most of them fled as soon as it was known that Forrest was on the battle-field. Those that were taken escaped.(?) The soldiers say they "lost them."[64]

This verifies the accounts of civilians participating in the pursuit and capture or execution of fleeing black troops. Union commanders had fettered black troops, preventing their unsupervised contact with civilians. Only acts by renegades could have fueled the wild stories of massive abuse. It was hysterical propaganda that fired fears and hates, entrenching ideas that anarchy and chaos would follow upon black emancipation, and justifying whatever force would be needed to curb it.

The number of black dead and missing were "only" about one fourth of the total infantry casualties, but their killed constituted 60 percent of the total dead.[65] The black death-toll added further to accusations that they were not allowed to surrender, and by the other side that they had been encouraged to fight to the death.

By this time, the commanders on each side were holding the others responsible and threatening greater retributions. The black flag (take no prisoners) could have been raised by both sides. Prisoners of war, even civilians, could have been executed as retribution. Forrest, who had been told that the oath had been taken in the presence of General Hurlbut, believed the black troops had been incited to take revenge. At Brice's Crossroads, their officers had supposedly called upon them to remember Fort Pillow. Forrest argued that the black troops had been sent out with their commanders knowing full well what was afoot.[66]

A series of exchanges and recriminations followed between the respective commanders. Each side claimed it would follow the rules of war, but only if guaranteed that the other would treat prisoners appropriately.[67] Washburn charged that if the Confederates would not treat colored troops as prisoners of war, "then let the oath stand, and upon those who have aroused this spirit by their atrocities ... be the consequences."[68]

Forrest responded that captured blacks would receive "kind and humane treatment," but would be treated not as prisoners of war but as captured property. Since Washburn was leaving "the matter entirely to the discretion of the negroes," he threatened to give orders that will "lead to consequences too fearful for contemplation." Noting that he held 2,000 prisoners as hostage, Forrest demanded a clear response of Washburn's intentions.[69]

All involved expressed a bloody mood.[70] Lee forwarded these exchanges to his commander, and fortunately indicated that he intended not to escalate things.[71] On July 3, Washburn responded to Lee in terms that were hardly conciliatory, but he too expressed a willingness to avoid further escalation.[72]

There the matter seems to have rested among the commanders. There are no records of what they might have tried to do to cool things among their troops. Incidents would continue as both sides suspected the worse of each other, but there was no further escalation of rhetoric among the commanders. Most importantly, no *carte blanche* given for revenge. Regardless, Forrest's raid and Brice's Crossroad had created a blood-feud atmosphere among the troops that equaled that already created between the Confederate partisans and the Federal's counter-partisan cavalry and by all the bloody revenges unleashed by guerrilla bands operating ostensibly for one side or the other.[73]

Black troops were caught in the middle, Germantown men among them. All total, 2,242 colored troops from West Tennessee were killed during the war, the vast majority during 1864 in confrontations with Forrest's troops. In return they had contributed to Forrest's 2,234 casualties. The casualty rate among West Tennessee's colored troops was 34 percent, almost half again greater than that for the colored troops from the entire state. In the defense of West Tennessee against Forrest, the partisans, and the guerrillas, they played a key role.[74] There will probably never be an estimate of how many Germantown area blacks were among these troops and casualties. We may never know if any of them came face-to-face with their former masters. Such, however, were the images that would linger in the minds of black and white alike as they sought to live together around Germantown through the following years.

Germantown Still in the Middle

Meanwhile, as soon as troops from the Brice's Crossroads disaster had returned to Memphis, significant Union advances south into Mississippi and Alabama were planned to put Forrest back on the defensive. In preparation to support one such expedition, the M&C was rapidly reopened to Grand Junction by July 1.[75] But the contraction of Federal bases tightly around Memphis meant that the line was increasingly vulnerable.

Sherman became convinced that as long as Forrest was alive, there would be no peace in the area. Consequently, on June 24 he launched an expedition to hunt him down.[76] One gets the impression from the exchanges among commanders that Germantown was considered on the frontier of their securely held ground.[77] Even so, occupation of the town seems to have been abandoned again before August.

Ironically, while this force was still out south and east hunting Forrest, he made his famous raid into Memphis on August 21. It seemed the Federals could hold nothing securely, while nothing could be permanently held by the rebels either. The M&C was again abandoned on August 29. Much of the cavalry still at La Grange had rushed back, Hurlbut's 1st Division returning to its headquarters at White's Station with the 12th Missouri and 2nd Iowa Cavalry reseated at Germantown by September second.[78] Once the defenses of the railroad were abandoned east of town, the Confederates wrecked the line between Germantown and La Grange "most effectively."[79]

Amidst all this turmoil, Federal occupation forces underwent changes. As a result of contraction of defenses around the city, Germantown and Collierville were again usually abandoned.

In September, the railroad was only in operation to White's Station, then abandoned on October 15. On September 29, The cavalry at White's Station was "making raids daily to Germantown." During November, Confederate cavalry were again tearing up the rail line from Germantown to LaFayette. On November 9, a sizable expedition of Union cavalry clashed with Confederate pickets inside Germantown. They left one wounded prisoner in the town for the locals to care for. On November 15, a Union patrol drove Confederates back through town into Collierville again. Never able to confront Federal troops significantly, the Confederates hit the railroad repeatedly.[80]

On November 17, the *Bulletin* reported, "the rebel Captain Thompson is making a sweeping conscription in the neighborhood of Germantown." He has a list of nearly every resident and compels all he finds to go with him or pay heavily to escape.[81] It is hard to believe any were left. Whatever life in Germantown had survived during 1863, protected by Federal occupation, was once again totally disrupted as skirmishers repeatedly fought their way through town. Citizens suffered another season of "drive-by shootings." The next clear record of an occupation at Germantown was of the 99th Illinois Regiment from late November to the end of the year.

p. 20 DeWitt Clinton Fort, Wikipedia. Vague early service in Confederate Cavalry in Virginia and Mississippi/Tennessee; Captain of Independent Scouts and unofficial guerrillas, 1864–65.

In addition to Confederate cavalry raiders, according to his memoirs, DeWitt Clinton Fort's command of Scouts ranged freely from the Mississippi border throughout south-west Shelby County into winter. Fort had begun his career as a scout under General Van Dorn. In March 1863, he applied to General Chalmers to form his own company-sized unit of "scouts." Such units were the only remnant of independent partisan operations. They had perhaps only local sanction, and they clearly challenged Confederate determination to end the partisan problem. Fort claimed Chalmers had given him "very wide discretion." Although Fort admitted that he pushed the limits of that discretion, Chalmers' satisfaction with him led to expanded authority to operate in November 1863. In his memoirs, Fort revealed himself a self-righteous, if not pathological egotist, which raises questions about the reliability of his self-serving descriptions. [82] He was, after all writing while awaiting a post-war trial for murder.

He countered the charges that they plundered the local population. Although he had "power and authority to conscript every man in the country, liable to service, and to break up the trade going on with Memphis, his "heart was unequal to the task. I have often seen poor women ... crying and begging for the privilege of going to Memphis to sell their own small produce and purchase supplies for their suffering little ones...."[83] His claim to have operated with humane discretion was a defense against charges of heartless guerrillas simply robbing the helpless.

At one time, one of his companies under Lieutenant Loftin was at Germantown. He remembers that during October, he had orders to maintain "reconnaissance" across an arc running from Collierville around north-east of Memphis to Raleigh and up the river to Randolph.[84] On December 4, a Federal patrol out the Germantown Road was unable to get any closer to Germantown than the vicinity of Ridgeway. They narrowly escaped an ambush by men "under Capt. Fort." Thirteen men were captured.[85] Fort operated comfortably around the town.

If Fort had semi-official endorsement, even worse creatures were afoot in the area. A local later told stories of "the band of one Capt. Davis" operating in the neighborhood.[86] This was undoubtedly Dick Davis, who, if he had ever had a commission, had long abandoned it for outright brigandry. According the historian of the 7th Indiana Cavalry who finally caught him, he had begun riding with the famous raider, General John Morgan, and later with Van Dorn in Mississippi. As leader of a guerrilla band operating near Memphis, he was captured, and while awaiting sentence in the Irving Block, bribed a guard and escaped. He rejoined his well-armed band of fifteen to twenty men, mostly deserters from both armies. Operating from the bottoms of the Wolf and Nonconnah, he ranged from White Station to Grand Junction for much of 1864. The secrecy of his bases depended on the disinclination of locals to inform, for like an evil twin of Robin Hood, he was *loved by a few and feared by many*. His band regularly robbed citizens coming and going from Memphis. "He made no distinction between loyal and disloyal, white and black, nor did he respect age, sex or condition." They struck at vulnerable Federal troops, they fired on a train between Germantown and Collierville. During the horrible retreat of Federal troops from Brice's Crossroads, near Germantown they captured and murdered a captain and six men. Finally, he was captured near the Cold Water, tried and hanged on December 23.[87] He was the kind that both armies had been trying to root out.

Meanwhile in December for a raid on Confederate supply lines General Grierson concentrated a Federal force of 3,500 cavalry, about 5,000 infantry, nine pieces of artillery, 300 pack mules at Germantown. The town was again overwhelmed by Union troops and their traffic.[88]

Heavy occupation would not last long, and the greatly reduced presence confined the benefits of protection to only the immediate town. Whatever recovery and stability the area had experienced had evaporated. If they had not already given up and been forced to seek refuge in Memphis or elsewhere, the poorer yeomen and landless farmers and laborers either left or resorted to more desperate means of self-support. As elsewhere, some felt entitled to take from those who still had means. The formerly wealthy had ceased charity or sharing and there was neither government aid nor law enforcement. According to a report in *The Nashville Daily Union* as early as the beginning of the year, "Throughout the entire South, the people . . . indulge in petty thefts and robbery."[89]

Social tensions that had smoldered below the surface before the war were fanned by Northerners who always believed the South was a decadent aristocratic atavism ready to collapse into social rebellion. In a call for class warfare, the short-lived Memphis *Union Appeal* advertised a rally against secession,

ILL. 13 Hand Grinding Corn Meal, *Harper's Weekly*, 10.10.1867. The destitute wives and widows of yeomen soldiers had to resort to such primitive means to feed their dependents the sparse food available.

calling on every "working men, mechanic and laborer" to turn out against the aristocrats who had disdained them. The effects of such appeals were mixed. Outbreaks of class conflict were sporadic.[90] Despite northern newspapers that reported daily riots in almost every southern city, nothing was reported in Memphis or surrounding towns.

For Germantown residents, this was perhaps the nadir of the war experience, worse even than the initial shocks of pillaging in 1862. Gone was both the support provided by the Provost Marshal and access to goods sold by a suttler. So to were any means to pay for such supplies formerly provided by boarding Union officers and families.[91]

The desperate wives of marginal families had been encouraging their men to desert, and all the lower classes felt especially aggrieved by the unfairness of conscripting the sole breadwinners of their families. Deserters found shelter among neighbors and conscription teams even encountered armed resistance.[92] Such tensions were also spreading through the ranks of the men away from home.

Before continuing the story of Forrest's expeditions, there is an extremely unique case of a Germantown area slave caught up in the Confederate Army, serving under Forrest. He was Preston Roberts, son of the previously described Schuyler Roberts and his slave-wife Mahalia. In his father's 1860 will, Preston had been alloted to Robert's white daughter, Sallie, who married Fernando Scott. As her half-brother, Sallie may have given Preston special treatment, he was Fernando's body servant, so Fernando took Preston with him to Somerville to enlist in Ed Porter's Company of the 2nd Partisan Rangers in 1862. Fernando soured on such service after only six months and deserted, returning home. Strangely, Preston remained loyal to the unit, which would eventually be incorporated in the 13th Tennessee Cavalry under Forrest. A very capable and trustworthy man, Preston rose in Forrest's trust to become his de facto Quartermaster, commanding 75 black cooks, with money and responsibility for purchasing supplies, and with authority to confiscate whatever that could not be bought. Preston once described himself as "one of the most importantest men in the army." In this final capacity, he was travelling with Forrest's Body Guard.[93]

Preston's story provides insight into the enigmatic nature of Southern attitudes about their black slaves, especially considering he served among men who had become extremely hostile to those former slaves serving in the Federal Army as "traitors." He was well respected and popular among the men with whom he served. They called him "Uncle Pres." After the war, 100 surviving veterans would endorse him to be the first black man to receive the Southern Cross of Honor. Perhaps we should label that aspect of Southern racial attitudes as "paternalistic affection." One romantically described him as a typical antebellum "darky."

Perhaps Preston also tells us about the complexity of black attitudes about their status in Southern society. Until his death, he would attend the reunions of Confederate veterans, and pursued and won that Southern Cross. Certainly the status he ultimately achieved helps explain his post-war behavior. But the dedicated service that got him to that status needs explanation. He had allegedly grown up working with his father in the company of white men. Perhaps he truly identified with "their cause." More significant would be the strong sense of brotherhood that develops among the members of a military unit, despite the differences in rank or status.

As for other blacks in Confederate service, "servants" commonly performed armed picket duty, and even went into combat armed. Some were glad to find themselves captured, but others escaped and rejoined their Confederate units. Blacks had learned to live with whites, and accept whatever was necessary to achieve a comfortable accommodation. Both before, during and after the war, such a mentality would largely determine who would find any kind of advancement in white society anywhere they settled. On the other side, the war certainly did not improve the racist mentality of the majority of American whites.

✦ ✦ ✦

Meanwhile in the midst of their relatively good year of campaigning, a considerable row developed over Forrest's troops within the Confederate command structure. Fortunately the resultant report tell us a good deal about life among the Tennessee cavalry containing Germantown area men, but especially their time as partisans.

In the investigator's report, some of the murky history of these units emerged clearly. It began, "the present organization of this command was irregular and without authority." Among the abuses listed, deserters from the infantry were accepted into his cavalry, seriously undermining discipline. Inspection revealed 654 deserters from the Army of Tennessee on Forrest's rolls. Only 200 of these men had "deserted" Forrest's command, apparently referring to the behavior of the irregular partisan rangers. Forrest had 200 of the infantry deserters returned to their commands. "All officers who had received them knowingly were arrested and charges preferred against them."[94] Later, Forrest would complain that the scare created by sending back deserters led to seriously damaged moral and desertions.[95]

From all this emerges a picture of the circumstances under which Germantown area men had been "riding with Forrest." Although they were eventually mustered officially into Confederate service, their origins had been diverse. Although many later arrivals had only served as volunteers or conscripts in regular Tennessee Cavalry regiments, others had begun earlier in Partisan Ranger service shifting back and forth from that to something more like privateers. They had "served" like Robin Hood's Merry Men with a sinister edge, moving freely in and out of semi-official status, ultimately ending as official cavalry under Forrest. Even then, they retained many of their old ways.

Their motivations for service were equally complex. Some had been drawn by the mixed appeals of partisan service. Some had volunteered only after the units became regular cavalry. Some reported dutifully after conscription orders were posted, even while under Federal occupation. Others responded to threats of punishment if they failed to report, while some were simply dragooned.

Untold numbers had drifted in and out of service, often more than once. Those who rejoined when their units swept back through the area were treated as simply having been home for "rest and re-equipment." Increasingly however, some had intended to give up permanently. A member of the 7th Illinois posted at White's Station in September reported, "I have not ... seen a Reb since I came back, only what comes in and gives themselves up. They are a coming in every day more or less."[96] Desertion is a harsh judgment. At some point, one came to believe he had done all he should be expected to do for a lost cause. Others had never been truly committed in the first place.

A member of the 7th Tennessee Cavalry reflected on the conversations among his fellows by autumn. The handwriting seemed on the wall.

> We had little else to do than sit around and discuss such subjects as when the war would end, how it would end, and how we should be treated, if finally defeated.... The federals had unlimited resources in men.... Many believed that ... the independence of the Confederacy was improbable, if not impossible.... We could only hope that

something would happen that would turn the tide. . . . It took moral courage, and plenty of it, for a man to make himself a target for bullets, when he had no very reasonable hope that, even by his death, he would save his country. While some abandoned the cause, it is to the everlasting credit of the men of the Seventh Tennessee cavalry that they stood by those who had the direction of affairs . . . in their hands.[97]

One must remember that for most Americans at that time, regular military service was not an obligation to which they were bound to respond. The concept of duty was more like that of the time-and-space limitations of militia service. Indefinite conscription and the indefinite extension of volunteer service violated American traditions. Defense of their homes or their region was primary. Service required to fulfill the military objectives of a Southern government could easily be seen as impinging on their inalienable rights and their family responsibilities. When the Confederate government failed to keep one's home and family safe and fed, one should go home to tend to it himself. Earlier ambivalences about secession resurfaced, at least until one went back home. There the realities of enemy occupation could reportedly change that. Over the entire duration, for many a sense of duty and honor transitioned to ambivalence then to apathy, and back again, perhaps several times.

✦ ✦ ✦

Meanwhile for the infantrymen with the Army of Tennessee, despite all the reverses, the year began with a display of determination. In January, most of the men of the 13th along with the rest of the Tennessee regiments in Georgia allegedly voted to remain in service for the duration.[98]

Soon however, the war went sour. In July, Jefferson Davis replaced the popular General Joseph Johnston with the Texan, John B. Hood. Hood had an inflated sense of Southern honor and berated his men whenever they failed to live up to his martial expectations. Before Atlanta, he had thrown them against Sherman with devastating results. He blamed them and expected them to reclaim their honor. While Sherman marched across Georgia, Hood embarked on a crusade to liberate Tennessee and sever Sherman's supply lines. Along the way, every frustration in his campaign led to further castigations of his men. Then in November, at Franklin he threw them into a disastrous frontal assault that produced only massive casualties. While enduring extremely bitter cold weather without adequate shoes and clothing, they suffered a last blow in front of Nashville. By December, his command was no longer an army in size or energy. Henry Dunavant of the 1st Tennessee Cavalry expressed the feelings of his compatriots about Hood. "All the men who Hood failed to see Slaughtered at the Battle of Atlanta on the 22nd of July 1864 he got rid of at the Battle of Franklin, Tenn. in his vain attempt to immortalize him self."[99]

After every major bloodletting, Tennesseans suffered demoralization. Many felt betrayed, especially when they suffered from poor military decisions that did not seem to serve the needs of family under occupation. Hood's debacle was the last straw. After the winter of 1864/65, another massive drift back home ensued from the Army of Tennessee. They simply left the ranks in despair and made their way home as best they could.

An interesting example of a man dealing with the disillusions of the war was Lieutenant Needham Harrison of the 13th Infantry. But the historian is confronted with vague and contradictory evidence. He was arrested near Germantown March 4, 1864, according to provost marshal records. Until March, he had been on convalescent leave in Mississippi from wounds received at Chickamauga. Since we know his wife had died before he finally returned home at the end of the war, if he had learned of her illness, he may have been trying to get home to her. After eighteen day's detention, the provost marshal simply decided to release him, which would have entailed his signing a parole. He mentioned none of this in his post-war responses to the veterans' questionnaire. His narrative of involvement runs consistently from 1861 through the Battles around Atlanta, then reaches the point where the 13th Tennessee crossed the Tennessee River in November 1864 for Hood's disastrous campaign. At that point he "resigned there on account of (illegible) of my Co.—(illegible words) connecting myself with Henderson's Scouts, a branch of Forrest's Cavalry, serving three months or until closing of war." At least four companies of such scouts served with Forrest, some formed of former officers who had been left without commands due to the consolidations. The rest of his narrative says that he returned home on horseback from Grenada.[100]

If the Provost Marshal had paroled him to go home to Germantown in March of 1864, he would have had to violate his parole when he returned to service. Perhaps he had the "encouragement" of McCulloch's "liberation" of Germantown in late March and got back to the 13th/154th Tennessee.

In any case, when first arrested in Germantown he had been listed as a "deserter" and the provost marshal treated him favorably. Even if he had truly "taken leave," the shame of "desertion" cannot apply. He was a man who fought through some of the worst battles of the war, was severely wounded, and perhaps worried about a seriously ill wife. Only after experiencing Hood's bloody leadership before Atlanta and on the eve of an offensive with a bedraggled and demoralized force did he "resign." Even then, he resumed service until the end. After the war, he would be honored by fellow veterans who obviously suffered no suspicions or held no grudges against men like him.

The stubborn remnants of the 13th/154th came under Johnston's command and in February 1865, marched into North Carolina. There along with the rest of the remnants of the Army of Tennessee, the consolidated and depleted 13th/154th ended up at Bentonville, NC, where it was further fused into the 2nd Consolidated Tennessee Infantry Regiment. It surrendered on April 26, 1865, and was paroled on May 2. Fewer than 50 officers and men remained out of the twelve hundred plus numbers who had mustered into the 13th during the war.[101] Out of the original 1100 men of the 154th, fewer than 100 survived the war.[102]

By this time the 4th/5th had also been so reduced it formed only Company D of the 3rd Consolidated Tennessee Infantry Regiment, and it also surrendered on April 26. After being paroled on May 1, the men gradually made their way back home.[103]

Meanwhile, at home the guerrilla war continued. DeWitt Clinton Fort implies in his memoirs that throughout the winter up to March 1865, his command of holdouts was operating as true guerrillas, without official military commission and in defiance of orders intended to curb guerrilla depredations. "For a while we were as much afraid of our own soldiers as of the enemy."[104] Both Federal and Confederate commands sought to exterminate them.

Prisoners of War

The fate of those who became prisoners rounds out the picture of the war experiences of Germantown's men. The suffering of Federal soldiers in Confederate prisons, especially the infamous Andersonville, is well known. The experience of Confederate prisoners of war was less severe than that, but the camps of neither side were humane by any modern standards. Germantown men captured in the eastern campaigns could end up in many different camps.

ILL. 14 Irving Block, Memphis, *Harper's Weekly*. 9.10.1864. The makeshift Federal prison in Memphis used to hold locals suspected of offenses and prisoners of war awaiting transfer to a regular prisoner camp in the North or to exchange at Vicksburg.

Those captured closer to home traveled a special route, particularly those swept up by the Federal expeditions, or caught in Chalmers and Forrest's expeditions. Irving Block in Memphis was their first stop, a way station before transit to prisoner camps. Irving Block was "three large brick warehouses with iron front, 120 by 75 feet, four stories high" on Irving Street off Court Square. It served as a general military prison for the city, housing not only Confederate prisoners, but Union soldiers and civilians under arrest. The first floor confined white male prisoners of all sorts. The second housed the kitchen, offices and holding cells. The third held the hospital and white female prisoners. The fourth was for "coloreds."[105] Germantown's male civilians arrested for espionage or smuggling ended in Irving, but the internment of such white females was not consistent.

Unless exchange or parole was being negotiated, Confederate prisoners were forwarded on as soon as possible. Nevertheless, overcrowding had become serious. When he had assumed office, Captain George Williams, Provost Marshal, reported very poor conditions which he tried to correct. By June of 1864, conditions had become scandalous., An inspection report noted that it was "the filthiest place the inspector ever saw occupied by human beings." As a result of subsequent improvements, by September a medical inspection gave a clean bill of health, except for the conditions of colored inmates.[106]

One of Williams' complaints had been the laxity of the guard details, which the inspection reaffirmed. That explains the stories of Henry Woodson and Joe Duke. Woodson could easily have escaped and Duke did. If Woodson had not been exchanged and Duke had not escaped, they would have been shipped north to a true prisoner-of-war camp.

An early report in the *Chicago Times* described conditions at Camp Douglas in the spring of 1862, before overcrowding. "All the prisoners are receiving the best of treatment, are allowed plenty to eat, and are quartered in warm, comfortable barracks."[107]

This rosy picture coupled with negative depictions of the poor conditions in

ILL. 15 Confederate Prisoners of War at Camp Douglas, *Harper's Weekly*, 4.5.1862. At this intermediate date, the camp was not as crowded as it would become.

the Confederate army was typical of prejudicial reporting in all wars. At least the author admitted that accommodations for the sick in the camp hospital were inadequate. Soon overcrowding would change every Federal prisoner-of-war camp for the worse.

Thereafter Union prisons were grossly inadequate, and stories of inhumane treatment abound. Inadequate food, clothing, shelter and sanitation facilities prevailed. Rock Island, Illinois was a prison known to have housed Germantown men. It was situated on a swampy island in the Mississippi River opposite Rock Island, Illinois. The first Tennesseans to arrive tell a horror story. Still in light-weight clothing they had to stand outside for hours in a December blizzard with temperatures below zero, awaiting processing. Some allegedly froze to death.[108]

In winter brutally cold, icy and snowy, the fourteen-acre square was surrounded by twelve-foot wooden walls. Inside the wall, was a twenty-foot "Dead Line," marked by posts. The prisoners who entered and ignored the single warning of a guard, would be shot. Sometimes the guards did not bother with that warning. The barracks were two-stories and wooden, so roughly put up that "the winter winds howl through the many crevices in the walls, sometimes covering the floors with a carpet of snow." With only one stove per room, "not more than a dozen, out of seventy-five inmates, can get close enough to feel its warmth." With only one blanket per prisoner, the rest had "to keep from freezing by constant exercise."[109]

Initially rations were good Care packages arrived regularly, with "clothing, provisions, books, and luxuries of all kinds" from the border states, and almost every northern city. The quality of rations began to deteriorate over time, however. In June 1864, the government ordered rations cut further as retribution for the suffering of Union troops at Andersonville.[110] Rations were not only scanty, but quality was well below standards for human consumption. Dog and rat meat became delicacies. Most prisoners returned home skin and bones. Concerning his time in the camp, Anderson Kirby reported, "If not for detailed service While in prison would have starved to death." He apparently referred to opportunities for work details to earn something to buy extra rations.[111] Lice ridden and without proper sanitation facilities, disease was rampant. Of the 12,000 total population, almost 2,000 died.

Alton Prison was established in an abandoned state prison also on the Mississippi River. Because Dorothea Dix had previously published an exposé of the unhealthy conditions when it had been a state prison, it had been shut down, but was recommissioned as a military prison in early 1862. It became quickly overcrowded with three men to the four foot by seven and a half foot cells. When a smallpox epidemic broke out, the sick were quarantined in an inadequate hospital on an adjacent island. There 1354 died, to be dumped in mass graves. During its three-year tenure, about 12,000 Confederates resided there.[112]

Camp Hoffman at Point Lookout, Maryland, had perhaps the worst conditions. Established after the Battle of Gettysburg, anywhere from 12–20,000 men existed in a camp intended to house 10,000. There were no barracks, only leaky, reject tents, despite Maryland's freezing, wet winters. Drinking water became polluted, and food was so poor that here too rats became a staple. 3,584 bodies have been found in a mass grave. The bitterest memory for many, however, was their treatment at the hands of the sadistic troops who guarded them.[113]

These three camps were the most frequently mentioned facilities holding men who served in the units that held Germantown men.

9

1865 · WINDING DOWN THE WAR

On January 1 after Grierson's expedition, the M&C was again completely abandoned, leaving Germantown cut off. Die-hard guerrillas and renegades remained stubbornly resistant to the very end, and Germantown experienced its share of continued hostilities, disrupting life and commerce. For instance, one P.P. Dunbar was apparently trying to do some kind of business in Germantown under a Federal commission when "Confederate raiders" confiscated all his money and merchandise.[1] Presumably this disrupted an effort to make merchandise available to residents. The area remained immersed in the total insecurity of a no-man's-land through February.

The land around Germantown and down into Mississippi was heavily infested with robber bands. Far to the south in Georgia and Alabama, even Forrest, as the commander responsible for order in West Tennessee and Mississippi, was sending what units he could spare into the area to suppress guerrilla-bandits and arrest deserters.[2] Across the countryside, blue and grey cavalry scoured the land looking for men pretending to serve the Confederate cause. Whether semi-official partisans living off the land, guerrillas without sanction, or just plain robber bands, they had become an intolerable source of disorder.

Anarchy grew from far more than the depredations of guerrillas, renegade soldiers, and the growing numbers of bandit gangs. Desperate whites who had lost everything showed no respect for private property as they sought to survive. Unoccupied, even inadequately defended homesteads fell prey to their needs. At least the Germantown area was free from the attentions of the vengeful Unionist home guards. Unionists had not suffered the persecutions in relatively harmonious Germantown that they had experienced elsewhere in the state. There were apparently few local grudges to be settled.

TABLE 5 Civil War Incidents in and around Germantown, 1865

11 February	raid into Mississippi launched from Germantown
March	regular, but light occupation resumed
3 March	major expedition into Mississippi launched from Germantown
28 March	incident at Germantown
9 April	Lee Surrenders
18 April	ambush near Germantown. The last combat in Tennessee
3 May	Guerrilla hunt launched from Germantown
4 May	Lt. Gen. R. Taylor surrenders the Confederate forces in Alabama
9 May	Forrest disbands his forces at Gainesville, AL
30 September	occupation of Germantown ended

The first three months were an especially rough transition from such anarchy back to the relative security of an occupied town. Germantown repeatedly served as a staging point for major and minor cavalry expeditions. For instance, on February 27, three entire cavalry divisions descended on the town, departing the town on the eleventh and returning on the twenty-sixth.[3]

Again on March 3, the bulk of a Cavalry Division coalesced at Germantown to mount another expedition. 1st brigade camped on the south of town, 2nd on the north and 3rd on the west. Distrust of both locals and his own men was apparently so high that the commander posted guards at "all the houses inhabited." Such a comment reinforces our image of how bad the life in Germantown had become, with many houses obviously uninhabited. The next day the Division moved on toward Collierville. Lieutenant Colonel Shelby of the 1st Brigade observed that there was "fine country, but no farming being done." Agricultural activity had degenerated again. The force that had descended on the town for two days consisted of 2,672 men and their horses, plus hundreds of pack animals. On the 11th, the expedition returned through Germantown.[4]

A reason for the commander's distrust both of the locals and his men became clear on March 4. Three of his men violated orders and strayed from camp to forage in a barn. Despite the presence of such a large Union force, some "bushwhackers" captured them. One managed to escape and reported that the other two had been murdered. These were the only casualties the unit suffered on the entire expedition.[5]

ILL. 16 Guerrilla Robbers, *Harper's Weekly*, 12.24.64. By the last year of the war, guerrillas and even partisan scouts had degenerated into robbers and terrorists.

Despite all the raids, guerrilla warfare continued to plague the area throughout February and March. Memphis newspapers frequently detailed the depredations. Increasingly, it was impossible to tell semi-legitimate partisans from bandits. Even the partisan bands had degenerated into open criminality. Although they continued to burn cotton, the *Bulletin* reported that their primary purpose was simple robbery. They took mostly money and other valuables. In the process, some allegedly employed torture and murder to uncover hidden treasure.[6]

On February 2, just beyond the sentries on State Line Road, a band of fifteen guerrillas had totally cleaned out McKnight's Store.[7] One small squad of guerrillas claiming to be part of Forrest's command had been operating along the south side of Nonconnah Creek stopping all traffic and confiscating anything of value. Confederate deserters pretending to block cotton trade were actually extorting the farmers, accepting payment in lieu of burning.[8]

The growing transition of guerrilla warfare into banditry came from the fusion of several elements. Companies of "scouts," ostensibly certified and attached to a Confederate cavalry unit south of the area had a dubious status. Most simply evolved into uncertified guerrillas—no discipline remained. They were joined by deserters from both armies. Not just outsiders, however, for many were members of the local communities cut loose as bonds and constraints dissolved. Even teenagers of all classes sought to replace lost bonds with those provided by a gang. Formerly respectable citizens had been criminalized by involvement in partisan ranging. They viewed most locals as collaborators. The brutality directed at their victims exceeded that once focused on hated enemies.[9]

DeWitt Clinton Fort had still operated as a legitimate partisan during 1863. Yet in his memoirs he admitted that his men exercised increased hostility toward suspected collaborators.

> The loyal citizens living between the military lines were often much abused and misrepresented . . . as sympathizing with the enemy. This accusation of civilian disloyalty was generally alleged by our own unscrupulous soldiers when caught doing something unmanly, or as an excuse for thefts and robberies. . . . [Others so encouraged would do the same] for the single purpose of committing further outrages upon their much slandered countrymen, who were already plundered to poverty.[10]

✦ ✦ ✦

On February 10, as part of creating districts for the military government of the conquered South. the Department of the Cumberland, to include Tennessee, was established under Major General George A. Thomas. On the 28th when Tennessee was divided into three districts, General Washburn at Memphis was given command of the District of West Tennessee.[11]

Finally Federal forces began to reestablish continuous occupation. To begin the process of securing the railroad, on March 25, Colonel Hasbrouk Davis of the 12th Illinois moved his headquarters to Collierville, with detachments guarding all bridges along the line. To defuse tensions, Davis admonished his men to treat the people as "under the protection of the Union forces. . . . All good soldiers will conduct themselves so as to give no just cause of offense." Troops were to be assessed for damages caused, and if the villlains could not be identified, their entire unit would pay. "All stragglers will be reported at these headquarters to be placed at work upon the railroad."[12] The military was doing its best to protect the locals, but it also had to keep its soldiers from straying into places where they could be caught by guerrillas.

The commander of the Cavalry Division headquartered at Memphis, Colonel E.D. Osband, issued an order that tells us both about the distribution of troops in the Germantown area and how unstable Union control remained. One regiment each of the 2nd Brigade was stationed at Germantown (11th New York), Collierville (12th Illinois) and La Fayette (Rossville) respectively. They were to avoid predictable patterns of their patrols, to prevent ambush, and to facilitate capture of prowling bands.[13]

With victory imminent, intelligent commanders down the line perceived the necessity for establishing some sense of normalcy among the civilian population.

Union commanders assessed the civilian mood. For example, General Stanley, at Huntsville, Alabama, argued for much more conciliatory practices. His analysis of the public mood divided the population into three groups: (1) open unionists; (2) "people who are timid about their persons and property, and might be said to be on the fence;" (3) and secessionists. "It is from this middle or kind of neutral class that we have much to expect." Local unionists had assured him that in the upcoming elections "conservative or reconstructionist" candidates could win against the secessionists. "Under this state of affairs I deem it sound policy to make as many friends as we can by a just and lenient course toward the people, and to give our enemies as few occasions as possible to bring the accusation of an unforgiving course against us."[14]

Stanley's analysis described the mood at Germantown equally well. In his area, the harsh policies then being pursued were like those experienced in Shelby County during 1862 and 1863. The provost marshal was examining persons on a list for possible expulsion, including even former pro-unionists who had succumbed to the wave of enthusiasm during the heyday of the Confederate cause. Such harshness needed modification. Washburn apparently considered Stanley's assessment as applicable to his district as well.

In addition to having survived such an early wave of harassment in 1862, the citizens of Germantown had endured the depredations of almost three years of occupation and guerrilla warfare. Among the "neutral middle," there were undoubtedly many simply wishing "a plague on both your houses." They yearned only for some return to normalcy. To see the return of their neighbors—soldiers, refugees and expellees. They wanted to live together again in harmony, regardless of former differences. Such secessionist sentiments as those expressed by J. Dix Mills were seen as simply impracticable.

Stanley described a desire to restore old community relations that existed in tightly knit, small communities. Unionists pleaded leniency for their secessionist neighbors who "used their utmost influence during the late Confederate occupation to protect the Unionists of this vicinity." Such neighborliness needed to be rekindled. Stanly's best argument was, "We who are engaged in this war have other homes to go to if we survive the war, but these people must live here . . . they desire to extend kindness to their neighbors."[15] Sadly, this understanding did not extend throughout occupation forces.

In December 1863, President Lincoln had issued an amnesty proclamation. The interpretation and application of such directives were the responsibility of officers with a wide range of temperaments grown from years of war and hostility that had reached the level of demonization of the enemy. While some prominent Tennesseans, who had vacillated back and forth during the early years of the war, found easy readmission to the rights of citizenship, the former work-a-day agents of local and state government were less likely to get the benefit of the doubt. Occupation officials, badly needing to reestablish local government, had to argue for inclusion of "sheriffs, constables, magistrates, county and circuit clerks, registers, coroners, &c."[16]

Despite its unionist bias, the *Bulletin* was probably capturing local sentiments better than the *Appeal*, still away in Georgia behind Confederate lines. On February 5, it reported that in the surrounding counties the "war feeling of those who have heretofore actively supported the rebellion is entirely played out. With scarce exception, that avow a desire for peace, and admit that . . . a prolongation of the contest can only benefit guerrilla thieves and must bring greater ruin to the Southern people. Some (even prominent rebels) are expressing hopes that law and order might be restored by the reconstruction of State government in Tennessee."[17]

The political leaders of Germantown had hardly been prominent rebel officials. They now revealed their desire for the reestablishment of order through government. Some had obviously taken the detested oath to serve in appointed offices and to stand for election. Regardless of one's sentiments, the desire for peace, law and order had become the prominent motivation.

Many southerners had resigned themselves to the inevitable. Surviving local farmers and businessmen especially wanted nothing more than to get back to business as usual. In Memphis, both the Southern merchants who had remained and a flood of Northern businessmen who had come in to take advantage of commercial opportunities were anxious to have trade barriers with the North removed and connections with the still rebellious states reestablished as soon as possible. The machinery of an interstate mercantile system had survived in Memphis veritably undisturbed. Such an opportunity for reconnecting it to market would have an especially heavy influence on the agriculturalists and businessmen of the surrounding area.

At Washington, led first by Lincoln and then Andrew Johnson, farsighted officials sought a quick reunion and reconciliation to get the economy going as a bond of national unity. Needless to say, powerful business and financial interest groups supported the cause, but radical politicians and suspicious or embittered military men put vengeance first. Consequently from March through June, it remained unclear just when and how a reconstruction process would develop. Wartime laws and military ordinances had erected barriers to North-South trade and economic activities within occupied territory.

Lincoln's assassination ignited more animosity and distrust while throwing his lenient amnesty plans into disarray. President Johnson cast about for excessively lenient solutions while local occupation authorities interpreted the evolving guidelines inconsistently.[18] Like the rest of the South, the people around Germantown hoped for the best but continued to encounter frustrating obstacles. The guidelines issued for screening the applicants for amnesty to insure "good faith" were clearly intended to cull out those who still harbored unacceptable convictions or merely sought to escape retribution. Such should be tried "for his former treasonable acts."[19]

✦ ✦ ✦

On February 11, the *Bulletin* reported that "deserters from the rebel army continue to come into our lines every day, sometimes to the number of fifteen at a time. Many former residents of Memphis have come in and they state that others are on the way or watching for an opportunity to desert. Regiments are thus becoming mere skeletons; this is particularly true of Tennessee regiments."[20]

For several months preceding formal surrender, increasingly area soldiers had accepted the inevitable and came home on their own initiative. Of course, they had to swear loyalty, and to accept such changes that had occurred during the war, especially the emancipation. Interestingly, this oath included an escape—they would not have to continue to respect emancipation if Congress or the Supreme Court nullified it. As of February 28, 1,045 men from Shelby County had reportedly entered the city.[21] The records kept by the provost marshal at Memphis for monitoring these men divided them into those who took the oath and those accepted "in lieu of the oath."[22]

The *Bulletin* commented positively on the quality of this new wave of deserters, while unfairly dismissing former deserters as "unsteady, unreliable fellows" who had given up on the cause so easily. "The deserters who are now coming in are of a much better class. . . ." They had fought on in a mistaken sense of honor for a bad and hopeless cause. There was nothing traitorous about their decision, and they could be trusted to keep their oath.

In Memphis, General Washburn was ahead of the curve in efforts to find accommodation with the "neutral or middle" elements of the population. He focused especially on reestablishing production, commerce and civil government, all of which required a pacified population. He liberalized restrictions on the operation of plantations. Owners who had remained were allowed to operate. They had to have contracts of employment with either their former slaves or freedmen. Registered plantation owners would be allowed to take out the necessary supplies.[23]

On March 10, a general order relaxed some of the more stringent aspects of martial law. "(C)itizens will be allowed to come freely to Memphis and dispose of their products and take back a limited amount of family supplies." The oath was still required. All products for sale had to be the results of free labor. Procedures were established to protect those bringing in products for sale from being exploited.[24] Deserters and parolees who took the oath were registered with Memphis' provost marshal, with physical characteristics and general place of residence recorded to facilitate monitoring.[25]

On March 21, Thomas sent Washburn orders, some of which he had already instituted, apparently on his own initiative. Thomas had requested that

> as far as practicable . . . you will endeavor to restore the confidence of the people of West Tennessee, and encourage them in any desire they may express to enforce civil laws against the outlaws and guerrillas who infest their counties. To this end you are authorized to occupy and

repair the Memphis and Charleston Railroad as far as LaGrange....
Encourage all the counties in West Tennessee to organize their county
courts and administer the civil laws, assuring them that they will not
be interfered with by the military authorities as long as they conduct
themselves in a manner loyal to the Government of the United States;
encouraging them also to cultivate their farms, with the assurance that
no more arbitrary seizures of private property of any kind, particularly
horses, mules, and oxen, will be permitted....and that they will be
permitted to carry to market and dispose of at Memphis... products
of their farms... without molestation."

They were to "keep themselves well informed of all offensive movements of the enemy... and inform the nearest military authority promptly...." The people were responsible for preserving peace and quiet.[26] Accordingly, Washburn continued to issue new directives to curb financial restrictions.[27]

Meanwhile by March 20, orders had been issued to reopen the M&C Railroad. Within four days it was open to Collierville, and throughout April and May, the more extensively damaged portions were repaired to Grand Junction.[28] This restored mail service to Germantown. On October 18, Monroe P. Webb was appointed Germantown's new postmaster, and civilian mail service fully resumed.[29] Former teacher and son of the Webb school founder, he must have been a firm unionist. He had to have credentials that satisfied the politicians in charge of reconstruction. They, after all, had the Postmaster General's ear in making appointments.

The 11th Regiment was specifically headquartered in Germantown March 28–April 18, and then at Collierville with elements in Germantown until mustered out of service on September 30. From May through June, it was the only regiment covering the entire area. Only companies L and M remained encamped at Germantown proper.[30]

Yet, defending the rail line remained a problem. Colonel Davis at Collierville reported that on March 28 the vedettes of the 11th New York Cavalry at Germantown were attacked by "four men." Two Union men were wounded, one mortally, and one of the rebels was captured.[31] Such a small "prowling band of soldiers" was operating without support—a futile gesture of defiance.

The memoirs of DeWitt Clinton Fort cast light on their mood.

> But so confident were my hopes of the success of our cause that my mind could not be brought to think or dream of failure. My patriotism was too sanguine. It over did the thing. I was so infatuated by its prompting that upon all topics connected with the success of our cause I was mentally blinded to all but one event—Success.[32]

Supplemented by a bloody anger, such a mood led him to continue guerrilla operations in defiance of orders. He defended their reputation against charges of being little more than bandits by wrapping them in patriotic colors. Their "motives" or compulsions were more complex. They saw no future in defeat. Their lives had become no different from that of outlaw bands. They had fought in a desperate style that could terminate suddenly and violently. They had lived for the moment and the few material and psychological rewards that their adventures brought. Their desperation produced behavior that has always led occupation forces to see partisan resistance against them as banditry or terrorism. Any men who had become involved in such die-hard resistance had crossed a line that would make reintegration into society almost impossible.

Fort boasted of his ability to camp right next to Union camps and spy upon them or steal their horses. He or his men could move in and out of Germantown despite the presence of Federal occupiers. Never mentioning anything about actions that caused suffering by civilians, he bragged of being able to rob and punish Union jayhawkers who preyed upon defenseless civilians. After a period of purely unsanctioned existence during the winter of 1864/65, on March 15, his command allegedly received a new commission to operate again legitimately. He gave no clues about the source of such a "commission." He boasted that his small detachment struck wherever he pleased, but always avoided likely damage to itself. He claimed he had the guard detachments along the railroad terrified. Even the garrison in Memphis was uneasy.[33] If not "terrified," clearly "uneasy" describes the state of affairs up to the very end. Throughout the winter and spring of 1865, Federal records report incidents of his successful ambushes of patrols, even concentrating 100 to 150 men to defeat more sizable Union forays.

General Lee surrendered his Army in Virginia on April 9, *and Johnston's Army of Tennessee in North Carolina surrendered April 26.* Lieutenant General Taylor finally surrendered his army in Alabama on May 4, and Forrest disbanded his forces on the 9th. Consequently there was time for one more skirmish at Germantown. This was the last reported incident in Tennessee and among the last east of the Mississippi, all minor skirmishes.[34]

Captain George W. Smith, 11th New York Cavalry based in Germantown, reported that on April 18 a patrol moving toward Collierville was attacked about six miles out of Germantown, which would place it near Bray's Station on present Poplar Avenue. The rebel force was estimated as from 60 to 100 strong of "Ford's command" (undoubtedly Fort), while the patrol consisted of only eighteen men under Lieutenant John H. Mills, D Company. Mills was pursued to within two miles of Germantown (approximately the present Oakleigh neighborhood on Poplar Pike). The report implies that stragglers may have been unnecessarily shot.[35]

In his report on the next day, Smith noted that General Washburn had ordered that no more patrols be sent out with fewer than fifty men. The captain complained that he had only 190 men at Germantown, out of which he had to maintain a picket of 32 men daily, a daily scouting party of 30 men, plus camping duties. He called for reinforcements so he could mount operations against the guerrillas.[36] He would have to wait several weeks.

Until May, Smith had kept his camp widely scattered because "the garrison was continually menaced by guerrilla bands," requiring them to occupy defensible points.[37] Imagine how the men of the 11th New York felt, knowing the war was over for all practical purposes, but that they could still die at any moment.

As for Fort, he disbanded Fort's Scouts at Holy Springs on May 7, but nevertheless, he and some of his men remained in the Holy Springs and Memphis area. On May 17 at Columbus, Mississippi, apparently remnants of the Scouts surrendered with the 2nd Missouri Cavalry to which they were "formally attached," thus escaping any retribution for their careers. Although he had talked of going west to join the holdouts in Texas, he remained at Holy Springs until arrested in March 1866. He would be tried and acquitted for murder and a plot to assassinate Tennessee Governor Brownlow. After release, he took his wife to Texas where he would return to his law practice until he was shot by a former fellow officer in 1868.[38]

Local tolerance for the more flagrant bandits had reached its limits. By April in response to Washburn's appeals and being free of any legitimate partisans, Germantown residents were reportedly "determined to clear out these robbers. A few days since they caught three of them, and, after a hasty trial, hung them to a limb of a tree. They were young men from Mississippi."[39]

Finally on May 3, Washburn launched "a guerrilla hunt." The detachment left from Germantown on the 4th, ordered to "beat up the country as far as the Cold Water," but to stop there and return to Germantown. This expedition focused on territory that remained a base for raiders and brigands despite Confederate efforts. Washburn gave orders, "Should the murderers Fort and Mat Luxton be caught they will be disposed of by a drumhead court-marshal. . . ."[40] By this time most of the people of Germantown undoubtedly appreciated such expeditions for the relief they promised. But it was too late for Captain Smith to catch Fort.

During the months prior to surrender, Forrest based in Georgia and Alabama had also been dispatching policing detachments into Mississippi and even West Tennessee. When called upon to surrender in May, the commander of such a detachment, Colonel J.F. Newsom operating in eastern parts of West Tennessee, would request, "In behalf of the citizens I ask that none of the men belonging to the command of Colonels Hawkins and Hurst be sent here. The feeling that exists between soldiers of these commands and the citizens is such that private malice and private revenge might be more the result of such a policy than the restoration of order."[41] In fact, these two infamous commanders were no longer leading the 5th and 6th Tennessee Cavalry U.S.A.[42]

Indeed, renegades from these Tennessee Cavalry U.S.A. were as bad as Confederate guerrillas. By May 13, from Eastport, Mississippi, General Hatch was reporting,

> Many bands are surrendering here under your order, among them one of the worst, Burt Hayes. I learn a Mr. Chandler, calling himself captain, a brother-in-law of Fielding Hurst, is levying contributions upon the citizens of McNairy County, Tenn., amounting to $50,000. Hurst has already taken about $100,000 out of West Tennessee in blackmail when colonel of the Sixth Cavalry (Union). What shall I do with Chandler, if he reports to me as ordered? If he does not report, shall I treat him as an outlaw?[43]

Thomas responded, "Summon Chandler to surrender, and, if he refuses, declare him an outlaw and treat him accordingly, and inform the people that hereafter all illegal bands will be regarded and treated as outlaws."[44]

> If I ever get through this war,
> And Lincoln's chains don't bind me,
> I'll make my way to Tennessee ---
> To the girl I left behind me.

The Germantown soldiers away from home remained scattered across the south-east. For them, the road home was long and difficult. For each, it was a different story, different experiences, different hardships, and different conclusions. Henry Woodson, who was in Georgia when it ended, recalled his experience.

> I left Columbus, Georgia, and started on my journey homeward, walking much of the way as there were only now and then short stretches of railroad in operation . . . only one train per day of open flat cars.
> On leaving Columbus, there were some two or three hundred paroled Confederates in our crowd, returning to their homes in various parts. . . . Our route was from Columbus, Georgia, via Montgomery and Selma, Alabama. At Selma I spent one night with my cousin . . . thence to Meridian, Jackson, Grenada, Oxford and Holly Springs, Mississippi. . . . When I arrived at Holly Springs. The crowd of two or three hundred . . . had dwindled down to three. . . . Early on the morning of May 19, 1865, these three weary, dirty, hungry Confederate soldiers, having slept in a vacant outhouse by the roadside, started on our last stretch of our homeward journey. Having gone about twelve miles, two of the boys took the road leading to Mount Pleasant, I alone went on to Rossville, Tennessee, on the . . . Memphis and Charleston Railroad, arriving there at eleven o'clock a.m. . . . About two o'clock p.m., I boarded a west bound train. The conductor asked for the fare to Germantown, I replied, 'I have nothing but Confederate money.' The conductor saw the situation and with the remark 'I will see you later.' passed on, but the kind-hearted man made it convenient not to 'see me later.' . . . I arrived at Germantown about 4 p.m. May 19, 1865. After a few minutes' walk I reached home and loved ones.[45]

As the end approached, Forrest's cavalry had assembled at Verona, Mississippi. A general and a senator addressed them in hopes of buoying morale, claiming that if Lee was forced to abandon Richmond, he would take the army west across the Mississippi to continue the war indefinitely. Such transparent nonsense backfired. It confirmed suspicions of imminent defeat, and desertions increased. When Forrest resorted to executions, that also backfired. His ranks were depleted.[46]

When the official news of Lee's surrender had broken, an officer of the 7th recalled that "many brave, strong men wept as children. Some indeed, were willing to prolong the fight, 'to the death,' but better councils prevailed...." They actually struck up friendly relations with their Federal counterparts, and drew plentiful rations for the ride home. They like Woodson were left to find their own way in small groups, but mounted, for they were allowed to retain their horses. Some reported assistance from sympathetic Union troops along the way.[47]

The men were issued parole passes which enabled them to return home. The Federal Quartermaster's Department was supposed to provide transportation, but that usually failed, because the railroad network was badly shattered. The parolee had to sign and carry an oath. "I . . . do solemnly swear that I will not bear arms against the United States of America, or give any information, or do any military duty whatever. . . ." The pass specified at least the state to which he could return, and specified that he could remain there "without molestation so long as he observes the conditions of his parole, and the regulations and laws

ILL. 17 Union Troops Sharing Rations with Defeated Confederates. A scene described by Germantown's own men.

in force at his place of residence."[48] Thus, these war-weary soldiers expected to return home without anyone throwing obstacles in the way of beginning anew.

The local men coming from North Carolina or Virginia had to make their way home across all of Tennessee. Under the terms of surrender, they were allowed to retain any weapons and horses that were their personal property, a concession essential to their livelihood. This posed serious problems for the Union commanders in these areas. Consequently Federal officials appointed Confederate officers to maintain command over units which were provided with rations and baggage wagons, and were allowed to retain one-fifth of their issued rifles. They, after all, were endangered by brigands. They had to make their way on foot across the mountains to Greenville where most would board trains.[49]

Coming across Tennessee they also had to deal with the occupation authorities, many of whom were having trouble with the concept of "amnesty" for offenders. On April 17, General Thomas began revoking some amnesties. His concern was the allegedly numerous, formerly devout rebels who now sought to escape any consequences and save their property. They had gone to other districts to take the oath where their history was unknown.[50] Presumably this did not apply to the parolees.

But then on April 25, Thomas issued another harsh directive that further reversed policies that were ameliorating conditions in Tennessee. "No more amnesty oaths will be administered to either soldiers or citizens, and all are repudiated and annulled which have been taken since the 15th day of December last."[51] This sounded like it included the parolees.

The realities of the situation hit home immediately. On April 29 from Chattanooga, General Steedman reported,

> There are large numbers of paroled rebel soldiers from Lee's army and Forrest's here and coming into our lines at all points, who are utterly destitute, and who will inevitably be driven to stealing and robbery ... unless they can be permitted to go to their homes or be provided for. ... What shall I do with them?[52]

From Knoxville, General Stoneman also asked for clarification.

> Your telegram received. Numbers of men have come into East Tennessee with authority from Gen. Grant to go to their homes, which are in

East Tennessee. Do your instructions include such persons; and if so, shall they be sent without the limits of the State?[53]

To them, Thomas responded, "By decision of the Attorney-Gen., no Confederate is entitled to come into a loyal State on his parole. He will have to take the oath of allegiance to the United States to enable him to return."

Thomas forwarded part of this directive to Washburn.[54] From all appearances, his intention was to dump most of the veterans who did not immediately take the oath on the still unoccupied states, along with the accumulated flotsam of both armies.

Confronted with such large numbers of Confederate soldiers, especially Tennesseans who would have been expelled south, Thomas revised his orders on May 6. "You are authorized to administer the amnesty oath to rebel soldiers, but not to officers or citizens. It is now too late for them to be reaping the benefits of the amnesty proclamation, after having maintained an attitude of hostility for four years."[55] It was as though he did not know that most of the field and company officers had been elected, not appointed for their convictions. The next day, he seemed to reverse himself and allow all paroled prisoners who had surrendered with Lee or Johnston who lived in Tennessee to return to their homes. Others who had previously been captured in battle would continue to be processed as prisoners of war.[56] From Memphis, that would mean shipment to Vicksburg for parole. Thomas and others were so vindictive and vague that they left local men uncertain as to their status.

At least for West Tennessee, Washburn's policies were slightly more tolerant. "Citizens who left our lines and sought refuge in rebeldom, and have resisted all persuasions to return until the present moment, will not be allowed to return to Memphis at present. Confederate officers . . . paroled from the armies of Lee, Johnson, and Taylor will not be allowed to wear their uniform. . . ." Paroled enlisted men had thirty days to get other clothing.[57]

POWs like John Kirby, discharged from Rock Island Prison on April 15, 1865, were sent home to Memphis by steam boat.[58] Although the most commodious form of transportation, if they in any way resembled those of the infamous, overcrowded Sultana taking Federal soldiers North from southern prisons, they were neither comfortable nor safe, though undoubtedly a relief from confinement.

In order to get released, prisoners like Kirby had to take the oath of allegiance. Those who refused remained in custody until the end of summer. Aside from steamboats, trains brought most prisoners home.[59] The depot at Germantown was a welcome sight, marking the end of a long ordeal but the beginning of a new life of uncertainty.

On May 9, Washburn continued local efforts to restore peace and a working society. The large numbers who had taken refuge in Memphis were a serious problem. They had "to return home and do something for themselves. Rations will no longer be issued, except to the aged and helpless and young children. There is employment for all in the country who are willing to work. ... (M)illions of acres are lying waste for lack of labor; those that can work must or starve, black or white."[60]

Unfortunately, putting the agricultural economy back in shape involved much more than putting pressure on the idle. In reality, this effort might have merely diverted the pressure of supporting the uprooted on to the destitute countryside and towns like Germantown.

Meanwhile, Washburn still had to arrange the surrender and security of the remaining Confederate forces inside his part of Tennessee. One such was that under Colonel J.F. Newsom in the vicinity of Brownsville where they had been suppressing guerrillas and brigands. Newsom was sent copies of Confederate surrender orders giving terms.

> Confederate soldiers reporting to you will be paroled and allowed to go home, and such as desire to take the oath of amnesty will be allowed to do so.... You will keep record of all such and report to the provost marshal here. Officers and citizens will not be allowed to take the amnesty oath without first obtaining permission of the department commander....[61]

At least some officers and citizens were now being given an opportunity for amnesty. May 29, President Johnson issued another amnesty proclamation clarifying who qualified to take the loyalty oath and achieve an amnesty.

✦ ✦ ✦

The physical condition of the soldiers who had to "bum" their way home over hundreds of miles was undoubtedly poor. They must have looked gaunt. According to the Tennessee veterans' questionnaires, most were left with a lasting sense of the futility and horror of war. They would not add their voices to those who would romanticize the war. Undoubtedly bitterness at defeat would plague many. Initially, however, most were more interested in getting on with their lives and reestablishing themselves with families left behind.[62] Nevertheless, even those most focused on restoring a world of normalcy would soon encounter a long list of problems.

The Civil War equivalent of post-traumatic stress disorder left many haunted and hard pressed to resume a productive life.[63] Broken spirits and shattered minds often sought recourse in drink. As always, those with shattered bodies faced a more difficult future. During the war, each southern state sought to provide the numerous amputees with artificial limbs. After the war, those who had served the Union cause, continued to have such support from the Federal government which promptly established an "Artificial Leg Office" in Memphis to serve local veterans. Confederate veterans, however, had to endure a more uncertain support. By the spring of 1866, for Tennessee veterans a Benevolent Society of Tennessee organized to provide disabled Confederate soldiers with artificial limbs. It was dependent on donations and fund-raising events.[64] At least one local man had lost a leg.[65] There was no support for psychological damage, however. It continued well after the war.

✦ ✦ ✦

Meanwhile in April and May, Federal authorities removed trade restrictions on materials that could not be used for military purposes. After authorization of the resumption of trade with the "insurrectionary states," on May 11, General Washburn allowed stores to be reopened to sell supplies in nine communities outside Memphis. Collierville was one, but not Germantown. Presumably Germantown could be added since rules provided a procedure for merchants to apply for a permit, but aside from Union veterans, only established citizens who had long been loyal were granted permits. On May 13, Washburn terminated the requirement for passes to enter and leave Memphis. The city and its trade were open to all who took the loyalty oath.[66]

No matter how badly they wanted to resume a normal economic life, some locals could not stomach the idea of that oath. Some felt it was treason to bow to the invader. Others felt insulted that they should have to swear loyalty like traitors rather than people who had stood up for their presumed constitutional rights. Increasingly, however, most bowed to the inevitable. They headed for the Provost Marshal or the U.S. Treasury offices in Memphis, took the oath and began to do business. Between May 15 and June 26, almost three thousand oaths were turned in at the Memphis office of the Bureau of Refugees, Freedmen, and Abandoned Lands. Small farmers represented the largest numbers.[67] They had mere survival to worry about. They continued to pay the highest price for a war to preserve the Southern way of life focused so heavily on the slavery from which they had not benefited.

One planter and veteran who successfully broke through the barriers against major slave holders gaining an amnesty was John W. Quenichet. More typical of the local population, he had originally been ambivalent about secession, but like most was soon caught up in the "cause," and had joined the 154th Volunteer Regiment. Its constant connection with the 13th Regiment kept him in close contact with the neighbors of his plantation of over one thousand acres, located in the Germantown area south of Nonconnah Creek. Although excluded from the terms of President Johnson's amnesty of May 1865, he applied for an exception in June and was pardoned in October.[68] Undoubtedly one's original position on secession heavily shaped one's willingness to leave the "cause" behind and resume life and business as soon as possible.

✦ ✦ ✦

Finally on June 14, the Cavalry Division began its staged withdrawal from the area, although elements would remain until January 1866.[69] On July 3, martial law was lifted in West Tennessee, undoubtedly a date chosen to give locals a reason to celebrate the Fourth.[70]

Well before then, however, for some the story of Germantown and its occupiers had ended on a sweeter note. The Memphis *Argus* reported that on May 15, Germantown was the site of a gala, day-long social event involving a pleasant mingling of citizens and soldiers. "It was indeed pleasant to see the cordial and harmonious commingling of those who were so lately arrayed against each other in bitter hostilities." When the reporter asked several of "the most prominent citizens of Germantown in regard to the conduct of the troops," they responded that the men of the 11th New York Cavalry had "deported themselves with the utmost decorum."[71]

Yet from the article emerges an incongruous set of images. Although the event was held on the lawns of the home of Mr. Molitor, where "the ladies of Germantown were busy in spreading tables," who staged the event and why was not elaborated. Captain Smith played the role of host, the tickets to bring the guests from Memphis were provided by the railroad, and some of the special treats for the party were provided by the Memphis company of Mepham & Bros. In addition to the reporter invited to cover this apparent PR event, the primary guest of honor was General Washburn. To start the festivities, the guests, the members of the band and all the company's officers took a horseback excursion the three and a half miles to the "shady banks of the Wolf River. ... The ladies of the company enjoyed the ride exceedingly." Among them was Mrs. Smith, the commander's wife who must surely have resided in one of the Germantown homes.

> We passed through a deserted lawn, in which once had stood the pleasant house of some one; the rose bushes still bloom, and the woodbines still cling to the (illegible), but the tall Lombardy poplars weep over a heap of ruins that mark the old hearthstone spot. We plucked a few of the fragrant flowers, and the ladies of the party bound up a few bouquets as memorials of the visit to a deserted home, and then passed on our way. [72]

A romantic interlude amidst a ruin brought by the war?

Throughout the day, General Washburn's headquarters band, provided lively entertainment. In the evening, "All the delicacies and luxuries of the season" were placed upon the long tables set up on the lawn. "After becoming satisfied with strawberries, ice-cream, cake and confectioneries, it was soon made manifest that our entertainers had made some other provisions for our creature comfort," sparkling wine provided by Messrs. Mepham & Bros. Although the main course was described as "the plane essentials of life," one wonders how such a feast with delicacies from outside went down with the locals below the level of "the most prominent citizens of Germantown." If any remained, did they even have many of "the plane essentials of life" by this date? "One of the old citizens proposed a toast to Major General C.O. Washburn, whose actions and policy had proved so beneficial and instrumental in bringing about the present condition of affairs." After the banquet, the general was presented with "a splendid bouquet on behalf of Miss Lou Parish and Miss Nannie (Ann) Woodson, young ladies of Germantown."

Why was Germantown, the town so recently "menaced by guerrilla bands," chosen for this gala event? Sherman's "dirty hole" of guerrilla conspirators had evolved to the point that its most prominent citizens had become thankful and convivial to their occupiers. Were they limited to the old pro-unionists, or had so many of the "middle" come to accept the new order? Mrs. Molitor had been active in the women's auxiliary in 1861, but by 1863 was having convivial relations with boarding officers. The state of their mill is unknown, but they had suffered extensive confiscations. Miss Woodson's father had been an "old line Whig, a strong Union man, was opposed to secession and voted against it, but when his adopted state, Tennessee, seceded from the Union, he cast his lot with her; and all his sympathies and efforts were given to the south." Although he had not served, his son had, and he also had "given all that was in his power to aid the cause."[73] (At least, so ran the family's post-war accounts of allegiance to the lost cause.) Clearly General Washburn's policies constituted changes that had actually made "the present condition of affairs" so much better than the desolation of 1864 and the severance of all trade with the city.

One has to wonder, however, were similar "PR events" held in other communities? This was a carefully staged event by occupation authorities and not some spontaneous local display of harmony. The reporter's presence was arranged and the article was atypical for the *Argus*. The paper itself was an official organ of the occupation authorities. Washburn and his staff displayed considerable sagacity in their efforts to build up the public mood.

During the relative security of the occupation of 1863, accompanied by the major defeats at Gettysburg and Vicksburg, ardor for the cause had cooled among many. As occupation authorities curbed rapacious confiscations, familiarity also curbed the peoples' hostility. The returned chaos during 1864 had reinforced the longing for order and security instead of fueling a renewed zeal, despite if not because of Forrest's successes. That year must have brought something like the highs and lows of a manic-depressive. By May 1865, the happy participation of the leading ladies in this festive event reflects what one student of their writings has described as "Women's growing sense of self-interest shaded into self-indulgence. . . . As hardships mounted, escape seemed all the more desirable. . . . (L)ong years of war had to some degree hardened southerners' feelings and had left them insensitive to others sufferings." This increased the gap between them and the less comfortable.[74] Nevertheless being "grateful" (if not just "relieved") probably applied to much of the area's population.

On May 14, the *Bulletin*, published a reliable effort to ascertain the mood of the area. Careful to keep his disposition and intentions secret, the enquirer drew people out in casual conversation. He found only one man "who did not frankly and heartily express a desire for peace and order." They were all weary of war and anarchy, and wanted to get back to work, but greatly needed mules and farm hands. The great majority of those who had served as soldiers wanted to work their farms or find employment. "Those planters, who had dealt fairly with their blacks and had paid them for their work, were all doing well and satisfied with their future prospects. The railroad, now open, is doing its best to accommodate the public."[75]

Those who had stayed home and endured occupation had accepted the new reality. Many deserters and parolees, many of the refugees who were returning sought accommodation. Among the expellees and soldiers who had held out to the end, sentiments must have been much more complicated. Many were undoubtedly resigned and focused primarily on getting on with life. Others retained their self-righteous indignation against Northern oppression, were bitter and humiliated in defeat, and resentful of those who too easily sought accommodation. Finally, as in all wars, returning veterans felt an emotional divide from the civilian population who would never understand their experiences.[76] As this mix amalgamated, they all soon endured the conflicts of Reconstruction.

The periodically malnourished civilian population had been especially vulnerable to disease. The full occupation of 1863 may have provided some relief, but most of 1864 undid all that. During the last two years of the war, families continued to produce children in the face of such uncertainty. From the greatly reduced population, five old resident families birthed children who survived the war. Susan Rutland lost her husband and his namesake who had been born on the eve of the war. They had replaced him with William before her husband's death. Nevertheless, mortality undid any such growth. Emily Lucken Mills lost her first son. Elizabeth Woodson had a child, but both she and it would die in the summer of 1865. Something wiped out the entire family of William Wilson, his wife Adeline and two of their infants. Only little Lucy remained in the care of the John Callis family.[77]

The returning soldiers or their widows set to work restoring their farms. Neglected fields, destroyed equipment, the loss of draft animals and disrupted labor supplies made 1865 a year of minimal recovery. Nevertheless, commerce and subsistence agriculture struggled back to life. The M&C Railroad reopened in May, with a daily train leaving Memphis for Grand Junction. Operations required considerable caution on the much damaged line, however, for it took a full eleven hours to travel the fifty odd miles. Federal construction on the railroads had been stopped by an order of April 28, but the line was not turned over to the railroad company to begin repairs until September 12.[78] Nevertheless, by November, one train per day was running between Memphis and Stevenson, Alabama, a twenty-four hour trip. At least, this had reestablished the old connections with southern and north-eastern cities. Passengers and freight were again moving in and out of Germantown.[79]

Political order and self-government came even slower. As late as December, Shelby County remained the only county in the state to have no civil government outside the city of Memphis. Civil District Eleven was without any magistrate, and, without a charter Germantown had no official government. The resumption of both political and economic life would be entangled in Reconstruction politics.

PART SUMMARY

When it comes to contentious issues, a given population divides itself into three groups. Two will be aligned on the opposite sides of the issue. Rarely does either side constitute a majority. Between the opposition, the middle is often at least a plurality, ambivalent but rarely indifferent, until something brings about an overwhelming shift. This was the situation in Germantown and most of Tennessee before Lincoln's election. Even after the Deep South states seceded, the majority remained opposed to secession. Although almost uniformly fearful of abolition, even many slaveholders were ambivalent about slavery, and even those who were not saw no need for secession to "protect" it.

The fearmongering rhetoric of the rabid secessionists had its effect however. It precipitated secession in the Deep South. Then once Lincoln announced the use of force to suppress the revolt, a strong majority of Tennesseans demanded secession to defend against invasion. Typically declaration of war unleased a wave of martial fervor and an even stronger shifts in sentiments. Any opposition became unpatriotic, even treason. The ambivalent middle rallied to the new cause, defense against "Northern aggression." Even most of the remaining opposition either caught the infection or quietly submitted to the consensus. That consensus grew more than anything from the community's relative social harmony. Such was the result in all of Shelby County. No one in Germantown openly opposed enough to vote against secession, although some remained known as unionist. Only slowly did the community dissolve as it underwent the shifting tides of war.

The first year was one of martial, romantic enthusiasm mixed with concerns about possible invasion. Families contributed directly to the cause by buying bonds, women's groups made uniforms, flags and equipment, private businesses converted to military production, and most Germantown men volunteered at least for home defense. A growing number enlisted in Tennessee's volunteer regiments, prepared to serve wherever needed. Many who had volunteered for home defense, however, soon found themselves incorporated in Confederate regiments, especially as successive drafts were made from the militia to fill "volunteer" regimental ranks. This was a forerunner of draft laws that would expand subsequently to all able-bodied men ages 16 to 45.

As the war extracted more and more life and property from the people, the privileges of the few and the disproportionately heavy burdens that fell on the ordinary and poor became increasingly obvious. Those with the least property to loose hurt the most, but especially when the soldier was the sole breadwinner. The faith in social opportunity and sense of community that had prevailed in antebellum Germantown would erode.

1862 brought months of impending doom, then the chaos of living in a no-man's-land between federal forces in Memphis, Confederate forces harassing from Mississippi, and growing numbers of undisciplined Partisan units. Those who had not gone off to war were helpless to defend themselves. Acts of guerrilla defiance by a few brought retribution on the town. Federal troops were allowed a few days to destroy, confiscate or pilfer property in an orgy of retribution. Soon the town's factories and mills that had supported the Confederate cause were destroyed. The town experienced successive running firefights. Even if it had been possible to work the fields, the men and many slaves were gone and the remaining slaves increasingly self-assertive.

1863 brought a restoration of order at the price of occupation by numbers of soldiers and animals far exceeding the native population. Law and order was imposed and communications restored, but with extreme constraints on freedom. One could once more eke out a living, or get welfare from the occupiers. Yet the all-important support of religious life was disrupted and education became a problematic activity. Occupying forces found themselves uncertain about the population they hoped to pacify. Could they trust the seeming friendly or the coolly indifferent? Were only the openly hostile the likely "bushwhacker," spy or saboteur? Women were hardly above suspicion. Initial tense and hostile relations between civilians and their occupiers gradually wore away, however. A division took on the shape of rage at the humiliation and personal loss suffered on the one extreme, and a resignation to paying the price for secession. As the tides of war repeatedly swept over the town, "the middle," probably a growing majority, wished "a plague on both your houses," and yearned for restoration of some modicum of the former harmony.

With so many men gone into the army and the more fearful in flight, the remains of the population had to adapt at least to passive collaboration. Consequently, the town seems to have acquired the reputation of being defectors. They survived by providing services to the occupiers in return for the means of subsistence. Some even enjoyed convivial social relations. Then, 1864 brought a resumption of turmoil and depravation—caught again in a no-man's land without any protection from occupying troops. But, as the war wore down, the occupiers returned and rewarded towns-folk with a celebration of reunion. Ultimately in one way or another, however, the Germantown area had lost perhaps two-thirds of its population.

✦ ✦ ✦

As for the town's soldiers, away from home for an increasingly long time, they fought on and suffered depravation with that determination of men feeling a mix of commitment to a cause and to the brotherhood forged in combat. Periodically, however, some were overwhelmed by a combination of senseless sacrifice, a growing sense of injustice, and the need to return home and provide for and protect one's own. Finally the senseless decimation of the Tennessee regiments in 1864 took its toll. More men drew the inevitable conclusions. Even before formal surrender, many simply returned to their families. By this time, fewer wives and mothers experienced any sense of shame at their arrival. Entire communities defended their returnees from arrest and punishment.

The combat soldiers had experienced the severe traumatic stress of war that some can absorb better than others, yet all carried the scars. Charging in the face of massive, aimed rifle fire and grapeshot, entrenching ever deeper to escape exploding artillery shells, they experienced the most bloody war of the nineteenth century and conditions that presaged World War I. It was that next "great war" that introduced post-war society to the term "shell-shocked veteran." Today we know it as post-traumatic stress disorder of PTSD.

✦ ✦ ✦

The civilian population that awaited them had also suffered the traumatic stress of guerrilla warfare, subjected to the behavior of the combatants on both sides. Theirs had been a most uncivil war. The community suffered more than the physical scars of war, however. Open sores carried into the years of recovery.

Now even the staunchest had to accept defeat. Some stubbornly refused to accept the consequences, but most just longed to get on with life. They intended to build on whatever remained, and naively expected to be able to do so without retribution. In November, the *Appeal*, back in Memphis, resumed publication. The once ardent supporter of the cause, nicknamed "the Voice of the Confederacy," now expressed the majority sentiment.

> We have no unmanly excuses to make, no stultifying recantation of opinion once honestly entertained, but the stern logic of events has practically compelled their renunciation. We frankly and truly accept the interpretation that has been stamped with the red verdict of war on the Constitution, of the indestructability of the Union of States and people which makes us, for all time, a mighty and indivisible Republic. We recognize and abide by the logical sequence of the late, unhappy Civil War of destruction, now and forever, of the institution of African slavery.[80]

The previously held belief in the constitutional right of secession had been annulled by a failed test far more forceful than any Supreme Court ruling. The crucible of war had forged an indivisible Union. At this point, there was hope that slavery was the only truly lost cause. That could be accepted. To the defeated Southerner, none of this failed test seemed any more treasonable than a failed test in a court of constitutional law. The former proclamations denouncing an intolerable dictatorship and insufferable threats to a Christian way of life, issued in the heat of the moment, had lost their meaning. They hoped that bygones would be bygones.

But unfortunately, the war had intensified racial fears in the white population, while raising expectations among the blacks. Fears had turned to resentment and even hate among many whites, while black resentments were part of a more complex set of attitudes. All faced a settlement of such issues with unease.

PART III

THE AFTERMATH

For a decade after the war, the Germantown area struggled through a gradual but incomplete recovery. The war was not fully responsible for the town's relative decline in economic prominence and population. Before the war, Collierville already had advantages in its position on the local roads that had led to a shift in the flow of commerce. The war damaged both communities severely, but Collierville's recovery was much more vigorous. Yet, Germantown was also recovering economically, and by the 1870s seemed on its way to perhaps outpace Collierville by absorbing an emerging suburban sprawl from Memphis. A uniquely troublesome mosquito nipped that in the bud, however, and with it Germantown's recovery.

Perhaps more interesting than the story of a frustrated recovery is that of the social and psychological impact of the war and Reconstruction on what had apparently been a relatively harmonious and peaceful pre-war community. In this regard, Germantown was probably not too unique among area communities, but that aspect of the post-war experience for such communities has not been well explored. What follows here is, one proposes, a useful case study.

10

RECONSTRUCTION

Reconstruction in Tennessee

As before, the larger picture of state politics and regional economy is prerequisite to understanding local conditions and politics. Unfortunately, the contentious issues involved in understanding the phenomena of Reconstruction far exceeds what can be handled within the limits of a local history. The complexity of the social and cultural components of that story are perhaps more contentious and complex than the origins of the Civil War.

In contrast to negative views of Reconstruction, an empathetic view of the radical effort to reconstruct Southern society, including that of broader American society and politics has only emerged in the last half of the twentieth century.[1] In summary, one can argue that the sincere effort at radical reconstruction was doomed to failure at any level of American society. It ran head on into the brick wall of the deeply entrenched American consensus about white supremacy. Reformers sought to replace the power of an atavistic aristocracy *in the South* with a more democratic political system. They sought to institute everywhere political-legal equality for African-Americans. Once that "more backward" part of this country had been reconstructed, the spores could spread throughout the nation. The spirit of human rights implicit in the Constitution could be fulfilled. Unfortunately belief in human rights and human equality cannot be separated.

Because of the inevitable consequences of their radical agenda, there was no national base strong enough to support the revolution from above that they sought to impose on the South. The American people were too enmeshed in the assumptions of white supremacy. Inevitably Southerners would see efforts to impose such reforms on them as hypocritical. They were the work of vindictive victors. The Southerners were the ones who would "suffer the consequences" of living in forced equality with a mass of "inferior people." Not so, hypocritical Northern reformists.

One of the "lessons of history" seems to be that all revolutions imposed from above produce powerful reactionary forces. They can retard effectively, at the expense of any potential beneficiaries, the progress sought by those reforms. They can even be powerful enough to produce successful counter-revolutions. Nationally, radical Reformation of the South foundered on conservative and moderate liberal instincts. In the South, reactionary forces prevailed. They created and preserved a cultural history that embraced the Southern perspective of both the war and Reconstruction. It is mostly the Southern, and specifically the local perspective which must be explored empathetically in this history, with no intention of apology. That Southern perspective and that of Germantown's white people in particular is adequately revealed in the contemporary local press and other surviving sources.

◆ ◆ ◆

The Reconstruction experience in Tennessee was unique. The state contained the largest white, unionist presence among any of the Confederate states. In the east, they had a strong position but were a minority elsewhere. Even in the West, the old "non-secessionist" element had reemerged to cooperate in a "reunion." In 1862, Andrew Johnson, future Vice-President and President, was appointed Military Governor of the occupied state.[2] Thus, Tennessee's Reconstruction efforts began at that point. As the war ground down, unionists dominated the state convention and restored a civil government. Tennessee's readmission to the Union came early, July 24, 1866, so it did not fall under the post-war military controls established elsewhere in 1867. Usually without Federal troops to enforce his programs, Radical Governor William G. Brownlow had to rely on a shaky base. The disfranchised white majority was already restive when Tennessee became the first former Confederate state to enfranchise all African American men in 1867.[3] As a consequence, Tennessee remained in turmoil from 1865 to 1870, after which Reconstruction wound down in the state. What emerged was a significantly modified restoration of the status quo ante. Legal slavery was gone, social and political white-supremacy was not.

◆ ◆ ◆

When Johnson left for Washington to become Lincoln's Vice-President, a self-appointed Radical Unionist convention assembled to form a loyal government in Nashville, January 9, 1865. Its first acts nullified all acts of the secessionist state government since May 6, 1861, repudiating secession and the debts incurred, and approved the amendment to abolish slavery. With a loyalty oath required, only ten percent of the 1860 electorate could vote. So in February, the amendment passed, and the Radical Unionist William Brownlow was elected governor in March.[4]

Until 1869 when the Democrats reorganized formally, there was only the Republican Party. It, however, was divided between the Radical and Conservative Unionists. In addition to a true reconstruction, the Radicals were intent on punishing the ex-Confederate majority for its treason and the havoc their war had brought. The Conservatives were mostly those who had opposed secession, but had also originally opposed emancipation, and afterward urged a conciliatory treatment of ex-Confederates. Although the Conservatives often collaborated with ex-Confederates in anti-Radical efforts, the Radicals controlled the state government. They disfranchised all involved in the Confederate cause with franchise laws of June 1865 and May 1866. They were on the horns of a dilemma. If they allowed a democratic vote, reactionary Southern sentiments would block reforms. Those who had just lost the war should not regain power.[5] Nevertheless often, the anti-Radical coalition managed to thwart Radical intentions, and in many parts of the state, dominated local government and law enforcement.

On January 11, 1865, Radical Senator Almon Case was assassinated in Obion County by a former Confederate guerrilla. North-West Tennessee was a hotbed of murderous anti-Radical sentiments, they threatened in every part of the state.[6] In the countryside, guerrilla bands maintained their activity well into 1866. Their less-than-righteous motives were reinforced by a smoldering sense of righteous indignation at the victor and his collaborators, but they had generally lost most of the popular support. Ex-Confederates were not the only problem, for disbanded Tennessee Federal cavalrymen and some ex-slaves also contributed to lawlessness.[7]

Despite the continued threat of armed bands, in April General Thomas disbanded the state's Home Guard and turned over responsibility for combating criminal gangs to the civil authorities. Of course, he promised military support "as far as possible." As replacement, he approved raising state troops, which he promised to arm.⁸ Theoretically, they could be formed from citizens more interested in law and order than revenge.

The Radical legislature took up the assignment. The assembly proclaimed any armed plunderer "are hereby declared Guerrillas and Highway Robbers and Brigands, and upon his or their conviction, shall suffer death by hanging." Former Union soldiers and all loyal citizens were allowed to wear side-arms to protect themselves. With the Sheriffs Act of 1865 allowing them to create County Guards, the state government sought to combat the brigands, but in West and Middle Tennessee, local prejudices guaranteed that the sheriffs could not or would not effectively enforce Radical policies. Likewise the massacre of blacks in Memphis in May 1866 made it clear that more authority was needed there but also in Nashville and Chattanooga. The resultant Metropolitan Police Act gave Brownlow the power he needed to curb anti-Radical, anti-Reconstruction activities. Ultimately the Radical response was the State Guard Act of February 20, 1867. The army that the governor could raise theoretically consisted of one or more regiments for each of the eight congressional districts.⁹ Nothing that great ever emerged, however.

On February 25, Brownlow proclaimed his intention to mobilize the Guard and use it forcefully in counties that failed to keep the peace and enforce laws. On the same day, he signed the act granting blacks the vote, creating yet more racial hostility and white resentment. The suspicion that this law grew more from the Radical's need for an electorate that would support them than from any commitments to legal equality provided white-supremacists with a claim to righteous opposition.¹⁰ Inevitably, polling stations became a point of violence and intimidation.

Raising militia companies in West Tennessee proved difficult, although local unionists were desperate for protection.¹¹ None were formed in Shelby County. There, however, the presence of federal troops in Memphis was sufficient to insure that 4,000 votes were safely cast for the Radicals.¹²

This Radical victory demonstrated a strong pro-Radical power to which local Conservatives responded by biding their time and resorting to passive resistance. Of course, the Conservatives and unrepentant Confederates blamed the victory entirely on the black vote, especially in the city. Despite the *Appeal*'s shrill criticisms of the futility of Conservative efforts to woe the black vote, the Conservatives had some black support. Among the delegates Shelby Conservatives sent to their May 8 convention were seven identified as "colored."

The language of papers like the *Appeal* was racist and just plain Afrophobic, especially concerning the alleged gullibility of "the sons of Ham" for Radical "pie-in-the-sky promises."[13]

In response during 1867, the Ku Klux Klan evolved rapidly into a political-terrorist organization. The State Guard was deployed in West Tennessee, but in August and September, driven by financial pressures, the government reduced its militia army twice. Finally, they were demobilized in February 1868.[14]

After the 1868 electoral victory of the Radicals, the Klan reached full force, and incidents of terrorism mounted. For the national election of November 1868, beatings, shootings and lynchings, home and church burnings were among the hundreds of incidents in West Tennessee. Local sheriffs, if not complicit, were cowed into submission. Bellicose proclamations by Nathan Bedford Forrest, Grand Wizard, fanned the flames.[15]

In September, the Radicals in Nashville responded. An Act to Preserve the Public Peace essentially outlawed the Klan. Then a new militia law included a cumbersome procedure for imposing martial law. Fortunately to head off a racial civil war in Tennessee, President Johnson made Federal troops available to enforce the law. This was more acceptable to anti-Radicals than a pro-Radical militia. Unfortunately the Army proved too over-extended and indifferent to the Radical cause and the fate of black victims. Thousands of terrorized blacks stayed away from the polls, and Radical returns declined, reducing their strength in the government.[16]

In January 1869, the Radicals mobilized for war on the Klan, by this time running rampant. Yet in West Tennessee, initially no county met the stringent requirements for martial law. Only whites were mustered into the remobilized Guards, but the threat of black enrollments was held out. These threats of stern enforcement worked. Many counties promised to clean themselves up, but most importantly, Forrest, issued his disbandment order at the end of January. Despite the decentralized and independent nature of the Klan, many dens complied.[17]

Then the tide began to turn. On February 25, 1869, DeWitt C. Sentner replaced Brownlow as governor when he moved on to the U.S. Senate. A less extreme Radical, Sentner was more conciliatory in general. The Klan seemed to have drawn in its head in Middle Tennessee, and only minimal trouble erupted in the West. With the Klan underground and local citizens refusing to identify its members, the frustrated Guard seemed superfluous. So in March, reduction of the militia began again. The incidents of lawlessness that occurred seemed independent of the Klan, except in Gibson County.[18]

Primarily, financial and political pressures brought the second Guard mobilization to an end. The Radical party began to disintegrate and Reconstruction in Tennessee began to wind down. Their internal fighting even led Governor Sentner to use his authority to nullify enforcement of the disfranchising law in order to beat his rival. Ex-Confederates regained their franchise. The Democrats would soon repeal the anti-Klan legislation and the governor's authority to raise a State Guard.[19] Reconstruction in Tennessee had ended by 1870 with the passage of a new state constitution and the subsequent election of a Democrat, John C. Brown, as governor, a former Confederate general and Klan member.[20]

The elite leadership of the Klan had achieved their political goals of reestablishing Democratic and white dominance and knew that continued lawlessness would only undermine recovery. Forrest increasingly denounced the acts of the rabble that remained. Although elsewhere in the South, the Klan continued its reign of terror, in Tennessee, its threat was more significant than its actions. Until its resurrection in the twentieth century, the Klan was a "ghost" of its former self, a spirit around which lynch mobs and local bullies could occasionally rally.

In short, Reconstruction in Tennessee was short-lived. Radical "excesses" had certainly been galling, but most of their achievements were soon reversed. Blacks had held few significant political positions, only twenty held state positions betwen1868 and 1876.[21] Their short-lived force as voters was quickly blunted. The old racial social order had not been seriously challenged. Both the distribution of landed wealth and political power returned to something like pre-war norms. Nevertheless, the struggle at both state and local levels had been intense and generated bitter memories that exaggerated racial antipathies.

None of the truly progressive goals of the Radicals prevailed, and the South could resist them for the next hundred years. Radical threats to white supremacy, plus their necessary resort to anti-democratic tactics to prevent a return to power of the old establishment, fueled a rabid opposition to every aspect of the Radical and Republican agenda. Republicans took the blame for the perhaps unpreventable corruption and post-war opportunistic exploitation of the hardships of the population. Southerners would preserve all of that in a myth of the horrors of Reconstruction. The prevalence of white supremacy, both North and South, would facilitate that mythic distortion.[22]

The Status of "Persons of Color"

The situation of the newly freed slaves in Tennessee requires elaboration before a picture of post war life around the town can be painted. The Tennessee General Assembly had quickly ratified the Thirteenth Amendment to the U.S. Constitution, and then the Fourteenth, which specified that no state should "deprive any person of life, liberty, or property without due process of law." Legal access to full involvement in the economy was theoretically available. African-American men in Tennessee also gained the franchise even before Congress passed the Fifteenth Amendment. Black Tennesseans were able to take positions in local and state government.

Of course, in no parts of this nation did racial discrimination and prejudices abate. The Tennessee environment might not have been much different had it not been for the hostilities generated by the war and then Reconstruction, and especially the presence of blacks in such large numbers, which generated extra fears. In the minds of threatened whites this required the repression of blacks in ways more obvious than elsewhere in the Union.

Actually, the revised state constitution gave the "free-Negro" few rights, while most of the former constraints on freemen remained in place. In May 1866, while trying to legislate legal equality for African Americans, the state legislature insured the perpetuation of race consciousness and ethnic separation with the passage of the Act to define the term "Persons of Color," and to declare the rights of such persons as a separate category of human being. As a clear expression of the pervasive fears of miscegenation and the purportedly negative effects of mixed blood, persons of color were defined as "all Negroes, Mulattoes, Mestizos, and *their descendants, having any African blood in their veins*" (emphasis provided.)[23] Thus was imposed a "racial" identity that has survived to this day, and has become a badge of reversed pride for those defining themselves as African-American, regardless of mixed ancestry.

Originating as a term for young mules, Mulatto had become the designation for persons of mixed "Negro and Caucasian" parents. Mestizo had originated in Spanish settled areas for any person descended from Spanish or Portuguese mixed with Native Americans.

On the plus side, this legislation provided

> That persons of color have the right to make and enforce contracts, to sue and be sued, to be parties and give evidence, to inherit, and to have full and equal benefits of all laws and proceedings for the security of person and estate, and shall not be subject to any other or different punishment, pains or penalty, for the commission of any act or offense, than such as are prescribed for white persons committing like acts or offenses....
>
> That all free persons of color who were living together as husband and wife in this State, while in a state of slavery, are hereby declared to be man and wife, and their children legitimately entitled to an inheritance in any property heretofore acquired by said parents, to as full an extent as the children of white citizens are now entitled, by the existing laws of this State.[24]

Thus was annulled any complications resulting for the denial of legal marriage to former slaves.

> On the other hand, the act specified,
> *Provided*, That nothing in this act shall be so construed as to admit persons of color to serve on the jury:
> And *provided further*, That the provisions of this act shall not be so construed as to require the education of colored and white children in the same school.[25]

There would be no jury of peers for blacks, and whites would have no fear of being judged by their "inferiors." Legal segregation in schools added another limitation on equal opportunity.

Severe laws imposed social segregation to defend white blood. Miscegenation was not only a punishable offense, but it was also considered "contrary to good morals." As with most sexual mores, violations were common, but white persons exposed for the crime could be tried and publicly disparaged.[26] Enforcement against white males was, of course, problematic. Far worse would befall any black man even suspected of such intentions.

Segregation was proclaimed immediately for the public schools, and there were no ideas about separate-but-equal. The 1867 Act to Provide for the Reorganization, Supervision and Maintenance of Free Common Schools provided that districts were to establish "special schools for colored children," but only when their number exceeded twenty-five. If the average of those attending fell below fifteen *in any month*, it became the *duty* of the Board of Education to discontinue such a school for up to five months. No such constraints applied to white schools. This was a severe penalty for black families holding children out of school seasonally to help in the fields—a common requirement in rural families of any color. Parsimonious board members could convince themselves that they should not squander public funds on families that did not "appreciate the advantages of a common school education." Such funds saved were supposed to be reserved for "the education of such colored children,"[27] presuming that authorities audited diligently. The language of the legislation implied that only the most elementary level of schooling was required.

In this respect, Tennessee's Reconstruction experience differed significantly from much of the rest of the South, which experienced more Federal interference and for a longer period. Public schools in many states, ostensibly "integrated," producing higher levels of literacy among blacks initially.[28]

Indeed, the newly emancipated blacks were by no means merely passive recipients of the mix of paternalistic and negative attentions. They established their own communities and institutions. They created banks, churches, cemeteries, fraternal societies and collectives and schools for themselves. Initially, the Freedman's Bureau was helpful with schools, but poor funding and local opposition limited its effectiveness. Black schools created by the Bureau were turned over to the state in 1869, and the Bureau terminated its educational activities in 1870. In Germantown, public schools for blacks actually resulted from black initiatives faster than those for whites.

The local Freedmen's Bureau helped negotiate between black workers and white employers and provided legal advice. Yet the Bureau and its agents could also be paternalistic, moralistic, and authoritarian with its well-intentioned efforts. The generally favorable comments in the *Appeal* about the local Bureau indicate that when it erred, it did so in favor of efforts to condition blacks to become better disciplined as an agricultural work force in a "free" plantation economy. The planters merely needed to honor their contracts, which most of them could be *trusted* to do. In contrast, the Bureau even enforced a rule that forbade contracted blacks from leaving the plantation for purposes of entertainment without the owner's permission.[29] As early as May 1866, Bureau courts for settling labor disputes in Tennessee were discontinued. Assistant

Commissioner Carlin insisted that justice was nevertheless being administered regarding labor contracts.

By 1866 in Tennessee, half the labor contracts of freemen were for a share of the crop. Those working for wages received $150-$180 a year, which included the purported value of any clothing and housing provided by the employer. The transition to a stable work environment was disrupted in 1868 as Klan violence erupted, but by the following year most freedmen were again working under contract. The Bureau served only to settle claims until it was abolished in 1872.[30]

The role of blacks in the evolution of the new plantation economy was not one-sided. When employed in the "gang" system, blacks resented a return to the format of slave labor. Families were still concentrated in the former slave quarters. Black resistance forced many planters into the tenant system regardless of their desires. Likewise, dispersal of housing onto tenant plots was often a product of black family initiative. They erected their own shanties and benefited from both removal from owner supervision and the convenience of living on the land they worked. Soon, planters also saw dispersal as more desirable and began erecting houses to rent to tenants.[31]

Nevertheless, some of the positive side-effects of planter paternalism survived or was forced as concessions to get labor. The Sabbath and holidays were observed, along with half-day Saturdays. Tenants had hunting, fishing and gathering rights in the owner's woodlands, streams and ponds. Medical care and the convenience of the owner's store were available on credit, which could be both a blessing and a debt trap. At least some planters felt obliged to provide the feeble elderly with shelter and basic sustenance until death.[32]

While blacks tried to take advantage of their new civil rights, many were stripped from them before they could be fully exercised. Contrary to law, civil courts dispensed harsh sentences for petty offenses and prevented blacks from testifying in court, requiring the Freedmen's Bureau to establish Bureau Courts to guarantee justice for blacks. When the Assembly allowed black testimony, the Bureau discontinued its courts in May 1866. Even so, Assistant Commissioner Carlin complained that "the enforcement of the laws in criminal cases has been very imperfect."[33] Violence could erupt between whites and blacks as they worked out their new economic relationships. In such cases, whites usually had the whip hand. The whites' habit of exercising "righteous" violence combined with their perception of injustice in the constructive efforts of

Reconstruction generated an environment that would plague life in the South. A "poll tax" appeared in Tennessee's new state constitution of 1870. Although it was repealed three years later, it would reappear in 1890.

♦ ♦ ♦

Before the war, all over America negative racial stereotypes, hostility and fear had been well entrenched. During the war, conflicts between white and black soldiers had been common in the Union Army. Fears of "African savagery" evolved into phobic hostility, North and South. For southerners, the departure of "unfaithful servants" was one provocation. Undoubtedly nothing matched the ire raised by the sight of blacks in the blue uniform. Such "treason" was exceeded only by the insolence of assuming a position of equality against their "superiors." On both sides, any incivility towards whites by black soldiers, but especially any abuse of power, became a provocation that far exceeded similar behavior by white Union soldiers. Offended whites vented their spleens in newspapers—even those of unionist bent were not free from expressions of concern about the "proper order" of things being upset.

In April of 1864, the *Appeal* reprinted such expressions from Union-occupied Louisville and Nashville papers with stories of the crimes of black troops. One writer was "happy to record" an incident when "one of these uniformed sons of Ham" took a shotgun blast "that sent his adventurous spirit to mingle with the shades of Hades."

> If a few more of the arrogant scoundrels meet with the same summary disposal, it will be better ... and decidedly more satisfactory to all who prefer the superiority of the white race. ... I have only to say that, had I authority ... I'd end this insolence of negro soldiers ... very suddenly.[34]

Although white citizens on both sides decried the depredations of white soldiers, no one proposed mass shootings as the solution. In contrast, it is not farfetched to argue that nation-wide there was a strong feeling that vigilante violence might become necessary to keep blacks in their place.

After the war, newspapers always identified a criminal or disruptive black person as black. When the offender was white, no emphasis on color was felt necessary. The net effect of the language employed, especially of vivid descriptions and editorial comments about the black man's criminal act, was to enhance the awareness of "African savagery" and reinforce fears. Such fears were growing by December 1865, when the Freedmen's Bureau received wide-spread rumors especially in West Tennessee about impending black insurrections. When conflicts between white employers and black laborers erupted into violence, and the white man was killed or beaten, it was always a horrible or brutal crime. When the black man "had to be killed," it was always justified, and usually because the unreasonably belligerent villain had refused to work as he was contracted to do. There was never a question about what conditions precipitated the black man's forceful rebellion.[35] After centuries of suppression, some "violent" black men now asserted the right to defend their dignity and honor the way white men always had.

Few southerners actually lamented the passing of slave labor—mostly just the financial loss and labor problems. As the war had worn down and the owners foresaw slavery's inevitable doom, many began to realize that it was far more burdensome than it was worth. The women, left at home to manage and fear slaves, often reached that conclusion.[36] During 1864, to solve their manpower problems, the Confederate High Command had been considering arming blacks, to be granted freedom. Jefferson Davis finally put forward the idea in November. Young black slaves would be purchased from their owners. Robert E. Lee endorsed the idea, but it came to naught. Too many feared such limited emancipation was a slippery slope. Four generals and a dozen regimental commanders of the Army of Tennessee recommended a program of emancipation as the salvation of the Southern cause.[37]

For what it is worth, the vote in Shelby County against the constitutional amendment to abolish slavery in the state was a total of 6 out of the 879 restricted voters, many of whom had held slaves.[38] Regardless, many would subsequently recite romanticized images of the loving relations that had allegedly existed between masters and slaves and bemoaned their passing—replaced by undisciplined liberality.

Southerners could accept the "freedom" of the black man, but they felt that with that freedom came responsibilities that required the black man to go much more than half way in solving the problems of his inclusion in a white world. A widely circulated editorial revealed an absolute certainty about how few reciprocal responsibilities were required from whites. The "undeniable" mental and moral differences between black and white, and the superiority of the latter formed the basis of all arguments. "Uneducated, surrounded by bad advisers, and completely unsettled by their sudden changes of status, (black) ideas of the rights and privileges of freedom have assumed a wild, exaggerated form."[39]

The author of this assertion then addressed the contentious issue of this imbalance of power. The planter can be <u>trusted</u> to do justice. But while the whites should abandon their "improper prejudices," the negro must learn that the secret of his independence is labor. It is a fraud on society to get something without useful toil. Labor is not degrading, it is what will raise the negro up from "the prison of his low estate."[40]

It was as though the black man had sole responsibility for overcoming all the admitted deficits inherent in the lack of preparation for his admission into the white man's society, its economy and legal system. And all this without access to any of the economic resources he had helped to build during his centuries of slave labor.

Political Reconstruction in and around Germantown

With the broader picture of reconstruction politics and race relations established, we can turn to an examination of developments around Germantown. The last significant military presence in the area ended in February 1866 when the District of West Tennessee was discontinued. Only the 3rd United States Colored Heavy Artillery Regiment remained at Fort Pickering, plus a small white contingent.[41] Unfortunately the black presence preserved a lingering resentment, contributing to the Memphis Massacre shortly thereafter. Race and politics became inseparably intertwined. The political history around Germantown will tell us as much about race relations there as any other source, but we will still have to examine economic, cultural and interpersonal elements for balance.

As an economic center tied to the national economy, Memphis accommodated itself to part of the new order of things better than the rural sections with less hope of a rapid recovery. So perhaps Memphis took most of Shelby and adjacent counties with it and avoided the worst extremes of anti-Reconstruction activity. Even the so-called 1866 "race riot" would be more a product of socioeconomic conflict between the Irish and black elements than of overt political opposition. But of course, it is impossible to separate such efforts to reassert white supremacy from political opposition to Reconstruction. After the dust had settled by late 1866, Shelby County avoided the imposition of martial law and more extreme Home Guard enforcement actions in western

Tennessee in 1867 and 1869.[42] Consequently Germantown experienced significantly less severe conflict and external interference, although its political leadership would be heavily involved in the struggles over county government.

◆ ◆ ◆

Well before the end of official hostilities, local government had begun to re-emerge in Shelby County. In September, 1864, without the benefit of elections the county attempted to resume its governing court, with safely occupied Memphis as the new, de facto county seat. It began with a judge pro-tem appointed by Governor Johnson, Judge Thomas Leonard, and also an appointed clerk and a sheriff who was the only elected official.[43] It was during this period that the previously-described vote fraud in Germantown's district eleven was rigged by some Radicals.

Amidst the continued disruptions of guerrilla activities, there was little hope of reestablishing stable legal and political operations. By January 1865, "the peculiar circumstances of the times" had prevented an assemblage of the magistrates to properly elect a judge-chairman, and the judge pro-tem had to continue in office. Only two magistrates had been elected from the districts in any case, and, of course, Brownlow refused to allow formerly elected justices to resume office in districts that had not been able to hold a vote, even if they had not "committed any act of Treason." In April, the state legislature was forced to pass a special act to enable Shelby County to appoint its court chairman to perform constitutional duties.[44]

On the authority of the Act for the Protection of Sheriffs of 1865, Sheriff Winters had regularly employed posses of up to twenty-five men to enforce the law in the county. Apparently in response to some mounting tensions and persisting lawlessness, in December 1865, Judge Leonard relied on the emergency clause of the same act to call up and arm a County Guard of one thousand men.[45] Whatever they did was not effective in the countryside.

Only two civil districts outside Memphis had magistrates for the Quarterly Court. There was neither a justice nor constable for Germantown. Bridges, roads and public buildings remained unrepaired. Governor Brownlow's appointee, Judge Leonard, forwarded recommendations to the governor, whose appointments included magistrate for Germantown's District Eleven, W. P. York.[46] His name occurs in neither the 1860 nor 1870 census for the district—probably an outsider sent in to enforce Brownlow's policies.

The county elections of 1866 certainly revealed opposition to the governor's appointments in many districts, but especially in Germantown's. Judge Leonard had exacerbated affairs by vacillating over whether or not to include his office in the election or to continue in his appointed seat. He initially announced that he would run and surrender his appointment if he lost. Then he recanted. Most papers took him to task, noting elections for judges should fall in that year, and not be determined by his date of appointment. The coroner, who was responsible for holding elections, committed publically to doing so, preserving the results so disputes could be settled by the courts. Leonard's position was contested, and he lost by 77 votes. He was even beaten in the city, and received no votes at Germantown. Nevertheless, as threatened, Leonard continued to serve until 1867. Across the county, the votes in the districts outside Memphis were unanimously against Brownlow's ticket. Although Sheriff Winter won reelection, primarily on the city vote, he lost everywhere else. In Germantown, it was 74 to 3 against him.[47]

As conservative opposition to Brownlow's regime organized locally, Germantown's political leadership reemerged. By January 1866, when the county's Conservative Party appointed its standing committees for each civil district, William H. Walker, Finley Holmes and James Morgan served District Eleven, and for District Ten there were Thomas C. Bleckley and Benjamin Cash, both living around Forest-Hill. In the spring, such Conservatives formed the Johnson Club, as supporters of President Andrew Johnson's conciliatory approach to reconstruction. At the April 5th meeting of Shelby County's club, William H. Walker, Henry T. Jones and Lonallen Rhodes were selected to canvass District Eleven for membership.[48]

Over the next years, most of these men would serve as local leaders in the reformation of the Democratic Party and hold positions in county and district government. Thomas Bleckley, a resident since 1832 and former small slave-owning farmer, represented District Ten. He had served as magistrate for many years before the war. A leading Conservative in the county, he reemerged as magistrate-justice for District Ten and frequent chair of the county Circuit Court. He claimed to have been a "very strong Union man," who had changed his allegiance only after his farm had been pillaged by Federal soldiers. In his sixties, he would remain prominent in county Democratic politics. William Walker had also been a pre-war magistrate. He remained in town and after the war returned to his former business as dry goods merchant. Despite his role in the district's 1861 secession meetings, he too seemed to have established pro-Union credentials during the occupation. Henry Jones, also a small farmer, had served as magistrate-justices for District Eleven. Lonallen Rhodes, former wagon maker turned dry goods merchant, would regularly hold various appointed and elected district offices. George W. Small was district constable, usually uncontested in elections.[49] Small had also been a small slave-owning farmer. To be able to vote and hold office, although most had been ostensibly active in the secession movement, all these men must have reestablished their loyalty before 1865.

Infighting in the county among Republicans must have involved more than the division between Radicals and Conservatives, apparently limiting Brownlow's control. The two county representatives to the state assembly had resigned, requiring new elections in December 1865. S. P. Walker and W. K. Poston, emerged as the overwhelming favorites of county voters. Yet they must have been unsatisfactory to the Brownlow faction. When another election was ordered at the end of March, an even more overwhelming result returned them. During this process, all the voters of Germantown were disenfranchised. There was also "no poll" in three other civil districts. All had been unable to get their electoral judges certified, a problem that definitely confronted other districts at times. A form of voter suppression. Still dissatisfied, Brownlow ordered another election in December, which was won by two new men, with a much lower turnout, apparently also because of uncertified election judges.[50] It would seem the governor finally got the results he wanted.

It quickly became obvious to radical Reconstructionists that neither Memphis city nor Shelby County government officials could be relied upon to enforce the new order. The massacre of May 1866, the role of some city officials in inciting the worst extremes of that event, and the failure of the entire city government to investigate and punish the culprits made this patently clear. Especially the role of police and firemen of the city in the rapes, pillaging and murders was ignored.[51]

The response was the "Act to Establish a Metropolitan Police District, and to Provide for the Government Thereof," passed on May 14. Shelby County became the prototype for a Metropolitan Police District of the State of Tennessee, reforming police government and discipline. The act abolished the Memphis police and removed police authority from the Board of Mayor and Aldermen. It sought to create a professional police establishment for Tennessee cities, and indeed had salutary long-range effects. It established Commissioners of the Metropolitan Police and a Board of Metropolitan Police. The police had the authority to operate in any part of the state. Specifically they were to "enforce every law . . . ordinances, or resolution of the Board of Aldermen of Memphis, or of town or village authorities in other parts of the district in relation to police, health or criminal procedure."[52]

The city and county had to bear the tax burden for this force, which was directly answerable to the governor.[53] Nevertheless, divisions among Board members prevented Brownlow from exercising the sort of control over Memphis that he had elsewhere.

If anything around Germantown aroused the suspicions of the Board, special patrolmen might appear on the scene to do whatever the sheriff or district constable was not doing to their satisfaction. The mere threat probably encouraged local tendencies to make the transition relatively peaceful.

Germantown lacked anything near the explosive combination of economic and racial tensions that erupted in Memphis. Although the occupation forces for the entire area had been heavily black during 1865, with an entirely white unit occupying the town, the racial hostilities there had been far less extreme than in Memphis.

The tinder for violence in Memphis lay in the presence of 16,000 freedmen and demobilizing black soldiers in conflict with the large, Irish immigrant population that saw them as rivals for jobs and depressants on wages. The Irish had dominated in the city's police and fire departments. While Blacks had been part of the breakdown of law , the papers overemphasized their relative contribution. Increasing efforts by blacks to seek unilateral justice for abuses directed at them simply added to the general population's sense that strong measures were needed to keep them in their place.[54]

Readers of the *Avalanche*, however, must have thought Germantown had its own experience, and that "the Radical ideas . . . (were) being attempted by negroes" there. It reported that a detail of soldiers were escorting three black prisoners to the prison at Nashville. "When the train reached Germantown . . . an attack was made on the guard by a party of negroes, for the purpose of forcing the prisoners' release from custody." Firing ensued and one of the prisoners was killed while the other two escaped.[55]

In contrast, the more detailed report in the *Argus*, mostly corroborated by a sketchy one in the *Appeal*, presented a very different version. After the train had passed the town by about one mile, the three prisoners simply jumped from the box car to escape, and one was shot.[56] There was no ambush or shootout involving armed blacks. Germantown readers of the *Avalanche* must have wondered how they had missed all the action. Their paper of choice was the most virulent in propagating hysteria over the black threat.

◆ ◆ ◆

Unhappy with Judge Leonard's continued rule, the majority of county magistrates struck out against him. With Bleckley, Walker and Jones active among the leadership, in January 1867 they ordered a thorough examination of his "financial position." This was expanded to all his appointed revenue officers. Yet all they could find as pretext for a censure was his having allotted funds for emergency pauper relief without the court's formal approval. They drafted a petition to the State Legislature to abolish the "expensive" office of County Court Judge as an unnecessary burden on the taxpayers.[57]

Not everyone in the county approved the leadership style of these magistrates. Even those who opposed Leonard found the Germantown magistrates obstreperous. A voter from another district described them as rejecting

> every account, however just, if it comes from Memphis, and vote for everything that purports to come from Raleigh or Germantown. Representing one-seventh of the wealth and population of the county, these Squires control twenty-five-thirtieths of the power of the County Court.... Instead of attending to public business, they spend nearly all their time in jowering and in badgering the judge.[58]

Somehow Germantown and Raleigh's magistrates managed to build a network for controlling 25 magistrates.

Brownlow struck back. In March, to replace the untrustworthy county government, the Radical legislature abolished the Shelby County Quarterly Court as its governing body and replaced it with an appointed County Commission. The county justices challenged the constitutionality of the act in vain. Of course, Justices Bleckley, Jones and Walker were active in the challenge, and most locals never accepted the Commission's legitimacy. Proponents argued that the smaller body of five commissioners and a lawyer would be less costly and more efficient. Opponents countered that the former court of magistrates, two from each civil district, consisted of men thoroughly familiar with the needs of each locality. They knew the state of their roads and bridges, and all specific issues that county government had to attend. Indeed when the commissioners met on April 1, they noted that they needed a map of the county to acquaint themselves with its specifics.[59] It would be two years before they got it.[60]

Brownlow proceeded to appoint the Commission consisting of a president, Barbour Lewis, and four other commissioners. The *Appeal* ran an anonymous editorial ending with the cry, "let the public know the load that has been saddled upon us by the Brownlow clique."[61] It did not help matters that Barbour Lewis, former Captain of the 1st Missouri Cavalry, had headed the U. S. Civil Commission governing Memphis during Federal occupation. He had obviously established such important contacts in Memphis that after the war, he returned to practice law.[62]

One of the early acts of the Commission was to repeal the censure of Judge Leonard and terminate the suits against him. Instead it commended his promptness and humanity in assisting the poor during the cholera epidemic. In their desperation to fight back, the anti-Brownlow faction had taken a specious shot out of frustration, making them look petty and uncharitable. As we shall see, charity was not a high priority among these worthies.

Nevertheless in the face of such hostile opposition, to get its work done, the Commission had to rely heavily on members of the old social and political establishment of prominent planter, farmer, merchant and professional families, including the elected justices like Bleckley, Jones and Walker.[63]

In the elections of 1867, the people of the county, especially the disfranchised, rallied behind the Conservative Party. Since most could not vote, they could merely campaign. The Conservative platform embodied the sentiments of those citizens seeking only reconciliation. It called for both loyalty to the Union and resistance to the oppression of radical politicians. The rights of disfranchised citizens were to be restored while those of "the colored race" were to be assured. "Military despotism" was to be brought to an end, and President Johnson's efforts at reconciliation were endorsed. The less reconciled supporters, however, denounced the black vote as a tool to be exploited by hypocritical Radicals.[64] For the moment, the Conservatives were their only political option.

A stumping tour of speakers arrived in Germantown on July 24, but the Radical speaker did not bother to visit the town, telling us something about its irrelevance to Radical power. Strangely, the Conservatives were not yet well organized with only a couple of clubs in the city. The civil districts like Germantown's had made no such moves either.[65] The Conservatives predominated among the 66 voters of the district, and only 10 supported the Brownlow ticket, which nevertheless won.[66]

By 1868, opposition had intensified with the Democrats reemerging in the county, titling themselves Democratic Conservative. The *Appeal* referred to the party as the "white man's" Conservative Party of Shelby County. Elections for county offices came in May, with Conservative expectations of further victories. The Conservative convention met first on February 14, with representation heavily favoring the city wards, but each civil district, such as the tenth and eleventh, had two representatives. Local voters were to choose their representatives on February 8. Germantown, however, was well ahead of the curve, and on January 18, the local branch met to choose its delegates. L.A. Rhodes chaired with Thomas Nelms serving as secretary. They chose Walker and Henry Jones as delegates.[67]

Several districts like the Eleventh had assembled early because of Brownlow's efforts to restrict voter registration, specifically in Shelby County. They intended to make everyone aware of the need to apply for certificates of registration in time to vote. The drum beat was, of course, to get every eligible white man registered. Previously, Brownlow had replaced the Shelby County registering officer and nullified all of his registrations, because he had certified voters guilty of sympathizing with secessionists. Such an act had some justification, for there had been a flagrant marketing of illicit and defunct registrations. Now, there were allegations that the registration process was being delayed and manipulated to serve Radical ends. According to the *Appeal*, on February 28, the Commissioner registering votes in the county allegedly refused to accept any more "white" and "Conservative" voters, despite their having been vouched for by federal officers. Conservative monitors claimed that not more than half the eligible citizens of the county had received certificates. To counter potentially illicit Radical voters, the Conservatives called on their supporters who knew their neighbors to monitor the polls closely and have violators arrested.[68]

The Radicals hoped to keep a tight lid on the county elections in March 1868. The officers whom the Commissioners appointed to supervise the polls at Germantown for District Eleven were Monroe P. Webb, Wm. Hack, A. L. Thompson as Judges, and Henry Fulton as Deputy Commissioner.[69] Only one appointee was a resident. William Hack was not the elderly former merchant by that same name who had lived in the district since before 1850. That appointee was, instead, the Radical William Hack of the Commission. Webb, of the Webb School family, was, however, the federally appointed Germantown postmaster with appropriate connections, he was probably a Conservative. The others seem to have been typical outsiders guaranteeing Radical interests.

A total of 23 men had registered and voted, among whom Conservatives formed the vast majority. Only 2 men voted for Lewis for Commissioner, while 21 supported Kelly. Lewis won with more than half the vote county-wide. Only Germantown and Collierville, which only turned out 9 voters, had such a predominantly Conservative showing.[70]

In June, Shelby County Democrats held a convention to appoint delegates to the state convention in preparation for the national convention of the Party. All Conservatives and Democrats were invited to attend and a complete reorganization of the county body was called for. Among the resolutions that the county forwarded to the state convention were an acceptance of emancipation, but a denial of the freedman's right to vote and have other aspects of full citizenship. Of course, they decried the disenfranchisement of so many white citizens.[71] The influence of the unreconciled was growing.

The Shelby County Democrats then proceeded to reorganize themselves as the Democratic Club of Shelby County. But the representatives appointed for Civil District Eleven to help in the formation of its club were J.B. Abbington, B.C. Bledsoe, who were not residents. Consequently dissent erupted against party members in the city presuming to lead in organization. Specifically a citizen of White's Station bemoaned the loss of equality that had existed before the war and criticized the presumptuousness of Memphians.[72] So, Germantown's Democrats took it upon themselves to form their local branch, ignoring the Memphis appointees.[73]

The Democrats refined strategies to outmaneuver the Radicals, especially their reliance on black voters. For its part, the *Appeal* proclaimed the right of former Confederates to defy the law against their carrying pistols. While carefully denying any affiliation with the Klan, it championed their right to make peaceful torchlight parades through the city at night. Even more effective, all good men were called upon to deny employment to any black man who voted Radical.[74]

The official posture of the Democrats was a restoration of national harmony while denouncing Radical Reconstruction and the black vote. Implicit was a need to defend and preserve the "white race" and to undo the "disharmony" of black equality. In response to the July convention in New York, the town of Center Hill, Mississippi, converted what was to be a social and cultural celebration by its various societies into a political demonstration. They intended to "give a democratic tone to every meeting which is *white* and *decent*, and it was determined that the occasion should be seized on to ratify the doctrines of the Democracy...." People came out from Memphis on special trains to Germantown and Forest Hill, where they joined residents for conveyance down the Center Hill Road. There they endorsed the National Democratic Platform and nominees. This was promptly followed by the band playing Dixie.[75] The "unreconstructed Rebels" had the bit in their teeth.

From all indications, the Republican presence around Germantown was predominantly black, or was certainly seen as such. As the party prepared for the presidential election, a correspondent to the *Avalanche* reported that on October 1, "Beaumont, Dr. Toles and two other colored orators, of your city, came out to our quiet village to enlighten us in Radical politics, to the interest of None." They spent four hours in town, mostly "at a negro blacksmith shop," but allegedly nobody black or white came to hear them. "General W.J. Smith and about twenty of his colored friends came out from the city to speak to the darkies in Smith's interest. They had drum and fifes, with which they made much noise about the depot, drawing up about twelve or fifteen country darkies . . ." He disparaged the speakers and concluded, "There was no disturbance."[76]

In contrast, the *Evening Post*, presented a different picture. Inclement weather had indeed dampened attendance. But the affair was chaired by Captain W.H. Wood and the first two speakers were white, one a former Confederate soldier. Both reporters agreed that the thrust was to rally the blacks to vote, or lose their freedoms.

Predominant in the *Post*'s version was the role of white hecklers. The leader was Squire Bleckley, interrupting "in a very excitable manner." "The speaker was interrupted by Blakely (*sic*) and others frequently . . . ; so much so that the chairman appealed to the crowd of white listeners to accord to the speakers common decency and courtesy. . . . But for the indecent interruptions of the unreconstructed, everything passed of (*sic*) very pleasantly."[77]

This singular picture of black and white politics in the town reveals an image darkly. Local blacks exercised their franchise with uneven openness.

Some turned out boldly. The blacksmith Grant Allen and perhaps his teenage helper Arena Andrew were in the thick of things, perhaps inadvertently. Consequently, men like them had to endure quietly verbal harassment. Other blacks would turn out to receive Republican political enlightenment. One speaker alluded, however, to the behavior of many others. "He may promise to vote the Democratic ticket, yet it was not made in good faith, and he yet would vote for Grant."[78] The economic threats of landowners and employers against black Republican voters might elicit promises, but could not compel conformity. More importantly, however, they more likely could keep a black employee from registering or voting.

As an interesting parallel, while the town's Democrats were forming their club in July, they proclaimed their goal "to encourage emigration of the . . . freedmen North, to reduce the numbers South."[79] On this point, the main difference between them and the racial policies of many Radicals was the latter's preference for emigration back to Africa.[80] Neither was enthusiastic about a large black presence among them, and the Southerners sought to turn the tables on the North with a flood of "black savages."

Not satisfied with even their own level of Democratic organization, on September 12 locals intensified organizing efforts. They formed a "Seymour and Blair Club to support the presidential candidacy and the party platform. This time the leaders were P. W. Stephenson, Thomas "Blakely," and A. T. Cornelius, and they immediately recruited sixty members.[81] More about Cornelius' problematic character later.

In the November presidential election, Grant took Tennessee by 71,539 over Seymour's 50,376, while in Shelby the ratio was an even higher.[82] Registered voters attending the polls at Germantown had increased to 53. This election is the only one for which a list of area voters has survived, enabling clouded estimate of the relative numbers of white and black voters in the Germantown area. Although "race" was uniformly listed as "unknown," comparison with the census lists allows partial identification. Of the 56 voters, 25 cannot be found on any census, which makes it impossible to determine black or white. No more than four of the remaining 31 were black. Although the high percentage of whites among those identified should not be taken as a representative ratio of the entire list, the black turnout seems to have been disproportionately low, even if most of the unidentified were short-term black residents. Furthermore, the almost total unanimity of votes, 52 for Etheridge and Cooper as electors to

3 for Harrison and Sentner and 53 Democratic to 3 Republican in most other cases, shows that local voters favored Conservative politics, regardless of color. Germantown's Democratic majority stood firmly against Grant.

The probable disproportionate representation of white voters in District Eleven may indicate that local intimidation of black voters was effective, whether economic or terroristic. Klan terrorism was at its peak in 1868. Even Grant Allen, the blacksmith, had failed to vote. The secret ballot was no ally of the black voter either. The *Appeal* had encouraged Democrats, whenever they doubted the true intentions of a voter (black tenants implied), they should accompany him to the polls, procure the right ticket, put it in his hands, and see that he deposits it in the ballot box."[83] Whatever the causes, the preponderance of white over black voters apparently became a stable factor in District 11 politics.[84]

✦ ✦ ✦

If the newspapers provide an accurate picture, the Ku Klux Klan emerged in Shelby County in the spring of 1868. While the *Bulletin* viewed it with alarm, the *Appeal* only reported occasional incidents attributed to the Klan, and by and large played it down, or treated it humorously. It featured a few letters and articles that depicted the KKK largely as a Radical myth. The *Ledger* even published occasional, boastful pronouncements allegedly produced by the Klan, but also tended to downplay its seriousness. The *Avalanche* was openly favorable in its coverage, frequently carrying cryptic advertisements for its meetings and approving its impact on Radicals and blacks. The Klan was formed by and served the interests of prominent citizens. Prominent Memphians attended its 1867 convention in Nashville where they openly proclaimed themselves a patriotic league to uphold the Constitution and restore law and order.[85]

Although no incidents in the immediate Germantown area appear in the papers, there was involvement. On October 24, 1868, J.W. Wells and Thomas Reasonover were tried for membership in the Klan. Although Reasonover was discharged, Wells was bound over for the Criminal Court's next term.[86] The Reasonovers were Confederate veterans from DeSoto County Mississippi who had settled on a sizable farm south of Forest Hill after the war. As we shall see, Thomas, who had been severely wounded during the war, was prone to violent involvements with whites as well. Wells, also a Confederate veteran, was the son of the former overseer William Wells. The social structure of this Klan was not unlike that of the new Klan of the early twentieth century. Quite prominent citizens were known to be in high leadership positions and frequently appeared in the ranks. They postured as disapproving of killings, church burnings, etc. Such "unacceptable" behavior was always attributed to an uncontrollable element whose "unfortunate excesses" were accepted as "necessary evils."

Typically, the son of one of Germantown's Baptist ministers, a family opposed to guns and violence, would later comment almost dispassionately on racial violence and the Klan. "There was much excitement and bitterness, culminating in the determination of the white people to regain control of the state and county government at any cost." Immediately across the border in Mississippi where Reconstruction turmoil continued well into the 1870s, fears of the "negroes rising" led to much violence. "It was not uncommon to see negroes parading with fife and drum. At times the white people had to keep the streets patrolled at night." Some of this mood had spilled over into Germantown as we shall see.[87]

The conspiracy of silence about the Klan grew out of more than complicity. Even powerful people found discretion advantageous, while others feared ostracism and/or retaliation. One former resident of the town, who after the war had moved across the Wolf to Sangin Church (Cordova), had the misfortune of being impaneled for an inquest into a lynching. For whatever reasons, he participated in the typical ruling "death by persons unknown."[88]

During the last of Brownlow's efforts to enforce Radical Reconstruction policies in 1869, the people of Shelby County felt threatened by potential martial law and militia enforcement, because local Radicals had allegedly exaggerated the Klan threat. Sheriff Curry had publicly denounced what he described as rampant Klan abuse. Both the *Appeal* and offended citizens countered that there had been only one such event since the previous autumn—the shooting and burning of a negro man who had run away with a white girl—freely reported and condemned in the press.[89] However, there was at least another, the above-listed lynching inquest somewhere in the county.

Klan activity in Shelby County is a shameful story, but around Germantown there is no indication that it was focused on political terror during these early years. There was only that one lynching mentioned by the *Appeal* close to the town before 1880, and in 1893 an anonymous black man was lynched at Forest Hill. In subsequent years, however, the county became notorious for its lynchings. Between 1877 and 1950, the number of lynchings attributed to the county, the highest in the state, is set at 21. Ten occurred between 1892 and 1894 alone.[90] The resort to lynchings was escalating, but long after the war and its immediate effects. They were part of the growing white-supremacy movement toward the turn of the century that spread across the entire nation.

The one lynching near Germantown occurred in January 1869. Sensationally, both the *Appeal* and the *Ledger* initially reported that a teenage white girl living between Bartlett and Germantown had run off with a black man. Alert citizens in Germantown apprehended her, and returned her to her father. The man escaped only as far as Collierville. Approvingly, the *Appeal* reported that "the darkey ... was made to 'dance on nothing,' suspended on the limb of a tree." In contrast, the Nashville *Union and American* reported that after his captors had crossed the Wolf, an armed group of Klansmen intervened, seized and shot him. Also, it reported that the girl had merely paid him to help her escape her father. Nevertheless, it was always a death sentence for a black man to have any dealings with a white woman. A few days later, the girl's father killed a relative of the black man "in self-defense."[91]

✦ ✦ ✦

Meanwhile, voter registration at Germantown continued to grow. In May, 1869, the *Appeal* announced that the Registrar had enrolled sixty voters there, 38 whites and 22 blacks. Nevertheless, the *Appeal* continued to post allegations of flagrant abuses by the Radical Registrar, Williams. Although he had promised to visit all the major communities so planters could register without disrupting their work, he allegedly did so only selectively. He was at places like Bartlett where large numbers of blacks and Radical whites were expected, while at Whites Station and Collierville, he failed to bring enough certificates for white voters, but had more than enough for blacks. Unfortunately what happened at Germantown was obscurely passed over—he "made a very brief visit." Such alleged chicanery reportedly produced two black voters in the county for each white voter. Given such an atmosphere, contested elections became common. As a point of interest, two such hearings were held in Germantown, drawing an interested crowd from the city. Contested election hearings were held in a different county from that contested, so it is extremely difficult to uncover possible cases for Districts Eleven or Ten.[92] One desires more sources than the *Appeal*.

Prior to the gubernatorial election of August, the new Registrar Mr.

Boughner dutifully visited all points of the county, including Germantown. He registered black and white alike. Still, the *Appeal* reported gross attempts at voter fraud by the Radicals. Efforts were allegedly directed at stuffing the ballot boxes in the city by importing black voters, but were generally frustrated. One recruiter sent out on the M&C out as far as Collierville reportedly found black interests in voting in return for "a little snack and a dram" on the wane. But most specifically, the four cars sent out to Germantown the night before to pick up about 500 "negro voters" were surreptitiously uncoupled, leaving them cussing and unable to vote because only twelve were known locally as voters and allowed to vote. The remainder were residents of Mississippi. They allegedly assembled at flag stops along the line between Germantown and Collierville, trying in vain to flag down another train. Since "officers of the road were not willing to assist the contemplated fraud in the election, they failed to arrest the train. . . ." Assuming the accuracy of this account, Moses Rhodes, the local conductor, and Joseph Rhodes, the depot clerk, would have been among those who frustrated the fraud. The subsequent vote at the town was 242 for Sentner and only 4 for Stokes, "showing a decided turning of the tables, and affording the first evidence of the full growth of the liberty of the white man."[93] For whatever reasons, Germantown blacks must have voted overwhelmingly for Sentner as well.

Perhaps out of dissatisfaction with trends in election results, the Radical's County Commission reorganized the civil districts. It reduced the old twenty-seven districts and wards to twenty-five new districts, consolidating Memphis' ten wards into four districts. A new polling place at Forest Hill for new District 20, diminished Collierville's District 12 by loss to the new Forest Hill district. The borders of Germantown's district were changed only slightly.[94] Exactly what the Commission hoped to achieve is a mystery. Regardless, it did not last. One legitimate reason was reorganizing Collierville's' former District 10 into two districts, separating Collierville from Forest Hill. This acknowledged the increased population of former District 10, and doubled the number of justices.

Once the tide had turned and the Radicals' new County Commission was replaced by return to the old county court system, the victors immediately proceeded to repudiate all warrants issued by the "usurped authority" of the commission. Bleckley was unanimously elected chairman in 1869, and Germantown area magistrates resumed their leading roles in county government.[95]

The redistricting was abandoned in the following year and the civil districts resumed their old numbers with some border changes.[96]

In the county elections of August 1870, Democratic voters prevailed in Germantown, but Radicals still represented a strong minority: in the vote for the Supreme Judges, 178 versus 108. For the district magistrates, however, the popularity of Walker and Jones obliterated the opposition. Unfortunately first names are hard to find in the reports. There was the politically active local R. Weir, and a Mr. Anderson, who was probably Charles L. Anderson. Walker's support seems to have weakened a little.[97] As we shall see, he had strong personal conflicts with a few local Democrats. His popularity passed its peak in 1872 when he was being touted for state senator. He was also beaten in an election for Chancellor in that same year.[98] In both cases he faced county voters outside Civil District Eleven.

As the Tennessee Constitutional Convention of 1870 approached, the officials appointed to manage the polls at Germantown were familiar names in district politics, Lonallen Rhodes, R. Weir, J.C. Callis, J.P. Winford, M.P. Webb and William Carter. Again all were established pre-war residents, but clearly a bipartisan mix..[99]

By the gubernatorial and congressional election of 1870, the Democratic Party was triumphant in West Tennessee, but had by no means obliterated the Republican base. Brown ran for governor as a Democrat against Wisener, the Republican. For the congressional seat, Vaughan ran against Smith for the Republicans, and Edward Shaw for the Colored Republicans. When Vaughn spoke at Germantown, the turnout was overwhelmingly favorable. Democrats won both races by about a 5 to 2 margin. When Germantown's vote came in, the margin was closer at 160 to 62. As elsewhere, Shaw failed even to garner black votes, seen by most as a lost cause.[100] Such electoral results paint an interesting picture of the town's political atmosphere and the lines along which party affiliation were drawn.

By the elections of 1872, the relatively greater growth of Collierville's reestablished Tenth District resulted in the recreation of two polling places, giving some credence to the County Commissioner's aborted effort to divide the district. The western half of the 10th district, more oriented toward Germantown, began polling again at Forest Hill.[101]

The political differences between the neighboring districts 10 and 11 continued, however. For instance, they split over the effort of the more eastern parts of the county to secede and form with parts of Fayette County a new county to be named Nashoba. At least according to the *Appeal*, Collierville provided strong support, but, "At Germantown the white population are in the majority, and are against the new county for various reasons." The rest of the article implied that the proposal originated from people interested in having more control over their blacks by separating from the city. It reported the rumors being spread by the opposition designed to strike fear among blacks over their fate if the new county was formed. Of course, there was no unity in either district, because one of Germantown's "more correct and upright magistrates" was "leaving no stone unturned to accomplish the success of Nashoba" and was openly intimidating the opposition.[102] Presumably this was Walker. One would love to uncover the real motives and interests of both sides as well as the political divisions within Germantown's district. The internal contradictions within the *Appeal's* analysis do not help.

This move to secede from Shelby County was the second such attempt. The first in 1844 excluded Germantown from the proposed new county. This one was to include Germantown and the other eastern districts as far north as Eads. Collierville was apparently to be the new county's seat. Both times the state Legislature authorized the creations, but for unexplained reasons, never took effect.[103]

Germantown's citizens continued to expand their influence in county government. Charles L. Anderson began running for county sheriff in 1872, and was ultimately elected in 1874, representing a shift in influence from the city to the country, which was, of course, appropriate since the city had its separate law enforcement. The ticket that he led was referred to as the Bartlett Convention, an apparent effort of factions within the Democratic Party to wrest control from the city. Anderson would serve two terms until his death in 1878.[104]

In the presidential election of 1872, the town's national vote turned Republican in sharp contrast to its otherwise Democratic posture. Grant won 268 over Greeley's 175, a victory which the *Appeal* attributed to Grant's previously overwhelming victory in key northern states. The logic behind this editorial explanation seems to have been that Democrats were either too resigned to the inevitable to waste their votes or voted for the winning side.[105] The *Appeal* could not comprehend Grant's popularity.

By the time of the 1874 county elections, the Democrats mobilized a fiscal conservative, anti-tax campaign, always accusing Republicans of irresponsible taxing and spending. Among the 10 candidates running for the 3 positions as delegates to the party's county convention, there were many new entries into political activity.[106] The aged Squire Bleckley had passed and other old stalwarts were facing competition and/or grooming new blood.[107]

For the state elections of November 1874, Germantown returned a Democratic majority of 76 votes out of the 345 total. These numbers when compared to the 1872 votes hardly support the *Appeal*'s claim that Grant won because of voter indifference. But in all these elections, the *Appeal* continued its drum beat of the threat of illegal black voting purchased by the Radicals. During the local elections of the previous summer, it warned that a large number of Mississippi blacks had once again been hired to vote in Shelby County. They were to appear at Collierville, Germantown, Whites Station and Memphis. All election officials were to be on guard against this "prospective invasion of the ballot box."[108] It's hard to take this purported threat seriously.

As the Democrats assembled for their county convention in 1876, Memphis still dominated the floor with each of its wards having three to four times as many delegates as the civil districts in the country. Collierville's District Ten with Forest Hill had five, while Germantown's District Eleven had four. Nevertheless, Germantown, with its Forest Hill share of District Ten's magistrates, still managed to play a disproportionate role in the governing County Court.

♦ ♦ ♦

Fifteen years after the war, the area was divided on partisan lines between Democrats and Republicans, as it had been before between Democrats and Whigs. Also as before, the Democrats had the majority. It does not seem that the divide was as clearly "racial" as the *Appeal* always insisted so shrilly. At least as early as 1868, the blacks of Memphis had organized Conservative meetings, while blacks in the countryside were voting Conservative and then Democrat. Although the Radicals had elected Edward Shaw, the prominent black political leader, to the short-lived County Commission in 1869, dissatisfaction was growing among the blacks over the scarcity of appointments and other unfulfilled promises. Typically the *Avalanche* branded Shaw "a Northern negro ... a representative of the ultra-wing of the party." Shaw, actually born in Kentucky, had moved to Memphis in the 1850s and was a local businessman as well as a political activist. He was a source of tension in the Republican Party, leading efforts to get a better share of political power and economic opportunity for blacks, even sabotaging the campaign of General W.J. Smith for Congress in 1870. Smith was an outspoken obstacle to black appointments. Shaw's internal dissension culminated in his run for governor as an independent Republican in 1876. The power of black voters had peaked in 1867, and declined thereafter, but especially after 1870 outside Memphis. The Republicans increasingly lost interest in their cause. By the 1880s, black support had shifted significantly to the Democrats, and Shaw even campaigned briefly for Democratic candidates.[109]

Nevertheless, around Germantown, blacks would make a respectable turnout for the district election of 1880. The baton continued to pass, for Walker had finally resigned and A.B. Ellis had moved away. C.M. Callis and James Brett won their seats. Although Callis won a clear victory, Brett beat W.F. Mitchell by only 10 votes, and a "colored" John Graham garnered 87 votes.[110]

✦ ✦ ✦

As for Germantown without a town charter, its sole source of local administration were the officials of Civil District 11. Because of the loss of local records, politics within District Eleven and the town remain mostly below our radar. While Collierville recovered and reacquired its charter in 1869, Germantown apparently languished until 1880 without a town government. Although most local historians refer to a new charter granted as early as 1871, there are no such records in any of the published Acts or county court records. In 1878, the *Public Ledger* made a clear reference to the town's lack of a charter. Although it certainly could have gotten one during the 1870s, apparently the locals saw no need for anything beyond district management of its affairs. The town seems to have preferred spontaneous citizens' meetings to deal with more mundane issues as they arose, rather than paying extra taxes for public services. Goodspeed reported, "It was reincorporated, however, in 1880," omitting any reference to any 1871 charter.[111]

11

SOCIAL AND ECONOMIC RECOVERY

Conditions in Tennessee

Despite all the destruction, the economic prospects for Tennessee in general were not gloomy, at least according to economic interest groups in the state. Looking forward to the end of the war in February 1865, a correspondent from Nashville published an optimistic essay in the *Times*.[1] Its purpose was to encourage northern immigration.[2]

The author began by describing conditions and emphasizing an ongoing shift in the population that, nevertheless, only affected Germantown minimally. "Since the commencement of the war, at least ten thousand citizens of the North have permanently located themselves on Tennessee soil. Nearly all the cotton baled in this State last season was raised by Northern men. Thousands of acres of land are now for sale in different sections of the State." But what was really needed to exploit the potential was northern investment.

Memphis proper had suffered relatively little from the war. Physical damage had been minimal, and the city's institutional and commercial structures were intact. River and rail transportation were quickly restored, business recovered, and the population expanded rapidly, although overcrowding and inadequate housing and worsening sanitation came with that growth. The immediate benefits to Germantown, however, would be slight.

Two major deficiencies would plague the area for some time: a shortage of capital and white labor—at least from the point of view of white employers. Eastern financiers invested relatively little in the South, and local banks could do little more than meet the credit needs of cotton planters. Thus while the city's commercial and industrial ventures were credit starved, at least the farmers in Germantown got the seed money they needed to begin anew, but only with cotton that local financial interests saw as profitable. Then, the bank failures of 1868 brought another setback, and banking remained unstable into the 1880s.[3] The entire country wallowed in a Great Depression throughout much of the 70s.

✦ ✦ ✦

For more agrarian communities like Germantown, the economic consequences of the war were significant on several counts. A statistical study of eight counties from across the state revealed that "The median value of real estate per white farm household fell during the 1860s by from one-half to three-fifths. Former slave-holding families ... suffered financial loss ... of more than 275,000 slaves." A loss of hundreds of million-dollars.[4]

The financial losses caused by emancipation had uneven effects. Ironically it seems to have been the non-slaveholding, small property owners who suffered worse. Yet it represented the greatest redistribution of wealth in the country's history. Former slaveholders lost the value of their slaves who could not be sold to pay debts or raise cash. More problematic, they had to find substitute labor. More important, the former slaves now owned their own labor. It was the wealth or value of labor that was redistributed from owner to freeman. If the new freeman was not self-sufficient, however, he was simply a factor in the "labor market" that they had to negotiate. Land-owners were in a better position to manipulate the new system of "free" labor.[5]

Because of its slave-holding history, West Tennessee was the most severely affected part of the state, but the impact was unevenly spread as a comparative analysis of the 1860 and 1870 censuses will show. Equally uneven was the competence of the heads of household to deal with the problems and stresses they now faced.

Although the wealthiest former planters were severely hit, many reemerged socially and economically dominant. The distribution of land and its use was altered. Land-ownership became more inequitable. Of course, all of this had been greatly skewed by the addition of the large propertyless black population.

The most truly revolutionary force of change was emancipation. Far beyond its economic impact, it radically affected perceptions of human relationships. Beyond being a seemingly indispensable part of the economy, as we have seen, slavery had been the foundation of beliefs in white supremacy and black subordination. Those beliefs still prevailed. The ideology and pseudoscience of racial differences continued to bolster them. While whites still demanded deference from blacks, it required both new forms of enforcement and readjusted expectations within black society. Ultimately, where black and white society overlapped, a pro forma deference would have to prevail. But a different world evolved within black society to deal with it.

Blacks confronted the reality of a minimally changed social-political relationship. Following in the footsteps of the army's previously described management of contraband labor, the Freedmen's Bureau initially preferred to organize blacks into gang labor for plantations as the best way to employ them. That coupled with the freedmen's searches for separated family members had significant effects on the emancipated population both physically and psychologically.[6] Some were fortunate enough either to avoid paternalistic interference or had enough ingenuity and resources to establish themselves. Across the state, the most self-reliant and fortunate 10 percent of ex-slaves acquired their own farms.[7] Those who had been trained in crafts were either readily employed or established themselves independently. Most, however, had never gotten a whiff of autonomy or responsibility for themselves, and had been denied achievement of any sort. They were less prepared to operate in a world of white standards shaped by white convictions that blood explained everything rather than conditions created by slavery. Blacks were indeed vulnerable to the predatory instincts of those hoping to recreate a de facto system of slavery.

The landowners had to solve the problem of lost labor. Some hoped to entice northern and foreign workers into their fields, but few came. Many planters tried to maintain the old system by using "gangs" of hired black workers under the supervision of "drivers." Between 1865 and 1880, however, the planters negotiated the transition to the New South plantation system. Although they still owned the land, much was subdivided into smaller farms worked by families under several different arrangements.[8] By 1880 when the dust had settled in Tennessee, over one third had entered into a variety of tenant farming arrangements. However, in Shelby County less than 12 percent of farms were sharecropped.[9]

Renters had to have the means to operate a farm independently—draft animals, tools and equipment, and the costs of seeds, etc. Economically, this put them only slightly below the landowning yeoman farmer of the same means. Next to the bottom of the ladder were the "sharecroppers." With little or no means of their own, they remained basically farm labor, working under the authority of owners who provided everything and paid with a share of the crop. Between renter and sharecropper, was the "share tenant," owning some of his own implements and livestock. Such a tenant and the owner split the other costs of operation, such as seeds and ginning, on a set percentage basis. Consequently, the share-tenant's share was greater than the sharecroppers'.[10]

Tenant farming had already been a preferred arrangement for white farm workers before the war. As we have seen, during the war, it was extended to some slaves whose owners were desperate to keep them on. Although tenant farming would soon constitute one of the worst forms of exploitation, it was actually a step up for white field hands who previously had to compete against slave labor. They had their own leased homes and lands, and a percentage of what they produced. The same was even truer for black tenants, for they were now free.

Below the croppers lay the farm laborer. For whites, things probably had not changed much, except for the alleged unfairness of cheap black labor driving wages down. Most of the blacks benefitted less. In so many ways, the chains of the past remained. They could only earn wages as farm hands, often while supporting preexisting families.[11] The experience around Germantown involved variations of these four relationships: renter, tenant, cropper, landless laborer.

Social-Economic "Reconstruction" of Germantown

By 1870, the official population of the town proper was only 162 whites and 35 blacks, down from somewhere around 500 whites, plus 80 odd slaves. Despite the 1850s decade of growth, during the 1860s decade of war, the town's population had plummeted to well below 1850 levels. Now an unincorporated village, the town was a shadow of its former self. The rest of the Eleventh District held 663 whites and 1143 blacks. Numbers of the white population outside town had only declined by about fifty, despite the fact that many families and all farm laborers had been replaced. The gross inaccuracies of the 1860 slave schedules complicate comparisons for the blacks. Their story will be told below.

Residents, Old and New

Many survivors and returnees sought about for a new life. They explored many options—different forms of livelihood. Those who left sought to sell or rent whatever land they still owned. The Reverend Phillip Tuggle's church appointments were relocated deeper into Mississippi in 1868, so he had moved south. Now an appointment elsewhere seemed more promising. From all appearances, the devastation inflicted on the farmers south of Nonconnah, in no-man's land, had been worse. The Memphis papers were full of ads selling farm and timber land, business establishments, and homes throughout the entire district.

Both the major merchants, Henry Boardman and Samuel Cole, owner of Cole & Co. store, had given up and left after paying their federal back taxes in 1866.[12] William Hack had abandoned his store and turned entirely to working his farm. Their businesses had probably been too thoroughly pillaged and denied opportunities to resupply.

Young Henry Woodson described initial efforts following his return to the family farm.

> As there appeared to be no opportunity for business of any kind, I went to work in the field, with a few of my father's former slaves who were still on the place, and made a little crop of corn, split rails, and rebuilt fences and outhouses, all of which had been utterly destroyed.... I was married ... on November 15, 1866, to Miss Maria Louise Ford of Germantown, Tennessee, daughter of Lloyd Ford and Malvina Scruggs.

By January 1867, the new couple sought greener pastures in Devall's Bluff, Arkansas where he "engaged in the mercantile business."[13]

His father's fate was even harder. His home had been plundered, but at least the house had been saved because it had been "occupied" by Union officers. Boarding them had provided more benefits than just income. According to family traditions, "(T)he close of the war saw him stripped of all his property except" his house and land, "and with no means whatever of supporting his family and the few negroes who still remained on the place, and whom he felt as much bound to care for as if they had not been emancipated." He went to Memphis and "secured a position, at a salary of $200 per month, in the shoe store of A. H. Borcher." One trouble followed another. On June 24, his youngest child, an infant, died. "Within a few days thereafter, his beloved wife who had been his efficient helpmeet in all the vicissitudes ... was taken ill and died July 4, 1865."[14]

His partnership in the burned cotton gin factory left him with debts to northern manufacturers, suspended by the Confederate government during the war.[15] They now came due, and he refused the dishonor of bankruptcy. In 1867, he even sought to make ends meet as an agent selling butter churn dashers in town at $3.00 each. Remarried in 1868, he sold the home and farm in 1869 to pay his debts, and in 1871 bought another farm near Senatobia where he lived out the rest of his life.[16]

Stephen Truehart, Woodson's former partner and now a 40 year-old veteran, suffered the same financial problems. He, on the other hand, had more modern ideas about capitalism and took bankruptcy in January 1868.[17] He would hold on and remain one of the town's respected citizens. It is never clear what induced someone like Truehart to cling to his hometown while others abandoned it for some new environment.

George W. Trueheart, his father and a lawyer, apparently found it necessary to relocate to Memphis in his sixties. In April 1866, the *Appeal* announced that Mr. G.W. Truehart was their authorized agent for expanding the paper's circulation outside the city, accepting subscriptions and advertisements.[18] He was one of several professionals to depart and not be replaced, reflecting the decline as a center of legal and commercial activity.

In town, only twelve of the thirty-seven white households held over from the 1860 census. With the exception of a pastor, two merchants, a mill owner and two physicians, the town's elite was gone. Molitor's mills had at least been rebuilt. Lucken's resources had been greatly reduced and he may have given up inn keeping, while his son Frederick listed himself as a painter. Both the Southern Star and Hurt's gin factories had been totally demolished, as had the Bliss book business. There are no further references to a brick factory. All but two of the shopkeepers and craftsmen were gone, so too all pre-war employees and laborers.

Among the soldiers returning, not all gave up. Needham Harrison found himself a widower. He had married Eliza Neely shortly before the war. With deep roots, the bereaved man immediately set to work on his 320 acres three miles south of town. While recovering, he deepened his roots, marrying his deceased wife's sister in January 1866. They eventually had seven children, five of whom would survive. Like his successful planter predecessors, he diversified, also functioning as a "merchant," and served as County Register from 1886.[19]

Tracing the fate of Nathan Booth, one uncovers a rare story, that of a small farmer survivor. In 1860, he had been a farmer-renter with only $400 in non-real property. By 1870, he was supporting his family as a well digger.

Nevertheless, he continued to farm sixteen acres, producing $500 in crops, while modestly increasing his non-real wealth. His wife further supplemented their income with boarders, among whom were a widow, who worked as a cook, and her teenage son as a laborer, plus another laborer and a teenage girl of undefined status. Mary Booth must have been running a boarding house. The Booths truly exhibited determination.[20]

Among the town's old guard, Pastor Evans remained for life and continued to teach for extra income, although he had retained much more than modest wealth. William Harrison's widow presided over their former plantation. Also Cary Harrison's widow, Elizabeth, still held much of his estate, but perhaps as an absentee landlord.[21] Isaac Bliss was all that remained of the book agent consortium. He had lost everything. At first, he made his living as a carpenter, apparently renting a small house in which he and his wife struggled on alone. He returned to something more familiar, for by 1880 he described himself as a "huckster." Neither a shady business man nor a simple peddler, he was probably more like a sales representative.[22]

Most of the town's holdovers barely clung to respectable middle class status. In contrast, Lonallen Rhodes, the former wagon maker now ran a dry goods store and would soon expand into hotel ownership. William Walker and Shephard's widow Sallie apparently combined their resources to open a general store. Gin manufacturer Berry Hurt would temporarily support his family as a blacksmith before rebuilding his factory.

Finally, as for black "holdovers," it is known that at least 8 men, some with intact families, definitely either stayed through the war or returned after. Additionally, relying only on 1870 black households with family names of former area slave holders, and correlating them with the 1860 slave schedules, one finds as many as 60 "likely" such cases, and another 21 possible such cases.[23] One only wishes for the true stories of all who actually decided to return to their pre-war "roots" and why. Among the "likely," fifty-three year old Isham Stout and his wife Harriet (and 9 children probably working as farm laborers) were living with Dr. Stout.

✦ ✦ ✦

The majority of the new white residents, including even many immigrants, had moved to the area after having lived somewhere else in the southern states. Only five people had moved south from northern states. The community even increased its immigrant mix, but they may not have added the same degree of "cosmopolitan" flavor that former "foreigners" had provided. There were three new people from England, three from Ireland and two from Scotland, two Germans, two Dutch, and ten Swedes. One exotic old woman had been born in Java. Among all 23 immigrants, 21 had no measurable wealth. They provided various forms of skilled, semi-skilled and unskilled labor. Only one man born in Ireland possessed some means—the blacksmith, Arthur O'Neill. Actually, he and his family had settled in town in 1861, on the very eve of the war.[24]

There is only one clue as to what brought immigrant workers to Germantown. As part of a concerted effort to recruit immigrants from among arrivals in New York City late in 1865, Memphis city leaders had sent agents there to recruit. The agents simply paid their fare, and by January 1866, they were arriving by the scores.[25] As a member of the Committee on Immigration and major employer in the city, William Greenlaw undoubtedly employed many, and brought ten Swedes and two Dutch to service his operation in Germantown.[26]

Financially all old residents in town and country were eclipsed by this newcomer William Greenlaw and his son Eugene. They, like other newcomers, affected the town's social structure and milieu. In the 1870 census, the senior Greenlaw had listed $550,000 in properties, more than quadruple that of all but one other local land-owner, also new. His son, also financially well endowed, was described as an "insurance clerk."[27] These Greenlaws were among the more prominent and wealthy families of Memphis, active in real estate development and investment in railroads and insurance, and major owners of property in the city and plantations in Mississippi.[28] William himself had been an active secessionist and official of the Memphis Committee of Safety. He fled the city after its occupation, but by 1863 had returned and taken the oath under the threat of losing his property. Greenlaw needed to collect rents in the city and to bring his cotton to market.[29] Although seemingly a defector and profiteer, he may have collaborated with the Confederate spy, Belle Edmondson, facilitating movement through the lines between Memphis and his lands around Senatobia. His older brother had died in the service, while his two sons, one riding with Forrest, served to the end of the war.[30]

His having a home around Germantown was part of the growing trend to flee the city's filthy and unhealthy environment. For relocation, Germantown was favored for its convenient rail connection. The men could commute daily, or stay in their city houses, joining their families on weekends and holidays.[31]

P. 21 Greenlaw House, 1870s, courtesy Walter Wills. Typical Victorian Town House of the sort being built in Memphis; the Germantown family home of the prominent William Greenlaw.

Such families could still benefit fully from the city's social and cultural life by rail.

The home, built in 1870 off the State Line Road was a substantial Victorian neo-Gothic of the sort favored in the city.[32] It differed notably from typical local simplicity and neo-classical styles. Additionally, it also housed several employees. Among the non-family residents were another insurance agent, two laborers and two Dutch carpenters. An adjacent house held the Johnson family of nine—the Swedes. All the adults worked in service as gardener, cook and house servants. Two other adjacent buildings housed two black households with female heads—a cook, laborer, nurse (for children), and wash woman. This family empire had a significant social, economic and political impact on the town and surrounding area. His local estate operated as something of a diverse, model truck farm compared to the mono-cropping around them. Greenlaw was highly influential in county government which relied on him for advice and services relating to finance.[33]

An even greater intrusion into land-ownership was James H. Anderson, who had bought 100,000 acres, mostly outside the district. He was apparently a land speculator, who had consolidated such massive holdings around 1869, and was gone by the 1880 census. Such speculators could take advantage of the needs of the broken-spirited and bankrupt former farmers and planters or their widows. He probably benefited from sales of this land generated by the urban flight before the bubble burst.[34]

Not all new names were true outsiders, however. One such was Dr. John Thompson. Illinois born but not new to the area, he had married Florida Pettit, the former teacher and daughter of Judge Pettit. They had married in 1860 and settled in Mississippi where she had her first son in 1861. They subsequently returned, probably by 1862, when she had her next child.[35] Certainly a tumultuous time to be moving a family.

Another new resident of professional status was Dr. Richard Martin who arrived in 1868 with his family from Mississippi. He was typical of the highly mobile Americans of the 1840s and 50s. Born in North Carolina in 1816 and trained in Philadelphia, he had joined a mass migration of neighbors in 1847, settled temporarily at Somerville, Tennessee, then Red Banks, Mississippi, before Germantown, always practicing medicine and acquiring considerable means. He acquired land north-east of town and built a fine home, quickly becoming a prominent citizen and elder of the Presbyterian Church.[36]

Robert Scruggs was a new dry goods merchant with a general store, but given the name one wonders if he did not have family connections to build on. Nelms Madison, another new grocer had also moved around quite a bit. He was born in Ohio around 1823. Julia, his much younger wife was born in North Carolina in 1845. His oldest son had appeared in Mississippi in 1854, by an earlier wife. He may have settled in Germantown by 1867. Railroad contractor William Gilmer and his family of five had come from Mississippi. Edward Gorman, another grocer and his family of four had resettled from elsewhere in Tennessee, as had Pennsylvania-born Samuel Gardner and his wife. To supplement his income as a plasterer, Gardner ran a profitable little farm. Then there was Mary Rhoads, a widow of some means in both land and other resources, who had moved to town from Texas sometime after 1866. Perhaps she had inherited her estate from one of the prewar families. Two of her sons were employed by the railroad as a conductor and an office clerk, while the oldest clerked for a riverboat.

Previously one dividing line between the respectable middle class, and those below them had been their ability to have either white domestic servants or slaves as such. Even under reduced economic conditions, the presence of a pool of cheap black labor enabled many to maintain that status image. As before, a young white woman or girl was occasionally living in a household, also playing such roles.

Further down the economic scale respectively, but still middle status, were Thomas Chambers, an attorney who had brought his family from Mississippi between 1866 and 1869. Then there were William Miller and Thomas Webb who partnered as druggists. William Mitchell was a wagon maker. Susan Burnley, another widow, must have relied on leasing her farm lands to tenants. Robert McKay, physician, had apparently arrived with limited resources to support his family of six, but by 1876 the *Tennessee State Gazetteer* listed him as one of the town's prominent physicians. Finally Thomas Sanders, who had brought his family from Louisiana after 1868, described himself simply as saloon keeper. Among the non-property-owning middle class, who are harder to assess for social status, was Charles Anderson, a superintendent with the M&C.[37] Clearly, the railroad was now one of Germantown's significant sources of employment. All these persons in the 1870 census, many of whom would have occupied positions in the old town's elite, were apparently just recovering from wartime losses or just getting themselves established. As in the cases of Dr. McKay and Mr. Anderson, they would soon rise to local prominence, but overall, the townsfolk, new and old, suffered relative loss of economic standing compared to the greater rural landowners.

The remaining new white households were those of skilled, semi-skilled and unskilled laborers who earned enough to rent a house for their families. Below them were the single workers, male and female who boarded.

Among the town's black households in 1870, only two were headed by men with resources to be self-employed. On the edge of town was James Scott, a carpenter of reasonably good financial resources who apparently owned his house and shop. Sixty-five year-old Grant Allen, a blacksmith, at least owned his own tools, but apparently rented a modest shop. The remaining black households were occupied by families whose members worked as servants in the white homes, or as employees for the various businesses or mills. Five such families were headed by women.

As for the future of these black townsfolk, by 1880, among them there would be two blacksmiths, a carpenter and a shoemaker. All were new names, although one may have been Allen's heir. Unfortunately, since the 1880 census does not list indicators of wealth, we cannot tell how well they were doing. The old propertied carpenter was gone, while the new one boarded with a white brick mason, so he was probably an employee. In the household of one family, older teenage sons were supplementing family funds as farm laborers.[38] It is hard to tell how blacks in the town proper had fared over the decade of the 70s.

✦ ✦ ✦

In the districts outside town, according to the 1870 census, whites often lived and worked side-by-side with over 2,753 blacks. Only about twenty-six of the former white farm households had reestablish themselves. The rural population was even less persistent than the townsfolk. Those who stayed sought to resume life as quickly as possible, rebuilding with the same self-reliance as the original settlers. Among them, 7 widows and a couple of widowers struggled on alone, the more fortunate with older children to help. A few others quickly found new mates. The regular appearance of new children testified to the drive to resume life as before. The greatly reduced number of physicians since 1860 may or may not have affected the quality of obstetrical care. Two black woman now listed themselves as midwife. White women so practicing would not have listed such an occupation, only house keeper.

The continuation of the family names of many of the more prominent planters provided some continuity in the old social order—the Bradleys, Brooks, Callises, Carters, widow Cogbill, the Dukes, Ellises, the Hacks, both Harrisons, Kimbroughs, Massys, Neelys, and Mrs. Walker. Several, however, had declined significantly in wealth, if not social status. Although Samuel Mosby still held his lands, he had apparently moved his residence elsewhere. Likewise, the family of the deceased Allen Rutland. The Burns estate had been inherited by Caroline, now married to a newcomer, Thomas Moore. It is difficult to tell, without family histories just how many other apparent newcomers were tied into old families either by marriage or inheritance.

Below them, the old respectable farmer families were still represented by the Carters, Featherstons, Myricks, Rodgers, Shepherds, Thompsons, and Winfords. This economic group was joined by numerous new-comers, including several black households. They replaced almost all the former yeomen families of lesser means who had left. That element had been more thoroughly decimated than the others. Below them, absolutely none of the landless white poor had persisted.

In the countryside, the property damage and confiscation of livestock, especially draft animals, had completed the destitution of the farmers. For several years, those who held on survived on the margin. Planters who managed to remain were reduced temporarily to the standard of living of the former middling yeoman; the yeoman to that of the poorest landholder. Wives and children worked the fields alongside their men, if they still had them.

♦ ♦ ♦

By 1870, things had begun to stabilize. Most surviving families retained their acreage, but its value had declined. Yet in a few cases, their real wealth had increased, in some cases significantly, undoubtedly by expansion of holdings bought from former neighbors. Otherwise, most families' productive acreage had been reduced. As late as 1870, their cleared acreage had dropped by 33–50%, reverting to scrub. The loss of slaves and livestock had significantly reduced everyone's non-land wealth. Even by 1870, the surviving agricultural households were perhaps more than a half million dollars below their 1860 total holdings.[39] Their horses and mules were fewer, there were hardly any oxen, and the flocks of sheep were so badly thinned there was no wool produced for market, just homespun. Even the pig herds had not recovered.

A legal and financial problem faced by returnees was reestablishing ownership of property forfeited for back taxes, or held by the Freedmen's Bureau as abandoned lands.[40] Additionally new taxes piled on top of old, with cash income often insufficient to pay. By 1866, the federal direct taxes levied during the war on "insurrectionary districts" were overdue in Germantown. One hundred fifteen citizens of District Eleven paid the tax plus 50% penalty for late payment. With the largest plantation, the Kimbroughs paid over $60 plus over $31 in penalties. The Nashoba Tract cost Sylvia d'Arusmont $95.50 plus $47.25 in penalties. Most of the debt was paid between March and May, but a total of $213.73 still remained unpaid.[41] At least some of these must have led to forfeitures.

Compared to the lackadaisical local tax collecting of the prewar years, the tax man had become something to fear. When state taxation resumed, initially things seem to have been disorganized enough that land owners had a short reprieve, but a new tax law had teeth. On September 18, 1868, the tax collector arrived in Germantown for state and county taxes. If not paid by November, there was a two and one half percent penalty. In December, it went up to five percent, and in January ten percent. If the tax collector had to seize and/or sell the property, there was an additional fifty percent fee. To redeem one's property, one had to pay all taxes and fees with cash, and if not done before a year had lapsed, another fifty percent penalty was added.[42] Once sucked into such a maw, one could quickly become hopeless. For all the signs of progress in the papers, announcements of bankruptcies and foreclosed-sales painted a contrary picture. The names of Germantown citizens in such proceedings were not uncommon.[43] Hard luck would also strike continuously. In December 1866, James Armstrong's woolen mill burned. In 1872, Molitor's mill burned. Even after insurance, he lost $4,000. The Featherston home burned in 1875, uninsured. Ben Owen's grocery store in Forest Hill with all his stock was lost without insurance in 1879.[44]

Even the formerly most prosperous plantation family, the Kimbroughs, had been significantly reduced. They had apparently sold several hundred acres. The entire family and its plantation inexplicably escaped the attention of the census takers in 1870. Nevertheless, we know that James passed in 1867, but his wife Mary continued to preside as matriarch until 1882. The fates of the oldest son, Syrus, and his younger brother Buckley are obscure. William eventually returned to farm some of the family's lands, but also had business ventures around Memphis. Albert G. Kimbrough continued to live at Cotton Plant, and served as a prominent citizen of the county and town. The other brother, John, also eventually returned to live in the family home, operating one of the town's stores.[45]

The former Duke compound had declined considerably, not only from loss of its slaves, but also the value of its land holdings. Robert, the son who had stayed home to manage the estate and family now presided over more than half of the lands, while Britton's widow Mary ruled over her share. With her lived the youngest son, Joe.

Several newcomers intruded significantly into the upper crust. Of course, James H. Anderson's 10,000 acres well out-paced the old guard. After the Greenlaws, he represented the most significant intrusion into the social order. Also another new touch of class was a wealthy settler from the West Indies, Charles Patton and his French-born wife, Adriana. John Hunt, John Quenichet

TABLE 6 Comparative Wealth, 1870 Census[1]

Total Wealth	Households	Cumulative Total	Notes (planters and/or farmers assumed)
Over $100,000	3 households, 0.6%	$825,000	1 financier, 1 speculator, 1 planter
(Below $100,000 4 households 0.8%)			(Brooks, Kimbrough, Mosby & Massey)
Below $50,000	15 households, 3.2%	$243,403	1 miller
Below $10,000	21 households, 4.4%	$134,389	1 black household/owner; 4 professionals, 1 grocer, 2 employees (Cornelius omitted)
Below $5,000	9 households, 1.9%	$39,130	2 merchants, 2 mechanics
Below $4,000	11 households, 2.3%	$38,130	1 black household; 1 doctor, 1 merchant, 1 contractor
Below $3,000	14 households, 3%	$40,528	6 black households/2 owning; 1 attorney, 1 mechanic
Below $2,000	35 households, 7.4%	$80,213	20 black households; 2 professionals, 1 druggist, 2 mechanics
Below $1,000	80 households, 16.9%	$52,040	64 black households/1 owning; 1 merchant, 2 mechanics
Below $500	76 households, 16%	$24,346	61 black households; 1 doctor, 4 mechanics
(lowest annual agricultural income $150)			
	Total: $1,506,516		

Total Wealth	Households	Cumulative Total	Notes (planters and/or farmers assumed)
Wage or Salary Earners without any Wealth Indicated			
			16 persons employed as skilled or white-collar workers (3 blacks) (4 households; 12 boarding; 1 family member)
			14 persons employed as semi- or unskilled workers (6 blacks) (6 households)
			52 persons employed in service roles (44 blacks) (24 households; 43 women; 44 blacks)**
Farm Households without Land or Other Wealth Indicated			
			83 households 17.5%, head listed as "Farmer" (77 black households)*
			35 households 7.4%, head listed as "Farm Laborer" (12 women heads of household; 30 black households)*
			44.3% living entirely on salaries and/or subsistence farming
			10 households 2% with no indicated means of income (7 women heads of household; 4 black households)
	Total Households 474		

and George Bennett also joined the old elite, although Quenichet had owned his Germantown lands before the war. Among the many other new names that acquired farm holdings were a number of widows. The stories of these people, what brought them with the means to buy lands would add much color to this account if they were available. One is greatly impressed by the spunk of those widows who pulled up roots and came to a new community.

Among the northerners, only two or three had the means to set up as land-owning. Widower Theodore Thompson from Ohio rented or was a tenant farmer. Another from Ohio, thirty-four year-old Joseph Thompson, had to give up and sought a position as superintendent. He was ready to pack up and move again with his wife and two young children.[46] All the foreign-born immigrants came without resources and worked for others.

A New Hierarchy

As the above implies, one of the more significant changes around Germantown was a new socioeconomic hierarchy with a more greatly skewed concentration of wealth. Unfortunately accessing the distribution of wealth by 1870 is complicated.[47] Despite such problems, it is worthwhile to use available evidence to attempt an analysis. A comparison of the available data in Tables 1 (1860, p.62) and 6 shows a much greater concentration at the top, a reduced middle, and grossly expanded lower economic classes, many of whom might have been considered a dangerous under-class. The wealth of the townspeople vs landowners had seriously declined.

Among the agricultural land owners, 10,904 acres were owned and operated by 69 resident families, three of which were black. The remaining 4,845 was apparently rented or cropped by 196 families, of whom 174 were black.[48] Since some owners held significant acreage outside the district, and much acreage in

TABLE 6 (*continued*)

1. The data are problematic because in some cases the agricultural census differed significantly from the population census. In all such cases, the highest recorded total wealth was accepted. In other cases, only agricultural wealth from that census was available. Two very prominent planters, Brooks and Kimbrough, and the Buster and Stout families were missing from both censuses, as were the Cornelius family. Many of the same problems that plagued the reporting in the 1860 census also apply to 1870.

*"Farmer" supposedly meant one owning less than 5 acres. Some households contained members designated "Farm Laborer" able to earn additional income.

**Some were members of otherwise designated households, contributing to the household income either by their own labor or by paying board.

the district was owned by outsiders, this is not a measure of land distribution in the district. Rather a measure of landed wealth held among its residents. Among non-landowners, any acreage they farmed was owned either by the other land-owning residents or absentee landlords.

No longer was there a relatively smooth transition down from the elite through a significant middle of yeomen farmers to a poor minority. Landed wealth now concentrated in the hands of the top five percent of families while the bottom thirty-six percent were landless laborers. Large tracts of recently bought lands were also rented or cropped out by absentee landlords, especially below the old state line.

When other forms of wealth are factored in, the result is still a much more skewed distribution of wealth than before the war. Together the Greenlaw and Anderson "magnates" (0.45% of the households) possessed more wealth than all the rest of the known holders of wealth combined. However, the absence from the full census data of four major landholders, Brooks, Kimbrough, Massey and Mosby, makes an accurate ranking of the top ten percent impossible. Among those included, however, that ten percent held at least 50% of the wealth. The lowest 41% held only 5% of that wealth. Thirty-seven percent of the households appear to have had no tangible wealth, living entirely on income. Admittedly, the census taker omitted any wealth reported below $100. Regardless of the questionable accuracy of these statistics, the reality behind them was absolutely one of a grossly imbalanced distribution of wealth. The shock of such a change from 1860, and its effects on the society and culture must have reduced harmony and increased social tensions.

Given the likelihood that the agricultural census taker apparently included the value of rented and even cropped property in the wealth of the renter or cropper (at least in many cases), this makes it likely that the actual distribution of real-estate wealth was even more badly skewed than these tables indicate.[49] Especially among the lowest 163 households in the above table, it is impossible to distinguish with certainty between renters and croppers who were included among them. Among the most likely croppers, 11 families worked more than 50 acres, 7 of whom were black. Another 9, 6 of whom were black, worked 40 acres. 79 families operated 39 to 20 acres, and 95 operated 18 or fewer. The value of the leasees' livestock ranged widely, determining how well they ate beyond what they could produce for the market. Few operating below the 30 acre level had any other non-real property such as livestock, farming implements or tools of a trade. Seven black women were among those trying to support a family on 20 acres or less. Among those scrambling to live off 15 to five acres, 15 had to do so without any draft animals to pull the plow. These black and white families lived and farmed side by side and shared all the same hardships. At the lowest levels, even race would not have advantaged the white families. For some of those white families, this would have generated increased racial hostilities. For the others, there might simply have been a sense of shared misery.

As many as 108 householders, men and women, many supporting families, survived as landless farm labor, while an additional 62 farm laborers, men and women, boys and girls were either working family members or boarders. The census records that only $9,233 was paid out in 1870 as agricultural wages to these 170 families and/or individuals, an average of $60 to feed and clothe several mouths. Nationally, a farm laborer earned an average of $15.50 per week or 90 cents a day. A full work-week was 66 hours, a 12 hour day in a 5 ½ day work-week. From all indications, local farmers paid as low as $1.92 a week, with $5.77 being the maximum, taking advantage of a glutted labor market.[50] The families, at least, usually had kitchen gardens to supplement their diets, while some of the boarders got meals in the owners' homes for whom they worked, but earned one-third less income to cover room and board. Many people obviously had to find other sources of income in addition to their farm labor. Absolutely none of these people possessed any non-real property. Here was a sizable and a truly poor population.

Among the top agriculturalists, annual incomes over several thousand dollars were restoring some positions despite hard times. Below that level, income dwindled down to less than $100 worth of corn and cotton going to market for the year. Two to three bales were scraped out by hard scrabble labor, sometimes without benefit of horse or mule. A decent horse or mule was valued at about $100 or more, but many had to do with animals of much less quality. Many of the poorest could hardly feed and clothe themselves adequately. Consequences of all this will be explored in the next chapter.

✦ ✦ ✦

The serious obstacle for agriculturalists at all levels was greatly reduced diversity—they concentrated exclusively on corn and cotton as the only cash crops. Greenlaw was the only man with resources to afford a fully diversified farm.[51]

Only one other farmer brought any wheat to market in 1870. Such a risky concentration was undoubtedly forced by their creditors focused on the cotton market. Even that cotton would not provide the financial rewards of the antebellum era. Cotton production did not return to its pre-war levels until 1879.[52] The total reliance on the cotton merchants and bankers and local merchants for credit between crops kept many on the brink of bankruptcy. Such reliance on only two crops greatly enhanced the danger from crop failures.

The problem of credit-and-lender-influenced cropping raises the question of the town's merchants and their place in the area's economy. Although most merchants in Germantown belonged to the "below $1000" wealth rank in the community, a few had far-reaching economic connections tied to Memphis businesses. Yet town merchants played vital roles as owners of gins and mills, as middle men in local produce trade, and controllers of local credit. The numerous small holders and renters were more likely beholden to local merchants rather than to larger Memphis firms. The croppers were primarily beholden to their land owners. Germantown certainly had no Will Varner, providing his debtors' every need and dictating agricultural practices. Basically the town's merchants were merely part of the overall, ineffective and often malfunctioning system of credit. It appears that the network of creditors, city and town combined, had the smaller farmers under their thumbs.[53]

Wide variations in the recorded production of cotton relative to acreage indicate that there was some resistance to mono-cropping pressures. For some, productive energies must have gone elsewhere. This would have been true of both blacks and whites for different reasons. Some blacks eschewed that crop so associated with their enslavement. Enforced mono-cropping was tantamount to a return to gang labor. The whites who had once been independently-minded yeomen or aspirants to that status would have suffered a special blow to their self-images if they were forced to devote a large percentage of their acreage to a cash crop. Since self-sufficiency had been at the heart of their identity, formerly they had carefully minimized devotion of acreage to market crops. Acreage and investment in livestock devoted to subsistence production provided them a more satisfactory sense of wellbeing, and greater independence.[54] As before, true poverty grew from insufficient self-sufficiency. Loss of self-sufficiency would have been another major source of social resentment for the former yeoman who were forced into mono-cropping to get loans for seed money or to pay off debts. The cropper who had no choice would have been totally controlled by the owner.

✦ ✦ ✦

The large, free-black population is of special interest. Though a problematic exercise, correlating the 1870 population census with that for agriculture in three of the town's surrounding districts produces interesting results.[55] There were 10 black land-owning households. According to the agricultural census, William Carter owned 216 acres, Green Galloway 200, John Bufford 100, while George Nelson and Isaac Harrison, living together, collectively owned 100 acres. Alexander Lee held 98, and Erasmus Freeman 75 acres. The agricultural census implies that 322 others were either renting complete farms of widely varying acreage, or they were tenants or croppers. Unfortunately that census did not distinguish between, owners, renters or croppers, so the actual status of most black farmers cannot be precisely determined. Four households worked total agricultural property valued between two and three thousand dollars; and 20 fell between two and one thousand dollars. So if they were cropping, they had enough resources to be share tenants. Another 63 with total property below a thousand dollars were in the same position but usually working less than forty acres. Perhaps as many as 61 were worse off, often simple croppers. More problematic were the 194 black households the heads of which were listed as "farmers," but not reported in the agricultural census, implying they owned or worked less than 3 acres. They and their dependents over age ten, had to supplement income as seasonal laborers. Lowest of all, 205 black men, and women were clearly landless farm laborers, but all of their children over 8 or 10 years of age were also seasonal laborers. This makes it impossible to determine the truly greater number of people in the glutted, landless, seasonal-labor market. In addition, all dependents of croppers or "farmers" with no designated occupation, 574 over age eight worked on their family farms, at least seasonally.

Despite the extreme financial differences among blacks, there is an indication that aspirations for a higher status remained strong at every level. Among both black and white households, all aspired to the same symbol of status with few exceptions. They listed their wives as "keeping house" in the census reports as opposed to "farm laborers." As we shall see, that was an initial, early black aspiration for self-esteem.

Evaluating the productivity of black farms is especially problematic since they were all self-reported and few kept books. According to the agricultural census, Isaac Harrison's 80 acres produced 36 bales of cotton generating $4,000 income. He also paid $40 in wages. William Carter's 75 cleared acres generated only $1,700 income, from which he paid $60 in wages. Lewis Jones got 9 cotton bales and generated $1,150 from his 35 cleared acres, but had to pay $650 in wages to do it. Other more incongruous statistics discredit the accuracy of the census, but they clearly show the success of some local black farmers. As already suggested, some differences among renters and owners may have indicated greater preference for devoting acreage to self-sufficiency. Also some of them held acreage that was more than they and their families could handle, so they employed hands just like comparable white farmers. Most of these relatively successful blacks had several horses or mules, plus cows, pigs and even a few sheep.

Erasmus Freeman was one about whom we have more than census records. As a slave, he had lived in Mississippi where he and his wife had four children. He served in the 55th USCI Regiment, receiving a wound in the shoulder, which always troubled him. In 1866, he and his Matilda resettled near Germantown, buying seventy-five acres. Shortly thereafter they had another girl. In addition to his land, he had about $280 in livestock. After his wife died, he married Lou, who brought three additional children who had been born in slavery. He and Lou had two more children, and everybody worked the land from an early age. By 1880, the value of his land had dropped considerably, but his livestock and agricultural production had increased. Neighbors later described the quality of his land as too wet and poor to support the family, and he suffered too greatly from his old wound to continue working. By his death in 1905, they had lost most everything of value except the land, and lived mostly on his pension.[56]

Seemingly, the local blacks did not come off as well initially as the states' average of 15 percent who owned their own lands. Nevertheless, 322 former slave families now rented or cropped several thousand acres of land, so they fared better than the average black elsewhere. Whether living as renters, tenants, and field hands, all at least had their freedom, legal rights (with growing limitations to be sure), reasonable degrees of autonomy in their family affairs, some possible educational opportunities for their children, and, therefore, a chance for advancement. In the face of what was essentially a conspiracy against their advancement, they would work hard to take advantage of whatever opportunities. Over the next decade, some of these advantages would accrue.

Among the most successful were the sons of the previously discussed white planter, Schuyler Roberts, and his slave-wife Mahalia. Roberts had held about 50 slaves, at least 7 of whom were his own children. After the war, the previously described "Confederate veteran," Preston, was initially renting in the Germantown area, but by 1880 had moved to the Bartlett area where he owned a 100 acre farm with a large mixed orchard of several hundred trees, and $300 in livestock. In 1879 he had paid $150 in wages to laborers.

His brother Quinton was especially determined to advance himself in every way. He had earned money during the war selling farm goods to the federal troops. In the 1870 census, he was either renting or owning 80 acres. Between 1873 and '83, he had been able to buy 72 acres of his white father's land, which he was working with his 20 year-old son. His wife, Alice Walker had belonged to Squire Walker, who had trained her as a seamstress and house keeper. Five of their school-aged children were attending regularly. While son Walter was learning to read and write, he was sharing it with his father, ambitious to learn well enough to become a Bible scholar. He became a deacon of the New Bethel Baptist Church. By 1887, he owned over 140 acres.

Brother Jack was missed in the 1870 census, but according to family traditions was share cropping successfully enough to acquire some of his father's land. By 1880, he was renting 175 acres, but passed in 1881. He was reportedly less diligent about the pursuit of education for his children, but if true, they would overcome such a handicap. Both Quinton and Jack had maintained large intact families from their time as slaves. The descendants of these sons of Mahalia would become prominent members of the Memphis area African-American community.[57]

From the slaves of the brothers Tuggle, perhaps 20 males remained initially in the area, although 9 of them had apparently departed by 1880. Charles Tuggle, who had earned $500 as janitor on the Reverend Phillip Tuggle's church, by 1880 had parlayed it into a 160 acre farm. According to family traditions, he eventually owned a 500 acre farm three miles south of town, with $3640 of total agricultural resources, generating $1275 in annual production. Too much for one man, he joined the white land-owners who were hiring field hands and employing household servants. He operated a gin, had a sizable stock of animals, and three orchards with a cider mill. He too had maintained an intact family since the time of slavery. Ultimately he rose to the status of preacher in the local Christian Episcopal Methodist Church, and would send his eldest son, Haywood, to Rust College.[58]

Of the other Tuggles, in 1870 Lewis and his wife were farming 60 acres with four children from an intact family, plus four orphans. By 1880, Lewis may have died. Robert Tuggle may have been their son, who with his wife Millie was supporting his mother and sister, who helped with the farm work. John and Mattie lasted through both decades farming 18 acres in the area. She brought two children to the marriage.

A typical black farm family would have two to five children, but eight was not uncommon. Those with children born in slavery had fortunately kept intact families, or they had been reunited, often with the help of the Freedmen's Bureau. Some 358 households had least retained some children, but some older children may have been sold away, or gone off on their own. In 101 cases, only the mother (or grandmother) was holding the family together, but in a couple of cases it was a single father. A few households held three generations. However, one tenant household clearly testified to permanent loss of family connections. Eighteen year-old George Jenkins was listed as head of household, with seventeen and twelve year-old boys as residents, all working as farm laborers—all with different family names. These were teenagers cut adrift by the backwash of slavery. In every household, husband and wife bore the same family name, indicating the high degree to which they had sought legitimate and Christian family status as quickly as it became available.

Occasionally a family got some extra income or extra hands from boarding farm laborers, or perhaps they simply sheltered an extended family member. Some like 75 year-old Frank Piggie and his wife Rhoda (age 65) were still trying to survive under the new system, with only the assistance of a teenage daughter. The Piggies were a good example of the relative lack of social support for the under-classes. There was no such thing as retirement unless a landowner felt an obligation to provide old, faithful hands with a cottage, garden plot and light labor for some income.

It was not unusual for a man in his sixties to attempt a solution by marrying a much younger woman and beginning a family late in life. With luck he could produce some sons in time, but if his strength failed, his wife and young children were in trouble. When both partners were advanced in age and childless, they had to rely on boarders who were willing to share in the field labor. Such problems faced the elderly tenant farmers, white as well as black. They worked until they fell. Older women without families had to find a family, white or black, to take them on as cook or house keeper.[59]

Certainly this picture of black industry belies the wide-spread complaints about their unwillingness to earn their positions by hard labor. Many led a life of hard scrabble and depredation, but it was pursued determinedly. They may have shunned wage slavery and gang labor, but they were willing to pay the price in self-employed hardship, if they had any means of obtaining it.

❖ ❖ ❖

Returning to the overall population, as before, family households of both colors provided what passed for social services—nursing, asylum or orphanage. Harriet Winn, housed a widow, a former slave, Ruben Winn, classed as an "idiot." In addition, ten-year old Frank Winn was there as well, perhaps an orphaned former slave, or a child separated from its parents. One of the black land-owners, William Carter and his wife had an eight-year old son, also classed as an "idiot."[60] Long-time resident, William Hack and his wife Caroline housed two other white families, Lucy Daily and her two small children, and sixty-seven year-old Sophia Harris, "Deaf and dumb." Mrs. Harris had a teenage daughter. Perhaps they were relatives of the Hacks. Next door in a cabin, resided Asthen Hack and her teenage son. She was a blind former slave of the family.[61] Undoubtedly the local churches, both black and white, aided the "deserving" unfortunates as far as their meager resources allowed, but more about problems with charity in the next chapter.

The Problem of Labor: Black and White

Since most of this picture relies on the 1870 census for data, we may never have a clear picture of what transpired locally during the transition to the new agricultural labor system before 1870. These were troubled and rocky years during which many land owners gave up and left. From the point of view of newspapers, North and South, this resulted from the unwillingness of blacks to work the fields as before. That was, of course, the obvious role for them to find their "proper place" in the economy. No sympathy was felt for the frustrated aspirations of the former slaves to have a place that corresponded to their contributions in creating this economy. As though they had not worked hard as slaves, they were now expected to prove they deserved the place of landless farm laborer.[62]

Although the belief that blacks would not work was clearly wrong, for the first two years after the war there was considerable dislocation and uncertainty among blacks, with the effect of limiting their involvement in the work force. The efforts, during the war by the military and immediately after by the Freedmen's Bureau to contract them, often forcefully, into plantation labor were obviously like a return to the old ways. They resisted. Furthermore, newly emancipated men were indeed "wandering the country side," looking like a vagrant threat. Some, however, were searching for their wives and children, trying desperately to reestablish their families. Others searched for more suitable opportunities. Ex-soldiers hoped for pension lands. Some vainly awaited the promised forty acres and a mule.[63] With the Klan compounding uncertainties, it took more than two years for the dust to settle.

Through 1867, the lack of labor for resuming production was a major concern. In response, there were hopes of bringing in labor from elsewhere. Agencies sprang up to serve as middlemen promising to bring workers.[64] As we have seen, a very few foreigners joined the ranks of farm laborers. Instead poor native whites and many more blacks became the area's tenant farmers and workers. There is no way to tell what percentage of the area's black residents were new, arriving as part of the massive relocation after the war. The state of birth of their post-war children does provide a hint of a family's previous locations. The majority were from somewhere in Tennessee.

The 1870 census reveals a large cluster of black families who had clearly moved together from South Carolina to settle in block as renters or croppers on one planter's lands. Other smaller clusters of families seem to have arrived together from Mississippi.[65] Such mass migrations may imply that West Tennessee had a better reputation than other plantation regions.

To find support for black orphans, from 1865 into the summer of 1866, the Freedmen's Bureau arranged apprenticeships for the large number of such children for farm work, their "proper place." Also included in these apprentice arrangements were the children of single black mothers unable to support them. Since this included taking children too young to be meaningfully productive, there was some element of charity involved. As one example of possibly mixed motives, John Stout got five orphans in August 1866, four boys, ages 4-14, for farm work, and one girl, age 4, for house work. Obviously the four-year-olds

ILL. 18 Colored Orphan Asylum, Memphis, *Harper's Weekly*, 5.5.1866. A mixed blessing, it provided temporary housing and care for orphans and other children without adequate means of support until they could be apprenticed until age twenty-one into "career training" for work considered "appropriate" for Blacks.

were not profitable as workers. However, the others significantly augmented Stout's labor force of the one large black family of Isham and Harriet Stout who apparently stayed with the elderly John and Rhoda. Isham and Harriet had 12 children aged from 1 to 24.[66]

For some, this was a good way to replace lost slave labor. Some planters casually took on apprentices, because children and teenagers were traditionally considered productive hands.[67] Thomas Bleckley got back into the apprentice business in January 1866, taking on three children for farm work. They were Calvin, Malvina and James "Blakely" (*sic*).[68] But perhaps Bleckley was not simply crass. He had sought out their mother, Milley Bleckley, to arrange for their apprenticeship.[69] In the 1860 slave census, he had a twenty year-old female slave and several children, three of whom might have matched these children. In other words they were probably his former "charges." Perhaps he had a sense of obligation for their welfare. By the 1870 census, Malvina and James were living in his house with his son and several white employees.

Also, Mrs. M. J. Eddins took on Frank Eddins, age 8, in 1865. Significant numbers of these young black apprentices bore the same family name as their sponsors, and were usually indentured with their mother's permission. One has to consider that sentimental ties to former slave families played some role in these arrangements. The very tender ages of many of those apprenticed for housework or work in businesses, mills, and craft shops made at least the earlier years of such an arrangement a charitable/investment.[70]

Some Signs of Progress and Improvement

By the end of the 70s decade with all its financial ups and downs, agricultural labor and land ownership issues had worked themselves out. The 1880 agricultural census provides much more clear pictures of the farming population, revealing the distribution of total agricultural wealth among owners, renters and tenants. Among the residences in Civil District 11, 7 held from $5000 to over $6000. Another 7 ranged from $5000 to $4000. 13 from four to three thousand; 18 from three to two; 38 from two to one; 19 from one thousand to $500; 7 below $500.

The presence of some prosperous land renters affected this distribution. R. J. Stephens, rented 515 acres and possessed $5710 in total agricultural wealth. He paid $1569 dollars for labor and produced $3238 for that year. Another 46 renters worked agricultural wealth ranging as widely as $3000 to $500; 13 below $500. Seventy-two others rented lands ranging from 125 to about 25 cleared acres. Nevertheless, this was still an inequitable bell curve much skewed toward the greatest numbers at the lower level of wealth.

The inequality becomes more apparent when share croppers are factored in. Nevertheless there are a few surprises in their statistics. Two men worked total agricultural wealth of over $2000. An additional 13 were over $1000; the remaining 40 ranged down to below $500. This 21% of farm families involved in sharecropping locally represented a considerably higher percentage than the less than 12% for Shelby County in that census.[71]

These men cropped anywhere from 65 to 20 cleared acres. Although the landowner took one quarter to half their production, many had additional income from livestock, and other means to reduce total dependence on the landlord. The total agricultural resources of 14 ranged from above $3000 to $2000, but 39 ranged for above $500 to below $500. Production of cash crops varied widely at all economic levels, and some diversified from only cotton and corn. Daniel Thornton produced $2924 in that year. The rest ranged from $1320 down to Minnie Jones at $217. Several even had to pay labor to bring in their crops. Some share tenants were doing as well or better than many renters, despite the share taken out. Four croppers were white, mostly in the lower levels of resources, but with mid-levels of productivity—$765 to $315 for the year.

Men, women and children lived in households consisting entirely of farm laborers without any means other than their labor. There were over 750, plus a few scattered as boarders in other households. As in 1870, 20 other households were headed by men described as "farmer," but possessing, renting, or cropping three or fewer acres in the agricultural census.[72] Nine were white men. In reality, these were essentially farm labor households, adding 55 more to the labor pool totaling 766, not counting persons who were boarding in farmer's houses. If the census is correct, a total of $36,703 was divided among them in 1880, but not evenly. The few cases in which wages were itemized gave ranges from $5.77 to $2 for a six and one-half day work week, although most averaged between $3 and $4. Obviously the labor market was still glutted by 1880, and the farmer held a whip hand. Since 52 laborers were white, this was a true underclass regardless of color.

✦ ✦ ✦

Between 1870 and 1880, changes in the wellbeing of the area's blacks present a very mixed picture. The 288 households and the total black population of 1143 contrasts clearly to that of 394 households and 2043 people by 1880. Many blacks continued to migrate into the area out of the Deep-South.

Predictably almost all former croppers and laborers had gone elsewhere in search of something better. Some 15 other agricultural households carried over from 1870. On the seemingly plus side, there were now 25 owners. Renters had declined to 38 and croppers to 64, with only 17 holding the ambivalent status of "farmer." These, however, are much more precise numbers, thanks to the improved clarity of the 1880 census. Nevertheless as before, the financial well-being of a household did not necessarily correlate with the different forms of "land-holding." An owner could hold fewer than 40 acres of mixed land, while another could be working well over 100. A renter could be working far more mixed acreage and producing more than many owners. Even some croppers were as well set as some owners or renters. Many owned implements and livestock sufficient to enable them to achieve tenant status. They were free from landlord pressures to monocrop in cotton. This seems to reveal significant progress for those who had been able to manage their affairs well. Cropping was not always a dead end. Regardless of a family's relative control over land, wives children and other family members, at least 75 all total, worked their family land seasonally and even did extra labor on neighboring farms to earn a little cash. Nevertheless, they were far better off than the family members of landless, farm-labor households.

Of the 749 farm laborers, there was little improvement over their predecessors. They, including all dependents 8 years old and above, lived off of seasonal employment. The more fortunate could supplement income by boarding other laborers. A few wives and other dependents could really add support as cooks and servants for white households, and in even a few black farm-owner or renter homes. The black community had its "elite" for them to serve.

Compared to the 1870 census, how black versus white framers described their wives reveals negatively changed self-perceptions. Clearly a shift had occurred among the black population. In white households, the wife was still almost always listed as "house keeper" even in a few farm-labor household. In contrast, in black households in District 11, about 240 wives (of the 260) were listed as "farm laborers," usually along with elder family members. While white sons, 16 or older, usually worked alongside their fathers as laborers, only 3 daughters reportedly did so. Of course, many white "housekeepers" and daughters nevertheless took to the fields with their families on occasion. It was a matter of both social self-perception and reality that accounts for the changed labeling. White small-farm families preserved their former sense of dignity in describing the status of the wife. Although blacks had initially sought such an image of self-esteem upon emancipation, by 1880, at least locally, it had mostly succumbed to reality.[73]

Although white households were occasionally headed by widows, women as heads were much more common among blacks, and sometimes adolescents of either sex had that responsibility, 49 in 1880. In one extreme case, twenty-four year-old widow, Martha McLemon, worked as farm laborer and servant of a white farm family. Her ten year-old son and seven year-old daughter worked as field hands beside her, all together trying to support her other 6 under-age children, the youngest of whom was 4 months.[74]

Clearly some white families lived and worked in poverty. It is more obvious that at least three quarters of the blacks lived under the tightest circumstances, many simply living hand to mouth. Nevertheless, land ownership among blacks had grown considerably during the 1870s. This may have exceeded the average for the state, but unfortunately the comparative data are vague.[75]

Interracial Relations

After the initial period of hysterical rumors about a black uprising had settled down, whites learned to live with what many considered a dangerous underclass. Whites able to employ blacks voiced a complaint that continues through the ages, "One just can't get good help these days." Whether employees worked any less diligently than the former slaves is not determinable, they just could not be beaten. White-black management-labor relations remained colored by racist assumptions. Also, one has to suspect that, like workers in similar conditions, some blacks proclaimed, "They pretend to pay us, so we pretend to work."

Croppers, of both colors, had a way of conveniently settling their debts when they felt exploited. They simply skipped out without paying. With few personal possessions, it was easy for such a family to disappear overnight. Even if located, recovery was like squeezing blood out of a turnip, so the effort was hardly worth it. The owner could lose a hundred dollars in a season from just one such misadventure.[76] Since both parties usually felt aggrieved, such results of gross inequity continued to inflame social and racial distrust.

On the other hand, some unexpected cases of very close, kind and friendly contact appear in the 1870 census. Some white land-owners lived close by their mostly black tenant families and workers—as neighbors, which had to involve some amicable familiarity. A few still had live-in black servants, but mostly relied on the wives and daughters of tenants for domestic labor. More unconventional living arrangements tended to occur within the tenant and farmhand households. Several single white farm hands boarded in black households. One of them, eighteen year-old Franklin Harrison may have been the survivor of an old area family. One white tenant in his twenties had a young black woman living with him as cook, and a young black farm hand as boarder. Two white children, ages one and two, were being raised in the home of a mulatto tenant farmer and his black wife along with their infant daughter. Inexplicably, the white children had the same family name as a white couple living nearby. Whatever, the black family had apparently assumed the care of orphaned children of their former owners. More strikingly, as late as 1880, the eleven year-old "mulatto," Mary Owens was living in the home of a white widower farmer, not as a servant, but listed as adopted daughter.[77] In many cases, blood ties created under slavery bridged the racial divide.

Such were the complexities of racial relations. People had grown up, lived, worked and played together, so they knew each other as people. Some of the sexual relations had been amicable. Such understandings existed side-by-side with racial prejudices and widely-held stereotypes to produce complex interracial relations. Even so, the war and emancipation had upset all former norms producing an always potentially explosive relationship.

One surprising occurrence is that former slaves who served in the Union Army came back and settled after the war. Of the 168 men in the 1870 census of an age to have served, 93 have names that match men who served in black units. Unfortunately the National Park Services registry gives only names and no other information with which to verify identity. Nevertheless, given that there were several hundred matches for those 93 names it seems highly likely that many had served. Furthermore, at least 29 names belonged to companies or batteries that enlisted in Germantown or Memphis, where locals were most likely to have gone. An additional 18 may have served in other units. As many as 19 new residents may also have served.[78] We have already discussed one definite case, Erasmus Freeman.

One even more surprising is Allen James Walker, the survivor of the Fort Pillow Massacre. According to one source, he returned to Germantown. If so, he was missed in the 1870 census, but appears in 1880 as a farm laborer with a wife Easter, a son and a daughter. As previously noted, he lived among one or more white men who might have participated in the massacre.

Considering the bloody hostility directed at these "traitors" during the war, their presence is most surprising. As Federal veterans, they could legally carry sidearms for protection, if they could acquire and keep them. Yet, their willingness to return, speaks to a triumph over racial hostilities by the immediate desire to get on with life, to forgive and forget among neighbors. Their return also speaks to the power of the familiar in determining where to live.

Platus Lipsey's recorded memories speak clearly of typically mixed white attitudes. There were blacks of whom he had fond and warm memories of close relations. In contrast, he revealed intense fears of blacks he did not know.[79] Living and working side-by-side, blacks and whites usually sought convivial relations. Exploitation, fear and resentment, warm feelings and charity coexisted. One incident at Germantown captures such juxtapositions. On March 21, 1871, Nathan Bedford Forrest arrived with a team of speakers courting subscriptions for the construction of an inter-city railroad being proposed at the time. One can only imagine the enthusiasm with which the town's white veterans turned out to welcome him. On the team with him was former governor Isham Harris, but also Robert Gleed, "(colored) State Senator from Lowndes County Miss."[80]

Rebuilding the Infrastructure

The town's place in the transportation network was still its primary hope. The first step was to rebuild that network. The second was to capitalize on how it tied the town to Memphis and the world. During the war, the infrastructure of roads and bridges had badly deteriorated. Although the Quarterly Sessions Court had resumed its old task of assigning overseers to maintain area roads, they had a lot of deterioration to catch up with. Again overseers were appointed for all roads. Without slaves for "hands," all land owners, black and white, were legally obligated to the corvée. Surviving photographs of the crews, however, were heavily black, indicating either white collusion in drafting and assigning "hands" and/or a practice of hiring one's replacement for service. Many of the bridges had been destroyed. This included Germantown's Wolf River bridge. Throughout 1865, a ferry had to suffice. Most of the bridges over the Wolf and Nonconnah were rebuilt during the summer of 1866. Yet as late as 1870, the county was still rebuilding bridges. Unfortunately the new bridge over the Wolf must not have been substantial. It washed out in an 1871 flood.[81]

Once again, in 1869 the responsibility for the State Line Road was turned over to private management, the Shelby County Turnpike Company, "as far beyond White Station as deemed practicable, upon the bed of the old Germantown Plank Road." The old company's charter elapsed during the war, and the road had fallen into disrepair. According to the new company's president, once the roads left the city, "there is not a road or a drive that three miles an hour can be made on, in ordinary weather." His company competed for investment resources with the many railroads.[82] Both the State Line and the M&C were the town's main arteries. Unfortunately, the turnpike fared less well than the railroad. By 1880, its improvement had advanced only five miles from

Memphis. The company was being sued for having erected two illicit toll gates, charging for use at both.[83] The *Ledger* was bemoaning the terrible state of all local roads, calling for an extension of this road to Germantown or Collierville. It encouraged farmers along such routes to take the initiative and form stock companies to build them.[84]

After the Federal forces turned the M&C over to former management, it was able to find sufficient funding and equipment to resume reasonable operations by 1866. For passenger service, it announced there would be three trains leaving Memphis eastbound, and three returning daily for passengers from Germantown to Memphis. The eastbound trains again made connections with practically every major city to the east, and were served with "Elegant Sleeping Cars on all night trains." For freight, Germantown was beginning to feel a squeeze. From the north, it competed with the Memphis and Ohio Railroad, and the Wolf's limited bridging also made access to that area problematic. To the south, the State Line Road from Mississippi into Collierville provided better access than the lower quality Center Hill and Hernando Roads leading to Germantown's depot. The Pidgen Roost Road funneled traffic away from town on a more direct route into Memphis. Such road patterns account for Collierville's displacement of Germantown as the major commerce center for south-east Shelby County and North Mississippi. Another advantage, Collierville had less competition from depots on the Memphis & Ohio which ran farther north of Collierville.

Even if Germantown was losing out to Collierville as a cotton depot, the railroad offered another advantage. To rebut the constant complaints, including many from vocal Germantown citizens, about the taxes involved in railroad building, the *Appeal* showed its progressive face. It painted a picture that would come true, but only after another century.

> The city of Memphis, within ten years, will overspread the whole elevated broad plateau between Wolf and Nonconnah, and Memphis and Germantown. This broad district will be converted into a vast productive garden, the cost of living will be reduced to a minimum.... Cheap food, a genial climate, cheap, healthful homes, away from the dust and crowds and vices of the city.[85]
>
> Such are the facts affecting property along railway lines.... We propose to extend the city far into the country ... and Memphis is

destined to overspread ... until Germantown becomes a delightful, gas-lighted, manufacturing suburb. The whole country will share advantages with Memphis and Germantown, the home of our (complaining) correspondent.[86]

The Benefit of Suburban Expansion

Many area citizens took advantage of their location on the rail line. In 1867, part of the defunct Forest Hill Seminary land went on sale in forty-one, two to three acre lots.[87] The seminary had closed down following a fire. These lots were offered as residential and commercial lots in the little hamlet. All along the line, the desperate and/or ambitious could sell their land at prices that covered their debts and funded new opportunities.[88]

By the spring of 1868, the *Avalanche* reported that a developer named "Almond" (*sic*; Ammons) had purchased "Forest Hill" (the troubled school) with plans to open it "as a place of resort." Other Memphians had purchased nearby lands, putting in orchards and other amenities. The paper touted the project. "Being only eighteen miles from town, it is a convenient place for business men to make their summer quarters. Many families have already prepared to go there ... when the hot summer months set in".[89]

Soon the *Public Ledger* announced that William Ammons, a prominent and wealthy Memphian, had settled at Forest Hill as proprietor with plans to restore the academy and grounds. His goals for the academy were a bit vague, for he announced the opening there of a summer resort within the next month. Nothing could be "more inviting" than a "retreat from the din and turmoil of city life."[90]

To draw attention to his project, Ammons used the hall and dining facilities to host dinner dances that would attract Memphians out to his planned summer resort. With the help of some Forest Hill and Germantown families, he inaugurated his program with two May Balls. The first evening of dining and dancing ended at dawn, when the special train took participants back to the city. Unfortunately, there were only about one hundred participants many local, because entertainments in the city provided too much competition.[91] That was Ammons' one and only promotional venture. He filed for bankruptcy. In 1871, "Forest Hill" went up for sale.[92]

Although his development scheme never took off, the land from White's

Station through Germantown and Forest Hill was being settled by both seasonal residents and for market gardens, providing an economic boost. During the sixties and seventies, the city's unhealthy environment deteriorated further. The large landholder of Ridgeway, Sam Mosby subdivided his lands to capitalize on the demands. From 1868 through '73, he was constantly advertising cottages for rent or sale along the M&C line.[93]

To accommodate a growing commuter population seeking escape, the M&C increased its attention to passenger service as far east as Moscow and Somerville. By 1868, that service had settled into a convenient routine that presaged modern-day commuter lifestyles. The Somerville Accommodation delivered passengers to Memphis in the morning in time to begin a work day, and brought them back home at a late afternoon hour. The less conveniently timed express mail train stopped at stations like Germantown, or flag stops. The evening freight hauled a passenger coach to accommodate Germantown commuters who needed a full day in the city. The car was left at the town, and picked up and returned by the morning freight that reached Memphis at 7:50 AM. By 1871, there was a dedicated Germantown Accommodation train stationed overnight in the town.[94]

As before, train service also greatly facilitated social ties between Germantown and Memphis. Ladies coming out could catch the noon train for a weekend stay with friends or relatives, while Germantown ladies who had been visiting in Memphis could return.[95] Both the Germantown and Somerville Accommodations paused at every little flag stop in the style of a true commuter train.

In 1872, the *Appeal* ran an editorial that described the impact of all this on the Germantown area.

> The prettiest farms in Shelby county, with few exceptions, lie along the line of the Memphis and Charleston road, between Memphis and Germantown. Annual railway tickets and the reduction of charges on local travel to a minimum have made the country densely populated. Messers. Sam Mosby, Greenlaw, Davy, Townsend, Goodyn, the stock farmer, and many others, have most attractive country homes and conduct most profitable farming and gardening operations along our great eastern road. Two lawyers of the city, like Cicero, find a Tusculum in Germantown.

> Esquires Bleckley and Jones report that Germantown and the surrounding country are flourishing in a remarkable manner.... The people out there are bound to prosper no matter what the other parts of the country do.[96]

If the Yellow Fever epidemic of 1868 in Memphis had encouraged the flight to the suburbs around Germantown, events of 1873 fueled it further. It was especially bad with a winter bout of small pox, followed in the summer by a "malignant type of Asiatic cholera" and then another devastating yellow fever epidemic.[97] At end of year, Florida Thompson wrote to a friend, "Mrs. Johnson has no boarders now, but during the Yellowfever the house was packed and crammed.—I only had sister Emma...." In addition to the hotel, boarding houses had sprung up in town, but many residents also had city relatives seeking shelter.[98] Enterprising people were offering houses in town to rent for the summer. If one preferred to own such property, entire plantations were being subdivided.[99]

A revealing image of the progress of "suburbanization" comes in the form of two surviving tract maps of Shelby County, 1869 and 1888. They attempted to depict an accurate picture of property ownership.[100] Before 1869, the division of lots into less than 10 acres had reached White's Station. Thereafter, through Ridgeway, they tended more toward approximately 100 acre farm-sized strips, but clearly positioned specifically on the State Line or old Plank Road. From there through Germantown, nothing had yet happened, although someone unnamed may have had plans for a sizable strip north-east of town. Beyond the town, some more well-positioned small farm-sized strips began to reappear as the road approached Forest Hill.

The boom at Germantown soon followed, and the 1888 map reveals what had happened. By then, the community now called White Station had been so extensively subdivided and the population of other suburbs east of Memphis had expanded so much that a new District 16 had absorbed the northwest section of Germantown's old District 11 as far east as Ridgeway. The former Greenlaw lands, now owned by William Messick, were subdivided into smaller farm-sized lots, and closer toward the center of town, more clearly residential and commercial lots abounded, also along the Germantown Road running north and south. Interestingly, a string of eight residential lots had emerged where that previously mentioned "sizable strip" had been laid out.

This development had apparently given birth to Hot Tamale Road (modern old Dogwood). This little road connected to the old Germantown-Macon Road at about the juncture of Dogwood and Poplar today, providing a better connection than the old route. Also, William Carter had subdivided his lands along the M&C/State-Line into 10 and 20 acre parcels, one of which held his cottage more conveniently located for travel to the city than his old plantation house. A couple of speculators had also bought up sizable well-located acreage that still awaited development. Perhaps they had missed the bus.

Economic Revival

As early as 1867, the *Avalanche* reported that, "a company is soon likely to be formed, of planters and others, in the vicinity of Germantown, to establish a cotton factory."[101] This sounds like a cotton mill for making yarn. If so, nothing apparently came of that scheme, probably for lack of funding. Nevertheless, the spirit of creative enterprise was obviously alive.

The Southern Star Cotton Gin factory was back in operation. Barry Hurt and his sons had taken over management. It maintained the Neely family connection, for its main sales agent was the firm of Brooks, Neely & Co., the eldest Neely son's booming Memphis mercantile venture. In 1875, Fred W. Flynn's cotton-gin feeder was being marketed in the city at Payne's Gin Factory. It had the advantage of being operable by "any man, boy or girl . . . a person of the most ordinary intelligence."[102] Unfortunately, Hurt's gin factory failed to capitalize on the opportunity. Perhaps there was insufficient capacity to pursue an expansion of its production.

Along with sewing machines (and the employment of a couple of residents in their sales), other aspects of the modern home were developing. In 1868, Germantown's William S. Morrison patented a washing machine, but who knows how well it fared in the crowded market for such home appliances.[103] Certainly any who could afford them would have been anxious to do so and reduce his wife's drudgery.

There were other signs that the town was regaining some of its economic vitality. In 1878, the offices of the Bluff City Insurance Company and the Hernando Insurance Company relocated to Germantown.[104] New elements of commercial life arrived to serve a reviving area.

Although there were many signs of recovery, it was neither evenly spread nor consistent. As late as 1871 one resident complained, "No weddings on hand—boys too poor...."[105] Yet by 1872, after the Hurt family had reestablished the gin factory, they erected a fine two-story home well back from the M&C on the Pike, investing at least $1800. Mr. Garner and Mrs. Shepherd also added town houses and Dr. McKay rebuilt his recently burned home. Mrs. Evans boasted, "our society is improving here every year, and if were not so near Memphis I would have hopes of being a large place."[106] She apparently did not understand the advantage of that nearness for the town's growth. In December 1873, Dr. Thompson's wife commented, "Dr. doing a good practice but getting little money. I am planning and contriving to make one dollar do the work of two."[107] A farmer's wife living outside town complained that 1874 had been a year of near total crop failures and poor health. "We owe Dr. McKay $52... besides Dr. Leek of Collierville, and Dr. Richmond, and other expenses. We bought a very fine coffin for Mother and her shroud was beautiful."[108]

Such little tidbits provide peaks into both change and consistency. Although some families were flourishing by the early 1870s, others continued to operate on the fringes of the cash economy. Those who served them had to accept credit. Fluctuations in the national economy and banking cycles disrupted the cash flow putting pressure on credit. A succession of bad crop years or market fluctuations hit some much harder than others. Correspondents also spoke of seasons of especially unusual sickness and deaths. Infant mortality and deadly childhood diseases remained as common as before. But the continued move away from home-made coffins reflected a broader shift toward manufactured goods, as did the growing reliance on sewing machines and other appliances.

Despite the influx from the city that added a larger consumer base to the local economy, agriculture remained the primary resource for most residents. After 1870, a decline in the agriculture market, especially cotton, became an increasing deficit.[109] A goodly number of farm and town families sought advantages by turning to scientific farming and rational management. The Grange Movement provided support. Between 1872 and 1874, the movement exploded in Tennessee. General Vaughan organized the town's Grange No. 19 on May 26, 1873, which held meetings in the hall over Owen's store in Forest Hill. Membership grew rapidly to "about sixty—twenty ladies and forty men." Both farmers, businessmen, professionals, and their wives became active. A major goal was becoming "a cash paying people" by stopping their store credit accounts, retrenching expenditures, and intensifying their agriculture. Fewer but more productive acres, better cultivated and manured, would increase productivity and replenish the land. Several young ladies invested in one hundred chickens for the next year's market plus expansion to turkeys and goose eggs. Grape vineyards and additional acres of wheat for both consumption and the market could reduce cash outflow. Some infection had apparently hit the hogs for several years, so the Grange planned to collectively import enough sheep to build flocks. The ladies intended to recycle and economize on clothing.[110] A combination of industry and economy boded well for the future, but only if relatively good fortune prevailed.

Such improvements had clearly had their effect by 1880. Local farmers had liberated themselves from total dependence on corn and cotton for market crops. Their livestock produced butter, cheese, eggs, beef, various fowl, mutton and pork. Wool production had resumed. New specialties like broom corn had appeared along with considerable tobacco. Peas, beans, potatoes and many fruits had returned to most farms' market production. Some oats as well as wheat were back to the market, and even a little rice, while sorghum was supplementing honey as sweetener. One experimented with vineyards, marketing 15 gallons of wine. Forest products augmented almost everyone's income. Unfortunately, smaller farmers could not diversify, and tenants were largely restricted to the cotton seeds the owner preferred to provide.

In addition, improvements in communication arrived in town to support such trends. In 1873, the town post offices became one that would post the Signal Services' daily weather reports and forecasts for "the benefit of agriculture."[111] Freeze and storm warnings could help save crops.

Unfortunately, improvements in technology did not advantage all local business. The town's gin factory would soon succumb to a shift in the planter's preference away from maintaining his own mill as opposed to larger commercial operations. As the market for the Star Gin was drying up, their ads emphasized "a low price" and their availability for rebuilding saws and gins. In September 1881, Hurt's factory "burned to the ground" at a loss of $12,000 to $15,000 against only $2000 of insurance. There was no incentive to rebuild. No further mention of gin factories appear in the *Tennessee Gazette* thereafter. Instead Kimbrough & Bradley would be operating their commercial cotton gin, representative of the transition.[112]

As the decade of recovery in the 1870s wore on, the forces of change were having uneven effects. Local inventiveness and progressive minds inevitably clashed with conservative, even reactionary moods. Technological improvements antiquate some businesses as often as they improve others. The relative benefits of the town's location on transportation routes diminished in favor of Collierville. The shaky national economy and the scarcity of capital were retardants. Such problems seemed unimportant, however, compared to the town's reputation as a suburban shelter attracting seasonal and permanent residents, agriculture and business. Yet, that recovery was fragile and depended on continued good fortune.

Cultural Renewal

The rebuilding of the churches and the town's other cultural institutions were integral parts of recovery. The process took a good six years, revealing how long the local population struggled to regain its economic position. From all indications, not only the Presbyterian Church and Masonic Hall, but most of the houses and some of the shops had survived. The Baptist Church had been dismantled with remains probably burned. The Methodist church had been so badly damaged that it had to be torn down and replaced. Until the churches could rebuild, the Presbyterians shared their facilities. The destruction of buildings suitable for public affairs left the Masonic Hall to serve such purposes, exempt from taxes.[113]

As the Methodists and Baptists rebuilt their churches, local correspondents reported on the progress. In September 1871, "The frame of the Methodist Church is up at last. As for the Baptists, they are both poor and slow and it is doubtful if they was to have a church."[114] As we shall see, this was probably a snide sectarian and/or classist shot. The Methodist's work, dragged on during the spring and summer of 1871. In July, one resident commented, "The Methodist Church is not yet completed, but will make a very fine appearance if they ever do get through."[115] It was a tall white-boarded structure with a steeple like the other churches. The reconstruction of both churches had been retarded by the loss of slave labor and the diminished financial resources now needed to pay for both manufactured materials and skilled labor. More than five years were needed before even families of some means would think of channeling family resources into church construction. Yet another indication of changes in the community that focused people more on self and family than community.

The Baptists began fund raising in 1869, but cash was still hard to come

p. 22 Germantown Baptist Church as rebuilt in 1871/72. Similar to original, but slightly larger; ball cap on steeple is from the original structure; bears bullet holes from probable Union soldiers' target practice.

by. Ed M. Cole was superintendent and contractor for the construction. He remembered charging about $800 for the labor, including constructing the pews. He paid carpenters between $1.50 and $2.00 a day. He thought about $2500 went into materials. Factory made nails cost $3.00 or $4.00 a keg of 100 pounds.[116] Fund raising dragged on.

In January 1872, Miss Kate Rhodes set about soliciting funds still needed to cover these costs. By April, Monroe Webb, the postmaster, offered a major contribution for a double-barreled project. He would donate an eleven acre lot on the condition that it would be used for the erection of a ladies academy. Since the Baptists already had a lot, the acreage was for the school, "on condition that other persons furnish fifteen hundred dollars . . . (for) a proper building on the (church) property." Unfortunately by combining efforts to raise stock for both projects, he aroused sectarian concerns. He then tried to separate the two projects, asking interested parties to form a Germantown Female School Company and contribute $500 for the church fund, and in exchange he would give title to the land for the school. "Let those who imagine sectarian bugaboos, come down with the *cash*, so that the aggregate of public spirit shall harmonize to consummate our project."[117] They did not, so nothing further was heard of the female school. Problems of community spirit and lack of harmony were as troubling as economic limitations.

The Baptists continued without Webb, and in January 1873, the congregation expressed indebtedness for completion to G.W. Thomas, a new resident. Even a year later the interior remained unfinished.[118]

Webb's enthusiasm to "make fame for the village and render it attractive and prosperous" had foundered on sectarianism, and he separated himself from both projects. Webb, about 70 years old and undoubtedly saddened, passed away in October.

On July 15, 1872, William Miller, pre-war postmaster and now Germantown druggist, had replaced Webb and resumed duties in his store as postmaster.[119] Germantown's post office had reopened well before Collierville's, while a new one at Forest Hill followed shortly thereafter. Its formal opening, however, may have come as late as December 1874, when William M. Perkins became its first official postmaster.[120] Perkins was a well-established local farmer who had settled there from elsewhere in Tennessee after the war.

As for the town's efforts to return to its former position as an educational center, the ups and downs of that story are best told in the next chapter.

12

THE TROUBLED REBIRTH OF A COMMUNITY

Changes in Social and Cultural Life

The spirit of recovery seemed strong among the town's citizens. Yet everyone faced persistent problems, and the community exhibited systemic disorders. Previous chapters have enumerated greater social and racial tensions during and after the war. The post-war community underwent a replacement of many old personal and community relationships with an influx of newcomers. Relations between blacks and whites had been inflamed and continued to be tested and unsettled. The community that had emerged was significantly different. The post-war experience was certainly worse than the anticipated return to normal.

The town, however, had become a seriously troubled community. Defeat and terrible personal losses produced depression, which manifested itself in diverse ways for years to come. The increased social tensions left many without the former sense of community support. Today's insights into "post-traumatic stress" and its symptoms help explain many of the unpleasant symptoms. All this mixed with a determination to get back to a normal life and to rebuild with all the limited sources available. We cannot tell how different this was for communities like Germantown elsewhere.

♦ ♦ ♦

Although the *Tennessee State Gazetteer* reported that the population had exploded from 245 in 1870 to 700 by 1876, that figure was exaggerated for the town proper. Since there was no longer a chartered entity, it's not possible to know what the *Gazetteer* used as the town's area. Nevertheless, there was significant growth and once again industry in the forms of a new gin factory, smithies and wagon making, plus the usual mills and artisans, numerous stores and at least one operating "hotel."[1] The town continued to benefit from the nearby mineral-springs. The accelerated "health flight" from Memphis was moving those who could afford it "to the suburbs."

There were other positive indicators. Perhaps the best measure of how quickly the local population generated some semblance of renewed vitality was the arrival of the new, great American pastime—baseball. During the occupation, New York soldiers had undoubtedly played the game, newly popular in the north, and they probably instructed the town's boys who would have gathered to watch. The American soldiers' habit of teaching baseball to the boys of occupied countries may have dated back to the origins of the sport. Considering what followed, before the end of occupation, the town may even have had an informal team of its own to play the "Yankees." As early as 1866, the fad of organized ball clubs in New York was copied by clubs in Memphis. By June of 1868, the *Appeal* announced that a Germantown Club was challenging the reigning champions, "Bluff City."[2] The sport thrived with a ball field somewhere in the town.[3]

But the town was never able to field anything that could compete with Memphis' premier teams. In 1876, they challenged the Memphis Reds, and were trounced 38 to nothing. Germantown, by then one of many "village clubs," was classed among the "rustic nines" in the tristate area.[4] One has to wonder, was there a massive commute by the town's supporters to their games in Memphis? What sort of festivities accompanied home games? Were uniforms worn, and, if so, what did they look like? Surely the town's pride would not allow them to appear in Memphis without something as easily made as a baseball uniform.

Despite this and other signs of positive social and cultural renewal, the wounds of war contained poisons. Although the war had little lasting effect relatively on the pattern of daily social life in each of the respective social classes, there were sinister changes in the underlying mood among them. Some of the social analysis previously explored suggests that class consciousness of the "lower orders" and animosity toward the privileged had increased significantly during the war. Likewise, the propertied had become more defensive. The exaggerated post-war economic gaps between the very rich, a much reduced middle, and the poorer intensified social discontent. All this was further compounded by racial tensions.

The trauma of war and the depressive nature of the immediate post-war environment had significantly negative psychological impact. Everywhere in the South, memoirs indicate that veterans suffered post-traumatic consequences: frightful dreams, the hollow stare, uncommunicative depressive withdrawal, and bouts of rage. They manifested unhealthy, dysfunctional behavior, including alcoholism, family abuse and increased violence.[5] For some their trauma continued after the war, the result of defeat in life and related degradation.

War-time trauma had hardly been limited to the combatants. According to letters and diaries, women all over the South suffered their own versions of post-traumatic stress that were compounded by the need to succor their damaged men folk and compensate for their frequently inadequate ability to cope with new economic problems. During the early years they described feeling drowsy, lethargic, and benumbed. They certainly did not seek liberation from their former position, however. If anything they sought the return of a romanticized version of both gender and race. Yet at the same time, they were more ambivalent about reliance on men who had failed to preserve their security or to restore their means after the war. Some of the public burdens they had assumed were freely shed. Self-interest eroded their former ideal of selfless service. They were more focused on family and self.[6]

Unfortunately, we have only hints of how much such mental conditions emerged among Germantown's women. Surely periodic emersion in the no-man's-land of guerrilla warfare, with all its traumas suffered with little male support, had affected local women. The only clues lie buried in their post-war letters almost all of which describe, more often, hardships, death and disease, or petty criticisms of other women. Reports of an individual's improvement are more mundane than joyous. The only clearly positive comments seem limited to signs of material improvements being made.[7]

The story for men is clearer. The abuse of children, spouses and lovers are symptomatic of PTS. For most of the years from 1840 covered in this book, the *Memphis Appeal* ran 8 articles about wife abuse before 1864 in the area. It ran 41 between late 1865 and September 1870 alone. The fewer surviving issues of the *Avalanche* exceeded that with 49 reports between 1866 and 1870. I have found only one newspaper report of abuse against local women, specifically at Collierville, but it had increasingly become a problem in Shelby County in general and Memphis in particular.[8] Another clear case of PTSD-related abuse occurred just north-east of the area. James Baxter of Davies Plantation had served in the 38th Tennessee Infantry in major bloody battles. On one occasion he attempted suicide unsuccessfully. His wife had to be defended by family members on several occasions when he threatened to shoot her. Because she sometimes sought solace with her family in Collierville, he threatened to kill all the horses she could use. She finally fled and got a divorce in 1867.[9]

The evidence for examples at Germantown lies buried in the private correspondence of women. Aratus T. Cornelius, called "Rat" by family and friends, had been a scion of the town's elite, marrying Julia Pettit, the judge's daughter. He was apparently among the earliest local men to be attracted to partisan service, enlisting with Edward J. Sanders' first company of Tennessee partisans in Shelby County in March 1862. They had been promised entirely independent and purely local service. But Sanders was ordered to report to General Albert Sidney Johnson's headquarters. So Cornelius, perhaps disillusioned about having to serve away from home, may have deserted. In whatever capacity, he was obviously back in the area for his marriage in July. Perhaps he joined some of Richardson's Rangers in the desired independent capacity. Whatever, in June 1863 with typical disdain for any service commitments, he showed up at Germantown with J. Dix Mills when they came to rescue their wives from Federal occupation. They settled safely behind Confederate lines in Mississippi, but then Cornelius had returned to somewhere in Shelby County by September, possibly scooped up in one of Richardson's conscription drives at that time. He served in the 12th Tennessee Cavalry as part of Richardson's Brigade under Forrest and would, therefore, have seen some of the nastiest aspects of the war. Perhaps his marriage to Julia had been one of those romantic unions made as the boys went off to war. After he returned, however, he soon became a notorious drunk and ne're-do-well. Former friends would not even trust him with the care of a puppy. By 1872, his wife's sister reported that he had "continued to drink and abuse her (Julia) until she could stand it no longer and she has finally left him. Mrs. Cornelius (his mother) is living with him—and although he has abused her shamefully she still hopes he may reform." Instead he duped his mother into borrowing money to finance a relocation for a new start, then "promptly used the money for a drunken bash in Memphis." On returning home, he "pretended to be crazy." A local gentleman stepped in to protect and house Julia and her children until she could find a position teaching.[10]

There were other probable examples. The wife of Matt Harrison, Louisa and her baby had to find shelter with Dr. Thompson's family. She was "another victim of imprudent marriage." When Mr. Carol Anderson died in 1873, Florida Thompson wrote that he had "died so poor that Bob Duke and Henry Madox had to pay his funeral expenses—and to think a few years ago he was a rich man. So much for whiskey."[11]

The correlation of drink with family abuse and the dissipation of resources was refueling the fires of the temperance movement. Germantown proponents participated prominently in one temperance event held in Collierville in 1876. An unnamed reverend from Germantown (perhaps Reverend Evans, or perhaps the Baptist minister) and a Mr. Perkins and Dr. M'Kay participated in a mock debate. The reporter commented that King Alcohol did not get an impartial trial. "The jury was not composed of his peers." The two debaters were probably Wilson Perkins, a sixty-six year-old farmer and Dr. Robert McKay, both of Germantown. Miss Fannie Burnley, the daughter of the widowed farm owner Susan Burnley, was also involved, as Germantown women continued to insert themselves more publicly in their causes.[12] Theirs was a voice of concern about what affected their families.

The presence in town of four reportedly outright saloons, as opposed to the former store/saloon combination, may indicate a behavioral shift. Inebriation would be less inhibited, given the absence of women and children from an environment devoted totally to drink. Old time residents remember being told by their parents that in post-war Germantown and Mid-South towns in general, women had to stay off the streets on Saturday nights because the town's saloon scene was so wild.[13]

There may indeed have been an effort by district officials to crack down on drunkenness. It may be remembered that a wit reported that the town was once "famous for drunken brawls . . . whiskey-shops, and . . . roaring old debauchees," before remedial measures had been taken. By 1872, such measures had allegedly shut down all but one proper saloon, thriving in a location convenient to the railroad.[14] If so, it was only one of several very temporary victories for temperance.

As the decade drew to a close, the battle over "demon rum" added to the town's social tensions, although it was probably the least serious social conflict.

One especially hostile participant described the opposite sides as "golden rule fellows, Mamma Pets and temperance lecturers" versus the "b'hoy's, Gander Pullers, and the Kangaroo Court." B'hoys were simply good-'ol-boys, but the other two seem to have referred to specific drinking cohorts in town. His references to members of the Kangaroo Court implies they had been prominent and respected community leaders, some of whom gave their lives in service during the epidemic of 1878. The temperance lecturers allegedly had little real effect except in so far as some of the Kangarooians "resigned on account of their 'girls.'"[15] The jocular nature of such reports makes it difficult to trace accurately the ups and downs of the movement's local success in cracking down on drunkenness during the 1870s.

✦ ✦ ✦

A more unnerving and glaring residue of the war, however, plagued everyday life for many years. The pre-war, peaceful and law-abiding atmosphere that had once prevailed locally had changed radically. Three factors were at work: fear of a perceived threat of a violent black underclass unwilling to accept their proper place; a truly criminalized element in both races; plus an apparent loss of the former sense of communal harmony and collective responsibility for dealing with problems affecting the unfortunate. In November 1865, while the area was still suffering guerrilla brigands, a violent confrontation just outside the town resulted in two deaths.

Amidst great uncertainty about how the masses of emancipated blacks would behave, wild rumors of a pending black armed uprising were spreading. One result was a rebirth of the pre-war phenomena of slave or vigilance patrols. At Germantown, this set the stage for that confrontation. In adjacent District Ten, a band of young men formed a vigilante band and set out to disarm local blacks rumored to be up to something. After passing through Forest Hill, they turned south and reached the farm of Monroe Harrison, two miles south of Germantown, which would have been below Nonconnah and near the border of the two civil districts. According to the first reports, they were drunken, disorderly and "knocked violently at the door." Why they were approaching white households was never explained. Harrison opened the door with pistol in hand, "expostulated with the marauders, but failing to check them, fired his pistol...." In the exchange that followed, both a Mr. Brown and Harrison were fatally wounded, and Harrison's father received a head wound.

The initial report in the *Appeal* concluded with the speculation, "Robbery was probably the leading motive, but there is an implication (word unclear) that a spirit of malicious vindictiveness, worse in the present unsettled condition of the country than thievish burglary, prompted the act." No one was arrested.[16]

On the following day, a reporter went out to Germantown and interviewed "citizens of the vicinity ... who are of a character to impart to their statements entire credibility," and they gave "a materially different version of the affair...."

> It was the result of an entire misunderstanding between the parties.
> ... It appears that the party which went to the house ... was made up of young men of the neighborhood of good character, between whom and the Harrisons there was not any (illegible word) existing misunderstanding, but on the contrary, on the part of most of them, an entirely friendly acquaintance.

The expedition was in response to local blacks shooting watch dogs south of Germantown in preparation for

> stealing and pillaging. These young men, it would seem, with the approval and countenance of elder citizens, had united together for the purpose of searching for and taking away arms in the possession of negroes suspected of having them in possession.... It is denied that they conducted themselves in a disorderly or offensive manner, either at Forest Hill or the several other houses of citizens they visited.

There were conflicts among the witnesses as to who fired first, for it was dark "and in the midst of excitement."[17]

Comparing this event with those that follow encourages a critical review of all reported aspects. The reporter's effort to interview "respectable" citizens but not either participants (more sensational informants) produced what seems suspiciously like a locally approved version of events and causes. Understandably the good citizens wanted to preserve the town's image of a respectable, harmonious community, and the *Appeal* was typically solicitous of community reputations and sensitivities. Their version which obfuscates and omits details while denying the negative versions makes one suspect the truth was lost. The community had no problems admitting that they were now plagued by a dangerous black underclass, whom they had an unquestioned right to disarm. But there could be no hints of disharmony, much less animosity among its good folk. We shall subsequently see more examples of such efforts to ignore or deny some serious problems, and to avoid responsibility for dealing with them.

Monroe Harrison was probably a veteran of either the 4th Infantry or the 12th Cavalry. He was truly comfortable with violent confrontation, and was living in an area threatened by bands of renegades and brigands. Nothing is known about the young men on the other side, or their true state of mind. Drinking would have been a common prelude to any such adventure. Nothing is reported about the results of any real efforts to disarm blacks, but rather visits to white households. If they had all been friendly and well acquainted, (assuming the "official" account was vaguely accurate) why would Harrison have fired, especially after having had time to talk with them? They were prepared to return fire quickly, even reportedly shooting the old father as he knelt over his son. All that is known about the results of this event is that Monroe Harrison's entire household was gone well before 1869.[18]

This was just one example of a total breakdown of law and order and community harmony. Before the war, never a day passed that Memphis papers failed to report crimes like theft, burglary, violent beatings and murder in the city. After the war there was a significant increase in such reports. Reports of crime outside the city had been rare before the war, while after there was a definite increase, specifically around Germantown.[19] The crimes committed by the regulars and partisans on both sides, ranging from plundering to murder, had helped to establish an environment. As the war wore on, the criminal activities of guerrillas and robber bands had increased.

The end of hostilities only brought a shift from groups disguised as guerrillas to outright robber bands. Although nothing as infamous as the James and Younger gangs appeared in Shelby County, the atmosphere that produced them west of the Mississippi also prevailed locally. Indeed during the 1870s, "Mr. Howard" (Jesse's alias) and brother hid in Nashville for several years and allegedly had "safe houses" in rural Tennessee counties provided by sympathetic parties who viewed crimes against the establishment as guerrilla class-warfare. Locally, the threat varied from robber gangs operating with impunity, through small teams of highwaymen, rustler gangs, and criminalized individuals.

In May 1866, a band of thieves had taken up residence in some woodland off the Germantown road. Men or women traveling to and from Germantown were regularly robbed. Farmers desperately trying "to make up a little of what they lost while the 'cruel war' was raging" were robbed of what they had earned after delivering to the city.[20]

Throughout 1866 and 1867, thieves were stealing so many cows, pigs and chickens from local farmers that the costs of such foods in the city were high and the farmers were "impoverished." One Councilman argued that outside the city, "murder, robbery, burglary, arson, and crimes of every character have become so prevalent as to render both life and property notoriously insecure. . . ." The Metropolitan Police got requests daily for patrolmen to come out to places as far afield as Germantown. Citizens' pleaded for an extra mounted sheriff's patrol to cover the fifteen mile radius around the city that included Germantown. Unfortunately when both the sheriff and the Superintendent of Metropolitan Police applied to the County Commission for such a force, it was denied for lack of a petition "from the citizens wishing such a force with a full knowledge of the cost." Since the appeal for law enforcement failed, a suspect was occasionally found hanging from a tree.[21] Despite the potential punishment, horse thieves continued to plague Germantown area farmers throughout the 70s. Two resident black laborers were apprehended while trying to sell the mules thay had stolen. More brazen local thieves even sold their stolen animals in the town itself.[22] For a while in 1876, the town also suffered an infestation of burglars.[23]

In 1867, a true outlaw gang was operating from the Loosahatchie bottoms like their partisan predecessors. By 1868, a well-organized gang of horse and cattle thieves were sweeping the river-tier counties of Tennessee and Mississippi, with bases in Cairo, Illinois, Jackson and Lafayette, Tennessee, and Grenada, Mississippi. Their operations had exceeded all previous depredations. This was a mixed gang of blacks and whites, with whites fencing the stolen animals. One prominent operator, John Niles, was black. Governor Brownlow got the blame for recently pardoning him in a reversal of the County Circuit Court. They had sent Niles to the penitentiary in 1866 for robbery near Germantown.[24] Brownlow had "played the race card" as we say today, by releasing Niles, further inflaming local hostilities.

In 1871, a mixed-race gang was discovered headquartered near Forest Hill, under the leadership of "a negro named Lindsay Hayes." They had regularly stolen widely from Memphis and stashed with Hayes who was the front man.[25]

By 1870, country folk were so dissatisfied with the Memphis-centric county efforts to curb crime that, as we have seen, they petitioned the state constitutional convention to divide Shelby County, separating Memphis and western districts to form a new county. City-oriented courts were so indifferent to their needs that it was not worth the time for country residents to prosecute a case. Consequently, "when things get too bad Judge Lynch steps in and gives a lesson or two."[26]

As for the threat of highwaymen. They operated along every major road, and the lesser byways. The network running out of Germantown was no exception. On September 9, 1867, the district's Constable Rhodes delivered to the Memphis jail one T. L. Hill, "a white lad, seemingly not more than eighteen years of age, but possessing a most sinister cast of countenance, charged with the double crime of attempted robbery and murder, on the highway." This "foot-pad," had been skulking around Germantown, scouting out the area roads for suitable places of ambush. In need of an accomplice, he approached a nearby black laborer. While pretending to cooperate, he immediately reported to his employer, who instructed him to go along and to keep him informed of plans. The farmer assembled a party to apprehend the criminal in the act. Somehow, the pretended accomplice was clever enough to "secretly withdraw the charges from a formidable revolver." Indeed when two suitable looking victims approached and Hill sprang out to "demand his money or his life" the white man seemed to resist. Hill tried three times in vain to shoot his victim. He was then seized by the vigilantes and turned over to the constable.[27]

Shortly thereafter, Sheriff Winter's deputy arrested a black man named John Ethling, also hiding on a plantation near Germantown. He had murdered Dr. M. R. Ramsey on the Raleigh Road, and was planning highway robberies in the neighborhood when a would-be accomplice reported him.[28]

In the previous year, a squad of Pinkerton detectives showed up near the town to arrest one of the men involved in the robbery of a Southern Express messenger in Memphis. He too had been hiding in a black man's cabin. This band of robbers had also included both white and black men.[29]

Undoubtedly the town's most notorious criminal was "Captain" John E. White, who had been operating a saw-mill at Tipton until 1870. In that year at Germantown, he married Sallie Reasonover, the young sister of the Reasonover brothers, living south of Forest Hill. His new neighbors saw his as "a pleasant man, who was supposed to be honest and honorable," and initially had doubts about his guilt. In fact, however, he had a murky past. His mill in Tipton had burned down, the fire rumored to have been set to get insurance. Shortly before, his brother was rumored to have attempted a murder. Then in August 1873, everyone was surprised when the Captain was arrested for horse theft. The evidence was overwhelming for an entire string of operations under his leadership.[30]

Then a bigger shock came on September 7 when his wife helped him escape from the county jail. On a visit, she smuggled in a pistol, then distracted the guard who was courteously holding the door for her to bid White goodbye. White pulled the gun, threatened the guard and bolted. Mrs. White grabbed the guard long enough for her husband to mount a horse and ride off before he could fire. The horse had been tied nearby by an accomplice. To round out the story, one of her Reasonover brothers had been staying the night before in the same Memphis boardinghouse as Mrs. White. The evening after the escape, when a lady suggested that he was the accomplice, he became irate.[31]

Meanwhile, the wife was arrested and jailed. Her's was a penitentiary offense, but the papers all opined that it was unlikely she would be punished. "She exhibits that devotion which the madness of woman's affection too often displays in behalf of unworthy manhood. She is of excellent social relations. . . ." They were correct, for she returned to her brother's farm. Meanwhile, her husband continued his notorious adventures. He was caught again, led an unsuccessful jail revolt in 1874, then a successful escape by a gang, again with smuggled arms, in January 1875. He was facing a fifteen year penitentiary sentence.[32] The papers continued to report Sheriff Anderson's efforts to catch him for the rest of the next year, in the process giving him the status of a clever anti-hero. Thereafter, his trail went cold. Such approval by locals of such criminals reveals underlying hostility toward establishment society.

Nevertheless, the citizens of the town manifested fear of criminals, often transients. The war had left so many men rootless and criminalized, like Captain White.[33] In March 1875, one man walking along the tracks from Collierville toward Memphis fell in with two others, and they were observed by some citizens camping by the tracks that evening. The next morning he was found dead, robbed of all valuable property. Unlike before the war, the townsmen simply buried his body where they had found it.[34]

Despite the *Appeal* and *Avalanche*'s constant, shrill efforts to propagate hysterical fear of black criminality, the involvement of Germantown's black citizens in crime seems hardly proportional to their numbers. Among them, during 1870 and 1871, there were three serious black on black crimes involving area blacks. Maryland Johnson had abandoned his family in Germantown to settle in Memphis where he killed another man. Steve Perkins had murdered an unnamed man in Germantown. Joseph Phillips had broken into the house of Henry Lewis to steal his gun and kill him, but was caught in time. Aside from the previously mentioned highwayman, the only incident of black violence against a white man "near Germantown" was a non-fatal shooting in 1870.[35]

Predictably, the fear of black crime often resulted in false accusations. In December 1878, D. C. Rhodes (sic; Rhoads) was "assassinated" one night while sitting in a storehouse. He was described conventionally as "a quiet, orderly man, highly esteemed by all who knew him." In this case also, the unknown assailants escaped. J. H. Alsup, who was probably the constable, reported to the sheriff that it was done by "negroes," but the *Ledger's* report implied that was not certain. A group had "stealthily approached the house and one of them fired at Mr. Rhodes." He was hit in the face and killed instantly. No motives were proposed, but he was involved in local business in ways that apparently produced serious conflict.[36]

The *Appeal* reported that seven men were arrested for the crime on December 10. The *Ledger* reported that "A. Wright, proprietor of the store in which Rhodes was killed, and John Newell, clerk, have been arrested for alleged complicity." The paper reserved comment pending investigation. The white men were released on five thousand dollar bonds, while the blacks were held without bail.[37]

James Fountain, Monroe and James Hunt, all "colored," were indicted, while two other suspected black men were released. Both Fountain and Monroe Hunt were found innocent at trail, while James Hunt was held in durance "to answer for deviltry in Mississippi."[38] If not a murderer, he was certainly some kind of "black devil." With the blacks exonerated, the alleged conspiratorial involvement of the white men remained unsettled. A presumption of black criminality distracted police investigation and resulted in another unsolved murder.

As before the war, violent acts relating to family honor, often a young lady's reputation, remained a part of life, but also escalated locally. Jack Johnson of Olive Branch wounded J. W. Cooney in such a confrontation just south of the town in 1874. In 1876, Thomas Reasonover killed Samuel H. Ellis on his way to the Masonic Hall in town. These were not duels, but nevertheless confrontations over family honor. Reasonover actually published a letter claiming self-defense. He contested newspaper reports that he shot Ellis in the back, and described him as a threatening, foul-tempered slanderer. Ellis had spread rumors defaming their young niece. Unfortunately for Reasonover, Ellis was found to have been unarmed. In its initial reports, the *Ledger* hinted that the Reasonovers' family connections were indeed a bit shady, reminding everyone about their connection with "the notorious Captain (John E.) White, the Shelby county horse-thief." Despite being lawyers, they were typical examples of the widely held view that blood and honor trumped the law. As in the Joyce incident before the war, the case became the source of great interest and contention. Reasonover and his brother were initially found guilty by a close margin, but then ruled innocent in a retrial.[39] The appropriateness of such violence remained a question in local minds, but many accepted it as justified homicide.

Another incident in 1876 had similar overtones. When a man named Sweeney was killed by one Hamilton, Magistrate Walker investigated and released Hamilton from custody. Sweeney's friends demanded justice, but the Judge released him on four thousand dollars bond after examining several witnesses. He would still have to answer any indictment preferred against him in the Circuit Court, but all authorities seemed to treat the affair lightly.[40]

Around Germantown, outright murder had become almost common. One man living just north of town murdered another in Bartlett. In addition to the black-on-black murders and attempted murders, even more killings and murders were committed by whites around town. In 1866, Christian Berger murdered Miss Mary Watt at Germantown. While awaiting execution, Berger died of "congestion of the brain,"—a hint at a possible source of his aberrant behavior.[41]

In May of 1867, while sitting in his parlor with wife and family, Smith Wilson was shot through a window by an unknown assassin. His farm had been subjected to pilfering for some time, and he had suspects. They apparently struck before he could expose them. It soon became certain that the killer was a W. T. Knowlton, "who under the name of Peebles, was formerly a United States military detective." Knowlton and his brother were post-war settlers, and his undercover role was certain to cast him in a dark light. Wilson, from Ohio, had also settled between Forest Hill and Germantown in the previous December. His neighbors petitioned the county court and the governor to post generous rewards, but Knowlton had immediately fled the area. Their references to Wilson as an "esteemed" citizen, and "a very quiet and worthy man," who "has never before had any difficulty with any person," implies that the locals had no problems accepting "Yankee" settlers into their community.[42] Unlike those who spoke for the community, however, the culprit and whatever accomplices apparently resented his economic success.

In 1880, W. F. Kimbrough was tried for the murder of a black man, William McCoy, whom he shot after McCoy called him a liar and struck him. Kimbrough had accused McCoy, a cropper on his lands, of selling his cotton on the side. Kimbrough left his family and fled.[43]

Unlike the pre-war violence, most of these were outright murders, some conducted stealthily. Compared to the one case of spontaneous homicide uncovered during the entire pre-war history of the town, there were four premeditated murders, two other killings of a more undefined nature, and at least two honor killings. Even if such an accelerated rate of violent crime and property theft were not unique to the Germantown area in Shelby County, for such a small community, they clearly add to other arguments for a definite change of atmosphere.

✦ ✦ ✦

The economic hardships of the post-war recovery had brought other signs of social conflict, specifically a defensiveness among the more comfortable classes coupled with a tendency not to see or tend to the problems and poverty of those around them. In 1868, J. Dix Mills published a voluble appeal in the *Avalanche* describing the hardships suffered by the "destitute" in and around the town.

> Indeed, I know of but few families that are not more or less destitute. I know of nothing that exceeds our poverty, but our pride—and dignity of Germantown.... When from the wars the planter returned to the charred remains of his once handsome home ... and by acts evinced a determination to bring from the earth the bread by the sweat of his brow, the merchant of Memphis ... extended to him the hand of help; placed within his reach the means to purchase the implements of husbandry, the means to purchase mules and horses, and provisions on which to live till time and labor could mature the crops. The crops failed in part, the products declined in price, and at the end of the first year ... the planter found himself in worse condition than at its commencement—in debt to the merchant....

The merchants came to their aid again, but the process repeated itself.[44] Up to this point, Mills had put a positive spin on the merchants.

Mills' description of the poverty in the area was accurate as we have seen, and such cycles of debt and failure plagued many locals. His published appeal was, however, actually a vain effort to defend himself against charges that he exaggerated both the number of impoverished farmers and claimed falsely that there was insufficient local charitable assistance. Instead he was allegedly profiting from a specious campaign to raise funds. In April, one anonymous "citizen" had published a charge that the shady "originator of this pauper excitement" had brought disgrace on Germantown—now to be called "Paupertown."[45] Mill's published defense began a series of public exchanges that revealed a community that had not or could not provide support for the misfortunate—the kind of support that had characterized its antebellum character. Whether out of guilt or embarrassment, prominent townsmen sought to paint him as an unethical opportunist and con man.

The Reverend J. (John) Dix Mills already lived under a cloud of suspicion in the community, but also had respectable defenders. By 1858, Mills was a "local preacher" of the Methodist Episcopal Church South. This was a unique position within the Methodist Church, ostensibly a first step to becoming an ordained pastor. They were licensed to preach and perform clerical services. Some like Mills, however, chose instead to pursue a secular occupation while retaining their semi-clerical status. Wherever they lived or traveled, they were expected to be available to local congregations to provide necessary pastoral services in the absence of their circuit rider. Mills also chose to use the prestigious title of reverend, even listing himself as such in censuses rather than giving his actual occupation. There are few clear indications of exactly how Mills made his bread. He had relocated in different cities after leaving his Kentucky home. He seems to have been an opportunistic entrepreneur, going from one opportunity to the next, traveling widely to do so.[46] Such a lifestyle raised suspicions among more traditional agrarians, especially since he performed a combination of business and clerical services simultaneously as he traveled. Opportunistic capitalism was not yet viewed favorably by most agrarians, and that would have repercussions.

During the spring of 1858, he had courted and proposed to Emily Lucken, the daughter of the popular innkeeper. After they married, he settled in Germantown as his base of operations.[47] The marriage provided strong local family ties. Nevertheless, he ran afoul of some in his district. In early 1862, they pressed charges at their district conference, which found him guilty, although there is no record of what. He was confident enough to appeal the decision to the Memphis Conference, which dismissed the charges for lack of evidence and reinstated him. This was not unusual, for the elders were sensitive to the problems of ministers, often victims of congregation politics.[48]

After this settlement and shortly before Federal occupation, Mills left the area "on business," and was "unable to return to his wife," during which time he had not volunteered or been conscripted. Then as previously described, he collected her, and they made their sojourn into "Dixie" where they settled down in residence. He pursued both his business affairs and a role in local religious services. When he came to the attention of local conscription authorities, after examination, they deferred him for heart problems.

After the war, Mills became concerned for the plight of many local farmers. Since January 1868, he had been drumming up local support for efforts to raise out-of-state funds for them. On April 18, his campaign had resulted in a meeting at the Presbyterian Church. In addition to Reverend Evans, T. Scott, William Mitchell and Dr. John Stout had been mobilized by concern over "twelve families in need of help." A motion was passed by a slim majority (15 to 13) to send an agent north "to solicit aid for the disabled." The dissenting minority promptly left the meeting. When the remainder selected "a proper person to go north," the choice fell on Mills.[49]

Members of the concerned minority called a more general meeting on April 25, to which 50 came. Led by local merchants, Harmand Furstenheim, William Walker and Henry Massey, they adopted a resolution to be published in Memphis and Louisville newspapers. They denied that the community was destitute and unable to relieve the "few people unable to work." No "contributions of neighboring states" were needed. They formed a committee "to inquire into the destitution of this community" and to solicit from the community whatever aid was needed. They impugned Mill's motives.[50]

Previously careful to speak highly of the role of such merchants, Mills now retaliated with words that inflamed the controversy. Among those who had thrived after the war, two "little fellows . . . to-day . . . are in a position to speculate upon the pressing needs of our suffering countrymen." The destitute around Germantown had the misfortune "to be so near a town holding . . . two or three stupid men, determined to rule or ruin every move of which they themselves are not the head and front—men noted neither for benevolence of character nor for courteous treatment of their fellow-men." He attacked an indirectly identified Memphis merchant as "one of the leaders." He had "repeatedly refused to accommodate good men, only on such terms as may possibly involve them in hopeless ruin." He focused specifically on the author of the word "Paupertown" whose supposed wit was designed to create an " excitement" that would discredit the good cause. To make this villain's identity known, without naming names, Mills associated him with a well-known, failed, local political maneuver.[51] This was William Walker, local merchant and magistrate. Furstenheim and Massey are good candidates for the Memphis merchants.

A storm broke about Mills. Anonymous comments appeared in the *Avalanche* criticizing him for referring to a firm of merchants "who are too well known for highest business capacity and integrity.... Perhaps Mr. Mills cannot even appreciate the worth of honesty or good breeding, and had better devote himself to the study of theology."[52] His former backers began to disassociate themselves.

William Walker proceeded to thoroughly blacken Mills' name. He "is a minister of the Gospel, of small usefulness in his clerical calling." He had been a rabid secessionist who not only failed to bear arms, but proceeded to speculate and profit in food and materials, even selling at high prices to a lone widow "on the Sabbath day." Perhaps this relates to the charges against him in 1862.

> He goes privately to a few gentlemen with his insinuations and deceptions; got them to certificate him for Kentucky. After an absence of six weeks he returns, with (an abundance of supplies), the bulk of which went to his home. Besides this, he sent home some money by express, and informed a party in this vicinity that he made $2,000 by the trip. Not a dollar had been given to the destitute ... for whom he went out to beg.

Noting that Mills had charged him with "a want of politeness to gentlemen," Walker responded, "I regret his reverence is not in a position to receive those little attentions due a gentleman." In other words, a duel. "With Rev. J. Dix Mills I have no further communication. If I have done him an injustice, his appeal is to the courts of the country."[53]

At this point, the editors of the *Avalanche* announced that they had washed their hands of the affair and urged the *Ledger* to do so also. The proclaimed intention of the people of Germantown to take care of their own should settle the matter. The press could not judge the merits of the case but respected the "old, influential citizens" of Germantown who had pronounced Mill's cause unfounded. "Mr. Mills' course, both in and out of print, has not been calculated to strengthen his position."[54]

Typically the publicity-shy local Methodists made no published proclamations in favor of either side. Unlike the other town churches, they never submitted letters to the editor or even notices of church activities. Meanwhile, Mills remained a certified local preacher of the Memphis Conference. Clearly the Methodist Conference leadership saw no substance to the accusations of fraud.[55]

The picture that emerges from all this is certainly unpleasant. By his actions, Mills made major enemies, and we will never know if he had the support of the others he claimed. His enemies tried to destroy whatever reputation he had. Although the good people of the town now assumed some responsibilities for some unfortunate neighbors, before Mills had created an embarrassing sensation they had been too distracted by their own problems to do so. Although the responsible committees had identified "a dozen" destitute families around each of Germantown and Collierville, all rhetoric about them referred to farmers and former planters. Considering the previous chapter's picture of local poverty, one wonders what contemporaries considered both destitution and worthiness in order to come up with only twelve such families. Black poverty clearly lay entirely beyond the pale.

The three or four "villains" Mills identified may have been as hard-hearted or indifferent as he claimed—country and city merchants who controlled local credit. Whatever his merits or demerits, by embarrassing the town in such a public manner and attacking a few of its leaders he insured his demise. Memphis' newspaper editors rallied behind their cause, not his. Polite society demanded discretion, especially concerning "respectable gentlemen." Identified as a Methodist, he could also have run afoul of emerging sectarian divisions.[56]

Clearly not everyone subscribed to the accusations against him, for he apparently did not become a town pariah. He could shelter in the Lucken's popularity, and his wife's correspondence reveals continued friendly relations with prominent families, including the Evans. By 1872, however, they had relocated to his family's holdings in Kentucky while Mills' business activities took him farther afield. Friends continued to correspond with Emily, enquiring into his wellbeing, and he returned to town occasionally on business. Perhaps they gave him the benefit of the doubt, knowing full well that he had run afoul of powerful men. Of course, he had embarrassed the town in general, which had lost its former social cohesiveness and much of its spirit of collective Christian charity.

If charity and a sense of communal responsibility had been undermined, one's social conscience suffered as well. Clear evidence surfaces in local probate records. Apparently aware that death was approaching, in November 1871, John Quenichet drew up his will, appointing Adrian Mayer of Marshall County, Mississippi, "my friend and their uncle," guardian of his two minor children. In addition to Mayer, he assigned his "friends," Nathaniel F. Lemaster and William P. Deadrick of Shelby County as executors, without security, "having the utmost confidence in their prudence, judgment, and honesty." Following Quenichet's death in December, the executors sold his home and land near Memphis for $7000, $4500 in cash and an interest bearing note for $2500. The twenty-year old son, John was given management of the 1162 acres a couple of miles southwest of Germantown. He collected rent from the tenants, mostly in cotton, applying it toward badly needed repairs. In August 1877, Mayer died "utterly insolvent," and the Probate Court appointed Minor Meriwether as guardian. When the children's grandfather had died in 1878, Mayer had received their $1600 as guardian. Those funds had disappeared in Mayer's insolvency. The executors turned over to Meriwether the $2500 note and two small uncollectable rent notes. Meriwether promptly did a thorough examination of the accounts and found the executors indebted to the estate for over $9000. The funds had been "squandered." He filed a bill in court to call them to account, but the case had not been settled by 1880. Lemaster had also mismanaged tax payments causing serious difficulties. They had also failed to register the trust deed on the outstanding note for $2500 or to collect interest. Meriwether had to file in the court in 1878 to secure it plus interest. Meanwhile that property had become entangled in debter's other debts requiring further legal actions that remained unsettled. In short, the two children had suffered serious losses. When John Quenichet reached majority in 1879, the Germantown area property was divided between the two children, apparently all they had left to support themselves.[57]

By 1880, the sister was renting or cropping out her share as an absentee. John also rented or cropped out some of his share, but personally farmed 105 of his acres for an income of $720. He continued to live in the community, betrayed by family friends and relatives. His status had seriously suffered.

❖ ❖ ❖

Incidents conducive to depression plagued locals. During the winter and early spring of 1866, one grim reminder of the federal occupation must have resurrected many a family's grief. As part of government efforts to find and properly rebury the Union dead, an agent scoured the counties east of Memphis for their remains. Along the heavily occupied course of the M&C RR alone thousands of casualties had been quickly interred, often where they fell. Hasty burials had often lined the roads. Despite his diligence, for years after the war, locals would uncover remains on their lands. Specifically at Germantown, his team disinterred 24 men from the town cemetery who joined the ranks to be reinterred in the Mississippi National Cemetery (Memphis National Cemetery).[58] The event had to bring up the sad awareness that Germantown's men lay in unmarked graves far away from home.

Other disturbing incidents like suicides speak to the pressures everyone suffered as well as symptoms of PTS. Between 1862 and 1870, the *Appeal* reported four times as many suicides as it had in the fourteen years before the war.[59] Locally in 1869, a derelict woman was found dying by the tracks, a consequence of escape into "the excessive use of opium or morphine." Shortly thereafter, a black man was found dead on the tracks. Samuel Meachum was ruled insane, supposedly resulting from "pecuniary affairs." Three months after he disappeared from his home, N. M. Young's body was found at the Seventeen-Mile Creek one mile from his home, a suspected suicide. The elderly Mrs. Roberts, living with the Isaiah Stout family, had been run over by the train while walking home from town. Recently widowed and losing property, "she had been heard to say that she was completely discouraged and was weary of life." The *Appeal*'s description was unusually graphic and gory. Two days later, a Mrs. Robinson, "a milliner from New York," threw herself under the train shortly after losing her husband. The last four of these incidents all coming within one three-month period must have cast a pall.[60]

Other possible suicides were probably kept quiet out of propriety. The death of William Greenlaw had been listed variously in the papers as caused by heart attack and or/dropsy. Although not a suicide, he had suffered great depression from the death of his wife, and serious stress because of a pending bankruptcy. Depression and financial crises ultimately killed this millionaire. More likely however, the related death of his son was a suicide. Eugene Alonso had reportedly just returned home from Memphis just a month after his father's death. He had been immersed there in the family's financial crisis which was probably consuming his own financial resources.[61] No newspapers carried any cause of death, nor was any coroner's inquest from Germantown reported. What had been a source of powerful influence for the town had evaporated with their fortunes.

The seemingly greater frequency of all these negative reports about Germantown in the papers differs greatly from their almost complete lack before the war. Admittedly that is impressionistic evidence. Clearly however, it at least speaks of an age of greater awareness of or attention to misfortune and a negative shift in the greater community's mood. Townsfolk now felt compelled to share these stories in the newspapers.

Having to rely on newspaper coverage as a barometer of the town's experiences is not entirely satisfactory. They generally covered the town's news when locals reported it, making coverage uneven. However, that also makes them a barometer of local feelings and attitudes. The newspapers' preference for humorous and entertaining exaggeration makes some of the accounts about town life suspect. Also the colorful stories lack clear references to specific times—describing conditions that might have been very time specific rather than covering decades. Also the papers seem to have shifted more toward sensational coverage than before, making it difficult to determine how much had changed as opposed to the news coverage—a problem that repeats itself today. Clearly the press' increasing emphasis on black crime is an example.

In contrast, one specific hole in newspaper coverage of positive developments creates an enigma. In September 1873, the *Appeal* published a report applauding achievements among towns within Memphis' commercial sphere. The commercial and industrial facilities and the agricultural potential of each town were detailed. The editors had sent invitations "to the best men in each place" to report such details, and "sent agents to inquire." Collierville reported a population of one thousand to twelve hundred, the rebuilding of a totally burned town with a fine new town square and commercial buildings, several of brick, a female college and a boys school, and five churches built or under construction. It sent twelve thousand bales of cotton to Memphis. Even little Lafayette reported a population of nearly one hundred. Germantown was not even mentioned.[62]

It seems unlikely that the editors had ignored the town. The "best men" must not have responded. Was there no pride? Could they not agree on how to depict the town, or was the prospect of a comparative report embarrassing? Collierville had obviously left the town far behind. Whatever reason, this seems symptomatic of problems within the community and its self-esteem.

By 1880, however, the community was finally willing to air its dirty laundry. The 1880 petition for a charter composed by the town's leading citizens paints a picture of a community completely in shambles, lawless and chaotic. They spoke of the need to be able to pass and enforce municipal laws

> for the suppression of drunkenness and other vices, to prevent careless and reckless shooting in the limits of the town to the endangering of life and to the great annoyance of the inhabitants, and as drunken fights are of frequent occurrence on the streets; and as they are subjected to profane and indecent language, to the great disturbance of peaceful and quiet citizens, there being no power to restrain these offenders; as dead stock is allowed to remain in their streets; to the great annoyance of the inhabitants and the endangering of public health. . . ."[63]

These were the conditions the town's residents had tolerated since the end of the war. Nothing more clearly reveals a complete loss of community pride and collective responsibility. None were willing to serve in public office or pay the taxes for road maintenance and the other community services so badly needed.

As we shall see, the devastating 1878 epidemic may have exaggerated post-war consequences, unleashing a full breakdown of the community. At least the community was finally ready to face up to its embarrassing problems, take forceful steps and pay the necessary taxes to do so. More about that later.

Meanwhile, even sectarianism had asserted itself. Initially the post-war community had even intensified its relative ecumenical harmony. The Presbyterian Church made its facilities available for the other congregations until they could reconstruct. When a pastor was away, members simply attended the services of another congregation where they had friends. To maintain regular Sunday schools, they even conducted a "union Sunday School."[64]

Despite this initial harmony, we have already seen indications that sectarian conflict emerged as war-time accommodations lapsed. Vituperative exchanges between Baptists and Methodists unleashed by the publications of Reverend J. R. Graves in Memphis were read by townsfolk. Graves went so far as to question whether Methodists were legitimate Christians. Finally, Germantown's

Baptist Reverend Lipsey invited Graves to "deliver a series of doctrinal sermons" in town. Attendance was high. Although the hall remained packed, some were put off by his attacks, offended by any examples of "sectarian hate."[65] Opinions about belief and faith became polarized.

Lipsey was emboldened to take on a Campbellite preacher named Lauderdale in the Methodist Church, perhaps neutral ground. A moderator insured "the orderly manner of debate." According to Lipsey's son, Platus,

> The differences between Campbellites and Baptists were thoroughly aired, attention was attracted and large crowds drawn from far and near. The people liked that sort of thing and I think got good out of it. ... At Germantown and probably most other places at that time there was a good deal of strong denominational sentiment and quite a bit of prejudice or bitterness. The lines were clearly drawn and feeling was strong."

Platus noted that his father's outspoken manner provoked controversy and antagonism.[66]

Young Platus freely expressed such religious convictions, and they apparently infected his personal relationships. He sought in vain to convert Dr. McKay's son, a Presbyterian. "I asked him if he didn't want to be a Christian and go to heaven. He tried to be funny by asking me if I had the key."[67] Of course, Lipsey's implication was that a Presbyterian was not a saved Christian. As Lipsey's comments indicated, the town was not only divided along sectarian lines, but also between those who harbored sectarian prejudices, and those who found that unchristian. Not everyone was infected. Some correspondence indicates that mixed-denominational families could maintain harmony.[68] Whatever sectarian friction there may have been, it was also symptomatic of other social tensions and prejudices.

If witnesses to pre-war conditions had denied significant social differences and tensions among whites, post-war witnesses and other evidence say things had changed. This supports the theory that the war had brought previously latent conditions to the fore. Young Lipsey put it bluntly.

> Farming was an honorable occupation, but almost any other occupation which required manual labor put a person below par. Marriages between families of what was considered more honorable

occupation and those less esteemed were not encouraged nor seemed desirable. The difference between a 'good family' and humbler people was more accentuated than now. The lines of demarcation were more distinct and harder to cross.[69]

As the son of a Baptist minister, he contended that he was more aware of the life of the diverse population to whom his father ministered. He expressed a mix of his own social and sectarian sentiments, "The Presbyterians had been the leading people here for a long time and it seemed to me rather resented the progress being made by Baptists." As we have seen, one Presbyterian expressed just such sentiments, "As for the Baptists, they are both poor and slow and it is doubtful if they was to have a church." The alleged social leveling influence of the churches was also insufficient even within denominations like the Baptists. When the Brooks family attended a special service north of the Wolf, after arriving in their fine carriage, no one invited them to dinner. When Mr. Brooks explained to his indignant wife that the simple folk considered them as "quality" and were too embarrassed to take care of them, she remained scornful.[70]

Many of the pre-war symptoms of a relatively harmonious community had been displaced by those of social tension, both within and among classes. Drunkenness, violence, and crime had increased. The successful could be the targets of violence, even murder. Every fire provoked rumors of arson, symptomatic of the fear of the "barn burner"—that vindictively resentful member of the underclass. The propertied were increasingly defensive and more parsimonious with their charity, which was probably more hurtfully just a "performance".

If the small farmer and the landless had grown increasingly resentful of the slave-owning class during the war, unequally shared post-war hardships and the increase in the gap between the rich and the rest of society further enhanced social tensions. Although some 40 families still represented a spread of "comfortable" wealth, another 60 or so occupied a more marginal place, while the rest of the population ranged down from "respectably poor" to "dirt poor." The bottom half of agricultural families did not control or even rent any property, as opposed to the 3 to 6 percent attributed to numbers elsewhere in the country. Many lived in poverty, black and white alike, although the numbers were heavily skewed against the blacks.

✦ ✦ ✦

Racial tensions worsened such developments. White rage focused on blacks who could vote when one could not. Irresponsible journalists fueled racist phobias. As one historian put it, Klan terror was unequal to "that of the other Western Hemisphere societies that abolished slavery in the nineteenth century. It is a measure of how far change had progressed that the reactions against Reconstruction proved so extreme."[71]

Whether they liked it or not, blacks and whites were integrated in a socio-economic structure that was badly skewed in the distribution of wealth, with a very large percentage of truly poor. Many whites had lost status and means. The previous chapter discussed the complexities of racial relations in general within the community. Perhaps more complex were those among the under-class. Seventeen white families lived among the black families who also rented or cropped. Most survived on a few hundred dollars income per year, one as little as $100. Another twenty whites were among the landless laborers. An additional three white widows had no apparent means of support. All these whites lived close by their black neighbors. Their reactions to such shared conditions were by no means simple. Many were hostile about competition with blacks and about how they threatened a fictitious racial superiority. Others, however, worked together, even occasionally mixing socially, with music as a common denominator. Finally, some of the above accounts of local crime reveal a shared participation in the under-class's disregard for law and property. Criminal teams, gangs and organizations were integrated. White outlaws found black safe houses.

✦ ✦ ✦

In addition to all these symptoms of a higher degree of disharmony in society than before the war, one unexpected area of relative harmony was between reinvigorated unionists and ardent secessionists, and between newly arrived Yankees and Southerners. As we have seen, even Confederate veterans coexisted with black Union veterans. Locally there were no indications that former anti-secessionists had been persecuted during the war, as elsewhere in West Tennessee. Afterward, few if any harbored desires for revenge.

As the war wore down, differences in attitude produced no apparent hostility. Union loyalists revealed themselves, took the hated loyalty oath, participated in the reestablishment of local government, or simply collaborated economically and socialized openly with the occupiers. Reverend Evans was probably the most prominent and influential among them. Benjamin Cash, a planter to the east of town, was another. In 1868, when William Hack sought restitution for confiscated property, these two men testified that Hack had been "at all times, an unconditional Union man . . . during the entire rebellion."[72] Josiah Deloach and Monroe Webb's appointments as postmasters did not hurt their local status and reputations. The ever popular Molitors, whose daughter had been courted by and married to a Yankee officer, had hosted the 1865 reunion picnic.

The successful integration of new Yankees into the community was a little more complex. Locals expressed positive sentiments for Smith Wilson, newly from Ohio, as an "esteemed" citizen, and "a very quiet and worthy man." In contrast, his murderer, W. T. Knowlton, a former United States military detective, seems less positively received, but probably because of his character. Young ladies might see Yankees as less suitable mates for their friends, but were apparently not hostile toward them. None of these Yankees bore the stigma of "carpet bagger." Only in family traditions that had morphed through successive generations does one find truly hostile, local references to carpet baggers who "swept into Germantown after the Civil War." All this reinforces the impression that, at the end of the war, all involved were most interested in a return to peace and normality. Even the short-lived experiences with radical Reconstruction seemed more focused on Brownlow enemies than local Republicans.

There were other positive contrasts to a totally stark picture of "reconstructed" Germantown. Despite all the disruptions and apprehensions about real and imagined threats and the turnover of population, the community retained some of its former cohesiveness. Despite indications in the Reverend Mills affair that citizens of means had become less sensitive to the needy poor before he embarrassed them, there was still some dedication to Christian charity. When yellow fever struck Memphis in 1873, townsfolk contributed to the relief fund.[73] One must be careful with generalizations about a collective loss of community spirit. Undoubtedly there were bigoted sectarians, but ecumenical sentiments also survived. Tightfisted businessmen mixed with the warm hearted and charitable still offering a helping hand. Unfortunately the reactionary white-supremacist world view infected everything.

Social and Cultural Reconstruction

The recovery of community social life also presents a mixed picture. Among the elite, their high life style and cosmopolitan contacts resumed quickly. Many young men returned to their college educations to pursue professional careers, but were also joined by an increasing number seeking greater opportunities than those offered by small scale agriculture. Young ladies still remained mostly confined to the level of finishing school colleges and academies. In Germantown at least their public activities expanded.

Even so, the world of the elite Victorian lady would change little before the next century, though it would be nudged by the suffragette movement, and more women would find activist roles in the prohibition movement. The issue of women's suffrage hit Tennessee and local politics first in 1869. In sharp contrast to its hostility to African-American suffrage, the *Appeal* came out in support when Senator Nelson submitted to the Assembly a bill to enfranchise women.

> In every part of the civilized world women are successfully advancing their claims to intellectual culture and freedom from the political restraints with which they have heretofore been surrounded. . . . They demand as reasoning human beings—certainly the superiors of the negroes who have been forced into political equality with the white race—they shall be hereafter admitted to vote, to say who shall govern States where their children are to be raised. . . .[74]

The paper acknowledge women's expansion into more public realms, but it seemed disappointed that the women of Tennessee and Memphis had yet to come out in support of Nelson's motion. In fact, Southern women's letters and diaries indicate a withdrawal of interest in politics, even a sense of its futility. The politics of Reconstruction were off putting and distasteful.[75] They allegedly even withdrew from political discussions around the dinner table. Female experiences during the war unleashed mixed responses. Some undoubtedly yearned for a complete return to pre-war gender roles and relations. Others realized some relations had fundamentally changed.[76]

If this argument about the withdrawal of women from interest in politics in the South applied to most Germantown women, one must wonder if there were exceptions. The early prominence of Memphis suffragettes in the national movement makes one doubt that the proximity of the city, and the constant social contacts of the town's more privileged women did not somehow infect some.[77] One can only hope for the appearance of some long-lost piece of correspondence providing a contrast to Emily Mills and her friends.

One must wonder how Germantown men in their gatherings responded to the prospect of women voting. Though legislators voted 12 to 9 in favor, it failed to pass with the two-thirds majority required to amend the constitution. If this vote is any indication, the idea must not have been too unpopular among men, especially since enfranchising their women could help the Democrats regain political control and end their own disenfranchisement.[78]

The diary of Martha Titus, a middle-aged spinster of a prominent Memphis family describes a conventional daily life in the town. She occasionally came out to Germantown to stay with relatives, while they came into Memphis to visit frequently. This enabled Germantowners to attend evening social and cultural events without the problems of hotel accommodations. The festivities and balls of the annual Mardi Gras was one such event. The ladies' daily life was much quieter, however. They spent their time visiting, attending church, some charity work, reading the latest novels, and corresponding with family and friends. Letter writing was almost a daily activity. Sewing, making their own dresses, could also be a social event affording an opportunity to show off their new sewing machines.[79] If only the finer homes possessed sewing machines before the war, over the next two decades they began to facilitate the labors of other women, who browsed the numerous ads in the papers and catalogs. By 1880, the much reduced town even supported two sewing machine agents.[80]

In contrast, the privileged ladies lead an ever more public life than before the war. As we shall see, Mrs. Miller's name would appear prominently alongside her husband's as managers of the girls' school, while the Baptist church's fund raiser was totally run and organized by the ladies, with names were proudly published in the papers. The respectable young ladies performed "on-stage" in a tableaux. Though still decorous and refined, they were public displays unlike their former performances limited to finishing school and home entertainments.

Their efforts to raise funds for the Baptist Church provide a vivid picture of social life. They advertised extensively a gala fund-raising event in the remaining Young Ladies Academy facilities at Forest Hill. As usual, a special train left Memphis at 6 PM. One dollar got a round trip, entertainment and supper. The entertainment lasted until 11 PM, consisting of "tableaux, singing, comic tragedy and burlesque.... The tableaux were very pretty indeed...." A tableau was elaborately costumed young ladies posing silently with backdrop. It depicted a well-known literary or historical moment or a famous painting. After the crowd applauded, the curtain would go down to prepare for the next tableau. "Afterward, a sumptuous supper ... besides all kinds of confectionary." The organizers were Miss Lou Parrish and Mr. Nasal Rhodes, while the meal was arranged by Mrs. Dr. Gray and Mrs. Vernon Rhodes. Other local young ladies featured in the papers were Kate Rhodes, Fannie Burnley, Susie Gray, plus Lizzie Perkins, Aggie Cash and Sallie Reasonover of Forest Hill.[81]

Of course, Germantown was a cultural satellite of Memphis for all who could afford train tickets. And as early as 1868, The New Memphis Theater sought to extend its audience, relying on the restored M&C service. The grand cost for the complete package of train and theater tickets for Germantown folks was $1.75 per head. Likewise, when the county's Old Folks at Home society held its annual meeting and ceremonies in 1870 at the Fair Grounds, the M&C provided a special train.[82]

By 1872, Memphis gave birth to its first Mardi-Gras. Special trains brought Germantown's celebrants in for the festivities, a spectacle open to all classes, in their proper places, of course. Like alcohol, however, such medieval revelry alarmed the more religiously restrained. Baptist and Methodist ministers exhorted against "worldly amusements," such as attending dancing parties, card playing, visiting theaters, circuses, county fairs; and "the chief of abominations—Mardi-gras." Some also condemned prize fighting, horse racing, and other "popular evils." As usual, the best insights into what people were actually doing are clerical condemnations.

The folk of the countryside were hardly dependent on the city for their social life. Suburban and rural entertainments were not necessarily of "common culture" either. The commencement or examination ceremonies, concerts and recitals of the Forest Hill ladies or Germantown academies provided the same level of sophistication as before. In 1872, both Germantown schools were holding "exhibitions," also as fund raisings for such as repairing the war-time damage done to the cemetery. There was also a debating society and other groups that sponsored events combining refined speeches and readings supplemented political orations, dances and barbecues. For one such in Center Hill, special trains carried passengers out from the city to Forest Hill and Germantown, from where locals joined them in wagon cavalcades down Center Hill Road. Social gatherings for dancing, music and food assembled at natural arbors and idyllic spots along the Wolf from Germantown to Collierville. The Nashoba Springs remained one such spot.[83]

The town's Masonic Lodge was reinstalled in 1873 with a grand affair drawing "five or six hundred of the best people of that well-to-do part of the county" and guests from the city. The ceremonies were held out at Brunswick Springs, followed by a barbecue and dancing until midnight.[84]

Black social life was equally rich. Much of it centered on the churches, with suppers, barbecues, fairs and excursions. The railroad facilitated such events. Local businessmen also organized secular picnics at places along the line, chartered five to ten cars, sold reduced-fare tickets, and "flooded the country with handbills." Of course, such affairs could be less than decorous. Fraternal organizations based in the city provided insurance against death and illness as well as social contacts.[85] Blacks were sometimes present at white events, sometimes segregated, sometimes not.

Unfortunately insight into Germantown's black social life escapes specific documentation except when the local papers found them occasions for denigrating humor. Typically, the *Public Ledger* reported events that revealed "black savagery." "Saturday night the negroes had a dance and a very festive frolic at Brae's station, above Forest Hill." Two "of the biggest, blackest bucks had a quarrel for the hand" of a woman. "To settle it they drew pistols, and did some indiscriminate badly aimed shooting. Only one nigger was shot. He got it in the back, and will most likely die."[86]

Undoubtedly, the Germantown area had its share of juke joints and "colored cafes." The event at Brae's Station may have been at one such. At first they occurred at private homes or any available building, or probably brush arbors. Enterprising blacks could begin a commercial occupation, and musicians and vocalists could earn income. Most importantly, they provided an exclusive and uninhibited African-American social and cultural environment that nurtured soul music. Unconventional "white boys" of any class could occasionally find accommodation, especially if they could make musical contributions.

The *Ledger* also liked stories that denigrated blacks for superstition. When Ralph Harrison, a marginal farmer, was bitten by a rabid dog, and on his death bed accused a neighbor of poisoning him, a "society" of Harrison's friends caned

p. 23 New Bethel Missionary Baptist Church.

the accused with hickory rods "in the most approved Ku-Klux style." The editors admitted that the whites would not normally notice such a black death, but they obviously found it irresistibly funny, especially to compare black behavior with the Klan. His severe wounds were also described with a wry chuckle.[87]

According to local and family traditions, the New Bethel Missionary Baptist Church traces its roots to a brush arbor that a white resident allegedly allowed slaves to have on her property to serve as a church in which they could also learn to read and write. This was Florida ne Pettit, Dr. Thompson's wife. The congregation reportedly had roots going back to 1843, which would be well before her time and before the Baptists sponsored separate black congregations. Florida had been a school teacher living with her parents until 1860 when she married and moved away until perhaps 1863 at the earliest. From all indications, they did not own the property in question until well after that date. At the earliest, it must have been a post-war accommodation.[88] In any case, this is when blacks especially sought to separate themselves from the authority of white ministers and needed land for gathering.[89] Getting such a story straight is characteristic of the problems created by oral traditions and fragmentary documentation. From here on, however, the story of local African American self-help is unquestionable.

From this brush arbor base, the self-reliant members of their community commenced efforts to build what would eventually become the New Bethel Baptist Missionary Church. In December 1869, black community leaders acquired from Eliza Cornelius two acres for two hundred dollars. The land was specifically designated for both a church and school. A sizable building was erected just north-east of town on a lane (present Southern) that ran north of the tracks. It was high-ceilinged and competently constructed with proper plank siding. Reverend Isaac Cotten became the first pastor, while the initial leadership for the new congregation were James Scott, Germantown carpenter, James Cornelius, a farmer living east of town in district ten, and Godfrey Goode, another farmer.[90]

Baptisms were held in an artificial pond on church grounds, rather than the conventional location on a natural flowing stream like the Wolf. Perhaps a peaceful and private place, free of possible harassment, was preferable.

The history of the African Methodist Episcopal Church during this period remains unwritten. Such congregations clearly existed.

❖ ❖ ❖

The story of the revival of education facilities in the post-war town casts further light on racial relations and white social divides. The Freedmen's Bureau had done nothing to help develop a black school in District Eleven. By the same token, area planters had not responded to the Bureau's plea to provide schooling.[91] In 1866, the Bureau had created Fisk University to train black teachers, turning out over 800 per year. There is no record of who did the earliest teaching at the little school. Malida Featherston, who worked as a cook, had somehow gotten her son Daniel schooling during the 1870s after which he was able to take over teaching. Possibly, his preparation occurred at the newly established LeMoyne Normal and Commercial School in Memphis.

Then in 1886, under the leadership of Phillip Cornelius, Ed Finch and Alf Hall, the church donated one of its acres to the Eleventh School District for the erection of a separate building for the Germantown School, providing the black community with its first official public elementary school. The initiatives of the black community exceeded local white efforts. They had "encouraged" the county to build a proper black public school by providing the land. In 1897, the church would acquire over fourteen acres from Mrs. Florida Thompson and expand their school buildings, eventually adding a public junior high and finally a high school. To distinguish it from the white Germantown School, it was renamed the Nashoba School.[92]

The recovery of local education for whites reflects the gap that had developed between the relatively privileged and others. White educational institutions recovered at varied rates—private schools coming first. At the higher levels that had brought the town cultural prominence, the names of two schools appear in newspaper advertisements. The "Germantown Male and Female English & Classical School," with boarders, advertised intentions to "reopen" in January 1866, with A. N. Plunkett as Principal. Also a "Shelby Male High School" was soon back in operation, apparently a continuation of the Shelby Military and Classical Institute, often referred to as Mr. Evans' School. The locations of both schools are unclear as are their duration. The "High School" (perhaps the Classical School?) had a sizable faculty consisting of young adults and perhaps some widows who had recently arrived to take the positions. As before, they were a transient population.[93] Perhaps the two schools had become consolidated by 1880.

The Young Ladies' Collegiate Institute of Forest Hill had been quick to get itself back in operation, announcing its first culminating "exercises" on January 2, 1866. Its facilities had survived unscathed. Reverend H. Miller was still Proprietor, while Mrs. C. F. W. Miller, his wife, had risen to the status and title of Principal.[94]

Unfortunately, surviving the conflagrations of the war provided the school with no insurance against calamity. On December 19, 1867, fire struck destroying the main building.[95] The school could not reopen. By the next year, as we have seen, developers had purchased the property with an eye toward creating a suburban resort and seasonal residence complex. Mr. Ammon, who bought the land for speculation allegedly wanted to have the school reopened "as soon as the necessary arrangements can be perfected." Unfortunately, his previously described promotional efforts had led to naught, and he did not demonstrate any true dedication to the institute. He tried to sell the desks and forms to cover his losses. Nothing came of other plans to restore the ladies institute.[96]

Until 1873, the elementary schooling for whites was purely private, the old common schools system being totally defunct. The Webb school house had been saved by the daughter's diligence. It is not clear whether Mary still taught after war, for she never listed herself as employed as a teacher in any of the censuses. Perhaps that was simply for reasons of social convention. Eventually, the Webb School relocated elsewhere.

Meanwhile, Tennessee had sought to revise its public school system for both "races" in 1867. The system of school districts based on the civil districts was to resume with local school boards as before. Now enumeration of both white and "colored youth" between the ages of six and twenty would determine relative funding. Each civil district's Board of Education was responsible for maintaining both elementary and high schools, employing teachers, building, and maintaining schoolhouses. They were required to maintain district schools of appropriate grades for at least every fifty students. There had to be at least one free common school each year for a period of five months of twenty school days per month. If state funds were insufficient, the Board was to submit a proposed tax to the district for approval. Teachers had to be examined and have certificates of qualification, while the Boards determined the studies to be taught.[97] Germantown's district was not only slow responding, but it also made no initial compliance.

The 1870 census indicates that there were 230 white and 420 blacks in district eleven between the ages of six and twenty. So there should have been at least four to five white and eight colored common schools or classrooms. That census, however, makes it clear that a large number of young people of both ethnicities were working in the fields. Although their numbers generated state funding, their unavailability for education greatly reduced the pressures on the district to comply. So did the white preference for private schools. This reticence on the part of local district authorities to establish public schooling, even for whites, is yet another example to the post-war decline in a sense of community responsibility for the needier elements.

Clearly the district had not gotten around to complying with the 1867 education act, reestablishing any common schools. In 1870, outside town nestled among the tenant farmers and land owners, resided Ms. Elizabeth Rosco, a thirty-three year-old widow and her 12 year-old daughter. She, a white woman, was listed as school teacher, but she was only one of many men and women who would cycle through the area, setting up short-lived private school operations Also according to town tradition, a "Miss Thompson" taught a more permanent school in the east wing of her home at present 7642 Poplar Pike.[98] This was Florida Thompson, who had bought the old Cornelius house and the same who had helped the black community. Unfortunately, when Miss Thompson's school opened is not a matter of record. But, it too was a private school referred to commonly as the "Thompson Place." Over the decade of the 1870s, at least two men and ten women would add to the roster of teachers. Two were the spinster daughters of ministers.[99] The appearance of some of them finally heralded the arrival of the first new public school for whites.

There was certainly a crying need for public education, among both blacks and whites. In addition to playing catch-up for the older white children, deprived during most of the war and immediately after, it was needed to serve the new generation of "scholars" that both black and white families were producing. In the 1870 census for the entire district, 25 white children over age 10 were illiterate or partially so, while 787 blacks were so classed. Disruption by the war was the most common cause for young white people to be illiterate, yet many families had worked to homeschool or otherwise educate their children under wartime conditions.[100] The high rate of illiteracy among blacks was to be expected, but a smattering of teenagers and young adults who had acquired literacy speaks to individual determination to overcome the lack of public education since emancipation.[101] When in 1870 the Legislature had ordered a scholastic census, only six districts complied, but neither the 10th nor 11th. In January 1871, the County Court chided the district commissioners for failing to make their annual report, noting that twelve still had no commissioners at all. Without the enumeration, the county could not get the funds allocated for public education. The commissioners then reported that they were unable to carry out the education laws, citing the general apathy of parents and guardians and community failure to provide facilities. Finally the 11th Civil District elected its commissioners in March. The district was just getting around to organizing itself.[102] By October, the Court charged the commissioners with failure to comply with the state laws, having appointed no County Board of Education to certify teachers.[103]

Finally, in 1873, Governor John C. Brown signed a bill that provided for a statewide system of public schools, and the legislature levied taxes to pay for new schools and teachers' salaries.[104] As before, there was now enough motivation for the community to pursue these funds for public education.

On December 9, 1873, Florida Pettit Thompson proudly wrote, "we now have a genuine free school."[105] Its first location is not a matter of record. Dr. Martin, Chairman, was advertising for "a regular graduate to take charge of the

Germanton High School." In 1878 still without a dedicated building, the town designated the Masonic Hall as the site of the free common school for whites, soon to be taught by the Baptist minister, Lipsey, and Reverend A. G. Parrott's twenty-nine year-old daughter.[106] One young student remembers that there were many larger boys, "some were practically grown men." The community was playing catch-up for its neglect. Nevertheless, the new school provided more than the old basic 3Rs. There was algebra, geometry and even Latin and Greek for advanced students with college and professions in mind. The county Board of School Directors provided a list of approved books with regulated prices. At Germantown, the merchant William Miller was the agent for official book sales.[107]

Between the opening of the school in 1873 and the arrival of the Lipseys, the appearance of a unique woman as teacher brought a short-lived potential to the town for something great. Miss Sarah (Sallie) Eola Reneau had been campaigning for higher education for women in Mississippi for over twenty years. An 1854 graduate from the Holly Springs Female Academy, in 1856 she had petitioned Governor John McRae for the creation of a State Female College. Then and again after the war, she sought and got state legislative approval to fund such schools, but they were never funded. After 1873, she accepted defeat, and returned to Tennessee—eventually to Germantown.[108]

Reneau was truly an independently minded woman with ideas that defied conventions. She was born in Somerville, TN in 1836, daughter of General Nathan S. Reneau, veteran of the Mexican War. More a capitalist than a planter, he was first involved in railroads and then mining interests in Mexico. He spent much time in Washington to further his interests. Sallie had grown up as much more than a conventional Southern belle. If she was anything near a Northern feminist in her makeup, she was clever enough to camouflage her objectives when dealing with Mississippi politicians. In her first petition, she promised that her school would not be "teaching young women to demand the rights of men nor to invade the phase of men," rather to rely on the appropriate men to protect their interests.[109] She appealed to the legislators' regional pride and prejudices by noting, if the state produced properly educated women teachers, it would "not be necessary to send to *New England* for a tutoress for a Southern institution or private family."

During the war, she displayed much more radical ideas. She proposed to the governor the creation of something like a Women's' Auxiliary Corps, to be uniformed and paid equally to the male volunteers. Although they would also tend to the sewing and knitting needs of the men, more shockingly they would perform as true nurses. She would have been America's Florence Nightingale. Of course, she proposed that an elderly physician or surgeon be assigned to provide proper accompaniment, but the ladies would also be armed with pistols to protect themselves. One can only imagine the reactions of the politicians who provided the inevitable rejection.[110]

In need of some meaningful role in education, she replied to Dr. Martin's advertisement for a graduate to take charge of the new public high school. In 1876, she was serving as a school teacher, but she is best known for her role as regular correspondent to the *Appeal* reporting regularly on the town's plight during the Yellow Fever epidemic of 1878. A reading of those reports do reveal a dedicated and loving teacher. Like so many other things, her death in the plague terminated what might have become the creation of educational institutions in the town to reestablish its former place as a cultural center.

As we shall see, she did subscribed sternly to Christian convictions and conventions. Sallie certainly was a rare progressive women in Germantown, representing a Southern brand of feminism. Indeed local women had been well ahead of conventions in their early pursuit of roles in the teaching profession, and early involvement in the temperance movement. But she had gone much farther in playing a public and political role prior to the war, and she had assumed the problematic social status of spinster to be free of dominance by a man. Undoubtedly most of the town's spinsters were not so by choice. Yet Miss Reneau offered a unique role model for a brief period.

Real progress in public education would not begin until 1882. By 1886, for Germantown students who could not afford to attend better schools in Memphis, the county public school system was their only recourse with the apparent exception of one private grade school. Clearly by the 1880s, the post-yellow-fever era had brought some sense of educational responsibility to the area.

CONCLUSION

In 1860, Germantown and its extended community were in many ways typical of southern agrarian communities. In some ways, however, it differed. The town had become something of a cultural gem. Its elite and middle class families had full access to the cultural and social life of Memphis. They also reached well beyond that horizon. But also, the entire population benefited from opportunities generated by their town's churches, fraternal orders, communal celebrations, and the rallies that combined political involvement with festive social mixing. Every home, even some of the poorer, constituted the center of a network of family and friends that reached well beyond the local community. The appeal of the local watering holes made the town's inns and Germantown-area homes attractive to visitors from far afield. Although the presence of private academies and collegiate institutions were not unique to such communities, Germantown's stood out, hosting regular cultural events that attracted attendance from as far as Memphis, and attracted numerous would-be educational entrepreneurs and book vendors to such an environment. For all classes, the level of education exceeded that normally associated with the South. Literacy was high. There were sectarian prejudices, but nothing that generated real tensions. There were the usual problems of excessive alcohol consumption, yet the level of crime and violence seems limited to the petty pilfering that never reached the newspapers, with two exceptions over two decades. The town was vibrant but peaceful. On the one hand, economically it was a typical center for an extensive agricultural community, but on the other it had nascent industrial development.

The area did not conform to the model of a community ruled by a plantation aristocracy, locked in a reactionary resistance to modernizing processes. Although Shelby County was part of the plantation South, Germantown clearly had more in common with the modernizing Border States, especially because of proximity to Memphis. Yet its citizens certainty subscribed to the conventional attitudes and values identified with the southern culture, and would defend them against the perceived, corrosive threats at work in the North. But, this conservative reaction to the less pleasant aspects of modernization was hardly sufficient to stifle progress

One such corrosive threat was certainly the abolitionists. Despite the ever-present brutality of slavery, local slave owners vacillated along a spectrum ranging from romantic denials of reality, through guilt-driven rationalizations, to an unquestioning acceptance of what seemed to be the natural and proper order of things. Some hoped for a day when slavery would dissolve somehow, but none were willing to cut the Gordian knot.

Theirs was not a unique historical conundrum. Historical societies have regularly been unable to correct their dysfunctional or inhumane socioeconomic or political institutions. As long as nation-wide racial phobias prevailed, Southerners could dismiss contemptuously "northern hypocrisy" and calls for abolition, the consequences of which Northerners would not have to suffer, because they were not threatened by a majority population of "savage blacks." Northern commerce, industry and finance were still benefiting from the products of slavery.

Likewise, slave owners made hardly any effort to devise an effective evolutionary end to the problem and to find a compromise with the abolitionist strategy. Immediate economic needs and interests were simply too powerful. The combination of "economic realities" and a veritably national, all-pervasive racist "consensus reality" prevailed.

Among the romantics were those who believed most owners truly cared for their slaves, who were basically happy with their lot and loyal to their masters and mistresses. They blithely built their own separate white world, supported heavily by black labor. With the little free time left them, the blacks developed a separate world of their own—built family lives and evolved an African-American cultural life. Although local slavery was comparatively less harsh than in the coastal and Deep South, the runaway rate around Germantown was significant. Then when the opportunity for slaves to "abandon" their owners came with the war, owners reacted with anger and a sense of betrayal. Until then, positive emotions about one's own slaves stood in stark juxtaposition to a general fear of black savagery. It took only one slave-revolt scare to bring out all the usual responses.

Another perceived threat was to the typically southern white family values and gender roles. Those roles were seen as biologically determined and properly protective of women and children. In self-justification, they focused on the "enslavement" of women and child laborers in the industrializing North, totally undermining all family values. None of this led locals to shun inventiveness and the industrial establishments that grew from it, however. Yet, because of slavery, the only place for the employment of poorer white women and children remained in occupations directly supportive of household economies. Only in the area of teaching, were Germantown women already more heavily involved than in most of the South.

Another purported threat to traditional family values was feminist ideas already infecting northeastern bourgeois family life. One feared that if women stepped outside their natural roles, they would not only disrupt the order but become vulnerable to exploitation. Nevertheless, Germantown area women were not as excluded from public involvements as were their sisters of the low country and Deep South. Easy and close social contact with Memphis introduced many "suburban" Germantown women to modernizing trends. At the same time, some of the less appealing aspects that they encountered in the city undoubtedly reinforced their determination to preserve traditional family values. However, in the allowed environment provided by their churches, they became involved in organized groups working on charitable and moral causes such as the temperance movement. Although they may not have been involved yet in leadership, the organized female activity was so familiar that when war erupted, it took little encouragement from the city's papers for them to take the next step and enter the public arena without male guidance. That became a training school for increased post-war visibility.

Whether unique in the South or not, area fathers were beginning to employ inheritance restrictions that would protect their daughter's property from imprudent husbands. That provided them with some financial security. Already, upon a husband's death, wives were legally entitled to one-third of his property. Husbands often allowed their wives to exercise independent financial actions. Although we have no measure of how common these erosions of traditional and legal paternalistic authority might have been around Germantown, there is evidence of their presence.

◆ ◆ ◆

If the plantation aristocracy ruled society elsewhere in the South, generating class hostilities, that was far too simple a picture of relations in and around

Germantown. The smooth continuity from wealthiest planter down through a majority middle to the poorer yet self-sufficient farmer contained no gaps that separated an elite from "the masses." Many young laborers had every expectation of moving up. Many were already sons of a property owning majority that had far more interests in common than not. Most others aspired to joining that majority. Many of those without significant means got helping hands from above. More often than not, that help did not appear as demeaning charity. The older citizens remembered the frontier environment, while most of the younger still worked hard to earn their modest comforts. Certainly any who had to compete against slave labor resented the system and those who benefited from it. Yet the relatively few "malcontents" hardly constituted a social problem, for they lay below the radar. Although hardly an egalitarian community that could weather severe economic crisis, it was far more meritocracy than aristocracy.

The same applies to the idea that the planters controlled politics. The early Whig planters like the Kimbroughs and Dukes lost whatever control they might have had over county and state politics to the allegedly broader based Democrats, so they changed allegiances. Party differences were not drawn along any clear class lines. The frequent differences in voting patterns between Collierville and Germantown's districts, despite identical socioeconomic populations, belie such arguments. As elsewhere, planters rarely ran for political office, leaving that to professionals, businessmen and ambitious slaveholding yeomen farmers. Although the planters undoubtedly had the ears of those office holders, they did not need to "control or manipulate" them. In most cases, shared interests prevailed.

As almost all students of the Old South have observed, slavery provided the tie that bound, even for those who did not share its alleged benefits. It had created a widely shared racist "consensus reality" or paradigm. Emancipation threatened far more than economic loss and the end of a more privileged life for the owners. If the slaves were ever freed, they would have to return to Africa, for they were too savage to share or even coexist in the white American society. Any equality in citizenship was out of the question. Indeed, such ideas were beyond the pale for almost all Americans, even most abolitionists, who envisioned a return to Africa as the final solution. Since such an exodus was unlikely, the poor farmer and laborer saw an even greater threat. In 1863, one West Tennessee diarist mournfully looked forward to the state of affairs when free blacks in large numbers would not only bring everyone's' wages down, but would compete with whites for jobs: "In this land a poor white man would have no chance to live. They are not willing to put themselves on an equality with the negro as a slave. Where can be the difference?"[1]

As the Civil War erupted around them, the people of Germantown abandoned their original good judgment in opposing secession, swept up by the collective jubilation of a newly proclaimed crusade against invaders bent on oppression. If they had been manipulated into secession, it was made possible by their harmonious sense of community. Once the radical course of war had become the accepted necessity, to deviate from it would have been an act of incivility, a cowardly retreat from communal responsibility, even heresy.

The evil institution of slavery ultimately demanded its own destruction. The price for the sins of the fathers would be inflicted upon all succeeding generations, North and South, black and white. The furor of a civil war, not just between North and South, but among Southners, created an uncompromising residue after the final defeat. Fearfully the Radical minority, who would reconstruct a new order, overplayed their hand, poisoned the well and refused compromise. Ultimately the majority responded and imposed a reactionary order as northern interference tired of the fight for abstract principals it did not fully embrace for itself. Whites had the political and economic power to push the pendulum back against what they feared was a biologically inappropriate human equality. Even so, the restoration of white hegemony required compromises with the new realities that emancipation and Reconstruction had created. It left cracks in the socioeconomic structure in which blacks could exist, and even find opportunities. Their perseverance, like the pressure of ice in the cracks of a granite face, would eventually lead to the current, relatively improved state of racial relations from which more progress seems hopeful, although painfully slow.

✦ ✦ ✦

Detailed studies of the writings left by southern white women present a complex and contradictory picture of the effects of the war and Reconstruction on them and their attitudes about their proper place in the world.[2] They were as determined as ever to preserve proper family and racial relationships. They would gratefully accept a restoration of security and order. Yet at the same time, they became acutely aware of the inability of their men always to provide the shelter, protection and sustenance once expected. Their experience with forced self-reliance had brought a contradictory mix of an awareness of their abilities with their inability to go it alone. Male management could not be left free of female input, yet it could not be too overtly challenged without rending the proper order. When the *Appeal* seemed disappointed that local ladies had not embraced the idea of suffrage, they failed to perceive female disillusionment with all current political possibilities. If political activity lay beyond their present conceptions of proper action, organizing for moral causes like temperance did not. Women had learned to organize themselves effectively and to enter the public forum.[3] There is no more obvious transition in the surviving records than this regarding Germantown area women.

If gender relations evolved more subtly, the war had a most marked impact on the area's socioeconomic structure. The resources for recovery were limited. Most of the town's middle-class economic base had been destroyed, requiring supplementation by newcomers with resources. Wealthy newcomers greatly exaggerated the former concentration of wealth at the top. Less well-heeled newcomers, however, were also looking for a place to start businesses and professions with the little they had. The former planters were also supplemented by newcomers with resources, while the yeoman class was almost totally decimated. There were fewer newcomers at that level. A much larger proportion of small farmers with only some means to pay rent now stood between the landowners and truly landless farmers. The middle had shrunk and the poor had become the vast majority. Most of all, such social-economic relations were complicated by inclusion of the new presence of the large, free black population. They increased greatly in numbers the farther down the economic scale one looked.

Such changes compounded war experiences that had seriously undermined the relatively peaceful harmony of the Germantown community. Whatever sectarianism had existed before soon erupted in conflict. How seriously it affected interpersonal relations is unclear, but it certainly generated interest and paralleled expressions of new social resentments. Although there were still some examples of Christian charity, people had become more focused on the needs of their families than those of the community. Charity began at home. Alcoholism, depression and suicide became more visible phenomena. Worse, lawlessness, robbery and murder now supplemented the also more frequent honor-related violence and killings. Additionally, racially directed terrorism was the order of the day, if economic pressures failed to prove sufficient to control the blacks. The ravages of war left sores that would take a long time to heal—scars that would continue to throb down to today.

The already complex relationship that had existed between blacks and whites underwent severe stress from the experiences of both groups during the war and Reconstruction. Clearly fears and animosities grew. For whites, the Radical's overturning of racial relations was more embittering because it appeared to be directed at punishing and destroying the South. It seemed less a product of well-intentioned reforms than of the pursuit of nefarious vested interests. It seemed as if Radicals had not just enfranchised black men, but had incited them with promises of reward and even revenge. Few on any side in this story seriously intended for the blacks to get any proper reimbursement for their years of slave labor. Economic justice was out of the question. Radical legislation would only go beyond granting the right of freedom to the point of enfranchisement. The political spectrum of the general white population ranged from conservative to unregenerate Rebel, resentful of any change in racial relations, unwilling to concede the franchise. Almost all, driven by old fears, felt the need to keep the blacks "in their place." Such sentiments did not divide the white classes.

Blacks had gained little more than emancipation. The American ideal of "a society of justice for all" would have to continue its head-on battle against deeply rooted social and cultural conventions which the decade of the 1860s had entrenched further. Nevertheless in communities like Germantown, blacks and whites inevitably lived and worked in close proximity. Familiarity can breed the opposite of contempt. While negative stereotypes clouded the minds of both blacks and whites, abstractions often crumbled wherever real individuals encountered each other. Neither property, influence nor respect was entirely denied the blacks. Even the constrained opportunities truly benefited some, both within their own economic subset and in dealings with fair whites. Most would persevere and hope for better. Although an underclass, most blacks were not excluded from all the benefits of the society in which they had to function. Although usually blamed on the blacks, the increased levels of crime were not simply race related. No greater percentage of the blacks than of the white population chose to function outside the law where the risks of criminal activity were no more costly than those of ordinary life. In criminal ventures, disadvantaged blacks and whites could often find themselves collaborating.

The African-American subculture generated its inevitable counter-racism and maintained a conflicted, initial black preference for segregated schools, which they themselves built. Even if allowed to compete in a white-run educational system, they would have usually "failed." They had to struggle to overcome centuries of denied education with the illiteracy and other problems that entailed. They had to build from scratch a qualified teaching profession with the limited resources of the new black universities. They had to be taught by their own to have a fair chance.

Likewise, they expanded their own church congregations and denominations to provide strong spiritual and social systems of self-support. Unable to rely on a sufficient number of "fair" white business and professional men, they created their own business and professional community in the city that could reach out to the country and towns. Out there, they evolved their own professional class of teachers, and clergy and their own "mechanics" to serve them locally, who in turn could reach back for support to the even stronger black establishment in Memphis. Most of all, they generated a rich and vibrant African-American culture, especially music, that became a major conduit for the future integration of American society.

Young, sometimes other-minded whites intruded into this black world to share in the exuberant music. Black nannies continued to have their impact on young white minds—sometimes a lasting impact. Black and white children played together, often in defiance of both sets of parents. Although adolescence inevitably drove wedges between them, continued familiarity eroded the prejudices that drove those wedges. More cracks worked away at the granite face of racism.

✦ ✦ ✦

Everywhere in the South, the war had both divisive and cohesive effects on the population, but the latter effects were unique. If the scars of a fratricidal war fought at your door and the destruction of so much of your means had not been enough reason, the humiliation of Reconstruction with its allegations of treason guaranteed that Southerners would never forget "the War." Anyone who feels his acts were legitimate or justified, feels unjustly punished, even abused, when he suffers from the consequences of those acts. One's responsibility for the consequences of his acts fades in comparison to the responsibility of others for such consequences. Already in 1869, letters to the editor in the newspapers reflected the range of feelings among whites. All expressed a sense of injustice. The Confederate soldiers who had expected to return home to peace and the lawful pursuit of their lives saw themselves as in the hands of a vengeful and rapacious faction, who controlled the state, flaunted the Federal and state constitutions, oppressed the defeated, abused authority and took advantage of every opportunity for corruption. Of course, these "victims" failed to see any reason for enforced changes.

Indeed even well-intentioned Radicals inevitably obstructed a reconciliation of the unionist and secessionist factions of society. The harsh punishment they imposed was for what they saw as "treason," but such a charge simply defied every other southerner's sense of what had happened. Worse, as an insecure minority, the Radicals resorted to flagrant abuses of power to stay in control. The economic corruption of the "scalawags and carpetbaggers" defied control, and had little to do with any Radical agenda. Both the perceived harshness of Radical Reconstruction policies and the overturning of what was seen almost unanimously as "proper racial relationships" produced determined and bitter reactionaries.

No matter how many soldiers had come home resigned to defeat and determined to get on peacefully in the new order, no matter how many civilians felt the same, Reconstruction soured such hopes. The loss and damage of property and other economic obstacles to recovery were bad enough. They could not understand being treated as traitors, losing their franchise and any voice in local, state and national politics. They could not stomach being lorded over by those they had considered traitors and by outsiders who had all the rights they had lost. Perhaps worst of all, the former slaves now purportedly had all those rights. The need to "set things right" prevailed.

As a backlash, the smoldering old "Southern patriotism" flared up with a vengeance. If the disillusionments of the war and defeat had originally cooled the ardor of former secessionists and intensified the sentiments of old pro-unionists, the Reconstruction experience undid most of that and brought them back together. Even ardent unionists who had joined the Federal army, fought against secession, and had been post-war Republicans became as embittered as the Confederate hard-liner.[4] Even more so did the former unionist who had reluctantly supported secession. Likewise the secessionist, war-time defector from the cause. All were welded together by a common reaction. As early as 1866, the commander of the garrison at Memphis, Major General

George Stoneman, noted that locals had become "less loyal than they had been six months before."[5]

The "injustices of Reconstruction" became as powerful a myth as the Lost Cause. In Tennessee, Reconstruction only lasted four to five years, was never fully effective, and quickly gave way to something that too closely resembled the old order of things.

Behind this powerful sense of injustice lurked the psychological scars, not just of defeat, but of the horrors of combat and of living with the threats to unprotected loved ones about which one could do nothing. The guerrilla war theater had intensified all that. On top of all the hardships, southern women, equally scarred, had to resume old relationships with a manhood that was greatly damaged. Some students of southern women attribute the growth of the Lost Cause movement to local women's organizations that memorialized the fallen, lionized the military leadership and the heroic and honorable service of every Confederate soldier. They supported a cultural and literary movement to write history as it needed to be seen for the self-respect of a defeated people.[6]

Nostalgia over the "Lost Cause" grew as Southerners memorialized their dead. Soon, only heroes had served—there had been no disillusioned, deserters or slackers. There had been no unwilling draftees. Memories of the bitter civil war among themselves that pitted Southerners against each other evaporated. The ghosts of the many, black and white, who had fought for the Union were entombed in the ubiquitous statues to the Confederate soldier in every community. Eventually all who had vacillated remembered only their moments of support. Any who had deserted remembered and glorified only their service. Veterans remembered their hardships but not their loss of morale. The real combat veterans eschewed the popular romanticizing of the war, but even most of them cherished the camaraderie of the experience. The cultural and literary movement actually enabled the losers to write history for a change. Such was the Southern cultural unity that was reemerging before the 1870s. All were bonded by it. Unregenerate Southern patriotism helped to plaster over some cracks and provided some crutches for the more severely scarred. It provided a badly needed sense of common identity for a more badly divided society. On the one hand, it also preserved, even intensified, the old consensus reality about proper racial relations that had to be maintained, but on the other, that Southern common identity was not sufficient to plaster over newly felt social inequalities.

For Germantown in particular, these generalizations about a cohesive Southern culture have to coexist with symptoms of discord. The extensive breakdown of law and order, increased violence and abuse, especially within families, alcoholism and suicide were accompanied by other symptoms of social as well as racial tensions, even open sectarian conflict. Even more striking was an apparent inability or unwillingness of the community to acknowledge, much less try to deal with its problems. The former sense of communal harmony and social responsibility seems to have been badly eroded.

When post-war Germantown was struck by a new disaster in 1878, an unusually open infighting would focus entirely on internal differences that coexisted with unity in support of the Lost Cause. Our conclusions about Germantown's Civil War era experiences require a special postscript. A severe shock may have been required for the white community to share fully in a "plastering over" of social divisiveness.

POSTSCRIPT

YELLOW JACK—WHAT DOESN'T KILL YOU...

The town was clearly on the road to economic recovery as the decade of the 70s wound down. Even its declining advantage in the area's commercial transportation network was not sufficient to dampen other developments. Recovery evaporated, however, in 1878. The fatal blow came with the great Yellow Fever Epidemic, the worst in American history—the first one to reach Germantown. Because it totally destroyed the town's image as a healthy retreat/resort, it terminated the urban flight that was fueling the town's recovery. Conventionally this crisis is seen as a veritable death knell for the recovery of the town.

Its impact on the community was indeed severe, both immediate and long-term. It also exaggerated the prevalent local social tensions and hostilities, yet it may have subsequently refocused the community on the need to solve its problems. It brought out the worst and the best in people, perhaps to the town's long term advantage. In regard to the sense of community spirit and social responsibility, it may have saved the town.

✦ ✦ ✦

Although Memphians knew their filthy city was dangerous, they had done nothing significant to address the problems.[1] Every summer they feared the return of yellow fever, and warmer El Nino years had been encouraging the responsible mosquito population that immigrated often into New Orleans and then up river. The disease had struck Memphis hard in 1867 and especially again in 1873. This time however, the disease strain was more virulent than ever before with a three-time greater mortality rate.[2] As the season of 1878 approached, Memphis papers expressed a mix of apprehension and complacency. For those

ILL. 19. Quarantine Stop on the Railroad. Such a stop at Germantown for travelers coming into Memphis on the M&C at the beginning of the epidemic. Germantown people proclaimed that they did not subject later refugees from Memphis to the same treatment.

who could afford it, the response remained family retreats to resorts like Germantown, encouraged by the M&C with reduced fares.[3]

In July, word came that the disease was in New Orleans and bound to come up river. That prompted the Memphis Board of Health to impose a quarantine. They established posts on President's Island south of the city for river traffic, at Whitehaven Station south on the Mississippi and Tennessee RR, and, for some reason, at Germantown on the M&C. There, the metropolitan police with shotguns stopped anyone coming to Memphis with symptoms of fever, plus all shipments suspected of carrying the disease. On the M&C, an agent went out as far as Grand Junction to warn passengers. Germantown might be their last stop. Cargo could be stopped at Germantown also.[4] At this time, the embargo was on traffic entering the city, and no Memphians seemed concerned about how Germantown could accommodated a possible quarantined population of infected transients. That exact problem never materialized.

Despite such efforts, numerous cases had developed in Memphis by late July, and it was officially recognized on August 13. By August 15, the papers reported that every seat on trains out of the city were booked days in advance. Panic ensued; 25,000 fled. The desperate clogged outbound roads. Everyone sought safety. The myth of the healthier climate of the ridge running east drew many out along the M&C and the State Line Road toward Germantown and Collierville. Refugee camps were established along the rail lines within ten miles of the city. Further out, refugees sought shelter in accommodations in the country—roon-and-board, refuge with friends and family if they had them, otherwise they erected temporary shelters. This time, however, the devastation followed them.[5] Rail lines like the M&C and its links transported the little mosquito along with its hosts to every town on the way to Chattanooga and Atlanta.

Reverend Evan's day-book tells of the growing apprehension. By mid-September, it was rampant in Germantown and Collierville, with people dying daily. Before it was over, 81 people in Germantown fell ill. Of them, 45 would die.[6] Many others would flee, some permanently.

Thanks to the previously mentioned Miss Sallie Enola Reneau, who began forwarding regular reports to the *Appeal* beginning September 16, we have a blow-by-blow description. The school teacher valiantly nursed the sick until she too succumbed.

She began, "Our town is in unusual distress—eight (*sic*; seven) deaths within ten days past, and there are now twelve to fifteen cases of sickness of the same kind." She seemed reluctant to name the disease, for indeed one or more deaths were among people already suffering from other ailments, and "lack of sufficient nursing" also contributed. On the fifth, "Professor R. B. Simmons, of the public school, died of congestive chill, or yellow-fever—reports conflict." . . . "On the fifteenth Mr. Moore, a Memphis refugee . . . died of yellow-fever, as reported."[7]

> It matters not about the name of the disease, since the fatality, unprecedented in this usually healthful place, has become alarming to all who are not sustained by strong powers and unwavering faith. On the thirteenth "the storm" of excitement began to blow, and on the fifteenth (*sic*; fourteenth) it burst in . . . a general stampede of . . . many citizens. Our railway and express agent . . . left us in haste. Our indefatigable postmaster and druggist . . . Mr. Wm. E. Miller . . . remains faithful to his many duties . . . ; nothing but death or severe sickness will drive him from his post.

Reluctance to name the beast was not just an act of denial, for Yellow Fever was hard to diagnose, at least in its early stages. The high fever, head and body aches were typical of many ailments. The telltale yellow skin and eyes and the bloody black vomit only appear in the terminal last days.

The rest of her report is especially valuable for its insights into the sentiments and divisions that emerged quickly in the town.

> Among those who have thus far been faithful to the humane and Christian work of administering to the sick and burying dead, (thirteen individuals or families) are prominent. There are also several colored men, whose timely help in burying the dead is worthy of remembrance. All who are brave and faithful during an epidemic and panic deserve special mention, for the temptation to fly or hide from danger and duty is surely great, and still greater and more demoralizing is the example of the many whose animal instinct of self-preservation is more than heathenish . . . ! An epidemic, like war, develops the latent strength and weakness . . . of human nature, while it proves . . . that a coward cannot be a christian or a soldier. . . . Germantown has at no time taken part in the wicked farce of quarantine; all refugees and citizens, have been, and are yet, free to come and go at will.

In another letter on September 18, she reported:

> The 14th of September, 1878, a day long to be remembered by the few who were left here to bury the dead, while the panic-stricken many were flying for personal safety, as if there is safety save in God. . . . I was present at three burials during the day, the greatest number of internments I ever witnessed in a single day. . . . So few are the well ones left here to nurse the sick and bury the dead . . . no bells are tolled, when one is to be buried. When we see a light wagon and two or three persons passing slowly through the street we instinctively recognize the wagon as hearse. . . . If one desire to join that small procession we can do so, as it passes the house. (On one such occasion) in the peaceful evening twilight, Mr. Evans offered a most feeling prayer. . . . The village church yard, in the rear of the Methodist Church . . . has not the awfully gloomy appearance of the average country grave-yard.[8]

On the twentieth, she reported extensively on the selfless nursing care being provided by family and community members, many of them women, some losing their lives as a result.[9] The individual's constitution was obviously more relevant to survival than any known treatment. Traditional ministrations could be harmful. Some were properly distrustful of the doctors. In addition to bleeding, the severe purgatives that doctors usually favored actually contained poisons like lead and arsenic, totally debilitating their patients.[10]

By that same date, however, Miss. Renaeu's published opinions provoked a local response that provides stark insight into the dispositions of town folk. A new, anonymous correspondent calling himself Maxey began offering some strongly contrary but colorful observations. First he defended his friend, the railway and express agent whom Miss Reneau had castigated for abandoning his post. Most of all Maxie took exception with her claims that it was only the true Christian souls who stayed to face death and administer care. "There has been no Christian or any one who makes any pretensions to religion, waiting and nursing upon the sick, with the exception of our most notable minister, Bro. R. R. Evans.... Those who sit up in the amen corner and sing the loudest ... were the first to leave, and that before the 'morning train.'"[11] He then took angry shots at some she had praised. Thus began, amidst the horror and stress, an exchange of back biting and finger pointing, exposing to the world the town's decayed spirit of community and social harmony.

Maxie provoked Ms. Reneau to counterattack. In a letter of September 23, she exposed Maxie as DeWitt Rhodes, accusing him of shamefully bringing improper attention to the suffering. She also dropped a few indirect shots at his character. Then she launched into another diatribe about how it was the Christians of the community who did God's work of selfless service.[12] Unfortunately no DeWitt Rhodes appears in any of the 1870 or 1880 censuses for either Civil District 10 or 11. He is, however, mentioned in at least two other newspaper reports, including one of hers in which he is listed as selflessly nursing the ill.[13]

Meanwhile, Collierville had appealed for assistance from the Howard Association, a relief organization working in Memphis.[14] In this context, Miss Reneau's next letter of the 25th forms an interesting comparison to the town's previous turmoil over communal and charitable responsibilities in the J. Dix Mills episode. Also she was primly avoiding direct response to Maxey's shots across her bow while deftly counter attacking. To contradict him, she announced that the town had indeed formed a relief fund to which 39 had made contributions ranging from $10 to 10 cents. Its officers were A. L. (*sic*; Lon Allen) Rhodes, A. J. Wright and Reverend Evans. She asserted

Of the white population of Germantown and vicinity there is but one dependent family, and that family has required very little material assistance; hence the relief committee is in receipt of funds sufficient for present purposes. The citizens are prepared to contribute whatever amount may be required, unless visited by affliction far greater than the community has yet suffered. The committee has not asked nor received assistance outside the community. Two nurses were sent . . . by the benevolent Howard Association of Memphis, but, as their services were not required . . . they were immediately dismissed.[15]

While the town retained its prideful insistence that it needed no outside charity, those few residents who had remained to serve now indeed demonstrated an especially strong return to communal and charitable commitments. The 39 family contributors may well have represented the population that had stayed behind or not retreated into rural isolation. What distinguished "the faithful from the cowardly," however, became increasingly a point of contention.

In contrast to Miss Reneau's discrete report that the Howard nurses being dismissed because their service was not required, Maxey's letter had charged that they were "too fond of 'lager juice.'" One was so unsympathetic that Mr. Weir sent her packing.[16] Maxey aired scandal freely and offensively trashed the Howard nurses' heroic services.

At the same time, Maxie, penned another report describing local behavior far more disdainfully than had Miss Reneau.

> Your correspondent had an occasion to go across country this afternoon, and it is quite amusing to see the folks stand with mouths, ears and eyes wide open and listen so eagerly to hear the news, and the least move . . . toward them will cause a general stampede. . . . Now for them. Whenever . . . can smell sulphur and camphor, with asafetida, you can bank on casting your optics soon on a Germantownite, with Sulphur on his boots and a ball of camphor in his bread-basket, and immediately on discovering you he pulls out a bottle of turpentine and sticks it in to his or her proboscis, and will stand at a very respectful distance. . . .[17]

When he asked an "old 'canebiter'" to bring him a drink of water from his well, he "wanted to know 'whar' I was from." I was told to fetch it myself, for "he was 'not gwine nigh' me." The Nonconnah bridge was being quarantined by a fellow with a big shotgun, allegedly a bluff that no white man would take seriously. Despite his good-ol'-boy demeanor, his ridicule of local country folk reeked of social disdain. Likewise, his reference to "christian burials" in quotation marks, was probably a shot at the lack of attendance by fellow congregants. Here was another expression of the tension between the local areligious element and their perception of the community's "self-righteous churchy" contingent. Nevertheless, like all others, he expressed gratitude for the town's two doctors, Thompson and MacKay.

Even some medical professionals still believed the source was inhaling miasmas. The majority, however, had come close enough, believing the disease was indirectly contagious; its source was transferred on the contaminated personal effects or cargo accompanying the infected—indeed the mosquitoes nested in such places. Many also agreed, however, with Ms. Reneau on the importance of faith in God for survival.[18]

Needless to say, Maxey provoked a retort. One "Woon Chong" accused Maxie of being out of sorts because Miss Reneau had failed to include his name among those she had honored for their services. Nevertheless, he also took shots at other residents by name. Typically avoiding any mention of the "villain's" name, this anonymous citizen proceeded to castigate Maxey and demean his character in terms reminiscent of the vitriolic exchanges between the participants in the affair of J. Dix Mills. He had avoided any risks while providing his "services," loved "too much 'John Barleycorn," and "would have left (town) if he could have gotten some one to carry him for nothing."[19]

On the twenty-seventh, Max responded, bemoaning the airing of "personal matters and egotistical blowings." Otherwise, he restricted himself to honoring the newly dead.[20] Perhaps he had pulled in his horns in the face of scorn for his behavior, and pretended to being above exchanging personal attacks.

By the twenty-ninth, another anonymous reporter began taking shots at Ms. Reneau both for her reluctance to accurately report yellow fever as the cause of some deaths, and for inaccuracies with victim's names. He also had to give it a nasty personal edge, "She is of that uncertain spinster age, not mentionable, and is, as I think, quite presumptuous. . . ."[21]

Then for some reason, Maxey shifted his voice from the *Appeal* to the *Avalanche*, while mitigating his insults to the Howard nurses (who were black) by publishing a praise for the Howard Dr. Sinclair who had selflessly sacrificed his life in service to the town, dying on October 7. Nevertheless, he could not resist an opportunity to offer one of his typically humorous stories about how he and a friend had treated a refugee to a hot mustard bath and generous doses of castor oil and calomel. So "he jumped the town again, going North." Maxey was proud of his clever form of vigilante quarantine.

A brief survey of the reports to the papers from the other communities contained nothing as discordant as those from Germantown. Some did angrily criticize those who abandoned neighbors by flight, even attacking prominent men by name. But others even praised the departed for sending aid and supplies back to their neighbors. Most generally limited themselves to reporting their suffering, mourning their dead, and praising positive behavior. Germantown stands out like a sore thumb for airing its disharmony.[22]

Meanwhile the starch had finally been taken out of the town's prideful denial of the community's inability to handle its problems. On the twenty-eighth, Miss Reneau reported that with Dr. M'Kay down and only Dr Thompson left, the town had finally called on the Howard Association. They dispatched a Dr. Howard from Texas and four colored nurses, distributed to four heavily infected families. On October 12, the Association began sending out special trains along the M&C to every affected community, bringing Germantown money, medicine and supplies.[23]

By October 3, Ms. Reneau reported twenty-six dead, "all white," including two refugees from Memphis. Like reports from most of the other affected communities, she asserted that Germantown had suffered per capita more severely than any other town. In the previous five years the town had never averaged more than two deaths per year, so her nearsightedness was excusable. Then on October 14, Miss Reneau's death was reported to the papers.[24]

On October 18, as hope grew that the pending frosts would end their ordeal, someone signing "I.N.S." noted that the flight had almost depopulated the town. No more than 75 persons remained, white and colored. Of them about 60 were infected, with 37 succumbing. He/she argued that "the name of 'Woman'" should be written in a high place in the role of honor in the history of the epidemic.[25] Before the war, women, who had eschewed the dirty work of nursing and left it to servants and lower class nurses, now did it all. Nevertheless at the end, when persons of importance were named as the town's most honored servants, they were predominantly male.

After the October frosts, most of the remaining infected slowly recovered, but a few continued to die. By November 17, Florida Pettit Thompson had recovered sufficiently from the shock to write her friend Emily Lucken Mills, relating the tragedy. She enclosed a clipping from the *Appeal* dated Germantown, November 14 listing names of 40 dead, three of whom were "colored."

> I can't begin to give you an idea of the times we have been through in the last two months—death on all sides and that too without the kindness and attention of friends. The fever was brought here first by a Mr. Roper from Memphis whose children were boarding at O'Neils. At first we did not think it would spread but in a little while our friends fell thick and fast. I sent my children to Cas Galoways and stayed here to take care of Dr. __ (Thompson, her husband). He worked day and night for six weeks then took the fever himself. It proved to be a light case, though even yet he has not regained his strength. Poor Dr. McKay worked three weeks and died. His wife had recovered before he was taken sick—all of his children was taken in three days after he was— had fearful attacks but got well.[26]

Among the prominent dead were Joseph Molitor and his wife Mary. Typically, their younger children were then sent to Arkansas to live with relatives, and some of the older children apparently followed later. The only survivor of this once prominent family to stay was a daughter, Della, who married a Mr. Strickland.[27] William Miller, the druggist, passed in November after the worse was over, but was preceded by his wife in October. They too left orphans. The Berry Hurt family left none except for two or three older children who were apparently living out of town, for the other five or six family members all died. Several families lost their mother and/or one or more children. The family of Dr. Richmond, well south of town, went unscathed. Although Dr. Richmond's name was left off the honor rolls cited above, family traditions insist that he came in to attend the sick, quarantining himself from the rest of the family so they remained safe. A Dr. St. Clair, a new resident, had died early.[28]

In addition to the doctors who died fighting the fever, long-time political leader Lonallen Rhodes and L. B. Rainey gave their lives attending to the sick and their families. Rhodes' political cohort, William Walker recovered from the fever, but not his wife. The town also publically honored J. H. Clark, Reverend Evans, D. C. Rhodes, and Joe Weir for steadfast service.[29] Whether it was brave or foolhardy to stay as the fever broke out, it was heroic to serve others as well as tending one's own family. Was this D. C. Rhodes Maxie? If so, what irony!

In contrast to the honored, again one especially hostile Germantown wit disparaged those who fled as being predominantly the self-righteous "golden rule fellows, Mamma Pets, and temperance lecturers" who left behind the targets of their former criticism. It was allegedly the hale fellows who stayed and served the afflicted, often at the cost of their own lives.[30] Perhaps no refugees had even sent back money and supplies as they had in Collierville, for there were no mentions of such. Of course, not everyone was condemning those who fled. One A. Johnson, noted, "Several families of this village left when the fever broke out, nor do we blame them; it would have been well if more had gone, for I cannot call to mind but one family in this place that has entirely escaped."[31]

Miss Reneau's reports of burial services attended by those free to do so contradict the frequently told stories that the dead were buried in secret at night to avoid hysteria. According to that tradition, Reverend Evans had made the rounds with a lantern in hand. A black helper drove the wagon and dug the grave, while Evans performed the last rites. Also according to tradition, the town cemetery contains unmarked mass graves where bodies were quickly interred to avoid contagion.[32] It is unlikely there were any truly "mass graves," since deaths averaged less than two per day. But there may have been some graves containing more than one family member. It is also doubtful that anyone thought that solitary night burials could avoid contributing to the town's panic. That was impossible. Mixed emotions were at work. Indeed. blacksmith, Arthur O'Neill, with the help of an elderly black man quietly buried his daughter Mary without ceremony or a marker. When rebuked by another daughter, his expressed sentiment was disapproval of ostentatious display.[33] Not just fear, but the endless shock of losses and the demands of nursing the living consumed everyone's energy. Church services had been suspended, so it was typical for proper memorial services to be held many months after the deaths. It was October 1879, a full year after the end of the plague, before the Presbyterians gathered to memorialize their four lost members.[34]

Given the operation of occasional criminals out from Memphis, this was not the first time that Germantown residents felt that undesirable elements from the city represented a threat. Attitudes changed after Miss Renau's earlier reports. The flood of refugees seeking shelter, camping on their lands and looking for water became alarming. Those who had initially been hospitable became infected. Doors and gates were soon closed. The town eventually set up a vigilance committee to post quarantine guards at the depot, reversing the barrier. Maxie reported that the cures to which refugees were subject upon arrival encouraged them to move on. When papers arrived from Memphis, they were exposed to the sun before being read. Although country stores would sell to refugees, they went to ludicrous extremes to avoid any direct contact with them. Locals even tore up the bridge over the Wolf between Collierville and Fisherville to stop traffic.[35] Locally mobilized safety patrols scoured the countryside to arrest refugees camping in the area and to prevent anyone from stopping.

Being removed a short distance from the town saved families like the Dukes. Their house lay west of town and well back from the road closer to the Wolf, so they barricaded themselves in and avoided expeditions to stores. "They couldn't get out to buy flour. . . . They thought, sometimes, yellow fever was spread through flour, or salt meat. They had a mill on the place . . . so they ground their own meal. . . . But they all said they were so tired of eating cornbread, they didn't want to see another piece as long as they lived."[36]

Fortunately for them and others, the carrier-mosquito species rarely ventured far from populated areas or the rail lines that carried their hosts or a cargo in which they might nest. They were inefficient fliers. Capleville below the Nonconnah reported no locals being infected, only refugees from the city. Fortunately they had brought no mosquitoes with them. Even Forest Hill, right on the M&C and close by Germantown, reported mostly refugees being infected.[37]

When the disease hit Memphis again the next year, Germantown people were terrified. Platus Lipsey recalled, "I cannot forget the look on peoples' faces in the afternoon when the train came bearing the afternoon papers with the big headlines: 'THE SCOURGE AGAIN.'" Everybody talked of the horrors of the previous year.[38] Fortunately the town was spared a repeat of anything near the previous.

After the plague reappeared at Memphis, it was determined that it had not come from elsewhere.[39] It had apparently regenerated locally, a few hardy mosquitoes managing to winter over. By mid-August, the fever was reported at Germantown, but perhaps it was actually only Bailey Station, seemingly also a spontaneous generation. By September, one had died, and a second case broke out. The Howards had sent out a nurse. Without previous indigenous infection, nearby Capleville preserved its status as disease free. [40]

Being the source of its generation, Memphis soon limited most of its quarantine efforts to the infected neighborhoods, controlling traffic in and out of the city. Many businesses shut down. Every other city that usually had commerce with Memphis shut down all contacts with that city. The result was a near total disruption of all its commerce. Meanwhile, multiple, local quarantine efforts had become so severe that Max, now reporting from Collierville, bemoaned the fact that the town had been so completely cut off from supplies that the community was suffering economically, "while such places as ... Germantown, are enjoying a liberal trade, with full stocks of goods in their houses. ..."[41] The usually polemical Max probably did not have the entire picture. The ups and downs of all this are hard to follow from the fragmented reporting in the papers. In support of Maxie's assertion, on October 14, the *Appeal* reported that the M&C had permission "to run a daily train down as far as Germantown, instead of Grand Junction, as formerly." Anyone trying to return to the city would be arrested.[42] They thought the plague could come to Memphis from points to the east beyond Germantown. Regardless, the bottom line is that in both years the economic effects compounded the human suffering greatly. The local cotton harvest was seriously disrupted with much loss, as were business activates of all sorts in area communities.

Meanwhile the devastated and frightened community sought solace in religion. The new Baptist minister, John Lipsey, previously residing in Coldwater until 1879, had been "cut off from his appointments" in Germantown, Collierville and Whites Station during the '78 plague until early fall when contagion ended. When he assumed his ministry in the town, people were still dying. After moving his family to town in '79, he held four weeks of revival meetings and brought his membership up to 96 souls with baptisms at the Wolf. Cynics commented, "yellow fever converts." Reverend Evans kept his distance from these less decorous affairs. Instead, the Presbyterians and Methodists combined their thinned ranks and held joint meetings.[43] The town's sectarian and social divisions were hardly healed by the plague.

In the aftermath, at least fifty percent of the town either died or moved away.[44] By the 1880 census, the town had recovered to only 223 people, while the district had 2,917 total.[45] The town had lost its reputation as a healthy retreat. Meanwhile, Memphis eventually got its health and sanitation act together. It cleaned up sources of contagion and employed effective quarantine procedures. After stringent measures, the city also solved its financial problems and improved other aspects of its infrastructure.[46] There were no longer so many reasons to eschew city life for bucolic Germantown. Some of the city's elite and seasonal settlers even abandoned their residences around the town.

As previously noted, expanding and improved transportation routes favored Collierville. In 1872 for instance, Germantown drew just under 2,000 bales while Collierville exceeded 7,000. Fewer people were arriving and departing through Germantown's depot. In that same fiscal year, only 5,535 passengers came through Germantown compared to 8,608 through Collierville.[47]

The previously mentioned shift from privately owned, small cotton gins to commercial operations terminated the town's sole industry other than lumber processing. The town's commercial cotton gin was duplicated in every community.

Another factor in the decline of the town was the inability of the local mineral springs to compete. None of them matched their rival at Raleigh, and there seems to have been no effort devoted to their marketing. Nashoba continued to draw locals into the twentieth century, but offered in facilities only a picnic ground. The Brunswick Springs became a relatively private preserve of Dr. Richard Martin's family.[48] In contrast, the Raleigh Springs were extensively commercialized and promoted in local papers. The mineral content of each of its springs was published in 1866, and a light rail line from the city was chartered in 1885. Railroad advertisements also hawked the more distant and prestigious springs such a Hot Springs, Arkansas, and White Sulfur in West Virginia.[49] The fact that the Yellow Fever epidemic reached and devastated the town eroded its myth as a healthier retreat.

There were fewer and fewer reasons for anyone outside the civil district to come to town, much less to stay overnight. As previously noted, by at least 1888, the size of the civil district was also reduced. Its eastern border had moved appropriately to the Seventeen Mile Branch, closer to Forest Hill. Its western border above Nonconnah Creek had been gobbled up by the new district, centered on White Station, running out past Ridgeway to the Duke and Messick properties, almost to the town's limits. The new Forest Hill Post Office and Memphis Offices drew off many former regular visitors, as did churches south of Nonconnah. The old "Greater Germantown" had been significantly reduced.

Prognosis

Germantown would not die. It would not even lapse into a coma, but it would certainly have an extended nap for recovery. Although the recovery of its population is usually given as the reason for the town's reincorporation in 1880, it never achieved anything near its pre-plague levels. Even a decade after the plague, Goodspeed gave it as only about 200. In any case, an 1880 petition for incorporation was signed by twenty prominent citizens, merchants, professionals and entrepreneurs.[50]

Their petition might be seen as a reassertion of life, an expressed determination to prevail. Actually their request for incorporation reflected more of a plea to empower them with both the authority and responsibility to overcome the sorry state of affairs that still prevailed. They needed incorporation

> for the purpose of enforcing order and quiet in their midst, that they may secure themselves against things which are obnoxious and troublesome, and which cannot be reached by any other power than the municipal laws of an incorporated town for the suppression of drunkenness and other vices, to prevent careless and reckless shooting in the limits of the town to the endangering of life and to the great annoyance of the inhabitants, and as drunken fights are of frequent occurrence on the streets; and as they are subjected to profane and indecent language, to the great disturbance of peaceful and quiet citizens, there being no power to restrain these offenders; as dead stock is allowed to remain in their streets; to the great annoyance of the inhabitants and the endangering of public health; and as they have no power to prevent persons from districts infected with contagious diseases coming into their midst bringing the seeds of disease with them, from which they have suffered greatly in the past; as their streets need the care which can only be had from a system of municipal laws, and as all these troubles and grievances can be reached and removed only by an incorporation, therefore the petitioners respectfully prey that a charter be granted them....[51]

Although the post war problems of organized gangs and rampant crime had almost abated by the 1880s, local theft and one murder continued to be reported in the papers.[52] The general deterioration of the community's harmonious and civil environment had continued unabated. However, the 1880 petition reveals that the town's good citizens had finally faced up to their embarrassing problems and gone public in an effort at correction. They determined to take the solutions of these problems on themselves, and to attend to other community problems affecting safety and health. They would once again accept the responsibility of taxing themselves to finance the means to do so—they would devote their time to serve in the necessary public offices.

The respectable citizens obviously intended to impose decorum on their own, while bringing the "lower orders" under control. They purchased an iron, temporary-holding cell so the constable could restrain overnight any obstreperous party. Goodspeed's 1887 history of Shelby County probably reflected the renewed image they sought to achieve.

> Germantown, comprising about 200 inhabitants, is situated about fifteen miles southeast of Memphis on the Memphis & Charleston Railroad.... The place was incorporated about 1854 but the charter was allowed to lapse during the war. It was reincorporated, however, in 1880. ... The principal business firms of the present time are C. M. Callis, G. W. Thomas, W. E. Miller, E. W. Gorman, Hatcher & King and Tuggle & Kimbrough.... Germantown is well supplied with churches, Methodist Episcopal Church South, Presbyterian and Baptist. Each of these denominations have good houses of worship. The Presbyterian Church alone escaped the ravages of the war. The membership of these churches is about 50, 75 and 125 respectively. The most distinguished divine in this vicinity is Rev. Evans, of Germantown, who has been administering to the spiritual interests of his flock for more than a quarter of a century.... Present physicians are Drs. Williams and Yancy.... Germantown Lodge, No. 95, was instituted by dispensation in April, 1841, and was regularly chartered October 7, 1841.... Present membership, 34.... Caro Lodge No. 1664, Knights of Honor, was organized June 28, 1879, with thirteen members.... The present membership is forty-seven. This lodge also meets in the Masonic Hall.... The public schools of Germantown are taught in the Masonic Hall, first floor. The enrollment of pupils amounts to about 100. The school term lasts about five months. They are under control of Prof. B. J. T. Moss, with Mrs. Moss as assistant, and Miss Jessie Williams primary.[53]

Of course, this was only the white community of Germantown. There were at least two black churches, The New Bethel Missionary Baptist and the African Methodist Episcopal Church. The blacks had built schools for all grades and donated them toward fulfilling the district's educational responsibilities. If there were any social or fraternal organizations, they were as invisible as all other aspects of black achievement. Their children were enrolled under their own black teachers. The subsequent history of black-white relations there has yet to be told. Clearly however, the town was immersed in a county that acquired over the next decades the reputation of having one of the highest rates of lynchings.

Meanwhile, the little town would otherwise slumber peacefully for almost a century. A few stores and mills clustered around the depot. For some time, there was a coffin factory. The number of church denominations increased, but not their sizes. It became most famous for its horse show and was consequently misperceived as a town of rich "horsey people." That aura helped it attract a post-1960s urban flight. Building on that initial stimulus, it rapidly became again a cosmopolitan and cultured community. It has coped as well with race problems as any other American community. Perhaps even better at integrating "immigrants," than it had been before.

APPENDIX 1

DEFINING GERMANTOWN AND ITS PEOPLE

This exercise involves a number of problems inherent in the available data. First, the chartered town itself was a relatively small community of a few hundred people. It covered only half a square mile, irregularly shaped, and defined on its north side by the State Line Road (modern Poplar Pike). The full community of Germantown, "Greater Germantown," all those people who defined themselves as from Germantown or living near Germantown, occupied a much more extensive area—all of Civil District 11 and parts of districts 7, 9 and 10.

Since 1860 census schedules were separated by the post offices serving them but failed to separate the residents of the town proper from the rest of its civil district, that limits analyzing the chartered town's population to estimates. "Greater Germantown," to be studied here, included all those persons designated as living in the areas served by the Germantown post office.

There are problems maintaining consistency among subsequent censuses and with the population defined by the 1860 census. By 1870, two or three of the most prominent citizens were omitted from the District 11 census, possibly by an undocumented expansion of the adjacent district's coverage through Ridgeway, former Pea Ridge that, therefore, included them. It is also possible, however, they were accidentally omitted because of confusion about district lines. For whatever reasons, the prominent Kimbrough family was simply missed as were perhaps others.

Even for the slave schedules of 1860, problems for District 7 make it almost impossible to include its residents in Greater Germantown. Only an estimate was possible. Nevertheless, family names of probable 1860 slaveholders can be identified in the search for any former slaves by those names in the 1870 census who might have remained.

The 1880 census presents even more problems for comparisons. The districts shifted east. The district to the west definitely shifted to include Ridgeway. On the other hand, District 11 shifted east to include Forest Hill facilitating some consistency. Such inconsistencies occasionally require limiting the population analyzed to either that of District 11 alone or both District 10 and 11. Wherever that occurred, it is stated in the text.

Given these problems, it must be admitted that the results of most comparative estimates are at least as impressionistic as statistical.

APPENDIX 2

IDENTIFYING MEN WHO SERVED IN THE WAR

Of 271 white men of military age in Greater Germantown, perhaps 169 served in Tennessee's Confederate units. Many others joined regiments in other states, especially Mississippi—at least 19 did so. At least 2 served in the Federal forces, perhaps as many as 14. Although this estimate is based on a problematic process, it clearly shows more than half of the area's theoretically eligible white men served, perhaps as many as two-thirds.

Using the 1860 census as a base, and defining future military age as between 40 and 12 in those census schedules, a total population sample was established. A 12 year-old would have reached 16 before the end of the war, and many under-aged boys served. A few men are known to have served above the age of 45, but adding older and younger to the search would have taken it beyond a point of diminishing returns. The men for this sample were drawn from all of District 11 and those from Districts 7, 9 and 10, known to have lived in Greater Germantown. The digitized Family Tree compilations of Civil War soldiers' service records, *Tennesseans in the Civil War*, and *The Roster of Confederate Soldiers* were searched for the names of these men.[1] Some other sources identified a few that were not in either of these compilations or the census.

Several problems plague this process. The compilations of service records are not complete and neither are the census records. Names in both are not always accurate, spellings varied and frequently only initials or just first and last names are given. The results are, therefore, inexact, but in a few cases the identities were certain, but especially in the case of the 13th Volunteer Infantry Regiment.

In other less certain cases, many combinations of names and initials created multiple hits in different units thus increasing the chances that the individual in question served in one of those many units, but making it impossible to identify which. Whenever the search on an individual turned up in units that recruited in Shelby County, or the Germantown area specifically, these were counted as "probably served." In the case of two or more such hits, the assumption is for "high probability." Whenever the search simply hit Confederate units not recruited locally, they are listed as "may have served."

Counting the men who might have served in a particular unit is, therefore, especially problematic. For instance, cases where one man's name produced multiple hits in units known to have recruited in the Germantown area, that produced inflated numbers for men who *might* have served in some of those units, but increases the probability of their service.

Only two or three cases clearly served in the Federal cause, but a few men born in the North were absent from the 1870 census, which may tell us that they returned home in 1861, perhaps joining units there. A few such names turned up some possibilities in *The Roster of Union Soldiers*. Also, in order to gain release, some men who initially served in the Confederate army and were captured agreed to serve in the Federal Navy or units in the Indian territories for the duration of the war, so they served both sides. A few such cases offered themselves as possibilities.

Nevertheless, all this gives us some picture of how, where and when the men of the area served. Out of 271 of military age:

40 may have served in Tennessee units;
27 probably served;
40 very probably served
52 definitely served;
21 may have served in other states;
9 possibly served with the Union;
2 definitely served with the Union.

♦ ♦ ♦

The service of African-Americans is even more difficult to establish, since no names are given in the slave schedules. The names of men in the 1870 census can be correlated with the federal military records, but that involves even more problems than with white men. Using the 1870 census, it is possible to assemble all African American males in the area who were of an age likely to have served. If the last name correlates with an 1860 owner, we can surmise that the man was possibly a former slave in the area. (See Appendix 3.) This divides the sample into two groups, (1) possible former slaves of the area and (2) a mixed sample—either former slaves in the area (who did not adopt their master's family names) or post-war settlers.

Crosschecking their names against the service records involves the same problems as with whites. Also as with the whites, for men who were possibly former area slaves, if the service record of a named man is for a unit that recruited at Germantown or in one of the artillery units recruited at Memphis, it is assumed to be a probable hit. If the unit was one stationed at Memphis, it is assumed as a possible hit. For the later arrivals, names of men who served in locally recruited units are assumed as possibly former slaves who probably served. Also others with a significant number of hits in any Union units are assumed as new settlers who probably served. Finally, Shelby County pension applications identify a few men who were drafted to be servants in the Confederate Army, as does the memorial for the 13th Infantry written by its commander.

This produces a surprisingly large number of former black Union soldiers who may have settled down to live side-by-side with former enemies at arms. Of a total 168 of military age:

- 26 likely to have been former area slaves who enlisted in or around Germantown/Memphis
- 18 likely to have been former area slaves who served
- 9 likely to have been former slaves who probably served
- 17 new residents who may have served
- 1 new resident definitely served
- A total of 66 blacks in the 1870 census who served in Union ranks were living among Confederate veterans, plus:
- At least 9 area slaves who were servants in the Confederate Army, perhaps even as employees
- 1 area slave who definitely served in an office on Forrest's staff

APPENDIX 3

ASSESSING POPULATION, WEALTH, AND PROPERTY

The author makes no pretensions of having produced a scientifically valid socioeconomic analysis. He has neither the professional qualifications for such, nor had access to the kinds of necessary sources. Furthermore, the problems involved in defining proper population for such an effort are almost overwhelming. As explained in Appendix 1, the population chosen for this study was those served by the Germantown post office, but that was not a consistent area for the entire period from 1840 through 1880. For a short period during the 1860s, a temporary small office served the land south of the Nonconnah, but that change can be ignored for the sake of consistency. By the same token, the small section along the Pidgeon Roost Road sometimes served by the Memphis Post Office has been treated as included. In civil district 10, the area covered by the Germantown Post Office shifted with the opening of the Forest Hill post office in the 1870s, and a different service covered the residents north of the Wolf River also previously covered by Germantown. Finally, by the time of the 1880 census, if not sooner, the borders of CD 11 had been moved to the east toward Forest Hill, while the developing residential tracts around White's Station to the west through Ridgeway had been lost due to redistricting.. Every effort has been made to compensate for these changes

Although a variety of miscellaneous sources have provided occassional insights, the bulk of information available has been the U.S. Censuses, 1840 through 1880—not just the general data in the published reports, but also the more specific individual population, agricultural and slave schedules, providing data on all individual residents. In a few cases the mortality schedules, and even the industrial and social cultural schedules are available, but problematic, as described below. Adding to the complexities of defining the population, the population schedules used for the census were not properly marked. Although each sheet in a district's schedules was clearly identified as belonging to a specific post office, that was obviously not entirely accurate. Every line of each sheet was completed by the census taker regardless of the location of households served by a specific post office. One suspects that the census taker even failed to place households in proper postal districts, in some cases, even civil districts. Simply filling sheets took priority, so no blank lines exist at the end of any sheet. In many cases, households spilled over into adjacent sheets designated for a different post office.

Beyond that, there are numerous other problems with census data. It is readily apparent that the assistant census marshals in these districts did not conscientiously follow the very specific instructions given in their Special Instructions. They did not distinguish the residents of the chartered town from the rest of the civil district. They did not distinguish hotels or boarding houses from private homes, or clearly identify the relationships among persons with different family names residing within a household or boarding facility. Regular residents temporarily absent were often omitted. The status of mechanics was not designated appropriately as master, workman or apprentice. The denomination of ministers usually fails as does the level taught by teachers. Worst of all, in the population sheets the term "farmer" is frequently used for men who do not appear in the agricultural census as producers of any crop, yet farm laborer is properly used in other cases, leaving one uncertain about the accuracy of "farmers." The term could only have applied properly to men occupying less than 3 acres. Finally, no occupational category is provided in many cases for either some adult members of a family or persons with a different family name living within a household. Thus many residents defy categorization. Such problems were only corrected in the 1880 censuses.

Also, the data covered changed with each census. The 1840 census provides little individual data, only the names of heads of households. The 1850 census gives for each individual only names, ages, gender, occupation, place of birth, and value of real property. That of 1860 adds other personal wealth and school attendance. 1870's census adds race and literacy, omitting school attendance. In 1880, it restored educational information but dropped any information on property or other wealth, adding marital status and parents' place of birth. It was not until the 1880 census that deputy marshals were appointed without local favoritism and were properly trained to follow instructions. Even then, the census bureau admits that 10% errors are common in census data. It was obviously much worse before that census.

Agricultural censuses for 1860 through 1880 become increasingly detailed as to the nature and value of acreage farmed by the individual, the values of other aspects of agricultural property, ownership or lease status, types of production and its value. This makes comparisons over the decades difficult. Finally, one is frequently left guessing about the consistency among the marshals in their definitions of the terms employed. Of course, a major problem is that most data is self-reported, and therefore depends on the interviewees' understanding of the terms and the kinds of records they kept, if any.

One serious discrepancy between the agricultural and population schedules is that individuals appearing in the agricultural census are often missing from the population schedules, or the names do not correlate well. This especially makes it impossible to determine the ethnic identity of such farmers, because that is only noted in the population schedules.

In many cases, the acreage and land values in the ag schedules cannot be squared with the real property and non-real property values in the pop schedules. The value of production is neither consistent nor given for all products. This leads one to conclude that the expectations for these censuses were unrealistic, especially since the constable had to rely entirely on the estimates or assertions of the owner. Presumably, the value of a house was to be included under real property, which implies that anyone without real property was a renter. However, the large percentage of such cases defies logic, especially in cases of people of significant wealth otherwise.

Although agricultural production was supposed to include both production for market and consumption, the latter would escape any calculation since record-keeping was highly unlikely. Likewise, that bartered between households was never a matter of record at any level of society. So much of this was under the radar that evidence is lost of the wealth and productivity of the "poorer" subsistence farmers and their standard of living. On farms, production of less than $100 was omitted, as was that of small or kitchen garden plots of farm laborer families. Even that of many mechanics and laborers with kitchen gardens, a milk cow and some poultry could be overlooked or assumed too insignificant to be reported in the schedules.

The availability of two Shelby County track maps for 1869 and 1888 do provide some tests for the acreage figures in the agricultural censuses of 1870 and 1880. They gave the total acreage figures for persons who also were renting or cropping out land that they were not personally farming. This is a valuable contrast to the agricultural census sheets which apparently speak only to what the owner was personally operating. Unfortunately, the eight year difference between the 1880 census and the 1888 map leaves families that left during that period without matching data and includes numerous new-comers. On the other hand, both maps provide a better sense of the continued turnover of property and a clearer picture of the amount of property owned by absentee landlords. Last of all, these maps clearly reveal the conversion of farm lands into residential property during the suburbanization along the line out through White's Station to Germantown and Forest Hill.

Although it is generally accepted that there is a 10% error in all censuses, those for Shelby County, Civil District 11 have proven to be much more problematic. For the slave schedules for 1860, far more than 10% were missed. The agricultural census for 1860 is even more incomplete. In the 1870 and 1880 population and agricultural censuses, the huge estates of some of the most prominent planters were completely overlooked in one or the other. Although it is understandable that census takers could overlook farms well off the beaten path, those missed were located on major thoroughfares. Finally the reporters do not seem to have accurate knowledge of the borders of the districts, frequently misreporting the location of a residence. As previously mentioned, the biggest problems with the 1880 agricultural census are significant internal contradictions. The total cash value of production also seems highly erratic when similar farms are compared. Rarely do entries for total acreage tilled equal totals of those listed for the specific crops of corn and cotton, plus what had to have been used for other crops.

The more routine errors to be expected are misspelled names, incorrect first names, missing middle initials, ages and place of birth, and on rare occasions, even gender. In such questions as literacy or school attendance, the attention of the takers to such issues was obviously erratic or perfunctory. It also seems that they were even less attentive about such accuracy when dealing with black families, and perhaps also poorer white families. They may have chosen to label their children as farm laborers rather than students, for their attendance was erratic due to cropping needs.

Unfortunately the slave schedules were not intended to provide any significant information about the slave population except to achieve a numerical count so important for the Southern states' claims to congressional representation. No names are listed, only age, gender and black or mulatto identified. As for ages, they were usually just estimates. Slave parents might know their children's ages, but they might not have been consulted. The older the slave the less likely age was known. Former slaves interviewed after the war reveal the problem in their answers. A few proudly claimed great antiquity with ages over 100. Others casually admitted they did not know their age. Unfortunately age is the primary indicator for identifying a post war freedman among the unnamed "property" of a former owner's population. This makes identifying former slaves who remained in the area extremely difficult when other sources of information are not available. One is left relying heavily on family names which correspond with owners. That is extremely unreliable, since many freedmen, military officers, and Freedmen's Bureau personnel disdained that practice and preferred to create new surnames.[1]

This leaves one groping for some way to estimate those who either stayed "home" during the war, or returned, perhaps to family, after the war. Since one can only begin by using the family names of former area slave-holders, and correlate those with the ages, gender, and "color" of listings on the slave schedules, one can only achieve a problematic ball-park number. It would exceed such cases based only on the family name, but miss many cases that did not identify with the owner's name. For what they are worth, the resulting numbers from such an exercise are given in the text. There are a few known case. Otherwise those with ages within one to three years of the schedule are counted "likely." Others off by 4-5 years are counted as "possible."

There are, however, two other interesting details called for in the schedules, which should have been useful: number of escapees for each owner during the year, and number of his slave quarters. Unfortunately, as mentioned in the text, the number of escapees seem seriously underreported. Perhaps the owners were embarrassed. There are no reported escapees in District Eleven for the period 1859 through 1860, which is clearly in error.

For extracting the data, the worse problem is occasionally poor quality of the microfilm of the schedules. It varies from clear to totally illegible. The writing can be too faint and the reproductions so badly scratched or exposed that data is obscured. The same person's handwriting can vary from distinct to highly problematic even numbers.

Unfortunately the schedules for mortality, industry and social-cultural are not readily available, even on microfilm and those that are can be totally unreadable. One is completely in the dark for details about non-agriculturalists except for the value of real and non-real property listed in the pop schedules. Also many persons who were probably clerical, industrial or service workers were simply not identified as to activity, especially when employed in family businesses.

The bottom line is that the analyses of population, wealth and property, and some characteristics of that population can often be more impressionistic than statistical. Statisticians say, GIGO—garbage in, garbage out, if the data being compiled is not clearly and consistently defined. However, I certainly feel that, despite statistical mushiness, the impressions derived are far better than "garbage." They provide a relatively good impression of social-economic differences and moods within the community, if not statistical accuracy about them. Since the reader is forewarned of its limitations, s/he should be forgiving of any consequent inaccuracies in detail. One hopes that this first attempt at a close case study of one Tennessee town will provoke more refined and comparative academic efforts.

All things considered, the census data for 1850 through 1880 have to be the primary sources for many of the social and economic aspects of this study. Generalizations about comparative wealth and social structure have been derived from the population and agricultural schedules. Equally important, insights into the more intimate details of a family's life and even community relations can occasionally be deduced from those sources. Each line of household entry is a picture of that family and their clients in that year. The places of birth of the parents (and in 1880, grandparents) plus those of each child and their ages tells one the history of that family's migrations, and sometimes approximately when it settled in the area. Frequently family ties between households with different family names can be deduced. One can surmise when a family is caring for one or more of its elders, or the orphans of relatives or friends. The presence of nannies, cooks or servants in residence or housed in adjacent houses speaks clearly of status. Sometimes it is hard to resist exercising a novelist's imagination.

To avoid excessive and repetitive footnoting, one reference to this appendix has been made at the beginning of long passages dealing with social and economic generalizations. Only where more specific insights have been deduced, references to the specific schedule sheets have been given. Otherwise footnoting would have become excessive.

The author has indulged in numerous generalizations and conclusions that are not footnoted. They are the result of well-founded impressions based on digesting a wide range of sources, primary and secondary. Any effort at footnoting would be impossible and tedious. Impressionism is an inescapable aspect of good history, as opposed to pretensions of scientific accuracy.

NOTES

Introduction

1. James S. Matthews, "Sequence Occupation in Memphis, Tennessee: 1819–1860," *West Tennessee Historical Society Papers*, (hereafter WTHS), 73, Figure 6, 65.

Part 1

1. *Acts of the State of Tennessee* (hereafter Acts), 1841, chap. 30, sec. 12, 29, for the first charter issued by the State Assembly; County Court Minutes Book 6, 1850, No. 788, 436–38, Shelby County Archives (hereafter SCA), contains the town's petition for a charter in conformance with the act of the Assembly, January 7, 1850 (Acts, 1849–50, chap. 17), which was approved by the county's Quarterly Sessions Court; Shelby County Map, 1839, TNGenWeb; and John M. Keating, *History of the City of Memphis Tennessee*, 1888, p. 133, Google Book Search (hereafter) GBS.

2. County Court, Minute Book 9, No. 788, July 1, 1850, pp. 437–38., SCA.

Chapter 1

1. On the problems and use of census data, see Appendix 3.

2. Mills to Martha, Feb. 17, 1864, Mills Family Records, Valentine Richmond History Center (henceforth VRHC).

3. Steve Baker, "Agriculture, Race, and Free Blacks in West Tennessee," WTHS, 48.

4. Pere Magness, *Past Times*, 1994, 54–60, provides a vivid description of the life of one such early family of wealthy settlers.

5. U.S. Census, 1860, pp. xxxiii-xxxiv; and "Germantown Pioneers," *Germantown News*, July 28, 1977, 4B.

6. Baker, "Agriculture." WTHS, 48.

7. *Memphis Tri-Weekly Appeal*, June 26, 1846, 2, col. 2.

8. Isham R. Howse's Journal, July 23, 1852; and July 25, 1853, Mississippi Valley Collection, Special Collections, McWerther Library, University of Memphis (hereafter MVC).

9. The Nashoba Tract was intended to be a model for the emancipation of slaves. The story of Wright's project precedes this period under study. Interested readers may consult Celia Morris Eckhardt, *Fanny Wright: Rebel in America* (Cambridge: Harvard University Press, 1984).

10. Howse's Journal.

11. Census 1860, Agriculture, p 136; Agricultural Schedules, 1860, Roll 10, Shelby County, CD 11; and 1860 census, slave schedule, CD 11.

12. Thomas Perkins Abernethy, *Frontier to Plantation in Tennessee*, 1955, 289; records in the Wills/Kirby collection giving examples of these conditions.

13. Rachel Brooks Hord, *A Little History of the Brooks Family*, correspondence, p. 48, Wills/Kirby collection.

14. Abernethy, *Frontier*, pp. 289f.; and William J. Cooper and Thomas E. Terrill, *The American South*, 1991, pp. 197–99.

15. E.g., credit problems between John Grey and James C. Anderson, 1848, Shelby County Court of Quarterly Pleas and Common Sessions, loose papers 1849/20/4658, SCA.

16. Hord, *Brooks Family*, correspondence, p. 48, Wills/Kirby collection.

17. Robert A. Lanier, *History of the Memphis and Shelby County Bar*, n.d. p. 7.

18. Thornton, J. Mills, III. "The Ethics of Subsistence and the Origins of Southern Secession" in Carol Van West, ed. *Tennessee in the Civil War*. Vol. I. Nashville: Tennessee Historical Society, 2011, p. 10.

19. See Appendix 3.

20. Alan N. Miller, "*West Tennessee's Forgotten Children* " WTHS, 36 (1982): 29–31, 36f, and 40.

21. Ibid, pp. 134–37.

22. Elizabeth Fox-Genovese, *Within the Plantation Household*: 1988, 63–64.

23. Drew Gilpin Faust, *Mothers of Invention*, 1996, 4, 10, 20–22, 27, 31–32., 56, and 78; and George C. Rable, *Civil Wars: Women and Crisis of Southern Nationalism*, 1989, 1–30.

24. John to Sottie, Head Quarters 52nd Ill. Infantry, Germantown, TN, August 22nd, 1863, Historic Sites folder/Civil War/Germantown Regional History and Genealogy Center (hereafter GRH&GC).

25. Fred Arthur Dyer, and John Trotwood Moore. *Tennessee Civil War Veteran Questionnaires*. 1985, 1032 and 1300.

26. Loose Papers, 1857, box 35, #2087, Road Order—James Kimbrough (overseer) Germantown-Hernando Road,; and 1849, box 17, #000, Tuition Payment, 11th CD, SCA.

27. Faust, *Mothers*, 53–56 and 63–64.

28. Rable, *Civil Wars*, 22–24; Will of W. C. Harrison, August 3, 1868, Harrison File; Will of John H. Harrison, January 11, 1859, GRH&GC; and description of 1877 deed left to Laura F. Brett by her parents in St. John Waddel to John A. Kirby, July 14, 1898, Wills/Kirby collection.

29. Although literacy is not recorded in the 1860 census, that of 1870 indicates female literacy was still high among property holders despite wartime disruptions.
Rable, *Civil Wars*, 18.

30. Platus Iberus Lipsey, "Memories of His Early Life, (1865–1888)," pp. 13f-14, 18–19., and 22 Tennessee State Library and Archives (hereafter TTSL&A)

31. Ibid, 11f–12, 23

32. Ibid, 21, and 31–32.; and Bertram Wyatt-Brown, "Community, Class, and Snopesian Crime": in Orville Vernon Burton and Robert C. McMath Jr., eds. *Class, Conflict and Consensus* 1982, 164f.

33. George B. Ayers, *Descriptive Railroad Handbook of Great Southern Route between New Orleans and Washington*. Memphis: 1858, 22f; *Weekly Appeal*, Oct. 2, 1846, 3, col. 4; Feb. 9, 1858, 3, col. 1; and Apr.15, 1872, 4, col. 6.

34. Howse journal, Apr. 5, 1853; and May 9.

35. Hord, *Brooks Family*, correspondence, p. 49, Books/Kirby collection.

36. Shelby County, Tennessee Soil Map (1916), TSL&A.

37. History of Education in Tennessee, Tennessee Department of Education web page: state.tn.us.education/edhist.htm; and "History of Education in Washington County," *Oak Hill School Teachers Resource and Curriculum Guide*.

38. *Acts*, 1851, chap. 133; and 1856, chap. 114, 127.

39. Fred Arthur Bailey, *Class and Tennessee's Confederate Generation*, 1987. 43–49, and Appendix 2, tables 8 and 12, 151n., and 154.

40. Dyer and Moore, *Veterans Questionnaires*, vol. 3, p. 1032.

41. Loose Papers, Tuition Payments - 11th CD, 1845, box 10, #000; 1846, box 11, #000; 1848, box 14, #000; 1849, box 17, #000, SCA.

42. Duke Papers, Memphis and Shelby County Room, Benjamin L. Hooks Central Library, Memphis (hereafter M&SC); Loose Papers, 1855, box 30, #000, School Fund Payment–11th CD—Mary Emma Pettit (Germantown), SCA.

43. Howse journal, April 10, 1853; May 11; July 8; and 10; and August 20.

44. Loose Papers, 1854, box 28, #92, Scholastic Population–11th CD, SCA.

45. Dyer and Moore, vol. 3, 1032 and 1300; but cf. Loose Papers, 1847, box 13, #000, tuition payment to Benj. C. Harrison, showing extremely erratic attendance during a 60-day session, SCA.

46. Young, *Standard History of Memphis*, 1912, 401, GBS; and Godspeed's *Standard History of the City of Memphis*, 1912, "Shelby," p. 840; Loose Papers, 1854, box 28, file 77, 1855, box 30, file 99, and 1856, box 32, file #000.

47. Loose Papers, teacher payments, 1855, box 30, #000; 1860, box 42, teacher and tuition payment files #2, 3, 4, and 5, SCA; and see Appendix 3.

48. Loose Papers, 1861, box 46, teacher payment, files #1 and #3, and passim, SCA.

49. Faust, *Mothers*, 82–84.

50. Loose Papers, 1848, box 15, #20; 1854, box 28, #92; and 1856, box 32, #117, Scholastic Population, 11th CD; 1860, box 43, #156, School Fund Distribution—CD 1–11; and 1860, box 42, #s 1 and 5, tuition, SCA.

51. Loose papers, 1849, box17, #000, teacher payment to Geo. C. Furber, SCA.

52. Census Statistics, 1860, p. 506.

53. Anita Ledsinger, "The Nurenberger's—city's oldest house," reprinted in Historic Germantown 2010 supplement, *Germantown News*, 3.

54. "Germantown Pioneers," *Germantown News*, August 18, 1977, 2; and 1850 census, District 10, 184A.

55. Letter, Dr. Leslie L. Thompson to Mrs. Clarence A. Smith, April 17, 1981, Hughes Papers/GRH&GC.

56. Linda McGregor Scott, *History of Germantown*. MS, n.d., chap. 3, 10, GRH&GS; Ayers, *Handbook*, p. 23; and 1860 census, Dist. 10, 361A.

57. *Enquirer*, January 20, 1838, p. 3, col. 5, and July, 21, p.3, col. 4; and *Tri-Weekly Appeal*, October 3, 1846, p. 2, col. 7; and census 1850, CD 10, p. 183B.

58. Emily Lucken Papers, GRH&GC, family files.

59. Duke papers, part IV, M&SC.

60. *Appeal*, June 6, 1855, 3, col. 2; and Ayers, *Handbook*, 23.

61. *Appeal*, July 18, 1854, 2, col. 5.

62. Census 1850, District 10; and Tom Phillips, "History prepared and read by Squire Tom Phillips," transcribed by Margaret Harrison Owen, March 27, 1938, Germantown Presbyterian Church Archive (hereafter GPC).

63. *Appeal*, June 6, 1855, 3, col. 2.

64. Ibid.

65. *Appeal*, March 8, 1855, 3, col. 1; July 14, 2, col. 6; and *Manual of Public Libraries, Institutions and Societies in the United States*, 1859, GBS.

66. *Appeal*, July 23, 1857, 3, col. 1.

67. *Appeal*, April 11, 1857, 3, col. 1; and Ayers, *Handbook*, 23.

68. Acts, 1857–58, chap. 59, 124.

69. Ibid, 125–26.

70. Census Statistics, 1860, 509–10.

71. 1860 census, Searcy, White County, Arkansas, 4.

72. *Appeal*, August 23, 1856, 2, col. 7; Ayers, *Handbook*, 23; Acts, 1857–58, 262; Scott, chap. 3, 10; and Corgan, "Towards a History of Higher Education in Antebellum West Tennessee," WTHS, 39, 65.

73. *Appeal*, January 3, 1857, 4, col. 3.

74. *Appeal*, July 15, 1859, 1, col. 4, and frequently thereafter

75. Woodson, *Genealogy*, 471.

76. Emily Lucken-Mills correspondence, 1854–58, GH&GS

77. *Appeal*, August 26, 1873, 1, col. 3; November 9, 1854, 3, col. 1; and November 10, 3, col. 2.

78. Hall, 12 and 14; E. Smith, 7; Hughes lecture; and *Appeal*, September 10, 1861, 3, col. 2.

79. Howse journal, May 14 and 15, 1853; August 17 and 18, and 28.

80. Pictures of typical local Methodist churches of the period, West historical file, Germantown United Methodist Church Archive (hereafter GUMCA); Dye, 106.

81. "United Methodist Church Development, Shelby County, TN, 1820–1990," 14, Memphis Conference Archives, United Methodist Church (hereafter MCA).

82. Maurice A. Crouse, "A Sketch of Early Germantown History," typescript, Cloyes files, GRH&G, np.

83. Lipsey, "Memories," 9f., and 34.

84. National Archives, In the court of Claims, Germantown Baptist Church of Germantown, Tennessee, vs. The United States, No. 11,688 Cong., depositions, November 3, 1904 (hereafter, NA/No. 11,688 Cong. Depositions), Medicus J. Turner.

85. Surviving membership records of Germantown Methodist Church; Faust, *Mothers*, 186; and Rable, *Civil Wars*, 13–15.

86. Howse journal, July 22 and 25, 1853.

87. Ibid, July 18, 1852.

88. Ibid, July 10, 1853; and e.g., July 4, 1852; November 28; January 16, 1853; and March 20.

89. Ibid., July 9, 1852; July 29; November 3; December 19; January 16, 1853; July 22; August 1; and September 25

90. Bernice Taylor Cargill, and Brenda Bethea Connelly, eds. *Settlers of Shelby County, Tennessee and Adjoining Counties*. Memphis: The Descendants of Early Settlers of Shelby County, Tennessee, 1989, 24.

91. Emily Lucken/Mills correspondence, Armistad to Emmie, May 2, 1858, GRH&GC.

92. *Appeal*, April 15, 1872, 4, col. 6.

93. An act to abolish and discontinue Spring Musters . . . , January 25, 1842, Acts 1861, 96f.; chap. 21 February 5, 1850, repealing compulsion to bear arms; and chap. 29, 114f. abolishing militia duty, February 15, 1857.

94. *Appeal*, September 6, 1852, 3, col. 1.

95. Appeal, September 24, 1852, 2, col. 1.

96. Emily Lucken/Mills correspondence, Armistad to Emmie, May 2, 1858, GRH&GC.

97. Nollan, "Troublous Times: The Civil War Letters of William J. Armstrong, M.D., March 1863-September 1865, WTHS, 60 (2006): 26.

98. H. H. Cunningham, *Doctors in Gray: The Confederate Medical Service*, 1958. 15.

99. Census 1860, CD 11, 165.

100. Susan Taylor, "Welcome to Germantown," *Midsouth Magazine, Commercial Appeal*, Feb. 24, 1974; Hall, *Germantown*, 96.

101. Bill to Britten Duke from Dr. Thos. M. Dupree, November 1854, Duke Papers, M&SC Room, MPL.

102. Howse journal, June 30, 1852; and January 17, 1853.

103. R.L. Scruggs, M.D., "Medical and Obstetrical Cases," *The Western Journal of Medicine and Surgery*, March 1847, 196–97, GBS.

104. Ibid, 197–98

105. Ibid, 198–200.

106. Scruggs, "Typhoid Fever, as it prevailed in Germantown, Tennessee, during the fall of 1847," *The Medical Examiner: A Monthly Record of Medical Science*, 4, 1848, 79–83, GBS.

107. Schedule 3, districts 10 and 11, Shelby County.

108. Census Statistics, 1860, 29, 213, 239–44, 247, 250, 252 and 258.

109. Faust, *Mothers*, 124–29; and cf. Rable, *Civil Wars*, 9, and 55–56.

110. Census statistics, 1860, 240, 258–59. Schedule 3, districts 10 and 11, Shelby County.

111. Kimbrough family cemetery, Church File/GRH&GC.

112. Schedule 3, district 11, Shelby County.

113. Howse journal, June 30, 1852; March 24, 1853; and passim.

114. *Appeal*, October 25, 1863, 3, col. 6.

115. Terry Isbell, "The Victorian Way of Death: How Our Ancestors Buried Their Dead, "Old Shelby County, 3–4.; Harrison account for Britton Duke, n.d., MVC 388, box 1, folder 13; and Hughes interviews.

116. Isbell, 4–5.

117. Ibid, 7–8.

118. Tim Schick, "13 Buildings in Germantown Cited for Historical Significance," *Press Scimitar*, Sept. 22, 1977;typical, surviving Germantown area homes, Hall, 88, 93, 95, 96, 114, 127; and Dye, 118.

119. Scott, chap. 3, 7; and E. H. Smith, *History of Germantown Baptist Church*, 1981; copy available at GRH&GS, 6 (e.g., Thomas Rutherford Baptist deacon until 1856).

120. "Cotton Plant," typed notes with attached photograph, dated June 1, 1982; and typed copy of title records, January 30, 1845; private collection of Carolyn Gates.

121. Interview, Walter Wills, March 29, 2011.

122. Hord, *Brooks Family*, correspondence, 47 and 50, Wills/Kirby collection; and Wills interview, October 29, 2011.

123. Wills interview, March 29, 2011.

124. *Avalanche*, March 10, 1862, 4, col. 7.

125. Charles S. Aiken, *The Cotton Plantation South since the Civil War*. (1998), 12–13.; Wills interview, October 29, 2011; and plan of Kirby Farm, Wills/Kirby collection.

126. Agricultural Schedules, 1860, Roll 10, Shelby County, CD 11.

127. Howse journal, January 9, 1853; January 18; February 1; February 15; March 24; and May 16.

128. 1850 Census District 11, 193a; Old Circuit Court Minutes, book 12, reel 29, pp. 120f., SCA; *Eagle & Enquirer*, January 27, 1855, 2, col. 2; *Appeal*, January 28, 1852, 3, col. 1; July 13, 3, col. 1; July 16, 3, col. 2; July 17, 3, col. 1; July 19, 3, col. 1; and October 8, 3, col. 1.

129. Old Circuit Court Minutes, book 12, reel 30, 261–64, SCA.

130. Cf. Wyatt-Brown, *Honor*, 364–66.

131. Old Circuit Court Minutes, book 12, reel 30, 291, 295–97, 380–83, and 401–402, SCA.

132. Index to Inmates of the Tennessee State Penitentiary, 1851–1870, tn.gov/tsla/history/state/inmate4.htm.

133. Howse journal, July 14, 1852; and June 2, 1853 on another duel elsewhere.

134. Ibid.

135. For a thorough analysis, Wyatt-Brown, *Honor*, 350–61.

136. McKibben, Indexes, subject duels.

137. Wyatt-Brown. *Honor*, 368–71.

138. "125 Years Ago," *Commercial Appeal*, January 11, 1977.

139. E.g. Loose Papers, Box 45, 1860, Merchant Bond, William Essmann, #5531; and Tippling Bond, #5552, SCA.

140. *Appeal*, March 30, 1852, 3, col. 2.

141. *Eagle & Enquirer*, March 5, 1852, 3, col. 1; and *Appeal*, March 5, 1852, 3, col. 1.

142. *Appeal*, July 12, 1860, 3, col. 2; and Nashville, *Union and American*, July 15, 3, col. 1.

143. Loose papers, Box 42, 1860, file #000, Pauper Burials, Unknown, by C.K. Holst, SCA.

144. Lipsey, "Memories," 32.

Chapter 2

1. *Appeal*, May 9, 1861, 4, col. 4.
2. Ibid.
3. *Union and America*, (Greenville, TN) July 15, 1860, 3, col. 1.
4. Bailey *Class and Tennessee's Confederate Generation*, 3–19 for a historiographic

summary; subsequently, Fox-Genovese, *Plantation Household*, and Faust, *Mothers*, come down on the side of stronger social elitism, while Cooper and Terrill, *American South*, favor social harmony; Thornton, "Ethic of Subsistence" for a sophisticated synthesis.

5. Subsequently published by Fred Arthur Dyer and John Trotwood Moore. *Tennessee Civil War Veteran Questionnaires*, 5 vols., 1985.

6. Bailey, 18–19.

7. Ibid, 19.

8. "October 25, 1861—Captain A.O. Edwards, in Germantown, too his sister in Tullahoma," TCWSB.

9. According to both the 1860 census and the 1866 federal tax assessment, Judge Pettit was only in the lower-middle wealth range.

10. Bailey, appendix Tables 4 and 5, 148–49.

11. See Appendix 3.

12. The story of Wright's failed, utopian project to prepare salves for emancipation precedes this period under study. Interested readers may consult Celia Morris Eckhardt, *Fanny Wright* 1984.

13. Clark. *The Tennessee Yeomen, 1840–1860*, 1932.

14. Bailey, 26–29; Howse's journal confirms this seasonal pattern, as do the agricultural schedules for censuses.

15. Clark, *Yeomen*, 16–17.

16. Howse journal, June 30, 1852; August 12; November 2; November 26; May 11, 1853; June 29; and September 12.

17. The Howse journal extensively documents this social and cultural lifestyle.

18. As indicated in Appendix 3, the lack of any personal wealth recorded for these professionals and mechanics seemingly resulted from the carelessness of the census takers.

19. Census 1860, CD 10, 361A.

20. Genovese, *Political Economy*, 13, 23–26, 28–31, 180–201, 206–8; and Wyatt-Brown, *Honor*, 176–77, and 189.

21. The 1860 census gives both occupation, landed wealth, non-real property, and place of birth.

22. These and subsequent such analyses are based on comparisons of the population censuses for District 11 in 1860 and 1870, and the slave schedules for 1860.

23. Abernethy, *From Frontier to Plantation in Tennessee*, pp. 285–86; see Appendix 3.

24. Cooper and Terrill, *South*, 211–14.

25. See Appendix 3; and Bailey, 25, and appendix Table 19, 158.

26. Ibid, 26.

27. Fox-Genovese, 224 and 235.

28. Dyer and Moore, xvi.

29. Ibid, vol. 3, 1032 and 1300.

30. Ibid.

31. Bailey, 160, Appendix Table 23, tabulates ranks achieved by respondents to the Tennessee veterans questionnaire. In the volunteer regiments, officers and NCOs were elected, and there was a surprising degree of opportunity for the poor and small-holder to achieve company grade sergeant and officer's ranks. Not unexpectedly for any society, field officer

and general's ranks fell to those who already had proven managerial or military command experience. Also table 20, 159 on political advantages.

32. Howse journal, e.g., July 20, 1852; July 23; and August 8, 1853.
33. Ibid., July 21, 1853
34. Bailey, appendix, Tables 17 and 19, 157–58.
35. Cf. Rable, *Civil Wars*, 21.
36. Bailey, appendix, Table 12, 153–54.
37. Bailey, appendix, Table 11, 152.
38. Bailey, appendix, Table 13, p. 155.
39. Bailey, appendix, Table 17, p. 157.
40. Jennifer K. Boone, "'Mingling Freely': Tennessee Society on the Eve of the Civil War," *THQ*, 51 (fall 1992), 3: 137–146.
41. Ibid, p. 142; and Wyatt-Brown, *Honor*, 67–68.
42. Boone, 143.
43. Ibid, 144–45; and Fox-Genovese, *Plantation Household*, 233–35.
44. Emily Lucken Mills Correspondence and Mills Family Records, GRH& GC.
45. Clark, 11.
46. Boone, 142, Table 2.
47. Ibid, 11–12.
48. Wyatt-Brown, *Honor*, 63–64, and 66–69.
49. Wyatt-Brown, xii.
50. Emily Lucken/Mills correspondence, letter to father, October 1, 1852, GRH&GC.
51. Census 1860, 467, see Appendix 3.
52. Census, 1850, 574–75, and 1860, 467.
53. Steve Baker, "Agriculture, Race, and Free Blacks in West Tennessee," *WTHS*, 48 (1954): 107–117.
54. *Tennessee Blue Book*, p. 414; Harkins, *Metropolis*, 43–45; Lamon, *Blacks*, 22; and Young, 25–26.
55. John Dougan, "Why They Chose to Stay: The Petitions of Free Persons of Color to Remain in Shelby County, Tennessee, 1843–1853," *WTHS*,
    48 (1994): 118–25; Loose Papers and Minutes of the County Court, passim, SCA; and e.g., *Appeal*, September 19, 1860, 2, col. 2.
56. Loose Papers, 1853–28–0715.
57. The Dred Scott Case; in the United States Supreme Court, December Term, 1856, 9, loc.gov.
58. Wyatt-Brown, *Honor*, 3–4.
59. Estes and Hamlett, *Short History of Memphis Annual Conference*, p. 13, MCA; L.H. Coleman, "The Baptists in Shelby County to 1900," *WTHS*, 15 (1961), 12–13; Holly Reed Harrison, "'Our Relation to persons of African Descent Has Been Less than Ideal ...': The Southern Baptist Convention, the Christian Life Commission, and Race Relations," *WTHS*, 53 (1999): 119f.; Elton Watlington, "Glimpses of Methodist History in the Mid-South," *WTHS*, 56 (2002): 129; and *Appeal*, February 13, 1861, 2 col. 3; and June 15, 4, col. 1. For a more thorough discussion of the complexities of each denomination's positions on slavery,

Herman A. Norton, *Religion in Tennessee, 1777–1945* (Knoxville, University of Tennessee Press, 1981), 57–61.

60. Lewis, 32–5, for a precise overview of local Jewish attitudes about and participation in slavery.

61. Minutes of Annual Conferences, 1854–1867, MCA; 1860 Census, District 11, 179; and slave schedules 1860.

62. Howse journal, May 12, 1853; and June 26.

63. Evan's Presbytery notebook, GPC; Minutes of the Annual Conferences, MEP, 1854, 526, MCA.

64. Coleman, "Baptists," *WTHS*, 15 (1961): 16; cf. Harrison, "Relation," *WTHS*, 53 (1999): 22; and Estes & Hamlet, *Short History*, 13;

65. Minutes of the Annual Conferences, MEP, 1844–1860; and Lamon, *Blacks*, 17.

66. Genovese, *Jordan*, 215–84, for an extensive analysis, including African elements of beliefs and practice; and Cooper and Terrill, 236–38.

67. Cooper and Terrill, 234–35.

68. Chaplain John Eaton, Jr., to Lieutenant Colonel Jno. A. Rawlins, 29 April, 1863, cited in Berlin, *Families*, 157.

69. Berlin, *Freedom*, Ser. I, Vol. III, 686; and Douglas Egerton, *The Wars of Reconstruction* (New York: Bloomsbury Press, 21014), 78–79.

70. Wills interview, October 29, 2011.

71. Hord, *Brooks Family*, correspondence, 46, and 48, Wills/Kirby records.

72. Scruggs, *The Medical Examiner*, vol. 4, 1848, 79–83, GBS.

73. Lamon, *Blacks*, 18.

74. Fox-Genovese, *Plantation Household*, 165–68, 172–74, 176–81, 183–86.

75. Ibid, plus pp. 143–44, 148f, 151f, 156, 191.

76. Saunders, Richard L. "The Racial Demographics of West Tennessee: An Essay Based on U.S. Census Data, 1830–2000," WTHSP, 61, 131.

77. Sutcliffe, e.g., 77–20; and Fox-Genovese, *Plantation Household*, 287–89.

78. Lamon, *Blacks*, 28.

79. Fox-Genovese, *Plantation Household*, 151, 153–561, 163–64; and Cooper and Terrill, 214–15, and 224–25.

80. "The Nurenberger's - city's oldest house," *Germantown News*, February 24, 2010, 3, reprint of original Anita Ledsinger, article.

81. Faust, *Mothers*, 73.

82. There are indications that the deputy marshal was either careless in noting mulatto status, or sensitive to owner's public image, since the deputy was a local.

83. 1860 slave schedules, CD 11, 1–2, and CD 10, 1.

84. *Appeal*, November 8, 1860, 2, col. 3; and Census 1860, x and 467.

85. Ancestry.com reports, Roberts name file, GRH&GC.

86. He is missing in the censuses of either 1840 or 1860 in Civil District Ten where his plantation was located. He appears in the 1840 and 1850 censuses for Madison Tennessee, where he owned more farmland. It is unclear how he could appear in both places in the 1850 population census. His absence from all 1860 censuses resulted from his 1859 death and his

estate being unsettled. Both he and his slave count were passed over creating accuracy problems for this narrative.

87. Marriage Bonds, Licenses, 1833–42, no 751–1400, SCA.

88. Annie C. Tuggle, *Another World Wonder*. Self-published, 1973. Copy available GR H&GC. 2; Arthur L. Webb, "From exile to excellence: the Roberts family," *Tri-State Defender*, May 29, 2002; and Dr. Paula E. Young, "The Roberts Family," typescript, and "The Plantation," hand-written notes, Roberts name file, GRH&GC.

89. Webb; Young; and typed inventory, "Transfer of Slaves of S. H. Roberts (February 1860), Roberts name file, GRH&GC. No Kincanon or Roberts are listed as slave-owners in the 1860 slave schedules, perhaps because the estate was still unsettled at the time it was taken.

90. Excerpts from Howse diary, APC/GRH&GC.

91. "Germantown Pioneers," Germantown *News*, June 23, 1977, 4B.

92. Lamon, *Blacks*, 17.

93. Minutes of the County Court of Shelby County, book 10, 35, SCA.

94. A.W. Montague, "My Experiences as a Confederate Soldier," MVC, Acc#89–52, MS 54–127, 17.

95. *The Western Journal of Medicine and Surgery*, March 1847, 198–99, GBS.

96. Ibid, 200.

97. Bill to Briton Duke from Dr. Thos. M. Dupree, November 1854, Duke Papers, M&SC Room, MPL.

98. SCA.

99. Census Statistics, 1860, 281–83 and 519.

100. "The Slave Laws of Tennessee," esp. Jones v. Allen, 38 Tenn., 627, 1858, genealogy trails.com/tenn/slavelaws.html

101. E.g., loose papers, 1850, box 20, #933, Inquest for Negro "Frank," JT Mason owner, Ledbetter, Sept 1849, SCA.

102. "Slave Laws of Tennessee."

103. Ibid,; and Cooper and Terrill, 224–25, 233–34.

104. Tuggle, 1.

105. Durham, *Railway* 58f-59 and n. 29, 102.

106. Census 1860, xv-xvi and 33–38.

107. 1860 Census, xv-xvi.

108. *Appeal*, September 25, 1856, 2, col. 6; February 5, 1857, 2, col. 7; and November 15, 1860, 1, col. 6.

109. *Appeal*, November 15, 1860.

110. Nashville *Union and American*, April 17, 1860, 3, col. 2, citing Brownsville *Atlas*.

111. *Appeal*, October 20, 1858, 3, col. 1.

112. *Appeal*, November 5, 1856, 3, col. 1; e.g. *Fayetteville Observer*, December 4, 1856, 2; and Lamon, 20, 22–24.

113. "The Slave Laws of Tennessee;" and Cooper and Terrill, 209–10.

114. *Nashville Union and American*, February 20, 1856, 2; February 26, 2; December 14, 2; and December 23, 2.

115. Quarterly Court loose papers, SCA.

116. "Tracing the 'roots' of Black Germantown," *Tri-State Defender*, April 23, 1977.

Chapter 3

1. There is no primary evidence for the town's naming. Traditions are questionable. One argues the name grew from the early presence of several German merchants in the town. That was hardly a unique situation in the area around Memphis. Another is that the surveyor of the first town plots was named German. Also unlikely that later residents would even be aware of his name, much less honor it. More likely is the story that the citizens originally proposed the name of Luckenville after its most popular inn keeper and brewer, who modestly declined. If true, "Germantown" was the next best way to honor him. That is a Lucken family tradition recorded by his granddaughter.

2. *Appeal*, August 26, 1873, 1, col.3.

3. Eric C. Albertson, et al, *Terrestrial and Submerged Cultural Resources Survey along Approximately 6 KM of the Wolf River, Shelby County, Tennessee*. Report for Corps of Engineers, Memphis District. Memphis: Panamerican Consultants, Inc., 2001; 18, 20–21, and 23; William F. Currotto, *Tracking the Wolf* (Memphis: self-published, n.d.), 10 , quoting anonymous ms, M&SC; Ronald W. Waschka, "River Transportation at Memphis before the Civil War," *WTHS*, 45 (1991): 1–18; Lawrence G. Gunderson, Jr., "West Tennessee and the Cotton Frontier, 1818–1840," *WTHS*, 52 (1998): 25–43; and Dorothy Rich, *Fayette County* (1989), 28–29.

4. Joe Curtis, "Wolf River Carried Own Steamers Once," *Commercial Appeal*, January 28, 1954, 36 quoting memories of John Johnson; and Nelson Diary, *WTHS*, 64 (2010): 131.

5. County Court Minutes, Shelby County, Tennessee Book I, 1820–24, 6 May, 1823, 172, reprinted in *Memphis, Shelby County Tennessee, the Early Years*, Selected Court Records & Survey Book, 1820–1850.

6. Ronald W. Waschka, "Road Building in and Near Memphis," *WTHS*, 43 (1997): 51

7. *The Public Statutes of the United States from 1789 to March 3, 1845*, Sess. V, Ch. 172, 276, GBS.

8. Acts, 1847–48, 401, and 403404; and John Linn Hopkins, "Brief History: Turnpike Companies Related to Old Poplar Pike," Hughes Papers, GRH&GC.

9. Acts, 1859–60, Ch. 72, Sec. 1, 55.

10. Loose Papers, 1844, box 10, #417; 1845, box 11, # 482 & 483, bridge construction payments, SCA; and Howse journal, e.g., December 23, 1852; and February 4, 1853.

11. Waschka, "Road Buliding," 52–5, and 60; and cf. J.M. Stafford, "The Cretaceous and Superior Formations of West Tennessee," *The American Journal of Science and Arts*, 2nd Series, vol. 37, May 1865, 360–61, GBS.

12. Acts, 1849–50, Ch. CXLIV, Sec. 6, 473.

13. *Appeal*, August 6, 1848, 3, col. 1; and Booth, "Germantown Pioneers."

14. Acts, 1847–48, 402.

15. John M. Keating, *History of Memphis Tennessee*, 1888, 281, GBS; County Court, Minute Book 9, 1858, 1, SCA; Hopkins, Hughes papers, GRH&GC.

16. Hopkins, "Kirby Farm."

17. Acts, 1859–60, Ch. 159, Sec. 1, 500; and Appeal, June 16, 1860. 3, col. 2.

18. Cloyes Interview; and Hughes interview.

19. *Appeal*, March 5, 1852, 3, col. 1.

20. *Daily Globe*, January 7, 1854, 8.

21. *Tri-Weekly Appeal*, May 19, 1849, 2, col. 7. No Furber appears in any of the 1850 or 1860 censuses, but other sources indicate his presence during the 1850s.

22. Loose Papers, Box 47, 1861, #2446, SCA; and 1860 census, Dist. 11, 164.

23. Loose Papers, 1860, box 42, # 9, Petition to County Court for new road from Germantown Plank Road to Raleigh Road; and 1860, box 41, #000, Jury of View—W. Moore (juror), SCA

24. E.g. Petition, n.d., County Court Loose Papers, 1860–42–0000, SCA.

25. Loose papers, Box 42, 1860, file # 9, SCA.

26. For a general history of the early M&C RR, John C. Mehrling, "The Memphis and Charleston Railroad," *WTHS*, 19 (1965): 21–35; and, Paul Harncourt, *A Biography of the Memphis and Charleston Railroad* (San Jose: Writer's Club Press, 2000). *Appeal*, July 24, 1852, 2, col. 6; and September 17, 3, col. 1.

27. Howse journal, August 2, 1852; and August 6.

28. Paul Harcourt, *Biography of the Memphis and Charleston Railroad* (2000), 93 and 237, Appendix B. This contradicts all previous depictions of the first engine into Germantown, usually described as an antiquated 0–4-0 with a vertical boiler on the back and the engineer siting up front like a wagon driver. This misunderstanding resulted from confusion with the "Best Friend of Charleston" which had been brought to Memphis to run out to Germantown for an historic celebration. It was a replica of the engine run on the first railroad out of Charleston in the 1830s, not the later M&C RR.

29. *Appeal*, August 10, 1852, 3, col. 2.

30. *Appeal*, July 27, 1852, 3, col. 1; and August 4, 1852, 3, col. 1.

31. *Appeal*, September 9, 1852, 2, col. 2.

32. *Appeal*, September 18, 1852, 2, col. 5.

33. Harcourt, *Biography of the Memphis and Charleston*, 105–106, citing *Appeal*, September 16, 1852, and *Huntsville Southern Advocate*, 10 November and 15 December.

34. Harcourt, 251, Appendix F.

35. Jack Daniel, *Southern Railway from Stevenson to Memphis* (1996) 24, 33, and 320; and Stewart Interview.

36. Howse journal, April 5, 1853; April 15; June 10.

37. 1860 census, District 11; in 1859, the agent was J.T. Tenbrooke, gone by 1860, *The Shopper's Guide: Containing a Complete List of all Railroad Stations . . .* , 1859, 122, GBS.

38. Mehrling, 31; and *Appeal*, February 6, 1855, 3, col. 1.

39. The relevant records are probably held by the Southern Museum, Archives and Library, Kennesaw, Ga., but have yet to be processed; correspondence from Dick Hillman, October 5, 2011.

40. *Appeal*, September 23, 1855, 2, col. 1; and October 4, 1855, 2, col. 7.

41. Mehrling, "Memphis & Charleston," 31–32; and *Appeal*, July `14, 1861, 3, col. 1.

42. *Appeal*, September 23, 1855, 3, col. 7; and April 16, 1861, 4, col. 5.

43. Annual Report of the Memphis & Charleston RR, July 1, 1861, csa-railroads.com/Essays/Original Docs/AR/Ar,_M_a_C_7-1-61_S.htm;; and Headquarters Third Division, Huntsville, April 11, 1862 (Captured M&C RR Locomotives) NA/RG94/159.

44. *Appeal*, October 15, 1852, 3, col. 1.
45. *Appeal*, January 25, 1853, 3, col. 1; September 26, 1854, 3, col. 1; and January 9, 1857, 3, col. 1.
46. Nashville *Union and American*, November 11, 1860, 3, col. 1.
47. M&C, Chief Engineer's Report, July 1, 1860, Daniel, 27, 29; and 35.
48. Annual Report, July 1, 1861.
49. Daniel, "Southern Railway," 69.
50. Mehrling, "Memphis & Charleston," 33–35; and Ayer's *Handbook*, 22–23.
51. Daniel, 55.
52. Interview with Jennifer Lynch, Senior Research Analyst, Postal History.
53. Ibid; and Postmaster Finder.
54. *The United States Postal Service*, 11–15.
55. Ayers, *Descriptive Handbook*, 22–23.; Weekly *Appeal*, August 8, 1845, 1, col. 5; and *Appeal*, April 15, 1872, 4, col. 6.
56. 1860 Census, District 11, 165.
57. *Tri-Weekly Appeal*, May 19, 1849, 2, col. 7.
58. Dye, 61.
59. *Appeal*, December 12, 1845, p2, col.2 and 3, col.7; and *Tri-Weekly Appeal*, January 22, 1846, 3, col.2.
60. *Tri-Weekly Enquirer*, August 20, 1846, 2, col. 3; and *Enquirer*, April 7, 1847, 2, col. 3; May 14, 2, col. 5, and June 3, 2, col. 3.
61. J. Curtis, "Wolf's Little Flood Recalls Bigger Ones," *Appeal*, January 22, 1947, 18.
62. Scott, chap. 2, 14; Hughes interview, June 30, 2010; Howse journal, July 9, 1853; July 13; July 16; July 30; August 2; and *Appeal*, November 5, 1856, 3, col. 8.
63. *Ledger*, April 25, 1874, 3.
64. Hord, Brooks Family, correspondence, 50, Wills/Kirby collection.
65. Schroeder-Lein, *Hospitals*, 37–38; and Goodspeed, "Shelby," 915–16.
66. "Germantown Pioneers," *Germantown News*, July 21, 1977, 16B.
67. *Appeal*, March 5, 1852, 3, col. 1.
68. Loose papers, 1860/42/0, jury of view, J.J. Todd; 1861/47/2462, and 1862/48/2534, road overseer, SCA
69. 1860 Census, CD 11, 171.
70. Census 1860, 471.
71. Beverly Booth, "Germantown Pioneers: Traces of Germantown Settlers Obscured by Time," *Germantown News*, July 14, 1977, interview with Molly Molitor Nowlin; and cf. 1860 Census, Germantown, 170. It is not entirely clear that all the children listed in the household in this census and born in Mississippi and Tennessee at various dates were Francis'. Family traditions related by Mrs. Nowlin do not speak of a Charles or Martha.
72. *Appeal*, January 21, 1858, 3, col. 3.
73. 1860 census, District 11.
74. "History prepared and read by Squire Tom Phillips," transcribed by Margaret Harrison Owen, March 27, 1938, 2, GPC.
75. *Appeal*, July 21, 1852, 2, col. 6 and July 18, 1854, 2, col. 5.
76. *Appeal*, May 19, 1855, 3, col. 5; and July 18, 1854, 3, col. 1.
77. *Appeal*, June 4, 1857, 6, col. 3.

78. Allison, *Notable Men of Tennessee*, 36.

79. U.S. Census, 1860, Agriculture, xi.

80. *Appeal*, October 31, 1855, 3, col. 1.

81. Hughes interview, June 30, 2010; *Journal of the Franklin Institute*, vol. 37, 1859, 372, GBS; Scott, Ch. 3, 9–10.; Ayers, *Handbook*, 23; Harrison's mill, *Appeal*, November 14, 1868, 1, col. 1; and Mills to Martha, February 17, 1864, describing pre-war Germantown, VRHC.

82. Emily Lucken/Mills correspondence, letters to Emily, March 15, 185(4?) and December 9, GRH&GC.

83. Available at GRH&GC, Shelby County Room, MPL, and SCA. From all indications, the vast majority of tracts indicated applied to a much earlier date, prior to 1840. There are at least three versions of this map: one a preliminary draft, and two printed versions, one not including the lands absorbed from Mississippi below the old state line. There are many contradictions among these versions and the names of known major landowners in the 1850 census. Some of these may relate to legalities grown from purchases made on credit. For instance, The Kimbrough lands had been bought from James Titus in 1838, instalments to be paid out by 1843. Those lands appear in the names of Titus and others in all drafts of the "1850" maps. The un-divided holdings of N.B.S. (Nicey Sheppard) appear where the town center was well developed by 1850. Both the lands of Dr. Cornelius or Brooks, long-standing residents, do not appear in their names. Only a part of the Duke lands are in their names. Most inaccurate, the Nashoba Tract appears as subdivided among several owners, which it never was. The 1850 date seems grossly anachronous. Nevertheless, despite their peculiarities, all versions show a massive and rapid change of land ownership and the land speculation involved from whatever earlier date it portrayed.

84. Howse journal, January 11, 1853; and August 20.

Chapter 4

1. See Oaks, *Freedom*, for an analysis of the abolitionist strategy as a real and growing threat to the long-range survival of slavery.

2. Wooster, *Politicians*, 45.

3. Atkins, *Parties, Politics, and the Sectional Conflict in Tennessee, 1832–1861*, 81–82.

4. Ibid, 82–88; Wooster, *Politicians*, 48f.; and Thornton, "Ethic of Subsistence," pp. 6 on regional, political, economic and demographic differences between the parties.

5. Thornton, "Ethics of Subsistence," especially for the development of this aspect of local political inclinations.

6. *Enquirer*, May 8, 1840, 1, col. 1, June 27, 1848, 2, col. 2, June 29, 2, col. 2, and May 30, 1849, 2, col. 3.

7. *Appeal*, August 4, 1843, 2, col. 1; and *Tri-Weekly Appeal*, August 9, 1845, 2, cols. 1 and 3.

8. *Appeal*, August 4, 1844, 2, col. 2.

9. *Appeal*, November 4, 1852, 2, col. 1.

10. Thornton, "Ethics," 21–22.

11. *Appeal*, July 17, 1852, 2, col. 2.

12. *Appeal*, June 15, 1853, 2, col. 1.

13. *Appeal*, August 9, 1844, 2, cols. 1 and 3; August 16, 2, col. 2; and June 15, 1853, 2.

14. *Appeal*, September 24, 1852, 2, col. 1.
15. *Appeal*, April 15, 1872, 4, col. 6.
16. *Tri-Weekly Appeal*, December 1, 1849, 2, col. 3.
17. TSLA website www.tn.gov/tsla/history/newspapers/tn-paper.htm; and Thomas H. Baker, "The Early Newspapers of Memphis, Tennessee, 1827–1860," *WTHS*, 17 (1963): 20–46.
18. Howse journal, December 21, 1852; February 3, 1853; and May 11.
19. *Appeal*, August 9, 1844, 3, col. 2.
20. Sterling Tracy, "The Immigrant Population of Memphis," *WTHA*, 4 (1950): 72–73.; and Harcourt, *Biography*, 95 and 101–102.
21. Keating, *History of the City of Memphis Tennessee. . . .*, 245, GBS.
22. E.g., *Semi-Weekly Appeal*, August 16, 1844, 2; *Weekly Appeal*, August 1, 1845, 2;
23. *Semi-Weekly Appeal*, August 16, 1844, 2, col. 3.
24. Faust, *Mothers*, 10–11.
25. *Weekly Appeal*, August 1, 1845, 3, col. 6; *Tri-Weekly Appeal*, August 2, and August 5;
26. *Appeal*, December 5, 1855, 2, col. 4
27. Cooper & Terrill, *South*, 316–17.
28. *Appeal*, August 7, 1855, 3, col. 2.
29. *Whig*, August 6, 1855, 1, col. 3; and *Appeal*, February 10, 1855, 2, col. 1; and December 5, 2, col. 4.
30. *Appeal*, February 10, 1855, 2, cols. 1 and 5; September 29, 2, cols. 1–4; and November 5, 1856, 3 col. 1.
31. Howse journal, July 6, 1852; December 2; September 8, 1853.
32. Ibid.
33. Census Statistics, 1860, lvi and lviii.
34. *Boston Investigator*, October 4, 1848, Issue 22, col. D, citing the *Chicago Tribune*.
35. Scott, chap. 3, 3.
36. "Memories of the City's Settlers," *Germantown News*, June 16, 1977.
37. Howse journal, May 7, 1853.
38. Eckhardt, 273.
39. Nelson Diary, *WTHS*, 64 (2010): 125–26.
40. *Appeal*, June 25, 1852, 2, col. 5; July 9, 2, col. 2; and July 20, 2, col. 1.
41. *Appeal*, July 20, 1852, 2, col. 1.
42. *Appeal*, September 6, 1854, 2, col. 3; and on the yard, Walter Chandler, "The Memphis Navy Yard, an Adventure in Internal Improvement," *WTHS*, 1 (1947): 68–72.
43. Smith, *Germantown*, 7; and *Appeal*, June 30, 1853, 2, col. 2, and 3, col. 1.
44. *Appeal*, July 6, 1853, 2, col. 2; and July 19, 3, col. 2.
45. Norton, *Religion*, 56–57.
46. *Appeal*, February 10, 1855, 2, col. 5.
47. Howse journal, July 30. 1853.
48. Wooster, *Politicians*, 85, 99–102; and Quarterly Court Minutes, SCA.
49. Acts, 1836, Ch. 1.
50. Sheriff's declaration, May 13, 1837, (County Court Minutes, SCA); and Wills/Kirby Farm collection.

51. Loose Papers, 1849, box 19, #473, County Court Chairman Payment, Ledbetter, Samuel W.; 1850, box 21, #552, Coroner Bond, Ledbetter, S.W.; 1854, box 29, #797, Justice of the Peace Bond, Pettit, J.W.A.; 1855, box 31, #4231; 1856, box 32, # 130; 1856, box 34, # 4552; 1858, box 36, # 689; 1858, box 37, # 869, County Court Payment, Pettit, J.W.A.; 1860, box 41, #000, Justice of the Peace - Resignation, and Judge—John W.A. Pettit, Oath of office, SCA

52. *Appeal*, November 17, 1859, 3, col. 3.

53. Wooster, *Politicians*, 99.

54. Minutes, Quarterly Sessions Court, book 4, 560 and 576, SCA.

55. Report of returns, March 15/60, RG-87B/1860–61, TSA&L.

56. See Wooster, *Politicians*, Tables 6e, 7e, ad 8e, for state legislators.

57. Minutes, Quarterly Sessions Court, book 4, 616; and Loose Papers, 1842, box 8, #368, constable bond, SCA.

58. Loose Papers, 1845, box 11, #444, constable bond, SCA; and 1850 census, population schedules, District 11, p. 198B.; Loose Papers, 1844, box 10, #418, Job Lewis, deputy sheriff bond, SCA.

59. Loose Papers, 1848, box 16, #516; 1854, box 29, # 762; 1856, box 32, # 892; 1858, box 37, # 1001, Constable Bond; and County Court, minutes Book 9, 1860, 506, SCA.

60. Duke papers, folder IV, M&SC Room, MPL.

61. Ibid, draft of article of agreement, n.d.

62. Loose papers, 1848, box 15, #000; and 1856, box 32, #000, Electors Common School Commission, SCA.

63. Fleming, "Education;" Loose Papers, passim; 1846, box 11, #000, School Payment (misc.) 11th CD, Thomas Moore; and 1838, box 14, #000, School Payment, Eugene Magevney, SCA.

64. Loose papers, 1848, box 15, #000, election report; and passim, 1849–53, SCA.

65. Loose papers, 1854, box 28, #77, commission report, July 21, 1854; and census, box 28, #92, SCA.

66. In reporting these appointments, Pettit felt compelled to assert their legality, report, August? 28, 1854, loose papers 1854, box 30, #98, SCA.

67. Loose Papers, 1856, box 32, #000, Common School Commission Election, SCA.

68. *Appeal*, March 20, 1861, 3, col. 1.

69. County Court, Minutes Book 9, 1860, 526, and 1861, 704, SCA.

70. Howse journal, February 28, 1853.

71. Thornton, "Ethics," 15.

72. Acts, 1841–42, Ch. XXX, 26–29.

73. E.g., Acts, 1859–60, Ch. 72, 55.

74. Acts, 1849–50, Ch. XVII, sec. 2, 37–38.

75. Acts, 1841–42, Ch. XXX, sec. 2, 27.

76. Acts, 1849–50, 38.

77. Genovese, *Political Economy*, 13, 23–24, 28; and Wyatt-Brown, *Honor*, 70–87.

78. Wooster, *Politicians*, 126–29, and Tables 6e, 7e, and 8e; and Atkins, Table 1, 7 and Table 2, 8.

79. Cooper & Terrill, *South*, 323–24, 330.

80. Ibid, 313–15.

81. Atkins, *Parties*, 206–212, and 216–17.
82. *Appeal*, October 20, 1859, 2, col. 1, October 21, 2, col. 1, October 25, 2, col. 1, October 26, 2, col. 1, November 5, 2, cols. 1–5, and November 16, 2, cols. 4–5.
83. Atkins, 218–21.
84. Ibid, 224–28.
85. *Appeal*, November 8, 1860, 2, col. 1.
86. Howse journal, November 30, 1852.
Part I, Summary
87. See Cooper and Terrill, 323–33 on regional differences in southern industrialization as well as evidence against the argument that the slave economy and culture so stifled modernization that it was self-destructive.
88. Ash, *Occupied South*, 4–5.
89. Wyatt-Brown, "Snopesian Crime."
90. Colin Woodward, *American Nations: A History of the Eleven Rival Regional Cultures of North America*. One problem involved with applying his analysis to our subjects is that census data about origins is limited to state of birth rather than the "nations" he identifies which are especially mixed among settlers in social-geographic Appalachia.

Chapter 5

1. *Appeal*, February 10, 1861, p.2, col. 1; and February 21, 2, col. 7.
2. *Appeal*, February 8, 1861, p. 2; March 8, p. 2, col. 1; and Baker, "Early Newspapers," WTHS, 17 (1963): 44.
3. Lufkin, "Secession and Coercion in Tennessee, the Spring of 1861," THQ, 50 (Summer 1991), 2: 98–109.
4. *Appeal*, April 19, 1861, 2, c. 3.
5. *Appeal*, April 19, 1861, 2, c. 3.
6. *Appeal*, April 14, 1861, 3, c. 2.
7. *Appeal*, April 21, 1861, 3, c. 5.
8. *Appeal*, April 14, 1861, 2, col. 1.
9. *Appeal*, April 17, 1861, 2, cols. 3–4 for Collierville; April 24, 2, col. 4 for Germantown.
10. *Appeal*, April 17, 1861, 2, col. 3; and April 21, 2, col. 2.
11. Acts, 1861, Extra Session, chap. 1, 13–18, chaps. 3 & 4, 21–23.; *Appeal*, May 11, 1861, 1, col. 1; *War of the Rebellion: Official Record of the Union and Confederate Armies*. Washington: The Government Printing Office, 1881–1898. A compilation of military reports and correspondence on both sides (hereafter OR), ORIV, 1:296–98; and Acts, 1861, Extra Session, chap. 2, 19–21.
12. *Appeal*, May 21, 1861, 2, col. 3. "T.W. Trueheart" was undoubtedly G.W. Trueheart.
13. *Appeal*, April 17, 1861, 3, col. 2; April 19, 1861, 3, cols. 2, and 3; *Avalanche*, April 17, 2, col. 2; and OR vol. 52, pt. II, 67, 134–35., and 154.
14. *Avalanche*, April 16, 3, cols. 2 and 3; and April 27, 2, col. 5
15. *Appeal*, April 19, 1861, 3, col. 3.
16. Lufkin, "The Northern Exodus from Memphis during the Secession Crisis." *THQ*, 42 (1988): 6, and 9.

17. ORII, vol. 2: 1368–70.

18. Grievances and Memorial of the Greenville Convention," quoted in Oliver P. Temple, *East Tennessee and the Civil War* (1899), 565.

19. "Vote for Separation from the Union," June 8, 1861, 2, and for Report for Shelby County, RG 87/roll 1861–2, TSL&A.

20. OR, vol. 51, pt. I, 383.

21. OR III, vol. 1, 299f.

22. Ben H. Severance, *Tennessee's Radical Army*, (2005), 3–4.

23. *Acts*, 1861, chap. 30, 115–16; and *Appeal*, e.g., December 8, 1860, 3, col. 3; April 10, 1861, 2, col. 2; April 16, 2, col. 2; April 17, 3, col. 3; April 18, 3, cols. 2 and 3; April 23, 3, col. 2; April 28, 3, col. 4; April 30, 3, col. 3; May 4, 3, col. 2; May 14, 3, col. 2; and June 18, 2, col. 2.

24. *Appeal*, April 23, 1861, 1, cols. 2–3; strangely, neither Alsup, Coles, Cross, Rogers or Shepherd show up in the 1860 census for either District 11 or 10; but Cross was present in 1850, Dist. 11. The absence of some of these men appears to be a product of the inaccuracies of the 1860 census.

25. E.g., *Appeal*, December 12, 1861, 2, col. 6.

26. *Appeal*, April 23, 1861, 2, col. 2.

27. Ibid, 1, cols. 2–3.

28. Arnold, "Baptism of Fire, Forging of Veterans: The Thirteenth Tennessee Infantry and the Battle of Belmont," *WTHS*, 52 (1998): 96; and Wigfall Grays historical marker, Collierville.

29. *Appeal*, April 23, 1861, 1, cols. 2–3.

30. Ibid.

31. *Appeal*, April 28, 3, col. 4, for the Shelby Grays.

32. *Appeal*, April 26, 1861, 2, col. 3.

33. Faust, *Mothers*, 17–27.

34. Rable, *Civil Wars*, 138–40; and Faust, *Mothers*, 24–25.

35. *Appeal*, August 17, 1861, 3, col. 2.

36. On the planters' and urban wives support for the war, Whites, *Civil War*, 12–13, 21–24.

37. *Appeal*, May 9, 1861, 2, col. 9 and 3, col. 3; and May 15, 3, col. 1 and 2.

38. Company Muster Roll, Co. C, 13 Regiment Tennessee Infantry, May 5, 1863, NARA, M-268/169; and Arnold, "Thirteenth," *WTHS*, 52 (1998): 96.

39. Vaughan, *Personal Record of the Thirteenth Regiment Tennessee Infantry*, 1897, 9, and 49–52, GBS; and West, "The Thirteenth Tennessee Regiment—Confederate States of America," *Tennessee Historical Magazine*, 7 (October 1921): 180–89.

40. Vaughn, 49; and Lindsley, 320.

41. John B. Lindsley, ed, *Military Annals of Tennessee* (1886), 9, 48–49, 66–67, 69, and 75.

42. Acts, 1861, chap. 17, January 31, 1861, 37, and Militia Laws, chap 30, March 22, 1860, 115f.

43. *Appeal*, December 8, 1860, 3, col. 3; April 16, 1861, 2, col. 2; April 23, 2, col. 2.

44. Advertisement, *Appeal*, April 1, 1862, 3, col. 3, and *Tennesseans in the Civil War*, vol. 1, 27–28.

45. Aden, "In Memoriam, Seventh Tennessee Cavalry, C.S.A.," *WTHS*, 17 (1963): 109.

46. Hunt, p. 96; and Scott, chap. 4, 2.
47. Goodspeed, "Shelby," 826, 830–31 and 835.
48. *Appeal*, April 23, 1861, 2, col. 2;
49. *Appeal*, May 4, 1861, 3, col. 2; May 7, 3, col. 3; and July 7, 2, col. 7; and cf. Acts, 1861, 98.
50. Acts, 1861, chap. 3, 25 and 30; Minutes of the County Court of Shelby County, book 10, 41–42; and Loose Papers, 1861, Box 48, #0, Home Guard Regulations, n.d., SCA.
51. Acts, 1861, chap. 3, 25.
52. Loose Papers, Box 48; and County Court, Minutes Book 10, 1861, 80, SCA.
53. Minutes Quarterly Sessions Court, book 10, 41–42, 46, and 59; and Loose Papers, Box 48, SCA.
54. Loose Papers, 1861, box 48, #000, Home Guard, Tuggle, J.J, 11th CD; Minutes of the County Court of Shelby County, book 10, p. 43, SCA; and 1860 Census, District 11.
55. Minutes, book 10, 43; and 1870 census, District 11, household 382.
56. *Appeal*, August 13, 1861, 4, col 7.
57. *Appeal*, August 17, 1861, 3, col. 2.
58. Vaughn, *Personal Record*, 9–11, and 52; Arnold, "Thirteenth," *WTHS*, 52 (1998): 95–98; Scarbrough, "Camp Journal," WTHS, 66: 128–38; and OR, 7, 691–92.
59. *Appeal*, October 18, 1861, 2, col. 5.
60. Vaughn, 12–13 and 51; Arnold, 98–100; Lindsley, 315 and 320–21; and *Appeal*, November 13, 1861, 2, col. 5.
61. Rable, *Civil Wars*, 64.
62. McPherson, *Cause & Comrades*, 33–36.
63. OR, 4, 449f-50, 560–61., and 564;
64. Letter December 6, 1861, Frederick Bradford Papers, TSLA, 1, TCWS.
65. Nashville *Daily Gazette*, December 4, 1861, citing Memphis *Argus*; and *Daily Appeal*, December 18, 1861, 2, col. 1.
66. Bailey, *Class.* appendix, Table 23, 160.
67. Ibid.
68. William C. Nelson to Maria C. Nelson, 23 June 1861, UMiss, CWC.
69. Stith Nelson, "Excerpts from the Diary of Stith Nelson, University of Memphis Special Collections." *West Tennessee Historical Society Papers*. Vol 64. (2010): 119–133, 14 June 1861.
70. Nelson, 21 May 1861.
71. *Personal Record*, 80–81, GBS
72. Bailey, *Class*, 104.
73. ORI, vol. 52, pt. II, 127–28.
74. *The United States Postal Service*, 14; and interview with Jennifer Lynch.
75. Clarksville, *Chronicle*, January 10, 1862, TCWS
76. CSA-RR, NP, MAP 1/2/1861; NP, WTW, 7/11/1861; and NA, RR 7/9/1861.
77. CSA RR, NP, RD 11–18A-61.
78. Minutes, book 10, 41, SCA.
79. *Appeal*, May 30, 1861, 3, c. 1.
80. *Appeal*, July 19, 1861, 3, c. 2.
81. *Appeal*, June 15, 1861, 4, col. 1.
82. County Court, Minute Book, 10, 1861, 82, SCA.

83. County Court, Minute Book 10, 1862, 162 and 182, SCA.

84. *Appeal*, May 9, 1861, 2, col. 9; May 16, 3, col. 2; and late reference, December 9, 1861, OR, vol, 7, 749.

85. OR, vol. 51, pt. I, 383.

86. *Appeal*, September 26, 1861, 4, col. 2.

87. *Appeal*, October 31, 1861, 2, col. 8.

88. Nashville, *Union and* American, October 19, 1861, 3, col. 2.

89. *Tennesseans in the Civil War*, Vol. 1, 252; and SOR, Ser. 79, 238–51.

90. Allison, *Notable Men of Tennessee*, 36.

91. Barbieri, *Scraps from the Prison Table at Camp Chase and Johnson's Island*, 1868, 219, GBS.

92. Faust, *Mothers*, 126–27. and 146–48; and Rable, *Civil Wars*, 19394.

93. "October 25, 1861—Captain A.O. Edwards, in Germantown, to his sister in Tullahoma," TCWSB.

94. McFarland, *Medicine*, 23–24; and Cunningham, *Doctors*, 165–66, and 188–90.

95. Glenna R. Schroeder-Lein, Glenna R. *Confederate Hospitals on the Move* (1994), 43.

Chapter 6

1. *Appeal*, January 1, 1861, 2, col. 1.

2. *Appeal*, March 4, 1862, 2, col. 7, and 3, col. 4; *Avalanche*, March 10, 1862, 2, cols. 5 and 8, and 4, col. 4.

3. *Appeal*, March 25, 1862, 2, col. 8.

4. CSA RR, NP, ASCY 2/8/1862.

5. OR, vol. 10, 297–98; *Appeal*, March 7, 1862, 1, col. 7; March 9, 1, col. 3; *Avalanche*, March 10, 2, cols. 1 and 5.

6. Harncourt, *Biography*, 139; and OR, vol. 10, pt. II, 304.

7. OR, vol. 10, 298.

8. William Frank Zornow, "State Aid for Indigent Soldiers and Their Families in Tennessee, 1861–1865," *THQ*, 13 (1954): 298–99.

9. *Appeal*, March 20, 1862, 1, cols 1–2.

10. OR, Vol. 10, pt. I, 409.

11. OR, vol. 10, pt. II, 425.

12. Company Muster Roll, Co. C, 13 Regiment, May 3, 1863, NARA, M-268, roll 169.

13. 1860 census, CD 11, 169.

14. SOR, Ser. 78, 645.

15. *Appeal*, April 20, 1863, 1, col. 2; April 24, 1, col. 5, and 2, col. 4; and Faust, *Mothers*, 116.

16. McPherson, *Cause & Comrades*, 133–34., 139; and Faust, *Mothers*, 118, 243f.

17. Vaughn, 15–19; but cf. Arnold, 101, whose casualty figures for Shiloh differ.

18. Stanley F. Horn, ed. *Tennessee's War, 1861–1865* (1965), 98.

19. *Appeal*, April 27, 1862, 2, col. 5.

20. Harncourt, *Biography*, 181, citing M&C Asst. Superintendent's report, 19 June 1862.

21. Affidavit, Minnie Duke, April 5, 1941, Register of Deeds, Book 1675, 214, SCA.

22. ORIV, vol. 1: 1062.

23. ORIV, vol. 1: 1061–62; and vol. 2: 727–28.

24. McPherson, *Cause & Comrades*, 9.

25. ORIV, vol. 2: 728–29.

26. Albert Burton Moore, *Conscription and Conflict in the Confederacy*, New York: MacMillan, 1924; reprint 1963, University of South Carolina, for the classic study; and Faust, *Mothers*, 54f-55.

27. OR, vol. 29, pt. II, 601.

28. OR, vol. 24, pt. III, 1024.

29. *Appeal*, May 11, 1862, 1, col. 6.

30. Sherman, *Memoirs*, 257.

31. Aden, pp. 110–111; and Nathan K. Moran, "'No Alternative Left': State and County Government in Northwest Tennessee during the Union Invasion, January-June 1862," *WTHS*, 46 (1992), 24 and 31.

32. OR, vol. 10, pt. I, 650f-51

33. John M. Hubbard, *Notes of a Private* (1911), 32; OR, vol. 10, pt. II, 382, 465f, and 516; and Aden, 109, and 111.

34. Ash, *Yankees*, 16–22.

35. Ibid, 10, 14, 19–20., 31–33, 157, 223; and Rable, *Civil Wars*, 156–58.

36. Rable; and OR, vol. 17, pt. II, 10–11.

37. *Appeal*, 13 June 1862, 2, col. 2.

38. *Argus*, June 21, 1862, 2, col. 8; *Appeal*, July 11, 1862, 2, col. 1.

39. E.g., *Appeal*, March 30, 1864, 1, col. 1.

40. *Appeal*, June 23, 1862, 2, col. 7; Lew Wallace, *Smoke, Sound & Fury: The Civil War Memoirs of Major-General Lew Wallace*, (1998), 145–46.; and Stephens, 113–14.

41. OR, vol. 17, pt. II, 14.

42. OR, vol. 17, pt. II, 15.

43. Grant, *Memoirs*, vol. I, 171–72.; Sherman, *Memoirs*, 258; and Gary L. Donhardt, "On the Road to Memphis with General Ulysses S. Grant," *WTHS*, 53 (1999): 1–15.

44. OR, vol.17, pt. I, 10–12; pt. II, 638–39.; and *Appeal*, July 2, 1862, 2, cols. 1 and 4.

45. SOR, Ser. 65, 65; ORII, vol. 5: 323; *Grant Papers*, 158–59n.; and *Appeal*, July 2, 1862, 2, col. 1.

46. OR, vol. 17, pt. I, 11.

47. Grant, *Documents*, 179 n. 1.

48. OR, vol. 17, pt. II, 44.

49. Sutherland, *Savage Conflict*, 58–63, 80–2, 97, 126–29, 145–46, and 154–56.

50. OR, vol. 17, pt. II, 36–37.

51. Map, "Memphis and Vicinity, surveyed and drawn by order of Major General W.T. Sherman," circa 1862/63, MVC; General Topographical Map, plate CLIV, *OR Atlas*; Shelby Co. map, 1888, M&SC; and Hall, 19 and 21. To the north, of course, the Old and New Raleigh Roads were employed for operations.

52. OR, vol. 17, pt. II, 78.

53. OR, vol. 17, pt. II, 55.

54. Grant, *Documents*, 188.

55. OR, vol. 17, pt. II, 33, 40–41., 44, 55–56, and 60; SOR, Ser. 19, 599; Ser. 29, 46; and Ser. 53, 140–43.

56. Daniel A. Masters, "'Pen Lever': The Civil War Letters of Charles Edward Bliven of the Army Telegraph Corps." 52 (2016): 76–97, 85–86.

57. SOR, Ser. 19, 600.

58. OR, Ser. I, vol. 17, pt. I, 10–72, and pt. II, to 142; for the Confederate side, e.g. 692f-93, 696–98,

59. OR, vol. 17, pt. II, 45, 49 and 79; and *Appeal*, July 4, 1862, 2, col. 1.

60. *Appeal*, July 7, 1862, 2, col. 1.

61. *Appeal*, March 14, 1862, 3, col. 6.

62. Ibid, and March 30, 3, col. 3.

63. *Appeal*, April 1, 1862, 3, col. 1.

64. OR, vol. 10, part II, 372.

65. Ibid.

66. *Tennesseans in the Civil War: A Military History of Confederate and Union Units with Available Rosters of Personnel.* 2 vols. (1964), Vol. 1.

67. OR IV, 1008; and Rutherfurd, "Partisan Ranger Act," 816–21.

68. Rutherford, pp. 21f; SOR, Ser. 44, 283; and *Appeal*, June 10, 1862, 2, col. 1.

69. SOR, Ser. 44, 283.

70. *Appeal*, April 22, 1866, 2, col. 7.

71. For a thorough exploration of these developments, Sutherland, *Savage Conflict*.

72. *Appeal*, April 29, 1862, 2, col. 6; April 30, 2, col. 6;

73. SOR, Ser. 44, 282.

74. OR, vol. 10, pt. I, p. 591; and *Appeal*, July 4, 1862, 2, col. 1.

75. Ibid; and OR, vol. 10, pt. II, 592.

76. *Appeal*, July 4, 1866, 2, col. 1, quoting the *Avalanche*.

77. *Appeal*, July 25, 1862, 2, col. 7.

78. *Appeal*, November 4, 1866, 2, col. 1 quoting the *Bulletin* of October 31.

79. *Bulletin*, October 25, 1863, 2, col. 2; and October 11, 2, col. 3.

80. ORII, vol. 3: 664.

81. Rutherfurd, 821; and specifically on July 6, General Bragg wrote Halleck complaining of Federal soldiers wantonly destroying the property of secessionists and threatening to have them shot. ORII, vol. 5: 136.

82. Rutherfurd, "Partisan Ranger Act," 807–809, and 828–31.

83. ORIII, vol. 2: 402.

84. ORII, vol. 5: 948.

85. OR, vol. 47, pt. II, 69.

86. Wills interview.

87. *Appeal*, June 23, 1862, 2, col. 1.

88. Lipsey, "Memoirs," 34.

89. OR, vol. 17, pt. II, 16, 81 and 87–88; and Special Correspondence of the Chicago *Times*, from Shiloh, May 23, 1862, 3, TCWS.

90. OR, vol. 17, pt. II, 9–10, and 237; and Sherman, *Memoirs*, 256–59.

91. OR, vol. 17, pt. II, 22.

92. Sherman, *Memoirs*, p. 258; and OR, vol. 17, pt. II,.79.

93. OR, vol. 17, pt. II, 121.

94. *Appeal*, July 25, 1862, p. 2, col. 6; and July 26, 2, col. 3.
95. *The Ottawa Free Trader* (Illinois), August 16, 1862, 2, col. 4.
96. *The Athens Post* (Tennessee), August 1, 1862, 1, col. 2.
97. Masters, *"Pen Lever,"* 90.
98. Mills to Martha, Germantown, February 17, 1864, Mills Family Records, VRHC.
99. OR, vol. 17, pt. II, 99f., p. 106, 109, 118f., 121–23, 128, 142, 149f., and 171; and Sherman, *Memoirs*, 259.
100. OR, vol. 17, pt. II, 143–46; and vol. 24, pt. I, 4. Periodically Sherman's forces were greatly reduced when he had to dispatch significant forces, for instance Hurlbut's entire division, to deal with major Confederate threats to the east and south.
101. OR. Vol. 17, pt. II, 311, 337 and 341.
102. OR, vol. 17, pt. II, 182.
103. McLeary, *Humorous Incident of the Civil War*, 9.
104. OR, vol. 17, pt. II, 681 and 701 for Van Dorn's negative opinion of partisans and especially those operating as small independent commands.
105. OR, vol. 52, pt. II, 391; and *Appeal*, July 18, 1862,.2, col. 8; July 22, 1, col. 2; and August 7, 1862, 2, col. 2.
106. OR, vol. 17, pt. II, 681.
107. *Appeal*, November 20, 1862, 2, col. 8.
108. OR, vol. 17, pt. II, 605, 611, 616f, 621f, and 743; emphasis added.
109. OR, vol. 17, pt. I, 23; and ORII, vol. 4: 211f.
110. Thorndike, *Sherman letters*, pp. 162 and 167, September 22 and October 6, 1862,
111. OR, vol. 17, pt. I, 55.
112. *Sun*, October 14, 1862, 2, genealogybank.co/gbnk/newspapers/doc/v2:1134300.
113. OR, vol. 17, pt. I, 461f.
114. OR, vol. 17 pt. I, 144f, 235f, and 240.
115. SOR, Ser. 3, pp. 315–18.
116. *Fremont Journal* (Ohio), November 28, 1862, 1, col. 3.
117. SOR, Ser. 33, 316.
118. Moran, "Military Government," 94.
119. OR, vol. 17, pt. II, 855.
120. *Appeal*, 20 November 1862, 1, cols. 1f.
121. *Appeal*, October 23, 1862, 2, col. 3.
122. *Appeal*, October 27, 1862, 2, col. 4, citing the *Bulletin* of October 24.
123. Jarret Ruminski, "'Tradyville' The Contraband Trade and the Problem of Loyalty in Civil War Mississippi," *Journal of the Civil War Era*, Vol. 2 (2012) : Issue 4, 511–37, provides a compact analysis and summary of the problems of trade out of areas like Memphis.
124. Ibid. 511.
125. Ibid, 519.
126. SOR, Ser. 44, 286.
127. *Appeal*, October 27, 1862, 2, col. 4.
128. Sigafoos, *Cotton Row*, 44.
129. Sherman, *Memoir*, 266–68, Sherman to Secretary of Treasury Chase, August 11, 1862.
130. *Appeal*, July 16, 1862, 2, col. 2.

131. OR, vol. 17, pt. II, 261 and 272–73.

132. OR, vol. 17, pt. II, 351; and for a critical analysis of Sherman's policies, Fisher, "Prepare Them," 90–102.

133. OR, vol. 7, 65455; and *Memphis Union Appeal*, July 6, 1862, TCWSB.

134. *Daily Union*, October 29, 1862, 3, col. 2.

135. *Appeal*, November 10, 1862, 2, col. 6, quoting *Bulletin*.

136. *Rebel Picket—Extra!*, 1864 broadside, Duke papers, M&SC Room, MPL.

137. Woodson, *Genealogy*, 471–72.

138. Ibid, 472 and 475.

139. "Soldier's Furlough" form, 1865, Woodson papers, MVC, MS 114, box 1, folder 5.

140. OR, vol. 52, pt. II, 391; vol. 17, pt. I, 797; pt. II, 743; Tennesseans *in the Civil War*, Vol. 1, 38, 80; and Loving, 8–13.

141. Loving, 14 and 101.

142. OR, vol. 52, pt. II, 391.

143. OR, vol. 17, pt. I, 485.

144. Vaughn, 20–23.

145. SOR, Ser. 78, 646; and West, "Thirteenth," 187.

146. Vaughn, 23–28 and 49; and *Daily Appeal*, 24 January 1863, 1, col. 2.

147. OR, vol. 17, pt. II, 361.

148. *Philadelphia* Inquirer, December 5, 1862, 1; and Bear, 14n. 11, citing *Chicago Daily Tribune*, Dec. 2, 1862.

149. OR, vol. 17, pt. II, 513, and 516; and SOR, Ser. 33, 316.

150. Sanderson interviews.

151. OR, vol. 17, pt. I, 10 & 72, pt. II, 13, 39, 64, 144.

152. *Sanderson Letters*, extracts in TCWS.

153. Family traditions passed down by Carrie Callis Sullivan relate that the Baptist Church was "expected to be burned." Beverly Booth, "Germantown Pioneers: Memories of the City's Settlers," *Germantown News*, June 3, 1977, 4B.

154. From notebook of A.H. Holden, Germantown, 1942, Cloyes files, and Dean interview, 7.24.2007, GRH&GC; and E. Smith, *Germantown*, 8.

155. Browder, "The Burning of Germantown" *WTHS Papers*, 2017, 107–20.

156. Ibid.

Chapter 7

1. OR, vol. 17, pt. II, 510.

2. OR, vol. 17, II, 522–23.

3. SOR, Ser. 31, 606.

4. OR, vol. 17, pt. II, 499, 504, 513 and 524. Quinby's official orders to relocate to Memphis were dated December 25 (OR, vol. 17, pt. II, 486), so he was already in Memphis on December 30 (Ibid., 506).

5. NPS regimental histories; and *Annual Report of the Adjutant General of Missouri*, 1866, 138, GBS.

6. OR, vol. 17, pt. II, 513, and 516; *Annual Report of the Adjutant General of Missouri*, 146;

Report of the Adjutant General of the State of Illinois, vol. 3, 1900, 209, GBS; and *Report of the Adjutant General and acting Quartermaster General of the State of Iowa*, 1047, GBS; SOR, Ser. 31, 451; Ser. 33, 317; and Ser. 66, 124 and 130.

7. Frost, *Tenth Missouri*, 104–105

8. Ledsinger, Anita, "Talk Offers Look into City's Past," *Germantown News*, Oct. 29, 1981.

9. Pomeroy diary, TCWSB; and Sutherland, *Savage Conflict*, 58, 97, 113, 133–34, and 173.

10. OR, vol. 24, pt. III, 68, 141–43.

11. NPS regimental histories.

12. OR, vol. 24, pt. III, 35, 50, 92 and 140; and Jeffrey N. Lash, "'The Federal Tyrant at Memphis:' General Stephen A. Hurlbut and the Union Occupation of West Tennessee, 1862–64," *THQ*, 48 (Spring 1989), 1: 15–28.

13. OR, vol. 17, pt. II, 565, and 576–78; and vol. 24, pt. III, 20–29.

14. *Appeal*, January 12, 1863, 2, col. 2.

15. OR, vol. 24, Pt. III, 40 and 75.

16. Ibid, 88–92, 673.

17. OR, vol. 17, pt. II, 524–25.

18. OR, vol. 24, pt. III, 74 and 179.

19. OR, vol. 17, pt. II, 526.

20. *Times-Picayune*, January 15, 1863, 1.

21. OR, vol. 17, pt. I, 79–80.

22. OR, vol. 24, pt. I. 428; and Pomeroy Diaries, March 10, 1863.

23. OR, vol. 24, pt. III, 654.

24. OR, vol. 24, pt. III, 696–97

25. OR, vol. 24, pt. III, 111.

26. Loving, 19–20.

27. OR, vol. 24, pt. I, 498.

28. OR, vol. 24, pt. III, 27.

29. OR, vol. 24, pt. III, 746.

30. OR, vol. 24, pt. III, 764–65.

31. OR, vol. 24, pt. III, 814–16.

32. *Appeal*, April 27, 1863, 2, col. 2.

33. OR, vol. 24, pt. III, 185 and 189.

34. OR, vol. 24, pt. III, 253–57; and SOR, Ser. 19, 669; and Ser. 21, 629, 660, and 678–79.

35. OR, vol. 24, pt. III, 381–82, 398–99, and 452–56; and vol. 30, pt. III, 27.

36. E.g., SOR, Sers. 19–21, and 28–29 contain frequent references to such arrivals.

37. OR, vol. 24, pt. III, 406 and 965; and *Bulletin*, June 16, 1863, 1, col. 6.

38. June 24, 1863, OR, vol. 24, pt. II, 487.

39. OR, vol. 24, pt. III, 702–5; and *Tennesseans in the Civil War*, Vol. 1, 118–21, and 133.

40. OR, vol. 24, pt. III, 1024.

41. *Bulletin*, June 26, 1863, 3, col. 2.

42. OR, vol. 24, pt. III, 512.

43. OR, vol. 24, pt. II, 683.

44. *Bulletin*, July 30, 1863, 2, col. 3.

45. Wyeth, 254.

46. OR, vol. 52, pt. I, 72.
47. OR, vol. 30. pt. IV, 718.
48. OR, vol. 30, pt. II, 759; and *Tennesseans in the Civil War*, Vol. I, 80–90
49. See Appendix 2
50. Memories of the City's Settlers," *Germantown News*, June 16, 1977, B.
51. E.g., OR, vol. 30, pt. III, 83, Colonel Mersey to General Hurlbut, from Corinth, 20 August, 1863; and vol. 31, pt. I, 244.
52. OR. Vol. 30, pt. III, 26f.
53. OR, vol. 24, pt. II, 487–88, 492–96, and pt. III, 682–83.
54. OR, vol. 30, pt. III, 82–83, and vol. 31. Pt. I, 822.
55. OR, vol. 30, pt. III, 161.
56. OR, vol. 30, pt. III, 170, 622–23.
57. NPS regimental histories.
58. *Report of the Adjutant General of the State of Illinois*, vol. 3, 1900, 65 and 96, GBS; and SOR, Ser. 20, 303 and 477.
59. E.g., *Bulletin*, July 31, 1863, 2, col. 2.
60. OR, vol. 30, pt. IV, 581–82; Harrell described his location as 12 miles south-east of Memphis which would put him within the present borders of the city of Germantown, probably within a mile or two of the old town proper. Nevertheless, no Harrell is reported on the 1860 census.
61. OR, vol. 30, pt. II, 733 and 757.
62. OR, vol. 30, pt. II, 731, and 759f.
63. OR, vol. 31, pt. II, 569–70.
64. OR, vol. 30, pt. II, 732 and 760–61, and pt. IV, 279.
65. OR, Ser. I, Vol. 30, pt. II, 790–791; SOR, Ser. 5, 707, and 710; and *Appeal*, quoting unidentified source from Memphis, October 24, 1863, 2, col. 3.
66. OR, vol. 30, pt. IV, 278–79; and Nashville *Daily Union*, October 17, 1863, 2, col 4.
67. *Appeal*, December 8, 1863, 2, col. 6.
68. *Daily Union*, October 27, 1863, 2, col. 4.
69. OR, vol. 30, pt. IV, 304–305.
70. OR, vol. 31, pt. I, 690.
71. OR, vol. 30, pt. II, 734, and pt. IV, 305, and 407.
72. OR, vol. 31, pt. I, 33, 673, 677, and 690.
73. OR, vol. 31, pt. III, 592.
74. OR, vol. 31, pt. I, 247, and pt. III, 597.
75. OR, vol. 31, pt. I, 242–49, and Pt. III, 31.
76. OR, vol. 31, pt. III, 33.
77. OR, vol. 31, pt. III, 580.
78. OR, vol. 30, pt. II, 787–89.
79. OR, vol. 31, pt. I, 248–49.
80. OR, vol. 31, pt. III, 689.
81. Lloyd's New Map of the United States, the Canadas and New Brunswick, from the last surveys, showing every Railroad & Station finished to June 1863, LC, www.loc.gov/item/98688332.

82. OR, vol. 31, pt. I, 253; and pt. III, 678–79, and 684–85.
83. OR, vol. 31, pt. III, pp. 132f, 544f, and 566f.
84. OR, vol. 31, pt. III, 641; and 694, and 730.
85. OR, vol. 31, pt. III, 730–31.
86. OR, vol. 31, pt. III, 731.
87. OR, vol. 31, pt. III, 469.
88. OR, vol. 31, pt. III, 336.
89. OR, vol. 32, pt. III, 366 and 386.
90. OR, vol. 31, pt. III, 395; and Pt. I, 607.
91. OR, vol. 31, pt. III, 494 and 517.
92. OR, vol. 31, pt. I, 620; and John Johnson, "Forrest's March out of West Tennessee, December 1863, Recollections of a Private," WTHS, 12 (1958): 146.
93. OR, vol. 31, pt. I, 620–21.
94. ORIII, 5: 63 and 586.
95. OR, vol. 31, pt. I, 620–21.
96. County Court, Minute Book 10, 1862; and Minute Book 10 ½, 1 and 50; Minute Book 11, 1864, 256, SCA; and OR, I, III, 148–49.
97. Records of the U.S. Civil Commission at Memphis, 1863–1864, NARA #410/reel 78/1; and for an overview of the complex evolutions of civil and military government in Memphis during occupation, Lanier, WTHS, 66 (2012); 27–64.
98. Robert A. Lanier, "The Memphis Legal Community," WTHS 66 (2012), 33.
99. *Papers of Andrew Johnson*, Vol. 6, 112–13, and n. 1 & 7, TCWS; *Bulletin*, December 27, 1862; and on the disrupted election, Nathan K. Moran, "Bullets and Ballots: Nathan Bedford Forrest and the Congressional Election of 1862," WTHS, 58 (2004): 2–31.
100. *Bulletin*, June 19, 1863, 2, col. 8.
101. *Bulletin*, September 1, 1863, 3, col. 6; and October 12, 2, col. 1; and "Regulations for the Collection of Direct Taxes . . . , Instant Archive: archive.org/details/regulationsforcounit.
102. *Bulletin*, October 25, 1863, 1, col. 6.
103. General Orders No. 100, April 24, 1863, Instructions for the Government of Armies of the United States in the Field, Sec. I, Martial Law; OR, III, vol. 3, 148–51; and Ash, *Yankees*, 82–84, 87–88.
104. Ash, *Yankees*, 59.
105. *Bulletin*, September 1, 1863, 4, col. 3.
106. Petition of William Hack, 13297, April 26, 1872, GRH&GC.
107. Claim of Agnes Brooks, April 1, 1901, Wills/Kirby collection; and Cargill and Connelly, *Settlers*, 22.
108. Edward A. Davenport, ed, *History of the Ninth Regiment Illinois Cavalry Volunteers*, (1888), 406, LC
109. Wills interview.
110. OR, vol. 24, pt. III, 162.
111. OR, vol. 24, pt. III, 382.
112. Fortress Germantown file, GRH&GC. This site has been partially reconstructed in a park know as "Fortress Germantown."
113. Diary of Fletcher Pomeroy, January 26, 1863, TCWSB.

114. NPS Regimental histories.

115. Green, *Letters*, 49. The date in the published version of February 20 seems strangely inconsistent with her descriptions of the weather and types of trees and flowers in bloom. Indeed, given her ending of the letter, it would have had to have been early March when blooming roses and honeysuckle were not possible.

116. Ibid, 53.

117. Ibid, 54.

118. Ibid, 55.

119. Albert Sydney Witherington III, *History of Germantown: Utopia on the Ridge*. (Germantown: self-published, 1997); copy available at GRH&GS, 62, citing Fletcher Pomeroy's War Diary.

120. Frisbee, "'Remember Me to Everybody,'" WTHS, 55 (2001): 41.

121. Witherington, 63, citing Webster Moses.

122. Davenport, *Ninth Regiment*, 429–50, LC.

123. John to Sotie, August 20 and 22, 1863, Historic Sites folder, Civil War, GRH&GC.

124. Wills interview.

125. Journal, Emily Lucken Mills, Mills Family Records, VRHC; and cf. ELM/GRH&GC.

126. Ibid.

127. Green, *Letters*, 41.

128. Woodson, *Genealogy*, 306.

129. Wills, Brook's family papers.

130. Woodson papers, MVC, MS-114, box 1, folder 9.

131. *The United States Army and Navy Journal and Gazette of the Regular and Volunteer Forces*, vol. III, 1865-'66, 7, GBS; and *Daily National Intelligencer*, November 11, 1863, 3; *Bulletin*, November 7, 2, col. 1

132. Faust, *Mothers*, 205–207.

133. "Germantown Pioneers," *Germantown News*, August 25, 1977, 3B.

134. Faust, *Mothers*, 198–201, and 205; Ash, *Yankees*, 61f.; and *Appeal*, 27 June 1863, 2, col. 3.

135. E. Susan Barber and Charles F. Ritter, "'Physical Abuse . . . and Rough Handling' Race, Gender, and Sexual Justice in the Occupied South," in Whites and Long, 49–51.

136. Ibid.

137. Dunaway, June 11, 1864.

138. "Memoirs of the City's Settlers," *Germantown News*, June 16, 1977, B

139. Walter F. Fraser, Jr and Mrs. Pat C. Clark, "The Letters of William Beverly Randolph Hackley, in *WTHS*, 25 (1971): 25–106, 96.

140. *Bulletin*, June 19, 1863, 2, col. 8.

141. Ash, *Yankees*, pp. 78–80; and *Bulletin*, November 7, 1863, 2, col. 1.

142. NA/No. 11,688 Cong. Depositions, Philip Cornelius.

143. Journal Emily Lucken Mills, 1, VRHC.

144. Jennie Mills to Uncle and Aunt, March 22, 1863, ELM/GRH&GC.

145. Mills to Martha, February 17m 1863, Mills Family Records, VRHC.

146. Jennie Mills to Aunt Emma and Uncle John, February 15, 1863, ELM/GRH&GC.

147. *Bulletin*, June 14, 1863, 2, col. 1.

148. Based on a comparison of 1860 and 1870 censuses.

149. Nolan, "Troublous Times," WTHS, 60 (2006): 25–28, and 32.

150. James B. Jones, Jr., "The Struggle for Public Health in Civil War Tennessee Cities," WTHS, 66 (2007): 69–85.

151. *Bulletin*, August 9, 1864, 4, col. 3.

152. NARA, M-598, roll 98, Memphis, TN, Military Prison, book 1, 86.

153. Emily Mills journal, 24–25, Mills Family Records, GRH&GC.

154. *Bulletin*, September 1, 1863, 3, cols. 1 and 4.

155. Ibid, 3, col. 3.

156. *Bulletin*, September 1, 1863, 4, col. 3; September 17, 1, cols. 4–5.; and October 30, 3, cols. 2 and 5.

157. OR, vol. 31, pt. III, 160.

158. S.A. Steele, *The Sunny Road: Home Life in Dixie during the War*.

159. Loose Papers, Box 48, W.P. Moore, Oath of Allegiance, Provost Marshal Germantown, 1863, # 71, SCA.

160. *The Roster of Union Soldiers*; and Census 1860 and 1870, CD 7.

161. OR, vol. 31, pt. III, 160–61

162. Dunaway, *Letters*, August 4, 1863, and July 20, 1864.

163. Thompson to Smith, April 17, 1861, FH/GRH&GC.

164. Capleville Methodist Church Bulletin, May 27, 1851, "History," 2–3, GUMCA, West File.

165. Faust, *Mothers*, 184–86.

166. *Fremont Journal* (Ohio), December 25, 1863, 1, col. 5.

167. Thoroughly exposed in the most recent literature, e.g., Oaks, *Freedom*; and Downs, *Sick from Freedom*.

168. Berlin, *Freedom*, Ser. I, vol. III, 622–23, and 692.

169. James Oaks, *Freedom National*, (2013), 415.

170. *Appeal*, 19 August 1862, 2, col. 1 for a summary of one of Sherman's early orders for employing "negroes" and the rights of their owners; 10 April, 2, col. 7; and Sherman, *Memoirs*, 265–66.

171. John Cimprich, "Military Governor Johnson and Tennessee Blacks, 1862–65," THQ, 39 (Winter 1980), 4: 462.

172. Berlin, *Freedom*, 623, and 890–899.

173. Foner, *Reconstruction*, 81, and n. 9.

174. McKinney, "Ned and Rose Kearney," WTHS, 64 (2010): 135.

175. Whites, *Civil War as Crisis*, 7.

176. Ash, *Yankees*, pp. 154f, 165–68.

177. NA/No. 11,688 Cong. Depositions, Philip Cornelius.

178. NA/No. 11,688 Cong. Depositions, Quinton Roberts.

179. *Bulletin*, July 30, 1863, 3, col. 4.

180. Berlin, *Families*, 35.

181. E.g., Brigadier General [Augustus L. Chetlain] to Lieutenant Colonel T.H. Harris, 12 Apr. 1864, cited in Berlin, *Families*, 35–36.

182. Ibid, 686.

183. *Bulletin*, October 30, 1863, 3, col. 2; and Berlin, *Freedom*, 709–10, and 714–15.

184. Berlin, *Freedom*, Ser. I, Vol. III, 621–22.

185. Jim Downs, *Sick from Freedom* (2012), 47.

186. Ibid, 686 and 689–91.

187. Ibid, 686 and 689.

188. *Appeal*, 20 January 1864, 2, col. 3f.

189. Lieutenant Col Jos R. Putnam to Brigadier General W.D. Whipple, 30 Jan. 1865, in Berlin, 78.

190. Ibid, 690.

191. Bobby L. Lovett, "The West Tennessee Colored Troops in Civil War Combat," *WTHS*, 34 (1980): n.1, 53; and cf. *Tennesseans in the Civil War*, vol. 1, 366–67., 396, 407–9, and 436.

192. E.g., OR, vol. 24, pt. III, 406,

193. ORIII, 3:117, 122, and 1190.

194. ORIII, 4:164; and *Tennesseans in the Civil War*, Vol. 1, 366–67, 369–70.

195. Andrew Ward, *River Run Red* (2005), 73.

196. NPS, Soldiers and Sailors System.

197. Ward, *River*, 64.

198. ORIII, 3: 212.

199. *Tennesseans in the Civil War*, Vol. 1, 407; and ORIII, 4:165.

200. NPS, Soldiers and Sailors and System.

201. http://www.tngenweb.org/civilwar/usainf/usa61c.html.; and Tennesseans in the Civil War, vol. 1, 408.

202. OR, vol. 31, pt. I, 577.

203. OR, vol. 31, pt. I, 578.

204. ORRIII, 4:165.

205. NPS, Soldiers and Sailors System.

206. Ibid, 820–21.

207. Lieutenant Col John Foley to Lieutenant Colonel T. Harris, 11 Jan. 1865 in Berlin, *Families*, 75–76.

208. Captain T.A. Walker to Captain J.S. Lord, 34 Jan. 1865 in Berlin, *Families*, pp. 76–77.

209. ORIII, 3:1190.

210. Berlin, *Freedom*, Series I, Vol. I. 776–77.

211. *Appeal*, 19 August 1862, 2, col. 3.

212. *Appeal*, March 17, 1863, 1, col. 5.

213. Dyer and Moore, *Questionnaires*, vol. 3, 1300.

214. *Bulletin*, October 11, 1863, 4, col. 1.

215. McPherson, *Cause & Comrades*, 11.

216. Ibid, vol. 5, 2255.

217. Ibid, 13, chap. 2, and 94–97.

218. Ibid, 9, 35, 88–89, 97, and 102–103.

219. NARA, M-598, roll 98.

Chapter 8

1. OR, vol. 32, pt. II, 77.

2. *Appeal*, 8 December 1863, 2, col. 1; 4 January 1864, 2, cols. 1f.; 20 January, 1, col. 3; 2 March, 2, col. 2; and 6 May, 2, cols. 3f.

3. E.g., *Bulletin*, March 22, 1864, 2, col. 2; and New York *Times*, June 16, 1862, TCWSB
4. *Daily Illinois State Journal*, February 22, 1864, 4.
5. Mills to Martha, February 17, 1864, Mills Family Records, VRHC.
6. Ibid.
7. *Appeal*, April 2, 1864, 1, col. 2, citing *Argus*.
8. *Appeal*, March 30, 1864, 1 col. 3, citing the *Bulletin*.
9. *1860 Census—Tennessee*, 5 vols, Nashville: Byron Sistler & Associates, 1981; and *1870 Census -Tennessee*, Nashville: Byron Sistler & Associates, 2 Vols, 1985.
10. *Bulletin*, March 9, 1864, 3, col. 3.
11. *Wisconsin Daily Patriot*, March 28, 1, quoting *Argus*, March 19, 1864, and *Chicago Times*.
12. *Ledger*, January 23, 1868, 3, col. 3.
13. *Bulletin*, March 4, 1864, 2, col. 6, and March 9, 2, col. 1, and 3, col. 3.
14. Loose Papers, 1863, box 49, #71, SCA.
15. Evans to Woodson, November 28, 1864, GPC.
16. *Appeal*, 27 January 1864, 1, col. 5; and *Tennesseans in the Civil War*, Vol. 1, 410–11, including General Order Number 29, September 14, 1863.
17. *Bulletin*, March 22, 1864, 2, col. 2.
18. *Bulletin*, March 22, 1863, 2, col. 7.
19. *Bulletin*, August 9, 1864, 3, cols. 3 and 6, 4, col. 3.
20. OR, vol. 32, pt. II, 67–68.
21. *Papers of Andrew Johnson*, vol. 6, 648–50, TCWSB.
22. OR, vol. 32, pt. III, 117–19; and for a clarification of the extortion of Jackson indicating that the regimental fine may not have been justified, Blankenship, "Hurst," *WTHS*, 34 (1980): 79–80.
23. OR, vol. 32, pt. I, 152; and pt. II, 119.
24. *Appeal*, February 5, 1864, 1, col. 7.
25. OR, vol., 32, pt. I, 173–79; and pt. II, 493.
26. OR, vol. 32, pt. I, 179–80.
27. OR, vol. 32, pt. I, 171–72, and 174–75; and pt. II, 229, 240, 242, 258, 297, 302, and 493.
28. OR, vol. 32, pt. I, 348; and pt. II, 485.
29. OR, vol. 32, pt. II, 505.
30. OR, vil. 32, pt. I, 269; and ORIII, vol. 5: 63, and 586.
31. OR, vol. 32, pt. I, 346–47.
32. OR, vol. 32, pt. I, 351–52, and 355.
33. OR, vol. 39, pt. II, 640–44.
34. OR, vol. 32, pt. I, 208.
35. OR vol. 32, pt. III, 609 and 635–36.
36. OR, vol. 32, pt. III, 665.
37. Galbraith, 103, Edmondson diary entry Monday, March 28; and *Appeal*, April 28, 1864, 2, col. 2, quoting Cairo *News*, of April 10.
38. Nashville *Daily Union*, April 10, 1864, 3, col. 6.
39. OR, vol. 32, pt. III, 253.
40. I find Andrew Ward's *River Run Red* a well-balanced and well-researched source.
41. OR, vol. 32, pt. I, 610.

42. McPherson, *Cause & Comrades*, 148–53, based on soldiers' letters.
43. Stanley, F, ed. Horn, Tennessee's War (1965), 257; and Hubbard, 101–102; and cf. Lufkin, "Thirteenth," 136–39.
44. OR, vol. 32, pt. I, 602–603.
45. *Appeal*, April 28, 1864, 2, col. 5.
46. OR, vol. 32, pt. I, 589, and 592; and Ward, *River*, 275.
47. OR, vol. 32, pt. I, 611.
48. Ward, *River*, 74–78, and 80–83.
49. Ibid, 78, 128 and 152.
50. Ibid, 128–29; c.f. Cole, Custerman website for much larger figures for Union men present, www.custerman.com/DixieBoys/FtPillow.htm.
51. An impressive effort to create a complete analysis of killed, wounded and captured can be found at Steve Cole's website, www.custerman.com/DixieBoys/FtPillow.htm.
52. Ibid, 249–50, 287–94 and 296–98.
53. Ibid, 23–39, 249, and 299–300.
54. Waldon Loving, *Coming Like hell!* (2002), 79–81; and Ward, *River*, 140 and 143.
55. *Appeal*, April 26, 1864, 2, col. 6, citing unidentified Northern papers.
56. OR, vol. 32, pt. I. 588.
57. OR, vol. 39, pt. I, 85–86.
58. OR, vol. 39, pt. I, 94 and 125–26.
59. OR, vol. 39, pt. I, 109 and 127.
60. OR, vol. 39, pt. I. 183.
61. OR, vol. 39, pt. I, 129; and pt. II, 119.
62. OR, vol. 39, pt. I, 215.
63. *Daily South Carolinian* (Columbia), June 29, 1864, issue 154, col. A.
64. Ibid.
65. OR, vol. 39, pt. I, 95.
66. OR, vol. 32, pt. I, 586, 589, 592–93, 600; and cf. Lovett, "Colored Troops," *WTHS*, 34 (1980): 59–60.
67. OR, vol. 32, pt. I, 587.
68. OR, vol. 32, pt. I, 588–89.
69. OR, vol. 32, pt. I, 591, and 593, for two different versions of their exchange.
70. OR, vol. 32, pt. I, 599–601.
71. OR, vol. 32, pt. I, 606.
72. OR, vol. 32, pt. I, 603–604.
73. See Sutherland, A *Savage Conflict*, chap. 11.
74. Lovett, "Colored Troops," *WTHS*, 34 (1980): 70.
75. ORIII, vol. 5: 63 and 586; and OR, vol. 39, pt. II, 208.
76. OR, vol. 39, pt. II, 142.
77. OR, vol. 39, pt. II, 149–50. and 165.
78. OR, vol. 39, pt. II, 318, 333 and 368.
79. OR, vol. 39, pt. I, 368.
80. OR, vol. 39, pt. I, 901, and 919; pt. II, 885; pt. III, 912; vol. 45, pt. I, 919 and 1228; and ORIII, vol. 5: 63 and 586.

81. *Bulletin*, November 17, 1864, 2, col. 1.
82. Laurier B. ed. *Fourteen Letters to a Friend*, Self-Published, 2007, 68–72.
83. Ibid, 95.
84. Lois D. Bejack, "The Journal of a Civil War 'Commando' DeWitt Clinton Fort," WTHS, 2 (1948): 24–29.
85. OR, Ser. I, 45, pt. I, 93.
86. *Ledger*, April 16, 1869, 2, col. 2.
87. Cogley, 188–204, LC
88. ORIII, vol. 5: 63 and 9909; and OR, vol. 42, pt. I, 866.
89. *Nashville Daily Union*, "Union Spy in the South," January 21, 1864, 4.
90. Ash, *Yankees*, 177–84, 204.
91. Ash, *Yankees*, 112–13; Faust, *Mothers*, 235–38, 242; and Rable, *Civil Wars*, pp. 222–24.
92. McPherson, *Cause and Comrades*, 9, 101f, 138, 168; and Faust, *Mothers*, p. 243.
93. *Springfield Republican*, 28 February 1904, 20 (original from *Pittsburg Gazette*); Rodriguez, *Black Confederates*; and miscellaneous notes in Roberts family, African-American descendants file, RH&GC.
94. OR, vol. 39, pt. II, 640–44.
95. OR, vol. 39, pt. II, 683.
96. Civil War Letters Written by William Dunaway, 7th Illinois Cavalry. MVC- 3540, September 18, 1864 (hereafter Dunaway Letters).
97. John Milton Hubbard, *Notes of a Private* (1911), 80–82.
98. *Appeal*, 20 January 1864, 2, cols. 2–5.
99. Bailey, 92–93; and Dyer and Moore, vol. 2, 734.
100. Dyer and Moore, vol. 3, 1032; and NARA, M-598, roll 98, 88.
101. Vaughn, 29–34; but cf. Goodspeed , "Shelby," 829; and *Appeal*, 12 September 1863 2, col. 5. Cf. *Tennesseans in the Civil War*, 202–203.
102. Goodspeed, "Shelby," 829; and Harkins, 75–76.
103. Goodspeed, "Shelby," 831.
104. Bejack, "Journal," 30–31.
105. OR, Ser. II, vol. 7, 404–408, and 920–22.
106. Ibid.
107. *Appeal*, March 9, 1862, 1, col. 3, quoting *Chicago Times*.
108. Dyer and Moore, vol. 3, 1300.
109. *Appeal*, April 29, 1864, 1, cols. 4–6, reprinting "Prison Life on Johnson's Island. By an Exchanged Prisoner Returned to Mobile," from the *Advertiser and Register*.
110. Ibid.
111. Dyer and Moore, vol. 3, 1300.
112. Webb Garrison, with Cheryl Garrison. *The Encyclopedia of the Civil War*. (2001), 9; and CensusDiggins.com/prison, "Alton Civil War Prison."
113. Charles T. Loehr, "Point Lookout," *Southern Historical Society Papers*, vol. 18 (Jan.-Dec. 1890): 114–20; Rev. J.B. Traywick, "Prison Life at Point Lookout," *Southern Historical Society Papers*, vol. 19 (January 1891): 432–35; Garrison, 193; and CensusDiggins.com/prison, "Point Lookout Civil War Prison."

Chapter 9

1. *Argus*, September 3, 1865, 3, col. 1.
2. *Bulletin*, February 16, 1865.
3. Dunaway, Letters, February 27, 1864.
4. OR, vol. 49, pt. I, 76–78, 80–81.
5. OR, vol. 49, pt. I, 82–83.
6. E.g., *Bulletin*, February 28, 1865, 3, col. 2; and March 1, 3, cols. 1 and 2.
7. *Bulletin*, February 2, 1865.
8. *Appeal*, March 1, 1864, 1, col. 8, citing Chicago *Times*.
9. Ash, *Yankees*, 204–208; and Sutherland, passim.
10. McDonald, *Fourteen Letters*, 73.
11. OR, vol. 49, pt. I, 2–3.
12. OR, vol. 49, pt. II, 31 and 83.
13. OR, Ser. I, vol. 49, pt. II, 120.
14. OR, vol. 49, pt. I, 718–19.
15. Ibid.
16. OR, vol. 39, pt. II, 133–34.
17. *Bulletin*, February 5, 1865.
18. Patrick W. O'Daniel, "Loyalty a Requisite: Trade and the Oath of Allegiance in the Mid-South in 1865," *WTHS*, 60 (2006): 35–47.
19. OR, vol. 49, pt. I, 865–66.
20. *Bulletin*, February 11, 1865.
21. *Bulletin*, February 28, 1865, 3, cols. 3–4.
22. NARA, M-598, roll 98, book 3.
23. *Bulletin*, February 28, 1865, 3, col. 5; and March 1, 2, col. 5.
24. OR, vol. 49, pt. I, 890–91.
25. NARA, M-598, roll 98, book 3.
26. OR, vol. 49, pt. II, 169.
27. E.g., OR, vol. 49, pt. II, 356.
28. ORIII. Vol. 5: 63 and 586.
29. Postmaster Finder; which unfortunately contradicts *Tennessee Postoffices and Postmaster Appointments, 1789–1984*, 714, which gives the year as 1863.
30. NPS regimental histories; and SOR, Ser. 53, 491, and 507–508.
31. OR, vol. 49, pt. I, 507.
32. Beach, 31.
33. Lois D. Bejack, "The Journal," WTHS, 2 (1948): 32.
34. OR, vol. 49, pt. I, 4.
35. OR, vol. 49, pt. I, 512–13. In fact, if these were Fort's men, they were a separate detachment, probably much smaller than described. Fort described his "last battle" as occurring on April 2 at Cold Water Creek in north Mississippi when an attempt launched from Collierville failed to capture him. McDaniel, 153–57.
36. OR, vol. 49, pt. I, 512–13.
37. *Argus*, May 16, 1865, "Visit to Germantown," 4, col. 2.

38. McDonald, *Letters*, 158, and 182.
39. *Daily Illinois State Journal*, April 22, 1865, 4.
40. OR, vol. 49, pt. II, 557.
41. OR, vol. 49, pt. I, 1057–58; and pt. II, 711–12.
42. Blankenship, "Hurst," *WTHS*, 34 (1980): 85.
43. OR, vol. 49, pt. II, 750, and 800.
44. OR, vol. 49, pt. II, 791.
45. Woodson, *Genealogy*, 475.
46. Montague, "Experiences," MVC, Acc# 89–52, MS 54–127, 15.
47. Aden, "In Memoriam," 116; Montague, "Experience," MVC, Acc# 89–52, MS 54–127, 17–18; and Hubbard, *Notes of a Private*, 194–95.
48. Woodson papers, MVC, MS 114, box 1, folder 5.
49. Bailey, *Class*, 107–108.
50. *Argus*, May 2, 1865, 2, cols. 1 and 4.
51. OR vol. 49, pt. II, 905.
52. OR, vol.49, pt. II, 518.
53. Ibid.
54. Ibid, 518–19.
55. OR, vol. 49, pt. II, 671.
56. *Bulletin*, May 14, 1865, 3, col. 3.
57. OR, vol. 49, pt. II, 671.
58. Dyer and Moore, *Questionnaires*, 1300; and Kirby family papers, copy of loyalty oath and steamboat ticket.
59. Bailey, *Class*, 111–12; and Ibid.
60. OR, vol .49, pt. II, 692–93.
61. OR, vol. 49, pt. II, 770.
62. Bailey, *Class*, 104, 113–14., and 116.
63. McPherson, *Cause & Comrades*, 43–44.
64. *Appeal*, 6 May 1864, 2, col. 2; 8 November 1865, 2, col. 9; and 30 March 1866, 1, col. 4.
65. *Ledger*, August 9, 1870, 3, col. 2.
66. *Bulletin*, May 14, 1865, 3, col. 7; and *Argus*, May 16, 1865, 1, cols. 6–7.
67. Patrick W. O'Daniel, "Loyalty a Requisite: Trade and the Oath of Allegiance in the mid-South in 1865," WTHS, 60 (2006): 35–47, 35–36, 42–43, and 46.
68. Petition 9 June 1865, Quenichet name file, GRH&GC.
69. OR, vol. 49, pt. II, 996; and NPS, regimental histories.
70. James D. Davis, *History of the City of Memphis, Being a Compilation of the Most Important Historical Documents of the City and Early Settlement* (Memphis: 1873), 43–44, TCWSB.
71. Weeks, 76; and *Argus*, May 16, 1865, 4, col. 2.
72. Ibid.
73. Woodson, *Genealogy*, 306.
74. Faust, *Mothers*, 244–45.
75. *Bulletin*, May 14, 1865, 3, col. 2.
76. McPherson, *Cause & Comrades*, 141.

77. Based on comparison of the 1860 and 1870 censuses.

78. *Argus*, May 2, 1865, 1, col. 8; and ORIII, 5: 990.

79. *Argus*, May 20, 1865, 4, col. 3; *Daily Appeal*, November 10, 1865, 3, col. 10; and freight receipt, M&C RR, December 9, 1865, Woodson papers, MVC, MS 114, box 1, folder 6.

80. Originally from the Appeal, November 5, 1865; no copies have survived; reprinted November 14, 2, col. 4.

Chapter 10

1. The preface to Eric Foner's *Reconstruction, 1863–1877: America's Unfinished Revolution* (New York: Harper & Row, 1988), vxii-xxvii could serve as a preface to the rest of this book, perhaps even the entire work.

2. Acts, 1865, i-ii.

3. Acts, 1865, iii; and Foner, *Reconstruction*, 43–45.

4. Acts, 1865, iv-vii and x-xiii; and Foner, Reconstruction, 44–45

5. Acts, 1865, Ch. XVI, 32–36; and Ben Severance, *Tennessee's Radical Army* (Knoxville: University of Tennessee Press, 2005), xii-xiii, and 5–6.

6. Severance, *Radical Army*, 1; and Charles L. Lufkin, "A Forgotten Controversy: The Assassination of Senator Almon Case of Tennessee," WTHS, 39 (1985): 37–50.

7. E.g., *Appeal*, Feb. 9, 1866, 3, col. 2; and May 25, 1869, 2, col. 2.

8. *Argus*, May 2, 1865, 2, col. 4

9. Acts, 1865, chap. 4, 19; chap. 24, 43–44; chap. 21, 41–42; Acts 1865–66, chap. 335, 52–62; Acts 1866–67, chap. 24, 24–25; Acts, 1868, 8; and Severance, *Army*, 15–16, and 20.

10. Acts 1866–67, chap. 26, 26–33; and Severance, *Army*, 23–24.

11. Severance, *Army*, 36–38, 52, and 55.

12. Ibid, 89–112, 135.

13. E.g., *Appeal*, May 2, 1867, 3, col. 4; and Aug. 3, 2, col. 3.

14. Severance, *Army*, 147–49, 155, 157–58, 168–72, and 175.

15. Acts, 1868, chap. 2, 18–23 and chap. 3, 23–25; and Severance, *Army*, 175–76, 178–79, 183–84 and 186–88.

16. Correspondence between Gov. Brownlow and Gen. H. Thomas, Acts, 1868, 5–8; and Severance, *Army*, 188–89.

17. Severance, *Army*, 193–98.

18. Ibid, 202, 206, 208–209., 216, and 218–23.

19. Ibid, 226–27., and F. Wayne Binning, "The Tennessee Republicans in Decline, 1869–1876," THQ (Winter 1980),4: 471–84.

20. Paul Bergeron, *Paths of the Past* (Knoxville: Univ. of Tennessee Press, 1979), 68.

21. Egerton, *Reconstruction*, 267.

22. Foner, *Reconstruction*, 384–90.

23. Acts, 1865–66, chap. 40, 65.

24. Ibid.

25. Ibid.

26. E.g., *Appeal*, Jan. 16, 1868, 3, col. 2.

27. Acts 1866–67, chap. 27, sec. 17, 39; emphasis added.

28. Foner and Brown, *Forever Free*, pp. 162–63.

29. E.g., *Appeal*, 8 Nov. 1865, 2, col. 1; 3, col. 2; 25 Nov., 2, col. 2; and 26 Dec., 3, col. 4.

30. Field Offices, Tennessee, Bureau of Refugees, Freedmen, and Abandoned Lands, 1865–1872, NARA, M 1911/reel 77/3–5.

31. Charles S. Aiken, *The Cotton Plantation South since the Civil War* (1998), 17–21.

32. Ibid, 27.

33. Field Offices, Tennessee, Bureau of Refugees, Freedmen, and Abandoned Lands, 1865–1872, NARA, M 1911/reel 77/4.

34. *Appeal*, April 3, 1864, 1, col. 6

35. E.g., *Appeal*, Nov. 25, 1865, 2, cols. 1 and 4; Dec. 5, 3, col. 2; Dec. 21, 3, col. 1; Dec. 28, 2, col. 2; Jan. 7, 1866, 3, cols. 1–2, and 3; Feb. 25, 3, col. 1; April 3, 3, col. 1; April 5, 1, col. 2; May 3, 3, col. 2.

36. Faust, *Mothers*, 60, 62, 70–74.

37. Douglas R. Egerton, *The Wars of Reconstruction* (2014), 85–87; and *Appeal*, 3 April 1864, 1, col. 3; and Jan. 10, 1866, 2, col. 4; and OR vol. 52, pt. II, 586–92.

38. TSL&A, RG-87, Statewide Referendum on Amendment to the State Constitution Abolishing Slavery, Feb. 22, 1865, folder 43.

39. *Appeal*, Jan. 18, 1866, 1, col. 4.

40. Ibid.

41. *Appeal*, Feb. 9, 1866, 3, col. 1,

42. Severance, *Radical Army*, 117 and 207.

43. On Thomas Leonard's career during and after the war, Lanier, WTHS, 2012, 44–45, and 54.

44. TSL&A, RG-87, Special Elections and County and Local Elections, 1865, folder, 80; and County Court, Minute Book 11, 1865, 88, SCA; and Acts, 1865, chap. 1.

45. *Appeal*, Dec. 21, 1865, 3, col. 1.

46. *Appeal*, 9 Dec. 1865, 2, col. 2; 10 Dec. 3, col. 1; and 26 Dec. 3, col. 1.

47. Minutes County Court, March 12, 1866, 280, SCA; *Appeal*, March 1, 1866, 3, col.3; March 3, 3, col. 1; and March 6, 3, col. 2.

48. *Avalanche*, April 6, 1866, 3, col. 2.

49. *Avalanche*, Jan. 1, 1866, 3; April 6, 3; July 21, 3, col. 1; Jan. 8, 1867, 3, col. 1; *Evening Post*, Sept. 14, 1868, 3, col. 1; and *Ledger*, Oct. 11, 1871, 3, col. 2; Bleckley's name was rarely spelled the same; Jones seems to have been missed in both the 1850 and 1860 censuses; Rhodes' name would come up as Jonathon L. Rhodes in the 1870 census.

50. TSL&A, RG-87, Special Elections & County and Local Elections, 1866, folders 29, 56 and 67.

51. "Report of an investigation of the cause, origin, and results of the late riots in the city of Memphis made by Col. Charles F. Johnson, Inspector General States of Ky. and Tennessee and Major T. W. Gilbreth, A. D. C. to Maj. Genl. Howard, Commissioner Bureau R. F. & A. Lands," Records of the Assistant Commissioner for the State of Tennessee Bureau of Refugees, Freedmen, and Abandoned Lands, 1865–1869, NARA, Microfilm M999, roll 34.

52. Acts, 1865–66, chap. 25, secs. 1–40, 52–62.

53. Ibid, sec. 9, 55.

54. For a thorough analysis of the massacre, Stephen V. *A Massacre in Memphis: The*

Race Riot that Shook the Nation One Year After the Civil War (2013); *Appeal*, Feb. 25, 1866, 3, col. 1; May 1, 3, col. 1, May 2, 3, col. 1; and May 3, 2 col. 1, and 3 col. 2.

55. *Avalanche*, May 3, 1866, 3, col. 1.

56. *Argus*, May 5, 1866, 3, col. 4; and *Appeal*, May 3, 1866, 3, col. 2.

57. Minutes County Court, Book B-13, 1867, pp. 231f, and 303f.

58. *Ledger*, Jan. 26, 1867, 3, col. 2.

59. *Avalanche*, March 22, 1867, 3, col. 2; *Appeal*, March 22, 1867, 3, col. 5; March 28, 3, col. 3; and April 2, 3, col. 3; and Minutes County Court, Book B-13, 1867, 384, SCA

60. See Appendix 1.

61. Minutes County Court, Book B-13, 1867, 384–88, and 448; and *Appeal*, April 2, 1867, 3, col. 3. The William Hack on the Commission was not the Germantown area resident by that name.

62. Records of the U.S. Civil Commission, NARA, T-410/reel 78/ 1; and on Barbour Lewis during and after the war, Lanier, WTHS, 2012, 41, 47f, and 58

63. Minutes County Court, Book B-13, 1867, 502, and e.g., 455–56 and 535, SCA

64. *Appeal*, April 27, 1867, 2, cols. 1 and 3; May 1, 1, col. 4; May 3, 2, col. 3; May 11, 2, col. 2; Aug. 1, 1, col. 4, and 3, cols. 3–4.

65. *Appeal*, July 7, 1867, 3, cols. 2 and 3.

66. *Ledger*, Aug. 2, 1867, 3, col. 5.

67. *Appeal*, Jan. 15, 1868, 3, col. 3; and Jan. 16, 3, cols. 2 and 3; and Jan. 18, 3, col. 4; and *Ledger*, Jan. 21,3, col. 2.

68. *Appeal*, Jan. 25, 1868, 2, cols. 2 and 3; Jan. 26, 3, col. 5; Feb. 14, 2, col. 1; Feb. 21, 3, col. 3; and Feb. 29, 3, col. 3.

69. *Appeal*, March 6, 1868, 2, col. 5.

70. *Ledger*, March 9, 1868.

71. *Appeal*, June 1, 1868, 2, col. 1; June 2, 3, col. 3; and June 3, 3, col. 5.

72. *Appeal*, July 2, 1868, 3, col. 3; July 6, 1868, 3, cols. 4 and 5; July 7, 1, col. 2; and July 11, 1. col. 2.

73. *Avalanche*, July 19, 1868, 2.

74. *Appeal*, July 7, 1868, 1, col. 3; July 21, 1868, 2, col. 1, and Aug. 8, 2, cols. 1–2.

75. *Appeal*, July 23, 1868, 4, cols. 4–6.

76. *Avalanche*, Oct. 4, 1868, p. 3.

77. *Evening Post*, Sept. 14, 1868, 3, col. 1.

78. Ibid.

79. *Avalanche*, July 19, 1868, 2.

80. Lamon, *Blacks*, 35.

81. *Appeal*, Sept. 17, 1868, 1.

82. *Appeal*, Nov. 14, 1868, 1, col. 4.

83. *Appeal*, Nov. 1, 1868, 2, col. 2.

84. *Appeal*, Jan. 21, 1872, 4, col. 3.

85. *Appeal*, July 14, 1868, 3, col. 6; Aug. 29, 3, col. 3; 9.30.68, 3, col. 3; Oct. 15, 3, col. 1; and Oct. 9, 2, col. 2; *Ledger*, April 24, 1, col. 3; and Young, 150–52.

86. *Appeal*, Oct. 25, 1868, 3, col. 1.

87. Lipsey, "Memories," 17.

88. *Appeal*, Feb. 8, 1871, 3, cols. 3–4.

89. *Appeal*, Jan. 28, 1869, 2, col. 1; and Jan. 29, 2, cols. 1–3.

90. "Lynching in America," Equal Justice Initiative, 2015, eji.org/files/EJI Lynching in America SUMMARY.pdf; and "Shelby County's Shame," anonymous pamphlet, 1896, archive.org/stream/shelbycountyssha00slsn#page/n3/mode/2up.

91. *Appeal*, Jan. 16, 1869, 3, col. 2; *Public Ledger*, Jan. 15, 3; and Nashville *Union and American*, Jan. 21, 1.

92. *Appeal*, May 2, 1869, 3, col. 2; May 5, 2, cols 1–2; May 27, 4, col. 4; May 31, 4, col. 2; and July 20, 4, col. 4.

93. *Appeal*, July 25, 1869, 4, col. 5; Aug. 6, 4, cols. 4–5; and Aug. 7, 2, cols. 1 and 3.

94. Commissioner's Minute Book, E, 223f-24; and Map of Shelby County, Tennessee, Compiled and Published by J.H. Humphreys, Civil Engineer. Sears & Smith of the Memphis Abstract Co., 1869 (courtesy of Walter Wills III), SCA.

95. County Court Minutes, Book G, Oct. Term 1871, 3 and 50; and *Appeal*, Oct. 8, 1874, 4.

96. County Court Minutes Book F, April Term 1870, 6.

97. *Appeal*, Aug. 5, 1870, 1.

98. *Appeal*, April 15, 1872, 4; and Aug. 3, 1872, 4.

99. *Appeal*, Nov. 20, 1869, 3, col. 3; and Dec. 30. 3, col. 5.

100. *The Morning Republican* (Little Rock), Nov. 9, 1870, issue 158, col. B; but cf. Nashville *Union and American*, Nov. 9, 1870, 1, col. 2; *Ledger*, Oct. 7, 2, col. 1.

101. *Appeal*, July 30, 1872, 3, col. 6.

102. *Appeal*, Jan. 21, 1872, 4, col. 3.

103. *Tennessee Atlas of Historical County Boundaries*, 255 and 418; and Plan showing Bel County (Tenn.) as laid down according to the act of Dec. 20, 1870, TL&A.

104. *Appeal*, Oct. 8, 1874, 4, col. 5; and June 24, 1, col. 2; and *Ledger*, July 3, 1874, 2; and Aug. 8, 1878.

105. *Appeal*, Nov. 6, 1872, 1, col. 1, and 4, col. 2; Nov. 7, 2, col. 1.

106. *Ledger*, June 1, 1874, 2, cols. 2–4.

107. *Appeal*, Oct. 8, 1874, 4.

108. *Appeal*, Nov. 4, 1874, 1, col. 2; and July 31, 1, col. 1.

109. *Avalanche*, Feb. 24, 1868, 3; Feb. 25, 2, col. 1; March 12, 3; Lamon, *Blacks*, 46–52; and David M. Tucker, "Back Politics in Memphis, 1865–1875." Reprinted, 73 (2019): 151–57.

110. *Ledger*, April 14, 1880, 4, col. 4.

111. Helen M. Cappock, and Charles W. Crawford, eds. *Paul R. Cappock's Midsouth*. (1992 & 1993), vol. 2, 382; Darnell, *Germantown News*, July 3, 1986; and cf. Goodspeed, "Shelby," 915.

Chapter 11

1. New York *Times*, Feb. 16, 1865, TCWSB.

2. Acts, 1867–68, chap. 15, 11–13.

3. Robert A. Sigafoos, *Cotton Row to Beale Street*, (1979), 49.

4. Robert T. McKenzie, "Reconstruction." *Tennessee Encyclopedia of History and Culture*. tennesseeencyclopedia.net/entries/reconstruction.

5. Ibid.

6. Downs, *Sick from Freedom*, 57–60, 63–64., 123–24, 133–34; and Egerton, *The Wars of Reconstruction* (2014), 79–83.

7. McKenzie, "Reconstruction."

8. E.g., *Avalanche*, April 15, 1872, 1, col. 2–3; and Charles S. Aiken, *The Cotton Plantation South since the Civil War.* (1998), 16–22.

9. Ibid.

10. Aiken, *Cotton Planation South*, 29–35; McKenzie, "Reconstruction;" and Cooper and Terrill, *South* map, 428.

11. McKenzie, "Reconstruction."

12. Regulations for the Collection of Direct Taxes in Insurrectionary Districts.

13. Woodson, *Genealogy*, 475.

14. Woodson, *Genealogy*, 306–307.

15. Lanier, WTHS, 29.

16. Ibid; *Appeal*, Dec. 20, 1867, 4, col. 2; and Dec. 14, 1869, 1, col. 6.

17. *Appeal*, Jan. 22, 1868, 3, col. 9.

18. *Appeal*, 3 April 1866, 3, col. 1.

19. Dyer and Moore, vol. 3, 1033.

20. 1870 census, District 11, 304A; and 1880, 230B; by 1880, Mary was a widow listed as having a 35-year-old daughter by a different name and an 18-year-old son. This is indicative of census data problems. The 1880 deputy was supposedly better trained and more diligent than in the previous decades. The best explanation is that the 1870 deputy missed the older daughter and confused the gender and name of the son.

21. The woman listed as Elizabeth G. Harrison may be a name error.

22. Census 1870, CD 11, 311A; and 1880, CD 11, 230B.

23. See Appendix 3.

24. Mrs. John Scruggs, notes, O'Neill name file, GRH&GS.

25. *Appeal*, Jan. 21, 1866, 3, col. 2.

26. Sigafoos, 0.

27. 1870 census, District 11, 313A.

28. Peggy Boyce Jemison, *Greenlaw Rediscovered*, (1919), 4–5.

29. E.g., Records of the U.S. Civil Commission at Memphis, 1863–64, NARA T-410/roll 1/ 27, & 83.

30. OR, vol. 32, pt. III, 634; Galbraith, 182 and 201; and Jemison, 4–5.

31. *Appeal*, June 26, 1870, 4, col. 1, rental advertisement.

32. Wills Interview, Oct. 1, 2011.

33. E.g., County Courts Minutes, April Term, 1871, 414–17.

34. Cf. 1870 and 1880 censuses and 1869 Shelby County property map which was compiled from records preceding his intrusion.

35. Ibid, 312A; and Shelby County Marriages, 1860, book 2, 70.

36. Marie Goodman Jenkins, *Church of Six Generations: A History of the Red Banks Presbyterian Church.* Holy Springs, (1955), 12–13.

37. *Ledger*, July 3, 1874, 2, col. 1; and *Gazetteer*, 1876, 149.

38. Census 1880, CD 11, 234A, 235A, 242A, and 250 A.

39. Based on comparative 1860 and 1870 census data on non-real property, including approximation for Kimbrough and Brook's holdings.

40. Woodson papers, MVC, MS 114, box 1, folder 6, Redemption Certificate No. 347.

41. Assessment List of the United States Direct Tax . . . , 37–40.

42. *Appeal*, Aug. 6, 1868, 1, col. 5.

43. E.g., *Appeal*, July 12, 1868, 3, col. 5; March 2, 1869, 3, col. 6; Sept. 23, 1871, 1, col. 7; and Oct. 25, 1874, 3, col. 8.

44. *Appeal*,1, col. 6; and *Ledger*, Jan. 10, 1867, 1, col. 4, July 12, 1875, 3, col. 2, and Feb. 3, 1879, 4, col. 5.

45. Comparison of 1860 agricultural census with 1869 property map; Hall, 10–11. and 88; Hunt, 15; Kimbrough family cemetery survey, GRH&GC; and census 1880, CD 11, 241 A&B.

46. *Appeal*, Jan. 2, 1874, 4, col. 1; and Census, 1870, CD 11, 308B.

47. See Appendix 3.

48. Much of this acreage lay outside District 11, much of it in Mississippi and some in Arkansas. By the same token, much of the acreage in District 11 was owned by absentee landlords. The difference between ownership and cropping is indeterminate in this census. Further problems of determining property ownership are explained in Appendix 3.

49. See Appendix 3 concerning contradictions between agricultural and population censuses and the 1869 plot map. The census taker seems to have been ignoring guidelines.

50. U.S. Department of Labor, *History of Wages*, 226–7. Local pay based on 1880 census.

51. The absence of the Kimbroughs and Brooks from the agricultural census obscures the possibility that they were also free from the pressure to monocrop.

52. Cooper and Terrill, *South*, 385, 436–39.

53. Ibid, 429–34; and Foner, *Reconstruction*, 406–8.

54. Foner, *Reconstruction*, 108, and cf. 408–9.

55. See Appendix 3. Especially problematic for determining the lands farmed and or owned by blacks is the number of households in the agricultural schedules that are missing from the population schedules. Ethnicity is not identified in the agricultural schedules.

56. Civil War Pension Records, Lou Freeman pensioner, Cert. No. 598229, NARA

57. Annie C. Tuggle, Another *World Wonder* (1973). 2–3.; Arthur L. Webb, "From exile to excellence" *Tri-State Defender*, May 29, June 6, and June 12, 2002; and 1880 Shelby County Platt map.

58. Tuggle, 1–3.

59. E.g., 1870 census, District 11, 290A-293A, 296Af, 300A, 302A, and 303Af.

60. 1870 census, District 11, 294B, and 304 B.

61. Ibid, 307A.

62. *Appeal*, 7 Jan. 1866, 3, col. 4; and 18 Jan. 1, col. 4.

63. Foner, *Reconstruction*, 81–84.

64. *Appeal*, 9 Dec. 1865, 2, cols. 1–2; 23 Jan..1866, 1, col. 7; and 3 April, 3, col. 9.

65. 1870 census, District 11, 305a-b.

66. Miller, *Apprentices*, 138–44; and census 1870, CD 10, 255A.

67. Freedmen's Bureau Indenture Bonds for Shelby County, Tennessee, FB

68. Miller, p. 145; and census 1870, CD 10, 274A.

69. Quarterly Court, Loose Papers, 1829–0028, SCA.

70. Freedmen's Bureau Indenture Bonds for Shelby County, Tennessee, FB

71. Cooper and Terrill, *South*, 428.

72. An additional three seem to have been missed in the agricultural census as were either owners or renters.

73. This confirms Foner, *Reconstruction*, 85–87.

74. 1880 census, District 11, 252A.

75. Lamon, *Blacks*, 37.

76. E.g. First and Second Reports of William Meriwether as Guardian of John H. and Susie E Quenichet (*sic*), 27 Jan. 1880 and n.d., Probate Court Loose Papers, 1880, SCA, available in Quenichet name file, GRH&GA.

77. 1870 census, District 11, 295b, 300a, and 303a; 1880 census. District 11, 251B.

78. NPS, Soldiers and Sailors System; and *The Roster of Union Soldiers*; and see Appendix 2.

79. Lipsey, "Memories," 11, 17, 33, and passim.

80. *Appeal*, March 10, 1871, 4, col. 6.

81. County Court, Minutes Book 11, 1865, 364; Book A-12, 1866, 324–25, 507, 509, 512, SCA; Book K, 1870, 562; and April Term, 1871, 429.

82. *Appeal*, June 7, 1870, 4, col. 6; and Hopkins, Hughes Papers, GRH&GC.

83. *Appeal*, Feb. 22, 1880, 4.

84. *Ledger*, May 18, 1880, 2.

85. *Appeal*, June 5, 1870, 2, col. 2.

86. *Appeal*, Dec. 20, 1871, 2, cols. 1–2.

87. *Appeal*, April 14, 1867, 2, col. 5.

88. *Appeal*, Dec. 14, 1869, 1, col. 6; and June 26, 1870, 4, col. 1.

89. *Avalanche*, March 27, 1868, 3, col. 2.

90. *Ledger*, April 8, 1868, 3, col. 4.

91. *Avalanche*, May 6, 1868, 3, col. 5; and *Ledger*, May 4, 3, col. 3; May 13, 3, col.4; and May 20, 3, col. 2.

92. *Ledger*, Aug. 22, 1870, 3, cols. 3–4; and Aug. 26, 1871, 3, col. 1.

93. *Ledger*, Nov. 16, 1868, 3, col. 5, and frequently thereafter.

94. *Appeal*, Feb. 21, 1868, 3, cols. 2, and 8; Nov. 22, 3, col. 8; and Jan. 31, 1871, 4, col. 9; and *Ledger*, Nov. 27, 1871, 1.

95. Martha Titus Diary, March 8–18, 1873, MCV.

96. *Appeal*, May 24, 1872, 4, col. 2.

97. Young, *Memphis*, 157.

98. Emily Lucken/Mills correspondence, Florida to Emily, Dec. 9, 1873, GRH&GC; and *Martha Titus Diary*, M&SC.

99. E.g., *Appeal*, May 29, 1873, 4, col. 1; and Aug. 4, 4, col. 7.

100. Available at SCA and GRH&GA, among others. As explained in Appendix 3, it was impossible to keep track of the constantly changing ownership, and each map was significantly out of date by publication.

101. *Avalanche*, March 2, 1867, 3, col. 1.

102. *Appeal*, Aug. 27, 1879, 2, col. 5.
103. Census 1880, CD 11, p. 233A.Census 1880, CD 11, 233A.
104. *Ledger*, Sept. 11, 1878, 1, col. 4.
105. Emily Lucken/Mills correspondence, J. C. L. to Emily, Sept. 15, 1871, GRH&GC.
106. Ibid, Mrs. Evans to Emily, April 2, 1872; Florida to Emily, July 18, 1872; and Dec. 9, 1873.
107. Ibid., Florida to Emily, Dec. 9, 1873.
108. Ibid, Jenny to Emily, April 30, 1875.
109. Bergeron, *Paths of the Past*, 69.
110. Nashville *Union and American*, Dec. 30, 1874, 4, col. 4; *Appeal*, May 26, 1873, 8, col. 2; and *Ledger*, Feb. 3, 1879, 4, col. 5.
111. *Ledger*, Sept. 10, 1873, 2, col. 3.
112. *Appeal*, July 23, 1880, 2; and Sept. 13, 1881, 2, col. 4; and excerpts of Gazette, 1887 and 1890, *Germantown News*, Feb. 23, 2011, 16.
113. Quarterly Court Minutes, April Term, 1871, 346; and Assessment Lists of the United States Direct Tax . . . , 38.
114. Emily Lucken/Mills correspondence, J.C.L to Emily, Sept. 15, 1871? GRH&GC.
115. Ibid., Florida to Emily, 1872.
116. NA/No. 11,688 Cong. Depositions, Ed. M. Cole.
117. Smith, *Baptist Church*, 8; *Appeal*, Jan. 31, 1872, 4, col. 3; April 17, 4, col. 3; April 20, 4, col. 2; April 30, 3, col. 3; and May 29, 4, col.
118. *The Baptist-Memphis*, 2 and 10 Jan. 1874, typed notes of Elisabeth P. Hughes, GRH&GC, Baptist Church folder.
119. Postmaster Finder.
120. *Appeal*, 23 Jan. 1866, 1, col. 3; and Dec. 25, 1874, 4, col. 1.

Chapter 12

1. *Gazetteer* entries for 1876, 1887 and 1890, *Germantown News*, February 23, 2011, 16; and Census 1870.
2. First notice, *Appeal*, January 4, 1867, 3, col. 3; and June 26, 1868, 3, col. 3.
3. Lipsey, "Memories," 29.
4. *Appeal*, August 15, 1876, 4, col. 2; and September 5, 1, col. 4; and Lipsey, "Memories," 26.
5. Faust, *Mothers*, 252.
6. Faust, *Mothers*, 195, 238, 242–43, 256–57.; and Rable, *Civil Wars*, 222–26, 230.
7. The largest collection of letters are correspondence of Emily Lucken Mills, GH&GC.
8. Indexes to *The Memphis Appeal, 1843–1870*, and the *Memphis Avalanche*, 1860–1870, compiled by Joyce McKibben, Reference Librarian, The University of Memphis formerly available at tn-roots.com/tnshelby/newspapers/index.htm. Currently not available.
9. Joanne Crawford, "The Davies Family," *Old Shelby County*, No. 52:9–10.
10. On Sanderson's organization, Browder, "Richardson," 66–69; Emily Mills Journal, 1863, Mills Family Records; Emily Lucken/Mills correspondence, Dix to Julia, July 29, 1870; Florida to Emily, January 17, 1872; and October 19, GRH&GC; and Loving, p. 159.
11. Ibid, Florida to Emily, December 9, 1872.
12. *Appeal*, June 2, 1876, 4, col. 5.

13. Interview with Nancy Thompson, *Germantown News*, March 3, 1977, 7; and Lipsey, "Memories," 26.

14. *Appeal*, April 15, 1872, 4, col. 6.

15. *Appeal*, Oct. 21, 1878, 2, col. 3.

16. *Appeal*, Nov. 7, 1865, 3, col. 1; and Nov. 8, 3 col. 1.

17. Ibid, Nov. 8.

18. Shelby County Tract Map, 1869; and US Census 1870.

19. McKibben, *Index to Appeal*.

20. *Appeal*, May 31, 1866, 2, col. 2.

21. *Appeal*, Jan. 17, 1866, 3, col. 2; Nov. 30, 1867, 3, col. 3; Dec. 7, 3, col. 4; and Dec. 12, 3, col. 2; and *Bulletin*, Nov. 3, 1867, 4, col. 1.

22. *Appeal*, June 26, 1868, 4, col. 4.; Jan. 6, 1870, 1, col. 6; and Aug. 29, 1873, 4, col. 2; and *Ledger*, March 1, 1871, 3, col. 5, July 3, 3; and Dec. 20, 1879, 4, col. 6.

23. *Ledger*, May 11, 1876, 3, col. 4.

24. *Avalanche*, April 18, 1868, 3, col. 2.

25. *Ledger*, Aug. 21, 1871, 3.

26. *Appeal*, Jan. 12, 1870, 4, col. 4.

27. *Appeal*, Sept. 10, 1867, 3, col. 5.

28. *Appeal*, Sept. 20, 1867, 3, col. 3.

29. *Appeal*, Feb. 11, 1875, 4, col. 4.

30. *Appeal*, Sept. 8, 1873, 4; and *Ledger*, Sept. 8, 3.

31. Ibid.

32. *Appeal*, Sept. 8, 1873, 4; *Ledger*, April 23, 1874, 3; Oct. 5, 1874, 2; and Jan. 13, 1875, 3.

33. Although there were numerous John Whites in Confederate military records, including specifically a John E. serving as a private in the 45th Mississippi, I have yet to find a "Captain" John E. White.

34. *Appeal*, March 20, 1875, 4, cols. 2–3; and March 21, 1, col. 5.

35. *Appeal*, June 27, 1870, 4, col. 2; June 11, 1871, 4, col. 3; and Sept. 9, 4, col. 2; and *Ledger*, May 10, 1870, 3, col. 4.

36. *Memphis Public Ledger*, Dec. 9, 1878, 4, col. 4; and 1870 census, CD 11, 310B.

37. *Appeal*, Dec. 11, 1878, 4; and *Ledger*, Dec. 10, 4.

38. *Ledger*, Dec. 24, 1878, 1, col. 1, and Feb.5, 1879, 4, col. 3, and Feb. 13, 4, col. 5.

39. *Appeal*, March 13, 1874, 2, col. 4; May 25, 1876, 4, col. 2–3; and May 28, 4, col. 8; *Boston Journal*, May 27, 1876, 1; and *Ledger*, May 26, 1876, 3; June 22, 1877, 3, col. 5, July 30, 1878, 1, col. 7, and July 31, 3, col. 7.

40. *Ledger*, July 9, 1876, 3, col. 3.

41. *Ledger*, Jan. 10, 1867, 1, cols. 2–3.

42. *Avalanche*, May 3, 1867, 3, col. 2; May 5, 1; and 3, col. 2.

43. *Appeal*, Oct. 23, 1880, 4; and *Ledger*, Dec. 6, 4, col. 5.

44. *Avalanche*, April 29, 1868, 1, cols. 2–3.

45. *Avalanche*, April 21, 1868, 3, col. 1.

46. Based on Emily Lucken/Mills correspondence with Dix and others, GRH&GC.

47. They appear in the 1860 census with him misnamed Richard Mills, minister, age 29, born in the District of Columbia.

48. Memphis Conference Minutes, 1862–67, 16.
49. *Avalanche*, April 22, 1868, 3, col. 4.
50. *Avalanche*, April 29, 1868, 1, col. 3.
51. *Avalanche*, April 29, 1868, 1, cols. 2–3.
52. *Avalanche*, May 2, 1868, 2, col. 2.
53. *Avalanche*, May 2, 1868, 3, col. 3.
54. *Avalanche*, May 13, 1868, 3, col. 1.
55. Certification, May 6, 1871, signed Lorenzo D. Mullins, Mills Family Records, VRHC.
56. Norton, *Religion*, 76.
57. Quenichet will, Nov. 4, 1871; undated Meriwether petition to County Court; First and Second Meriwether Reports to Probate Court, 27 Jan. 1880 and n.d., Loose Papers, SCA.
58. Nancy Freemen, McEntee, *Haversacks, Hardtack, and Unserviceable Mules*, 260, 263, 269, 271–72, and 274–75.
59. McKibben index.
60. *Appeal*, Feb. 21, 1871, 4, col. 2; March 28, 1875, 4, col. 3; June 8, 1, col. 4; June 9, 4, cols. 2–3; and June 11, 1, col. 3; and *Ledger*, April 3, 1869, 3, col. 3; December 14, 3, col. 3; June 10, 1871, 3, col. 3; June 9, 1875, 3, col. 2;
61. Sigafoos, *Cotton Row*, 30; Jemison, *Greenlaw*, 4; and Register of Death in the City of Memphis, 1875, file # 17131, SCA; *Appeal*, August 3, 1875, 4, col. 3; August 24, 2, col. 1; and Sept. 26, 1, col. 3, and 4, col. 7; and *Public Ledger*, Aug. 24, 2, col. 2.
62. *Appeal*, Sept. 1, 1873, 3.
63. *Appeal*, March 4, 1880, 4.
64. *Martha Titus Diary*, March 9 and 16, 1873; and "Germantown Methodist Church," anonymous, 1, GRH&GC, Germantown History Collection, Churches.
65. Norton, *Religion*, 76; on Graves, *Appeal*, May 12, 1875, 1, cols. 1–3; Aug. 17, 1873, 4, col. 3; a disputation, May 4, 1871, 4, col. 3–7; and Lipsey, "Memories," 35.
66. Lipsey, "Memories," 35.
67. Ibid, 31 and 35.
68. Emily Lucken/Mills correspondence, Florida to Emily, Oct. 9, 1872, GRH&GC.
69. Lipsey, "Memories," 22.
70. Ibid 22, 29, 34; and Emily Lucken/Mills correspondence, J.C.L to Emily, Sept. 15, 1871? GRH&GC.
71. Foner, *Reconstruction*, 425.
72. Petitions, Hack folder, GRH&GC.
73. *Appeal*, May 3, 1870, 4, col. 4; and Oct. 21, 1873, 4, col. 4.
74. *Appeal*, Jan. 14, 1869, 2, col. 1.
75. Rable, *Civil Wars*, 230; there are absolutely no references to politics in the extensive Emily Lucken/Mills correspondence, GRN&GC.
76. Faust, *Mothers*, 256–57; and Whites, Civil War, 21–24.
77. Prescott, "Woman Suffrage," THS 73: 200–207.
78. *Appeal*, Feb. 8, 1869, 3, col. 5.
79. *Martha Titus Diary*, March 8–18, 1873, MVC; *Ledger*, February 23, 1878, 3, col. 7; and Emily Lucken/Mills correspondence, Florida to Emily, Jan. 17, 1872, GRH&GC.
80. Census 1880, CD 11, 233A.

81. *Appeal*, June 22, 1869, 1, col. 6; and June 26, 4, col. 3; and *Ledger*, June 25, 3, col. 4.
82. *Appeal*, Dec. 3, 1869, 2, col. 5; and Sept. 22, 1870, 4, col. 5.
83. *Appeal*, Aug. 12, 1869, 1, col. 4; Dec. 22, 1872, 2, col. 4; and *Ledger*, July 27, 1874, 3, col. 4.
84. *Ledger*, June 2, 1873, 3, col. 3.
85. Lamon, *Blacks*, p. 45; and *Ledger*, June 14, 1880. 1, col. 1.
86. *Ledger*, June 21, 1869, 3, col. 4.
87. *Ledger*, Oct. 7, 1872, 3.
88. *New Bethel Missionary Baptist Church*, Germantown, no publisher, n.d.; *Guide to Church Vital Statistics in* Tennessee, 388; Census 1860, p. 166, and 1870, District 11, p. 312; and Shelby County Marriages, 1860, book 2, 70.
89. Foner, *Reconstruction*, 89–95, for a summary of the post-war black religious experiences and relevant literature.
90. *New Bethel Missionary Baptist Church*, copy of County Register's purchase, Book 73, p. 374; Katharine Bennett, "New Bethel Has Rich History," *Commercial Appeal*, Oct. 25, 2009, B7; and *New Bethel Missionary Baptist Church*, n.p.
91. *Appeal*, Dec. 5, 1865, 3, col. 2.
92. Ibid.; and 1860 & 1870 censuses, District 11
93. *Appeal*, Jan. 10, 1866, 2, col. 7; Smithsonian Institution, *List of the Institutions, Libraries, Colleges, and Other Establishments in the United States*, 1872, 214, GBS; Emily Lucken/Mills correspondence, J.C.L. to Emily, Sept. 15, 1871, Florida to Emily, July 18, 1872, and Oct. 19, GRH&GC.
94. *Appeal*, 18 Jan. 1866, 1, col. 7; and Dec. 21, 1867, 3, col. 4. C. F. W. Miller was listed a Synthia E. W. Miller in the 1860 census.
95. *Ledger*, Dec. 20, 1867, 3, col. 2; *Appeal*, Dec. 21, 3, col. 4; and Dec. 22, 3, col. 4.
96. *Avalanche*, March 27, 1868, 3, col. 2; Nov. 18, 3; and Sept. 13, 3, col. 1.
97. Acts, 1866–67, chap. 27, 33–42.
98. Crouse, "A Sketch" typescript, Cloyes files, GRH&G.
99. Booth, "Germantown Pioneers: Memories"; Census 1880, CD 11, 230A, 234A, 235A, 246B, and 247B.
100. 1870 census, District 11, 290A, 293B, 294B, 297A, 299Af., 301B.
101. Ibid., 290A–291A, 292B, 293A, 295B, 297B, 301A, 304A, 306B, 312A, and 313A.
102. County Court Minutes, Jan. Term, 1871, 324–25; and Goodspeed, 838.
103. County Court Minutes, Oct. Term, 1871, 47–48.
104. Goodspeed, 839–40.
105. Emily Lucken/Mills correspondence, Florida to Emily, Dec. 9, 1873, GRH&GC.
106. Lipsey, "Memories,", 28; Census, 1880, CD 11, 230A; Goodspeed, 839; and Crouse, "A Sketch" typescript, Cloyes files, GRH&G.
107. Lipsey, "Memories," 28; *Appeal*, Dec. 31, 1873, 3.
108. Sheldon S. Kohn, "Men and Women of Mississippi, You Have a Jewel!: The Establishment and Funding of Mississippi's Industrial Institute and College," typescript, 2–5.
109. Ibid, citing Reneau's "Address to the Legislature of the State of Mississippi, Jan. 1856."
110. Ibid.

Conclusion

1. Spence, *Diary*, November 10, 1863, TCWSB.
2. Rable, *Civil Wars*, chapter 13.
3. Faust, *Mothers*, 253; Rable, *Civil Wars*, 230–38.
4. E.g., *Appeal*, May 27, 1874, p. 2, col. 2.
5. Young, *Memphis*, 146.
6. Faust, *Mothers*, pp. 252-f.; Rable, *Civil Wars*, pp. 236–39; Cooper and Terrill, *South*, 454–58 and Whites, *Civil War: Gender*, chap. 6.

Postscript

1. For a vivid contemporary description, colored by the prevalent prejudices, J. M. Keating, *A History of the Yellow Fever: The Yellow Fever Epidemic of 1878, in Memphis, Tenn.* (Memphis: Printed for the Howard Association, 1879; reprinted London: FB&c Ltd., 2015), 101–105.
2. Molly Caldwell Crosby, *The American Plague* (2006), 14–15, and 42–45.
3. *Ledger*, August 9, 1878, 3, col. 6.
4. Mildred, ed. Hicks, *Yellow Fever and the Board of Health: Memphis, 1878*. Memphis: The Memphis and Shelby County Health Department, 1964. 6, and 10–11; and Crosby, *American Plague*, 47–50.
5. *Avalanche*, September 15, 1878, 1, cols. 4–5; September 21, 1, col. 3; Keating, *Yellow Fever*, 94.
6. Notes on Evans' day-book, May 3, 1973, EHC/GRH&GC; *Appeal*, September 28, 1878 1, cols. 4–5; Hicks, 20; and Crosby, pp. 51–55; c.f. Keating, *Yellow Fever*, 239–40, naming 42 dead.
7. *Appeal*, September 18, 1878, 1; with corrections on September 24, 1.
8. *Appeal*, September 24, 1878, 1.
9. *Appeal*, September 25,1.
10. For a contemporary description of the wide and contradictory range of proposed treatments by medical professionals, the only valid ones of which were efforts to reduce fever, full bed rest and fluids, Keating, *Yellow Fever*, 46–73.
11. *Appeal*, September 22, 1, col.3.
12. *Appeal*, September 28, 1, col. 2.
13. *Appeal*, September 25, 1, Col.3; and *Avalanche*, October 18, 1, col 5.
14. *Avalanche*, September 28, 1, col. 5.
15. *Appeal*, September 28, 1.
16. *Appeal*, September 22, 1.
17. *Appeal*, September 27, 1.
18. Keating, *Yellow Fever*, 16–45.
19. *Appeal*, September 29, 1.
20. *Appeal*, October, 3, 1.
21. *Avalanche*, October 4, 1868, 2, col. 1.
22. E.g., *Avalanche*, October 6, 1868, 2, col.1; October 9, 2, col.1.

23. *Appeal*, October 4, 1; and October 16, 1, col. 3; Notes on Evans' day-book, May 3, 1973, EHC/GRH&GC;

24. *Appeal*, October 4, 1; October 15, 1; and October 20, 1

25. *Appeal*, October 20, 1.

26. Emily Lucken/Mills correspondence, Florida to Emily, November 17, 1878, GRH&GC.

27. Beverly Booth, "Germantown Pioneers: Memories of the City's Settlers Obscured by Time," *Germantown News*, July 14, 1977, interview with Molly Molitor Nowlin.

28. *Avalanche*, October 4, 1878, 2, col. 1; October 16, 1, col. 2; October 18, 1, cols. 4–5; and Scott, *Germantown*, chap. 5, 8 and 11

29. *Avalanche*, October 18, 1, col 5.

30. *Avalanche*, October 21, 2, col. 3.

31. *Appeal*, October 19, 1; and October 13, 1.

32. "How It Began;" and Hughes interviews.

33. Scott, *Germantown*. chap. 5, p. 9

34. *Appeal*, May 23, 1879, 2; and Notes on Evans' day-book, May 3, 1973, EHC/GRH&GC.

35. Lipsey, "Memories," 27; *Avalanche*, September 28, 1878; and October 10, 1878, 2, cols. 1–2.

36. Interview with Louise Duke Bedford, "Memories of the City's Settlers," *Germantown News*, June 16, 1877.

37. *Appeal*, September 26, October 3 & 13, 1878, 1;

38. Lipsey, "Memories," 30.

39. *Appeal*, July 20, 1879, 1, col. 1.

40. *Knoxville Daily Chronicle*, August 19, 1879, 4, col. 2; *Morristown Gazette*, August 20, 2, col. 7; *Knoxville Chronicle*, September 3, 1, col. 4; and *Appeal*, September 7, 2, col. 2.

41. *Appeal*, September 7, 1879, 2, col. 2.

42. *Appeal*, October 14, 2, cols. 1–2.

43. Lipsey, "Memories," p.30; and Smith, *Germantown*, p. 9.

44. Goodspeed, "Shelby", 915; Cf. Magness, "Germantown," 124.

45. Census 1880, 338.

46. Dowdy, *Memphis*, 55–63.

47. M&R RR, Superintendent's Report for year ending June 1872, Statement 7, Passengers, and Statement 9, Bales of Cotton, Brooks/Kirby collection.

48. Interview with Mary Martin, "Victorian Romance: A Germantown Love Story," *Germantown News*, July 21, 1977, 16B; and Hughes and Kirby interviews.

49. *Appeal*, July 25, 1867, 1, cols. 4 -5; February 14, 1868, 2, col. 5; and Goodspeed, Shelby, 797 and 911f.

50. *Tennessee State Gazetteer*, 1887, reprinted in *Germantown News*, February 23, 2011, 16; and *Appeal*, March 4, 1880, 4.

51. Ibid. Although difficult to interpret, the description of the town's new borders reflected a slight reorientation to new residential and business areas with the depot at the center and an apparent reduction in size to 160 acres.

52. *Ledger*, December 6, 1879, 4, col. 5; and December 20, 4, col. 7.

53. Goodspeed, "Shelby," 915–16.

Appendix 2

1. Family Tree, ancestry.com, U.S. Civil War Records and Profiles; *Tennesseans in the Civil War*, Pt. II.; and *The roster of Confederate Soldiers 1861–1865*, ed. Janet B. Hewett (Wilmington, NC: Bradfort Publishing Co., 1995).

Appendix 3

1. Egerton, *Reconstruction*, 61, 84–85.

BIBLIOGRAPHY

Primary Sources

ARCHIVES AND PRIVATE COLLECTIONS

Germantown Presbyterian Church, historical display. Referred to as GPC.
    Rev. R.R. Evans, Letter to Henry Woodson, November 28, 1864.
    Rev. R.R. Evans, Notebook, Records of the Memphis Presbytery, 1855–1860.
    Rev. R.R. Evans, Notebook, Record of Tuition Paid, 1870s
    Phillips, Tom. "History prepared and read by Squire Tom Phillips," transcribed by Margaret Harrison Owen, March 27, 1938.
Germantown Regional History and Genealogy Center. Referred to as GRH&GC.
    Cloyes, Harry scrap books. Church Files
    Dean, Adelaide Sullivan, interview, 7.24.2007.
    Hughes, Elizabeth Collection.
    Germantown History Commission Interviews.
    Map Files
    Mills, Emily Lucken, correspondence
    Personality Files. Referred to as folder name/GRH&GC
    Pouncey, G. Andrew Collection.
    Pouncey, Andrew, "Civil War and the Baptist Church: United States vs. Germantown Baptist Church, U.S. Claims Court No. 11688."
Germantown United Methodist Church, Archive. Referred to as GUMCA.
    Browder, George C. "The Early History of the Germantown Methodists and their Church."
    History of Germantown United Methodist Church File.
    Historical File of Elizabeth West.
    Warranty Deeds File.
    West, Betsy. "A Short History of the Germantown United Methodist Church." typescript, revised 1982.
    Wilson, Karen, "The History of the Germantown Methodist Church." typescript, May 3, 1979.
Memphis Conference Archives, United Methodist Church, Jackson, TN
    Minutes of the Annual Conferences, 1773–1958
    Journals of the Memphis Annual Conference, 1862 to current.
    Estes, Lud H. and Earl G. Hamlett, *A Short History of the Memphis Annual Conference of the Methodist Church*, n.d., n.p.

Memphis and Shelby County Room, Benjamin L. Hooks Central Library, Memphis, TN. Referred to as M&SC, MPL
   Britton Duke Papers
   Civil War Letters and Diaries
   M.T. Williamson, Historical Map Collection
Mississippi Valley Collection, Special Collections, Ned R. McWerther Library, University of Memphis. Referred to as MVC.
   Ayers, George B. *Descriptive Railroad Handbook of Great Southern Route between New Orleans and Washington*. Memphis: 1858.
   Dunaway. Civil War Letters Written by William Dunaway, 7th Illinois Cavalry. MVC-3540.
   Freedmen's Bureau Papers, MVC-107
   Martha Titus Diary, 1873, Shelby County, TN., MSS 54–84
   Montague, A.W., papers, Acc#89–52, MS 54–127. MS, "My Experience as a Confederate Soldier," by A.W. Montague
   Nashoba Research Files, MVC-388.
   Howse (Howze), Isham R. *Isham R. Howse's Journal*, Book 8, June 1852- September 1853. M 5388, Box 1, Folder 10.
   Neely, Mrs. R.P., Memoirs, MVC-240, Box, 1, Folder 1.
   Woodson Family papers, MS 114.
National Archives and Records Administration, Washington, D.C. Referred to as NARA.
   M 268, Compiled Service Records of Confederate Soldiers who Served in Organizations from the State of Tennessee
      Twelfth (Green's) Cavalry, A-I, roll 50
      Thirteenth Infantry, A-D, roll 169
   M 598, Selected Records of the War Department Relating to Confederate Prisoners of War, 1861–65, Roll 98, Memphis, Tennessee, Provost Marshall
   M 1911, Records of the Field Offices of the State of Tennessee, Bureau of Refugees, Freedmen, and Abandoned Lands, 1865–1872.
   RG 15, Records of Department of Veterans' Affairs, 1773–2009; Case Files of Approved Pension Applications of Civil War Veterans, 1861–1910
   RG 77, Civil War Map Files.
   T 227, Assessment Lists of United States Direct Tax Commission for District of Tennessee
   T 410, Records of the United States Civil Commission at Memphis, 1863–64.
      Microfilm, 1860 Census of the United States, Shelby County, Tennessee.
         Free Persons Forms, roll 278.
         Slave Schedules, roll 279
      M 1135 Agriculture Schedules, roll 10
      Manufactures Schedules, roll 31
      Social Statistics, roll 37
   T 655 Mortality Schedules, roll 27
      Microfilm, 1870 Census of the United States, Shelby County, Tennessee Population Schedules

    M 1135 Agricultural Schedules, roll 15
        Social Statistics, roll 38
    Microfilm, 1880 Census of the United States, Shelby County, Tennessee, Population Schedules
    M 1135 Agricultural Schedules, roll 27
        Manufactures Schedules, roll 35
        Social Statistics, roll 40
    T 655 Mortality Schedules, roll 30
Shelby County Archives. Referred to as SCA.
    Cemetery Inscriptions
    Death Records, 1848–1958
    Election Voter Lists, 1868
    Map Collection
        Map of Shelby County, Tennessee. Compiled by J.B. Humphreys, Civil Engineer, Sears & Seoth of the Memphis Abstract Co., 1869
        Topographical Map of Road from Moscow to Memphis Tenn., by order of Maj. Gen. W. T. Sherman, n.d. (1863)
        Topographical Map of the Environs of Moscow, La Grange & Grand Junction, Tenn. By order of Maj. Gen. W.T. Sherman, n.d. (1863)
    Marriage Records, 1820–1929
    Memphis City Directories, 1859–1901
    Naturalization Records, 1856–1906
    Shelby County Circuit Court Minutes
    Shelby County Court of Quarterly Pleas and Common Sessions
        Minutes
        Records—referred to as Loose Papers
    Shelby County Probate Records
Tennessee State Library and Archives (TSLA).
    Lipsey, Platus Iberus. "Memories of His Early Life, (1865–1888)," typed MS reproduced by Julia F. and John J. Lipsey, Colorado Springs, CO, 1949.
    Robert Boyte Crawford Howell Papers, Mf.1270, roll 3.
    Tennessee Election Returns, State, County and Local Elections RG 87.
    Historical Maps, digital
    TSLA and Duke University. *Tennessee Agricultural and Manufacturing Census Records for the years 1850, 1860, 1870 and 1880*. Nashville: Tennessee State Library and Archives, 1990.
    Agricultural Schedules, 1860, Roll 10, Shelby County
    Agricultural Schedules, 1870, Roll 84, Shelby County
    Agricultural Schedules, 1880, Roll 95, Shelby County
Valentine Richmond History Center (VRHC)
    MS. C 27, Mills Family Papers, 1828–1945. (Available at Germantown Regional History and Genealogy Center)
Wills Family papers/Kirby Farms collection, Germantown, Tennessee. (Wills/Kirby Collection) Courtesy of Walter Wills.

Hopkins, John L. "The Kirby Farm House: A Brief History." Typescript, April 1, 1987.

Hord, Rachel Brooks, composed and compiled by. *A Little History of the Brooks' Family of Pitt North Carolina and includes some descendants in Tennessee, Arkansas, Louisiana, Texas*. Crescent City, FL, 1990.

Miscellaneous Materials & Notes

Tagg, Susan. "Wilks Brooks: Early Germantown Settler and Community Builder, 1785–1849." Typescript, n.d.

ON-LINE COLLECTIONS

Confederate Railroads, www.csa-railroads.com (CSA RR)
   Maps
   Essays and Documents
   Memphis and Charleston www.csa-railroads.com/Memphis_and_Charleston.htm.

The Freedman's Bureau Online, Tennessee. Referred to as FB. http://www.freedmensbureau.com/tennessee/index.htm.

GenealogyBank.com.
   Google Book Search, providing an extensive on-line library of publications now in the public domain and dating to the period under study. Referred to as GBS.

Germantown Museum, The (Virtual Museum) https://germantownhistory.org (GM)
   Browder, George C. "Anton H. Lucken." /people-and-places/personal-stories/anton-h-lucken.
   Parker, Susan. "Wilks Brooks: Life and Times of an Early Germantown Settler, February 11, 1875-March 9, 1849."/peoples-places/personal-stories/wilks-brooks.

Library of Congress, Digital Collections
   Chronicling America, historical newspapers: in addition to the *Daily Appeal*, the *Memphis Public Ledger*, plus several other period Tennessee papers and innumerable papers of other states.
   Civil War Documents: Contemporary literature referred to as LC

Missouri Digital Heritage
   Frost, M.O. *Regimental History of the Tenth Missouri Infantry*. Topeka, KA: M.G. Frost Printing Company, n.d. http://sos.mo.gov/mdh.

National Park Service, Soldiers and Sailors System. www.itd.nps.gov/civilwar/soldiers-and-sailors-database.htm

Regulations for the Collection of Direct Taxes in Insurrectionary Districts under the Act Entitled "An Act for the Collection of Direct Taxes in Insurrectionary Districts within the United States, and for Other Purposes." Washington: Government Printing Office, 1863. Instant Archive: http://archive.org/details/regulationsforcounit.

Shelby County, Tennessee Genealogy and History, http://www.TNGenweb.org (TNGenWeb).

Smith, Trevor Augustine, "Pioneers, Patriots, and Politicians: The Tennessee Militia System, 1772–1857." PhD diss., University of Tennessee, 2003. http://trace.tennessee.edu/utk_graddiss/2661.

Tennessee Blue Book. https://www.tn.gov/sos/bluebook/.

Tennessee Civil War Source Book, http://www.tnsos.net/TSLA/.cwsourcebook.
   A digitized collection of primary sources. Referred to as TCWSB. Includes selected excerpts from the following, plus numerous period newspapers.
   Papers of Andrew Johnson, Vols. 4—6, Knoxville: University of Tennessee Press.
   Pomeroy, Fletcher. *The 7th Kansas Cavalry in the Civil War: The Diary of Fletcher Pomeroy*. Topeka, Kansas: Kansas Historical Society, 1997.
   Sanderson, Jr., William F. *The Civil War Letters of Colonel William Lawrence Sanderson*. Np: 1997.
The United States Postal Service: An American History, 1775–2006. Publication of the U.S. Post Office. https://www.usps.com/cpim/ftp/pubs/pub100.pdf.
University of Mississippi, Civil War Collection, Digital Archive. http://egrove.olemiss.edu/civ-war (UMiss, CWC)

PUBLISHED DOCUMENTS

Acts of the State of Tennessee. 1839, 1841–42, 1851, 1854, 1855–57, 1859–60, 1861, 1862, 1865, 1868, 1869, 1871 and 1880 (Acts, year, page).
Bear, Henry C. *The Civil War Letters of Henry C. Bear: A Soldier of the 116th Illinois Volunteer Infantry*. Harrogate, TN: Lincoln University Memorial Press, 1961.
Berlin, Ira and Leslie S. Rowland, eds. *Families & Freedom: A Documentary History of Afro-American Kinship in the Civil War Era*. New York: The New Press, 1997.
Berlin, Ira, et. al., eds. *Freedom: A Documentary History of Emancipation, 1861–1867*. Cambridge: Cambridge University Press, Series I—II, 1986–2012.
Dyer, Fred Arthur and John Trotwood Moore. *Tennessee Civil War Veteran Questionnaires*. 5 vols. Easley, SC: Southern Historical Press, Inc., 1985.
Green, J. Harvey and Rachel. *Letters to My Wife: A Civil War Diary from the Western Front*. Complied by Sharon L. D. Kraynak, Comp. Apollo, PA: Closson Press, 1995.
Horn, Stanley F., Ed. *Tennessee's War, 1861–1865: Described by Participants*. Nashville: Tennessee Civil War Centennial Commission, 1965.
Hubbard, John Milton. *Notes of a Private*. (Company E, 7th Tennessee Regiment) St. Louis: Nixon-Jones Printing Co., 1911.
Hicks, Mildred, ed. *Yellow Fever and the Board of Health: Memphis, 1878*. Memphis: The Memphis and Shelby County Health Department, 1964.
Lacy, Eric Russell, ed. *Antebellum Tennessee: A Documentary History*. Berkeley, CA: McCutchan Publishing Corporation, 1969.
Memphis, Shelby County, Tennessee, The Early Years: Selected Court Records & Survey Books—1820–1850, Brunswick, TN: The Tennessee Genealogical Society, n.d. Referred to as *Selected Court Records*.
Minutes of the Memphis Conference of the Methodist Episcopal Church, South for the Years 1862,-1867, The. Mobile: AL: M. A. Publishing, 1984.
Simon, John Y., ed. *The Papers of Ulysses S. Grant*. Vols. 5–6. Carbondale, IL: Southern Illinois University Press, 1973, 1977. Referred to as *Grant Papers*.
Supplement to the War of the Rebellion. Wilmington, NC: Bradford Publishing Company, 1994–2000. Supplemental reports to OR Series I, and records of events by unit. Referred to as SOR.

Sutcliff, Andrea, ed. *Mighty Rough Times, I Tell You: Personal Accounts of Slavery in Tennessee*. Winston-Salem, NC: John F. Blair Publisher, 2000.

Thorndike, Rachael Sherman. *The Sherman Letters: Correspondence between General and Senator Sherman from 1837 to 1981*. New York Charles Schreiber's Sons, 1894.

U.S. CENSUSES

Statistics of the Population of the United States at the Tenth Census (June 1, 1880). Washington: Government Printing Office, 1883. Cited as Census 1880.

The Statistics of the Population of the United States Compiled from the Original Returns of the Ninth Census (June 1, 1870). Washington: Government Printing Office, 1872. Cited as Census 1870.

Population of the United States in 1860: Compiled from the Original Returns of the Eighth Census. Washington: Government Printing Office, 1864. Cited as Census 1860.

Statistics of the United States, (including mortality, property, & c.) in 1860; comp. from the original returns and being the final exhibit of the Eighth Census. Washington: Government Printing Office, 1866. Cited as Census Statistics, 1860.

The Seventh Census of the United States: 1850. Washington: Robert Armstrong, Public Printer, 1853. Cited as Census 1850.

Population and Agricultural sheets, Shelby County TN, Districts. 7, 9, 10, 11. Available on microfilm

U.S. Department of Labor, Bureau of Labor Statistics, *History of Wages in the United States from Colonial Times to 1928*. Washington, D.C.: U.S. Government Printing Office, 1934.

War of the Rebellion: Official Record of the Union and Confederate Armies. Washington: The Government Printing Office, 1881–1898.

A compilation of military reports and correspondence on both sides.

Series I, vols. 3, 4, 7, 10, 17, 24, 30, 31, 38, 39, 45, and 49 covered reports and correspondence of both sides in West Tennessee about troop dispositions, operations and combat, and many general aspects such as dealing with the people of the occupied territories. Referred to as OR, vol. #, part #, page(s).

Series II includes correspondence and reports concerning prisoners of war, suspect civilians and violations of the conventions of warfare. Referred to as ORII, vol.#, page(s).

Series III includes Federal correspondence and reports concerning personnel and recruitment, including "colored troops," railroads, telegraphs, hospitals, etc. Referred to as ORIII, vol.#, page(s)

Series IV includes Confederate reports and correspondence concerning defenses, ordinance and transportation. Referred to as ORIV, vol.#, page(s).

CONTEMPORARY REPRINTS

Ayers George B. *Descriptive Railroad Handbook of great Southern Route between New Orleans and Washington*. Memphis: 1858.

Davenport, Edward A. Ed. *History of the Ninth Regiment Illinois Cavalry Volunteers*. Chicago: Donohue & Henneberry, 1888.

Goodspeed's *History of Tennessee: From the Earliest Time to the Present*. Nashville: The Goodspeed Publishing Company, 1887.

Goodspeed's History of Hamilton, Knox and Shelby Counties of Tennessee. Reprinted from Goodspeed's History, 1887. Nashville: Charles and Randy Elder Booksellers, 1974.

Keating, J. M. *A History of the Yellow Fever: The Yellow Fever Epidemic of 1878, in Memphis, Tenn.* Memphis: Printed for the Howard Association, 1879; reprinted London: FB&c Ltd., 2015.

Tennessee State Gazetteer and Business Directory for 1876–77. Nashville: R.L. Polk and Co., 1876.

Wright, General Marcus J. *Tennessee in the War, 1861–1865.* New York, NY: Ambrose Lee Publishing Co., 1908. (LC)

NEWSPAPERS

Memphis Daily Appeal 2.27.1847–11.8.1890
Memphis Tri-Weekly Appeal 4.1845–5.1862
Memphis Weekly Appeal 4.21.1841–11.8.1890
Memphis Union Appeal 7.-8.1862
Memphis Daily Avalanche 1.12.1858–3.4.1866 [continued as *Memphis Avalanche* 1866–1890]
Memphis Weekly Avalanche 1.19.1858–11.6.1890
Memphis Daily Argus 5.1859–12.1866
Memphis Bulletin 9.1.1855–12.31.1868 [7.3.62–6.65 replaced the suspended *Avalanche*]
Weekly Memphis Eagle 1.1848–12.9.1851
Daily Memphis Enquirer 1847–12.1.51 [merged with *Daily Eagle.*]
Tri-Weekly Memphis Enquirer 1841–12.9.1851
Memphis Daily Eagle and Enquirer 12.10.1851–6.30.1858
Memphis Weekly Eagle and Enquirer 12.16.1851–1861
Memphis Evening Ledger. 10.3.1857—1859?
Public Ledger. 7.18.1865—8.31.1893.
Weekly Public Ledger. 3.8.1870—8.26.1890.
Memphis Evening Post. 4.1868—9.1869.
Memphis Morning Post. 1.15.1866—4.27.1868.
Daily Memphis Whig 4.1852–7.1856

MEMOIRS AND AUTOBIOGRAPHIES

Barbieri, *Scraps from the Prison Table at Camp Chase and Johnson's Island*, 1868, p. 219, GBS.

Cumming, Kate. *A Journal of Hospital Life in the Confederate Army of Tennessee from the Battle of Shiloh to the End of the War: With Sketches of Life and Character, and Brief Notices of Current Events during that Period.* Louisville, KY: John P. Morton & Co., 1866.

Grant, Ulysses S. *Personal Memoirs of U. S. Grant.* The Project Gutenberg EBook, 2004. www.gutenberg.org/files/4367/4367-pdf/4367-pdf.pdf

McDonald, Laurier B. Ed. *Fourteen Letters to a Friend: The Wartime Ordeal of Captain DeWitt Clinton "Clubfoot" Fort.* . . . Edinburg, TX, Self-Published, 2007.

Nelson, Stith. "Excerpts from the Diary of Stith Nelson, University of Memphis Special Collections." *West Tennessee Historical Society Papers.* Vol 64. (2010): 119–133.

Sherman, William T. *Memoirs of General William T. Sherman.* Vol. I. New York: D. Appleton and Company, 1875.

Wallace, Lew. *Smoke, Sound & Fury: The Civil War Memoirs of Major-General Lew Wallace, U.S. Volunteers.* Jim Leeke, ed. Portland, OR: Strawberry Hill Press, 1998.

REFERENCE MATERIALS

Albertson, Eric, C. Andrew Buckner, Michael C. Tuttle, and Michael C. Krivor, *Terrestrial and Submerged Cultural Resources Survey along Approximately 6 KM of the Wolf River, Shelby County, Tennessee.* Report for Corps of Engineers, Memphis District. Memphis: Panamerican Consultants, Inc., 2001.

Allison, John, ed. *Notable Men of Tennessee; Personal and Genealogical with Portraits.* Atlanta: Southern Historical Association, 1905.

Cargill, Bernice Taylor and Brenda Bethea Connelly, eds. *Settlers of Shelby County, Tennessee and Adjoining Counties.* Memphis: The Descendants of Early Settlers of Shelby County, Tennessee, 1989.

Cole, Steve. Battle of Fort Pillow. www.custerman.com/DixieBoys/FtPillow.htm

Civil War Centennial Commission. *Guide to the Civil War in Tennessee.* Nashville: Civil War Centennial Commission, 1960.

Garrison, Webb with Cheryl Garrison. *The Encyclopedia of the Civil War.* Nashville: Cumberland House, 2001.

Guide to Church Vital Statistics in Tennessee. Nashville: War Services Section, 1942.

Hewett, Janet B. ed. *The Roster of Confederate Soldiers, 1861–1865.* Wilmington, NC: Broadfoot Publishing Co., 1995-

———. *The Roster of Union Soldiers, 1861 to 1865.* Wilmington, NC: Broadfoot Publishing Co., 1997.

McKenzie, Robert Tracy. "Reconstruction." *Tennessee Encyclopedia of History and Culture.* tennesseeencyclopedia.net

McKibben, Joyce. *Index to Early Memphis Newspapers.* No longer available.

———. *Index to the Memphis Appeal.* Memphis: Memphis Public Libraries 2003–2006.

Miller, Alan N. *West Tennessee's Forgotten Children: Apprentices from 1821 to 1889.* Baltimore: Clearfield Company for Genealogical Publishing, 2006.

Rodriguez, Ricardo J., Ed., *Black Confederates in the Civil War.* Nashville: Tennessee Library and Archives, n.d.

Tennessee Atlas of Historical County Boundaries. John H. Long, ed. New York: Charles Scribner's Sons, 2000.

Tennesseans in the Civil War: A Military History of Confederate and Union Units with Available Rosters of Personnel. 2 vols. Nashville: Civil War Centennial Commission of Tennessee, 1964.

Interviews

Harry Cloyes, Germantown, Tennessee, July 7, 2010.
Adelaide Dean, Germantown, Tennessee, May 14, 2010.
Elizabeth Hughes, Germantown, Tennessee, June 30, July 1, 2010, September 20, 2011.
Jennifer Lynch, telephone, Washington, D.C., December 7, 2010.
Jane Sanderson, Memphis, February 11, March 4, 2012.

Frank Stewart, Memphis, Tennessee, August 5, 2010.
Susan Thompson, Germantown, Tennessee, June 2012, August 2, 2012
Walter D. Wills III, Germantown, Tennessee, September 31, 2011; March 29, 2013.

Secondary Sources

Abernethy, Thomas Perkins. *From Frontier to Plantation in Tennessee: A Study in Frontier Democracy.* Memphis: Memphis State College Press, 1955.

Aiken, Charles S. *The Cotton Plantation South since the Civil War.* Baltimore: The Johns Hopkins University Press, 1998.

Ash, Stephen V. *A Massacre in Memphis: The Race Riot that Shook the Nation One Year After the Civil War.* New York: Hill and Wang, 2013.

———. *When the Yankees Came: Conflict and Chaos in the Occupied South, 1861–1865.* Chapel Hill: University of North Carolina Press, 1995.

Atkins, Jonathan M. *Parties, Politics, and the Sectional Conflict in Tennessee, 1832–1861.* Knoxville: The University of Tennessee Press, 1997.

Bailey, Fred Arthur. *Class and Tennessee's Confederate Generation.* Chapel Hill: The University of North Carolina Press, 1987.

Bergeron, Paul H. *Paths of the Past: Tennessee, 1770–1970.* Knoxville: The University of Tennessee Press, 1979.

Brown, Myers E., II, with the Tennessee State Museum. *Images of America: Tennessee's Union Cavalrymen.* Charleston: Arcadia Publishing, 2008.

Cappock, Helen M. and Charles W. Crawford, eds. *Paul R. Cappock's Midsouth.* Vols. II & III. Memphis: The Paul R Cappock Publication Trust, 1992 & 1993.

Cary, Bill. *Runaways, Coffels and Fancy Girls: A History of Slavery in Tennessee.* Nashville, TN: Clearbrook Press, 2018.

Clark, Blanche Henry. *The Tennessee Yeomen, 1840–1860.* Nashville: Vanderbilt University Press, 1932.

Clinton, Catherine. *The Plantation Mistress: Woman's World in the Old South.* New York: Pantheon Books, 1982.

Cooper, William J. and Thomas E. Terrill. *The American South: A History.* New York: Alfred A. Knopf, 1991.

Coulter, Frederick Lee. *Memphis, 1800–1900. Vol II. Years of Crisis, 1860–1870.* New York: Nancy Powers & Company Publishers, 1982.

Crosby, Molly Caldwell. *The American Plague: The Untold Story of Yellow Fever, the Epidemic that Shaped Our History.* New York: Berkley Books, 2006.

Crouse, Maurice A. "A Sketch of Early Germantown History," *Germantown News, Germantown Festival Annual-1973,* September 15 and 16,

Commercial Appeal, Memphis. Numerous articles by local historians and references to historical articles in the Memphis *Appeal.*

Cunningham, H.H. *Doctors in Gray: The Confederate Medical Service.* Baton Rouge: Louisiana State University Press, 1958.

Currotto, William F. *Tracking the Wolf: One Hundred and Seventeen Miles Mostly from an Armchair, 1828–1997.* Memphis: self-published, n.d.

Daniel, Jack. *Southern Railway from Stevenson to Memphis: A History of the Memphis Division Southern Railway System*. Germantown: Grandmother Earth Creations, 1996.

Darnell, Dr. J. Millen, "A brief Chronological History of Germantown until the Civil War," compiled for the *Germantown News*, 1990.

Davis, Burke. *The Southern Railway: Road of the Innovators*. Chapel Hill: University of North Carolina Press, 1985.

Dowdy, Wayne. *A Brief History of Memphis*. Charleston, SC: History Press, 2011.

Downs, Jim. *Sick from Freedom: African-American Illness and Suffering during the Civil War and Reconstruction*. New York: Oxford University Press, 2012.

Durham, Walter T. *The State of History in Tennessee in 2008: The Underground Railroad to 1865*. Nashville: Tennessee State Library and Archives, 2008.

Dye, Robert W. *Images of America: Shelby County*. Charleston, SC: Arcadia Publishing, 2005.

Eckhardt, Celia Morris. *Fanny Wright: Rebel in America*. Cambridge: Harvard University Press, 1984.

Egerton, Douglas R. *The Wars of Reconstruction: The Brief, Violent History of America's most Progressive Era*. New York: Bloomsbury Press, 2014.

Faust, Drew Gilpin. *Mothers of Invention: Women of the Slaveholding South and the American Civil War*. Chapel Hill: University of North Carolina Press, 1996.

Fisher, Noel C. "'Prepare Them for My Coming:' General William T. Sherman, Total War, and Pacification in West Tennessee." In Carroll van West, ed. *Tennessee in the Civil War: The Best of the Tennessee Historical Quarterly*. Vol. I, pp. 90–105. Nashville: Tennessee Historical Society, 2011.

Foner, Eric. *Reconstruction: America's Unfinished Revolution*. New York: Harper and Row, 1988.

——— and Joshua Brown. *Forever Free: The Story of Emancipation and Reconstruction*. New York: Alfred A. Knopf, 2005.

Fox-Genovese, Elizabeth. *Within the Plantation Household: Black and White Women of the Old South*. Chapel Hill: University of North Carolina Press, 1988.

Genovese, Eugene D. *The Political Economy of Slavery: Studies on the Economy and Society of the Slave South*. New York: Random House, 1967.

———. *Roll, Jordan, Roll: The World the Slaves Made*. New York: Pantheon Books, 1974.

Germantown News. Numerous articles by local historians, especially Beverly Booth's Germantown Pioneers series based on interviews with old town residents.

Gibson, Christine. "Who Gets to Let States Back into the Union?" American Heritage.com.

Graebner, William. *A History of Retirement: The Meaning and Function of an American Institution, 1885–1978*. New Haven: Yale University Press, 1980.

Hall, Russell S. *Images of America: Germantown*. Charleston, SC: Arcadia Publishing, 2003.

Harkins, John E., Dr. *Historic Shelby County: An Illustrated History*. San Antonio: Historical Publishing Network.

———. *Memphis Chronicles: Bits of History from the Best Times*. Charleston: The History Press, 2009.

———. *Metropolis on the American Nile: Memphis & Shelby County*. Memphis: The Guild Bindery Press.

Harncourt, Paul. *Biography of the Memphis and Charleston Railroad*. San Jose: Writer's Club Press, 2000.

Jemison, Peggy Boyce. *Greenlaw Rediscovered: A History.* Memphis: Metropolitan Inter-Faith Association, 1979.

Jenkins, Marie Goodman. *Church of Six Generations: A History of the Red Banks Presbyterian Church.* Holy Springs, MS: The South Reporter Printing Co., 1955.

Jordan, General Thomas and J.P. Pryor. *The Campaigns of Lieut.-Gen. N.B. Forrest, and of Forrest's Cavalry, with Portraits, Maps, and Illustrations.* Reprint. Dayton, OH: Press of the Morningside Bookshop, 1973.

Lamon, Lester C. *Blacks in Tennessee, 1791–1970.* Knoxville: The University of Tennessee Press, 1981.

Lanier, Robert A. *The History of the Memphis & Shelby County Bar.* Memphis: Memphis & Shelby County Bar Association, n.d.

Ledsinger, Anita. "Talk Offers Look into City's Past." Report on lecture by Betty Hughes. *Germantown News*, October 29, 1981. Referred to as Hughes Lecture.

Lewis, Selma S. *A Biblical People in the Bible Belt: The Jewish Community of Memphis, Tennessee, 1840s-1860s.* Macon, GA: Mercer University Press, 1998.

Lindert, Peter H. and Jeffrey G. Williamson. "American Incomes 1774–1860." NBER Working Paper Series, Working Paper 18396. Cambridge, MA: National Bureau of Economic Research, 1212.

Lindsley, John Berrien, ed. *Military Annals of Tennessee: Confederate.* Nashville: J.M. Lindsley & Co., 1886.

Loving, Waldon. *Coming Like hell!: The Story of the 12th Tennessee Cavalry, Richardson's Brigade, Forrest's Cavalry Corps, Confederate States Army, 1862–1865.* San Jose: Writer's Club Press, 2002.

Mackey, Robert R. *The Uncivil War: Irregular Warfare in the Upper South, 1861–1865.* Oklahoma City: Oklahoma University Press, 2004.

Magness, Perre. *Past Times: Stories of Early Memphis.* Memphis: Parkway Press, 1994.

———. *Good Abode: Nineteenth Century Architecture in Memphis and Shelby County.* Memphis: Junior League of Memphis, 1983.

McEntee, Nancy Fessenden. *Haversacks, Hardtack, and Unserviceable Mules: The Civil War Journey of a Union Quartermaster in Tennessee.*

McFarland, Patricia LaPonte, and Mary Ellen Pitts. *Memphis Medicine: A History of Science and Service.* Birmingham, AL: Legacy Publishing, 2011.

McLeary, A.C. *Humorous Incidents of the Civil War.* Chapel Hill: University of North Carolina Press, 1997.

McPherson, James M. *For Cause & Comrades: Why Men Fought in the Civil War.* New York: Oxford University Press, 1997.

New Bethel Missionary Baptist Church: 135 Years, 1869–2004. Germantown: New Bethel MBC, 2004.

Norton, Herman A. *Religion in Tennessee, 1777–1945.* Knoxville: University of Tennessee Press, 1981.

Oaks, James. *Freedom National: The Destruction of Slavery in the United States, 1861–1865.* New York: W.W. Norton & Co., 2013.

Old Shelby County Isbell, Terry. "The Victorian Way of Death: How Our Ancestors Buried Their Dead." 2–9.

Press Semitar, Memphis, Numerous articles by local historians.

Rable, George C. *Civil Wars: Women and Crisis of Southern Nationalism*. Urbana and Chicago: University of Chicago Press, 1989.

Rich, Dorothy. *Fayette County*. Memphis: University of Memphis Press, 1989.

Rosenbloom, Joshua L., and Gregory W. Stutes. "Reexamining the Distribution of Wealth in 1870." NBER Working Paper Series. Working Paper 11482. Cambridge, MA: National Bureau of Economic Research, 2005. http://www.nber.org/papers/w11482.

Ruminski, Jarret. "'Tradyville' The Contraband Trade and the Problem of Loyalty in Civil War Mississippi." *Journal of the Civil War Era*, Vol. 2: 4, pp. 511–37.

Russel, Clarene Pinkston. *Collierville Tennessee: Her People and Neighbors*. Collierville: Town of Collierville, the Collierville Chamber of Commerce, 1994.

Rutherfurd, Winthrop. "The Partisan Ranger Act: The Confederacy and the Laws of War." *Louisiana Law Review*, Vol. 79, Number 3 (Spring 2019), pp. 807–37.

Scott, Linda McGregor. *History of Germantown*. MS, n.d. Copy available at GRH&GS

Severance, Ben H. *Tennessee's Radical Army: The State Guard and Its Role in Reconstruction, 1867–1869*. Knoxville: The University of Tennessee Press, 2005.

Sigafoos, Robert A. *Cotton Row to Beale Street: A Business History of Memphis*. Memphis: Memphis University Press, 1979.

Schroeder-Lein, Glenna R. *Confederate Hospitals on the Move: Samuel H. Stout and the Army of Tennessee*. Columbia: University of South Carolina Press, 1994.

Smith, Eugenia H. *History of Germantown Baptist Church*. Germantown: Germantown Baptist Church, 1981. Copy available at GRH&GS.

Smith, Gerald. *Fort Germantown Historical Park*. Germantown: City of Germantown, 1985. Copy available at GRH&GS.

Southern Historical Society Papers Referred to as SHS

    Loehr, Charles T. "Point Lookout," vol. 18 (Jan.-Dec. 1890): 114–20;

    Traywick, Rev. J.B. "Prison Life at Point Lookout," vol. 19 (January 1891): 432–35

    Stephens, Gail. *Shadow of Shiloh: Major General Lew Wallace in the Civil War*. Indianapolis: Indiana Historical Society Press, 2010.

Steele, S. A. "The Salt Problem" from *The Sunny Road: Home Life in Dixie during the War*. 10–22.

Tennessee Historical Quarterly Referred to as *THQ*.

    Binning, F. Wayne. "The Tennessee Republicans in Decline, 1869–1876." 39 (Winter 1980), 4:471–84.

    Boone, Jennifer K. "'Mingling Freely': Tennessee Society on the Eve of the Civil War." 51 (Fall 1992), 3: 137–146.

    Cimprich, John. "Military Governor Johnson and Tennessee: Blacks, 1862–65." 39 (Winter 1980), 4: 457–70.

    Lash, Jeffrey N. "'The Federal Tyrant at Memphis:' General Stephen A. Hurlbut and the Union Occupation of West Tennessee." 48 (Spring 1989), 1: 15–28.

    Luflin, Charles L. "Secession and Coercion in Tennessee, the Spring of 1861." 50 (1991), 2: 98–109.

    Zornow, William Frank, "State Aid for Indigent Soldiers and Their Families in Tennessee, 1861–1865," 13 (1954): 297–300.

Thornton, J. Mills, III. "The Ethics of Subsistence and the Origins of Southern Secession"

in Carol Van West, ed. *Tennessee in the Civil War*. Vol. I. Nashville: Tennessee Historical Society, 2011.
Tuggle, Annie C. *Another World Wonder*. Self-published, 1973. Copy available GR H&GC.
Vedder, O.F. *History of the City of Memphis and Shelby County, Tennessee*. 2 vols. Syracuse: D. Mason & Co., 1888.
Ward, Andrew. *River Run Red: The Fort Pillow Massacre in the American Civil War*. London: Viking Penguin, 2005.
———. *The Slaves War: The Civil War in the Words of Former Slaves*. Boston: Houghton Mifflin, 2008.
Warner, Ezra J. *Generals in Gray: Lives of the Confederate Commanders*. New Orleans: Louisiana University Press, 1959.
Webb, Arthur L. "From exile to excellence: The Roberts family." *Tri-State Defender*, May 29, June 6, and June 12, 2002.
Weeks, Linton. *Memphis: A Folk History*. Little Rock: Parkhurst, 1982.
West, Carroll Van. *Tennessee in the Civil War: The Best of the Tennessee Historical Quarterly*. Vol. I. Nashville: Tennessee Historical Society, 2011.
West, James, "The Thirteenth Tennessee Regiment—Confederate States of America," *Tennessee Historical Magazine*, 7 (October 1921): 180–89.
Western Tennessee Historical Society Papers. Referred to as *WTHS*.
   Aden, Mrs. R.F. (Capt. F.F. Aden), "In Memoriam, Seventh Tennessee Cavalry, C.S.A." 17 (1963): 108–117.
   Arnold, Mark L. "Baptism of Fire, Forging of Veterans: The Thirteenth Tennessee Infantry and the Battle of Belmont." 52 (1998): 95–104.
   Bailey, Robert. "The 'Bogus' Memphis Union *Appeal*: A Union Newspaper in Occupied Confederate Territory." 32 (1978): 32–47.
   Baker, Steve. "Agriculture, Race, and Free Blacks in West Tennessee." 48 (1994): 107–117.
   Bejack Lois D., "'The Journal of Civil War 'Commando' DeWitt Clinton Fort," in WTHS, 2 (1948): 5–32,
   Blankenship, Gary. "Colonel Fielding Hurst and the Hurst Nation." 34 (1980): 71–87.
   Browder, George C. "Robert V. Richardson and the First Tennessee Partisan Rangers." 66 (2012): 65–97.
   ———. "The Burning of Germantown: The Case of Germantown Baptist Church." 71 (2017): 107–120.
   Coleman, L.H., "The Baptists in Shelby County." 15 (1961): 8–39.
   Donhardt, Gary L. "On the Road to Memphis with General Ulysses S. Grant." 53 (1999): 1–15.
   Dougan, John. "Why They Chose to Stay: The Petitions of Free Persons of Color to Remain in Shelby County, Tennessee, 1843–1853." 48 (1994): 118–125.
   Dunn, Durwood, "Apprenticeship and Indentured Servitude in Tennessee before the Civil War." 36 (1982): 25–40.
   Ellis, John H. "Henry Morton Woodson Confederate Veteran; Historian; Memphian." 14 (1960): 74–91.
   Gunderson, Lawrence G., "West Tennessee and the Cotton Frontier, 1818–1849," 52 (1998): 25–43.

Harrison, Holly Reed. "Our Relation to Persons of African Descent Has Been less than Ideal . . .'": The Southern Baptist Convention, the Christian life Commission, and Race Relations." 53 (1999): 118–134.
Jones, James B., Jr. "'The Reign of Terror of the Safety Committee Has Passed Away Forever': A History of Committees of Safety and Vigilance in West and Middle Tennessee, 1860–1862." 63 (2009): 1–28.
———. "The Struggle for Public Health in Civil War Tennessee Cities." 60 (2007).
Lanier, Robert A. "The Memphis Legal Community under Federal Occupation 1860–1870." 66 (2012): 27–64.
Lovett, Bobby L. "The West Tennessee Colored Troops in Civil War Combat." 34 (1980): 53–70.
Lufkin, Charles L. "A Forgotten Controversy: The Assassination of Senator Almon Case of Tennessee." 39 (1985): 37–50.
———. "The Northern Exodus from Memphis during the Secession Crisis." 42 (1988): 6–29.
———. "Not Heard from since April 12, 1864? The Thirteenth Tennessee Cavalry, U.S.A." 45 (1986): 133–51.
Maness, Lonnie E., "Forrest's New Command and the Failure of William Sooy Smith's Invasion of Mississippi." 40 (1986): 55–72.
Masters, Daniel A, "'Pen Lever': The Civil War Letters of Charles Edward Bliven of the Army Telegraph Corps." 52 (2016): 76–97.
Matthews, James S. "Sequent Occupance in Memphis, Tennessee: 1819–1860." Reprinted 73 (2019): 57–80.
McKinney, John B. "N ed and Rose Kearney: My Dear Friends." 64 (2010): 134–142.
Mehrling, John C. "The Memphis and Charleston Railroad." 19 (1965): 21–35.
Moran, Nathan K. "Military Government and Divided Loyalties: the Union Occupation of Northwest Tennessee June 1862-August 1862." 48 (1994): 91–106
Nollan, Richard. "Troublous Times: The Civil War letters of William J. Armstrong, M.D., March 1963–September 1864." 60 (2006)
O'Daniel, Patrick W., "Loyalty a Requisite: Trade and the Oath of Allegiance in the mid-South in 1865," 60 (2006): 35–47.
Prescott, Grace Elizabeth. "The Woman Suffrage Movement in Memphis: Its Place in the State, Sectional and National Movements." Reprinted, 73 (2019): 200–220.
Saunders, Richard L. "The Racial Demographics of West Tennessee: An Essay Based on U.S. Census Data, 1830–2000." 61 (2007): 122–154.
Scarbrough, L. Alex, Jr., Vincent L. Clark, ed. "Camp Journal of Corporal Lemuel A. Scarbrough, Sr. Company E 'Dixie Rifles.'" 66 (2012): 123–47.
Thornton, J. Mill, III, "The Ethics of Subsistence and the Origins of Southern Secession." See above under Thornton.
Tucker, David M. "Back Politics in Memphis, 1865–1875." Reprinted, 73 (2019): 151–57.
Waschka, Ronald W., "River Transportation at Memphis before the Civil War," 45 (1991): 1–18.
———, "Road Building in and Near Memphis," 47 (1993): 50–64.

Watlington, Elton. "Glimpses of Methodist History in the Mid-South." 56 (2002): 128–134.
Whites, LeeAnn. *The Civil War as a Crisis in Gender: Augusta, Georgia, 1860–1890*. Athens, GA: University of Georgia Press, 1995.
———. *Gender Matters: Civil War and Reconstruction in the Making of the New South*. New York: Palgrave Macmillan, 2005.
———, and Alecia P. Long, eds. *Occupied Women: Gender, Military Occupation, and the American Civil War*. Baton Rouge, LA: Louisiana State University Press, 2009.
Witherington, Albert Sydney, III. *History of Germantown: Utopia on the Ridge*. Germantown: self-published, 1997. Copy available at GRH&GS.
———. *The History of the Wolf River: Diamond in the Rough*. Germantown: self-published, 1997. Copy available at GRH&GS.
Woodard, Colin. *American Nations: A History of the Eleven Rival Cultures of North America*. New York: Penguin Books, 2011.
Wooster, Ralph A. *Politicians, Planters, and Plain Folk: Courthouse and Statehouse in the Upper South, 1850–1860*. Knoxville: The University of Tennessee Press, 1975.
Wyatt-Brown, Bertram. "Community, Class, and Snopesian Crime: Local Justice in the Old South." In Orville Vernon Burton and Robert C. McMath, Jr., eds. *Class, Conflict and Consensus: Antebellum Southern Community Studies*. Westport, CN: Greenwood Press, 1982.
———. *Southern Honor: Ethics and Behavior in the Old South*. New York: Oxford University Press, 1982.
———, and Alecia P. Long, eds. *Occupied Women: Gender, Military Occupation and the American Civil War*. Baton Rouge, LA: Louisiana State University Press, 2009.
Wyeth, John Allen, *That Devil Forrest: Life of General Nathan Bedford Forrest*. Baton Rouge: Louisiana State University Press, 1959.
Young, *Standard History of the City of Memphis: From a Study of the Original Sources*. Knoxville: H.W. Crowe and Co., 1912

NAME INDEX

List covers residents of Greater Germantown area. Other important figures can be found in the subject index under headings such as Civil War and politics.

Page numbers in **boldface** refer to tables.

Allden, Andrew, 104
Allen, Grant, 365, 366, 384–85
Alsup J. H., 427, 510n24
Ammons, William, 407
Anderson, (Carol?), 420
Anderson, Charles L., 370, 371, 384, 426
Anderson, James C., 168, 494n15
Anderson, James H., 383, 387, 390
Angle, Mr., 17

Bedford, Julian, 17
Bedford, Virginia, 17
Berger, Christian, 428
Blair, Alexander, 108, 165, 260
Blair, William H., Dr., 37
"Blakely": Calvin Bleckley, 399; James Bleckley, 399; Malvina Bleckley, 399
Bleckley, Milley, 399
Bleckley, Thomas, 17, 74, 357, 360, 361, 364, 369, 372, 399, 409, 549n49. *See also* "Blakely"
Bliss, Hosea, 113, 158, 379
Bliss, Isaac W., 113, 158, 168, 379, 380
Boardman, Henry, 82, 378
Booth, Mary, 380
Booth, Nathan, 379–80
Boren, James, 121
Brett, James, 373, 43
Brooks, Agnes, 253, 439, 519n107
Brooks, Ann Elizabeth, 16

Brooks, Elijah, 173
Brooks, Elizabeth, 16
Brooks, Joseph, 14, 82, 201, 253, 410, 439
Brooks, Wilks, 22, 35, 43–44, 79, 111, 546
Brooks family, 14, 16, 42, 44, 202, 247, 256, 385, **388–89**, 439, 494n13, 506n83, 533n50
Brown, Matthew, 138
Buch family, 171
Bufford, John, 393
Burnley, Fannie, 420, 444
Burnley, Susan, (Mrs.), 161, 384, 420
Burns, Caroline, 86, 385
Burns, Jeremiah, Rev., 32
Buster, John, 164, 389n1

Callis, C. M., 373, 477
Callis, Carrie (Sullivan), 516n153
Callis, Clem, 164
Callis, Cleon (C.W.?), 164
Callis, John C., 336, 370
Callis, Lucy, 336
Callis families, 59, 336, 385
Carter, William (black), 93, 393, 394, 397
Carter, William (white), 168, 370, 410
Carter family (white), 385
Cash, Aggie, 444
Cash, Benjamin, 357
Chambers, Thomas, 384
Clark, Joseph H., 49, 138, 472

Clark families, 49, 66
Cole, Ed M., 414
Cole, J., 138,
Cole, Samuel, 156, 378
Cole, Wesley, 115
Cooney, J. W., 427
Cornelius, Aratus T. (Rat), 27, 365, 419
Cornelius, E. B., Mrs., 161, 178, 419
Cornelius, Edward, 17
Cornelius, Eliza, 447
Cornelius, James M. M., (Dr.), 47, 57, 82, 91, 107, 113, 126, 134, 137, 506n83
Cornelius, James, 447
Cornelius, Julia Pettit, 256
Cornelius, Philip, 447
Cornelius, Phillip, 260, 271
Cornelius family, 57, 389, 449
Cross, Joshua, Rev., 32, 510n28

Daily, Chaney, 93
Daily, James, 93
Daily, Lucy, 397
Daily, Mary, 93
d'Arusmont, Madam. *See* Wright, Frances
d'Arusmont, Sylvia, 101, 386
Davis, Charles, 190
DeLagutery, Eugene, 110
Deloach, Jonah, 113
Deloach, Josiah, 189, 267, 441
Dennis, John S., 137–38
Duke, Boelif (Rolfe), 164, 173, 217–18
Duke, Britten, 22, 37, 40, 88, 99, 121, 124, 130, 135, 136, 137
Duke, James, 164
Duke, Joel, 233, 312
Duke, Mary, 58, 68
Duke, Mattie, 116
Duke, Robert F., 27, 129, 164, 259, 420
Duke, William B., 132, 164, 183, 184
Duke family, 27, 37, 40, 58, 68, 70–71, 136, 385, 387, 456, 474, 476
Dunlap, David, 164, 171
Dunlap, Frances, 171
Dunlap, William, 164, 171

Eddins, Frank, 400
Eddins, M. J., Mrs., 400
Ellis, Adolphus, 164, 174, 280, 373
Ellis, Alf, 174
Ellis, Benjamin, 39
Ellis, Henry, 276
Ellis, Samuel H., 427–28
Ellis, Sarah, 39
Ellis, William, 164, 174, 218
Ellis family, 385
Essmann, William, 65, 114
Ethling, John, 425
Evans, Margaret, Mrs., 411
Evans, Richard R., Rev., 27–29, 32, 34–35, 61, 121, 131–32, 219–20, 255, 266, 288, 380, 420, 431, 440–41, 448, 467, 468
Evans family, 433

Featherston, Daniel, 447
Featherston, Malinda, 447
Featherston family, 385, 387
Ferguson, S. W., Mrs., 27
Finch, Ed, 447
Flynn, Fred W., 410
Ford, Lloyd, 378
Ford, M. L., 169
Ford, Mary, 169
Ford, Mary Louise, 378
Ford, Robert L., 164, 169
Fountain, James, 427
Frazier, Mrs., 134
Freeman, Erasmus, 393, 394, 404
Furber, George C., 100, 108, 121, 504n21
Furstenheim, Harmond, 160, 431, 432

Galloway, Green, 393
Galloway family, 264
Gardner, Samuel, 383
Gilmer, William, 383
Goode, (Mrs.), 161
Goode, Godfrey, 447
Goodrich, Thomas, 39, 171
Goodwin, Richard, 82
Gorman, Edward W., 383

Gray, John M., Dr., 59, 135, 139, 160, 287
Gray, Sarah, 444
Gray, Susie, 444
Greenlaw, Eugene Alonso, 381
Greenlaw, William, 381–82, 387, 390, 391, 408, 435
Griffin, George, 65

Hacher, James, 264
Hacher, Joseph, 264
Hack, Asthen, 397
Hack, Caroline, 397
Hack, William, 246, 362, 378, 385, 397, 441
Hall, Alf, 447
Hall, Joel H., 121
Hall, Theophilus, 48
Hammer, H. F., 121
Harrell, J. A., 235
Harris, Mrs. (Louisa?), 161
Harris, Sophia, 397
Harrison, Cary, 82, 163, 380
Harrison, Elizabeth, 163, 380, 532n21
Harrison, Franklin, 403
Harrison, Isaac, 393, 394
Harrison, James, 177
Harrison, Joel, 233
Harrison, Louisa, 420
Harrison, Matt, 420
Harrison, Monroe, 421–23
Harrison, Needham, 23, 164, 173, 280, 309, 379, 385
Harrison, Ralph, 445
Harrison, William C., 100, 116, 138
Harrison, William D., 163, 114, 173, 174, 385
Hayes, Lindsay, 242
Helley (Kelley?), James, 64
Hicks, (Mrs.), 161
Hill, T. L., 425
Holmes, Finley, 35
Holmes, Samuel, 24
Howse, Isham, 13, 21, 22, 24, 34, 40, 45, 47, 58, 59, 60, 71, 76, 76, 116–17, 132
Howse family, 13, 24, 40, 68
Hughs, John, 295

Hunt, James, 427
Hunt, Monroe, 427
Hurt, A. F., 177, 410–11
Hurt, Barry, 51, 52, 114–15, 380, 410
Hurt family, 411, 472

Jenkins, George, 396
Jenkins, Martha, 94
Johnson, A., 472
Johnson, Isaac, 276
Johnson, John, Dr., 165
Johnson, L. B., 27
Johnson, Maryland, 427
Johnson, Mrs., 405
Johnson family, 382
Jones, Henry T., 148, 357, 358, 360, 361, 362, 370, 409, 529n49
Jones, Lewis, 394
Jones, Minnie, 401
Jones, Sarah, 19, 58, 82
Jones, William B., 114–15
Joyce, Mary, 17,
Joyce, William W., 46–48, 428

Kelly, James, Jr., 48–49
Kelly, James, Sr., 49, 66
Kelly family, 48–49, 54
Keener, Mary, 85
Kenney, Lucy, 17
Kimbrough, Albert G., 387
Kimbrough, Buckley, 387
Kimbrough, James 43, 100, 101, 115, 120, 130, 135, 138, 177, 390, 456, 506n83
Kimbrough, John, 387
Kimbrough, Mary Elizabeth, 43, 387
Kimbrough, Syrus, 387
Kimbrough, William F., 429
Kimbrough family, 14, 39, 43, 247, 385, 386, **388–89**, 478, 533n51
Kirby, John A., 68, 163, 330
Kirby family, 57
Knowlton, W. T., 428, 441
Kuner, Maria (Mary) Louise, 85
Kuner family, 85

Lamb, James, 164
Ledbetter, Louisa, 17
Ledbetter, Samuel W., 74, 100, 107, 108, 113, 134
Lee, Alexander, 393
Lewellin, P. A., 48
Lewis, Henry, 427
Lewis, Job, 59, 107, 135, 143, 243, 287
Lipsey, John, Rev., 438, 450, 475
Lipsey, Platus, 404, 438, 474
Lucken, Anton H., 108, 123, 254, 260, 379, 433, 503n1
Lucken, Emily, 35, 36, 73, 30. *See also* Mills, Emily Lucken

Madison, Julia, 383
Madison, Nelms, 383
Madox, Henry, 420
Malone, Jane, 271
Martin, Richard, Dr., 383
Massey, Henry, 82, 385, **388–89**, 431, 432
Mattlock, A. J., 138
McCoy, William, 429
McKay, Robert, Dr., 165, 384, 411, 420, 438, 472
McKever, Rhoda, 271
McLemon, Martha, 402
Meachum, Samuel, 435
Mendenall, Telip/Telix, 64
Messick, William, 409, 476
Miller, Barnett, 29
Miller, C. F. W., Mrs., 448
Miller, H., Rev., 448
Miller, Lucius, 164
Miller, Robert, 164
Miller, William, 112, 384, 451, 466
Mills, Emily Lucken, 253, 336, 443
Mills, J. Dix, Rev., 32, 205, 261, 285, 320, 419, 429–33, 441, 468
Mitchell, Jonathan H., 116
Mitchell, William, 373, 384, 431
Molitor, Charles F., 113, 168, 252, 252–53, 333
Molitor, Cordelia, 113, 161, 252–53, 335
Molitor, Della (Strickland), 472

Molitor, Francis, 64, 113
Molitor, Joseph, 472
Molitor, Mary, 472
Molitor, Moore, 472
Molitor family, 113, 252–53, 441, 472, 505n71
Moore, Andrew, 164
Moore, Caroline Burns, 385
Moore, Thomas, 385
Moore, William, 104, 163
More, Lewis, 164, 171
More, T. M., 137
Morgan, James, 357
Morgan, William W., Dr., 47, 82, 100, 113, 121
Morgan Mary M., 161
Morrison, William S., 410
Mosby, Benjamin, 109–10, 388–89, 408
Mosby, Samuel, 385
Mosby children, orphans, 16
Moss, B. J. T., Prof., 478
Moss, Mrs., 478
Myrick, William, 168, 385

Neely, Eliza, 379
Neely, H. M. (Hugh?), 27, 177
Neely, James, 233
Neely, Joseph C., 51, 115
Neely, Moses, 115
Neely family, 385, 410
Nelms, Thomas, 362
Nelson, George, 393
Newell, John, 427
Niles, John, 424
Nunnemaker, W. B., 105

Owens, Ben, 387
Owens, Mary, 404

Parish, Lou, 334
Parrott, A. G., Rev., 451
Pass, Missinah, 85
Patton, Adriana, 387
Patton, Charles, 387

Perkins, Lizzie, 444
Perkins, Steve, 427
Perkins, William M., 415
Perkins, Wilson, 420
Pettit, Florida, 25. *See also* Thompson, Florida Pettit
Pettit, John W. A., 24, 113, 131,134, 135, 138, 157, 168, 178, 242, 243, 383, 499n9
Pettit, Julia, 25, 63. *See also* Cornelius, Julia Pettit
Pettit, Maria L., 24–25, 161
Pettit family, 53, 63, 69
Phillips, John Lewis, 90
Phillips, Joseph, 427
Pickett, Mrs. L. G., 262
Piggie, Frank, 396
Piggie, Rhoda, 396
Pittman, Thomas, Jr., 27
Plunkett, Achilles N., 25, 448
Plunkett, Adie, 161

Quenichet, John H., 434, 534n76
Quenichet, John W., 333, 387, 434
Quenichet, Susan E., 434, 534n76

Rafter, Alexander M., 27–29, 160
Rafter, Elizabeth, 29
Rafter, James, 27, 29
Rainey, L. B., 472
Ramsey, M. R., Dr., 425
Reasonover, Robert, 428
Reasonover, Sallie, 425, 444
Reasonover, Thomas, 366, 426, 427–28
Rehwoldt, Henry, 115
Reneau, Sarah (Sallie) Eola, 451–52, 466–73
Resten, Julius, 16
Resten, Mary, 16
Rhoades, D. C., 427, 472
Rhoades, Mary, 383
Rhodes, Dewitt, 468
Rhodes, Jonathan L., 529n49
Rhodes, Joseph, 369
Rhodes, Kate, 414, 444

Rhodes, Lewellen (Lon-Allen), 16, 64, 138, 157, 357–58, 362, 425, 468
Rhodes, Moses, 369
Rhodes, Nasal, 425, 444
Rhodes, Rachel, 16, 161
Rhodes, Vernon, Mrs., 444
Richmond, Leonidas, Dr., 37, 165, 411, 472
Robards, Waddie, 164
Roberts, Iris, 85
Roberts, Jack, 395
Roberts, Mahalia (Mahayley), 85–86, 395
Roberts, Mary Kenner, 85
Roberts, Missinah Pass, 85
Roberts, Mrs., 435
Roberts, Preston, 305
Roberts, Quinton, 271, 395
Roberts, Schuyler H. (Kirk), 85–86, 305, 395
Roberts, Waddy, 85
Robinson, Mrs., 435
Rochelle, Feraby, 39
Rochelle, Wiley, 39
Rodgers, James, 510n24
Rosco, Elizabeth, 449
Rutland, Allen, 336, 385
Rutland, Susan, 336
Rutland, William, 336

Sanders, Thomas, 384
Scales, Margaret, 93
Scott, Fernando, 305
Scott, James, 384, 447
Scott, T., 431
Scruggs, Malvinia, 378
Scruggs, Maria, 19
Scruggs, R. L., Dr., 37–38, 88
Scruggs, Robert, 383
Shephard, Nicey B., 95
Shepherd, George, 95, 508n24
Shepherd, Sallie, 411
Shetter, Jeremiah, 135
Shide, Anton, 29, 166
Simmons, R. B., Prof., 466
Sims, James, 168

Sinclair, Dr., 470
slaves (identified by first name only): Henry, 91; John, 91; Simon, 91; Taylor, 91
Slough, James, 164
Slough, John, 64
Small, George W., 358
Small, Mary, 164
Small, Richard, 164, 171
Solomon, M., Prof., 29–30
St. Clair, Dr., 472
Stephens, R. J., 400
Stevenson, Elizabeth, 39
Stevenson, Josephine, 39
Stevenson, William, 39
Stewart, A. C., 168
Stewart, Columbus, 59
Stokes, William, 183
Stout, Harriet, 380, 399
Stout, Isham, 380, 399, 435
Stout, John, Dr., 398, 431
Stout, Rhoda, 399
Stout family, **389n1**
Stratton, T. J., 168
Strickland, (Mr.), 472
Strickland, Moore Molitor, 472

Tate, William, 113
Tenbrooke, J. T., 502n37
Thomas, G. W., 415
Thompson, Florida Pettit, 409, 420, 447, 450, 471–72
Thompson, John, Dr., 471–72
Thompson, Joseph, 388
Thompson, Louis Lycurgus, 27
Thompson, Mary Webb, 27, 257, 265, 448
Thompson, S., 168
Thompson, Theodore, 388
Titus estate, 43, 506n83
Todd, Thomas H., Dr., 113, 130
Trammel, William, 46
Trezevant, Brooks, 27
Trueheart, George W., 168, 379, 509n12
Trueheart, Stephen D., 379
Tuberville, R. W., 168

Tuggle, Baltimore, 174
Tuggle, Charles, 90
Tuggle, Collins, 93
Tuggle, Dick, 174
Tuggle, George, 164
Tuggle, Haywood, 396
Tuggle, John J., 168
Tuggle, John T., 164
Tuggle, Joseph, 280
Tuggle, Lewis, 93, 396
Tuggle, Martha, 164
Tuggle, Mary, 164
Tuggle, Millie, 396
Tuggle, Palmer, 218
Tuggle, Phillip, Rev., 32, 61, 76, 82–83, 90, 93, 166, 266, 378, 395
Tuggle, Phillip, 164
Tuggle, Robert, 396
Tuggle, Thompson, 164, 170, 173
Tuggle families, 174, 395
Twyford, William, 97, 129

Vaden, William P., 120
Voorhees, James, 29

Walker, Alice, 395. *See also* Roberts, Quinton
Walker, James Allen, 276
Walker, Sarah (Sallie?), 82, 271, 276, 295
Walker, William H., 135, 160, 176, 243, 257, 287, 357, 360, 362, 370, 373, 380, 428, 431–32, 472
Warmell, William, 113
Watson, James, 65
Watt, Mary, 428
Weir, Joe, 469, 472
Weir, R., 370
Wells, J. W., 366
Wells, William, 65, 366
Webb, Amos, 84
Webb, Mary. *See* Thompson, Mary Webb
Webb, Monroe P., 63, 323, 362–63, 370, 414–15, 441
Webb, Randolph, 25–26, 84, 323

Webb, Thomas, 384
White, Eppy, 101, 134
White, John E., 425–26, 428
White, Sallie Reasonover, 425–26
Willett, Mrs., 233–34
Williams, Jessie, 478
Wilson, Adeline, 336
Wilson, John, 121
Wilson, Lucy, 336
Wilson, Smith, 428–29
Wilson, William, 336
Winford, John, 164
Winford, John P., 137–38, 370, 385
Winford, Martha, 164
Winford (Wainford), Sam, 164
Winn, Frank, 397

Winn, Harriet, 397
Winn, Ruben, 397
Woodson, Elizabeth, 336
Woodson, Henry, 164, 214, 312, 327, 328, 335, 378
Woodson, John M., 51, 114–15, 256–57
Woodson, Maria Louise Ford, 378
Woodson, Nannie (Ann), 334
Woodson family, 257, 288
Woodward orphans, 19
Wright, A. J., 427
Wright, Frances (Fanny) d'Arusmont, 13, 59, 109, 129, 491n9

Yancey, A. L., 137, 139
Young, N. M., 435

SUBJECT INDEX

This index is divided into four major categories: **African American Experience**, the most uniquely separate component of the Germantown community's story; **Civil War**, the event around which the story hinges; **Germantown**, the central story of the community as a whole; and **Political Environment**, the broader political contexts in which the story evolved.

historical parallels, xiii, 157, 193
sources and evidence, 486–92; availability problems, xi–xii, 5, 236, 285, 288, 388–89, 481–82, 486–92; interpretation, xiv, 145–46

African American Experience

SLAVERY

abolition, Abolitionist Movement, 74, 76, 117, 118–19, 127, 144–45, 156, 281, 454, 456
complex nature of the institution, 15, 58, 72–3, 74–77, 83–4, 87–90, 142, 149–50; Dred Scott decision, 75; rights, privileges, 86, 89–90; romanticizing of, 80, 83–84, 87–88, 149, 187, 306, 354, 370, 454; slave "communities," 79–80, 81–83
deaths, life expectancy, 89; autopsies, 89
escapes, 49, 73, 83, 90–92; numbers of, 73; reasons not to during the war, 84, 267–75
freemen, "free coloreds" pre-war, 73–74, 84, 157; apprenticed orphans, 17; as a threat, 74, 157
history of in Tennessee, 73–74, 89; Nat Turner and other revolts, impact of, 12, 74, 79

labor, diversity and nature of, 18–19, 53, 80–81, 84, 86
owners' attitudes about and practices of: discipline, 19, 86, 89; education, 79; maintenance, 38, 86, 87–89; marriage and families, 78–79, 81–83, 86, 93–94; rationalizations for slavery, 74–77; rebellion, 92; religion for slaves, 76, 77–78; sexual relations among, 82, 83; sexual relations with, 84–86; White Supremacy, 74–75, 150–51, 343, 349, 355, 375
resistance, 90, 92
sales, treatment as property, 15, 58, 86, 87, 93
self-assertion, 83–84
slave quarters, 45, 81–83
vigilance patrols, 90, 93, 168, 421, 451

FREEDOM

abandonment by owners, 269
ambiguous beginnings of, 267–68; contraband status, 268, 272; problems for Federal commanders, 268, 277–78; reluctance to flee, 83–84, 271–74
apprenticing, 398–400
black uprisings, white fears of, 117, 299, 353–54, 403, 421
Confiscation Act of 1862, 269
Contraband Camps, 272–73, 278
contrabands, use of the term, 268, 273
economic and social impact of, xii, 5, 9, 375; for blacks, 82, 86, 94, 267–70, 349–33, 352, 375–76, 397–98, 402, 404, 459; for landowners, 351–52, 354–55, 375–76, 398–400; for whites in general, 118, 375–77, 404, 456–57

Emancipation Proclamation, 269; exceptions for Tennessee, 269–70, 272; owner efforts to thwart, 271
escape/flight to freedom, 268–69, 270, 271; Confederate efforts to thwart, 271, 279; dangers and hardships, 94, 268, 271, 273–74, 278–79; incentives by owners to prevent, 270, 274–75; Southerner's responses to, 279
Freedmen's Bureau: 351–52, 354, 376, 386, 396, 398, 447; Carlin, Asst. Commissioner, 352; military service as opportunity, 275; paternalism, 376, 398; Walker, T. A. Capt. Superintendent, 278
self-assertion, acts of, 271

POST-RECONSTRUCTION

advancement, 349–50, 375, 384–85, 393–97, 401; frustrated aspirations, 349–50, 375–77, 393–94, 397, 402, 405, 459
civil rights, 352; franchise, voting, 363, 364–66, 368–69, 370, 372–73; poll tax, 353
crime, involvement in, 421, 424, 425, 426–27, 440; racial hysteria about, 421–22, 426–27, 428, 436
education, 350–51, 447–48, 449, 450
family structure, households, 350, 375, 396–97, 403–4; heritage of slavery, 378; survival of slave families, partially or intact, 395–96, 399; women heading households, 382, 384, 391, 402
lynchings, 347–48, 367–68, 425, 479
military service. *See* Civil War: U.S. Colored Regiments
occupations, diversity of, 384–85
orphans, apprenticing, 398–400

population, 3–4, 11, 377, 385; influx, postwar, 398, 401; problems assessing, 377; returned or remained, 379, 404
property, wealth, income and status, 90, 352, 375–77, 384, 388 table 6, 389–91, 393–97, 402, 405, 440, 458
social/cultural life, 445–47, 460, 478
white assumptions about black labor, 354–55, 376, 397, 403
White Supremacy as universal consensus reality, 74–75, 150–51, 343, 349, 355, 375; as barrier to all efforts for equality, 343–44, 375–76; propagated in public media, 344, 347, 353–54
work ethic, 392, 394–95, 396
Yellow Fever and local blacks, service, deaths and relative immunity, 470, 471, 472, 473

Civil War

animosities heightened, 200, 234–35, 282, 294–96, 297–300
bandits/robber gangs, 315, 317, 324–25
Blacks in Confederate service, 173, 174, 305–6, 354
body servants, 80, 173–74
conscription, 184–85, 187, 222, 231–32, 239, 240, 282–83, 284, 292, 293, 294, 301, 305–8, 310, 315, 317–18, 321–22, 419, 431
desertion/deserters, 170, 185, 187, 214, 239, 279, 281–82, 295, 307, 310, 328, 336
election of officers, 146–47, 163–64, 167, 172–73, 186, 499n31
location, significance of, 1, 95, 148, 192, 206–7, 407, 413; strategic importance of, 192, 205
moral, public, 160, 162–63, 175, 179, 187, 191, 208–9; soldiers', 183–85, 186, 217, 239, 281, 283, 307, 309–10, 327, 462
pacification, xii, 192–93, 213
parole policies: Confederate, 166; Federal as effort to control population and conscription, 188, 201, 226, 309, 322
pillaging, Federal efforts of control, 9, 180, 186, 202, 204, 208–9, 218, 223, 254, 256–57, 285, 305
post-traumatic stress disorder, xii–xiii, 5, 332, 339, 416, 418–20
surrender and parole, 310–11, 316, 324, 326–31
trade policies, Confederate, 180–81, 211–12
trade policies, Federal, 188, 210–13, 332
widow and family support, 176, 181, 252, 304

CONFEDERATE PARTISAN/GUERRILLA UNITS

2nd Partisan Rangers, 208, 228, 305; Looney, Robert F., Col., 216, 228
advantages in operation, 205–7, 248
advertised, 194, 196, 198
appeal of, 196–97, 201, 419
Ballentine's guerrillas, 200
Confederate policy, conflicts about, 194–96, 207, 228–32, 302, 315
criminality, degeneration into, 195–96, 207–8, 212, 302, 317, 423
Davis, Dick, Capt., 303
discipline, lack of, 195
Federal policy, conflicts about, 200–201, 213
Fort's Scouts, 302; Fort, Dewitt Clinton, Capt., 302–3, 310, 318, 323–25, 544n35; Loftin, Lt., 303
impact on community, xi, 9, 198, 208, 226, 234, 244, 248, 271, 282, 325, 338
Luxton, Mat, 326

nature of, 192, 194–96, 199, 205, 248, 306–7
no-man's-land, 204, 212, 315, 338
Partisan Ranger Act, 195
Partisan Rangers, 1st Tennessee, 215–16, 227–28, 233; Burrow, Reuben, 216, 236–37; Conscription, 231–32, 289, 419; Green, John, 216, 229, 233; Richardson, Robert Vinkler, Col., 215–17, 227–29, 231–33, 235, 238–40, 242, 263, 289, 290–91; Richardson's Brigade, 215, 291, 295, 419
Porter's 2nd Partisan Rangers Company, 200, 208, 305; Porter, Ed E., Capt., 196–200
Sanders, Edward "Ned," 194–95, 535n10
Sherwin, Captain, Independent Scouts, 198
Street, Mississippi Partisan Rangers, 212, 217
Thompson, Capt., 301

CONFEDERATE COMMANDERS

Beauregard, Pierre G. T., Gen., 186, 198
Chalmers, Gen., 185, 212, 229, 231–32, 235–39, 241, 263, 276, 279, 292, 302

Forrest, Nathan Bedford, Gen., 165, 183, 185, 189, 195, 234, 240, 289, 296–301, 305–7, 309, 327, 335; 1st raid into West Tennessee, 241–42, 263; 2nd raid into West Tennessee, 288–96; suppression of brigands, 315, 317, 326; surrender, 324, 327
Hood, John B., Gen., 308–10

Johnston, Albert S., Gen., 171–72, 195
Johnston, Joseph, Gen., 288, 241, 279, 308, 310, 324
McCulloch, Mo, Col., 292, 309
Pillow, Gideon, Gen., 156, 170–72, 215
Van Dorn, Earl, Maj. Gen., 223

CONFEDERATE UNITS

2nd Tenn. Volunteer Inf. Regt., 165
3rd Tenn. Cav. Regt. Forrest's, 165
4th Tenn. Volunteer Infantry Regt., 163, 177, 182, 280, 423; 4th/5th Regt., 217; Wigfall Grays, 160, 182
5th Military District, N. Miss. Chalmers, Gen., 231
  West Tennessee Cav. Brig. (Richardson's), 233, 235–37; 12th Tenn. Cav. Lt. Col. James L. Green, 233, 282, 419; 13th Tenn. Cav. (14th) Col. J. J. Neely, 233, 294–95, 315; 14th Tenn. Cav. (15th) Col. F. M. Stewart, 233, 235
7th Tenn. Cav. Regt. Col. Wm. H. Jackson, 165, 186–87, 231, 307; Logwood's Battalion Tenn. Cav., 165, 186
13th Tenn. Volunteer Inf. Regt., 163, 169–75, 214, 281, 309–10; Co. C, Secession Guards, 160, 162–63, 169, 182; uniform, 162
37th Tenn. Inf. Regt., 177
38th Tenn. Inf. Regt., 177, 419
39th Tenn. Inf. Regt., 177
154th Tenn. Volunteer Inf. Regt., 159, 164, 183, 218, 309–10
militia: Germantown Home Guards, 167; Minute Men, 167–68; mobilization, 80–81, 86

FEDERAL COMMANDERS

Grant, Ulysses S., Gen., 171, 189, 190–94, 201–2, 205, 211, 223, 225–27, 230, 234, 242, 245, 247, 267, 272
Grierson, B. H., Col., 192–93, 205, 209–10, 212, 215, 227–29, 285, 289–92, 297–98, 303
Halleck, H. W., Maj. Gen., 190–200, 202, 205
Hurlbut, Gen., 16th Corps, 203, 225–30, 235–38, 241, 243, 275–78, 288, 290–92, 295–96, 301
Hurst, Fielding, Col. 1st W. Tenn. Cav., 6th Tenn. Cav., 235, 289, 294, 326
McCrillis, La Fayette, Col., 221, 230–31, 234, 254–56

Sanderson, William L. Col., 219–20
Sherman, William T. Gen., 185, 190–94, 201–5, 208–13, 218, 221, 236–38, 262–64, 269, 290–91, 301, 308, 334; hostility toward Germantown, 190–91; tacit approval of pillaging of Germantown, 191–96, 203–5
Sturgis, Samuel D., Brig. Gen., 296–98
Thomas, George A., Maj. Gen., Dept. of Cumberland, 318, 322, 326, 329–30, 345, 356
Washburn, C. C. (C.O.?)., Maj. Gen., 289, 293, 299–300, 318–19, 322–23, 326, 331–32, 335

FEDERAL OCCUPATION FORCES

2nd Inf. Brig., Col. Ephraim R. Eckley, 224
7th Division, Brig. Gen Isaac F. Quinby, 224, 226, 514
8th Mo. Inf. Regt., 210, 218–19
10th Mo, Inf. Regt. Col. Samuel A. Holmes, 219, 224

16th Corps, Hurlbut, Gen., 225, 234, 276
  1st Cav. Div. Col. John Mizner, 230; 1st. Brig. Col. Lafayette McCrillis, 230–31, 234; 1st Ill. Lt. Arty. in Germantown fortifications, 234; 2nd Brig. Cav., McCrillis, 230, 290, 319; 2nd Iowa Cav. Regt. on Festival Grounds, 234, 301; 3rd Brig. Cav. Col. Edward Hatch on Nashoba, 234, 238; 6th Ill. Cav. Regt., Lt. Col. Lewis, at Germantown, 234, 257; 7th Kansas Cav. Regt., Kansas Jayhawkers, 209, 219, 222, 224–25, 230, 248, 257; 9th Ill. Cav. Maj. Ira R. Gifford in Germantown, 230, 247, 252–53; Herrod, Thomas, Maj., murder of Col. Loomis, 257
  3rd. Inf. Brig. Col. George B. Boomer, 224
  4th Inf. Brig. Col. W. W. Sanford in Germantown, 226, 230; 25th Ind. Inf. Regt. 238; 48th Ill. Inf., 110; 49th Ill. Inf., Col. Phineas Pease in Germantown, 110, 230; 59th Infantry Regt. Company F, 223; 119th Ill. Inf., 110;
  Cavalry Division, Col. A. L. Lee at Germantown, 226
  5th Division, Hurlbut's/Laumann's, 226
  72nd Ohio Cav. Regt. Lt. Col. Charles G. Eaton, 240, 267
  Cavalry Division, Col. E. D. Osband in Memphis, 319; 2nd Brigade, 319; 11th NY Cav., 319, 323, 325, 333; Co. D, Capt. George W. Smith, 325, 326; Cos. L & M, 32
  17th Iowa Inf. Regt., 224
  56th Ill. Inf. Regt., 224
  80th Ohio Inf. Regt., Camp Forest Hill, 224
  Lt. John D. Mills, 325
  Provost Marshal, Capt. W. P. More, 221, 226, 244–46, 258, 261–63, 271–72, 305
  Springfield Light Artillery Battery, fortifications commanding Germantown, 224
  West Tennessee Cavalry Regiment (1st), 6th Tenn. Cav., 235, 289, 294
  West Tennessee Cavalry Regiment (2nd), 235, 276

FEDERAL PRISONS

generally, 310–14
Alton Prison, 262, 313
Camp Hoffman, Point Lookout, Maryland, 314
Irving Block, 214, 233, 262, 303, 311
Rock Island, Illinois, 313, 330

SIGNIFICANT EVENTS, CIVIL WAR

Atlanta, Battle of, 308–9, 310
Belmont, Battle of, 171
Brice's Crossroads, Battle of, 297; retreat from, 297–98, 299, 300, 303
Collierville
  1st Battle of, 235–36; incidents at Germantown, 236
2nd Battle, 238
Fort Pillow, massacre, 292–95
Lee surrenders, 324
Memphis, Battle of, 185, 187
Murfreesborough, Battle of, 217–18
Nashville, Battle of, 309
Shiloh, Battle of, 165, 182–83

U.S. COLORED REGIMENTS

2nd Light Artillery Regt. (Memphis Lt. Battery), 275, 294–95, 296
3rd Brig. (Sturgis expedition), Bouton, P. Col., 297, 298
3rd Heavy Colored Artillery Regt. (1st. Regt. Tenn. Heavy Arty. [A.D.]), 275
6th Heavy Colored Artillery Regt. (1st Alabama Siege Arty.), 275, 276, 295

11th Infantry Regt., 275
59th Infantry Regt. (1st W.TN Inf. Regt. AD), 275, 276, 297
61st Infantry Regt. (2nd W.TN Inf. Regt. AD), 276–77
88th Infantry Regt., 275
casualties, 278–79, 300

Germantown

AGRICULTURE

corn, 1, 45, 97, 113, 304, 378, 391, 401, 412, 589
cotton, 1, 45, 74, 96–97, 118, 213; finance, 14, 111, 211, 374–75, 392; ginning, 44–45, 476; marketing, 4, 14, 99, 102, 104, 111, 175–76, 180, 188, 191, 200, 210, 212, 262–63, 288, 289, 381; mono-cropping, 382, 391–92, 401, 402, 533n51; production, 2, 391–92, 394; recovery, post-war, 392, 411
diversification, 44–45, 401, 411–12
Grange, 411–12
land, quality of, 12, 22, 394; clearing, 13, 14, 44, 386, 394, 400; depletion of, 12, 14
market crops, 120, 392, 412
Signal Service, weather forecasting, 412
vicissitudes of agricultural life, 12–13, 15

COMMUNITY RELATIONS

agricultural population: "farmer" census definition, 389n, 458; land owning, 54, 62, 65, 389, 397, 400, 401, 402, 403, 504n83; land renting, 54, 58–59, 62, 376–77, 379, 390, 392, 394, 395, 398, 400, 401, 402, 486–87; landless labor, 49, 54, 58, 62, 66, 147, 304, 377, 380, 385, 389, 390–91, 393, 394, 396, 398, 401–2, 404, 440, 456; overseers, 12, 19, 62, 64, 65, 84, 86, 88, 114, 164, 171, 185, 264, 270, 366, 394; planters, 11, 14, 19, 43–45, 52, 54–55, 58–59, 61, 62–63, 64–65, 67, 87, 88, 99–100, 107, 111, 114, 119, 120–21, 130, 135, 138, 141–42, 148, 151, 160, 173, 193, 198, 212–13, 270, 273, 336, 351–52, 375, 383, 385, 386, 387–89, 399, 433, 447, 458; share cropping, 270, 395, 400–402, 403; tenant farming, 52, 156, 352, 366, 376–77, 388, 393, 394, 398, 400–403, 412; women heading households, 19, 82, 244, 250, 261, 264, 354, 384, 388, 402; yeomen farmers, small holders, 12, 20, 52, 54, 56, 59–60, 66, 68, 69, 87, 111, 119, 124, 135, 138, 147, 148, 149, 156, 264, 304, 385, 390, 392, 456
apprentices, 16–17, 132, 398–400
charity, 10, 35, 71–72, 304, 361, 398, 434, 439, 441, 443, 456, 458
community spirit and harmony, 5, 17, 21, 23, 35, 50–51, 52, 67–72, 80, 121–22, 126, 128, 142–43, 145–46, 148–51, 156, 158, 160, 172–75, 267, 320, 337, 339, 436–37, 439, 453–57
dangerous underclass, 49, 149, 403, 439
disruptions by war, 175, 176, 183, 184–85, 261, 265, 267, 283, 304–5, 335, 437–39, 340–41, 457–60, 462
professional, industrial, and commercial population
attorney/lawyers, 12, 64, 74, 96, 112, 132, 141, 142, 388, 408, 428
contractor, 388
doctors/physicians, 12, 17, 37–39, 41, 52, 61, 62, 64, 82, 88, 96, 112–13, 134, 165, 184, 254, 379, 384, 385, 388, 468, 470, 472, 478; midwives, 19, 39, 385
domestic service: 54, 66, 73, 82, 384, 403; cooks, 18, 80, 269, 305, 380, 382, 397, 402, 403, 447; housekeepers, 385, 387, 395, 397, 402; nanny/nurse, 382, 460, 471; servants, 80, 174, 258, 382, 384, 402, 471

employees: 16, 63, 66, 115, 130, 190, 379, 382, 384, 399, 403; clerks, 62, 68, 104, 122, 138, 171, 265, 320, 369, 381; laborers: 12, 58, 62–64, 66, 71, 118, 122, 184, 304–5, 354, 379, 382, 384, 388–89, 456; seamstresses, 395; wash woman, 382
financier, 388
lawyers, 12, 64, 74, 132, 141, 142, 408, 428
machinists, 61, 64; miller, 388
mechanics/artisans, 12, 54, 63–65, 68, 71, 118–19, 128, 147–48, 305, 460, 487; blacksmiths, 12, 39, 41, 64, 80, 111, 116, 365, 366, 380, 381, 384, 385; brick layers, masons, 41, 116, 385; carpenters, 41, 64, 116, 380, 382, 384, 385, 414; wagon maker, 16, 49, 64, 66, 82, 116, 138, 168, 358, 380, 384, 417
merchants, 4, 12, 13, 14, 20, 36, 48, 52, 53, 54, 58, 61–64, 82, 111–12, 114, 119, 121, 128, 135, 141, 147–48, 156, 160, 168, 212, 259–60, 263, 321, 332, 357, 358, 361, 378–79, 383, 388, 392, 429–33, 451, 477; druggist, 112, 384, 388, 415, 466, 472; saloon keeper, 65, 111, 114
pastors/clergy/preachers (*see* Social/Cultural Life: churches and religion)
speculator, 62, 383, 388
teachers/educators (*see* Social/Cultural Life: education)
society, status, and distribution of wealth, 11–12, 54–59, 61–63, 64–66, 67–72, 142, 148–49, 173–74, 304, 360, 375, 376, 381–86, 387–91, 392–93, 400–401, 439–40, 453, 455, 458; problems assessing, 5, 145–46
symptoms of loss of harmony after war, 315, 340–41, 390, 413, 415, 416–40, 421, 422–23, 431–34, 439, 449, 450, 460, 463, 467–70; crime, 50, 149, 244, 423–29, 436, 439, 440, 453, 459, 477–78; honor killings, duels, 47–48, 429, 427–28; J. Dix Mills scandal, 431–34, 468; Maxie vs. Reneau, 467–70; murders and killings, 46–48, 205–6, 208–9, 257, 426–29; sectarianism, 414–15, 437–38, 453, 458, 475; suicides, 435–36, 458, 463
symptoms of resumption, 417, 418, 437, 440–41, 460–62, 463, 477–78; Lost Cause phenomenon, 288, 335, 462–63

ENVIRONMENT

generally, 1–3
Afton. *See* High Hill
Bridge Street (Germantown Road), 111
Brunswick Springs, 109, 163, 177, 224, 247, 445, 475
Capleville, 41, 266, 473–74
Church Street (McVay), 111
"Greater Germantown": scope of community, 2–3, 7–8, 73, 87, 156, 476, 481–82
High Hill (Afton), 41, 107
Hot Tamale Road, 410
Pea Ridge, 7, 23, 41, 95, 106, 134, 136, 481
Ridgeway, 99, 106, 112 173, 303, 408, 409, 476, 481–82
Spring Street (West St.), 31, 103, 111

GOVERNMENT

charter/incorporation, 1841 and 1850, 9, 139, 373, 491, 493n1; lapse of, 337, 372; 1880, 373, 427, 477, 491, 493n1, 538n51
town government: 130–41; authority of, defined by Charter 1850, 139–40; constable, 68, 140, 134, 135, 139, 142–43, 243, 187, 356, 358, 478; franchise, 141; structure, 139

SUBJECT INDEX · 573

OCCUPATION OF

generally, 180, 191–92, 193, 218, 219, 223–24, 225, 226, 230, 234, 238, 240, 248, 284, 290, 292, 301, 303, 323, 338
benefits of, 223, 245, 248, 258, 260, 263, 303, 338
boarding in homes, 249–50, 252–54, 305, 335, 378
Camp of Instruction, Sam Hays, 177–78
churches, federal abuse and use of, 219–21, 285
  Baptist, 219–21, 266
  Methodist, 219–21, 266
  Presbyterian, 219, 255, 266, 288
  services during, 255, 266, 338
collaboration, 189, 333–35
suspicions of, 237, 242, 339
confiscation of property, 191, 201, 212, 226, 234, 244, 245–47, 256, 258, 289, 335, 386
  federal efforts to control, 186, 202, 245, 247, 335
damages, 4, 5, 218–21, 225, 248, 251, 253, 254, 256, 338
effects of war and occupation, 5, 162–63, 338–40, 341, 458–59
fears and mutual distrust, 190, 191, 192–93, 223–24, 242, 251, 338
firefights through town, 9, 189, 193, 198, 210, 226, 338
fortifications, 234, 247–48, 249
fraternization, 252, 253, 262, 333–35
furloughs home for troops, 170, 188, 214, 234, 296
government, local, 213, 242–43, 244, 287, 320, 337
guerrilla resistance, local, 189, 190–91, 338

jayhawkers, 225
martial law, 213, 242–43, 263, 264, 289, 322, 333
military traffic, effects on town, 97, 230, 266, 285, 291, 303, 316
mood of public, changes, 5, 286, 305, 333–35, 339, 340
oath of allegiance, 188, 213, 238, 243, 255, 256, 259, 261, 262, 263, 284, 287, 288, 320, 322, 328–31, 332–33
observations of individual participants
  Booth, Louis F., Capt., 252–53
  Dunaway, William, 518n137, 519n162, 523n3
  Green, Harvey, Capt. and Mrs., 249–51
  Hackley, W. R. Fed. Treasury Agent, 259
  Pomeroy, Fletcher Pvt., 248–49, 251–52
  Shelby, Lt. Col., 316
pillaging of, 9, 180, 186, 202, 204, 208–9, 218, 223, 254, 256–57, 285, 305
population loss, 267, 285
Provost Marshall, 221, 226, 244–46, 258, 261, 262–63, 271, 305
quality of life during, 251, 253, 261–63, 264–67, 336
reprisals, 223, 226, 237–38
returning soldiers, 331–32, 336, 378, 379
robber bands guerrillas, impact of and reactions against, 315, 317, 325
service in Confederate Army, 482–83
service in Federal regiments, 264, 482–83
smuggling, 188, 214, 244, 262, 311
Suttler's store, 259–60, 271, 305
taxation, 243, 263

POLITICS IN

Civil District constable, 113, 134, 135, 140, 142–43, 243, 287, 356, 358
Democratic Association of Germantown, 121, 124, 126
education issues, 136–38
Germantown's predominance in county
politics, vii, 134, 360, 369, 372
Know-Nothing Movement, 125–27
  effects on local attitudes, 124, 125–28
Memphis Navy Yard, attitudes about, 130–31, 142
political leadership, 135, 370, 371, 372

post-war reemergence of, 357–58, 361, 362, 363, 365, 369
presidential election of 1860, votes, 144–45
property and power, 135, 141–43, 361
Quarterly Sessions Court, 8, 74, 132–34, 242, 356, 360, 405
secession, attitudes about, 2, 60, 76–77, 118, 123, 143, 145–48, 150–51, 156–59
stumping at Germantown, 122, 126, 131, 361, 364

taxation issues, 9, 22–24, 69, 120, 122, 129–30, 136–39, 142–43, 150, 243, 263, 353, 359–60, 371–72, 373, 378, 386–87, 406, 437, 449–50, 477
temperance, 20, 34, 48, 131–32, 143, 420–21, 452, 455, 458, 472
vote fraud, 286–88, 356, 369, 433
voters/voting, 177, 215, 365–66, 368, 370
Whig Party, 120–21, 124, 128, 130, 136, 145, 335

SOCIAL/CULTURAL LIFE

baseball, 266, 417
childhood and youth, 20–21, 33, 39, 49, 68, 80, 81–82, 265–66, 273, 278, 418, 455, 460
churches and religion, 21, 31, 70, 77, 266, 285, 468, 475
    church buildings, construction, 33; reconstruction, 413; Confederate use as hospitals, 178, 184
    pastors, ministers, 27, 29, 32, 76, 166, 265, 396, 367, 430, 433, 438, 444; positions on slavery, 76–77
    religiosity, 33–35, 468, 470, 475
    sectarianism, 35, 415, 437, 458
death and burial, 13, 38–40, 49, 53, 87, 104, 166, 169, 171, 178, 183–85, 262, 272–73, 467–68, 470, 471–75
denominations, 31–35, 77, 266, 479
    African Methodist Episcopal Church, 447, 494
    Baptist, 29, 31, 32, 33, 41, 42, 44, 70, 77, 76, 111, 131, 184, 219–21, 224, 254, 266, 285, 413–15, 420
    black, 351, 397, 445, 453, 479
    Campbellites, 33, 35, 438
    Catholics, 33, 35
    Episcopalian, 33, 70, 76
    Methodist, 31, 32, 40, 70, 76, 77, 111, 159, 178. 219–21, 413, 433, 467; Bethlehem Church, 33, 266; Chapel Hill Church, 33; New Bethel Baptist Missionary Church, 224, 395, 446–47, 479;
    Presbyterian, 31, 70, 76, 477
diseases, illness, 22, 30, 38–39, 178, 261, 273–74, 411, 473, 477
education, 22–30, 52, 61, 63, 65, 69, 79, 84, 132, 136–38, 142, 338, 350–51, 394–95, 442, 447–52
    attendance, 25, 69, 350, 449, 452, 487
    common schools, 23, 25, 69–70, 137–38, 350, 448–49
    District School Commission/ Board, 23–24, 69, 136–37, 141, 449, 450
    Duke School House, 23–24, 33, 140
    early academies, failure of, 4, 10, 27
    Forest Hill College Institute for Young Ladies, 29, 63, 407, 444, 448
    Germantown Male and Female English and Classical School, 448
    Nashoba School, 448
    public education, 22–23, 25, 132, 136–38, 450, 452
    Shelby Male High School, 27–29, 448; Shelby Military Academy, 28–29, 160, 166
    subscription schools, 23, 69, 137
    teachers, 23–25, 27, 29, 61–63, 137, 447, 449–50, 460, 478; quality of, 132, 447, 449–50
    Thompson Place, 447, 449–50
    Webb School, 25–27, 63, 221, 257, 265, 448–49
family life, 15–21, 81

gender relations/roles, 17–20, 21, 23, 25, 34, 82, 132, 148, 418, 442, 454–55
   progressive changes, 19–20, 148, 455, 458
housing, construction, quality, 54–57, 352
   Cotton Plant, Kimbrough house, 14, 43, 387
   outhouses, 43, 45, 378
   Woodlawn, 43–44, 201, 253, 256
Masonic Lodge, 31, 445
militia, Civil District 11 company, 35, 47, 93, 132, 133, 167
Nashoba Springs, 109–11, 163, 203, 232, 445, 476
Nashoba Tract, 13, 22, 109–10, 234, 236, 238, 247, 259, 386, 493n9, 506n83
newspapers, influence of, 100, 123–24, 125, 146, 155, 158, 159, 160, 353, 397, 436
   (Memphis) *Argus*, 123, 287, 335, 359
   (Memphis) *Eagle and Enquirer*, 60, 123, 125
   (Memphis) *Evening Post*, 364
   (Memphis) *Union Appeal*, 304
   Avalanche, The, 123, 146, 155, 157, 198, 359–60, 364, 366, 372, 426
   effects of the war, 188, 213–14, 320, 340
   Memphis Appeal, 28, 109, 115, 121–23, 125, 131, 144, 146, 155–56, 188, 194, 196, 198, 214, 279, 320, 340, 347, 351, 353, 361, 362, 363, 366, 368–69, 372, 406, 422, 426, 442, 458
   Memphis Bulletin, 123, 146, 232, 235, 284, 287–88, 320, 335, 366
   Memphis Daily Whig, 123
   Public Ledger, 373, 445
   Rebel Picket, 214
Odd Fellows, 31, 35, 285
population, 3–5, 7–9, 11–12, 53, 73, 87, 337, 37, 401, 416, 481–82
   character of, regional origins, 11–12, 48, 59, 61, 63, 118–19, 125, 150–51, 371, 374, 429, 439, 440–41, 509n90
   "Greater Germantown," 2–3, 7–8, 87, 156, 476, 481
   mobility of, 2–3, 186
   problems defining, 11, 73, 479–80, 481–82, 486–92
   remaining/returning after war, 253, 267, 336, 339
Post Office, 2, 4, 11, 41, 99, 107, 123, 132, 134, 412, 415, 476, 481–82
   mail delivery/service, 7, 107, 188
racial relations, post-war, 403–5, 440, 447, 457, 459, 461
suburban Expansion into, 341, 407–10, 413, 448
Temperance Movement, 20, 34, 48, 131–32, 420–21, 452, 455, 458, 473
Town Commons (the green), 111

TRANSPORTATION AND COMMERCIAL

bridges, 98, 241, 405
   maintenance of, 101, 132, 356, 361, 405
Businesses
   Ben Owen's Grocery, 387, 411
   Bliss book sellers, 113, 158, 379–80
   Bluff City Insurance Company, 410
   boot-maker, 16
   cabinet maker, 116
   Cole & Co., 156, 378
   Harrison & Nuland's Wholesale & Retail Grocery & Produce, 114
   Hernando Insurance Company, 410
   Lucken's Place/Inn, 35, 108, 111, 114, 123, 146, 257, 261–62
   recovery of, post-war, 206, 232, 337, 412–13, 416
   saloons, 7, 21, 46, 48, 65, 96, 111, 114, 123, 181, 420
   stores, 4, 48, 111–12, 114, 259, 332, 417, 478; credit, 13–15, 37, 39, 45, 47, 48, 111–12, 119, 352, 374, 392–93, 411, 429, 430, 433
Cherokee Trace, 98
county roads, 97–100, 132–33, 356, 361, 405
   maintenance of, 101, 133, 356, 361, 405

decline of economic position, 4–5, 341, 379, 380, 406, 436–37, 475
Germantown Plank Road Company, 100
industry, 4, 40, 41, 99, 111–16, 151, 166, 417, 476, 491
   Armstrong's Woolen Mill, 387
   Burdine & Moore's Southwestern Cotton Gin Factory, 114
   Hurt, Shepherd & Co., Cotton Gins, 51, 167, 379
   impact of war on, 166, 379
   Kimbrough & Bradley Cotton Gin, 412
   lack of census data, 489
   Molitor's Mill, 50, 111, 116, 379, 387
   Southern Star Cotton Gin Manufactory, 49, 51, 115, 166, 250, 379, 410
   Tennessee Terra Cotta Works & Pottery, 115
   wagon maker, 49, 64, 66, 82, 138, 384
Ledbetter & Furber's Hack Service, 100, 108
Memphis & Charleston Rail Road (M&C), 4, 101–7, 100, 226, 277, 300–301, 323, 336, 384, 405–6, 464–65
   accidents, 104–6
   American Standard Engine, 102, 504n28
   defense of, 191–93, 224–26, 230, 240, 242, 301
   Germantown depot, 21, 86, 103, 111, 123, 230, 262, 266, 277, 331, 364
   impact of war on, 176, 179–80, 187–89, 193, 205, 242, 260–61, 289, 291, 300–301, 315, 323, 336
   property values, impact on, 106–8, 408, 410, 441
   service, 102, 104, 176, 179–80, 260–61, 408, 441, 464–65, 474, 475; commuter, 106, 408, 410
Memphis and Germantown Turnpike Company, 98–99
plank roads, 99
post roads, 98
Shelby County Turnpike Company, 405
stage lines, 100
State Line Road (Alabama Road), 7–8, 95, 97–98, 181, 192–93, 405, 481; as toll road, 99, 406
Wolf River, 97

YELLOW FEVER EPIDEMIC IN

generally, 341, 452, 464–75
burials, 467, 473
conflict within the community, 468–71, 473
   Maxie/Maxey, 468–71, 475

flight from Memphis to, 464–65, 473–74
impact, 464, 475–76
return in 1879, 474

Political Environment

MEMPHIS

massacre of 1866, 346, 355, 358–60

Metropolitan Police Act, 358–59

NATIONAL

American Party (Know Nothings), 125–27
Democratic Party, 117, 119–32, 143, 145, 357, 370–71
John Brown's Raid, 144
Kansas-Nebraska Act, 143

bleeding/bloody Kansas, 143, 160, 209
National-Republican Party (Whigs), 117, 119–21, 123–25, 127–28, 130–31, 136–37, 142–45, 150, 335, 372, 456
Native American Party. *See* American Party

Presidential election
   1844 and 1852, 121
   1860, 144–45
   1868 and 1872, 364–65, 370–71
Republican Party, 117, 143, 145, 345, 372
slavery issue, 117, 124, 143–44

RECONSTRUCTION

Brownlow, Governor's manipulation of Shelby County elections, 344, 356, 358, 362
controversial nature of, 343–44, 345, 349
Democratic Party reemerges, 362–63
Enfranchisement, 344, 459
Home Guards, 288, 315, 345, 356
Ku Klux Klan, KKK, 347–48, 352, 363 366–68, 398, 440
   and lynchings, 425, 479
Metropolitan Police Act, 358–59

Republican Party divided
   Conservative Unionists, 267, 345–46, 357, 358, 361–63, 365–66, 372
   Radical Unionists, 344–70, 372, 457
results, consequences, 337, 353, 359, 371, 457, 459, 460–63
State and County Guards, 346–48
Tennessee, uniqueness of, in, 344, 348, 349, 351

SHELBY COUNTY

Academy, 25
Brownlow opposition in, 357, 359, 361–62, 441
Civil districts, vii, 7–8, 11, 122, 133, 356, 358, 362, 369, 370, 421, 449
   7th, 479
   9th, 479
   10th, 2, 8, 122, 156, 369, 421, 479
   11th, 2, 7, 122, 133, 156, 362, 421, 479;
      Germantown as seat of, 7
   20th, 369
Conservative Party in, 357, 361–62

County Commission, 360–61, 369–70, 372, 424
education, 69, 132, 137, 450
militia, 36, 133, 159, 163, 167, 169, 179
Quarterly Sessions Court, 8, 74, 93, 132, 134, 242, 356, 360, 405
Shelby County Turnpike Company, 405
Shelby Male High School, 27–29, 448
Shelby Military Academy, 28–29, 160, 166
Sherriff's Acts, 346, 356
Sheriff's office, 134, 243, 356–57, 367, 371
voters, racial representation, 36

STATE

Constitutional Convention, 1870, 370
Constitutional Union Party, 145
currency, banking, and market economy, 14, 119, 120, 122, 210, 375, 411
elections 1870 and 1872, 370
emancipation, 5, 9, 12, 267, 269–70, 271, 363, 375, 404
   Emancipation Proclamation, 269
   U.S. Constitution Amendments, 171
Jacksonian democracy, 119, 122, 130, 136, 137, 141
Johnson Radicals, 287
legislation

public education, segregation of, 350–51
racial, Persons of Color, 349–51
Lincoln Abolitionists, 138
Nashoba County, 424–24
re-admission into Union, 344
regional differences, 1–2
republican commitments, 119, 143
taxation and public works, 117, 120, 129, 132, 143, 150, 386–87
Tennessee, Declaration of Independence, 157
Unconditional Free State Union ticket, 287, 441